THE ROAD TO DEMOCRACY IN GERMANY

The Role of State and National Elections, 1946–2011

Lowell W. Culver

University Press of America,® **Inc.**
Lanham · Boulder · New York · Toronto · Plymouth, UK

To the State and Federal Executives

and Legislators of the Federal Republic Whose

Efforts Made Possible the Strong Democratic

System Which Exists in Germany Today

TABLE OF CONTENTS

List of Tables

STATE AND NATIONAL ELECTIONS FROM 1965 TO REUNIFICATION

STATE AND NATIONAL ELECTIONS FROM REUNIFICATION TO THE PRESENT

Preface

Following six years of war Germany lay in ruins, divided between four occupying powers, the United States, the Soviet Union, Great Britain and France, whose governments exercised total control over the defeated country's economic and political future. With no government in exile or legitimate group on which to confer authority, a new political order for the German State had to be created.

But, within months of the German capitulation, the anticipated cooperation between victors vanished, and, rather than one Germany, two emerged, one, encompassing the Soviet zone of occupation, modeled after Russian totalitarian communism, the other, encompassing the American, British and French zones, after the parliamentary democracies of Western Europe. Each part embarked on a markedly different path. In the West, the Allies favored a federal union as a check against the possible reemergence of undemocratic centralized authority. The Basic Law of 1949 created a decentralized structure under which the prerogatives of the states (*Länder*) were protected by a Federal Constitutional Court and by the direct representation of the *Land* governments in the *Bundesrat*, the upper house of the federal parliament, whose approval was required on all *Bundestag* measures affecting *Land* interests. The economic health of what became the Federal Republic of Germany was restored relatively rapidly under a free market system, and a stable democratic political order developed. Sovereignty was gradually regained as the West German state became integrated into West European economic and defense arrangements.

In contrast, the eastern part of Germany, what became the German Democratic Republic (DDR), evolved into a police state closely aligned with the Soviet Union. The democratic practices associated with western political institutions were strikingly absent. Industries and farmlands were placed under state ownership, and output was based on government determinations rather than on the demands of the market place. Although the economy languished for many years, by the late 1980s it afforded DDR citizens the highest per capita income in the Soviet bloc, albeit a level far below that of the West and at considerable cost to the local environment. Ultimately, the forces of change, including a more enlightened Soviet leadership, brought an end to the division of the two Germanies and to the existing police state in 1990.

Today, in the second decade of the 21st century, Germany stands reunited and free, a strong and vital member of the world community. However, 45 years of separation left a legacy of difference and mistrust between the two parts of the Federal Republic which are only gradually being overcome, helped by the successful economic and political institutions forged in the western part of the country after the war. (E. Wayne Merry sees the roots of the East's continuing alienation as stemming from the "enforced, prolonged isolation that its society endured during most of the Cold War" *Current History* (March 2010: 112-118). The existence of a federal structure, which allows for diversity within a larger unity, is helping to facilitate the healing process.

The evolution of German political institutions from their feeble beginnings in the three western zones over 65 years ago to their present status has been the subject of numerous studies, most of which have concentrated on national arrangements and the political forces which have shaped them. Only limited attention, however, has been given to regional political developments, in spite of their important contribution to the development of German democracy following twelve years of totalitarian rule.

A unique feature of German federalism, which gives to the German states (*Länder*) a direct voice in federal legislation through representation in the *Bundesrat*, causes every regional election to be at once a national and a regional poll because their outcomes determine which party or parties will control the *Land* ministries and, thereby, the federal upper house. Because of this relationship and the role of *Länder* in administering national policy, German politics cannot be completely understood without an appreciation of the contribution of *Land* elections to the functioning of the German state. In addition to covering all seventeen general elections, a major purpose of this study is to delineate more clearly the influence of regional election contests in the German political system. The investigation sees national and regional politics as so interwoven in a mesh of constitutional and political interdependencies as to be almost inseparable. Political developments on one level invariably influence those on the other. By focusing on the campaigns and outcomes of some 200 elections held in the West German states between 1946 and 1990 and in a reunited Germany since 1990, the study seeks to answer a number of questions about regional politics, and, through a comparison of political trends on the state and federal levels, to develop some meaningful generalizations about German politics in general. Its concern, then, is with the outcomes of both *Bundestag* and *Land* elections, their influence on the party system on state and national levels, on regional and national governments and on national political developments, and, conversely, with the legal and political forces which have shaped the various electoral decisions. In short, it is an analysis of the role played by regional and national election contests in the German political system and the influence of national politics on political developments in the *Länder*.

In spite of threats to regional autonomy posed by the coordination efforts of the national parties, especially during the early years of the Federal Republic, domination of regional politics has never been complete, and developments on one level continue to exert an important influence on party and governmental decisions on the other. The influence has never been one way. Just as the fate of the regional parties and governments has been strongly influenced by the success or failure of their national counterparts, shifts in party strength in regional contests, the election successes of new parties such as the NPD in the late 1960s, the Greens since the 1980s and the PDS/*Die Linke* since 1990 or changes in the existing government coalitions in the *Länder* have strong repercussions on the national coalition.

This inquiry traces the formation of the *Länder* and the initial governments in the three western zones of Germany after 1945, the outcomes of the elections held through mid-2011 and the ministries formed in the various states, the nature of early and current electoral arrangements, their similarities and differences, their influence on regional voting behavior and the party system in the *Länder*, the outcomes of the seventeen general elections, the development of the party system on regional and national levels, noting trends, pertinent influences and areas of party dominance; the coalition patterns in the *Länder* and in the federal capital, the influence of state elections on the politics of the *Bundesrat* and national influences on the party composition of state governments and political developments in general from 1945 to 2011.

An investigation as broad as the study of some 200 postwar elections in the German *Länder* and seventeen for *Bundestag* representatives is not without its limitations. First, the information available on the subject is so considerable that only a small portion of it could be consulted for the study. Even that which was consulted could have served as the basis for a volume much larger than the present work had much detail not been left out. Second, the information examined is open to differing interpretations, and what is included in this inquiry obviously reflects the judgment of this particular author. The study recognizes a network of interdependencies which promotes a constant interaction between state and federal affairs. It presumes a vital interest by the national parties in influencing the outcomes of regional election contests and the party composition of the *Land* governments because of the important role played by the *Bundesrat* in national legislation, and it assumes the predominance of national over local issues in most *Land* election campaigns, but with local issues playing a significant role in some elections such as in the setbacks for the CSU in Bavaria in 2008 and the SPD in the January 2009 rerun contest in Hesse.

The author is greatly indebted to the statistical bureaus of the various *Länder*, to the parliamentary offices of the *Landtage*, to the Federal Statistical Office in Wiesbaden, to *Die Welt* newspaper in Hamburg, which allowed him access to its archival files going back to 1946, to the parliamentary library of the Hamburg *Bürgerschaft* under Uwe Weissert and Ute Bärschneider-Reese; to Gerhard Vaupel, former assistant city manager of Langenhagen, who was helpful in providing information on the early regional elections; to Prof. Dr. Joseph Nyomarkay of the University of Southern California for his encouragement in the early stages of the study; and to the late Richard Hingst, former mayor of Reinfeld, Germany, who gave him the initial inspiration to include state elections in any study of German politics. I am likewise extremely greatful to my wife, Anke, for her patience over the many years that this singular work was in progress.

The principal parties provided assistance by making available newspapers and booklets concerning their programs and activities. Material in this volume is supplemented by personal interviews with party officials and by direct correspondence with the directors of the *Land* statistical offices and with various governmental officials. Where discrepancies existed in statistical sources, figures provided by the *Land* statistical offices and the *Bundeswahlleiter* have been relied on. The author takes full responsibility for omissions and for the interpretations which appear in the study. It is hoped that the study will serve not only to broaden the understanding of a very important aspect of German politics, but to encourage more definitive investigations.

Lowell W. Culver
Chicago, Illinois, 2011

Glossary of German Political Parties

AUD	Association of Independent Germans
BCSV	Baden Christian Social People's Party (Baden affiliate of CDU)
BdD	Federation of Germans
BDV	Bremen Democratic People's Party (merged with FDP)
BHE	Refugee Party
BIW	*Bürger in Wut* (Angry Citizens) in Bremerhaven 2007-2011
BP	Bavarian Party
CDU	Christian Democratic Union
CNG	Christian National Community (in the Saar)
CSU	Christian Social Union (Bavarian affiliate of CDU)
CVP	Christian People's Party (in the Saar)
DDU	German Democratic Union (in the Saar)
DFU	German Peace Union
DG	German Association
DKP	German Conservative Party
DNS	German National Rally
DP	German Party, Democratic Party
DPS	Democratic Party of the Saar (Saar affiliate of the FDP)
DRP	German Reich Party; German Rightist Party prior to 1949
DSP	German Social Party (in Lower Saxony)
DVP	Democratic People's Party (FDP affiliate in Baden-Württemberg)
DVU	Democratic Peoples Union
FDP	Free Democratic Party
FSU	Free Social Union
FU	Federalist Union (formed by BP and ZP for 1957 general election)
FW	*Freie Wähler* (Free or Independent Voters in Bavaria and other states)
GB/BHE	All-German Bloc (merger of German Bloc and Refugee Party)
GDP	All-German Party (merger of German and Refugee parties)
GVP	All German People's Party
HB	Hamburg Bloc (Party alliance of CDU, FDP, DP and BHE in 1953 *Land* election in Hamburg)
KP	Communist Party (in the Saar)
KPD/KDP	German Communist Party (outlawed in 1956, but reinstated after 1967)
LP	Liberal Party
Die Linke	An amalgamation of the PDS and WASG in various states beginning in 2005
NLP	Lower Saxony State Party (German Party after 1947)
NPD	National Democratic Party

NU	Lower German Union (party alliance of CDU and DP formed in Lower Saxony in 1951)
Pirates	Founded in 2006 in opposition to Internet surveillance and barriers to network entry
PDS	Party of Democratic Socialism (successor of the SED)
Republicans	A right-extremist party which has run candidates since 1988 and gained representation in several states
RSF	Radical Social Freedom Party
Schill Party	Law and order party formed by Ronald Schill to contest the 2001 *Bürgerschaft* election in Hamburg
SED	Socialist Unity Party (Communist Party in Berlin and East Germany prior to 1990)
SHB	Schleswig-Holstein Bloc (DP and Schleswig-Holstein Union in 1954 *Land* election)
SPD	Social Democratic Party of Germany
SPS	Socialist Party of the Saar
SRP	Socialist Reich Party (outlawed in 1952)
SSW/SSV	South Schleswig Voters' Association (Danish minority party)
STATT Party	Formed to contest the 1993 *Bürgerschaft* election in Hamburg
SV	Social People's Service
SVP	Saarland People's Party
VBH	Hamburg Native Alliance (CDU, FDP and DKP alliance in 1949)
WASG	Electoral Alternative for Social Justice formed in 2005
WAV	Economic Reconstruction Association (in Bavaria)
WdF	Voters League of Victims of Bombing (in Bremen)
ZP	*Zentrum* or Center Party

The Road to Democracy in Germany:
The Role of State and National Elections, 1946-2011

Introduction

State (*Land*) and national politics in Germany are intertwined as in no other federal system. While general elections determine the party composition of the *Bundestag* and the coalition possibilities of the national government, *Land* contests define the party makeup of the several state parliaments and the resulting ministries, which, in turn, control the decisions of the upper house of the federal parliament, the *Bundesrat*. The constitution of the *Bundesrat* as a delegative body, consisting of members appointed by and directly responsible to the *Land* governments, rather than as a Senate-type chamber with representatives popularly elected and responsible to the people, as in the United States and Australia, means that its party ratio can be altered with any change in the composition of a regional government, whether resulting from a decline in party strength at the polls or a falling out of the factions forming a coalition in the absence of a majority party. Since the federal upper chamber has a virtually absolute veto on stipulated categories of legislation affecting *Land-Bund* relationships and a general suspensive veto power, the use of which can be overridden only by the requisite *Bundestag* majorities, control of the *Bundesrat* through control of state politics is an inevitable goal of the national parties (Merkle, 1959, 732-741). This objective is magnified by the fact that by the early 1990s, the proportion of *Bundestag* measures requiring *Bundesrat* approval had risen to nearly seventy percent (Walker, 1991: 22).

The particular nature of German federalism, which causes national policies to be administered by the *Land* governments in a legislative-executive relationship provides an added incentive for the national parties to influence the outcomes of regional contests, since each *Land* election, in effect, determines which party or party grouping will administer policies laid down by the federal government. The intertwining of policy formulation and implementation institutionalizes a mutual interdependence, promoting a form of intergovernmentalism and a bargaining relationship which is unique among federal systems (Merkle, 1959: 732-741; Smith 1992: 42). The linkages that have evolved and the accommodations often required to gain concurrence of territorial interests, however, have made all but incremental administrative and policy change in the German Federal Republic exceedingly difficult (Katzenstein, 1989: 81).

Although the *Länder* were accorded by the Basic Law of 1949 the power to legislate in a wide range of areas, either exclusively or concurrently with the federal government, the reality of the immediate postwar period had a strong centralizing influence, since the major issues facing the three western zones of the German state demanded a unified, national approach—the resettlement of some 13,000,000 refugees and expellees from the East, the replacement of destroyed housing and transportation facilities, factories and machinery, the rebuilding of the economy, financial disparities between the *Länder*, the problems created by the division of the country and the East-West split-- solutions to which required close cooperation between the two levels of government. These and questions concerning the future of Germany in Europe (rearmament, membership in international arrangements, reparations for the harm inflicted by the Third Reich, etc.) came to dominate both regional and national balloting after 1949. Since reunification in 1990, new issues of national and international import have arisen to influence voting decisions on the two levels, including the financial and social burden of integrating the former eastern provinces into the Federal Republic, how best to rein in the costs of an overextended welfare state, the competitiveness of Germany's high-wage economy in a global setting, the influence of the global financial crisis on the stability of the Euro, the integration of non-Christian minorities into the German State, right-extremism and the threat of international terrorism, the question of political asylum, the participation of Germany's armed forces in international police actions, the division of powers between *Bund* and *Länder* and disparities in financial resources between the states.

Because of the impact of national issues on regional balloting and the interspersal of *Land* elections between *Bundestag* contests, seldom falling on the same date, the voting for *Land* representatives tends to take on a plebiscitary character, in a kind of running referendum on the actions of the national parties. This plebiscitary role gives added significance to regional election outcomes in the German political system. To illustrate, the sixteenth *Bundestag* election was held September 18, 2005. There followed *Land* contests in Baden Württemberg, Rhineland-Palatinate and Saxony-Anhalt March 26, 2006; in Berlin and Mecklenburg-Vorpommern September 17, 2006; in Bremen May 13, 2007; in Hesse and Lower Saxony January 17, 2008; in Hamburg February 24, 2008; in Bavaria September 28, 2008; in Hesse (a rerun) January 18, 2009; in the Saar, Saxony and Thuringia August 30, 2009; and in Brandenburg and Schleswig-Holstein September 27, 2009, the same day as the seventeenth *Bundestag* balloting. The *Land* election in North Rhine-Westphalia took place May 9, 2010. There will be seven state elections during the course of 2011, the first taking place in Hamburg February 20, 2011.

Occurring as they do at varying intervals between national elections, and influenced by the electioneering of the national parties, *Land* elections have the effect of serving as a continual barometer of public opinion, indicating shifts in public sentiment within a particular *Land* since the last *Bundestag* or regional election or between two or more consecutive elections in different *Länder*. In their plebiscitary role, *Land* elections act as both validating and alarm mechanisms, indicating, on the one hand, approval for the policies of the state or national coalitions or of the actions of the individual parties, or, on the other, dissatisfaction within the body politic or with the actions of the state or national administrations, allowing sufficient time before the next general election for the ruling coalitions to seek corrective measures or for the opposition parties to exploit public dissatisfaction. Moves to link regional contests with general elections or to hold large numbers of *Land* elections at one time would undermine this valuable function of regional elections in the German political system.

Since state governments determine representation in the *Bundesrat*, their party composition is of considerable importance to the national parties. The relationship between *Land* elections and the control of *Bundesrat* majorities has encouraged the intervention of the national parties in regional affairs to a degree unknown in other federal systems, resulting in each poll in the *Länder* being at once a regional and a federal election (Culver, 1966: 305). Not only do large delegations from Berlin take an active part in regional election campaigns, but once negotiations on the formation of *Land* governments get underway, considerable pressure is exerted on the *Land* parties by their national counterparts to influence the party composition of the ministries. Agreements are sometimes forged prior to the election.

The significance of *Land* elections is readily appreciated when one considers the possible fate of many of Konrad Adenauer's (CDU Chancellor from 1949 to 1963) policies had he been faced with a hostile majority in the *Bundesrat*. It was for this reason that he was particularly active in attempting to coordinate regional and federal politics and to force the coalition of *Land* ministries that replicated the Bonn cabinet as far as party make-up was concerned (Heidenheimer, 1958: 809-828). It mattered little that the largest party in the *Land* parliament was often frozen out of the government. Willy Brandt (SPD) and Helmut Schmidt (SPD) were less successful in creating supportive coalitions in the *Länder* and faced *Bundesrat* majorities controlled by the opposition throughout their chancellorships, and Helmut Kohl (CDU) had to contend with a *Bundesrat* controlled by the opposition Social Democratic Party during much of his tenure in office. Gerhard Schröder (SPD), federal Chancellor from 1998 to 2005, came to office with a comfortable *Bundesrat* majority, but a series of setbacks in regional election contests following the 2002 general election placed the upper house in the hands of the CDU and its allies in early 2003. The coalition of the two major parties in Berlin between 2005 and 2009 insured a *Bundesrat* majority on most questions. At the end of 2010 the CDU/CSU/FDP national coalition in Berlin could count on only 31 of the *Bundesrat's* 69 votes. Support for the national coalition was further eroded by the party turnover in Baden-Württemberg following the March 27, 2011 *Land* election.

The interaction between national and regional politics in Germany is clearly indicated in the pre-election campaigns in the *Länder*, in the electoral decisions, in the coalition negotiations which follow, and in attempts to secure support in *Bundesrat* decisions, even from party coalitions which do not reflect the make-up of the national government. While the plebiscitary character of *Land* elections has tended to undermine the autonomy of regional politics by causing the fate of regional parties and governments to be determined more by the success or failure of their national counterparts than by their own efficiencies/deficiencies, in the interplay between the two levels, the influence is far from being one way. Shifts in party strength at the polls, the electoral successes of new parties or changes in existing government coalitions in the *Länder* likewise have had strong repercussions on politics in Bonn and Berlin. The decision of the Christian Democratic Union (CDU) in April 1963 to settle the question of a successor to Konrad Adenauer as quickly as possible, for example, was precipitated by a series of party setbacks following the 1961 *Bundestag* election, and the formation of a coalition between the Union parties and the Socialists in Bonn in 1966 was partially influenced by the successes of the right-wing National Democratic Party (NPD) in Hesse and Bavaria in November of that year. Likewise was Chancellor Gerhard Schröder's decision to call early *Bundestag* elections following a series of party setbacks in regional contests, most notably in North Rhine Westphalia in May 2005, after the 2002 national election.

The efforts of the national parties to control *Land* election outcomes have, however, at times, so distorted the election results that they could hardly be called valid expressions of trends in public sentiment. This was clearly the case in the 1962 election for the Bavarian *Landtag* in which the CSU won an absolute parliamentary majority of seats in spite of the implication of its chairman, Franz Josef Strauss, then Federal Defense Minister, in the Spiegel Affair, which involved the arrest of several editors of the news periodical *Der Spiegel* on charges of treason concerning the publication of certain military information (*Die Welt*, October 28/29, 1962). During much of the Adenauer era, attempts to control *Bundesrat* majorities often meant freezing the Social Democratic Party out of government coalitions even when it was the leading parliamentary party in the *Landtag*. The SPD, however, turned the tables on the CDU/CSU in several states during that same period.

The existence of parliamentary systems in the *Länder* makes possible changes in the party make-up of the regional governments long after their initial formation. A party may withdraw from the coalition and make common cause with the former opposition to form a new government because of disagreement on local issues, or the move may be precipitated by party disagreements in the federal capital. Arnold Heidenheimer, for example, describes the upset of the government of Karl Arnold (CDU) in North Rhine-Westphalia in 1956 following the withdrawal of the FDP from the coalition, a move precipitated by a dispute with the Christian Democrats in Bonn over a national electoral law (Heidenheimer, 1958: 822-23). Whether a rupture in the *Land* coalition is precipitated by disagreement on local issues or by political developments in the nation's capital, the party ratio in the *Bundesrat* is altered thereby.

The coordination efforts of the national parties in their attempts to control *Bundesrat* majorities have encouraged a strengthening of the central party organizations at the expense of *Land* affiliates. The coincidence of interests between the upper and lower houses of the federal parliament during the Adenauer era reflected the degree to which the regional branches of the CDU conformed to the wishes of the party headquarters. This concentration of power during that period, however, was not without its benefits. It tended to limit the number of parties gaining representation in legislative bodies in spite of electoral systems which are basically proportional in nature. Because the formation of *Bundesrat* majorities requires the creation of large followings in all of the *Länder* and cooperation with other parties to build a government, the parties have been forced not only to maintain nationwide organizations and programs capable of appealing to the diverse make-up of the separate state electorates, but to modify their positions on many issues in order to maintain cohesiveness within *Land* coalitions. Parties lacking national organization and appealing to narrow ideological, religious or group interests have little chance of gaining control of *Bundesrat* majorities, let alone gaining representation in *Land* parliaments, as voters have ordinarily limited their votes to parties with national representation. Parties lacking national appeal or championing narrow causes, such as the National Democratic Party (NPD) or the German People's Union (DVU), may gain legislative representation in individual states, but they will be unable to gain control of the federal upper house.

The all-encompassing nature of the CDU early brought it into a position of dominance on both the national and regional levels, and, to remain competitive, other parties were forced to modify their programs to appeal to a broader electorate. The Social Democrats altered their party program in 1959, but were unable to prevent the CDU and its partner party in Bavaria, the CSU, from dominating every national balloting until 1972. The ability of the SPD to gain substantially larger followings in regional than in national elections, however, enabled it to control a number of *Land* governments beginning with the first postwar elections, and, by 1965, to achieve a position of near parity in votes with the Union parties on the *Land* level. It was however, unsuccessful in participating in the national government until 1966 and in gaining full control of the *Bundesrat* until 1990.

Reunification has significantly altered the political landscape in Germany. With the accession of the five eastern provinces to the Federal Republic in 1990, membership in the *Bundesrat* was increased to 69 members, nineteen of them representing the five new *Länder*. To offset the potential power of the less-populated eastern states in the *Bundesrat*, each of the four most populous *Länder*, North Rhine-Westphalia, Bavaria, Baden-Württemberg and Lower Saxony, all in the west, was awarded an additional vote, so that, together, with 24 of the 69 *Bundesrat* representatives, they would be able to block the passage of any measure requiring a two-thirds majority vote.

For the first forty years of the *Bundesrepublik* the outcomes of the election contests in the West German *Länder* and skillful coalition building enabled the CDU and its partners to dominate the *Bundesrat* even during the 1969-1982 period when the SPD was in the ascendancy in Bonn. From June 1990, after the

Socialists had replaced the Union-led government in Lower Saxony and gained the four *Bundesrat* votes of a united Berlin, and the October elections in the five eastern provinces, the SPD and its partners were able to take control of the *Bundesrat* for the first time. However, by gaining the upper hand in four of the five first elections held in the new *Länder* Union control was reinstated in the *Bundesrat*. That control was short lived, as Socialist successes in Hesse, Rhineland-Palatinate and Hamburg in the first half of 1991 enabled SPD-led governments to reclaim a majority in the federal upper chamber, a majority which the Socialists were able to hold until 2002. The alternation in control of *Bundesrat* majorities back and forth several times during the past two decades as a result of the volatility of *Land* election outcomes and reunification, indicates the difficulty in maintaining upper house majorities in today's altered political environment. Encouraged by reunification, there appears to be a growing readiness on the part of *Land* parties to cooperate among themselves regardless of the party line-up in Berlin, a tendency enhanced by the growing acceptability of the Greens and PDS/*Die Linke* as a coalition partner. Yet, even without a majority in the *Bundesrat*, the CDU/CSU-led federal government twice overcame Social Democratic dominance in 1992 by offering special favors to SPD-led *Land* governments (Sturm, 1993: 120, 124). Where regional interests are concerned, particularly in the distribution of federal monies, *Land* governments, regardless of party make-up, appear increasingly willing to go their own way.

Land elections provide the basis on which *Land* governments are formed and *Bundesrat* majorities built, and regional governments, whatever their party make-up, have the power to curb centralizing tendencies through their voice in the *Bundesrat*. However, the challenges of foreign policy, technological change, globalization, European Union expansion and mandates, protecting against acts of terrorism, financial disparities between the *Länder* and the need to resolve other problems of national scope, including fluctuating levels of unemployment, efforts to restructure the economy and the country's welfare system, the financial costs of reunification, and the burden of integrating both new and old immigrants exert strong centralizing pressures. *Land* elections will continue to play an important role in shaping German national policy in the coming decades, as they have in the past, by serving as expressions of public sentiment between national elections and by determining the party composition of the guardian of *Land* interests, the *Bundesrat*.

CHAPTER I

The Creation of the *Länder*

With the collapse of the Third Reich in 1945, the governments of France, the United States, the United Kingdom and the Soviet Union assumed supreme authority over Germany, and, in a joint declaration signed June 5, 1945, divided the country into four zones of occupation, one allotted to each of the four Powers. At the same time, Berlin was placed under four-Power control (*Documents*, 1955: 35). Under the Control Machinery Agreement, also dated June 5, 1945, each Commander-in-Chief became supreme in his own zone, and the four together constituted the Control Council, which, under instructions from their respective governments, was to be the supreme authority in matters affecting Germany as a whole. Decisions of the Council had to be unanimous, and the Council was to "ensure appropriate uniformity of action by the Commander-in-Chief in their respective zones of occupation and will reach agreed decisions on the chief questions affecting Germany as a whole" (*Documents*, 1955: 36-37).

What became the Soviet zone of occupation consisted of the eastern portion of Germany to the Oder-Neisse Line and included the five *Länder* of Brandenburg, Mecklenburg, Saxony, Saxony-Anhalt and Thuringia, formed between the end of 1946 and the beginning of 1947, but dissolved in 1952 and replaced by fourteen administrative districts. The northwest portion of Germany, comprising the present *Länder* of Schleswig-Holstein, Hamburg, Lower Saxony and North Rhine-Westphalia, was placed under British control. The American zone of occupation in the southern part of Germany included the *Länder* of Bavaria, Hesse, Württemberg-Baden, and, after January 21, 1947, Bremen. Prior to that date, Bremen had been part of the British zone of occupation without *Land* status, although it had been recognized as an American enclave in order that U.S. forces should have a North Sea port of their own (*Germany, 1947-1949*, 1950: 152). A French zone of occupation was created in the southwest out of the American and British areas, and consisted of Rhineland-Palatinate, Baden and Württemberg-Hohenzollern. The last two mentioned *Länder* were fused with Württemberg-Baden of the American zone in 1952 to form the present *Land* Baden-Württemberg following a plebiscite.

The Saar was also a part of the French zone of occupation, but France proceeded to effect a permanent separation of the Saar from Germany, granting the area an "international" political status inside an economic union with France, and undertaking responsibility for its foreign and external security. The Saar, in effect, ceased to be a German *Land*, with both the Americans and the British giving tacit consent to the French moves (*Documents*, 1955: 185). Following a plebiscite held October 23, 1955, in which the Saarlanders by a 67.7 percent majority rejected the European Statute which would have continued the Saar's autonomous international status until the conclusion of a peace treaty, the French declared their readiness to start negotiations with the West German government on a final settlement of the Saar question. In the *Land* election of December 18, 1955, the three parties associated with the *Heimatbund*, the CDU, SPD and the Democratic Party of the Saar, obtain 33 of the fifty seats in the *Land* parliament, and on January 31, 1956, the Saar *Landtag* resolved in a declaration of principles the attachment of the Saarland to the Federal Republic. The question of reunification was settled in the treaty of October 17, 1956 between France and West Germany, and on January 1, 1957, the Saar became politically incorporated into the Federal Republic with *Land* status, although economic ties with France continued until July 1959 (*The German State*, 1964: 43-44).

Of the *Länder* created in the three Western zones of Germany, only Bavaria, Bremen and Hamburg had roots in the past, Bavaria claiming a thousand year tradition and a previous status as an independent kingdom, Bremen and Hamburg as Hanseatic cities each dating from the Middle Ages. The remaining *Länder* were largely artificial creations, although Lower Saxony could point to its long Guelphic territorial and dynastic tradition. Lower Saxony was formed in 1946 from the former *Länder* Brünswick, Oldenburg, and Schaumburg-Lippe and the former Prussian Province of Hanover. Schleswig-Holstein had a tradition of a more complex kind, living in personal union with the Danish kingdom from 1460 to 1848, and, after 1866, governed as a Prussian province. Never previously having *Land* status, Schleswig-Holstein became a separate state entity for the first time in 1946. North Rhine-Westphalia was created in 1946 from the Prussian province of Westphalia, the governmental districts of Köln, Aachen and Düsseldorf (North Rhine), and the former *Land* Lippe. Hesse was formed in 1945 from that portion of the former *Land* Hesse on the right bank of the Rhine and the former Prussian provinces of Kurhesse and Hesse-Nassau with the exception of the four rural districts of Oberwesterwald, Unterwesterwald, Unterlahnkreis and St. Goarshausen which form part of the *Land* Rhineland-Palatinate. Other than the four rural districts just mentioned, Rhineland-Palatinate, created in 1946, includes the territory of the former *Land* Hesse on the left bank of the Rhine, the Palatinate and the governmental districts of Trier and Koblenz of the former Prussian Rhine province. The Saar included the Saar province in the Saar district as defined in the Treaty of Versailles and enlarged in 1946 by the addition of a number of adjacent rural districts of the former Prussian Rhine province in the northeast which contained lateral railways serving the Saar industries. The most artificial *Land* boundaries were found in the southwest part of Germany. When it was decided to carve a French zone from the original American and British areas, the upper portions of the former *Länder* of Baden and Württemberg were united into the *Land* Württemberg-Baden and placed in the American zone, and the two truncated *Länder* which became known as Baden and Württemberg-Hohenzollern, enlarged by the addition of the former Prussian enclave of Hohenzollern, were placed under French administration. The American attitude to the arrangement was determined entirely by the concern of the military authorities for communications and supplies, with German tradition and feelings counting for little. The division was satisfactory neither from an historical nor from an economic point of view, and was rectified in 1952 with the merger of the three *Länder* into the present *Land* of Baden-Württemberg.

Following the total military defeat of Germany in the Second World War, there was no government in exile to assume the responsibilities of government nor any group of officials who could be trusted to speak for the German people, making military government and occupation inevitable for an indefinite period of time. The Occupation Powers approached the task of reconstituting the political and administrative structure of the country in widely differing fashions as regards both to pace and method adopted. The Soviets were the first to encourage the resumption of political activity by ordering the establishment of anti-fascist parties and free trade unions in their zone and sector of Berlin on June 10, 1945 (*Documents*, 1955: 37-38). In July of 1945 various zone level administrations, later to be known as Central Administrations, were established for the coordination and restoration of the economy, transportation and communication services, and health and education matters (*Documents*, 1955: 64-66). By October 1945, the provincial and *Länder* administrations were given the right to issue laws and decrees having legal force (*Documents*, 1955: 82-83). As later developments proved, the steps were not taken for the purpose of establishing democratic institutions, but to ensure the complete domination of the Soviet zone population by Soviet authorities.

The original intention of the Western allies was to progress slowly in the reconstruction of German society, to forbid political parties for the first few years and to fill all political posts in government with independents. However, the actions of the Soviets in their zone and Berlin caused the Western Powers to make similar, yet uncoordinated, moves in their zones, not wishing to appear less democratic than the Russians. As early as May 28, 1945, the American Military Government for the *Land* of Bavaria set up a government, the first *Land* government to be established after the collapse of the Third Reich. In early September political parties were authorized in the American zone, and, on September 19, 1945, the creation of the *Länder* of Bavaria, Hesse and Württemberg-Baden was formalized by the American Military Government's Proclamation No. 2. In November, the American authorities transferred to the communes (*Gemeinde*) and counties (*Kreise*) the management of their own affairs.

The first political elections of the post war period were held in the American zone in January 1946 for the representative bodies of communities of less than 20,000 inhabitants and in April and May of 1946 for county and municipal councils. Delegates to the constituent assemblies of Bavaria, Hesse and Württemberg-Baden were popularly elected the middle of 1946 for the purpose of formulating constitutions for their respective *Länder*. These elections, held June 30, 1946, were the first *Land*-wide political contests of the post-war period. Before the end of 1946, *Land* constitutions had been adopted by the several constituent assemblies in the American zone and approved by plebiscite.[1] Elections for the first *Land* parliaments were held November 24 in Württemberg-Baden, and December 1 in Bavaria and Hesse, the same day as the constitutional plebiscites, making possible the formation of responsible governments on a parliamentary basis in these *Länder*. With the transfer of Bremen to American control, the *Bürgerschaft* or city council elected October 13, 1946, under the direction of the British Military Government, served as a constituent assembly and formulated a *Land* constitution which it adopted September 15, 1947. The constitution was ratified in a plebiscite held October 12, 1947, the same day that Bremen elected its first parliament under *Land* status. The October 12th election was necessitated by the incorporation of Bremerhaven (formerly Wesermünde) into Bremen. The size of the *Bürgerschaft* was raised from 80 to 100 representatives to accommodate the twenty delegates granted to Bremerhaven.

The British authorities were more reluctant than the Americans to establish elected representative bodies, and relied for a longer period on appointed officials from among the newly-constituted parties to serve as mayors and council members. The abolition of the State of Prussia cleared the way for the territorial reorganization of the area under British control and the creation in the second half of 1946 of the *Länder* of Lower Saxony, North Rhine-Westphalia and Schleswig-Holstein. The City of Hamburg was granted *Land* status. The first elections in the British zone were not held until September 15, 1946; however, the British had been the first of the occupying powers to establish councils at the two levels of local government (*Gemeinde* and *Kreise*) by appointing members from among the licensed political parties. The first elections in the rural areas and small towns were followed October 13, 1946 by elections in the large cities of the zone, including Bremen and Hamburg, and for seats on the county councils (*Kreistage*). *Land* parliaments were elected in Lower Saxony, North Rhine-Westphalia and Schleswig-Holstein April 20, 1947. The framing of permanent constitutions for the *Länder* was not considered by the British to be of primary importance until after the formation of an interzonal government.[2]

The French followed the British example of restoring political responsibility to the Germans on a step-by-step basis from the bottom up, also moving more cautiously than the Americans. However, the French were the last to authorize political parties and continued direct rule long after the British were governing through appointed officials. The French conducted the first elections in their zone September 15, 1946 for representative bodies in the rural areas and councils in all municipalities, regardless of size, followed October 13, 1946 by elections for county representative bodies. The results of these two series of elections determined the composition of the constituent assemblies in the French zone *Länder*. Delegates, rather than being popularly elected as in the American zone, were chosen indirectly on a quota basis by the municipal and county councils, of which the delegates themselves had to be members in addition to holding membership in one of the licensed parties. These assemblies reflected roughly the party composition of the local governments. For example, the 127 member body elected in Rhineland-Palatinate consisted of 70 CDU, 41 SPD, nine Communist, five Social People's Service and two Liberal Party delegates, corresponding to their relative strengths in the *Kreis* elections of October 13, 1946 (*Rheinland-Pfalz*, 1948: 21).

The constitutions drafted by the assemblies of the French zone *Länder* were submitted to referendum and approved in Baden, Rhineland-Palatinate and Württemberg-Hohenzollern May 18, 1947, the same day that the first *Land* parliaments in these *Länder* were elected. In the Saar, elections for all local representative bodies were held September 12, 1946, followed October 5, 1947, by the first *Land* level election. The latter election, in addition to selecting a *Land* parliament, served as an indirect referendum on a proposed constitution formulated by a constitutional commission headed by Johannes Hoffmann. The *Landtag*, consisting of an overwhelming number of representatives of those parties favoring the constitution, approved the document December 15, 1947. The document was strictly separatist in nature, providing for the economic integration of the area with France, while establishing autonomy in every respect with the exception of defense and foreign affairs which were a French responsibility. No provision, however, was made for the Saar's incorporation into France. This status continued until 1957 when the Saar was reintegrated into the West German state.

Berlin held a position different in many respects from the other areas under occupation. Not only was she divided into four sectors, each of which was under the jurisdiction of one of the Powers, Great Britain, France, the Soviet Union and the United States, but policies concerning the whole of Berlin required the unanimous concurrence of the Allied *Kommandatura*.

The Red Army had completed the conquest of the city on May 2, 1945, and for two months remained the unrestricted master of the city. By the time American, British and French troops had taken over their sectors of occupation in early July, the Berlin administration was largely staffed by personnel reflecting Soviet interests. On August 13, 1946, a temporary constitution for Berlin was promulgated by the four Powers, and on October 20, 1946, the first and only post-war election to be held in all sectors until 1990 took place. The crushing defeat of the Soviet-sponsored Socialist Unity Party (SED) and the futility of Communist efforts to effect a merger with the Social Democratic Party before and after the election broke Communist domination of the city. This led the Soviets to resort to a policy of frustrating the functioning of the

Allied Control Council and the *Kommandatura* for Berlin by vetoing their resolutions, and, finally, in 1948, after having walked out of both of these bodies, to attempt to force the Western Allies out of Berlin by imposing a blockade of the city.[3]

Repeated obstructionism in the municipal parliament and the threatening of elected parliament members by Communist demonstrators eventually forced the Berlin parliament to transfer its seat from the eastern to the western part of the city, without its complement of 26 SED members.[4] On November 30, 1948, the Communists set up a new municipal parliament in East Berlin, in direct contravention of the city constitution, and refused to allow the eastern part of the city to participate in the parliamentary elections of December 5, 1948, made necessary by the expiration of the two-year term of parliament members. The split of the city into two distinct parts was now complete.

Both the Federal Basic Law of 1949 and the Berlin constitution of September 1, 1950 expressly stipulated that Berlin was a constituent part of the Federal Republic as it then existed. A decision of the Federal Constitutional Court in May 1957 further asserted that as far as legal interpretation was concerned, Berlin's constitutional status was that of a *Land* within the Federal Republic (*The German State*, 1960: 60-61). In spite of these interpretations, there was a reservation that Berlin would not be governed through the *Bund*. In their statement approving the Berlin Constitution of 1950, the Western Allies specified that Berlin would possess none of the attributes of a *Land* and that the provisions of any Federal law would apply to Berlin only after they had been voted upon by the Berlin parliament and passed as a Berlin law (*Documents*, 1955: 509-510). Thus, although Berlin was treated as a *Land* of the Federal Republic and was integrated into the West German economy, her Four Power status prevented her from becoming a part of the *Bund* until 1990. The 22 delegates which Berlin sent to the *Bundestag* and her four representatives in the *Bundesrat* were not entitled to cast a vote prior to reunification.[5]

Months before the first *Land* parliaments were elected and governments responsible to them established, steps were taken by the Western Allies to devolve a wide range of powers to those proposed governments. In its directive of September 30, 1946, the American Military Government outlined the new relationships which would come into force between it and the German political authorities following the election of *Land* governments and the adoption of *Land* constitutions. The directive specified those areas in which occupation policies were to be considered "as superior to the authority of any German governmental agency, and to both statutory and constitutional law," the specific occupation purposes of the U.S. Government, reservations concerning governmental forms, including the establishment of an independent judiciary and a federated structure, and the right to "resume at any time full occupation powers in the event the purposes of the occupation are jeopardized." Military functions would be limited to observation, inspection, reporting and advising, and the disapproval of only such legislation as was found inconsistent with the objectives of the military occupation (*Documents*, 1955: 163-166). In effect, full legislative, executive and judicial power was granted to the American zone *Länder*, limited only by international agreements to which the United States was a party, quadripartite legislation and powers reserved to Military Government in order to effectuate basic policies of occupation. These conditions were further clarified in Military Government Proclamation No. 4, dated March 1, 1947 (*Germany*, 1950: 157-158).

The powers granted by the British to the *Länder* in their zone were more circumscribed than those passed on by the American authorities. The most important document for the devolution of powers to the Germans in the British zone was the British Military Ordinance No. 57 of December 1, 1946. This document stipulated four categories of subject areas: those matters which would be excluded from the competence of *Land* legislatures, those for which emergency powers would be exercised by the Military Government, those temporarily excluded from the competence of *Land* legislatures and those incumbent on *Land* legislatures. With respect to legislation on those subjects within the competence of *Land* governments, approval of the local Regional Commissioner was required before it could become effective (Ebsworth, 1960: 64). In general, military government legislation was limited to those matters intended to be reserved for the future central government, such as foreign relations, defense and currency, those subjects of an emergency nature such as price control, refugees and reparations, and temporarily excluded subjects as rationing and the planning of food production (*Documents*, 1955: 192-195).

The French took far longer to hand over important powers to the Germans than either the Americans or the British. Power of the *Länder* to legislate, in spite of Ordinance No. 95, was at first so restricted as to cause their governments to serve practically as executive organs of the occupying power. Moreover, the legislature had to accept that even the discussion of certain problems was forbidden (Arendt, 1948: 8 and *Documents*, 1955: 231-233).

With the completion of the first *Landtag* elections in the latter part of 1946 and the first part of 1947, the establishment of politically responsible governments in the *Länder*, and the circumscribed devolution of powers to the Germans by the Military governments, the *Länder* became the highest level of viable government. These state entities now concentrated their efforts on the creation of a unified West German State, a goal which was realized in 1949.

Endnotes to Chapter I

1 Württemberg-Baden's constitution was adopted by the constituent assembly October 24, 1946 and approved by the electorate November 24, 1946. The constituent assembly of Bavaria adopted the *Land* constitution October 26, 1946, and in Hesse the constituent assembly adopted a draft constitution October 29, 1946. The constitutions of both Bavaria and Hesse were ratified by their respective electorates December 1, 1946.

2 In contrast to the other zones, with the exception of Bremen, the constitutions of the British zone were formulated by the *Landtag* of their respective *Länder* rather than by

assemblies elected specifically for the purpose. The constitution of Schleswig-Holstein was approved December 13, 1949, that of North Rhine-Westphalia by plebiscite June 18, 1950, following adoption by the *Landtag* June 6, 1950, that of Lower Saxony April 13, 1951, and that of Hamburg June 6, 1952. Brief, provisional documents, however, had been in effect in these *Länder* prior to the adoption of permanent instruments. The absence of permanent constitutions in no way hindered the smooth functioning of government in the British zone *Länder* in this early period.

3 One of the Soviet vetoes prevented Professor Ernst Reuter in August 1947 from taking office as the city's Lord Mayor.

4 The move took place September 6, 1948. In reply to Marshal Sokolovsky's letter of November 29, 1948 concerning developments in Berlin, the Western Military Governors advised that "the actions of the Soviet authorities in permitting the disruption of the City Assembly by hooligan elements, their arbitrary dismissal of a number of duly-elected city officials without the consent of the commandants of the three western sectors, and their abandonment of the Allied *Kommandatura*, together with innumerable other unilateral breaches of the quadripartite arrangements for Berlin, have demonstrated the intention of the Soviet authorities to divide the city and to prevent the exercise of democratic rights and liberties in their own sector" (*Documents*, 1955: 347-348).

5 Prior to 1990 Berlin's 22 observers in the *Bundestag* were not elected directly as were other *Bundestag* representatives, but appointed by the Berlin parliament in proportion to the respective strength of the parties in that body. In the course of the arrangement whereby the *Länder* Heads of Government took it in turn to be President of the *Bundesrat*, Willy Brandt held that position during the 1957-1958 parliamentary year, Klaus Schütz 1967-1968, Dietrich Stobbe 1978-1979 and Walter Momper 1989-1990.

CHAPTER II

The First *Land* and *Bundestag* Elections

The 1946-1947 Elections in the American, British and French Zones

Scarcely three months after the ending of totalitarian rule in Germany, the Allied Powers in the Potsdam Declaration of August 2, 1945 committed themselves to a policy of restoration of German political life as rapidly as possible by lifting the ban on political activities and reconstituting local self-government on democratic principles as a means of preparing the Germans for political responsibility at higher levels. In accordance with the Declaration's statement on political principles:

> Local self-government shall be restored throughout Germany on democratic principles and, in particular, through elective councils as rapidly as is consistent with military security and the purposes of the occupation;

> All democratic political parties with rights of assembly and of public discussion shall be allowed and encouraged throughout Germany;

> Representative and elective principles shall be introduced into regional, provincial and state (*Land*) administration as rapidly as may be justified by the successful application of these principles in local self-government (*Documents*, 1955: 44).

The Soviets had already in June removed restrictions on the formation of anti-fascist parties and trade unions in their zone of occupation and Berlin, encouraging the organization and the development of a party press, while limiting the number of parties to four and directing their activity along lines desired by the Soviet authorities, including the forced fusion of Communist and Socialist parties. Hence, at Potsdam, the Western Allies found themselves faced with a *fait accompli* as far as Berlin and the Soviet zone were concerned.

The first parties in the American zone were authorized early in September 1945 with the British following a few days later. The French, however, did not officially lift the ban on political parties until December 13, 1945, although they had never taken the early prohibition on political activity seriously. France strictly limited the number of political parties which could be formed in her zone and closely regulated all expression of a political nature. She was motivated by a determination to prevent potential "anti-French" elements from exercising political power and to erect strong semi-autonomous *Länder*. In the early period of the occupation, political leaders were occasionally prevented from leaving the zone and others prohibited from entering it (Pollock, 1947: 202). Until July 1947 France refused to sanction affiliation of parties in her zone with parties in other zones; in the Saar this prohibition was kept in force for a decade.

The British relaxed prohibitions on political activities rapidly, not only allowing regional party organizations at an early stage, but taking the initiative in licensing party newspapers, considered indispensable to the development of viable political movements. The refusal of the American Military Government to follow the British example in its zone was a constant source of friction with the political parties in the early period of the occupation. In contrast to the French, the British placed no limitation on the number of political parties which could be formed, and even licensed some right-wing groups which could be classified as Neo-Nazi. It was felt that parties of this sort would draw off the less reputable leaders who had infiltrated the major parties. The British worked closely with the newly formed parties, especially with the SPD, whose leaders showed considerable willingness to cooperate with the military authorities, and devolved limited responsibility to the appointed local governments at an early stage.

Political groups were free to organize in the American zone if their character did not otherwise prohibit it. Parties whose programs did not call for a democratic form of government or whose activities were ascertained as militaristic, undemocratic, hostile to the United States and/or to Allied purposes, or prejudicial to military security and the maintenance of order would be refused licenses or have them revoked, as the case may be, by the Military Government. Political parties whose primary aim was judged to be the furtherance of expellee and refugee interests were prohibited in all zones, the Allied position being that the refugees and expellees should be assimilated into the other parties, making a refugee "interest" party unnecessary.

The general economic situation, the indifference on the part of the German masses toward anything political and the contempt for political parties did little to stimulate the development of party activity in the months immediately following the lifting of the ban. Few Germans could see the efficacy of political action under military government rule. After all, what could the political parties do about the acute problems of food, fuel, shelter, clothing and employment? The death of qualified and experienced leadership and the discouragement and disillusionment of those who survived the Nazi period, in addition to the absence of a party press in the American and French zones, likewise handicapped the organizational efforts of the political parties (Moscowitz, 1946: 535-561).

Out of this atmosphere of lethargy and indifference four major parties emerged, the Christian Democratic Union (Christian Social Union in Bavaria), the Social Democratic Party (SPD), the Communist Party (KPD) and the Liberals. In addition to these four, which were authorized in all three Western zones, there were a number of minor parties whose organizations usually did not extend beyond a single *Land*, such as the Economic Reconstruction Association (WAV) in Bavaria and the South Schleswig Association (SSV), party of the Danish minority in Schleswig-Holstein.

The oldest of the newly licensed parties was the SPD which furthered a program of social justice, civil liberties and responsible control of the basic industries through public ownership. It found its major source of strength among the industrial workers. The Communists, which were often among the first to obtain their licenses in the various zones, stressed close cooperation with the Soviet Union, social justice, public ownership of industry and working class unity. Realizing the weakness of its position, the major effort of the Communist Party in 1946 was to effect a merger with the Social Democratic Party. Although accomplished in the Soviet zone and Soviet sector of Berlin, merger in the Western zones was vigorously opposed by socialist leaders such as Kurt Schumacher, and Communist efforts failed miserably. Twelve years of constant anti-Communist propaganda and the conduct of the Red Army in the Eastern parts of Germany and Berlin from which many Germans had fled proved to be major liabilities to the growth of the party in spite of a noble effort of resistance during the Nazi period.

The most loosely organized, and, at first, the weakest of the four parties to be licensed in all zones, was a group of diverse *Land* organizations known as the Liberal Democratic Party in Hesse, the Democratic People's Party in Württemberg-Baden and Württemberg-Hohenzollern, the Democratic Party in Baden and Rhineland-Palatinate, and the Free Democratic Party in Bavaria, Bremen and all four *Länder* of the British zone.[1] This grouping, now known as the Free Democratic Party (FDP), purported to be heir of the liberal tradition of the old German Democratic Party, emphasizing the rights of private property and curtailment of church influence in public affairs. Although, in general, standing to the right of the CDU, its degree of conservatism varied considerably from *Land* to *Land* due to the party's federalistic character. Its appeal was mainly to Protestants, particularly to the merchant and professional classes and, in some *Länder*, to farmers, limiting its ability to attract a large following.

What was to become the most important single party in the early postwar period, the Christian Democratic Union (Christian Social Union in Bavaria), had its origins in efforts to establish a basis of cooperation between Catholic and Protestant groups and, at the same time, to thwart the revival of the Center Party in any form because of that party's role in granting powers to the Nazis in 1933 and its purely Catholic character. The party advocated a Christian basis for politics, supported the institution of private property and rejected totalitarianism in any form. As a federation of diverse elements, Catholics and Protestants, farmers, industrial workers and businessmen, factional rifts were to plague the party; yet herein rest its strength. It could not base its appeal on narrow philosophies of life, religious creeds or class or regional differences and still survive as a major party. In effect, it took on the character of Anglo-American parties concerned with the achievement of specific political purposes and compromised its differences to achieve the widest possible base of support.

Four minor parties are also worthy of mention: the *Zentrum*, German Party and South Schleswig Association in the British zone and the Economic Reconstruction Association in the American zone. The post World War II *Zentrum* (Center Party) was made up of those pre-1933 adherents of the party who did not join the CDU. Representing the left wing of the old *Zentrum*, it laid more emphasis on social policy than the CDU and favored such measures as the socialization of basic industries. Although authorized throughout the British zone, the strongholds of the party were in the Ruhr and Rhineland where it gained considerable support from Catholic industrial workers. The South Schleswig Association (SSV), later known as the South Schleswig Voters' Association (SSW), was authorized only in Schleswig-Holstein and represented the interests of the Danish minority. The Lower Saxony State Party, renamed the German Party (DP) in 1947 to widen its appeal, was founded in 1945 to carry on the traditions of the German-Hanovarian Party. Although originally a conservative agrarian party with a following limited to Lower Saxony, as it spread to other North German *Länder* under the DP label, it became the political home of numerous right-extremist elements. The Economic Reconstruction Association (WAV), authorized only in Bavaria, had no visible roots in the pre-Hitler past. Formed in 1945 by Alfred Loritz, it appealed to dissatisfied elements of the Bavaria lower-middle class and at first attracted many refugee adherents because of the party's demand for restoration of the pre-war German boundaries in the East (Office of the U.S. High Commission for Germany, 1950: 13-14).

The parties were given their first opportunity to exercise their primary function, the organization and holding of elections, when on October 17, 1945, General Lucius Clay, Deputy Military Governor, announced that elections for local representative bodies would be held in the American zone *Länder* in January 1946. In making his announcement, General Clay rejected the requests of German political leaders, including the three American zone Minister Presidents, that the elections be postponed until there had been adequate preparation for them (*New York Times*, January 21, 1946).

The first elections were held in two parts, the balloting on January 20, 1946, being limited to only seventeen *Landkreise* (rural districts) of less than 5,000 inhabitants in Hesse, while the elections a week later involved all communities of less than 20,000 inhabitants in Bavaria and Württemberg-Baden and 22 rural districts in Hesse which had not cast ballots the previous week. The electoral systems for these elections were left to the Germans to decide, resulting in the reintroduction of the arrangements which had been employed under the Weimar Republic with minor amendments in some cases. This meant the return of a proportional system in Hesse; however, Bavaria and Württemberg-Baden revived a multiple vote system which had been introduced into those *Länder* after the First World War.[2] The term of office for communal councilors was two years, with their numbers dependent on the size of the town. Campaigning was done mainly at small meetings and by door-to-door canvassing. Although campaign posters and handbills were permitted by the American Military Government, the lack of paper prevented their widespread use.

The results of these first elections indicated considerable differences in the political orientation of the three American zone *Länder*. While the Christian Social Union won an overwhelming victory in Bavaria, its sister party, the CDU, although outpolling the Socialists 30.8 to 20.0 percent in Württemberg-Baden, gained fewer votes than independent candidates.[3] In Hesse the SPD emerged as the leading party; however, the CDU/CSU was clearly in dominance in the zone as a whole, receiving 40.8 percent of the vote in contrast to 27.2 percent for the Socialists and 4.0 percent for the Communists. The relatively large vote for the Union parties was due as much to support from Catholics as to fears among the conservative farmers that the politically more active parties of the Left might come to power (Neumann, 1946: 756-758; *Time Magazine*, February 4, 1946: 29).[4]

Other characteristics of these first election contests were the large turnout, the large independent vote (amounting to 26.2 percent of zonal totals) and the relatively small number of invalid ballots. Although there had been predictions that political apathy among the Germans would result in a fiasco for these initial elections, General Clay's judgment was vindicated as 86.0 percent of the eligible electorate voted in the first free balloting in Germany in thirteen years. The large voting turnout was attributed by observers more to a tendency of a "shell-shocked" population to follow instructions than to any burning enthusiasm for the candidates. Attempts by former Nazis to sabotage the elections by urging voters to stay away from the polls failed in general. The independent vote, which reached a high of 37.0 percent in Württemberg-Baden, could be ascribed to several factors. Many Germans were unwilling at this time to commit themselves to any political affiliation or were unsure as to which party could represent them best. Moreover, on the local level popular community leaders could draw sufficient votes to gain election without the backing of parties, which at this stage of political development were still organizationally weak.

The first of a series of five elections to be held in the American zone before the end of 1946 could hardly be considered a reliable expression of German sentiment, taking place in rural areas which, for the most part, had not suffered from the devastation of war and postwar hunger and lack of housing. Moreover, the electorate was made up largely of older people and large numbers were disenfranchised because of former connections with National Socialism; only those candidates approved by the American military authorities were allowed to stand for election and there was at the time no free and independent German press. Because of the radicalism which was expected in the large cities of the zone, both Military Government and German political leaders alike desired to postpone elections there as long as possible. Furthermore, the January contests were not strictly political elections; party platforms were weak and observers noted that candidates, not issues, decided the results (*New York Times*, January 30, 1946).

The second series of American zone elections were held April 28, 1946 in all rural counties (*Landkreise*) for seats on the county councils (*Kreistage*). In general, the April elections involved the same electorate that went to the polls in

January. Although these were the Zone's first truly political elections involving a choice among parties, the relative positions of the parties remained unaffected as the CDU/CSU in Bavaria and Württemburg-Baden and the SPD in Hesse won clear victories.[5] In the Zone as a whole the Union parties polled over half the popular vote to remain the strongest party overall, with the Socialists firmly in second place. The gains registered by the parties, including the Communists and Liberals, were largely at the expense of the independent vote which all but disappeared. The improved organization of the parties and the increasing difficulty for independents to organize on a large scale where they were known only to a small percentage of the voters contributed to their decline. The influence of the political party was seen to grow as the distance from the immediate circle of local interests increased. But the growing role of parties contributed to a substantial decline in voting participation, notably in Württemberg-Baden where it dropped from 85.0 percent in January to 61.5 percent in April (Pollock, *et al*, 1949: 124; *Die Welt*, April 30, 1946).[6] (*Die Welt* first appeared April 2, 1946 under British license.)

The long-awaited elections in the 38 large urban districts (*Stadtkreise*) of the American zone, including Munich, Frankfurt, Stuttgart, Nuremberg and Mannheim, took place May 26, 1946. The large radical vote which was expected in these urban centers did not materialize as the Communists polled only 8.9 percent of the zonal total, with their greatest support coming in Württemberg-Baden with an 11.9 percent total. With its major strength centered in the urban areas, the SPD improved its position relative to the CDU/CSU by outpolling the Union parties in Hesse and in Württemberg-Baden, but, by virtue of its strength in Bavaria, the CDU/CSU remained the leading party in the Zone with 39.7 percent of the vote to the Socialists' 37.7 percent. The Communists continued to lead the Liberals in zonal totals, although trailing them in Württemberg-Baden (*Die Welt* and *New York Times*, May 28, 1946).

The first elections involving the total *Land* electorates were held in the American zone *Länder* June 30, 1946 to select delegates to the constituent assemblies (*Verfassunggebenden Landesversammlungen*). Since these assemblies would write the first postwar *Land* constitutions, the Germans, for the first time, had to face issues of far-reaching importance, including governmental forms and structure, electoral systems, the role of the church in education, denazification, the place of labor unions, social and economic reform, economic reconstruction and a host of other issues peculiar to the American zone as a whole or of a particular *Land*, such as the question of political union in Württemberg-Baden.

The results of the June elections only confirmed trends which had been indicated in the contests earlier in the year and which in many respects have continued to this day. The CDU/CSU maintained its dominant position in the zone as a whole with 46.4 percent of the total vote. Its major strength was centered in Bavaria where the party exhibited strong rightist tendencies. The SPD, with its major backing in Hesse, was the second strongest party in the zone with 32.4 percent of the vote. The Communist Party polled 7.3 percent, with its weakest following in rural Bavaria. The Liberals gained considerable support in

TABLE 2.1

LAND CONSTITUENT ASSEMBLY ELECTIONS JUNE 30, 1946

	Bavaria		Hesse		Württemberg-Baden	
Party	Percent	Seats	Percent	Seats	Percent	Seats
CDU/CSU	60.6	109	37.3	35	39.2	41
SPD	28.3	51	44.3	42	31.0	32
KPD	5.0	9	9.7	7	9.6	10
FDP/DVP/ LDP	1.7	3	8.1	6	16.1	17
Others	4.4	(WAV) 8	0.6	. . .	4.1	. . .
Totals		180		90		100

Württemberg-Baden, but their failure to gain a large following in Bavaria left them the weakest of the four major political groups with only 6.9 percent of the zonal total (Pollock *et al*, 1949: 125). A strong trend toward a two-party system was evident as the CDU/CSU and the SPD gained nearly eighty percent of the zonal total. The elections demonstrated that the Germans were not prepared for radical changes in spite of the depressing conditions.

The British and the French were more hesitant than the Americans in establishing elected representative bodies, and elections were delayed in their zones until the fall of 1946. These initial elections were held in two parts: September 15, 1946 for the representative bodies of rural communities and small towns of up to 20,000 inhabitants in the British zone and those of rural areas and of all municipalities regardless of size in the French zone; October 13, 1946, for county councils (*Kreistage)* in both zones and the major cities of the British zone.

The French, like the Americans, made no attempt to influence or change the electoral systems already in existence in the *Länder* of their zone of occupation in the pre-Hitler period. For the most part, this meant the reintroduction of proportional systems to the French zone *Länder*, although each area's system had its peculiarities. In Württemberg-Hohenzollern, for example, a voter could give up to three of his/her votes to a single candidate. In Rhineland-Palatinate, although involving an election between lists, the voter could strike out the names of various candidates on the list without replacing them with other names, creating the possibility of *Listköpfung* (beheading of the list), and enabling candidates low on the list to be elected in place of the order designated by the party (*Rheinland-Pfalz*, 1948: 17).

The first elections of the postwar period in the French zone were marked by a heavy turnout, amounting to 87.0 percent of the eligible zonal electorate, and, as in the American zone, a large independent vote. In Rhineland-Palatinate, for example, independents polled 22.8 percent and gained 39.1 percent of local council seats; the more rural the district, the greater the independent vote. The Christian Democrats won handily in all three *Länder*, with the Socialists running a poor second. The Liberals placed third in Baden and Württemberg-Hohenzollern, but did not compete in Rhineland-Palatinate, while the Communists trailed the Liberals in the first two *Länder* and placed third in the latter (*Die Welt* and *New York Times*, September 16 and 17, 1946).

In the *Kreis* elections of October 13, 1946, voting participation in the French Zone *Länder* dropped off sharply from the totals of the previous month, and the independent vote all but disappeared as party lists came to play a dominant role. Again, as in the *Gemeinde* elections, the Christian Democrats emerged as the dominant party in all three *Länder*, and, in contrast to the other two zones, there was no *Land* under French occupation that the Socialists could call their own. Moreover, the dominance of the CDU was much greater than in the American zone, the highest SPD vote total being gained in Rhineland-Palatinate with 30.2 percent, and, although the two-party vote was over eighty percent, there was little equality between the two major parties. In the zonal totals the Communists were third, the Liberals fourth (Pollock *et al*, 1949: 189).[7]

The first elections in the British zone, held September 15, 1946, produced a heavy turnout, but somewhat below that of comparable elections in the American and French zones.[8] As in the first elections in the other two Western zones, the British zone *Länder* experienced a large independent vote, but it did not reach the proportions of the American and French zone totals. This was due primarily to the small independent following in the highly urbanized *Land* of North Rhine-Westphalia, where it reached only 6.1 percent, in contrast to the rural *Länder* of Lower Saxony and Schleswig-Holstein where the figures were 21.3 and 21.5 percent respectively. Poor party organization in the rural areas, the contempt for parties after the Nazi period and the importance of personality on the local level all partially explained the substantial independent vote in these two rural provinces. In the zone as a whole, independents won more seats than any of the political parties (*Die Welt*, September 17 and 20, 1946).[9] In Schleswig-Holstein the Danish minority did not organize for the *Gemeinde* elections, but gave its support to independents, contributing to the large independent backing in that *Land*.

In these first elections the SPD emerged as the leading party in Lower Saxony and Schleswig-Holstein, the CDU as the leading party in North Rhine-Westphalia. The inability of the Communists to gain as much as ten percent of the vote in any of the *Länder* surprised most observers who had expected them to benefit from the general distress of the Germans, primarily the lack of rations.[10] Also significant was the poor showing of the *Zentrum* throughout the zone.

The elections of October 13, 1946 for county and municipal councils were the first true political elections in the British zone, and, as such, saw the almost complete disappearance of the independent vote. In the smaller communities where there was no reserve list, the independent candidates suffered no disadvantage, except that each had the responsibility of organizing his/her own campaign. In the *Kreise* and large urban areas, however, in which the reserve list played a much more important part, the independent was less fortunately placed, since no method could be devised to permit him/her to benefit from the reserve list. His/her only chance for a seat was to win a constituency outright.

The decline of the independent vote had little influence on the relative positions of the parties, as the SPD in Lower Saxony and Schleswig-Holstein and the CDU in North Rhine-Westphalia maintained their leading status. Gains by the CDU in Lower Saxony, however, enabled it to replace the indigenous Lower Saxony State Party (NLP) as that *Land's* second party. In the Hanseatic cities of Bremen and Hamburg the SPD emerged as the dominant party. The Communist Party made gains in all three *Länder*, but especially in the urban centers of North Rhine-Westphalia.[11] The campaign in Schleswig-Holstein was marked by the intense activity on the part of the Danish minority, organized in the South Schleswig Association (SSV), in the counties near the Danish-German border, to spur their drive to have South Schleswig placed under a Danish or international administration until a referendum could be held on the fate of the area. Food parcels were sent into the contested counties from Denmark in an attempt to influence the vote. While the SSV was reminding the electorate that "Prussia has only brought us misery," an SPD placard asked the voters to "eat Danish bacon, but vote German" (*Die Welt*, September 17 and October 17, 1946). The Danes succeeded in capturing the *Kreise* of Flensburg, Schleswig and South Tondern, but elected only three other representatives outside of these islands of strength.[12]

In contrast to the American and French areas of occupation, the British zone elections did not produce a single dominant party. The less stringent licensing policies of the British contributed to the splintering of the bourgeois vote, especially in Lower Saxony, and prevented the CDU from more than equaling the Socialists in zonal totals (*Die Welt*, October 17, 1946).[13]

One of the most significant developments of these first elections in the British zone was the introduction of a radically different electoral system which was to alter considerably the relationship of the German representative to his party. While the Americans and the French were willing to leave the decision of an electoral system to the Germans themselves, the British used their influence to prevent the reestablishment of a system of proportional representation based on party lists on which they partially blamed the weakness of the Weimar Republic. Although favoring a simple majority system, the British realized that it would be useless to force such a reform on the Germans without their cooperation. While disliking the unrepresentative character of the British system, the Germans agreed to a plan which combined proportional representation with the simple majority ballot (Ebsworth, 1960: 52-56). Once the size of the council of the community (*Gemeinde*) or county (*Kreis*) had been established, a determination

TABLE 2.2

KREIS AND MUNICIPAL ELECTIONS OF OCTOBER 13, 1946 IN THE BRITISH ZONE *LÄNDER*

Party	Bremen[a]		Hamburg		Lower Saxony	North Rhine-Westphalia	Schleswig-Holstein
	Per-cent	Seats	Per-cent	Seats	Percent	Per-cent	Per-cent
SPD	47.6	51	43.1	83	41.9	33.4	41.0
CDU	18.9	12	26.7	16	22.5	46.0	37.3
KPD	11.5	3	10.4	4	5.1	9.4	5.1
FDP	18.3[b]	12	18.2	7	8.2	4.3	6.1
NLP	---	---	c	c	19.4	---	---
SSW	---	---	---	---	---	---	7.3
ZP	---	---	---	---	2.0	6.1	0.1
Ind. & Others	3.7	2	1.6	---	0.9	0.8	3.1
Totals		80		110			

a Election totals for Bremen are included in the figures for Lower Saxony inasmuch as Bremen was not a separate *Land* at the time of the 1946 election.

b Totals in Bremen are for the BDV which subsequently merged with the FDP.

c The Lower Saxony State Party, although authorized in Hamburg, formed an electoral alliance with the FDP and did not enter a separate slate of candidates.

was made on the number of seats to be chosen through direct election. The remaining seats, usually numbering not more than 25 percent, would be distributed among the parties from a reserve list to which not only the votes of the losing candidates were credited (*Reststimmen*), but also the numerical differences between the winning candidates and the highest unsuccessful candidate in each constituency (*Mehrstimmen*). Moreover, each voter had from three to six votes depending on the size of the constituency. For example, for the *Bürgerschaft* election of October 13, 1946 in Hamburg, the city was divided into 21 districts, each of which elected four deputies, with each voter having four votes. In addition to the 84 seats filled by direct election, an additional 26 seats were distributed proportionally among the parties on the basis of the vote totals arrived at by the formula described above (*Hamburg*, 1947: 3-19).[14] In North Rhine-Westphalia each eligible voter had up to six votes and in Bremen from three to five votes depending on the size of the constituency. Bremen elected 64 deputies from sixteen multimember districts; two elected three deputies each, twelve elected four deputies each and two elected five deputies each. Sixteen additional seats were allocated from the reserve list on the basis of *Rest-* and *Mehrstimmen.*

Although the number of invalid ballots was less than five percent in the zone, the system would not have caused as much confusion had each voter been limited to one vote in single, rather than multimember, constituencies (Ebsworth, 1960: 55-61).[15] Rather than using the accustomed d'Hondt formula in determining the allocation of reserve list seats, the British made use of the Hare system, which proved to be as confusing to the Germans as the multiple vote. This British imposition was summarily abandoned. Moreover, the British listed candidates in alphabetical order on the ballots rather than blocking them according to party, the purpose being to institute a personality election rather than one based on party names. Contrary to expectations, most voters gave all of their votes to candidates of the same party. The degree of party discipline in Hamburg, for example, with all four votes going to the same party, was 86.0 percent, with SPD discipline the most consistent with 88.5 percent. Not only was the splitting of party candidates confusing to the voters, it was discriminatory between candidates of the same party on the alphabetical list, since those at the top of the list consistently received more votes than members of the same party at the bottom of the list.[16] In effect, the election was as much a battle of the alphabet as a battle between parties.

The British attempt to gain working majorities through their system met with more success, with a single party gaining a majority of seats in every major city of their zone with the exceptions of Hagen, Oldenburg and Solingen.[17] Of considerable significance for future developments was that the dominant party in every major city was either the CDU or the SPD with the single exception of Flensburg, where the Danish SSV gained a majority. In Hamburg the SPD won 83 of 110 *Bürgerschaft* seats, 76 by direct election, and in Bremen it gained 51 of eighty seats, 45 by direct election.[18]

The Berlin election of October 20, 1946 drew international attention, not only because of its Four-Power status, but because of the direct confrontation of ideologies which it involved. Following the capture of the city in 1945 the Soviets, in their two months of unrestricted rule, politically organized the city and staffed the most important administrative positions with trusted Communists. One of the major tasks of the Western Allies on entering Berlin was to loosen the political grip the Communists had placed on the city. The anti-fascist parties authorized in Berlin other than the Communists, namely the Social Democrats, Christian Democrats and Liberals, soon became strong supporters of the West. With their failure to fuse the Social Democratic and Communist parties in the Western sectors of Berlin into a new Socialist Unity Party (SED), as had been accomplished in their zone and sector of Berlin, the Soviets hoped to win the support of the Berliners through intimidation and flattery. In the last days of the campaign the Russians distributed millions of cigarettes and large quantities of liquor, shoes, coal and clothing to the city's inhabitants. Moreover, there was a continuous broadcast over Radio Berlin of the names of prisoners-of-war released by the Russians, names which also appeared in the columns of the *Tägliche Rundschau*, the Soviet Army-licensed newspaper. Electric power which came from the Soviet sector would be turned off intermittently in the Western sectors each day and attempts were made to hamper the campaigning of the Western-oriented parties in the Soviet sector. The Americans, not to be outdone by the Russians, developed a give-away program of their own in the form of shoes, automobile and bicycle tires, matches, cement, window glass and paper (*Die Welt*, October 19, 21 and 22, 1946; *Newsweek*, October 28, 1946: 40; *New York Times*, October 21, 1946).

However, few Berliners could forget the three weeks of looting, burning and raping by the Red Army after the capture of the city the previous year, in addition to their first-hand acquaintance with Russian rule, and the Soviet-sponsored SED was resoundly defeated, even failing to capture a majority of the vote in the Soviet sector, as 92.3 percent of the electorate went to the polls. In elections held the same day in the Soviet zone *Länder*, the SED failed to obtain an absolute majority of the vote in a single *Land*.

The Social Democratic Party emerged as the clear victor in the Berlin election, winning 48.7 percent of the vote and 63 of the 130 seats in Berlin's first elected municipal assembly, called the *Stadtverordnetenversammlung*. In contrast, the Soviet sponsored SED gained only 19.8 percent of the total vote and 26 seats.[19]

The election results in Berlin were not so much a victory for the democratic idea as it was a straight anti-Russian vote. This was to be the first and last election encompassing four sectors of Berlin until 1990. The stunning defeat of the SED and the failure of subsequent attempts of the Communists to merge with the SPD in Berlin foreshadowed the events of 1948 which were to effect a complete separation of the city into two parts.

In the latter part of 1946 the first *Landtag* elections and plebiscites on the newly drafted *Land* constitutions were held simultaneously in the *Länder* of the American zone. Balloting took place November 24, 1946 in Württemberg-Baden and December 1, 1946 in Bavaria and Hesse. The constitutions were approved in all three *Länder* by large margins;[20] however, in Hesse a great deal of controversy surrounded the voting on both the constitution and a proposal to socialize the mining, steel, gas, electric and transport industries in that *Land*. Because of the contentious nature of the socialization measure (Article 41), it was decided to submit it to the electorate in a separate referendum. Although both questions were approved, the number of invalid ballots reached 12.8 percent on the constitution and 13.0 percent on the socialization proposal (*Hessen, Heft* 1, 1947: 20). Opposition to the two questions was led by the conservative Liberal Democratic Party, which nearly doubled its June following, gaining most of its new adherents from the CDU which had cooperated with the Social Democrats on the socialization proposal.[21] Opposition to the constitution in

TABLE 2.3

FIRST *LAND* ELECTIONS IN THE AMERICAN ZONE *LÄNDER*, 1946 [a]

Party	Bavaria		Hesse		Württemberg-Baden	
	Percent	Seats	Percent	Seats	Percent	Seats
CDU/CSU	52.3	104	30.9	28	38.4	39
SPD	28.6	54	42.7	38	31.9	32
FDP/DVP/LDP	5.6	9	15.7	14	19.5	19
KPD	6.1 [b]	---	10.7	10	10.2	10
Others	7.4 [c]	13[c]	---	---	---	---
Totals		180		90		100

a With the addition of Bremerhaven to Bremen, a new election was held October 12, 1947 for the Bremen *Bürgerschaft* with the following results (seats in parenthesis): SPD 41.7 (46), CDU 22.0 (24), BDV (15), KPD 8.8 (10), FDP Bremen 5.5 (2), DP 3.9 (1).

b The Communists failed to obtain the required ten percent in an administrative district for representation.

c Economic Reconstruction Association (WAV)

Württemberg-Baden on the other hand was expressed through non-participation on the constitutional question of a large percentage of the electorate which had cast votes for *Landtag* representatives.[22]

The outcomes of the first postwar *Landtag* elections in the American zone showed few startling changes over the voting patterns registered in the June balloting for the constituent assemblies. The CDU/CSU remained the leading party in Bavaria and Württemberg-Baden, while Socialists outpolled all other parties in Hesse. The Liberals made extensive gains in all three *Länder*; in Bavaria and Hesse they gained support from those groups which were opposed to the draft constitutions.[23] The Communists made slight gains in the three *Länder*, but in Bavaria became the first victim of the *Sperr-Klausel* in the Bavarian constitution (Article 14) which required that a party obtain ten percent of the vote in at least one of the five administrative districts into which the *Land* was divided to be eligible for the proportional division of seats (*Bayern*, 1963: 122-125). Hesse had a provision in its new constitution that a party acquire at least five percent of the total *Land* vote; however, in contrast to Bavaria, all of the parties exceeded the five percent barrier.[24]

With the exception of Bavaria, where the WAV was an important factor, all of the first *Landtag* elections in the American zone were straight contests between the CDU/CSU, SPD, the KPD and the Liberals. The Liberals were the largest gainers over June election totals, polling 11.3 percent of the zonal vote to replace the Communists as the zone's third party. The Communists made slight gains to command 8.2 percent of the zonal totals, while the Socialists held their own with 33.1 percent. Although maintaining its position as the leading party in the zone overall, CDU/CSU support dropped by nearly three percentage points, as substantial losses were suffered in Bavaria and Hesse (*Die Welt*, November 26 and December 3, 1946).

The first politically responsible governments formed in the three American zone *Länder* were coalitions, even though in Bavaria the CSU held an absolute parliamentary majority. An all-party cabinet was established in Württemberg-Baden, an SPD-CDU government in Hesse, and a coalition which comprised the CSU, SPD and the WAV in Bavaria. Because of their opposition to the constitutions of Bavaria and Hesse, the Liberals were unacceptable coalition partners in those two *Länder*.

The first *Land* elections in the British zone were held in Lower Saxony, North Rhine-Westphalia and Schleswig-Holstein April 20, 1947.[25] Although British political observers predicted victory for the Christian Democrats in all three *Länder* under the new electoral system combining simple majority and proportional principles, the CDU sweep did not materialize as the party lost substantial support to other center and right-of-center parties.[26] The Socialists, on the other hand, while polling substantially the same percentage of the vote as in the elections of the previous October, maintained their leading position in Lower Saxony and Schleswig-Holstein and emerged as the strongest party in the zone. While the CDU outpolled the SPD in North Rhine-Westphalia, its total of 37.5 percent was 8.5 percentage points below its October following. Nevertheless, by winning 92 seats in direct election, 16 mandates more than its proportional entitlement, the CDU obtained 42.8 percent of the representation in the *Landtag* (*Die Welt*, April 22, 1947).[27]

In Lower Saxony the CDU entered into an electoral arrangement with the Lower Saxony State Party (NLP) in which it agreed not to contest NLP candidates in 38 constituencies, with the NLP agreeing not to run candidates against the CDU in 43 constituencies. In the remaining districts, where there was little chance of defeating the Socialists, both parties contested the election. The arrangement enabled the two parties to win 34 direct seats, 14 for the CDU and 20 for the NLP, but the alliance fell 4.1 percentage points below totals received in the election in October 1946 and failed in its purpose of defeating the Socialists in direct contests. The SPD not only won 58 direct and seven reserve list seats, but its 43.4 percent of the *Land* vote was a gain of 1.5 percentage points over October results (*Niedersachsen*, 1947).

The particular operation of the electoral system formulated for the first *Landtag* election in Schleswig-Holstein enabled the Social Democrats to win an absolute majority of seats in the *Land* parliament with 43.8 percent of ballots cast. Having been the stronghold of bourgeois parties, many people blamed the Social Democrat victory on the large number of newly arrived refugees and expellees who made up nearly forty percent of the population and which saw in the

TABLE 2.4

FIRST *LAND* ELECTIONS IN THE BRITISH ZONE *LÄNDER*, 1947

Party	Lower Saxony			North Rhine-Westphalia			Schleswig-Holstein		
	Per-cent	Direct Seats	Total Seats	Per-Cent	Direct Seats	Total Seats	Per-cent	Direct Seats	Total Seats
SPD	43.4	58	65	32.0	53	64	43.8	34	43
CDU	19.9	14	30	37.5	92	92 [a]	34.0	6	21
KPD	5.6	...	8	14.0	3	28	4.7	...	...
FDP	8.8	2	13	6.0	...	12	4.97	...	...
NLP	17.9	20	27	....	...	...	....	...	...
ZP	4.1	1	6	9.8	2	20	0.1	...	...
SSV	....	...	...	....	...	...	9.3	2	6
Others	0.3	...	...	0.8	...	...	3.2	...	...
Totals		95	149		150	216 [a]		42	70

a Sixteen of these seats are *Überhangmandate*.

Socialists their best hope for a redistribution of the wealth and a means of compensation for their losses in the East. Whatever truth there may have been in this assertion, the early difficulties faced by the CDU in making inroads in this heavily Protestant *Land* and the image of the SPD as a respectable party in an area which had held strong Nazi sympathies in an earlier period were also helpful to the Socialist cause.[28]

The only party other than the SPD and the CDU to obtain *Landtag* representation in Schleswig-Holstein was the party of the Danish minority, the South Schleswig-Association (SSV), which gained 9.3 percent of the *Land* vote and six seats while contesting only fourteen of the 42 constituencies. The campaign of the SSV in the border areas gave the election the character of a referendum and stimulated a high turnout, especially in Flensburg where 83 percent of the electorate voted in contrast to 62 and 63 percent in the constituencies in the southern-most part of the *Land*. Likewise, the number of invalid ballots was only 1.9 percent north of the Eider River compared with 4.2 percent in the southern counties. The Danish-Germans won both direct seats in Flensburg by absolute majorities (*Schleswig-Holstein*, 1947).[29]

Restrictive clauses were inserted into the electoral laws of all three British zone *Länder* in order to limit the splintering which characterized the Weimar period. In Schleswig-Holstein the restriction took the form of a direct seat requirement. Unless a party could win in at least one single member constituency, it would not qualify for seats from the reserve list no matter whether its total *Land* vote was three or twenty percent. Thus, in spite of the absence of a five percent clause, the FDP with 4.97 percent of the vote, the Communists with 4.7 percent and the German Conservative Party with 3.1 percent obtained no seats in the 1947 election because of their failure to win a direct seat.[30] The electoral law of Lower Saxony required that a party gain at least five percent of the *Land* vote or win one direct seat in order to qualify for reserve list seats. By virtue of its victory in a single constituency the Center Party gained five additional indirect seats, although it had polled only 4.1 percent of the Lower Saxony vote. In North Rhine-Westphalia the electoral law excluded those parties which did not receive at least five percent of the *Land* vote from the allocation of reserve list seats, regardless of whether they won a direct seat or not. Had this stipulation applied to Lower Saxony, the Center Party in that *Land* would have retained its single direct seat, but would not have participated in the distribution of reserve list seats (*Schleswig-Holstein*, 1947: 81-103).[31]

Reserve list seats were distributed according to one of two different methods. Schleswig-Holstein adopted the system previously employed in the major cities of the British zone, including Bremen and Hamburg, whereby both the votes of the losing district candidates (*Reststimmen*) and the excess votes (*Mehrstimmen*) of the winning candidates over the highest losing candidates were credited to the list. The totals arrived at for each party formed the basis for the proportional allocation of reserve list seats. The number of seats already won by direct election did not figure in the indirect entitlement.[32] The electoral arrangements formulated for the first *Landtag* elections in Lower Saxony and North Rhine-Westphalia employed an entirely new concept in distributing reserve list seats in that the total *Land* vote for each party entered into the allocation of reserve list seats. Indirect seats were distributed among the qualifying parties in such a manner as to correct any discrepancies caused by the results in the constituencies and to effect a proportional balance between them.[33]

Had the electoral system of either Lower Saxony or North Rhine-Westphalia been employed in Schleswig-Holstein in 1947, the manner in which reserve list seats were distributed would have cut considerably into the Socialist margin, with the party receiving only 36 seats under the former system and 38 under the latter. On the other hand, had the system of Schleswig-Holstein applied to Lower Saxony and North Rhine-Westphalia, the SPD in the former *Land* and the CDU in the latter would have gained absolute majorities in their respective *Landtage* in 1947.

In the zone as a whole the Socialists led the CDU by a comfortable margin, as the bourgeois vote was more fragmented in the British *Länder* than in the other areas of occupation, and the two-party vote amounted to only 68.8 percent, far below the totals in the *Länder* under American and French control.[34] The KPD, the third party in zonal totals, found its strongest support in the British zone *Länder*, particularly in North Rhine-Westphalia, where, aided by the food crisis, its total of 14.0 percent and 28 seats, three by direct election, represented

TABLE 2.5

FIRST *LAND* ELECTIONS IN THE FRENCH ZONE *LÄNDER*,
1947

Party	Baden		Rhineland-Palatinate		Württemberg-Hohenzollern	
	Percent	Seats	Percent	Seats	Percent	Seats
CDU/BCSV	55.9	34	47.2	48	54.2	32
SPD	22.4	13	34.3	34	20.8	12
FDP/DVP/DP	14.3	9	9.8 [a]	11 [a]	17.7	11
KPD	7.4	4	8.7	8	7.3	5
Totals		60		101 [b]		60

a Liberal totals in Rhineland-Palatinate include the figures for the SV which merged with Liberal forces.

b The size of the Rhineland-Palatinate *Landtag* was increased by one seat in September 1947 to allow for representation of the district Saarburg, which had previously been attached to the Saar.

the high point for the Communists in any election in the western part of Germany (*New York Times*, April 22, 1947). In contrast, the FDP found its weakest following in the British occupation area, where it ranked fifth in zonal totals.

Landtag elections and constitutional plebiscites were held in the three *Länder* of the French zone May 18, 1947. While only two-thirds of the electorate went to the polls in Baden and Württemberg-Hohenzollern, the controversy generated by the special referendum on state support for confessional schools brought out 77.9 percent of the electorate in Rhineland-Palatinate. Virtually identical proposals had been inserted in the draft constitutions of the two other French zone *Länder*, both with large Catholic populations, without arousing any particular opposition, but the high proportion of Protestants in Rhineland-Palatinate, 40 percent in 1947, and their hostility to the proposal, created the need for a special ballot on the question (*Rheinland-Pfalz*, 1948: 26-28). On the other hand, the provision in the constitutions of all three French Zone *Länder* for some degree of socialization, an issue which had aroused violent feelings in Hesse, stimulated little discussion in the French zone.[35]

Whereas the constitutions of Baden and Württemberg-Hohenzollern carried by comfortable margins,[36] in Rhineland-Palatinate the constitution was approved by only 53.0 percent of the voters and the school measure by 52.4 percent as Protestant areas voted heavily against both.[37] Opposition was also registered through ballot invalidation, amounting to 18.2 percent on the school question,

TABLE 2.6

ZONAL RESULTS OF THE 1946/1947 *LAND* ELECTIONS

Party	American Zone	British Zone	French Zone	West Germany [a]
CDU	43.5	32.1	50.4	37.7
SPD	33.1	36.7	29.1	35.0
FDP/DVP	11.3	6.6	12.3	9.5
KPD	8.2	10.4	8.1	9.4
Others	3.9	14.2	---	8.4

a The West German figures include results of the *Land* election of October 12, 1947, in Bremen, whereas American zone figures do not. British zone figures do not reflect the 1946 election in Hamburg whereas the West German figures do. Totals from the elections in the Saar and Berlin appear in none of these computations.

14.4 percent on the constitution and 10.6 percent in the vote for *Landtag* representation. The Socialists and Communists led the opposition on the school referendum, with the CDU supporting it. Liberal forces were split on the issue.

The CDU won absolute majorities in Baden and Württemberg-Hohenzollern and remained the leading party in Rhineland-Palatinate, with the Socialists running a poor second in all three *Länder*. The Liberals ranked third in all three contests. Of the four parties authorized in the French area of occupation, the Communists ranked last (*Die Welt*, May 20, 1947). Like the Americans, the French made no attempt to influence the writing of the electoral laws in their area of control, and proportional systems were introduced for the first *Landtag* elections in all three *Länder*.

In the French zone, where Christian Democrats continued to maintain their dominance, the elections were straight contests between the four major parties, due to the French policy of not authorizing minor parties. While the CDU found its greatest support in the French zone, the SPD found its weakest. In contrast, the CDU was weakest in the British zone where the SPD was strongest. The two-party vote was highest in the French zone where licensing policies were strictest, lowest in the British zone where numerous minor parties were authorized.[38] The Liberals had their greatest following in the French zone, the KPD in the British zone.

The first *Landtag* election in the Saar was held under French auspices October 5, 1947. In contrast to the other *Länder* under French control, the draft constitution, formulated by a commission representing all parties, was not submitted to the newly elected *Landtag* for ratification. In effect, the October election was an indirect referendum on the question of political autonomy and economic union with France; a vote for the parties favoring the draft constitution represented approval of the document. Of the four licensed parties, only the Communists opposed the proposed instrument, and in order for the voter to express opposition, the only alternatives were to fail to vote, to invalidate the ballot or vote Communist. Few voters desired to vote Communist in this heavily Catholic area, and the percentage of support for the KPD actually dropped from the total of 9.1 percent attained in the local elections of September 12, 1946, when there was no constitutional issue, to 8.4 percent in the *Landtag* election. In view of the turnout of 95.7 percent of the electorate, most opposition was expressed through invalidation of the ballot which amounted to 9.8 percent of the ballots cast.

In spite of precensorship of the press, the restrictions on party activity at the time and the lack of opportunity on the part of the Saarlanders to express their feelings on the constitution directly, there can be little doubt that most of the support for the parties supporting the constitution was genuine. The expectation of economic betterment through economic union with France dominated the balloting. Shortages of food and economic stagnation in the rest of Germany as opposed to a "favored nation" treatment in their own area made such a union appear advantageous.[39] The French were careful to distribute large quantities of wheat and other commodities during the campaign. Asked why the constitution was not placed to a direct vote, French Governor of the Saar, Gilbert Grandval, explained that "there were such complex and difficult questions involved that it was considered that the population was incapable of deciding on them through a referendum" (*New York Times*, October 6,1947; *Die Welt*, October 7, 1947).

The proponents of the constitution, led by the Christian People's Party (CVP), gained an absolute majority in the *Landtag* by winning 48 of the 50 parliamentary seats, with the opposing Communist Party receiving the remaining two seats.[40] On December 15, 1947 the three pro-French parties ratified the proposed constitution by a vote of 43 to 2, with only the Communist representatives expressing opposition.

The last of the first series of *Land* elections in the Western zones of Germany was held October 12, 1947 in Bremen. The city had elected a city council October 13, 1946; however, with her transfer to the American zone and the incorporation of Bremerhaven (formerly Wesermünde) into her territory, new elections encompassing the enlarged area became necessary. Following the practice of the other American zone *Länder*, a constitutional document was drafted and approved by the *Bürgerschaft* September 15, 1947 and then submitted to the electorate for ratification the same day as the *Bürgerschaft* election. In addition, a special ballot was held on the controversial Article 47 of the constitution which would grant certain management rights to labor councils. Although the constitution was ratified by a comfortable 72.6 percent majority, the labor council measure passed by only 109,841 to 100,354 votes (*Documents*, 1955: 165).

In the balloting, which brought out only 67.8 percent of the electorate in contrast to 85.2 percent the previous year, the Socialists won a clear victory, although somewhat diminished from the 1946 election.[41] The enlargement in the size of the *Land* parliament from 80 to 100 members, made necessary by the addition of Bremerhaven to the city, and the change from a mixed to a pure proportional system produced some rather exaggerated changes in the overall election results. The CDU, for example, doubled its representation from 12 to 24 seats with only moderate gains in its following, and the Communist Party increased its representation from three to ten seats while suffering a loss of 2.7 percentage points in its vote total. In like manner, the BVD gained three seats with a 4.4 percentage point loss of support (*Die Welt*, October 14, 1947).[42]

A five percent clause was incorporated into Bremen's new electoral system; however, the limitation applied separately to each of the two electoral districts into which Bremen is divided, namely, Bremen proper and Bremerhaven, not the *Land* as a whole. Normally, the German Party, which received but 3.9 percent of the total *Land* vote, would have been excluded from the proportional division of seats. However, it polled 14.7 percent of the Bremerhaven vote, giving it three of the twenty seats allotted to that district. In Bremen proper the party obtained 1.7 percent of the ballots cast and failed to qualify for seats. Had the five percent limitation applied to the total *Land* vote, or had the vote of the DP been equally distributed between Bremerhaven and Bremen proper, it would not have qualified for seats. By the same token, the FDP gained 10.7 of the Bremerhaven vote and two representations, but failed to qualify for seats in Bremen proper. Thus, we see an example of malrepresentation even under a proportional system: the FDP with 5.5 percent of the total *Land* vote obtained two seats, the DP with 3.9 percent of the vote, three seats (*Die Welt*, October 23 and 24, 1947).[43] (See footnote 41 of this chapter for a breakdown of election results.)

In surveying the results of the first parliamentary elections to be held in the West German *Länder* in the postwar period, it must be remembered that they took place under the most trying circumstances. Not only were there shortages of food, fuel, shelter, clothing and work, there were enormous material and technical difficulties connected with the holding of these elections. The preparation of voter lists proved especially difficult in the large cities where some streets and addresses were nonexistent; inhabitants lived where they could find shelter, whether it be in a cellar or in what was left of a former apartment house. Moreover, to complicate matters, people were constantly moving. In many cities voter lists had to be done completely in long hand, in most cases on the basis of ration-card lists. There was a critical shortage of paper, not only for campaigning, but for the printing of ballots. Ballot boxes were not always available nor was lumber for their construction. In some cities of the British zone, including Hamburg, empty munition cases were used for the purpose. Shortages of pencils, sealing wax and envelopes likewise plagued the administration of these elections, as did translation errors (from English or French into German) and the difficulty in finding suitable polling places.[44]

In view of the enormity of the situation and thirteen years of non-political involvement on the part of the German people, it is surprising that voting participation was as high as it was. The largest turnout was in Hamburg with 79.0 percent, the lowest in Lower Saxony with 65.1 percent. The turnout in these first

TABLE 2.7

**VOTING PARTICIPATION IN THE FIRST
AND MOST RECENT *LAND* ELECTIONS**

Land	Percent			Percent		
	Date	Voting	Invalid	Date	Voting	Invalid
Hamburg	1946	79.0	3.8	2011	57.3	3.0
Württemberg-Baden	1946 [a]	71.7	5.6	2011	66.3	1.4
Bavaria	1946	75.7	4.4	2008	57.9	1.5
Hesse	1946	73.2	7.6	2008	64.3	2.4
Lower Saxony	1947	65.1	4.5	2008	57.1	1.5
North Rhine-Westphalia	1947	67.3	4.9	2010	59.3	1.4
Schleswig-Holstein	1947	69.8	3.6	2009	73.6	1.4
Baden	1947 [a]	67.8	9.2	2011	66.3	1.4
Rhineland-Palatinate	1947	77.9	10.6	2011	61.8	2.1
Württemberg-Hohenzollern	1947 [a]	66.4	7.5	2011	66.3	1.4
Bremen	1947	67.8	4.5	2011	57.5	4.2

a The 2011 figures for the now defunct *Länder* of Baden, Württemberg-Baden and Württemberg-Hohenzollern are from Baden-Württemberg into which they were amalgamated.

elections under the most trying conditions stands in stark contrast to participation in the most recent series of *Land* contests which averaged eight percentage points lower, falling by as much as 16.1 points in Rhineland-Palatinate. The large percentage of invalid ballots in these first election contests compared to recent elections is not indicative of the greater skill of today's voters in marking ballots, rather the use made by the German voter in the 1946/47 period of the ballot as an instrument of protest, giving them up either blank or crossed through. This was especially true in the *Länder* of the French zone and Hesse, where, with the exceptions of Baden and Württemberg-Hohenzollern where opposition was less vocal, considerable controversy surrounded the approval of the constitution and special measures. In Rhineland-Palatinate the percentage of invalid ballots reached 14.4 percent on the constitutional plebiscite, and, in view of the closeness of the decision on the document (approved by only 53.0 percent), one can speculate that the constitution might not have been ratified had the invalid ballots been expressed in valid votes. In Hesse, Baden and Württemberg-Hohenzollern the margin of acceptance was large enough to have carried the proposed constitutions in any case. In the British zone where there were no constitutional instruments to pass upon, the percentage of invalid ballots was lower, as was voter turnout. Also in those *Länder* where there was a high degree of consensus on the fundamental law, the number of invalid ballots was low.

The licensing policies of the Western Allies, in particular the prohibition on expellee and refugee parties, limited most of the first elections to contests between four parties, the CDU/CSU, SPD, the Liberals and the Communists. Only in the British zone, where the authorities were less stringent in their restrictions, did large numbers of parties appear. Moreover, stipulations in the electoral systems of most of the *Länder* such as the direct seat requirement in Schleswig-Holstein, the ten percent requirement in an administrative district in Bavaria and the five percent of the total *Land* vote limitation in North Rhine-Westphalia and Hesse served to hinder the multiplication of parties characteristic of the Weimar period. In Schleswig-Holstein only three parties gained representation in the *Landtag*, in Baden, Bavaria, Hamburg, Hesse, Rhineland-Palatinate, Württemberg-Baden and Württemberg-Hohenzollern four parties, in North Rhine-Westphalia five parties and in Bremen and Lower Saxony six. The restrictive clauses did not always operate to limit the number of parties, as in Bremen and Lower Saxony; however, in Bavaria the Communist Party was excluded from representation by such a clause as were the Communists, the FDP and the German Conservative Party in Schleswig-Holstein. No independents won seats in any of the *Länder*, although provisions for their representation were provided for in a number of the electoral laws.

The CDU/CSU emerged as the leading party in Baden, Bavaria, North Rhine-Westphalia, Rhineland-Palatinate, Württemberg-Baden and Württemberg-Hohenzollern, the SPD as the leading party in Bremen, Hamburg, Hesse, Lower Saxony and Schleswig-Holstein. Parliamentary majorities were obtained by the CDU/CSU in Baden, Bavaria and Württemberg-Hohenzollern, and by the SPD in Hamburg and Schleswig-Holstein. With the exception of Schleswig-Holstein, the pattern of party dominance reflected in these initial *Landtag* elections remained through the first five election periods, although support for the two major parties often fluctuated considerably in individual *Länder*. In every *Land* the CDU/CSU and the SPD were either first or second in vote totals. The third party in Bavaria was the WAV, in Lower Saxony the NLP, in North Rhine-Westphalia the KPD, in Schleswig-Holstein the SSV, and in all other *Länder* the Liberals.[45] The Communist Party in polling 9.4 percent of the West German vote could do no better than a third place in a single *Land*, North Rhine-Westphalia. In all other *Länder* it was either the fourth or the fifth party. The Communists, however, gained representation in the parliaments of all *Länder* with the exceptions of Bavaria and Schleswig-Holstein, where restrictive clauses had excluded them, and participated in the first governments of several *Länder*. With 1,634,444 votes and 87 *Landtag* seats the Communist Party was at the peak of its postwar strength in West Germany, aided by the economic crisis of the period. After 1947 the party went into a steady decline as internal conditions in West Germany improved and relations with the Soviets deteriorated. The fall of Czechoslovakia in early 1948, the Blockade of Berlin, the expulsion of millions

TABLE 2.8

NATIONAL ELECTION TOTALS
FIRST *LAND* AND *BUNDESTAG* ELECTIONS

Party	1946/1947 [a] *Land* Elections		August 14, 1949 *Bundestag* Elections		Seats
CDU/CSU	6,560,477	37.7	7,359,084	31.0	139
SPD	6,089,631	35.0	6,934,975	29.2	131
FDP/BDV	1,658,107	9.5	2,829,920	11.9	52
KPD	1,634,444	9.4	1,361,708	5.7	15
BP	---	---	986,478	4.2	17
DP/NLP	448,709	2.6	939,934	4.0	17
ZP	593,503	3.4	727,505	3.1	10
WAV	225,404	1.3	681,888	2.9	12
DRP/DKP	64,972	0.4	429,031	1.8	5
SSW	99,500	0.6	75,386	0.3	1
Others	36,526	0.2	1,406,489	5.9	3
Totals	17,411,373		23,732,398		402

a These totals reflect the 1947 *Bürgerschaft* election in Bremen rather than the 1946 election held in that *Land*.

of Germans from the Eastern territories and the Bolshevization of the Soviet zone of Germany made an indelible imprint on the minds of the Germans. Moreover, in the fall of 1947 General Lucius Clay, U.S. Deputy Military Governor, commenced a campaign to educate the Germans to the totalitarian and brutal nature of Communist regimes.

The Union parties and the Social Democratic Party dominated the balloting in the first *Landtag* elections, polling 72.7 percent of the three zonal vote. Far behind with approximately one-tenth of the votes apiece were the Liberals and Communists. Together these four nationally-organized parties polled all but 8.4 percent of the ballots cast in the three Western zones, with the remainder going to a number of minor parties limited to a single zone or a single *Land*, including the Center Party, the Lower Saxony State Party, the Economic Reconstruction Association and the South Schleswig Association.

The Establishment of the Federal Republic of Germany

With elected local and state governments having been established in the three western zones of occupation in 1946 and 1947 the western military governors charged the executive heads of the various *Länder* in July 1948 with the responsibility of drafting a common constitution for that part of Germany under their control. However, because of the split between the western and Soviet zones of occupation the German leaders felt that the drafting of a common document should wait until an all-German arrangement could be established and German sovereignty reasonably reinstated. Refusing to wait, the military authorities urged the drafting of a basic instrument of provisional character to continue in force until a constitution for all of Germany could be adopted.

A constituent council was convened at Herrenchiemsee in August 1948 for the purpose of formulating a basic instrument. On September 1, 1948 a group of 65 representatives from six parties met in Bonn to consider the resulting draft. Dr. Konrad Adenauer, who was later to become Germany's first Chancellor, presided over the Parliamentary Council. In their deliberations, the delegates were determined to avoid the drawbacks that plagued the Weimar Republic.

A draft of a basic law for the three western zones was adopted May 8, 1949 by a vote of 53 to twelve. Following approval by the military governors and ratification by the parliaments of the several states, the Basic Law establishing the Federal Republic of Germany was promulgated May 23, 1949. The federal government went into operation following the first *Bundestag* election held August 14, 1949. Issues of importance facing the country as a whole could now be addressed in a common forum (*Facts About Germany*, Press and Information Office of the Federal Government, 1999).

The First *Bundestag* Election

Although the first *Landtag* elections of the postwar period revealed a number of significant political trends, they could hardly be equated with a national poll held simultaneously as was the first *Bundestag* election of August 14, 1949. Since the elections of the 1946/1947 period the electorate had been expanded by returning prisoners of war, by the continued influx of expellees and refugees from the East, [46] by the reenfranchisement of large numbers of individuals previously barred from voting because of former connections with National Socialism, and by the increment of youth voting for the first time. The higher level of voting participation in every *Land* with the exception of Württemberg-Baden and Württemberg-Hohenzollern accounted for only a small percentage of the increase of over six million voters. Although the CDU/CSU increased its following by nearly 800,000 votes and the SPD by nearly 850,000 votes in the first general election, both suffered large percentage losses over their *Land* election totals by failing to capture a comparable share of the enlarged electorate.

TABLE 2.9

FIRST *LAND* AND *BUNDESTAG* ELECTION COMPARISONS

Land	Year and Election		CDU/ CSU	SPD	FDP/ BDV	KPD	NLP	Others
Hamburg	1946	*Land*	26.7	43.1	18.2	10.4	---	1.6
	1949	*Bund*	19.8	39.6	15.8	8.5	13.1	3.2
Württemberg-Baden	1946	*Land*	38.4	31.9	19.5	10.2	---	---
	1949	*Bund*	31.1	25.2	18.2	7.4	---	18.2
Bavaria	1946	*Land*	52.3	28.6	5.6	6.1	---	7.4 (WAV)
	1949	*Bund*	29.2	22.8	8.5	4.1	---	20.9 (BP)
								14.4 (WAV)
Hesse	1946	*Land*	30.9	42.7	15.7	10.7	---	---
	1949	*Bund*	21.3	32.1	28.0	6.7	---	11.9
Lower Saxony	1947	*Land*	19.9	43.4	8.8	5.6	17.9	4.1 (ZP)
								0.3 (DRP)
	1949	*Bund*	17.6	33.4	7.5	3.1	17.8	8.1 (DRP)
North Rhine-Westphalia	1947	*Land*	37.5	32.0	6.0	14.0	---	9.8 (ZP)
	1949	*Bund*	36.9	31.4	8.6	7.6	---	8.9 (ZP)
Schleswig-Holstein	1947	*Land*	34.0	43.8	4.97	4.7	---	9.3 (SSV)
								3.1 (DKP)
	1949	*Bund*	30.7	29.6	7.4	3.1	12.1	5.4 (SSV)
Baden	1947	*Land*	55.9	22.4	14.3	7.4	---	---
	1949	*Bund*	51.1	23.7	17.4	4.2	---	3.6
Rhineland-Palatinate	1947	*Land*	47.2	34.3	9.8	8.7	---	---
	1949	*Bund*	49.1	28.6	15.8	6.2	---	0.3
Württemberg-Hohenzollern	1947	*Land*	54.2	20.8	17.7	7.3	---	---
	1949	*Bund*	59.1	18.9	15.3	5.2	---	1.5
Bremen	1947	*Land*	22.0	41.7	19.4 [a]	8.8	3.9	4.2
	1949	*Bund*	16.9	34.4	12.9	6.7	18.0	11.1

a This figure includes totals for both the FDP and BDV.

The Liberals, now nationally organized as the FDP under the leadership of Theodor Heuss, made the most spectacular gains by increasing their following by over a million votes. With the growing unpopularity of the Soviet Union and the improving economic situation, Communist support fell from 9.4 percent of the national vote to 5.7 percent (*Die Welt*, August 16, 1949).

The *Bundestag* results produced a number of significant changes in the political complexion of several of the *Länder*, with the most dramatic reorientation of political forces appearing in Bavaria, where the CSU total dropped from 52.3 percent in 1946 to 29.2 percent. The decline of the CSU was not the result of any sudden affinity on the part of the Bavarian electorate for the Social Democratic Party, itself a loser of 5.8 percentage points over 1946, rather of a splintering of the CSU's earlier base of support. A large portion of its earlier following was transferred to the strongly particularistic Bavarian Party (BP), led by Josef Baumgartner. Although formed in 1945, the BP did not actively enter the political arena until 1947, and first competed in a political election in the spring of 1948 when it gained 8.8 percent of the vote in Bavaria's second set of local elections. The BP success and the 12.6 percent won by refugee groups cut CSU support to 37.7 percent in the 1948 contests. The BP emphasized Bavarian tradition, federalism, and agrarianism and resented the presence of the large numbers of refugees in the *Land.* While it had much in common with the right-wing of the CSU from which it stemmed, personal rivalries and an unwillingness to cooperate prevented the possibility of merger. Better organized for the *Bundestag* election and espousing an extreme Bavarian nationalism, the BP polled 20.9 percent of the *Land* vote, a block which would ordinarily have gone to the CSU. In addition, the WAV, allied with refugee and expellee groups, gained a stunning 14.4 percent of the Bavarian total, in spite of the implication of its leader in a black marketeering scandal, to further fragment the non-Socialist vote.[47]

The strengthening of right-of-center groups, particularly the FDP and the German Party, hurt the CDU most in Northern Germany and Hesse. In North Rhine-Westphalia the party held its own and in Rhineland-Palatinate and Württemberg-Hohenzollern moderate gains were made. While slipping slightly from its 1947 *Land* election total in Baden, the CDU again obtained an absolute majority of the vote. The strict licensing policies of the French and their refusal up to 1950 to accept refugees on the grounds that France had not been party to the Potsdam agreement at which the movement of populations had been agreed to, prevented any radical changes from taking place in the political complexion of the *Länder* under their control.

While the CDU/CSU registered gains in two *Länder*, the SPD gained in only one and suffered its greatest losses in those states where it had earlier emerged as the leading party. Only in Schleswig-Holstein, however, did it lose its leading position to the CDU.[48] In North Rhine-Westphalia and the *Länder* of the French zone, the position of the SPD remained relatively stable in spite of a slight downward trend in all but Baden.

The Communists likewise lost ground. Although suffering a drop of 272,736 in its national total and percentage losses in all *Länder*, the KPD polled more votes in Bavaria, Bremen and Hamburg than in 1946. It experienced its greatest decline in North Rhine-Westphalia, its major stronghold, where support for the party was nearly halved.[49] The Communists obtained their highest total in Hamburg with 8.5 percent; however, even this figure was a drop over 1946 totals.

The Liberals recorded their most spectacular increase in Hesse, where their vote total jumped from the 15.7 percent registered in 1946 to 28.1 percent to outpoll the CDU and challenge the leading position of the SPD. Gains were made in five additional *Länder*, but in Bremen, Hamburg and Lower Saxony, where the party had to compete with a number of other right and right-of-center

TABLE 2.10

THE TWO PARTY VOTE IN THE *LÄNDER*

Land and Zone	1946/1947 *Landtag* Elections CDU/			August 14, 1949 *Bundestag* Election CDU/		
	CSU	SPD	Total	CSU	SPD	Total
American Zone						
Bavaria	52.3	28.6	80.9	29.2	22.8	52.0
Hesse	30.9	42.7	73.6	21.3	32.1	53.4 [b]
Württemberg-Baden	38.4	31.9	70.3	31.0	25.2	56.2
Bremen[a]	22.0 [a]	41.7 [a]	63.7 [a]	16.9	34.4	51.3 [b]
British Zone						
Schleswig-Holstein	34.0	43.8	77.8	30.7	29.6	60.3
Hamburg	26.7	43.1	69.8	19.7	39.6	59.3
North Rhine-Westphalia	37.4	32.0	69.4	36.9	31.4	68.3
Lower Saxony	19.9	43.4	63.3	17.6	33.4	51.0 [b]
French Zone						
Rhineland-Palatinate	47.2	34.3	81.5	49.1	28.6	77.7
Baden	55.9	22.4	78.3	51.1	23.7	74.8
Württemberg-Hohenzollern	54.2	20.8	75.0	59.1	18.9	78.0

a Figures for Bremen are for the 1947 *Land* election.

b The actual two-party vote in these three *Länder* in 1949 is slightly higher as the CDU was the third party. In Hesse the two-party vote would be 60.2 percent if figures for the FDP are used. In Bremen it would be 52.4 and in Lower Saxony 51.2 percent if figures for the DP are used.

parties for the conservative vote, it suffered modest losses.

The German Party, formerly the NLP, while confining its efforts to northern Germany, more than doubled its following, and in Bremen and Lower Saxony, with 18.0 and 17.8 percent of the vote respectively, replaced the CDU as second party. The German Rightist Party with 8.1 percent of the Lower Saxony vote and the Center Party with 8.9 percent in North Rhine-Westphalia contributed to the political fragmentation in those two *Länder* (*Die Welt*, September 18, 1949).

Better economic conditions, the worsening relations with the Soviets, the expansion of the electorate, the different character of issues created by the formation of a central government, the presence of an indelible record of the accomplishments of the parties in over two years of responsible office, and the emergence of new political groupings all had their influence on the outcome of the first *Bundestag* contest; yet the considerable variance between *Bund* and *Land* election results was to become an established pattern in West German politics.

The first national elections registered a move to the right, in spite of the fragmented nature of that movement as the Socialist parties suffered a loss of nearly ten percentage points. The results also represented a move away from the two-party alignment which appeared to be developing in earlier elections as the combined vote of the CDU/CSU and the SPD dropped from 72.7 percent in the 1946/1947 period to 60.2 percent in 1949. Only in Württemberg-Hohenzollern did the two-party vote increase, and only in three other *Länder*, Baden, Rhineland-Palatinate and North Rhine-Westphalia, did it remain relatively stable. In Bavaria it dropped by 35.7 percent and in Schleswig-Holstein by 22.5 percent. It was to take nearly a decade before the fragmenting forces in West German politics finally played themselves out.

The economic and political situation in Germany in 1949 gave strong support to proponents of a "grand coalition" between the CDU/CSU and the SPD. Most of the Minister Presidents of the *Länder* favored such a course. Karl Arnold, one of the most influential Christian Democratic leaders in the immediate postwar period and head of the coalition government in North Rhine-Westphalia which included Social Democrats, urged Adenauer to explore the possibility of forming a coalition with the SPD. However, sharp ideological differences between the parties and the marked personality clashes between Adenauer and Socialist leader Kurt Schumacher made such cooperation impossible, and Schumacher, fearing that a coalition with the CDU would involve the surrender of the SPD program in large measure, made it clear that he would not participate in such a government. A coalition of the CDU/CSU, the FDP and the German Party was formed to serve as West Germany's first national government, headed by Dr. Konrad Adenauer who was to retain the post of Chancellor for the first fourteen years of the new republic's existence.

Endnotes to Chapter II

1 The Bremen Democratic People's Party (BVD) which competed separately from the Free Democratic Party in the 1947 *Bürgerschaft* election subsequently merged with the Bremen FDP. This loose grouping of parties was amalgamated in 1948 into the Free Democratic Party under the leadership of Theodor Heuss. The party is referred to as the Liberals or as the FDP, although in Baden-Württemberg its affiliate continued to maintain the original designation, the DVP.

2 Under this system the voter is presented with a series of lists in each council area, and is given as many votes as there are councilors to be elected. He/she may either give his/her votes to the candidates on the same list (each party or group normally presenting a list with the same number of names as there are votes), or he/she can distribute his/her votes throughout the lists. An arrangement found in some districts was the accumulation

of up to three votes for any especially favored candidate. This same system was later allowed by the French in Württemberg-Hohenzollern and several districts in Rhineland-Palatinate. In Württemberg-Baden a voter was permitted to cross out some or all of the candidates and write in his/her own suggestions, a stipulation which caused considerable delay in the counting of ballots in the first local elections in that area (Ebsworth, 1960: 62-63).

3 The ill-advised appointment of Wilhelm Hoegner, a Social Democrat, to the premiership of Bavaria in September 1945 undoubtedly hurt the SPD and strengthened the CSU in that *Land* (Neumann, 1946: 756-758).

4 The CSU in its campaign in Bavaria made use of the slogan: "Do you want your barnyards, fields and cattle to remain your property? Then vote CSU" (*Time Magazine*, February 4, 1946: 29).

5 In Bavaria the CSU polled over two-thirds of the vote as the electorate reacted to the ban placed on CSU leader Friedrich Schäffer by American authorities on the eve of the election, reportedly for his Nazi sympathies. The ban prohibited him from either voting or holding office. The withdrawal of a pastoral letter critical of the U.S. denazification program which Catholic bishops had tried to circulate in the non-Bavarian sections of the Zone likewise influenced the election. By capturing most of the independent vote, which dropped from 37 to seven percent, the Christian Democrats gained 47.4 percent of the ballots cast in the election in Württemberg-Baden. Although the Socialists, Liberals and Communists all made moderate gains, their vote totals of 21.5, 10.5 and 5.7 percent of the vote respectively placed them far behind the CDU.

6 Note should be made that the first issue of *Die Welt* appeared April 2, 1946 under British license.

7 The French held local elections in the Saar September 12, 1946. Participation was high with 93.8 percent of the eligible voters casting ballots. The Christian People's Party (CVP) polled 52.4 percent of the vote, the Socialist Party of the Saar (SPS) 25.5 percent, the Communist Party (KP) 9.1 percent and independents 13.0 percent. These parties were authorized only in the Saar and had no official connections with any of the parties in the three Western zones of occupation (Saarland Statistical Office, 1949: 47-62).

8 In Lower Saxony 77.0 percent of the electorate cast ballots, in North Rhine-Westphalia 73.3 percent and in Schleswig-Holstein 77.2 percent. In contrast to the American zone, few members of the electorate had been declared ineligible to vote. Neither the British nor the French had gone into denazification with the crusading spirit of the Americans. Although a number of former medium and higher-grade Nazis had been excluded from the polls, the standards were far less rigorous than in the American zone.

9 Because of their strength in the small villages, independents won more seats in the zone than did any of the political parties with far fewer votes. The multiple vote and the allocation of nearly equal numbers of seats to the village councils regardless of size contributed to this seemingly unrepresentative result. In one *Kreis*, for example, independents received 101,051 votes and 1,226 seats, the CDU only 306 seats with 74,229 votes. In the British zone as a whole, independents received 23,870 seats with 2,649,179 votes, the CDU 19,129 seats with 6,637,664 votes and the SPD 17,122 seats with 6,379,136 votes (*Die Welt*, September 17 and 20, 1946).
Although the SPD outpolled the CDU 35.2 to 31.8 percent in Schleswig-Holstein, the strength of the Christian Democrats in rural areas enabled them to gain more council

seats. In Lower Saxony the SPD outpolled the CDU 37.1 to 15.0 percent, while the CDU gained 49.9 percent of the vote to the Socialists' 29.9 percent in North Rhine Westphalia. The indigenous Lower Saxony State Party in Lower Saxony was able to outpoll the CDU in that *Land*.

10 The KPD gained only 6.6 percent of the vote in North Rhine Westphalia, 4.0 percent in Lower Saxony and 4.4 percent in Schleswig-Holstein.

11 The Communist totals in the Ruhr and Rhineland increased from 6.6 to 9.4 percent and in nine cities of the region the party registered over twelve percent of the vote. In one, Solingen, its total of 22.9 percent nearly matched the figures of the CDU and SPD.

12 See "*Kopenhagens Südschleswigpolitik,*" *Die Welt*, September 17, 1946 and "*Die Dänen in Südschleswig,*" *Die Welt*, October 17, 1946. In Schleswig the German parties outpolled the SSV; however, their inability to work together enabled the Danes to win all direct seats.

13 Of the total votes cast throughout the zone, the SPD received 11,179,521, the CDU 11,029,953. The actual separation between the two parties was minimal inasmuch as each voter had from three to six votes.

14 See *Die Bürgerschaftswahl am 13. Oktober, 1946*, Hamburg Statistical Office, pages 3-19 for a complete description of the operation of the electoral system employed for the 1946 elections for municipal and county councils in the British zone *Länder*.

15 Hamburg changed to single member constituencies in 1949, while Bremen abandoned multimember constituencies completely for the 1947 *Bürgerschaft* election with the introduction of a pure proportional system. Raymond Ebsworth, a Military Government officer who participated in the deliberations on the British-imposed electoral system, noted that the goal of the British in establishing the multimember constituencies was to institute the principle of an annual turnover of a fraction of the councilors as in Britain, and so insisted that more than one candidate be elected from each constituency for this first election in order to establish overlapping terms (Ebsworth, 1960: 55 and 61). As soon as the Germans were given the right to devise their own electoral systems, the principle of annual elections was abandoned because of possible election-weariness resulting from *Land* and *Bund* elections in addition to local elections the same year.

16 See Figure 2 in Appendix I for an illustration of the influence of the alphabetical order on the election outcome in Hamburg's 20th District in the 1946 election.

17 Of the 21 major cities of the British zone where an absolute majority was obtained, the SPD won twelve, the CDU eight and the SSV one. In six of these cities the leading party also obtained an absolute majority of the votes cast.

18 Of the 84 direct seats in Hamburg the Socialists won 76, the CDU 8. In Bremen the SPD won 45, the BDV 9, the CDU 8 and independent candidates two of the 64 direct seats. Although fifteen independent candidates competed in the Hamburg election, none were successful in contrast to Bremen. Bremerhaven was not yet a part of Bremen for the 1946 election.

19 The only two other parties authorized in Berlin, the CDU and the FDP, obtained 22.2 percent and 9.3 percent of the vote respectively. Seats in the municipal parliament were distributed according to the principles of proportional representation from 20 districts into which the city was divided ("*Ergebnisse der Berliner Wahlen 1919 bis 1933*

und 1946 bis 1954," in *Die Wahlen am 5. Dezember in West Berlin,* Berlin Statistical Office, 1995: 46).

20 In Bavaria 2,092,385 voted to approve the draft constitution, while 871,027 opposed it; in Hesse 1,156,710 approved, 350,358 opposed the document; in Württemberg-Baden 921,181 voted for, 140,721 against the proposed constitution.

21 The Liberals obtained 14 parliamentary seats in contrast to the six gained with 8.1 percent of the vote in June. The LDP had been severely critical of the CDU for its support of the socialization measure.

22 Whereas 1,344,602 voters (71.7 percent) cast ballots for *Landtag* representatives, only 1,061,902 (56.6 percent) participated on the constitutional question. In Bavaria and Hesse voting participation was about the same for both the referendums and the election of members of the *Land* parliament.

23 In Bavaria the Liberals increased their vote from 1.7 to 5.6 percent, in Hesse from 8.1 to 15.7 percent and in Württemberg-Baden from 16.1 to 19.5 percent.

24 The Communists failed to gain representation in Bavaria even though they increased their following by 40,000 votes over the June election and gained 13,000 more votes than the FDP. The Liberals qualified for seats by virtue of the 10.9 percent following obtained in Upper and Middle Franken, even though their *Land* total was only 5.6 percent. The WAV, also with less than one-tenth of the *Land* vote, guaranteed itself representation by gaining 10.9 percent of the ballots cast in Upper Bavaria (*Wahl zum Bayerischen Landtag am 25. November 1962,* Heft 237, Bavarian Statistical Office: 122-125). For a complete description of the electoral system devised for the 1946 *Landtag* election in Bavaria, refer to page 220 of this study.

Whereas a *Sperrklausel* was placed directly in the newly written constitutions of Bavaria and Hesse, the basic law of Württemberg-Baden left the imposition of such a stipulation to subsequent legislation. As was the case with local electoral systems, the American authorities did not interfere in the formulation of the electoral systems for the first *Landtag* elections, and proportional arrangements were reintroduced into all three *Länder* of the American Zone. On the other hand, the innovation requiring a minimum percentage of the vote to quality for representation became a model for all other *Länder* and the national government.

25 Elections had been held in Bremen and Hamburg October 13, 1946; however, the future status of these two cities was not altogether clear at the time. No new elections were held in Hamburg until October 16, 1949, whereas in Bremen, with its transfer to the American zone and enlargement through the addition of Bremerhaven, new elections were held October 12, 1947.

26 Under the electoral laws devised for the first *Landtag* elections 95 of 149 deputies in Lower Saxony, 150 of 200 deputies in North Rhine-Westphalia and 42 of 70 deputies in Schleswig-Holstein were to be elected directly in single member constituencies with the remaining seats distributed among the qualifying parties according to various modifications of proportional representation. See Chapter VIII of this study for a full description of *Land* electoral systems.

27 When a party wins more seats by direct election than it otherwise would be entitled to under proportional representation, the excess seats are not lost to the party. Rather, the size of the *Landtag* is increased to equal the number of excess seats, known as *Überhangmandate.* The 1947 Christian Democratic success in single member constituencies in

North Rhine-Westphalia necessitated increasing the size of the *Landtag* from 200 to 216 seats.

28 The SPD failed to duplicate its 1947 following in Schleswig-Holstein until 1983, and, then only as the *Land's* second party, as the CDU gained 49.0 percent of the vote. However, in 1987, 1988, 1992, 1996 and 2000 it outpolled the CDU. In the 2005 *Land* election the CDU regained its earlier position as the state's leading party.

29 Food parcels from Denmark enticed many "*Speck Dänen*" (bacon Danes) to vote the SSV ticket. After 1947, support for the SSV (SSW) gradually receded, but increased to 4.3 percent in the 2009 *Landtag* election, for which it received four seats in the Schleswig-Holstein parliament. The exemption of the party of the Danish majority from the five percent clause has been widely disputed. In January 2005 the Supreme Administrative Court of Schleswig-Holstein ruled the exemption from the five percent restriction which applies to all other parties to be unconstitutional, a decision backed by the then CDU/SPD coalition in Kiel. A final settlement on the matter awaits a decision of the Federal Constitutional Court.

30 Since a party could conceivably have obtained 20 percent of the *Land* vote without gaining a single seat through failure to win a direct mandate or a highly concentrated party could win a direct seat with only three percent of the *Land* vote, the direct seat requirement, in effect, negated the proportional balancing function of the 28 reserve seats. The FDP, KPD and DKP would also have been excluded from representation under the electoral laws of Lower Saxony and North Rhine-Westphalia through failure to obtain five percent of the *Land* vote.

31 "*Gegenüberstellung der Landeswahlgesetze für Schleswig-Holstein, Niedersachsen und Nordrhein-Westfalen,*" in *Die Landeswahlen in Schleswig-Holstein vom 20. April 1947*: 81-103. Among the powers transferred to the *Landtage* of the British zone in the spring of 1947 was the right to formulate purely German electoral systems. Nevertheless, all of the *Länder* in question retained the principle of combining proportional representation with a simple majority system although removing certain annoying British-inspired stipulations. Hamburg, for reasons quite removed from any dislike for the British innovation, adopted a proportional system for the 1957 *Bürgerschaft* election. This system continued until the reintroduction of a mixed arrangement in 2004 under which 71 representatives are elected from seventeen multimember districts and fifty from party lists.

32 In contrast to the earlier elections held in the British zone, each voter in Schleswig-Holstein had only one vote and the allocation of indirect seats was determined by the d'Hondt formula rather than by the Hare system. Hamburg, by dropping the multiple vote and the use of the Hare system in distributing reserve list seats, held its 1949 and 1953 elections under a system not unlike that used in Schleswig-Holstein in 1947, minus the direct seat requirement. In 1950 Schleswig-Holstein amended its electoral law so as to make parties receiving at least five percent of the total *Land* vote or winning a direct mandate eligible for reserve list seats.

33 Once a proportional calculation is made on the basis of the total *Land* vote for each party, the number of seats won by direct election is deducted from each party's entitlement, with the balance representing the number of seats to be allocated to the party from the reserve list. If the number of direct seats won by the party exceeds its proportional allotment, the size of the *Landtag* is increased to allow the party to retain the excess seats (*Überhangmandate*).

34 In figures which exclude the results of the Hamburg election of October 13, 1946, the SPD polled 3,143,851 votes (36.7 percent), the CDU 2,744,537 votes (32.1 percent), the Communists 891,785 (10.4 percent), the Center Party 593,503 votes (6.9 percent), the FDP 568,159 votes (6.6 percent) and the NLP 440,467 votes (5.1 percent). Several splinter parties and independent candidates between them received 179,273 votes (2.2 percent). Had the Hamburg results been included in these totals, the position of the SPD in the British zone would have been even more favorable.

35 The large percentage of invalid ballots in Baden (9.2 percent) and Württemberg-Hohenzollern (7.5 percent) indicated a degree of opposition to the constitutions of those two *Länder*.

36 The constitution of Baden carried 296,959 votes to 140,188, in Württemberg-Hohenzollern 268,701 votes to 116,045.

37 In district Pfalz, where 55.1 percent of the population was Protestant, the vote against the constitution was 59.7 percent and against the school measure 63.2 percent. In administrative district Trier with a population 93.3 percent Catholic the opposition to the constitution was only 23.5 percent and to the school issue 17.2 percent (*Die Wahlen und Volksabstimmungen in Rheinland-Pfalz in den Jahren 1946/1947* [1948]: 7; 44-47).

38 Two-party totals amounted to 79.5 percent in the French zone, 76.6 percent in the American zone, 68.8 percent in the British zone and 72.7 percent for the three western zones as a whole.

39 By the time of the 1955 plebiscite, the western part of Germany had witnessed a remarkable economic recovery and its economy was outdistancing that of France. Even with the balloting taking place under radically changed conditions, 32.3 percent of the Saarlanders voted against union with Germany. A quite different result might have been expressed had West Germany not made such a spectacular recovery between 1947 and 1955. Many Germans at the time characterized the Saarlanders as a people that "bend with the wind."

40 The CVP gained 51.2 percent of the vote and 28 of the 50 seats, the Social Democratic Party of the Saar 32.8 percent and 17 seats, the Democratic Party of the Saar (DPS) 7.6 percent and three seats and the Communist Party, the only opponent of the constitution, 8.4 percent of the vote and two seats. Major changes over the local elections of the previous year included a gain of 7.3 percent by the Saar Socialists and the vote going to the DPS which had not organized for the earlier election ("*Die Wahlen im Saarland 1946-1949*," in *Die Gemeinderatswahl am 27. März 1949*; 1952: 47-62).

41 The SPD polled 41.7 percent of the Bremen vote and gained 46 of 100 seats in contrast to 47.6 percent and 51 of 80 seats in the election of the previous year. The CDU obtained 22.0 percent and 24 seats, the BDV 13.9 percent and 15 seats, the Communists 8.8 percent and 10 seats, the FDP 5.5 percent and two seats, and the German party, formerly the NLP, 3.9 percent and three seats. The only other party competing in the election, the Radical Social Freedom Party (RSF) received just 1.1 percent of the votes and no seats while independents obtained 3.1 percent of the vote.

42 In general, the election indicated a falling off of socialist support and a strengthening of the bourgeois parties, as the SPD and KPD together lost an 8.6 percentage share while the bourgeois parties gained an 8.1 percentage share. The addition of Bremerhaven had no influence on the SPD's 5.9 percentage loss as the new addition gave the Socialists a larger total (47.9 percent) than it had received the previous year in Bremen proper.

Without the addition of Bremerhaven the SPD would have suffered a loss of 15 rather than of only five seats.

43 In contrast to 1946 when two seats fell to independents, institution of a proportional system based on party lists prevented any independents from gaining a seat, although non-party candidates polled 3.1 percent of the vote.

44 A particularly interesting description of the difficulties surrounding the holding of the first *Bürgerschaft* election in Hamburg is found in *Die Bürgerschaftswahl am 13. Oktober 1946* (1947): 6-8.

45 In Bremen the totals of the BDV which subsequently merged with the FDP are considered in giving the Liberals a third place status in that *Land*. The Liberals failed to gain representation only in Schleswig-Holstein.

46 Between October 30, 1946 and December 31, 1948 a total of 1,372,000 expellees and 211,000 refugees settled in the three Western zones of Germany.

47 The founder of the WAV, Alfred Loritz, served as Denazification Minister in Bavaria for a period of six months prior to his being dismissed in July 1947 on black market charges. When refugees formed their own parties and the WAV became beset with internal strife, the parliamentary groups of the party in both Munich and Bonn disintegrated as most members deserted it. In the 1950 *Landtag* election the WAV faded to 2.8 percent of the vote and gained no seats. Its political death was marked by the 0.3 percent figure obtained in the 1952 *Kommunal* election in Bavaria.

48 The percentage loss in Schleswig-Holstein was 14.2 points, in Hesse 10.6 points, in Lower Saxony 10.0 points and in Bremen 7.3 points; in Hamburg the SPD's loss was limited to 3.5 percentage points. Refer to Table 2.9 of this chapter.

49 Some indication of the KPD's decline in public favor was registered in the *Kommunal* elections of October 17, 1948 in North Rhine-Westphalia when the party polled only 7.8 percent of the vote. Attempts of the Communist Party in April 1948 to change its name in the American zone to the Socialist Unity Party were rejected by OMGUS as a fraud upon the German people, intended to disguise the unpopular KPD. The British and the French likewise rejected such a redesignation, although activity of the party under the KPD label suffered no legal restrictions in any of the zones. See Seymour R. Bolton, "Military Government and the German Political Parties," *The Annals* (January 1950): 59.

CHAPTER III

The First Elections Under the New Federation

The Influence of the Establishment of the Bonn Government

The establishment of the Federal Republic in 1949 ushered in a new era in German politics, characterized by the increasing influence of national politics on political developments in the *Länder*. Prior to the formation of the central government the outcomes of regional contests were for the most part solely the concern of the often rather loosely-organized *Land* parties with coordination efforts limited to the zonal level. The policies of the occupying powers restricted any overall coordination in the first *Land* elections. The French, for example, refused to sanction any affiliation of parties in their zone with parties in the other two Western zones until after the initial regional elections had been held. Moreover, the major criterion in the formation of the first *Land* ministries was the establishment of a stable coalition regardless of its party composition. The all-party ministry in Lower Saxony, for example, contained groups ranging from the Communists on the left to the conservative German Party on the right. Even when a party held a parliamentary majority, as did the Socialists in two and the CDU/CSU in three *Länder*, it was reluctant to shoulder full responsibility for the acts of government in this critical period.[1] In most cases the ministries were continuations of the bodies which had been created by Allied appointment, and up to 1950 the dominant party pattern in the governments of the *Länder* was a "grand coalition" between the CDU/CSU and the SPD.

After 1949 the role and composition of the newly established upper house of the federal parliament, the *Bundesrat*, made it politically desirable for the parties comprising the national government to effect the coalition of ministries in the *Länder* reflecting the party make-up of the Bonn cabinet, and conversely, for the opposition parties, through control of the politics of the upper chamber, to establish a second line of defense in their attempts to frustrate the legislative program of the national coalition. As a delegative body directly responsible to the *Land* governments rather than to the separate *Land* electorates, the *Bundesrat* could be controlled only through the formation of favorable majorities in the *Länder*, making the outcomes of regional election contests and the party composition of the *Land* ministries of vital concern to the national parties. It was inevitable that the parties forming the national coalition, in order to assure the requisite *Bundesrat* majorities for their program, would attempt to coordinate the politics of the *Länder*.

The outcomes of the first popular regional election contests were for the most part determined by the economic-religious orientation of the *Länder*, by local conditions and by issues of local significance other than reactions to policies of the Occupation Powers. National policy, as in the areas of foreign relations, defense, foreign trade and resettlement of refugees, was the responsibility of the Western Allies, not of the first appointed *Land* governments nor of the politically responsible ministries formed in 1946 and 1947, and no German political party could be charged with the ineffectiveness of such a policy. With the establishment of the West German State in 1949, decisions of national and international significance became the responsibility of the Germans for the first time, and the parties of the national coalition became answerable to the electorate for their execution.

It is not surprising that national issues and foreign policy came to dominate *Land* election campaigns from the inception of the Federal Republic, since the problems facing the German people were primarily national, not local, in scope, and it was only in the *Bund* that the Germans, uncertain of their future and striving to maintain their identity as a nation, could assert themselves. Almost immediately such issues as the German contribution to Western defense, reunification and the pooling of Western Europe's coal and steel resources in the Schuman Plan were injected into the contests in the *Länder*. The outcomes of the elections in the fall of 1950 and the spring of 1951, fought precisely on these issues, indicated a possible loss of public support for Chancellor Adenauer's policies, causing Socialist leader, Kurt Schumacher, to call for new national elections.[2] With each successive *Land* election interpreted as a vote of confidence or non-confidence in the parties controlling the national government, the outcome of regional contests ceased to be merely the concern of the *Land* parties, but a concern of the whole party apparatus, and federal personalities came increasingly to take an active role in the campaigns in the *Länder* to support or condemn the policies of the national government and attempt to influence the electoral decision in favor of their *Land* counterparts. Rather than serving as expressions of sentiment on the effectiveness of the *Land* ministries, most regional elections since the establishment of the Federal Republic in 1949 have, in effect, taken on the character of a referendum on the national government.

The Politics of Political Fragmentation

The second series of *Land* election contests held between the 1949 and 1953 general elections were influenced by the same fragmenting forces which splintered the first *Bundestag* vote, reversing the earlier trend towards a kind of two-party system based on the bourgeois-socialist cleavage which had been developing in the *Länder*. Divisive forces, reflective of an unsettled political situation, which had been temporarily held in check for the first postwar *Land* elections by the restrictive licensing policies of the Western Allies, exerted themselves in the second regional contests with the lifting of most restrictions on political activity following the transfer of control over the regulation and authorization of political parties to the Germans.[3]

The unrestricted licensing of political groups produced a splintering of the political arena reminiscent of the Weimar period. *Land* elections ceased to be contests merely between the four original anti-fascist parties, but political battles between as many as twelve contending groups in some *Länder*. Fifteen separate parties gained representation in the various *Landtage* in the elections held between the first and the second *Bundestag* contests, and in Lower Saxony no fewer than ten parties gained parliamentary seats. The political splintering failed to be confined even by restrictive clauses now contained in most *Land* electoral systems, as five percent minimums proved no formidable barrier to the gaining of representation in the *Land* parliaments. In no *Land* did a single party obtain an absolute majority of the votes in contrast to three *Länder* in the 1946/1947 elections, and only in Hamburg and Hesse was a single party (the SPD in both instances) able to command a majority of parliamentary seats as opposed to five *Länder* in the first regional contests. In Bavaria and Schleswig-Holstein no party obtained as much as thirty percent of ballots cast, and, with the splintering of the bourgeois vote, the CDU/CSU total fell below twenty percent in five states, dropping to a low of 9.1 percent in Bremen.[4] Nationwide, nearly forty percent of the vote was polled by parties other than the CDU/CSU and the SPD. The rise of a powerful refugee movement beginning in 1950, the economic distress of a large section of the electorate, the initial lack of strong integrating forces on the national level and the absence of limitations on the formation of political groups contributed to the fragmentation of the period. After 1953 a backward trend set in; however, it was not until 1958/1959 that the appeal of various regional and interest type political movements had run its course and a stabilization began to take place around three national, multi-interest political movements.

The division of opinion expressed by the German voter in the second series of regional contests was most apparent on the right and more damaging to the interests of the Union parties than to those of the Socialists, and the CDU/CSU found itself having to "run with the pack" in competition for the bourgeois vote. As a result, the period from 1949 to 1952 marked the lowest ebb for the Christian parties in any series of *Land* elections and the only time, with the exception of the 1965-1969 period, that they did not outpoll the SPD in a series of *Land* contests.[5] Nevertheless, the greater ability of the CDU/CSU to attract coalition partners enabled it to maintain control of the *Bundesrat* during this period of flux.

While success of the Union's foreign and domestic policies and the growing personal popularity of Chancellor Adenauer enabled the party to achieve a position of supremacy on the national level as early as 1953, progress was more gradual in the *Länder*, where the absence of an integrating national campaign, the less restrictive nature of *Land* electoral systems,[6] the political peculiarities of each particular *Land* and the tendency of the German electorate at the time to give the CDU/CSU less support in regional than in national contests, hindered any spectacular Union advance on the *Land* level. Nonetheless, increased economic prosperity, the meeting of the needs of the refugee population, pensioners and war victims, and the widening prestige of Chancellor Adenauer for his efforts in regaining dignity and respect for the German people and as architect of the "New Germany" gradually won support for the Union in the *Länder* as voters came increasingly to base their decisions on the achievements of the national rather than of the regional parties. By 1956 the party was able to regain its earlier position of ascendancy on the *Land* level. The following year it polled an absolute majority of the third *Bundestag* vote and by 1959 its support on the *Land* level had expanded to over forty percent. This last year of the decade marked an early high point of Christian Democratic power in West Germany, as the following of the Social Democratic Party, effectively isolated by the success of Adenauer's and Erhard's policies, remained virtually stagnant between 1949 and 1959. The national totals of the SPD hovered around the thirty percent mark for the first three *Bundestag* elections, and its figure of 35.0 percent reached in the first series of regional contests was not exceeded on the *Land* level until 1958/1959. Not until the adoption of the Godesberg program in 1959 when the SPD dropped its Marxist ballast and transformed itself into a non-doctrinaire middle-of-the-road party could it become an effective challenge to the hegemony of the Union parties. The advance of the Social Democratic Party to a position of equality with the CDU/CSU on the *Land* level is discussed in Chapter V.

The 1949-1952 *Land* Elections

Between the 1949 and 1953 *Bundestag* contests ten parliamentary elections were held in the West German *Länder*, the first in Hamburg October 16, 1949, the last in the newly-created state of Baden-Württemberg March 9, 1952.[7] In addition to the influence of the establishment of the national government and the lifting of most restrictions on political activity on the outcomes of the second series of *Land* elections, parliamentary representation was affected by the presence of completely new or radically altered electoral systems in a number of the *Länder*. By 1948 the American zone provinces were beginning to take an interest in the mixed systems of the British zone, and for the 1950 elections both Bavaria and Hesse abandoned their earlier proportional arrangements for one which combined proportional and simple majority balloting.[8] Baden-Württemberg employed a similar system in 1952 for its first *Land* election.[9] While Rhineland-Palatinate, Schleswig-Holstein, Württemberg-Baden and, later, the new state of Baden-Württemberg were incorporating restrictive clauses in their electoral laws, requiring that a party obtain a minimum of five percent of the *Land* vote to qualify for representation, Lower Saxony deleted the requirement altogether, enabling no less than ten parties to gain seats in the parliament elected in May 1951.[10] Hamburg shifted from the four-man constituencies employed in the 1946 election to single member constituencies and changed the ratio between direct and indirect seats while retaining the system of *Mehr-* and *Reststimmen* in allocating seats from the reserve list. While Bavaria and Hamburg were increasing the size of their parliaments, from 180 to 204 members in the case of the former and from 110 to 120 seats in the case of the latter, both Hesse and Schleswig-Holstein reduced the size of their legislative bodies, from ninety to eighty members in Hesse and from seventy to 69 members in Schleswig-Holstein.[11]

The Bourgeois Alliances and CDU/CSU-SPD Rivalry

The first regional contests to follow the establishment of the Bonn government were characterized by the extensive use by the parties of the national coalition of electoral or party alliances. They were formed for the purpose of either strengthening their positions in certain *Länder* or breaking the political grip of the Socialists and thereby insuring a favorable majority for their programs in the *Bundesrat*. These alliances were most elaborate in the British zone *Länder* where Socialist strength was concentrated and the mixed electoral systems lended themselves to cooperative action.[12] The dominant form was an alliance between the CDU and FDP or DP; however, in Schleswig-Holstein all three parties cooperated against the SPD. The FDP, in addition to its bourgeois arrangements, also entered into agreements with rightist groups and the Refugee Party in several states, and the Refugee Party contracted similar arrangements with the German Association (DG) in Bavaria and Württemberg-Baden. While these arrangements did not appear in every *Land*, they all had a similar goal, to maximize the support of the parties making up the alliance and to minimize that of the other parties.

The efforts on the part of the bourgeois parties to defeat the Socialists and establish ministries similar in composition to the Bonn Government in as may *Länder* as possible met with varying degrees of success, but they resulted in the termination of most of the "grand coalitions" which had been in existence prior to the formation of the Federal Republic. The first of the bourgeois alliances, known as the Hamburg Native Alliance (*Vaterstädtischer Bund Hamburg-VBH*), was formed by the CDU, FDP and the German Conservative Party (DKP) for the election of October 16, 1949 in Hamburg.[13] Although the combination captured 34.5 percent of the vote and 40 seats, 22 by direct election, it failed to wrest control over the city administration from the Socialists, who utilized their majority in the 120 member *Bürgerschaft* to form a one-party government (*Die Welt*, October 18, 1949). While changes in the electoral law enabled the *Bund* parties to nearly double their representation over 1946, their support percentagewise fell below totals achieved in the earlier *Land* election and in the first *Bundestag* contest.[14] The electoral arrangement between the CDU and the FDP in North Rhine-Westphalia proved more successful, as the CDU won 93 direct seats, the FDP five, and the two parties together commanded 119 of 215 *Landtag* mandates (*Die Welt*, June 20, 1950).[15] The pre-election agreement between the two parties had encompassed 29 districts where their combined strengths were needed to defeat the Socialist candidates; in 12 districts the CDU refrained from putting up candidates and urged voters to support the FDP nominees, while the FDP supported Christian Democrat candidates in seventeen districts.[16] The FDP also made a similar arrangement with the DRP in certain districts, enabling three DRP members to gain *Landtag* seats over the FDP reserve list. Although the CDU-FDP combination held a sufficient number of parliamentary seats following the election of June 18, 1950 to form the right-of-center ministry desired by Chancellor Adenauer, Minister President Karl Arnold of the CDU's left-wing proposed a continuation of the existing coalition with the SPD, which held 68 seats in the new *Landtag*. A bitter political battle ensued between Adenauer and Arnold, eventually resulting in the breakup of the "grand coalition" with the Socialists, but in which Arnold asserted his independence by turning to the Center Party, which, with sixteen seats, enabled him to govern until 1954 with a three vote margin (Heidenheimer, 1958: 813-815).[17]

Three weeks following the decision in North Rhine-Westphalia the parties of the Bonn coalition, in an electoral bloc known as the *Deutscher Wahlblock*, won 31 of 46 direct seats to break the Socialist majority in Schleswig-Holstein.[18] Under an arrangement agreed to prior to the election, the CDU entered candidates in 24 constituencies, the German Party in twelve, and the FDP in nine. A single constituency in Flensburg was left uncontested, as all three parties supported an independent candidate in an attempt to defeat the Danish minority party representative.[19] By combining their strength the *Block* parties gained 44.9 percent of the mandates with only 36.4 percent of the vote, but failed to achieve the sought-for majority. Although the Socialists won only eight direct seats in contrast to 34 in 1947 and saw their count of mandates reduced from 43 to 19, they remained the single strongest party. The Socialist set-back enabled the bourgeois parties, following two months of bitter negotiations, to form a government with Waldemar Kraft's Refugee Party, marking the first major success for Adenauer's coordination efforts.[20]

Although the results in Schleswig-Holstein were widely interpreted as an expression of popular satisfaction with the domestic and foreign policies of the Adenauer government, the decline in Socialist support had less to do with Adenauer's policies than with the political reorientation taking place in this northernmost *Bundesland* as a result of the rise of a powerful refugee political movement.[21] Moreover, the combined vote of the parties of the national coalition in the Schleswig-Holstein election fell below that polled in both the 1947 *Land* and 1949 *Bundestag* contests (*Die Welt*, July 10 and 11, 1950).[22]

While the elections in the summer of 1950 witnessed the dropping of the Socialists from the coalition in Düsseldorf and the replacement of the SPD-led government by a bourgeois coalition in Kiel, the electoral decisions in the fall of 1950 were to enable the Socialists to turn the tables on the CDU. The November

TABLE 3.1

THE SECOND SERIES OF *LAND* ELECTIONS[23]

	1949 Hamburg			1950 North Rhine-Westphalia			1950 Schleswig-Holstein		
Party	Per-Cent	Direct Seats	Total Seats	Per-Cent	Direct Seats	Total Seats	Per-Cent	Direct Seats	Total Seats
SPD	42.8	50	65	32.3	52	68	27.5	8	19
CDU	a	a	a	36.9	93	93	19.8	16	16
FDP	a	a	--	12.1	5	26	7.1	8	8
KPD	7.4	---	5	5.5	---	12	2.2	---	---
DP	13.3	---	9	1.7	---	---	9.6	7	7
BHE	---	---	---	---	---	---	23.4	5	15
ZP	---	---	---	7.5	---	16	---	---	---
SSW	---	---	---	---	---	---	5.5	2	4
RSF	2.0	---	1	2.0	---	---	---	---	---
RSP	---	---	---	0.2	---	---	1.6	---	---
DKP	a	a	---	---	---	---	---	---	---
Others	34.5 [a]	22 [a]	40 [a]	1.8	---	---	3.4	---	---
Totals		72	120		150	215		46	69

a For the 1949 *Land* election in Hamburg the CDU, FDP and DKP formed a party alliance known as the *Vaterstädtischer Bund Hamburg*, which gained 34.5 percent of the vote and 40 seats. The CDU occupied 22 of these seats, the FDP 17, the DKP one.

campaigns in Bavaria, Hesse and Württemberg-Baden were dominated by the issue of West German rearmament, as the Western Allies attempted to work out a formula by which the Germans could make a contribution to European defense. Although endorsing some form of participation, Chancellor Adenauer was vague about how much and under what terms the German contribution would be made, giving the Socialists ample ammunition to exploit the issue to the fullest. SPD leaders demanded that the German people be given the opportunity to express their sentiment on the subject either through a national election or a special plebiscite. In Hesse the Socialists were aided by the Protestant Church which condemned the remilitarization program with a call for German neutrality (*Die Welt*, November 21, 1950; *New York Times*, November 20, 1950).

In contrast to the earlier elections in the British zone, no formal alliances between the CDU and the FDP were consummated in the American zone *Länder*, although the electoral systems of both Bavaria and Hesse lended themselves to beneficial cooperation. Local feelings between the largely Catholic CDU and the right-oriented nationalist Hessen FDP ruled out such cooperation in Hesse where the FDP formed an alliance with the Refugee Party. Hurt not only by the rearmament issue, but by dissension within the ranks of the *Land* party which was divided between those desiring a continuation of the relatively successful SPD-CDU coalition and those determined to institute a bourgeois government modeled after Bonn, the CDU total fell from 30.9 to 18.8 percent (Heidenheimer, 1958: 818-819).[24] The Socialists, on the other hand, aided by the new electoral arrangement which combined proportional representation with the simple majority ballot, won 44.4 percent of the Hessian vote and 47 of 80 *Landtag* seats. Backed by a legislative majority, the SPD terminated its earlier coalition with the CDU and formed an all-Socialist government.

The Württemberg-Baden election, held November 19, 1950, the same day as the contest in Hesse, registered a similar loss in Christian Democrat support and Socialist gains. Having replaced the CDU as the *Land*'s leading party, the SPD took action to drop the Christian Democrat ministers from the existing cabinet and continued in coalition with the Liberals, whose leader, Reinhold Maier. remained in the post of Minister President.[25]

Bolstered by their successes in Hesse and Württemberg-Baden, the Socialists continued to make rearmament the dominant issue in the Bavarian campaign one week later. In stark contrast to the poor turnouts in Hesse and Württemberg-Baden, 79.9 percent of the Bavarian electorate went to the polls. With 28.0 to the CSU's 27.4 percent the SPD outpolled the CSU in this stronghold of German conservatism for the first and only time in a *Land* election (*Die Welt*, November 28, 1950). However, because of differing fortunes of the two parties in the seven administrative districts into which the *Land* was divided and the ability of the CSU to win more direct seats than the SPD under Bavaria's new mixed electoral system, the CSU gained 64 to the Socialists' 63 seats, giving it the responsibility of forming the government.[26] Having lost its absolute majority in the *Landtag*, the CSU had to search for coalition partners, a task made difficult by the large bloc of seats won by the particularistic Bavarian Party. Whereas earlier elections had witnessed the breakdown of cooperation between the SPD and the Union parties, the fragmented political situation required such cooperation in Bavaria, and, after a protracted and bitter period of negotiations, a coalition comprising the CSU, SPD and Refugee Party was hammered out. Although the CSU and the Socialists controlled a majority of *Landtag* seats, the new coalition could not count on the complete loyalty of the CSU's right wing, which would have preferred a small coalition with the Bavarian Party to a grand coalition with the Socialists (Office of the U.S. High Commissioner for Germany, 5th *Quarterly Report*, 1950: 35).

To have attributed the increase in strength of the Socialists and corresponding loss in strength of the CDU/CSU in the three November elections solely to the rearmament issue as many political observers did at the time was to oversimplify the problem. Increasing prices, inadequate housing, vexation over shortages of sugar and coal, and the low voter turnout in Hesse and Württemberg-Baden, which amounted to 64.9 and 57.2 percent respectively, all played a role. But more significant was the rise of a refugee political movement in all three *Länder* and the success of the Bavarian Party in Bavaria. The refugee totals amounted to 14.7 percent in Württemberg-Baden, 12.3 percent in Bavaria and probably represented ten percent of the vote in Hesse, where the Refugee Party formed an alliance with the FDP. In addition to the entrance of a strong refugee party into the political arena in Bavaria, the Bavarian Party captured 17.9 percent of the vote, a bloc which would ordinarily have gone to the CSU. Appealing to the particularistic sentiment of the native Bavarian, the BP won sixteen direct seats and 39 seats overall.[27] There may also have been some credence in Adenauer's assertion that the Socialists had captured most of the former Communist vote, which virtually disappeared in Bavaria. In any case, the CSU bore the brunt of the political reorientation resulting from the entrance of two new parties into the election. Nonetheless, the interpretation of CDU/CSU losses as a rebuff of Adenauer's defense policies was to deal Allied defense plans a severe setback.

Construing their successes in the three *Land* elections held since remilitarization had become an active issue as an endorsement of their stand on the question, the Socialists pressed for nation-wide elections, holding that Adenauer no longer commanded the confidence of the German people. Kurt Schumacher, national leader of the Social Democrats, while not opposing German rearmament as such, demanded that three pre-conditions be met: 1) that the whole German population be given the opportunity to express itself on the question of remilitarization, 2) that German rearmament be carried out behind a shield of sufficient Allied force, and 3) that full equality be given to the German forces (*New York Times*, November 28 and December 3, 1950). Bitter memories of the war undoubtedly caused many Germans to have reservations concerning the rebuilding of German armed might, but the negative attitude of the Socialists to the question of German rearmament and to other international experiments as the Schuman Plan and the EDC was eventually to isolate the party and bring it a devastating defeat in 1953. Since the initiative for dissolving the *Bundestag* prior to the end of the legislative term resided with the Federal Chancellor and not with the Opposition, Schumacher's appeal for new elections came to naught.

The CDU continued to lose ground in the regional contests held in Bremen, Lower Saxony and Rhineland-Palatinate during the course of 1951. The Socialists, while also suffering percentage losses in all three *Länder*, however, were able to maintain a combined total of 145 seats in the three state parliaments.[28] In Rhineland-Palatinate the Union total fell 8.0 percentage points below the 1947 figure, but the SPD failed to topple the CDU from its leading position by its inability to make corresponding gains. Foreign policy continued to be the overriding issue in the campaign as the Socialists attacked the Schuman Plan for the merging of Western Europe's coal and steel resources, the Federal Government's remilitarization plan and other external policies. The

TABLE 3.2

THE SECOND SERIES OF *LAND* ELECTIONS (Continued) [29]

	1950 Hesse			1950 Württemberg- Baden		1950 Bavaria		
Party	Per- Cent	Direct Seats	Total Seats	Per- Cent	Total Seats	Per- Cent	Direct Seats	Total Seats
SPD	44.4	36	47	33.1	34	28.0	38	63
CDU/CSU	18.8	4	12	26.4	28	27.4	46	64
FDP/DVP	31.8 [a]	8	13 [a]	21.0	23	7.1	1	12
BHE/DG	a	---	8 [a]	14.7	15	12.3	---	26 [b]
KPD	4.7	---	---	4.8	---	1.9	---	---
BP	---	---	---	---	---	17.9	16	39
WAV	---	---	---	---	---	2.8	---	---
Others	0.3	---	---	---	---	2.6	---	---
Totals		48	80		100		101	204

a The FDP formed an alliance with the Refugee Party for the 1950 election in Hesse. Following the election results the eight BHE members elected on the FDP ticket formed their own *Fraktion* in the Hessen *Landtag*.

b Of the 26 seats won by the BHE-DG alliance, 20 were occupied by Refugee Party members, six by DG representatives.

FDP, although a member of the national coalition, also did not hesitate to criticize certain policies of the CDU/CSU. Free Democrat leader, Franz Blücher, had been only lukewarm toward the Schuman Plan and his party was strongly opposed to federal legislation on workers' codetermination with management (Office of the U.S. High Commissioner for Germany, *7th Quarterly Report*, 1951: 26).[30] Nevertheless, following the election in Rhineland-Palatinate the CDU broke up its existing coalition with the SPD and formed a government with the FDP on the Bonn model.

Rhineland-Palatinate was the first *Land* since remilitarization became an active issue where the results remained uninfluenced by a large refugee vote,[31] and as the FDP, not the Socialists, won away much of the CDU's former support, the outcome indicated less an endorsement of the stand of the SPD on the Bonn government's policies than an uncertainty and even confusion over those policies which appeared to many to be a groping in the dark, as is often the case in the initial stages of great international experiments (*Die Welt*, April 30 and May 1, 1951).

To strengthen their position for the election of May 6, 1951 in Socialist-controlled Lower Saxony, the CDU and the German Party combined in an alliance known as the Lower German Union (*Niederdeutsche Union – NU*). The combination's attempt to defeat the Socialists in the *Land's* 95 single member constituencies met with abysmal failure, as the SPD won 64 direct seats, six more than in 1947, with nearly ten percent fewer votes, while the Union parties gained only 35 seats in contrast to 57 seats in 1947.[32] The disappointing showing of the CDU-DP alliance could be blamed on two factors, the splintering of the political Right and the entry of the Refugee Party into the political arena to claim 14.9 percent of the Lower Saxony vote.[33] Moreover, the deletion of the five percent or direct seat requirement from the *Land* electoral law enabled four splinter parties to gain ten seats which otherwise would have been distributed among the larger parties (*Die Welt*, May 7, 1951).[34] Unable to form a majority on its own, the SPD negotiated an agreement with the *Zentrum* and the Refugee Party which had earlier supported bourgeois forces in Schleswig-Holstein (*Die Welt*, May 8, 1951).

In the Bremen election of October 7, 1951 the Christian Democrats registered their poorest showing in any election of the postwar period with 9.1 percent of the votes. Although never strong in Bremen, the CDU was again hurt by the splintering of the right-of-center vote in that *Land*, 14.7 percent of which went to the German Party, 11.8 percent to the FDP, 7.7 percent to the Socialist Reich Party and 4.3 percent to the Voters' League of Victims of Bombing (*Wählergemeinschaft der Fliegergeschädigten—WdF*).[35] The existence of a straight proportional system ruled out any advantage to be gained from an alliance with the DP and FDP, both of which outpolled Adenauer's party (*Die Welt*, October 8, 1951).

The SPD emerged from the election as the *Land's* strongest party, although it too suffered a percentage loss over its 1947 figure. While the SPD and the Free Democrats controlled sufficient seats to continue their existing coalition, moderate socialist *Bürgermeister* Wilhelm Kaisen brought the CDU into his cabinet.[36]

The last of the second series of *Land* elections was held March 9, 1952 in the area encompassed by the former *Länder* of Baden, Württemberg-Baden and Württemberg-Hohenzollern. The body elected was to serve as both a constituent assembly, charged with the purpose of framing a constitution for the new *Land* of Baden-Württemberg and as *Landtag*. National rather than local issues played the dominant role in the campaign, as the election became a foreign policy test of strength on Germany's contribution to Western defense by becoming a member of the proposed European Defense Community. Realizing that severe losses would weaken his hand on defense and strengthen the Socialist demand for new parliamentary elections, Adenauer made two trips to the new *Land*, and the two parties waged a vigorous campaign. Although the CDU suffered losses

TABLE 3.3

THE SECOND SERIES OF *LAND* ELECTIONS (Continued) [37]

Party	1951 Rhineland-Palatinate		1951 Lower Saxony			1951 Bremen	
	Per-cent	Total Seats	Per-Cent	Direct Seats	Total Seats	Per-cent	Total Seats
SPD	34.0	38	33.7	64	64	39.1	43
CDU	39.2	43	23.5	23	35	9.1	9
FDP/BDV	16.7	19	8.4	3	12	11.8	12
BHE	1.9	---	14.9	1	21	5.6	2
KPD	4.3	---	1.8	---	2	6.4	6
DP	---	---	a	a	a	14.7	16
SRP	---	---	11.0	4	16	7.7	8
ZP	2.1	---	3.3	---	4	---	---
DRP	0.5	---	2.2	---	3	---	---
DSP	---	---	0.8	---	1	---	---
WdF	---	---	---	---	---	4.3	4
Others	1.3	---	0.1	---	---	1.3	---
Totals		100		95	158 [b]		100

a For the *Land* election in Lower Saxony the CDU and the DP combined in a party alliance known as the Lower German Union (NU). The figures in this column represent the totals of the Union, not of either of the parties separately.

b The number of seats in the Lower Saxony *Landtag* was raised by nine as the SPD succeeded in winning nine direct seats in excess of its proportional entitlement (*Überhangmandate*).

over its 1946/1947 *Land* and 1949 general election figures in the three constituent *Länder*, in the Württemberg-Baden portion of the *Land* the party gained 2.8 percent while the Socialists absorbed a corresponding loss in comparison with totals in the 1950 contest when the rearmament issue was at its peak (*Die Welt*, March 11, 1952). The SPD made gains over its *Bundestag* totals in the three regions and duplicated the 1946/1947 *Land* election figures; however, the party's loss in the most populous portion of the *Land* was construed as showing that the Germans were not overridingly opposed to the rearmament policy of the Federal government, thus removing the psychological obstacles to West German ratification of the EDC.

Under ordinary circumstances the CDU, as the new state's leading party with 50 of 121 mandates, would have formed the government;[38] however, serious dissention within the CDU, resulting from opposition within its ranks to the formation of a single Southwest State, as well as the political adroitness of Reinhold Maier, *Land* leader of the Free Democrats and Minister President of the former *Land* of Württemberg-Baden, who resented the Chancellor's attempts to dominate his party, caused the FDP to side with the Socialists and the Refugee Party in the formation of a government, holding that an FDP-CDU coalition would prove too unstable. The establishment of the left-of-center coalition in Baden-Württemberg drastically altered the party composition of the *Bundesrat*, as the safe CDU states of Baden and Württemberg-Hohenzollern had been extinguished in the process, and more than offset the earlier party change in Schleswig-Holstein. While the national coalition had enjoyed a safe majority in the *Bundesrat* since 1949, it was now faced for the first time with the possibility of a hostile upper chamber on certain vital questions. Maier's action was assailed by party leaders of the CDU on both the *Land* and national levels as well as by the federal executive of his own party; however, it was not until October 1953, following Adenauer's overwhelming victory in the second *Bundestag* election, that the "sore" in the Southwest State was removed.[39]

In the ten regional contests held between the first and the second *Bundestag* elections, exclusive of Berlin and the Saar,[40] the Socialists made gains over their 1949 general election totals in every *Land* but Schleswig-Holstein and bettered their previous regional election totals in four *Länder*. Although polling a smaller percentage of the national vote than in the first series of regional contests, the poor showing of the CDU/CSU in these same elections enabled the Socialists to outpoll the Union parties in seven *Länder*.[41] In suffering losses over its 1946/1947 figures in every *Land* and over its *Bundestag* totals in all but North Rhine- Westphalia, where it duplicated its 1949 following, the CDU/CSU lost its leading position on the *Land* level to the Socialists.

The changing fortunes of the two main parties and the bitter antagonisms which had developed between them caused nearly every *Land* to witness a change in the party composition of its government between 1949 and 1953. The "grand coalitions" between the CDU and SPD were broken up in Hesse, Lower Saxony, North Rhine-Westphalia, Rhineland-Palatinate, Württemberg-Baden and Württemberg-Hohenzollern: in Hesse it was replaced by an all-Socialist government; in Lower Saxony by a Socialist-*Zentrum* cabinet in September 1950 and after June 1951 by a government comprising Socialist, Refugee Party and *Zentrum* ministers under a Social Democrat premier; in North Rhine-Westphalia by a coalition of the CDU and *Zentrum* headed by a Christian Democrat Minister-President; in Rhineland-Palatinate by a CDU-FDP ministry under a Christian Democrat; in Württemberg-Baden by an FDP-SPD coalition headed by a Free Democrat (1950 to 1952); and in Württemberg-Hohenzollern the coalition was dissolved upon the absorption of the *Land* into the new South-

TABLE 3.4

THE 1952 *LAND* ELECTION IN BADEN-WÜRTTEMBERG[42]

Party	Baden-Württemberg		Württemberg-Baden		Württemberg-Hohenzollern
	Percent	Seats	Baden Seats	Baden Seats	Seats
CDU	36.0	50	14 [a]	24	12
SPD	28.0	38	8	25	5
FDP/DVP	18.0	23	4	15	4
BHE	6.3	6	---	5	1
KPD	4.4	4	---	4	---
DG/BHE	3.1	---	---	---	---
SRP	2.4	---	---	---	---
ZP	0.9	---	---	---	---
Others	0.1	---	---	---	---
Totals		121 [a]	26 [a]	73	22

a The CDU won a single *Überhangmandat* in Baden, increasing the number of deputies elected from that portion of Baden-Württemberg from 25 to 26 and from the *Land* as a whole from 120 to 121. Baden filled 16 seats by direct election, Württemberg-Baden 45 and Württemberg-Hohenzollern 13 for a total of 74.

west State in 1952. Following the formation of Baden-Württemberg the all-CDU cabinet of Baden and the two above-mentioned governments of Württemberg-Baden and Württemberg-Hohenzollern were replaced by a ministry of the SPD-FDP-BHE headed by Free Democrat Reinhold Maier.

In Bavaria the complicated political situation necessitated the formation of a coalition between the CSU and the SPD where one had not previously existed since 1947. The new Bavarian government, headed by Christian Social leader Hans Ehard, also included the Refugee Party as a safety measure against the doubtful loyalty of the CSU Right-wing. Also in Bremen the CDU was brought into the existing SPD-FDP coalition, although Christian Democrat support was not required for a majority. In Schleswig-Holstein the all-Socialist government was replaced by a four-party cabinet which included CDU-FDP-DP and BHE ministers, headed by a Christian Democrat, and in Hamburg the Socialists formed a one-party government. In the nine *Länder* which existed following the formation of the Southwest State the SPD participated in six governments, the CDU/CSU in five; each party headed four governments, the Free Democrats one.

The Rise of Refugee Political Movements

One of the most significant political developments in the period immediately following the first *Bundestag* election was the emergence of a number of refugee political movements, most important of which was the BHE (*Block der Heimatvertriebenen und Entrechteten* – the Bloc of Expellees and Victims of Injustice). Prior to 1950 refugee and expellee parties had been prohibited in the hope that the newcomers from the East would thereby be more readily integrated into their new surroundings and find homes in the established parties. However, the failure of the major parties to develop an effective refugee program or to reserve seats for refugee leaders in their *Landtag* delegations caused the unassimilated newcomers to form political movements of their own. In 1950 the count of refugees and expellees inhabiting the three Western zones numbered 9,613,000 or 20.2 percent of the entire West German population.[43] Moreover, they were unevenly distributed, having been absorbed by the predominantly agricultural *Länder* of Bavaria, Lower Saxony and Schleswig-Holstein where a modicum of shelter could be found, but which were economically least capable of supporting their numbers. Although the population of these three *Länder* had represented only one-third of the inhabitants living in the area encompassed by West Germany in 1939, in 1950 they housed 56 percent of the refugees, and while their total population had increased by 38 percent (over fifty percent in Schleswig-Holstein), that of the remaining *Länder* rose by only eleven percent. In Schleswig-Holstein refugees accounted for 38.3 percent of the population, in Lower Saxony 32.6 percent and in Bavaria 23.7 percent. Those *Länder* economically most capable of absorbing the refugees lacked the necessary living quarters because of the extensive destruction in their cities. As housing and employment opportunities became available, however, large numbers of refugees were transferred to these more highly industrialized *Länder*, primarily to North Rhine-Westphalia which had a refugee population of only 12.8 percent in 1950. Since France up to 1950 refused to participate in the movement of populations on the grounds that she had not been a party to the agreement at Potsdam, refugees made up only 6.9 percent of the zonal population, placing the greatest burden on the economies of the American and British zone *Länder*.[44]

Prior to the formation of parties of their own, refugees supported those political groups which appeared to best further their interests. In Bavaria the Economic Reconstruction Association (WAV) attracted many refugee adherents in the first elections as it demanded restoration of Germany's pre-war eastern boundaries. In the constituent assembly election of June 30, 1946, the WAV polled 4.4 percent of the vote and gained eight assembly seats. In the first *Landtag* election in December it increased its total to 7.4 percent to command 13 *Landtag* seats. Its leader, Alfred Loritz, served as Denazification Minister in the first Ehard cabinet for a period of six months before being dismissed in July 1947 on black market charges. The party's support fell to 1.6 percent in

Bavaria's second *Kommunal* elections held in the spring of 1948, as independent refugee groups polled 12.6 percent of the *Land* vote. However, in the *Bundestag* election of 1949, the WAV, allied with these same refugee and expellee groups, gained 14.4 percent of the Bavarian vote and twelve *Bundestag* mandates. Beset by internal strife and desertions by its parliamentary representatives and abandoned by expellee and refugee groups which formed their own parties, the WAV's following fell to only 2.8 percent of the Bavarian vote in the 1950 *Land* election.[45]

While some refugees gave their support to the established parties during the period of prohibition, others formed independent *"Wählergruppen"* to contest local elections. Such associations met with considerable success in the local balloting in 1948; however, in Hesse the Minister of the Interior worded his instructions on the administration of the electoral law of 1948 so as to deny representation to refugee organizations. Organized as the Democratic Voters Association (*Demokratische Wahlgemeinschaft—DEWAG*) the refugees challenged the elections of April 25, 1948 on grounds that the implementation of the electoral law had discriminated against independent electoral groups. Their claim was upheld by the Supreme Administrative Court for the Bizonal Area, and elections were held in the disputed area March 20, 1949 under the new regulations. In that election the DEWAG outpolled both the CDU and SPD and won ten of 36 seats on the Waldek council, although running second to the Free Democrats. New elections under the revised implementation of the Hessian electoral law were also held in *Kreis* Alsfeld in which a similar group of "disenfranchised" elements called the Democratic Reconstruction Association (*Demokratische Wiederaufbau Gemeinschaft—DWG*) succeeded in capturing more votes than any of the other parties and eight of thirty *Kreistag* seats (*OMGUS 45*, 1949: 166-167).[46] In the 1949 *Bundestag* election the refugees could enter only individual candidates in the single member constituencies, as only qualified parties could take advantage of the *Land* reserve lists. In Hesse refugee candidates, running in only a few districts, polled 244,339 votes or 11.9 percent of the *Land* total, but elected no representatives (*5th Quarterly Report*, 1950: 33).[47] In Württemberg-Baden they succeeded in electing one candidate.

With the lifting of the ban on refugee political movements in 1950, the newcomers, badly housed, discriminated against by the native population, unemployed at a rate twice that of the natives, and hearing nothing but promises from the established parties, formed a number of political groups to secure direct representation for their demands. The refugees did not contest the election of June 18, 1950, in North Rhine-Westphalia and the campaign there was waged between the traditional parties. Although numbering some 1,700,000 in 1950 in the Rhineland and Ruhr, refugees made up a relatively small percentage of the area population and were quickly absorbed into the big cities of the *Land* where their separate identity went unnoticed. Moreover, unemployment in North Rhine-Westphalia was only half of the West German average.

Schleswig-Holstein presented a different situation. Not only did refugees make up nearly 40 percent of the population, but unemployment was high, amounting to 28 percent of those employable, the newcomers were made to feel unwelcome by the native population and most refugee families lived under the most sordid conditions. It is therefore not surprising that this *Land* with its discontented, unassimilated new arrivals should give political birth to the BHE, the most important of the refugee political movements. Led by Waldemar Kraft, a former SS officer, the party appealed to all "disinherited" elements of German society, including expellees, refugees, pensioners, war victims and war orphans, demanding an effective Equalization of Burdens Law (*Lastenausgleichgesetz*),[48] return of their homelands, and compensation of losses incurred by these groups. Its slogan "all Germans have lost the war together and together they must pay for its consequences" summed up the social claims of the party. In effect, the BHE was a special interest party, set on alleviating those conditions which formed the basis for its existence. The more successful it was in achieving its goals, the less there remained the need for its continuance. Its program was set upon committing political suicide.[49]

In the election of July 9, 1950 in Schleswig-Holstein the Refugee Party proved itself to be a force to be reckoned with in West German politics as it gained 23.4 percent of the vote and 15 of 69 seats to become the second strongest parliamentary group next to the SPD. Because of the fragmented political situation in the *Land*, no government could be formed without its cooperation. After prolonged negotiations undertaken with the Socialists on the one hand and the bourgeois parties on the other, agreement was reached on a coalition with the CDU, FDP and German Party, with refugee leader Kraft serving as Deputy Premier and Minister of Finance and his colleague, Adolf Asbach, as Minister for Social Affairs, Labor and Refugees (*Keesing's*, December 2-9, 1950: 11124). Although the BHE did not receive the total support of the refugee population in Schleswig-Holstein as it had hoped, the party's success was nevertheless of great concern to the Allied authorities, who had made strong efforts to dissuade the refugees from forming a separate party, and to the Bonn government, which was sensitive to the possibility of a refugee political movement sweeping the country and solidifying the unassimilated and often unemployed newcomers into a troublesome group. While the Schleswig-Holstein result compelled the Central Government and the Allied authorities to pay greater attention to the demands of the refugees, it also stimulated the refugees to attempt to duplicate their success in other *Länder*.

In Hesse the BHE group formed an alliance with the FDP in contesting the election of November 19, 1950. The combination gained 31.8 percent of the vote and 21 seats; however, in comparison with the *Bundestag* election the result was far from satisfying. The FDP had alone polled 597,081 votes in 1949 and refugee candidates, running in only a few districts, 244,339 in the same contest. In 1950 the combination polled 588,739 votes, or less than the FDP alone the previous year. Even the drop of 257,253 in the size of the electorate could not account for the poor showing. Of the 21 seats, eight were filled by BHE members who quickly disassociated themselves from the FDP parliamentary delegation (*5th Quarterly Report*, 1950:35). With an absolute majority in the

Landtag, the Socialists found no necessity in forming a coalition with the refugees or any other party.

In the election the same day in Württemberg-Baden, the BHE in alliance with the right-wing nationalistic German Association (*Deutsche Gemeinschaft—* DG), won 14.7 percent of the ballots cast and 15 of 100 *Landtag* seats. As in Hesse, the refugees were not brought into the government; however, the political situation created by the results of the election of November 26, 1950 in Bavaria, necessitated their participation. In the Bavarian campaign the BHE again combined forces with the nationalistic DG and succeeded in winning 12.3 percent of the vote and 26 seats, of which twenty were filled by BHE members and six by members of the DG, including its leader, August Haussleiter.[50] The election cost the CSU its *Landtag* majority, necessitating a coalition government. Personal antagonisms prevented CSU cooperation with the Bavarian Party and the uncertain loyalty of the CSU right-wing required a broader majority than the 127 of 204 seats controlled by a CSU-SPD combination. To secure refugee support for the coalition, the BHE was granted two state secretaryships, one dealing with economics and the other with refugees. The latter position was filled by Dr. Theodor Oberländer, who was to become Federal Minister of Expellees, Refugees and War Victims in the second Adenauer government.[51]

The BHE met with little success in the Berlin election of December 3, 1950, polling only 2.2 percent of the total vote and failing to qualify for representation. Not only were their numbers small, but those refugees choosing to remain in Berlin were quickly assimilated into the impersonal mass of the big city. The party was even less successful in Rhineland-Palatinate where its support amounted to only 1.9 percent. As a result of French policy, refugees made up only 6.8 percent of the Rhineland-Palatinate population as late as September 1950, and even after resettlement, the *Land* was to have the smallest percentage of refugees outside the Saar.

The large concentration of refugees in Lower Saxony, numbering 2,217,130 in a total population of 6,797,379 at the time of the 1950 census, enabled the BHE to gain 14.9 percent of the vote in the election of May 6, 1951; however, the party failed to maintain its earlier momentum as it obtained less than fifty percent of the potential refugee vote in contrast to percentages of over 60 percent given to refugee groups in Schleswig-Holstein, Württemberg-Baden and Bavaria. With 21 seats in the *Landtag*, the BHE remained the only acceptable coalition partner for the SPD other than the small *Zentrum*, as twenty seats were controlled by right-extremist groups and 35 by the Lower German Union, an alliance of the CDU and German Party, which had fought the SPD so bitterly in the campaign. An agreement was reached between the SPD, BHE and Center Party June 13 in which the refugees were given three cabinet posts: agriculture, economics and refugees, in a government headed by Socialist Hinrich Wilhelm Kopf. In concluding this line-up of political forces, SPD leader Kurt Schumacher went some distance toward meeting refugee demands concerning the equalization of burdens legislation then under discussion in the Federal

Parliament. The agreement underlined the willingness of the BHE to ally itself with either bourgeois or socialist forces for political advantage and emphasized the difficulty in labeling the party as either rightist or leftist in its orientation (*7th Quarterly Report*, 1951: 28).

Although refugees made up a relatively small proportion of the Bremen population, the BHE polled 5.6 percent of the vote in the *Bürgerschaft* election of October 7, 1951. By failing to meet the five percent requirement in Bremen proper, the party qualified for representation only in Bremerhaven where it gained two seats.

The election for the constituent assembly and first *Landtag* of the new state of Baden-Württemberg marked a falling off of refugee support in that area. In the 1950 election in Württemberg-Baden, refugee groups had polled 212,431 votes or 14.7 percent of the total. In the election of March 9, 1952, in that same portion of the *Land*, the combined total of all refugee groups competing in the election amounted to only 198,182, and this in view of an increase in the size of the electorate of 266,470, swollen in the main by the arrival of resettled refugees.[52] Unemployment in Württemberg-Baden was the lowest of any area of the Federal Republic at the time of the election, amounting to only 3.8 percent of the workforce; moreover, considerable progress had been made in meeting refugee demands in the period between the elections. In the *Land* as a whole, refugee support amounted to 9.5 percent, ranging from 13.0 percent in North Württemberg to 5.0 percent in Baden; however, the vote was split among three rival groups, the BHE, which polled 6.3 percent of the *Land* total to become the only group to qualify for representation, the DG/BHE which polled 3.1 percent and the DG which hardly made a dent in the statistics with 5,433 votes (*7th Quarterly Report*, 1951: 10). In April the refugees joined the widely criticized left-of-center coalition in the Southwest State which excluded the CDU, the *Land*'s strongest party. In the cabinet which included Socialist, FDP and BHE members, the Refugee Party member filled the post dealing with refugee questions (*10th Quarterly Report*, 1953: 206).

In the short span of less than two years refugee groups succeeded in gaining parliamentary representation in six of the nine *Länder*, cabinet positions in four *Länder* and polling the equivalent of 1,849,215 votes, 8.2 percent of the West German total.[53] Although its successes had indicated it to be a significant political force, the elections in 1951 and 1952 already demonstrated a weakening of its appeal as it entered the campaign for the second *Bundestag* election under a new designation which added the prefix "All-German Bloc" to its title (GB/BHE). The emergence of the BHE further fragmented the political arena, and being committed neither to free enterprise nor to socialism, the party could be completely opportunistic in efforts to achieve its goals, siding with either bourgeois or socialist forces as served its purposes. For a period of approximately a decade, the Refugee Party was to achieve an importance in certain *Länder* far out proportion to its size.

Early Postwar Extremist Parties

A second important party development in the period between the first and second *Bundestag* elections was the success of right-extremist elements in several of the *Länder*. It would have been foolish to have believed that the collapse of the Nazi regime in 1945 and the political reeducation of the Germans by the Western Allies in the immediate postwar period would eradicate all vestiges of Nazi sentiment in Germany. Because of the ban on parties whose purpose was to spread "nationalistic, pan-Germanic, militarist, fascist or antidemocratic ideas," whatever support existed for Nazi principles in the first *Land* elections in 1946 and 1947 had to be expressed through the most conservative of the licensed parties or it was allowed no expression whatsoever in the case of disenfranchisement. In the British zone *Länder* right-extremist elements gave their support to the Lower Saxony State Party, the German Rightist Party (DRP) or the German Conservative Party (DKP), only the first of which met with any success, appealing as it did to conservative, though not necessarily extremist, groups. In Southern Germany extremist support went either to the *Land* branches of what was to become the FDP or to the CDU/CSU. In the 1949 *Bundestag* election the DRP, competing only in the British zone *Länder,* distinguished itself by capturing 8.1 percent of the Lower Saxony vote and sending five deputies from that *Land* to the *Bundestag.* The national total of the party, however, amounted to only 1.8 percent (based on 429,031 votes) as it failed to duplicate its Lower Saxony success elsewhere. In January 1950 the German Rightist Party took the name German Reich Party (*Deutsche Reichspartei*—DRP) when it combined with the National Democratic Party of Hesse, a group which had gained 3.4 percent of the Hessian vote in the 1948 *Kommunal* elections and had concluded an electoral alliance with the FDP in Hesse to contest the 1949 *Bundestag* contest.[54]

With the lifting of Allied controls over German political life, extremist elements were free to form a wide variety of organizations representing their views, most important of which was the Socialist Reich Party (SRP), formed in 1949 in Lower Saxony. While neither the DKP nor the German Rightist Party prior to 1949 could be classified as genuine neo-Nazi movements, there could be little doubt about the fascist character of the SRP, whose founders were largely former Nazi party functionaries and SS and army officers who failed to reintegrate themselves satisfactorily into civilian life. The SRP met with little success until the 1951 *Land* election in Lower Saxony,[55] where high unemployment and large numbers of embittered refugees and farmers presented a more fertile ground for the preachings of the party. Proclaiming Nazi principles, calling for a restoration of "all that was good in national socialism," and invoking the ghost of Adolf Hitler whenever prudent, the party succeeded in gaining 366,790 votes or 11.0 percent of the total. Four of its sixteen seats in the 158 member *Landtag* were won by direct election. The success of the more radical SRP reduced three other extreme right parties, including the German

Reich Party, to near insignificance, limiting their combined following to only 3.1 percent. However, because of the deletion of the five percent clause from the electoral law governing the 1951 balloting, the DRP sent three and the German Social Party one deputy to the Lower Saxony *Landtag*.[56]

Because of the obvious totalitarian character of the Socialist Reich Party, the Bonn government announced two days before the decision in Lower Saxony its intention to institute proceedings against it under Article 21, paragraph 2 of the Federal Basic Law, which declares that "parties which, by reason of their aims or the behavior of their adherents, seek to impair or destroy the free democratic basic order or to endanger the existence of the Federal Republic of Germany are unconstitutional." The same Government order declared the party's uniformed storm troop organization, the *Reichsfront*, about 6,000 men strong, an illegal body, and called upon the *Land* governments to dissolve it and prohibit its activities (*Keesing's Contemporary Archives*, VIII, May 26-June 2, 1951: 11491).

Undaunted by the action taken against it, the SRP campaigned for the Bremen vote five months later, gaining 7.7 percent of the total and eight seats. In the Baden-Württemberg election held in March 1952 the party entered candidates only in Württemberg-Baden where it obtained 3.85 percent, or 2.4 percent of the total *Land* vote, and failed to qualify for representation. However, the SRP entered a slate of candidates late and waged a disorganized campaign.[57] Later in the year the Federal Constitutional Court in Karlsruhe declared the party illegal and action was taken to dissolve its *Fraktionen* in the Bremen and Lower Saxony parliaments. Although the appeal of right-extremist groups, most important of which were the SRP and DRP, in the period between the first two national elections was confined to a limited area, the nationwide total of 823,661 votes (3.6 percent) in this first wave of extremist activity was not exceeded until the period between the fifth and sixth *Bundestag* contests when the National Democratic Party (NPD), founded in 1964 by Adolf von Thadden, gained 5.1 percent of regionally cast ballots and 61 seats in seven *Land* parliaments (Jaeckel, *Wahlführer 1969*: 99-101).[58] These successes on the regional level were followed by a 4.3 percent share (1.4 million votes) of the 1969 *Bundestag* poll, insufficient to receive representation in Bonn.[59]

The outlawing of the SRP did not eradicate extremist activity in the West German *Länder*, but it dealt other extremist groups a severe blow, since from then on they had to be more careful about their activities to avoid similar action against them. The German Reich Party and German Party became heirs of some of the SRP's former support and attempts were made to infiltrate the BHE and FDP. The failure of extremist groups in the early years of the Federal Republic to gain widespread support did not mean that all former Nazi Party members had turned into good democrats or that extremist sentiment had vanished from German politics, rather that most Germans had found sufficient meaning for their lives under the existing democratic order which had given them position and material rewards and found no advantage in changing it. Outside of Bremen, right-extremist parties since 2001 have elected *Landtag* representatives only in the provinces of the former German Democratic Republic.[60]

Political Developments of the 1949-1953 Period

Of the 22,603,048 votes cast in the regional elections held between 1949 and 1952,[61] the SPD polled 7,325,883 (32.4 percent), nearly 400,000 more than in the 1949 *Bundestag* election and nearly a million and a quarter more than in the first series of *Land* elections, to become West Germany's leading party on the regional level as the forces of fragmentation hurt the Union parties more than the SPD. The equivalent of 6,338,912 votes (28.0 percent) fell to the CDU/CSU, a drop of over one million from its *Bundestag* totals and of over 200,000 from its total in the 1946/1947 *Land* contests.[62] The most consistent gainer in the second series of *Land* elections was the FDP, which bettered its *Bundestag* totals in five *Länder* and its previous regional election totals in six *Länder* to push the party's national following to 12.2 percent. A member of the national government coalition, but often taking a stand in opposition to the policies of the Chancellor, the party absorbed much of the support which had gone to the CDU/CSU in earlier *Land* contests.[63]

Hurt by growing East-West hostility, the Communists lost ground in every *Land* over both *Bundestag* and previous *Land* election totals. Whereas the party had been represented in all but two *Länder* with 87 deputies after the first regional contests, in 1953 it was represented in only five *Länder* (Baden-Württemberg, Bremen, Hamburg, Lower Saxony and North Rhine-Westphalia) by 29 deputies, a victim of restrictive clauses.[64] Its highest totals were reached in the Hansa cities of Hamburg and Bremen with 7.4 and 6.4 percent of the vote respectively, its lowest in rural Bavaria and Lower Saxony.[65] The 1.8 percent figure in Lower Saxony marked the poorest showing for the party in any election since the war, yet the deletion of the five percent requirement from the electoral law enabled the KPD to gain two deputies in that *Land*. The biggest blow to Communist hopes was the party's stunning setback in North Rhine-Westphalia where it gained only 5.5 percent of the vote and twelve seats in contrast to 14.0 percent and 28 seats three years earlier. Two events prior to the election strongly influenced the results. On May 4, 1950, the Soviet Union announced the termination of repatriation of German prisoners of war, and on June 6 the East German puppet government signed away German territories east of the Oder-Neisse Line (*Keesing's Contemporary Archives*, VIII, December 2-9, 1950: 11124). Nationwide, with 868,710 votes, half of what it polled in 1946/1947, the KPD total dropped from 9.4 to 3.8 percent.

The second series of *Land* elections fragmented the parliaments of nearly every *Land*. While only three parties gained representation in Rhineland-Palatinate and four in Hesse, five groups gained seats in the parliaments of Baden-Württemberg and North Rhine-Westphalia, six in Bavaria, Hamburg and Schleswig-Holstein, eight in Bremen, in spite of a restrictive clause, and ten in

Lower Saxony, where six parties would still have obtained seats even had the five percent qualification been retained.[66] The Socialists outpolled the CDU in six *Länder*, but held the largest delegation in only five parliaments because of the particular operation of the Bavarian electoral system. In the other four *Länder* the Union parties held the largest number of seats. In all, twelve parties other than the CDU/CSU/SPD/FDP gained 251 parliamentary seats in the 1949/1952 contests in contrast to only 21 seats gained by splinter parties in the 1961/1965 *Land* elections. Whereas the vote falling to other than the CDU/CSU/SPD/FDP amounted to 27.4 percent in the 1949/1952 period, it had declined to 6.4 percent by the 1961/1965 series of regional contests, indicating, at the time, a stabilization around two large and one small, nationally-organized parties. This fraternity of three was initially challenged by the NPD and later by the Greens and PDS/*Die Linke*.

Endnotes to Chapter III

1 Absolute majorities had been held by the CDU/CSU in Baden, Bavaria and Württemberg-Hohenzollern and by the SPD in Hamburg and Schleswig-Holstein after the first *Landtag* elections.
Only in Schleswig-Holstein did the majority party, the SPD, form a one-party government from the outset. The coalitions in Baden and Bavaria broke down some months after their formation, and the CDU/CSU had sole responsibility for the administration of those two *Länder* prior to the establishment of the national government.

2 *Dithmarscher Landeseitung*, November 20, 21 and 28, 1950, and May 7, 1951. Whatever propaganda Schumacher hoped to make from this appeal, he must have been aware that the initiative for calling new elections rested entirely with the Chancellor, who would take no move to jeopardize his position as long as he maintained a parliamentary majority. The first Adenauer government was based on the slim margin of 208 of 402 seats and was beset with internal dissention throughout its four-year life; yet it successfully withstood all attempts to bring it down.

3 U.S. authorities relinquished all control over the regulation and licensing of political parties to the Germans in November 1948, and similar actions were taken by the British and French early in 1950 (*Handbook of German Affairs*, Press Office German Diplomatic Mission; New York, 1954: 53).

4 A series of losses at the polls was the price that the CDU/CSU had to pay in the formative years of the national government for policies which often seemed utopian and contrary to the goal of eventual German reunification. Yet, these very policies were to form the basis for the Christian Democratic successes after 1953.

5 The national total of the CDU/CSU in the second series of *Land* elections dropped to the equivalent of a mere 28.0 percent of the regional vote in contrast to 32.4 percent for the SPD; yet its greater ability to attract coalition partners enabled it to maintain control of the *Bundesrat*.

6 Although restrictive clauses were included in the electoral laws of all of the *Länder* with the single exception of Lower Saxony, which did not adopt a five percent

requirement until 1959, the smaller the size of the constituency involved, sometime encompassing less than the entire *Land* as in Bavaria and Bremen, enabled regional and special-interest groups, incapable of building a national following, to gain minor successes and reduce the number of seats available for distribution among the major parties.

7 Between these two elections, regional contests were held in North Rhine-Westphalia, Schleswig-Holstein, Hesse, Württemberg-Baden and Bavaria in 1950 and Rhineland-Palatinate, Lower Saxony and Bremen in 1951.

8 In Bavaria a double balloting system was established in which each voter cast a ballot for one of the 101 district representatives, one for a candidate on the extensive party lists. The *Land* was divided into seven districts (*Regierungskreise*) for purposes of allocating the 103 indirect seats and creating a proportional balance between the contending parties which obtained a minimum of ten percent of the vote in at least one *Kreis*. In Hesse the simpler mixed system provided for the election of 48 deputies by direct election, 32 indirectly over the *Land* list. Both of these systems are covered in more detail in Chapter VIII of this study.

9 In Baden-Württemberg 74 of the 120 *Landtag* seats were filled by direct election, 16 from Baden, 45 from Württemberg-Baden and 13 from Württemberg-Hohenzollern. The remaining seats were distributed on a proportional basis within each of the three constituent *Länder*. The number of direct seats was reduced to 70 beginning with the 1956 *Land* election contest.

10 Under the 1947 election law in Lower Saxony parties could qualify for reserve list seats only if they won at least one direct mandate or obtained five percent of the *Land* vote. A five percent requirement was reinstituted in 1959.

11 The size of the Hamburg *Bürgerschaft* was increased to 120 members to make possible a more equitable division of direct and indirect seats and establish a 60:40 ratio between the two (72 direct; 48 indirect). The 1947 election law in Schleswig-Holstein had established a 60:40 ratio between direct and indirect seats (42 direct; 28 indirect). The 1950 law increased the number of direct seats to 46 while reducing the reserve list seats to 23 to establish a 2:1 ratio between the two categories of seats. The Bavarian and Hessian systems were described in footnote 8 of this chapter.

12 It is interesting to note that the electoral and party alliances formed in the postwar period have been almost exclusively between parties of the right. By 1957, however, the conclusion of such alliances had virtually ceased because of the ability of the CDU to stand on its own and the general decline in the number of parties. An informal, non-reciprocal type of alliance occurred in the 1966 elections in Hamburg and North Rhine-Westphalia where the DFU did not run a slate of candidates and recommended that its followers support the SPD to break the Christian Democratic grip on the state. Moreover, the combination of lists was declared unlawful by the Federal Constitutional Court in 1959.

13 The VBH had been licensed for the 1946 *Bürgerschaft* election, but formed an alliance with the CDU and did not take part in the contest independently. An alliance was also concluded between the FDP and the Lower Saxony State Party for the 1946 election.

14 Although polling 42.8 percent of the vote as against 43.1 percent in 1946, the Socialists received 18 less seats (65 in contrast to 83 in 1946) because of changes in the *Land* electoral system which gave greater weight to the allocation of seats indirectly. The

new system enabled the *Bund* parties, which had obtained only 23 seats with 45.2 percent in 1946 to gain 17 additional mandates in spite of a 10.7 percentage drop in support. The failure of the German Party to participate in the VBH possibly prevented the *Bund* from breaking the Socialist majority.

15 The size of the North Rhine-Westphalian *Landtag* was increased from 200 to 215 members because of the ability of the CDU to win fifteen direct mandates in excess of its proportional entitlement (*Überhangsmandate*).

16 *3rd Quarterly Report on Germany, April 1-June 30, 1950*, Office of the U.S. High Commissioner for Germany: 31-32.

A plebiscite on the *Land* constitution was held the same day as the *Landtag* vote. Although the draft contained a provision calling for the socialization of the Ruhr industries, this did not create the controversy caused by the article giving parents the right to decide whether local schools, while sponsored by the State, might be administered by the Church. The provision was strongly supported by the CDU, the Center Party and the Catholic Church, while opposition came from the SPD, FDP and KPD on the ground that it favored parochial as against interdenominational schools. In view of this opposition, it is surprising that the constitution carried by such a comfortable margin, with 3,627,000 voting for approval, 2,241,000 disapproving and 497,000 casting invalid ballots. The constitution also contained a section endorsing the economic co-determination rights of workers, granting workers in a factory the right to determine not only policies of welfare and working conditions, but economic-managerial policies affecting purchasing, production and salesmanship as well.

17 An account of this political struggle between Adenauer and Arnold is found in Arnold Heidenheimer, "Federalism and the Party System: The Case of West Germany," *American Political Science Review*, LII (September 1958): 813-815.

18 The CDU won 19.7 percent of the vote and 16 seats in its districts, the FDP 7.1 percent and 8 seats in its districts and the DP 9.6 percent and 7 seats in its districts. The bourgeois parties were prevented from participating in the division of reserve list seats through a clause in the electoral law governing the contest requiring that a party enter candidates in all 46 constituencies in order to qualify for indirect seats. This stipulation was challenged by the *Block* parties, but the Supreme Administrative Court in Lüneberg upheld the provision as not conflicting with the Bonn Basic Law. The restriction did not apply to the Danish minority party (*Dithmarscher Landeszeitung*, June 20, 1950).

19 In spite of this arrangement in the Flensburg-East constituency, the SSW candidate easily won the district as the pro-German vote was split by contestants of the BHE, DRP, KPD and SPD.

20 In contrast to the 60:40 ratio between direct and indirect seats which existed in 1947, the 1950 electoral law increased the number of direct mandates to 46 while reducing the number of indirect seats to 23 to create a 2:1 ratio between the two categories of seats. At the same time the size of the *Landtag* was reduced from 70 to 69 seats.

The appointment of Dr. Walter Bartram as Minister President of Schleswig-Holstein marked the first time that a former Nazi Party member had been elected to the premiership in any *Land* (*Keesing's Contemporary Archives*, VIII [December 2-9, 1950]: 11124).

21 The Refugee Party polled 23.4 percent of the vote which otherwise would have fallen to the established parties. See pages 57-61 of this chapter.

22 The combined vote of the *Block* parties had amounted to 38.9 percent in 1947 and 50.2 percent in 1949, but to only 36.4 percent in 1950.

23 Election figures are from *Die Wahl zur Bürgerschaft und zu den Bezirksausschüssen am 16. Oktober 1949*, Hamburg Statistical Office: 78-114; *Handbuch des Landtags Nordrhein-Westfalen*, (*5. Wahlperiode*): 295-297; and *Statistisches Jahrbuch Schleswig-Holstein 1950*: 77.

24 Werner Hilpert, *Land* chairman of the CDU and Deputy Minister President and Finance Minister of the existing SPD-CDU coalition in Hesse, desired a continuation of cooperation with the Socialists, inviting attacks from Adenauer and his Hessian party colleague, Erich Köhler. As a result of this dissension the CDU waged a weak campaign. This struggle is covered in Arnold Heidenheimer, *American Political Science Review* (September 1958): 818-819.

25 Reinhold Maier (FDP) continued in the post of Minister President in Wurttemberg-Baden. The change in Stuttgart marked the third occasion since 1949 in which CDU-SPD cooperation had broken down.

26 The CSU won 46 direct seats to the SPD's 38. The enlargement of the Bavarian *Landtag* from 180 to 204 members enabled the SPD to increase its parliamentary delegation from 54 to 63 members in spite of a modest loss over 1946 *Land* election figures.

27 The Bavarian Party, appealing to the particularistic sentiment of the Bavarian, registered outstanding successes in Upper and Lower Bavaria, winning nine direct seats in the former and seven in the latter, and gained 39 seats in the *Land* as a whole.

28 In Rhineland-Palatinate the SPD gained four additional seats with a 0.3 percent drop in support because of the large percentage of non-represented votes (parties which were excluded from representation by the five percent clause). In Lower Saxony the Socialists lost one seat; in Bremen, three. Its ability to win a large number of direct seats limited the SPD loss in representation to one seat in Lower Saxony in spite of a drop of nearly ten percentage points over its 1947 following.

29 Election figures are from *Handbuch des Hessischen Landtags*, (*V. Wahlperiode*): 104-206; *Die Welt*, November 20 and 21, 1950 and *Wahl zum Bayerischen Landtag am 25. November 1962*, Bavarian Statistical Office: 122-125.

30 *7th Quarterly Report on Germany, Office of the U.S. High Commission for Germany* April 1-June 30, 1951: 26. Codetermination is the right of industrial workers to share in the administration and policy-making processes of German industry.

31 The refugee backing had amounted to only 1.9 percent. French policy had strictly limited the number of refugees and expellees entering her zone up to 1950.

32 The CDU-DP combination polled only 23.8 percent of the vote as against totals of 37.8 percent in 1947 when the two parties competed separately and 35.4 percent in the 1949 general election. The number of direct seats for the Union parties amounted to 34 in 1947, 23 in 1951.

33 Including the Lower Saxony FDP, 32 seats and 22.4 percent of the vote fell to parties to the right of the CDU.

34 Four seats went to the *Zentrum* with 3.3 percent of the vote, three to the DRP with a 2.2 percent total, two to the KPD with 1.8 percent and one to the DSP with 0.8 percent of the vote. The 1947 electoral law had stipulated that a party must obtain at least five percent of the *Land* vote or win a mandate by direct election to be eligible for seats from the reserve list.

35 No less than eight parties obtained representation in the Bremen *Bürgerschaft* elected October 7, 1951. Although Bremen had adopted a five percent clause, it applied to Bremen proper and Bremerhaven separately. Thus, the WdF, while obtaining only 4.3 percent of the total *Land* vote, received four seats by satisfying the minimum requirement in Bremen proper.

36 Whereas an SPD-FDP partnership would have controlled 55 of 100 parliamentary seats, the combination with the CDU provided only 52 of 100 seats.

37 Election figures are from *Ergebnisse der Landtagswahlen am 18. Mai 1947 und 29. April 1951 sowie der Bundestagswahl am 6. September 1953*, Director of Elections of Rhineland-Palatinate: 2-10; *Landtagswahlen in Niedersachsen 1947-1963*, Lower Saxony Statistical Office, pages unmarked; and "*Bürgerschafts- und Bundestagswahlen 1947 bis 1963 nach Wahlbereichen*," appendix to *Die Wahl zur Bremischen Bürgerschaft am 29. September 1953*, Bremen Statistical Office.

38 In the 1950 *Land* election in Württemberg-Baden the SPD polled 33.1 percent of the vote, the CDU 26.4 percent. In 1952 that portion of the Southwest State gave 30.3 percent of the vote to the Socialists, 29.2 percent to the CDU.

39 Prior to April 29, 1952, when Maier appointed three SPD and two FDP delegates to the *Bundesrat*, placing Baden-Württemberg's five votes in the doubtful category, the CDU could count upon the three votes of both Baden and Württemberg-Hohenzollern, the SPD the four votes of Württemberg-Baden. The reduction in the size of the *Bundesrat* from 43 to 38 members with the formation of a single Southwest State and the political complexion which its government took, the national coalition under some circumstances could count on only 18 of the 38 votes. The difficulties in coordinating the divergent elements of the Maier coalition in Stuttgart and Bonn and its unrepresentative character led to the collapse of the SPD-FDP-BHE administration within one month after Adenauer's overwhelming national victory in September 1953.

40 Since Berlin did not participate in national election contests until 1990 and the Saar was not attached to West Germany until 1957, their election figures are not included in the totals.

41 Whereas the nationwide total for the SPD in the 1949-1953 regional elections dropped from 35.0 to 32.4 percent, the CDU/CSU total dropped from 37.7 percent in the first series of *Land* elections to 28.0 percent in the second. The Socialists outpolled the Union parties in Bavaria, Bremen, Hamburg, Hesse, Lower Saxony, Schleswig-Holstein and Württemberg-Baden; the CDU/CSU led in only Baden-Württemberg, North Rhine-Westphalia and Rhineland-Palatinate in the regional contests held between the first and second *Bundestag* elections.

42 Election figures were provided by the Baden-Württemberg Statistical Office.

43 Of this number the West German census of September 13, 1950, listed 7,977,600 as expellees, Germans forced to leave those areas of the pre-1937 Reich east of the Oder-Neisse Line and cultural Germans expelled from areas not belonging to the former Reich,

including Czechoslovakia, the Baltic States, Danzig, Poland, Hungary, Yugoslavia, Rumania and the Soviet Union, and 1,635,500 as refugees, Germans forced to flee the Soviet zone of Germany because of political persecution. See *Facts Concerning the Problem of the German Expellees and Refugees*, Federal Ministry for Expellees, Refugees and War Victims (Bonn, 1961). For purposes of this study, the word "refugee" will be used to refer to both groups unless the specific designation is called for.

44 See "Political Aspects of the Refugee Problem," *4th Quarterly Report on Germany, Office of the U.S. High Commission for Germany July 1-September 30, 1950*: 30-34 and 95 for a survey of the conditions which gave rise to the refugee political movements in West Germany.

45 Statistics are from diagram 12 and pages 122-125 of *Wahl zum Bayerischen Landtag am 25. November 1962*, and diagram 3 of *Kommunalwahlen in Bayern am 27. März 1960*, publications of the Bavarian Statistical Office.

46 *OMGUS Monthly Report* No. 45, March 1949: 11 and 46, April 1949, in *Germany, 1947-1949: The Story in Documents*, (Department of State, 1949): 166-167.

47 One of the best sources on the early political activities of refugee and expellee groups in West Germany is Jane Perry Clark Carey, "Political Organization of the Refugees and Expellees in West Germany," *Political Science Quarterly* LXVI (June 1951): 191-215.

48 An Equalization of Burdens law was eventually approved by the Federal parliament in 1952, imposing a 50 percent levy on all property assessed at 1949 values and payable in quarterly installments at a fixed rate of interest over a 30 year period. Over $18 billion was realized from the law by the end of 1979.

49 As the demands of the groups supporting the Refugee Party began to be met and they became integrated into the German society, the party declined in strength and ceased to be a factor in German politics after 1966.

50 The German Association (DG) was the creation of August Haussleiter, one-time deputy-chairman of the Bavarian CSU. It appealed to many of the same groups which the BHE attempted to attract, including refugees, air raid victims, returned German prisoners-of-war and other malcontented groups. During the course of the legislative period, four of the DG's six parliamentary delegates deserted to the Refugee Party.

Three other refugee groups, including the WAV which had gained considerable refugee backing in previous elections, between them polled an additional 3.9 percent of the Bavarian vote, but failed to gain representation. The WAV which had gained 14.4 percent of the total in the Bavarian election of the previous year was especially hurt by internal dissention in both Munich and Bonn.

51 Oberländer bolted the Refugee Party in 1955 to retain his position in the federal cabinet. He continued to serve as Federal Minister of Expellees, Refugees and War Victims until 1960.

52 The difference in voting participation between the two elections accounts for approximately 100,000 of the total. Figures are from *Die Parlamentswahlen in Baden-Württemberg seit 1952*, Baden-Württemberg State Statistical Office: 10. Comparative figures of refugee strength in Baden and Württemberg-Hohenzollern are not available as no *Landtag* elections were held in these two *Länder* between May 1947 and March 1952.

53 An exact figure of refugee support in Hesse is not available because of its alliance with the FDP in that *Land*, and the totals used in this summary are based on the relative strengths of the FDP and refugee groups demonstrated in the 1949 *Bundestag* election and in elections immediately following the 1950 *Land* contest. Of the 588,739 votes cast for the FDP-BHE combination, 412,117 are allotted to the FDP, 176,622 to the BHE. In order to avoid duplication, the results of the 1952 election in Baden-Württemberg are used, with the figures for the 1950 decision in Württemberg-Baden appearing nowhere in the totals.

54 *Germany's Parliament in Action*, Office of the U.S. High Commission for Germany (1950): 11, 14, 18 and 85-90.

55 The SRP made its first appearance in the June 1950 election in North Rhine-Westphalia, but obtained only 0.2 percent of the vote. The DRP was more successful in the same election. By concluding an electoral alliance with the FDP in which it abstained from running its own candidates in certain districts in exchange for having every seventh slot on the FDP reserve list allotted to its candidates, the DRP sent three of its members to the *Landtag* on the FDP ticket. In Schleswig-Holstein the following month the DRP polled 2.8, the SRP 1.8 percent of the *Land* vote. The lack of radical support in Schleswig-Holstein was surprising in view of the high percentage of unemployment and the large number of refugees. The emergence of the Refugee Party dissipated the potential strength of the DRP and SRP in that *Land*. In Hesse, Württemberg-Baden and Bavaria right-wing elements were absorbed by the established parties, although the DRP, competing in Hesse, managed to attract 2,010 votes. In Rhineland-Palatinate, where extremist sentiment was to run high as late as 1959, four extreme right groups, including the DRP, managed to gain only 1.7 percent of the *Land* vote.

56 *Die Welt*, May 7, 1951. One of the leaders of the SRP, Major General Otto Remer, had made a name for himself as a result of having remained loyal to Hitler at the time of the plot against his life July 20, 1944. Dr. Fritz Dorls, another leader of the party and member of the *Bundestag* until 1953, advocated a Mussolini-type corporate state.

57 *10th Quarterly Report on Germany, Office of the U.S. High Commission for Germany*: 41. An excellent survey of right-extremist movements in post-1945 Germany (up to 1962) is Richard S. Cromwell's "Rightist Extremism in Postwar West Germany," *Western Political Quarterly*, XVII (June 1964): 284-293. See also *Der Spiegel*, April 4, 1966: 30-44 for an early West German analysis of the NPD.

58 In the face of Chancellor Erhard's declining popularity and the growing inability to express dissatisfaction outside of three, seemingly look-alike, parties, the NPD in successive elections in 1966, 1967 and 1968 gained 7.9 percent of the vote and eight seats in Hesse, 7.4 percent and fifteen seats in Bavaria, 6.9 percent and four seats in Rhineland-Palatinate, 5.8 percent and four seats in Schleswig-Holstein, 7.0 percent and ten seats in Lower Saxony, 8.8 percent and eight seats in Bremen and 9.8 percent and twelve seats in Baden-Württemberg. The formation of a grand coalition between the CDU and SPD in 1966 was partially influenced by these NPD gains, but also gave the new party added appeal.

59 After 1969 the appeal of the NPD and other right-extremist parties subsided and it was not until a third wave, beginning in 1987, that a right extremist party (the DVU in Bremen) was able to gain representation in a *Landtag*. In the regional contests held between 2001 and 2005 right-wing groups, including the NPD, Republicans, DVU (German People's Union) and the Schill Party, polled 1,042,923 votes and gained

representation in four *Land* parliaments (Bremen, Brandenburg, Hamburg and Saxony). The Schill Party, playing on the fear of crime and terrorism, gained 19.4 percent of the Hamburg vote and 25 seats in the September 2001 *Bürgerschaft* election and participated in a coalition with the CDU until 2004 when conflict over the intolerant behavior of party leader Ronald Schill led to the calling of new elections and a stunning defeat for the party, which polled only 3.1 percent of the vote (see various issues of *Die Welt*, 2001 and 2004). In the regional elections held between the sixteenth and seventeenth *Bundestag* elections, the NPD succeeded in winning 7.3 percent of the vote in the 2006 state balloting in Mecklenburg-Vorpommern to place six representatives in the *Land* parliament. In Saxony it was able to retain a reduced delegation when its support fell from 9.2 percent to 5.6 percent in the 2009 state election. On the other hand, the DVU lost its six seats in the Brandenburg legislature when its following fell from the 6.1 percent share of the vote recorded in 2004 to only 1.1 percent in the 2009 election. In the 2009 *Bundestag* balloting right-extremist groups combined obtained only 2.0 percent of the national vote.

60 The NPD, nourished by a reaction to high unemployment, resentment against immigrants and their interpretation of the fire bombing of Dresden in 1945, calling it a "Holocaust of bombs" (*Der Spiegel on-line*, February 2, 2005), gained 9.2 percent of the vote and twelve seats in the Saxony *Land* election of 2004. In an election held the same day in Brandenburg the DVU received 6.1 percent of the vote and six seats in the *Land* parliament. It is noteworthy that the NPD was not able to follow up its Saxony success in any of the old *Länder*, receiving only 1.9 percent of the Schleswig-Holstein vote in the February 20, 2005 *Land* election and 0.9 percent of the North-Rhine Westphalian vote on May 22, 2005. The DVU's single seat in Bremen was gained in spite of the fact that it polled only 2.3 percent of the total Bremen vote in 2003. It obtained its seat by virtue of its 7.1 percent following in Bremerhaven, which is considered a separate voting district for the division of *Bürgerschaft* seats. The party obtained one seat in 2007 in like manner. In the 2009 provincial election in Saxony NPD support fell to 5.6 percent, causing the party to lose four of its earlier twelve seats in the state parliament, while the DVU following in the Brandenburg election of September 27, 2009 dropped to 1.1 percent, eliminating it from the legislature.

61 In order to avoid duplication, the figures for the 1950 election in Württemberg-Baden appear in none of these totals; rather, the party totals of the 1952 decision in Baden-Württemberg are used since that contest covered all three of the constituent areas of the *Land*.

62 Where party alliances were formed and only a single result is available for several parties, votes have been allotted to the constituent parties on the basis of previous performances (and in some cases future performances) in the *Länder*. Even had all votes given to the alliances into which the CDU entered in Hamburg and Lower Saxony been credited to the CDU, its national total would still have fallen short of the SPD figure.

63 The FDP gained over one million more votes in the second series of *Land* elections than in the first and increased its representation in the several *Länder* from 106 to 142 deputies. Major gains were made in North Rhine-Westphalia, Hesse and Rhineland-Palatinate.

64 In the 1952 election in Baden-Württemberg the Communist Party polled 4.4 percent of the total *Land* vote; however, the electoral law provided for representation for a party gaining five percent of the vote cast in any of the three constituent parts. The KPD's 5.1 percent total in Württemberg-Baden qualified it for four seats in that area, but

it failed to meet the five percent requirement in the other two areas. Restrictive clauses cost the KPD its representation in Hesse and Rhineland-Palatinate.

65 The KPD polled over 2,000 more votes than in 1947 and over 700 more votes than in the 1949 *Bundestag* election in Bremen; however, increases in the size of the electorate caused it to absorb percentage losses over both earlier contests.

66 The CDU/CSU-SPD vote ranged from 73.2 percent in Rhineland-Palatinate to only 47.2 percent in Schleswig-Holstein and amounted to a mere 60.4 percent in West Germany as a whole. In figuring the number of groups in each *Landtag* the CDU and DP are figured as separate parties in Lower Saxony, the CDU and FDP as separate parties in Hamburg, the FDP and BHE as separate groups in Hesse and the BHE and DG as separate groups in Bavaria.

CHAPTER IV

Elections in the Period of Christian Union Dominance

The 1953 *Bundestag* Election

No *Land* elections were held in the eighteen months which elapsed between the 1952 decision in Baden-Württemberg and the *Bundestag* vote of September 6, 1953 to indicate any significant shift in public sentiment since the second series of regional contests. However, *Kommunal* (local) elections held throughout 1952[1] and the results of work council polls in the Ruhr coal mines in April 1953 showed continued strong support for the Social Democratic Party, strengthening the opinion of many observers that the SPD might emerge as the leading, though not the majority, party in the 1953 general election. Moreover, the Berlin riots in June 1953 and growing unrest in the Soviet-controlled area of Germany gave added optimism to the Socialists who hoped to convince the voters that the chances for reaching agreement with the Soviets were never better and that support of such schemes as the European Defense Community would only serve to perpetuate the division of Germany. CDU/CSU leaders, in opposing the Socialists, relied heavily on the prestige of Chancellor Adenauer, his diplomatic successes, economic prosperity, and the manner in which their leader had identified himself with American foreign policy to bring victory to the party. While defending integration with the West, the Chancellor did not oppose German reunification; however, he was convinced that it could be accomplished only from a position of strength, which only time could build. His hope for victory was in persuading the Germans that their future lay in close attachments with the West rather than in neutrality and possible domination by the Soviet Union (*New York Times*, August 19, 1953).

The German electorate gave a clear indication of the course it wished to follow by giving Adenauer's party 45.2 percent of the national vote and an absolute majority in the *Bundestag*, firmly establishing the CDU/CSU as the dominant political group on the national level. No one had foreseen the immensity of the CDU victory which saw the party increasing its following in every *Land* and carrying every state with the exception of the Socialist strongholds of Bremen, Hamburg and Hesse.[2] An absolute majority of the vote was polled in Baden-Württemberg and Rhineland-Palatinate and only in Bremen did the Christian Democrat total fall below thirty percent.

TABLE 4.1

NATIONAL TOTALS
SECOND *LAND* AND 1953 *BUNDESTAG* ELECTIONS[3]

Party	1949/1952 *Land* Elections		September 6, 1953 *Bundestag* Election		Seats
CDU/CSU	6,338,912	28.0	12,443,981	45.2	244
SPD	7,325,883	32.4	7,944,943	28.8	150
FDP/DVP	2,746,680	12.2	2,629,163	9.5	48
GB/BHE	1,849,215	8.2	1,616,953	5.9	27
DP	718,466	3.2	896,128	3.3	15
KPD	868,710	3.8	607,860	2.2	---
BP	828,856	3.7	465,641	1.7	---
DRP/SRP/DKP	823,661	3.6	295,739	1.1	---
Zentrum	630,012	2.8	217,078	0.8	3
SSW	71,864	0.3	44,585	0.2	---
Others	400,789	1.9	389,201	1.3	---
Totals	22,603,048		27,551,272		487

The Union success was proclaimed a personal triumph for Chancellor Adenauer and a strong endorsement of his policy of close integration with the West. The results showed that there had been a considerable crossing of ideological and religious lines and that for the first time in postwar Germany the electorate voted for a personality rather than a program. The failure of the SPD to duplicate either its regional election totals in any *Land* or to exceed its first *Bundestag* following indicated that the SPD had overplayed the issues of rearmament and reunification and failed to appreciate the diplomatic successes of the Adenauer government. Yet, the tremendous victory of the CDU/CSU was accomplished not so much at the expense of the SPD, which polled one million more votes while suffering only a slight percentage loss over 1949, as of other center and right-of-center groups. The Bavarian Party, *Zentrum*, and the Union's two partners in the national coalition, the FDP and the DP, all suffered varying degrees of losses. Moreover, the party attracted a large portion of new voters.

Already the Refugee Party, competing for the first time in a national contest, showed signs of decline as it fell far below its regional election totals in every *Land*. Its largest following came in Schleswig-Holstein where its 11.6 percent figure was only half that polled three years earlier. Nevertheless, by exceeding the five percent requirement, it qualified for 27 *Bundestag* seats. The participation of the German Party in a number of beneficial alliances with the CDU and FDP enabled it to win ten direct seats and fifteen overall, while the CDU aided the *Zentrum* in gaining its modest representation. The elections were a strong rebuff of the extremist parties of the left and right. While the

TABLE 4.2

SECOND *LAND* AND 1953 *BUNDESTAG* ELECTION RESULTS [4]

Land	Year and Election	CDU/ CSU	SPD	FDP/ DVP	GB BHE	DP	KPD	Others
Hamburg	1949 *Land*	a	42.8	a	---	13.3	7.4	VBH[a] 34.5
	1953 *Bund*	36.7	38.1	10.3	2.5	5.9	3.8	RSF 2.0 2.8
North Rhine-Westphalia	1950 *Land*	36.9	32.3	12.1	---	1.7	5.5	ZP 7.5
	1953 *Bund*	48.9	31.9	8.5	2.7	1.0	2.9	ZP 2.7
Schleswig-Holstein	1950 *Land*	19.8	27.5	7.1	23.4	9.6	2.2	SSW 5.5
	1953 *Bund*	47.1	26.5	4.5	11.6	4.0	1.2	SSW 3.3
Hesse	1950 *Land*	18.8	44.4	31.8[b]	b	---	4.7	0.3
	1953 *Bund*	33.2	33.7	19.7	6.4	2.8	2.5	GVP 1.7
Württemberg-Baden	1950 *Land*	26.4	33.1	21.0	14.7	---	4.8	---
Bavaria	1950 *Land*	27.4	28.0	7.1	12.3	---	1.9	BP 17.9
	1953 *Bund*	47.8	23.3	6.2	8.2	0.9	1.6	BP 9.2
Rhineland-Palatinate	1951 *Land*	39.2	34.0	16.7	1.9	---	4.3	ZP 2.1
	1953 *Bund*	52.1	27.2	12.1	1.5	1.1	2.3	DRP 2.5
Lower Saxony	1951 *Land*	23.5[c]	33.7	8.4	14.9	c	1.8	SRP 11.0
	1953 *Bund*	35.2	30.1	6.9	10.8	11.9	1.1	DRP 3.5
Bremen	1951 *Land*	9.1	39.1	11.8	5.6	14.7	6.4	SRP 7.7
	1953 *Bund*	24.8	39.0	7.5	3.3	17.0	3.9	DRP 3.0
Baden-Württemberg	1952 *Land*	36.0	28.0	18.0	6.3	---	4.4	SRP 2.4
	1953 *Bund*	52.4	23.0	12.7	5.4	1.6	2.3	2.6

a The CDU and FDP combined in Hamburg in 1949 as the VBH.

b The FDP and BHE combined lists in the 1950 election in Hesse.

c The CDU figure in Lower Saxony represents the total for the NU, an alliance of the CDU and the German Party.

Communist Party fell into almost insignificance with 2.2 percent of the national vote to lose its *Bundestag* representation, rightist groups, which had been so successful in the second series of *Land* elections, fared even worse with 1.1 percent of the total.[5]

The 1953-1956 *Land* Elections

In contrast to the Weimar Republic when economic, social and political instability perpetuated a multiplicity of parties, a backward movement in the number of groups obtaining parliamentary representation in the *Länder* set in after 1953. The outlawing of the SRP in 1952 and the subsequent action taken against the Communist Party,[6] together with the general loss of support for all extremist groups as a result of growing economic and political stability, the tightening of election law requirements for parties to get on the ballot and to obtain representation, the integrating influence of national politics and the growing personal popularity of Chancellor Konrad Adenauer and acceptance of his program all contributed to this trend, and by 1957, other than the CDU, SPD and FDP, only the German and Refugee parties continued to play an important role in German politics. While the number of separate parties receiving representation in the various *Landtage* was reduced from fifteen to nine during the third series of regional elections, and only in Lower Saxony did more than five parliamentary groups gain seats, resulting in more manageable legislative bodies, no period witnessed such extensive jockeying for position among the parties, such political bitterness and unrepresentativeness of government.

The first Adenauer government had been based on the slim parliamentary majority of 208 of 402 *Bundestag* seats, yet in spite of dissention within the coalition and attacks from without, it successfully held its own for the four-year legislative period. The results of the second general election made it possible for the Chancellor to govern with only a single coalition partner; however, in order to establish a two-thirds, constitutional majority for his policies, Adenauer broadened his government to include the 27 member Refugee Party delegation to give him command of 334 of the 487 *Bundestag* seats. Whereas the ability of the SPD to dominate the regional election results between 1949 and 1952 had caused the CDU/CSU to work feverishly to maintain a bare *Bundesrat* majority during the first four years, following the 1953 general election, the Union parties hoped to capitalize on their national victory to create a firm two-thirds majority in the federal upper chamber. Success was to come rapidly, but the CDU/CSU's constitutional majority in the *Bundesrat* was to be lost and won back several times before the end of the second *Bundestag* period.

Within a month of the *Bundestag* decision, a cabinet reshuffle in Baden-Württemberg brought that *Land's* five *Bundesrat* votes safely into the CDU column,[7] and in November a victory for the parties of the national coalition in Hamburg, traditional Socialist stronghold, assured Adenauer control of 26 of the 38 *Bundesrat* votes, making possible the enactment of any constitutional amendment needed to implement his foreign and defense policies. Realizing the hopelessness of efforts to defeat the government of the popular Max Brauer on issues of internal administration because of its identification with Hamburg's remarkable postwar recovery, the CDU, FDP, German and Refugee parties, combined in an alliance known as the *Hamburg Block*,[8] fought the campaign on issues of foreign policy. The closeness of the election, in which the *Block* parties won 62 to the Socialists' 58 seats in the 120 member *Bürgerschaft*, was demonstrated by the equal distribution of the 72 direct seats between each of the two contending groups.[9] The Socialist total of 45.2 percent was the highest reached by the party in any election since the war and represented a solid vote of confidence on the record of the Socialist administration; however, national political considerations necessitated the exclusion of the SPD from the government. The strain within the *Block*, particularly after 1956, and the resulting decline in public confidence, was to make possible the overwhelming victory for the Socialists in Hamburg in 1957.[10]

The results of the elections in the summer of 1954 in North Rhine-Westphalia and Schleswig-Holstein enabled the Christian Democrats to continue their control over the administrations of those two *Länder*. In the former *Land* the CDU polled over forty percent of the vote for the first time in a regional contest to remain the *Land's* leading party, yet its inability to win large numbers of direct mandates in excess of its proportional entitlement (*Überhangmandate*) as in 1947 and 1950 cost the party three seats.[11] The loss of over 1,000,000 votes over its general election total and the faltering of the *Zentrum*, which, with only nine mandates,[12] left the existing coalition with 99 of 200 seats, seemed to indicate that Minister President Arnold had no alternative but to accept the SPD as his coalition partner, if he were to continue his left-wing orientation. Yet, in spite of bitter differences between the CDU and the FDP in North Rhine-Westphalia and the expressed willingness of the Social Democrats to enter into a coalition with the CDU, even going as far as to agree not to jeopardize the *Land's* five *Bundesrat* votes, Arnold fell into line with the wishes of the Federal Chancellor by bringing the Free Democrats into the *Land* government. Growing disagreement between the FDP and the CDU/CSU in Bonn, brought to a head by a proposed electoral law, designated "*Grabenwahlsystem*," which would have reduced the FDP to a satellite of the Union parties, eventually led to the startling turn of events in February 1956, when the FDP in North Rhine-Westphalia decided, as a means of enforcing retribution upon Adenauer, to dissolve its coalition with the CDU and form an alternate cabinet with the Socialists, who, anxious for revenge, forgot the differences which separated the parties.[13]

In the Schleswig-Holstein election the Social Democrats made significant gains to outpoll the CDU 33.2 percent to 32.2 percent, while obtaining the same number of seats as the CDU. In contrast to the 1950 contest in which the parties of the national coalition entered into an extensive system of agreements to defeat Socialist candidates in 31 constituencies, each group ran separately in 1954, with the exception of arrangements in Flensburg, established for the purpose of defeating the Danish minority party candidates, and in *Kreis* Pinneberg between the CDU and the FDP, enabling the Socialists to win 22 direct mandates compared to only eight in 1950.[14] The election result came just two weeks after the French rejection of the European Defense Community treaty, and as foreign policy had played a major role in the campaign, the extensive losses absorbed by the CDU over its *Bundestag* following of the previous year were regarded in some circles as a weakening of support for the Chancellor's international policies. The defeat of the EDC treaty was a severe blow to the Federal Government's defense plans, and the confusion thereby created undoubtedly hurt the CDU cause; nevertheless, the party could point to its gain of 12.4 percentage points over the 1950 *Land* election. A change in the political complexion of the Schleswig-Holstein government would have cost the national coalition its two-third *Bundesrat* majority; however, that majority was protected when the CDU formed a coalition with its partners in Bonn, the Refugee Party, the biggest loser in the election, and the FDP.[15]

The first major setback for Adenauer in his attempts to establish replicas of the Bonn coalition in the *Länder* came after the November elections in Bavaria and Hesse. Coming just after the Paris agreement on German sovereignty and membership in NATO and the European Statute for the Saar had been signed, the two contests were dominated by issues of foreign policy. Although the CSU emerged as by far the leading party in Bavaria, a position it had lost in 1950, and the Socialists only barely held their own with 28.1 percent of the vote,[16] the issue of confessional schools, the antagonisms between the CSU and the Bavarian Party, Refugee Party opposition to the Saar accord and the determination of the smaller parties to check the coordination efforts of the national CDU all played a role in the unholy marriage of the FDP, BHE (both members of the Federal coalition), and the particularistic Bavarian Party with the SPD.[17]

In Hesse Adenauer's attempts to remove the Socialists from power were also unsuccessful. Although the CDU and the FDP, which formed an electoral alliance for the election, succeeded in breaking the Socialist majority, they failed to win a majority for themselves, and, with seven seats, the Refugee Party held the balance between the two groupings.[18] Pressures were brought on the Refugee Party to join in a government with its national coalition partners, the CDU and the FDP; however, the BHE sided with the Socialists, finding its interests best served by countering those federal policies which it opposed through the *Land* governments. The events in Bavaria and Hesse were severe blows to Adenauer's coordination efforts, and he was determined to prevent such a recurrence in Lower Saxony.

In the Lower Saxony election of April 24, 1955, the CDU registered its sixth consecutive gain over totals of the second series of regional contests to exceed by eight the number of mandates which it and the German Party combined had won as the Lower German Union four years earlier. With the DP total of nineteen mandates, the two parties nearly doubled their 1951 representation. The SPD remained the leading party; however, it lost five *Landtag* seats in spite of a small percentage gain over the previous *Land* contest because of its inability to carry as many single member constituencies as in 1951. This loss coupled

TABLE 4.3

THE THIRD SERIES OF *LAND* ELECTIONS [19]

Party	1953 Hamburg			1954 North Rhine-Westphalia			1954 Schleswig-Holstein		
	Per-Cent	Direct Seats	Total Seats	Per-Cent	Direct Seats	Total Seats	Per-Cent	Direct Seats	Total Seats
SPD	45.2	36	58	34.5	65	76	33.2	22	25
CDU	a	a	36	41.3	85	90	32.2	19	25
FDP	a	a	16	11.5	---	25	7.5	---	5
GB/BHE	a	a	a	4.6	---	---	14.0	1	10
KPD	3.2	---	---	3.8	---	---	2.1	---	---
DP	a	a	10	0.0	---	---	5.1 [b]	---	4
ZP	---	---	---	4.0	---	9	---	---	---
SSW	---	---	---	---	---	---	3.5	---	---
DRP	0.7	---	---	---	---	---	1.5	---	---
BdD	---	---	---	0.3	---	---	0.8	---	---
Others	50.9 [a]	36	a	---	---	---	0.1	---	---
Totals		72	120		150	200		42	69

a Represents the alliance of the CDU, FDP, DP and BHE in the *Hamburg Block* which won 50.0 percent of the *Land* vote. Two splinter groups polled the remaining 0.9 percent of the total vote. The 62 *Block* seats were distributed as follows: 36 to the CDU, sixteen to the FDP, ten to the DP.

b The DP in Schleswig-Holstein concluded an alliance with the Schleswig-Holstein Association known as the Schleswig-Holstein Bloc (SHB) for the 1954 election.

with a drop in the number of seats won by the Refugee Party from 21 to seventeen cost the existing coalition its parliamentary majority.[20] The bourgeois parties also lacked a clear majority, and to have brought the six deputies of the right-wing DRP into either grouping was out of the question.[21] The continued fragmentation of the Lower Saxony *Landtag* gave rise to a number of coalition possibilities, including an SPD-FDP-BHE combination or a grand coalition between the SPD and the CDU. However, to insure the institution of a government on the Bonn mode and prevent a repetition of the Bavarian debacle a coalition between the CDU, DP, FDP and BHE was hammered out in Bonn long before the first session of the new *Landtag*. The establishment of a bourgeois ministry in Lower Saxony marked the first time since the war that a non-Socialist premier headed the *Land* government.[22]

Although the success of Adenauer's intervention tactics in Lower Saxony

TABLE 4.4

THE THIRD SERIES OF *LAND* ELECTIONS (Continued) [23]

| | 1954 | | | 1954 | | | 1955 | | |
| | Bavaria | | | Hesse | | | Lower Saxony | | |
Party	Per-Cent	Direct Seats	Total Seats	Per-Cent	Direct Seats	Total Seats	Per-Cent	Direct Seats	Total Seats
CDU/CSU	38.0	68 [a]	83	24.1	5	24	26.6	20	43
SPD	28.1	29	61	42.6	41	44	35.2	59	59
FDP	7.2	---	13	20.5	2	21	7.9	1	12
GB/BHE	10.2	---	19	7.7	---	7	11.0	---	17
KPD	2.1	---	---	3.4	---	---	1.3	---	2
DP	---	---	---	1.2	---	---	12.4	15	19
DRP	---	---	---	---	---	---	3.8	---	6
ZP	---	---	---	---	---	---	1.1	---	1
BP	13.2	2	28	---	---	---	---	---	---
BdD	0.5	---	---	0.5	---	---	0.3	---	---
Others	0.7	---	---	---	---	---	0.4	---	---
Totals		99 [a]	204		48	96		95	159 [b]

a The Bavarian electoral law did not allow for *Überhangmandate*, requiring the CSU to relinquish two of its direct mandates in Upper Bavaria and reducing the total number of direct seats from 101 to 99.

b Ten of the seats are *Überhang-/Ausgleichmandate* made necessary by the ability of the SPD to win more seats than its proportional entitlement.

restored a two-thirds majority for the Bonn coalition in the *Bundesrat*, the exclusion of the largest parliamentary group from the government and the necessity of coordinating the activities of four separate parties to maintain a working majority placed the new coalition on a very shaky basis from the very beginning. After surviving the "*Schlüter Affair*" in which the nomination of a crypto-Nazi Free Democrat was withdrawn following the resignation of eighteen members of the University of Göttingen faculty, a student boycott and nationwide protests,[24] and the subsequent withdrawal of the BHE and FDP from the national coalition, the right-of-center cabinet in Lower Saxony was eventually brought to an end in the fall of 1957 when the inevitability of a merger between the FDP and the right-wing DRP on a *Land* basis and the possible embarrassment it could create for the CDU/CSU both nationally and internationally caused Minister President Hellwege (DP) to dismiss his Free Democrat and Refugee Party ministers and

TABLE 4.5

THE THIRD SERIES OF *LAND* ELECTIONS (Continued) [25]

Party	1955 Rhineland-Palatinate		1955 Bremen		1956 Baden-Württemberg		
	Per-Cent	Total Seats	Per-Cent	Total Seats	Per-Cent	Direct Seats	Total Seats
CDU	46.8	51	18.0	18	42.6	48	56
SPD	31.7	36	47.8	52	28.9	20	36
FDP/DVP	12.7	13	8.6	8	16.6	2	21
GB/BHE	1.8	---	2.9	---	6.3	---	7
KPD	3.2	---	5.0	4	3.2	---	---
DP	---	---	16.6	18	---	---	---
BdD	0.7	---	1.1	---	0.6	---	---
Others	3.1	---	---	---	1.9	---	---
Totals		100		100		70	120

bring the Socialists into his cabinet (*New York Times*, November 13, 1957).

In the election of May 15, 1955, in Rhineland-Palatinate, the first to be held since West Germany became a sovereign state, the CDU marked its seventh consecutive gain by winning an absolute majority of *Landtag* seats. The Socialists suffered their second setback in as many contests. The victory meant a reconfiguration of the government's two-thirds *Bundesrat* majority which had been reestablished through the rebuilding of the government in Lower Saxony.[26] In the Bremen election later in the year the CDU nearly doubled its 1951 *Land* election total, but it failed to prevent the SPD from gaining an absolute parliamentary majority and the largest following won by the party in any election since the war.

Coming as it did within days after the ouster of the Christian Democrats from the government in North Rhine-Westphalia, the election of March 4, 1956, in Baden-Württemberg took on a new and vital significance for Adenauer's party, for a Socialist success would give the opposition control of the *Bundesrat*.[27] However, the CDU was able to guard its narrow margin in the federal upper chamber by increasing its previous *Land* election total by 6.6 percentage points and polling an absolute majority of the votes in the area comprising the former *Länder* of Baden and Württemberg-Hohenzollern.[28] In contrast, the Socialists barely managed to better their 1952 totals and even failed to outpoll the CDU in their stronghold of North Württemberg.

Although the CDU/CSU failed to realize the percentages of its 1953 *Bundestag* success in any of the regional contests held between 1953 and 1956, it bettered its previous *Land* election totals in all nine states. While its portion of the nationwide vote jumped from 28.0 percent to 36.7 percent, the Socialist figure increased only from 32.4 percent to 33.5 percent, enabling the Union parties to replace the SPD as the leading party on the *Land* level. In contrast to the second series of regional elections when its following fell below twenty percent of the vote in five *Länder*, only in Bremen did the CDU/CSU fail to exceed that figure in the 1953-1956 contests, and it polled over forty percent of the ballots cast in three *Länder* as against none in the earlier period. The Socialists, while bettering their general election totals in every contest and outpolling the Christian Democrats in five *Länder*, nevertheless lost ground to its major rival, which captured the three most populous states.[29] Moreover, although gaining over its 1949-1952 *Land* election figures in all but two contests, changes in electoral laws, its varying fortunes between elections in single member districts or the small total of the non-represented vote caused the SPD to lose representation in six *Land* parliaments.[30] Absolute majorities were won by the SPD in Bremen, by the CDU in Rhineland-Palatinate.

In contrast to the excessive fragmentation of the second series of *Land* elections when the CDU/CSU and SPD together polled a mere 60.4 percent of the nationwide vote and fifteen separate parties obtained parliamentary representation, the total of the two major parties in the 1953-1956 period increased to 70.2 percent of the West German balloting and the number of represented groups was reduced to nine, the representation of two of which was limited to a single *Land*.[31] Only in Lower Saxony, where the continued absence of a five percent clause enabled eight parties to gain legislative seats, were there more than five parliamentary groups in any of the *Landtage*.[32] The total number of seats won by other than the CDU/CSU, SPD and FDP declined from 251 in the second series of regional contests to 161 in the third, sixty of which were gained by the Refugee Party, marking a significant reversal of earlier trends as growing economic well-being and the integrating influence of national politics reduced the number of acceptable choices for the voters.

As the intervention efforts of the national CDU/CSU and the retaliatory efforts of the Socialists reached a new intensity in the period following the 1953 *Bundestag* election, in their attempts to control the politics of the federal *Bundesrat*, governments were established in over half the *Länder* which were not reflective of the voters' wishes and which were headed by premiers who were neither the most popular nor the most influential political leaders in the *Land*. The political jockeying which characterized the period left only Bremen, Hesse, Rhineland-Palatinate and Baden-Württemberg after October 1953 unscathed.[33] In Hamburg an alliance of the bourgeois parties known as the *Hamburg Block* ousted the government of the popular Max Brauer after the 1953 *Land* election even though the SPD was by far the most important single parliamentary group in the Hamburg *Bürgerschaft*. In North Rhine-Westphalia a right-of-center government comprising the CDU, FDP and small *Zentrum* was established following the 1954 regional contest; however, following a dispute with the CDU in Bonn over a new national electoral law, the Free Democrats, searching for a way to get back at Adenauer, withdrew from the Düsseldorf coalition in February 1956 and entered into a government with the Socialists and *Zentrum*, leaving the leading CDU and its respected leader, Karl Arnold, out in the cold. Both of these unrepresentative coalitions governed until the end of the legislative period, when absolute majorities ended any question of the representativeness of the government. Again in Schleswig-Holstein, although the SPD emerged as the leading party from the 1954 election, it was excluded from the ministry in Kiel by a coalition of the CDU, FDP and BHE; however, later in the year the tables were turned on Adenauer's party in Bavaria as the smaller parties combined against the CSU to place it in the opposition for nearly three years. The negative basis of the coalition and the necessity of coordinating such diverse elements as the SPD, FDP, Bavarian and Refugee parties did not contribute to positive government and in October 1957 the withdrawal of the BP and the BHE from the Hoegner (SPD) cabinet made possible an administration of the CSU, BHE and FDP before the end of the legislative period. A four-party ministry reflecting the political groupings in the Bonn government was formed in Lower Saxony following the 1955 election. Again, the aberrant basis of the coalition contributed to its demise in the fall of 1957 when Minister President Hellwege (DP) dismissed his FDP and BHE ministers and brought the SPD into his government.

The decline in the number of parties receiving representation and the ability of a single party to obtain a legislative majority limited the need for the type of intense political maneuvering that characterized the early 1950s, and from the end of 1958 to 1966 when the right-of-center coalition, which excluded the Socialists, was formed after the election in North Rhine-Westphalia, the leading parliamentary group was always represented in the governments of the *Länder*. A recent example of the leading party being excluded from the *Land* government occurred in Hamburg after the election of September 23, 2001 when the CDU with 26.2 percent of the vote and 33 seats in contrast to 36.5 percent of the vote and 46 seats for the SPD, formed a coalition with the right-wing Schill Party which had gained 19.4 percent of the vote and 25 seats and the FDP in the 121 member *Bürgerschaft*. Then in 2011 the leading CDU was excluded from the government of Baden-Württemberg by an alliance of the Greens and the Socialists.[34]

While the Union parties and the SPD gained in their nationwide vote totals, the FDP absorbed a moderate loss as its *Land* election figures fell behind 1949-1952 totals in six *Länder*. Predictions that the party would be given its death knell in Baden-Württemberg following its action in upsetting the CDU government in North Rhine-Westphalia and withdrawal from the Bonn coalition proved to be groundless as the party gained more votes in 1956 than in any previous election held in the Southwest State, while suffering a slight percentage loss.[35] These actions and the split in the party caused thereby, however, were to plague the party in the 1957 *Bundestag* race and in the regional contests to follow.

The Refugee Party, while gaining nearly the same number of votes as in the second series of *Land* elections and nearly 200,000 more votes than in the 1953 general election, lost ground in every *Land* but Baden-Württemberg, where it equaled its previous regional election total.[36] The most spectacular drop in support was registered in Schleswig-Holstein, the *Land* of its founding, where its total amounted to 14.0 percent in contrast to 23.4 percent in 1950. The party would have suffered an even greater nationwide loss had it not been for the over 320,000 votes cast for it in North Rhine-Westphalia where it did not compete in 1950. The inability of the BHE to gain representation in North Rhine-Westphalia, which had absorbed over two million of the newcomers by 1954, was indicative of the degree to which refugees and expellees had been assimilated into the West German State. Again, the Refugee Party demonstrated its non-ideological orientation by siding with the bourgeois parties in Lower Saxony and Schleswig-Holstein and with the Socialists in Bavaria and Hesse.

The 1953-1956 regional contests were the last in which the early Communist Party competed before being outlawed in August 1956. While bettering its 1953 general election totals in every *Land* but Hamburg, the KPD lost ground over previous regional totals in eight of the nine *Länder* and gained representation only in Bremen, where its 5.0 percent figure was the highest reached by the party in any election following the 1953 *Bundestag* contest, and Lower Saxony, where the absence of a restrictive clause enabled it to gain two seats. Nationwide the KPD increased its total from 607,860 votes (2.2 percent) in 1953 to 765,126 (3.0 percent) in the 1953-1956 regional contests; nevertheless, in 1956 the Communist Party in no way endangered the political stability of the national government nor the governments of any of the *Länder*, and the decision of the Federal Constitutional Court in that year to outlaw the party only obscured the gradual extinction of the party at the polls.[37]

The left-oriented *Bund der Deutschen* (Federation of Germans—BdD), the only new nationally organized party, led by former Reich Chancellor Dr. Joseph Wirth, was able to exceed one percent of the vote in only one of the eight *Länder* in which it competed and to poll a mere 104,623 (0.4 percent) of the West German vote in the 1953-1956 *Land* elections.[38] Right-extremist groups had no better success than those of the Left, and in contrast to the second series of *Land* elections when they polled over 800,000 votes, support for such parties declined to less than 200,000 followers in the regional contests following the 1953 general election, the largest portion of that total falling to the German Reich Party, which, however, competed in only three *Länder*.[39] Most gratifying to the Federal Government was the decline in right-extremist support in Lower Saxony from 14.1 percent in 1951 to a mere 3.8 percent in the 1955 *Land* election.

The 1957 *Bundestag* Election

In contrast to the 1953 *Bundestag* contest, when the eventual outcome was in doubt up to the moment the votes were counted, the only question in the 1957 race was the eventual margin of the CDU/CSU victory. Instead of concentrating on domestic economic and social policies, where the Chancellor was vulnerable, the Socialists again chose to emphasize foreign policy, as in 1953, when they met a devastating defeat, in particular on the issue of German reunification. The electorate was unimpressed with the Socialist arguments and gave Adenauer his greatest national victory with an overwhelming 50.2 percent of the vote cast and 270 of 497 *Bundestag* seats. The CDU/CSU success was a strong endorsement of the Chancellor's policy of close ties with the United States and NATO and his party's economic program which had brought unprecedented prosperity to the country. The SPD's failure to adjust its foreign policy to the realities of the postwar period, its "neutrality" towards the West and purely class character did not make it an acceptable alternative to the multi-interest CDU/CSU. The party's stunning defeat, which saw its rival winning every *Land* with the exception of Bremen and Hamburg, five by absolute majorities, made abundantly clear the need for reform within the party if it hoped to compete successfully with the CDU and end its stagnation at the polls. Although the SPD had gradually been changing its character since the war, the setback in 1957 gave added impetus to the movement to transform the party into a *Volkspartei*, a party of all of the people, not merely of a particular class.

TABLE 4.6

NATIONAL TOTALS
THIRD *LAND* AND 1957 *BUNDESTAG* ELECTIONS [40]

Party	1953-1956 *Landtag* Elections		September 15, 1957 *Bundestag* Election		Seats
CDU/CSU	9,400,990	36.7	15,008,399	50.2	270
SPD	8,591,171	33.5	9,495,471	31.8	169
FDP/DVP	3,024,297	11.8	2,307,135	7.7	41
GB/BHE	1,811,209	7.1	1,374,001	4.6	---
KPD	765,126	3.0	---	---	---
DP	621,661	2.4	1,007,347	3.4	17
BP	643,469	2.5	254,322 [a]	0.9[a]	---
ZP	316,426	1.2			
DRP	151,476	0.6	308,564	1.0	---
BdD	104,623	0.4	58,725	0.2	---
Others	220,004	0.8	91,364	0.2	---
Totals	25,650,452		29,905,428		497

a The Bavarian Party and the *Zentrum* combined for the 1957 *Bundestag* election as the Federalist Union (FU).

Only four parties gained seats in the third *Bundestag* as the *Zentrum*, competing with the Bavarian Party as the FU, and the Refugee Party failed to gain either five percent of the national vote or the necessary three direct mandates. The German Party, although polling far fewer votes than the Refugee party, gained seventeen mandates by virtue of its ability to meet the direct seat requirement, giving it national representation along with the CDU/CSU, SPD and Free Democrats. The biggest losers of the election were the FDP and the BHE, both of which had bolted the national coalition during the previous legislative period and suffered from factional splits. In addition to its general loss in appeal resulting from the integration of refugee and expellee families into the West German society, the BHE was especially hurt by the loss of its top leadership to the CDU and desertions within its *Bundestag* and *Landtage* delegations to the other parties.[41] The drying up of campaign funds to the FDP because of fears that under certain circumstances it might support the "red" SPD as it had in North Rhine-Westphalia was an added blow to Free Democratic chances. Although returning a reduced delegation to the *Bundestag*, the FDP remained in the opposition with the Social Democrats, and the national government was formed with the German Party, the CDU/CSU's most consistent ally.

The CDU/CSU as Dominant Party

The integrating forces which produced the CDU/CSU national victory in 1957 and reduced the number of parties obtaining national representation to four, continued the string of Union successes in subsequent regional elections and hastened the decline of non-national and interest-type parties on the *Land* level. Between 1957 and 1959 Chancellor Adenauer was at the height of his personal popularity, and, as the CDU/CSU's major drawing card, remained unchallenged within the party. None of the other parties had a leader of such prestige and proven ability to compete successfully against him. Moreover, while his rivals held sufficient strength in certain of the *Länder* to win an occasional victory against him, none of their programs was broad enough to challenge his party nationally. Yet, Adenauer's tight-fisted control over the CDU/CSU and his failure to make provision for a successor evoked resistance within the new leadership of the party which came to a head in the spring of 1959 when the question of a successor to President Heuss was to be decided. While the CDU/CSU faction favoring the candidacy of Ludwig Erhard, symbol of West Germany's postwar economic recovery, for the Chancellorship attempted to persuade Chancellor Adenauer himself to accept the Federal Presidency, arguing that he could assure the continuity of his foreign policy from this position, those close to Adenauer proposed the candidacy of Erhard to the position of head of state. While seeming to accept, Erhard later announced his withdrawal from the nomination, paving the way, after considerable pressure, for Adenauer's decision in April to relinquish the Chancellorship and seek the Presidency instead.[42] Adenauer, however, was unwilling to see Erhard succeed him

TABLE 4.7

THIRD *LAND* AND 1957 *BUNDESTAG* ELECTION RESULTS [43]

Land	Year and Election	CDU/ CSU	SPD	FDP/ DPS	GB BHE	KPD	DP	BdD	Others
Hamburg	1953 *Land*	a	45.2	a	a	3.2	a	---	HB [a] 50.0
	1957 *Bund*	37.4	45.8	9.4	1.5	---	4.7	0.4	DRP 0.8
North Rhine-Westphalia	1954 *Land*	41.3	34.5	11.5	4.6	3.8	0.0	0.3	ZP 4.0
	1957 *Bund*	54.4	33.5	6.3	2.5	---	1.6	0.1	FU 0.8
Schleswig-Holstein	1954 *Land*	32.2	33.2	7.5	14.0	2.1	5.1	0.8	BSW 3.5
	1957 *Bund*	48.1	30.9	5.6	8.3	---	3.8	0.2	SSW 2.5
Bavaria	1954 *Land*	38.0	28.1	7.2	10.2	2.1	---	0.5	BP 13.2
	1957 *Bund*	57.2	26.5	4.6	6.8	---	0.7	0.2	FU 3.2
Hesse	1954 *Land*	24.1	42.6	20.5	7.7	3.4	1.2	0.5	---
	1957 *Bund*	40.9	38.0	8.5	5.6	---	5.5	0.2	DRP 1.2
Lower Sax-ony	1955 *Land*	26.6	35.2	7.9	11.0	1.3	12.4	0.3	DRP 3.8
	1957 *Bund*	39.1	32.8	5.9	7.6	---	11.4	0.2	DRP 2.3
Rhineland-Palatinate	1955 *Land*	46.8	31.7	12.7	1.8	3.2	---	0.7	3.1
	1957 *Bund*	53.7	30.4	9.8	1.5	---	1.6	0.3	DRP 2.7
Bremen	1955 *Land*	18.0	47.8	8.6	2.9	5.0	16.6	1.1	BdD 1.1
	1957 *Bund*	30.4	46.2	5.8	2.0	---	13.8	0.3	DRP 1.4
The Saar	1955 *Land* [b]	25.4	20.1	24.2	---	6.6	---	---	CVP 21.8
	1957 *Bund*	54.5	25.1	18.2	0.3	---	0.7	0.4	DRP 0.6
Baden-Württemberg	1956 *Land*	42.6	28.9	16.6	6.3	3.2	---	0.6	1.9
	1957 *Bund*	52.8	25.8	14.4	4.7	---	1.3	0.2	DRP 0.6

a The CDU, FDP, DP and BHE formed a party alliance known as the *Hamburg Block* for the 1953 *Bürgerschaft* election in Hamburg.

b The 1955 *Land* election in the Saar was held under French auspices, the area not yet having the status of a *Land* in the Federal Republic. The figures from 1955 are used for comparative purposes.

as Chancellor, although next to "*Der Alte*" he was the party's most popular leader. The adamancy of the parliamentary party in its support of Erhard and Adenauer's reappraisal of the role of the Federal President in foreign affairs caused him in early June to reverse himself and remain in the Chancellorship, with Heinrich Lübke being nominated instead. This about-face was viewed as a rebuff to Erhard and opened wounds within the party which took a number of years to heal. Moreover, the personal image of Adenauer suffered considerably from the 1959 succession struggle, and his continuance in office was to become a major issue in the 1961 *Bundestag* race and in the regional elections that followed. The Union had witnessed an uninterrupted series of gains in regional competition after the 1957 *Bundestag* election, including achieving absolute parliamentary majorities in North Rhine-Westphalia and Rhineland-Palatinate, but starting in the fall of 1959 the party's appeal began to wane and it suffered a string of losses which, with a few exceptions, ran unabated until the spring of 1963 when the political liability which uncertainty over the Chancellorship posed to the CDU/CSU caused it to settle the controversy by naming Ludwig Erhard as Chancellor-elect.[44] Although factors other than the succession crisis contributed to the CDU decline after 1959, it was one of the more important.[45]

The first repercussion of the CDU/CSU national victory in 1957 was the collapse in October of the Socialist administration in Bavaria following the withdrawal of the Bavarian and Refugee parties from the coalition, making possible a government comprising the CSU, FDP and BHE. In November, in an election that was fought on the record of the administration of the bourgeois government rather than on issues of national policy, the Social Democrats won an absolute majority in the Hamburg parliament. Although a member of the previous government coalition, the CDU was the only *Block* party to hold its own against the Socialist tide.[46] The CDU came out considerably better in the election of July 6, 1958, in North Rhine-Westphalia, when it won one of its most impressive *Land* victories of the early postwar period with 104 of 200 *Landtag* seats. While the election campaign was dominated by the issue of nuclear arms for Germany, with the Socialists playing upon the fear of "atomic death," the greatest influence on the election outcome was the untimely death of former Minister President Karl Arnold (CDU) in the last days of the campaign.[47] The CDU victory enabled it to form a one-party government and bring to an end the unrepresentative coalition under Socialist Fritz Steinhoff which had governed the *Land* since February 1956. The SPD made a gain of nearly five percentage points, but this was overshadowed by the Union gain of nearly twice that much.

The Schleswig-Holstein election in September gave the CDU a further resounding victory in which it increased its following by a spectacular 12.2 percentage points and came within two seats of winning an absolute *Landtag* majority. In replacing the SPD as the *Land's* leading party, the Christian Democrats carried 32 of the state's 42 single member constituencies, thirteen of which were won away from the Socialists who recorded only a small percentage gain. In forming his government, Minister President Kai-Uwe von Hassel continued

TABLE 4.8

THE FOURTH SERIES OF *LAND* ELECTIONS [48]

	1957		1958 North Rhine-Westphalia			1958 Schleswig-Holstein		
	Hamburg							
Party	Per-Cent	Total Seats	Per-Cent	Direct Seats	Total Seats	Per-Cent	Direct Seats	Total Seats
CDU	32.2	41	50.5	92	104	44.4	32	33
SPD	53.9	69	39.2	58	81	35.9	10	26
FDP	8.6	10	7.1	---	15	5.4	---	3
GB/BHE	---	---	---	---	---	6.9	---	5
DP	4.1	---	1.6	---	---	2.8	---	---
DRP	0.4	---	0.5	---	---	1.1	---	---
SSW	---	---	---	---	---	2.8	---	2
ZP	---	---	1.1	---	---	---	---	---
BdD	0.3	---	0.0	---	---	0.5	---	---
Others	0.4	---	0.0	---	---	0.2	---	---
Totals		120		150	200		42	69

an earlier working relationship with the FDP. The CDU continued to thrust forward with large gains in the fall elections in Bavaria and Hesse. The campaigns in both *Länder* were dominated by the Soviet threat to turn its occupation rights in Berlin over to the East German Democratic Republic. The plea of Adenauer and his followers to the voters to demonstrate their support of Bonn's determination to resist Communist designs on the former German capital undoubtedly aided the Union's cause, and in Bavaria the party came within one seat of winning half the representation in the *Landtag*. The Soviet threat also helped the SPD, whose kinsman, Berlin's Mayor, Willy Brandt, was right at the center of the conflict, and the Socialists made substantial gains, though less spectacular than the CDU, in both contests, winning exactly one-half of Hesse's 96 parliamentary seats.[49] The existing government coalitions in both *Länder* were continued after the election, the CSU, BHE and FDP in Bavaria and an SPD-BHE government in Hesse.

Both of the two major parties pushed ahead in the elections of April 19, 1959 in Lower Saxony and Rhineland-Palatinate. In the former *Land* the SPD remained the largest party and formed a government with the FDP and BHE, while in the latter the CDU increased its existing *Landtag* majority by one seat.[50] These two elections in the spring of 1959 marked the end of an uninterrupted

TABLE 4.9

THE FOURTH SERIES OF *LAND* ELECTIONS (Continued) [51]

Party	1958 Bavaria			1958 Hesse		
	Per-Cent	Direct Seats	Total Seats	Per-Cent	Direct Seats	Total Seats
CDU/CSU	45.6	77	101	32.0	6	32
SPD	30.8	23	64	46.9	42	48
FDP	5.6	---	8	9.5	---	9
GB/BHE	8.6	---	17	7.4	---	7
DP	0.4	---	---	3.5	---	---
DRP	0.6	---	---	0.6	---	---
BP	8.1	1	14	---	---	---
BdD	---	---	---	---	---	---
Others	0.3	---	---	0.1	---	---
Totals		101	204		48	96

string of gains by the Union parties in regional contests which had begun in 1953, increasing their portion of the total *Land* vote from 28.0 percent in the 1949-1952 period to 44 percent to effectively dominate both national and regional politics. The Union was at a postwar zenith. Its leader, Dr. Konrad Adenauer, was not only the undisputed master of his own party, but the opposition parties had neither leaders of comparable stature to oppose him nor programs which could provide acceptable alternatives to the dynamic economic, social, foreign and defense policies of his party. German democracy was no longer in danger of a fragmentation of political philosophies and political instability, but of the hegemony of a single party on the national and state levels and the possibility of a stagnation of the political status quo, as the only party capable of providing an effective alternative to the CDU/CSU found itself ballasted by an outmoded economic program, unrealistic foreign and defense policies and a leadership which failed to inspire the masses of the voters. The SPD seemed doomed to the status of a permanent minority, incapable of presenting an effective check on the power configuration of the CDU/CSU until a group of articulate leaders, among them Herbert Wehner, Carlo Schmid and Willy Brandt, began to breathe new life into the party. The program adopted at Bad Godesberg in 1959 was to effectively end the party's class character and aligned it with the West.[52] Between 1959 and 1965 the SPD was to surge to a position of equality with the CDU on the regional level and to close half the gap which had existed between the two parties on the national level.

TABLE 4.10

THE FOURTH SERIES OF *LAND* ELECTIONS (Continued) [53]

| Party | 1959 Lower Saxony | | | 1959 Rhineland-Palatinate | |
	Percent	Direct Seats	Total Seats	Percent	Total Seats
CDU/CSU	30.8	20	51	48.4	52
SPD	39.5	65	65	34.9	37
FDP	5.2	1	8	9.7	10
GB/BHE	8.3	---	13	1.4	---
DP	12.4	9	20	---	---
DRP	3.6	---	---	5.1	1
BP	---	---	---	---	---
BdD	0.1	---	---	0.4	---
Others	0.2	---	---	0.2	---
Totals		95	157 [a]		100

a The size of the Lower Saxony legislature was raised by eight seats to compensate for the ability of the SPD to win more direct seats than its proportional entitlement.

Endnotes to Chapter IV

1 Although not the most accurate indicators of opinion because of the strength of independent electoral groups, *Kommunal* elections, nevertheless, become useful when other opinion indicators are lacking. The *Kommunal* election of March 30, 1952 in Bavaria had indicated little change in the political situation in that *Land* as the CSU and the SPD polled 26.5 and 26.1 percent of the vote respectively. In Hesse the relative positions of the two parties changed only slightly. In the November local election in Lower Saxony CDU support fell to 12.5 percent of the total *Land* vote, the lowest ever registered by the party in that *Land*, whereas the SPD gained 32.1 percent, only a slight drop from the 33.7 percent figure recorded eighteen months earlier. That same month the SPD overtook the CDU in populous North Rhine-Westphalia with 36.1 percent of the vote in contrast to the Union's 35.6 percent total. The CDU figure of 38.9 percent in Rhineland-Palatinate and the SPD's figure of 33.4 percent nearly duplicated the totals registered in the 1951 *Land* election in that state.

2 The CDU/CSU victory marked the first time in German history that a single party controlled a majority of seats in the national parliament. The issues and results of the 1953 *Bundestag* contest are carefully analyzed in James K. Pollock, *et. al., German Democracy at Work* (University of Michigan Press, 1955).

3 Figures for the *Land* elections are taken from publications of the *Land* statistical offices and for the 1953 *Bundestag* contest from the Federal Statistical Office.

4 Figures are from the *Land* Statistical offices and the Federal Statistical Office.

5 The DRP and the German National Rally, a combination of several right-wing groups, failed to meet the requirements for entering a list of candidates in several of the *Länder*, limiting their national following. The total vote received by these two groups amounted to 366,465

6 The action by the Federal Constitutional Court against the SRP led to the dissolution of its parliamentary groups in Bremen and Lower Saxony; the KPD had *Fraktionen* only in the same two *Länder* at the time of the 1956 ban against it.

7 The CDU, previously excluded from the cabinet, formed a four-party government with the SPD, FDP and BHE under Dr. Gebhard Müller to replace the ministry of maverick Free Democrat Reinhold Maier, which was held together for eighteen months primarily by its common opposition to Adenauer.

8 Unable to break the Socialist grip over the Hamburg administration alone, the CDU formed the *Hamburg Block* with the FDP and DP in September 28, 1953. The BHE, which had no chance of gaining representation on its own, joined the alliance shortly before the election.

9 *Die Welt*, November 2 and 3, 1953, and *Die Wahl zur Bürgerschaft und zu den Bezirksausschüssen am 1. November 1953*, Hamburg Statistical Office. The 1953 contest was the last in which Hamburg competed under a mixed electoral system until 2008. In that year 72 seats were elected from districts, 48 over the *Land* list.

10 *Liberale in der Verantwortung* (publication of the Hamburg organization of the Free Democratic Party), 1964: 64.

11 The CDU had won sixteen excess seats in 1947, fifteen in 1950.

12 The *Zentrum* gained parliamentary representation only by virtue of a stipulation in the 1954 electoral law making eligible for the proportional division of the *Land* list seats those parties obtaining at least one-third of the vote in at least one constituency. This provision was added to the law for the specific purpose of aiding the *Zentrum* which participated in the Arnold (CDU) cabinet from 1950 to 1954. By obtaining 33.39 percent of the vote in constituency Essen-Borleck, the party obtained nine seats with 4.03 percent of the total *Land* vote. In the same election the BHE with 4.62 percent of the vote failed to gain representation by failing to gain either five percent of the state vote, to win a constituency outright or to gain the one-third constituency total.

13 This sequence of events is discussed in *Liberale in der Verantwortung,* Hamburg FDP, 1964: 37, and in Edward Pinney, *Federalism, Bureaucracy, and Party Politics in West Germany: The Role of the Bundesrat,* (Durham, North Carolina: University of North Carolina Press, 1963): 105-109.

14 *Die Welt*, September 13 and 14, 1954, and *Die Landtagswahl am 12. September 1954*, Schleswig-Holstein Statistical Office: 50-52. In the 1954 election the German Party formed an alliance with the Schleswig-Holstein Association known as the Schleswig-Holstein Bloc (SHB) and gained 5.1 percent of the votes and four *Landtag* seats.

15 Better economic conditions and the resettlement of large numbers of refugees to the industrial *Länder* contributed to the decline in the refugee vote in Schleswig-

Holstein. The number of eligible voters dropped by 170,000 between 1950 and 1954 as a result of this emigration.

16 The CSU outpolled the SPD 38.0 to 28.1 percent and won 83 to the Socialists' 61 seats. The SPD total of mandates was two less than in 1950 when it gained 28.0 percent of the vote because of the party's inability to win as many direct mandates as in 1950. Moreover, the percentage of "lost" votes (votes cast for which no representation was received) amounted to only 2.7 percent in 1954 as against 7.3 percent four years earlier, reducing the number of unearned seats to distribute.

17 The exclusion of the largest parliamentary group, the CSU, from the Bavarian government virtually required the cooperation of all four parties in the coalition. The constant necessity of compromising divergent views prevented the coalition from more than administering established policies.

18 The SPD won 44, the CDU/FDP 45 seats in the 96 member *Landtag*. A move to the right by the refugee group would have given a clear working majority to the bourgeois parties just as its move to the left placed power in the hands of the Socialists.

19 Election figures are from *Die Wahl zur Bürgerschaft und zu den Bezirksausschüssen am 1. November 1953*, Hamburg Statistical Office: 128-178; *Handbuch des Landtags Nordrhein-Westfalen (5 Wahlperiode)*: 295-297; and *Die Landtagswahl am 12. September 1954*, Schleswig-Holstein Statistical Office: 50-52.

20 In 1951 the SPD had carried 64 constituencies, but only 59 four years later. In contrast to 85 seats in the previous legislative period, the SPD-BHE grouping held only 76 seats, whereas eighty were required for a majority.

21 The most puzzling result of the 1955 election in Lower Saxony was the almost complete disappearance of the right-extremist vote which had amounted to 14.1 percent in 1951. The DRP failed to become the heir apparent of that vote as it increased its political following from 2.2 percent to only 3.8 percent in 1955 (*Dithmarscher Landzeitung*, April 25, 1955).

22 Wilhelm Kopf (SPD) had served as Minister President of Lower Saxony since the establishment of the *Land* in 1946. In May 1955 Heinrich Hellwege of the German Party took over the premiership.

23 Election figures are taken from *Wahl zum Bayerischen Landtag am 25. November 1962*, Bavarian Statistical Office: 122-125; *Handbuch des Hessischen Landtags (V. Wahlperiode)*: 204-206; and *Landtagswahlen in Niedersachsen 1947-1963*, Lower Saxony Statistical Office, pages unmarked.

24 Herr Schlüter had been appointed Minister of Education (*Kultus Minister*). See *Liberale Studenten-Zeitung*, (Bonn), June 1955, for a description of the form of the protests against Schlüter's nomination.

25 Election figures are taken from *Endgültiges Ergebnis der Landtagswahl am 15. Mai 1955*, State Director of Elections, Rhineland-Palatinate: 1; "*Parteien, Bürgerschaft und Senat der Freien Hansestadt Bremen*," *Staatsbürgerkundliche Arbeitsmappe*: 310; and a specially prepared list of election results from the Baden-Württemberg Statistical Office.

26 *Die Welt*, May 16 and 17, 1955. The national coalition controlled 26 of 38 *Bundesrat* votes.

27 The SPD-FDP coalition formed in North Rhine-Westphalia in February 1956 reduced the Federal Government's delegation in the *Bundesrat* to 21 and a defeat in Baden-Württemberg would have given the Socialists control of 22 votes in contrast to sixteen for the Bonn coalition.

28 *Die Parlamentswahlen in Baden-Württemberg seit 1952*, Baden-Württemberg Statistical Office, 1964: 6, 7 and 10.

29 In North Rhine-Westphalia the CDU outpolled the Socialists 41.3 to 34.5 percent, in Bavaria 38.0 to 28.1 percent and in Baden-Württemberg 42.6 to 28.9 percent.

30 The SPD lost seven seats in Hamburg, five in Lower Saxony, three in Hesse and two each in Baden-Württemberg, Bavaria and Rhineland-Palatinate, while gaining nine mandates in Bremen, eight in North Rhine-Westphalia and six in Schleswig-Holstein.

31 Of the nine parties receiving representation, only the CDU/CSU, SPD and FDP held mandates in every *Land*; the Refugee Party was represented in five, the German Party in three, the Communist Party and *Zentrum* in two and the DRP and Bavarian Party in a single state parliament.

32 In Rhineland-Palatinate only three parties were represented, in Baden-Württemberg, Hamburg, Hesse and North Rhine-Westphalia four, and in Bavaria, Bremen and Schleswig-Holstein five.

33 In Bremen the SPD formed a government with the CDU and FDP in spite of its parliamentary majority and the CDU continued its partnership with the FDP in Rhineland-Palatinate even though it controlled 51 of 100 seats. In Hesse the Socialists coalesced with the Refugee Party and in Baden-Württemberg the all-party government of the CDU, SPD, FDP and BHE was continued after the 1956 *Land* election.

34 In Schleswig-Holstein after the *Land* election of February 20, 2005 the CDU with the largest delegation of thirty seats was locked out of the cabinet for two months when the SPD, a winner of 29 seats, attempted to govern in concert with the Greens through the forbearance of the Danish minority party's two representatives. Controlling only 33 of the *Landtag's* 69 seats, the SPD/Greens combination broke down in April 2005 when it was replaced by a grand coalition of the CDU and SPD under a CDU minister president.

35 The FDP polled 50,000 more votes than in 1952 and 86,000 more votes than in 1953; nevertheless, the 16.6 percent figure marked a 1.4 percentage drop over the 1952 *Land* contest.

36 The BHE had not competed in Hamburg and North Rhine-Westphalia in the second series of *Land* elections. The party gained 6.3 percent of the vote in both the 1952 and 1956 elections in Baden-Württemberg.

37 The gradual decline of the Communist Party from 1946 to 1956 is indicated in Table 9.1, page 251 of Chapter IX.

38 The *Bund der Deutschen* competed in every *Land* election held between 1953 and 1956 with the single exception of Hamburg.

39 The three *Länder* in which the DP competed were Hamburg, Lower Saxony and Schleswig-Holstein.

40 Figures for the *Land* elections are taken from publications of the *Land* statistical offices and for the 1957 *Bundestag* contest from the Federal Statistical Office (Wiesbaden).

41 The most important desertions from the Refugee Party were those of leaders Waldemar Kraft and Theodor Oberländer, who preferred the security of cabinet posts in the Adenauer government to an uncertain future with a rapidly declining party.

42 See Arnold Heidenheimer, *Adenauer and the CDU* (Den Haag: Matinus Nijhoff, 1960: 221-229) for a more complete account of the 1959 succession struggle.

43 Figures are from the several *Land* statistical offices and the Federal Statistical Office.

44 Setbacks were suffered in Baden-Württemberg, Bremen, Hamburg, Hesse, North Rhine-Westphalia, Rhineland-Palatinate and West Berlin, in addition to the 1961 *Bundestag* race, during this interval.

45 The ability of Dr. Konrad Adenauer to maintain himself as head of the CDU and as Chancellor through the difficult period from 1959 to 1961 is ably discussed by Peter H. Merkle in "Equilibrium, Structure of Interests and Leadership: Adenauer's Survival as Chancellor," *American Political Science Review*, LVI (September 1962): 634-650.

46 In 1953 the *Hamburg Block* had polled 50.0 percent of the vote and gained 62 seats of which 36 were distributed to the CDU, sixteen to the FDP and ten to the DP. In 1957 the CDU won 41 seats outright and the FDP ten; however, the DP with 4.1 percent of the vote failed to qualify for seats. The obvious losers in the election when compared to earlier elections for which separate statistics are available were the DP and FDP.

47 Arnold died June 29, 1958, of a heart attack, attributed to the rigors of the campaign, which had been extremely bitter. Arnold, leader of the CDU left-wing, had occasionally been mentioned as a successor to Adenauer, and next to the Chancellor and his Economics Minister, Ludwig Erhard, was probably the most influential Christian Democrat at the time.

48 Election figures are taken from *Die Wahl zur Bürgerschaft und zu den Bezirksausschüssen am 10. November 1957*, Hamburg Statistical Office: 86-92; *Handbuch des Landtags Nordrhein-Westfalen (5. Wahlperiode)*: 295-297; and *Ergebnis der Wahl zum Schleswig-Holsteinischen Landtag am 28.9.1958*, Schleswig-Holstein Statistical Office: 3-4.

49 The crisis in Berlin also had a strong influence on the election of December 7, 1958, in the Western sectors of that city. With the voters showing strong support for both their Socialist mayor and the national government, the SPD increased its following by 8.0 percentage points, the CDU by 7.3 percentage points. So complete was the confidence shown in the two parties that no other party was able to elect a candidate, and in view of the crisis the SPD and CDU formed a common government.

50 While the incorporation in the *Land* electoral law of a five percent clause reduced the number of parties receiving representation in the Lower Saxony parliament to five, the lack of any basis for a grand coalition of the SPD and CDU necessitated the formation of a three-party government of the SPD, BHE, and FDP. In spite of its precarious existence, the coalition withstood all attempts to bring it down during the legislative session.

51 Election figures are taken from *Wahl zum Bayerischen Landtag am 25. November 1962*, Bavarian Statistical Office: 122-125 and *Handbuch des Hessischen Landtags (V. Wahlperiode)*: 204-206.

52 H. Kent Schellenger, Jr. in "The German Social Democratic Party After World War II: The Conservatism of Power," *The Western Political Quarterly*, XIX (June 1966): 251-265, presents the thesis that the change in the Social Democratic program was not the work of rebellious Young Turks, but the result of a deliberate, evolutionary process under the control of the party hierarchy. "At no point was the evolution of the Godesberg Program significantly influenced by a generation or a faction new to the principles or the organization of the Social Democratic Party. At no time, at least until 1958 when the program was virtually complete, was it out of the control of experienced, professional party functionaries." Nevertheless, Schellenger notes that an important stimulus to the party's change in program were the SPD's electoral losses and changing political conditions in postwar Germany.

53 Election figures are taken from *Die Wahl zum Niedersächsischen Landtag am 19. April 1959*, Lower Saxony State Administrative Office for Statistics: 7-15; and *Endgültiges Ergebnis der Landtagswahl am 19. April 1959*, State Director of Elections, Rhineland-Palatinate: 1.

CHAPTER V

Party Stabilization and SPD Resurgence

The Transformation of Social Democratic Appeal

The steady decline after 1953 in the number of parties receiving representation on the national and regional levels and the apparent stabilization around a system of three nationally-organized groupings was one of the important features of political developments in West Germany in the early years of the Bonn Republic. A second significant development was the resurgence of the Social Democratic Party, isolated during the 1950s by an increasingly irrelevant economic program and unrealistic foreign and defense policies, as a powerful political force, making possible for the first time since 1949 an alternation of political power in Bonn and in a majority of the *Länder*.

The political history of most of the groups which obtained parliamentary representation in the *Länder* between 1946 and 1965 such as the WAV and the SRP was short-lived; a few were able to hold their positions for two or more legislative periods before sinking into oblivion. By 1959, other than the CDU, SPD and FDP, only the German and Refugee parties remained as important political forces. However, both the DP and GB/BHE, because of the narrowness of their appeal, found it increasingly difficult to compete successfully against the three nationally-organized, multi-interest parties, and in the period following the 1961 *Bundestag* election, they too met the fate of the numerous political groups which preceded them. In 1960 the DP group in the *Bundestag* disbanded after a majority of its members joined the CDU/CSU, and the following year the frantic effort of the party to maintain a foothold in the national political arena through a merger with the Refugee Party came to naught as the combination, known as the All-German Party (GDP), obtained only 2.8 percent of the national vote.[1] Following the GDP's poor showing in the 1961 *Bundestag* contest, it gradually broke up, although the Refugee Party, the better organized of the two constituent groups, maintained the GDP designation. The DP *Fraktionen* in Bremen and Lower Saxony were emaciated by mass desertions and the 1963 elections terminated the party's political life in those two *Länder*.[2] By 1964 the Refugee Party had lost its representation in the parliaments of every *Land* with the single exception of Hesse, where it held six seats until 1966.[3] The collapse of these two parties, the inability of such new combinations as the DRP and the German

Peace Union (DFU) to gain a foothold on either the *Land* or the national levels and the continued success of the Free Democratic Party in maintaining its national and regional representation appeared to assure the continuance of a three-party system in the Federal Republic into the immediate future.[4]

While the West German electorate was limiting its support to three parties, after 1959 it also became increasingly willing to break with traditional political loyalties as the Social Democratic Party, freed from historical party dogma, began to attract an increasing number of voters who had previously regarded the party as an unacceptable alternative to the CDU/CSU. Although the SPD's opposition to close political and military integration with the West had produced minor successes for the party on the regional and local levels between 1949 and 1952, the party soon found itself out of touch with the main currents of German political sentiment as the Christian Union parties, under their popular national leader, Dr. Konrad Adenauer, won parliamentary majorities on the national level in 1953 and 1957 and made significant gains on the regional level between 1953 and 1959. While the Socialists increased their national support by a mere 2.6 percentage points between 1949 and 1957, the CDU/CSU gained 19.2 percentage points over the same period, and although they remained the leading party in Bremen, Hamburg, Hesse and Lower Saxony throughout the eight-year period, they, nevertheless lost ground to the Union parties in total *Land* support. Unquestionably most Germans preferred security within the Western alliance to the uncertainties of neutrality with all the possibilities this would have opened up for Soviet pressure and Communist subversion, and Socialist opposition to Adenauer's pro-Western orientation did not enable the party to win the goodwill of the great bulk of the German electorate.

The disastrous national defeat for the SPD in 1957 stressed the need for change within the party if it were not to continue to stagnate as a political group. Although the SPD had effectively ceased to be a party merely of the working class under the leadership of Kurt Schumacher and had gradually shed most of its Marxist orientation in succeeding years, the party nevertheless continued to be haunted by its class image. The party bureaucracy appeared unable to comprehend the changed nature of German politics since the war, in particular, the importance of an all-encompassing program and a popular personality as its leader. While the SPD was blessed with an abundance of capable leaders on the regional level, its national leadership had been colorless and mediocre since the death of Kurt Schumacher in 1952. The gradual process of transformation into a modern "bourgeois" party found its culmination in the program adopted at Bad Godesberg in November 1959, which effectively freed the SPD from its Marxist ballast as it endorsed free enterprise, modified by the demands of social justice.

With this, the economic differences between the SPD and the bourgeois parties were to all but disappear. Gradually the SPD came closer to the position of the CDU/CSU on foreign and defense policy, and by the time of the 1961 national elections, all that separated them were differences in the social and financial spheres. Moreover, following the example of the Union, the Social Democrats presented a popular figure, Willy Brandt, whose position as Governing Mayor of West Berlin since 1957 had kept him in the spotlight as its top candidate in 1961 rather than the colorless Erich Ollenhauer, who, nevertheless, remained as party chairman until his death in 1963.[5] Under its new program and leadership, the SPD, using campaign techniques which were frankly American in style, surged forward on both the regional and national levels. Between 1957 and 1965 the party increased its countrywide following by 7.5 percentage points and its total *Land* following by 8.8 percentage points, as it made gains in 21 of 22 regional contests held during the eight-year period. The resurgence of the SPD, although its gains were not always coupled with CDU/CSU losses, was a healthy development in postwar German politics, since it presented the German electorate for the first time with the opportunity for a change of leadership on the national level without fear of a drastic change of course in either domestic or foreign policies. The gains by the SPD on the regional level after 1957 were a precursor of it becoming the leading party on the national level in 1972.

The 1957-1960 *Land* Elections

The move toward a more dynamic leadership within the SPD got under way following the 1957 general election when two nonconformists, Herbert Wehner of Hamburg and Professor Carlo Schmid of Tübingen University, were elected deputy leaders of the parliamentary party in Bonn. The two helped to engineer the party's overwhelming victory over the CDU in Hamburg, just weeks after the party's national debacle, bringing down the bourgeois coalition under Christian Democrat Dr. Kurt Sieveking.[6] The Hamburg organization refused to allow any participation in the campaign by the national party apparatus, fearing that it could only have an adverse influence on the outcome.[7] The campaign was fought on the issue of good government, on the performance of the administration of CDU mayor Sieveking, who had found himself unable to contain the actions of certain of his cabinet members. In contrast to the bourgeois record, the Social Democratic administration from 1946 to 1953 under Max Brauer had been unblemished by political scandals (*New York Times*, November 11, 1957).

The victory in Hamburg gave impetus to the demand for new leadership and an overhauling of the party position in economics and foreign and defense policy, which had proven themselves outdated and unacceptable to a majority of voters. Changes were not long in coming, and in February 1958 at the party congress in Stuttgart, although Erich Ollenhauer was reelected as national party chairman, Herbert Wehner, an ex-Communist who was probably the most dynamic force in the party at the time, and Waldemar von Knöringen were chosen deputy chairmen. At the same meeting, in an effort to widen its appeal to the middle-class voter, the party's economic program rejected nationalization of industry, proposed private ownership of the coal industry and public regulation of industry when necessary. This draft formed the basis of the Godesberg program adopted the following year.

While the reform movement failed to prevent the CDU landslide victory in North Rhine-Westphalia in July 1958, the SPD made substantial gains in the Ruhr and Rhineland in a regional contest for the first time since the war.[8] Moderate gains were made in the fall elections in Schleswig-Holstein, Bavaria and Hesse. In Hesse the party gained one-half of the parliamentary seats. However, in all three contests the SPD was outgained by the CDU. In December, the Berlin crisis, precipitated by the Soviet threat to withdraw its occupation obligations in Germany and demand to have West Berlin turned into a "demilitarized Free City," united the Berliners behind the SPD and the CDU to give the Communist SED a stunning defeat. While both of the two major parties made extensive gains, the Socialists won an absolute majority in the Berlin parliament, and its local leader, Willy Brandt, was brought to national attention by the crisis and kept in the spotlight by the German and world news media, circumstances which, notwithstanding his own natural abilities, were eventually to propel him into the position of national leader of the party within two years.

The results of the elections in the spring of 1959 in Lower Saxony and Rhineland-Palatinate showed gains of nearly equal proportions for the SPD and the CDU/CSU, as both parties continued to increase their followings at the expense of the smaller parties. The fact remained, however, that the Socialists up to the middle of 1959, in spite of gains in seven consecutive *Land* decisions, had lost ground to the CDU/CSU in the total *Land* level vote since the 1957 general election, as the popularity of the CDU/CSU and its leader Konrad Adenauer, was at its height. Several significant events following the decisions in Lower Saxony and Rhineland-Palatinate were to reverse this trend. Foremost was the controversy over a successor to Federal President Theodor Heuss and the blow which Adenauer dealt to his authority by deciding to seek the presidency and then, almost as suddenly, recanting his decision. This action not only fanned the fires of division within the party, but his prestige among the CDU voters was severely shaken. Rather than preparing a successor for his office as the situation now appeared to demand, *Der Alte* continued to act as if he would go on forever.[9] Secondly, the new leadership within the SPD, Willy Brandt of West Berlin, and Fritz Erler, Herbert Wehner and Carlo Schmid of the parliamentary party in Bonn, began to attract increasing attention, and gradual changes in the program of the party which were to come to fruition later in the year in the Godesberg program began to draw support from voters who had earlier found the party's economic policy repugnant.[10]

The first indication of a decline of the Union parties in public favor and a move to the SPD came in the Bremen election of October 11, 1959, in which the CDU suffered its first clear setback in nineteen regional contests and the SPD pushed its *Land* total from 47.8 to 54.9 percent. Neither the absence of the Communist Party from competition nor a switch of former CDU supporters to other bourgeois parties could explain the Bremen result, since the increase in Socialist support far exceeded support for the KPD in the 1955 *Bürgerschaft* election and the DP and FDP both lost electoral support.[11] A second successive setback was suffered by the CDU in Baden-Württemberg, where it lost five mandates in contrast to the Socialists' gain of eight. Moreover, the SPD won only one less seat than the CDU in the constituency competition. The large Socialist gain was attributed mainly to the active participation in the election campaign of West Berlin's Governing Mayor, Willy Brandt, who proved himself to be a big drawing card for the party. [12] The *Land* election of December 4, 1960, in the Saar was the last to be held prior to the 1961 *Bundestag* contest. While the unification of Socialist forces in the Saar enabled the SPD to increase its following by nearly ten percentage points over 1955 *Land* election figures,[13] the split in the Christian-oriented vote prevented the CDU from realizing its sought for majority. Although increasing its share of the vote by 11.2 percentage points over the 1955 balloting, the CDU total was 10.6 percentage points less than the combined CDU/CVP following five years earlier when the two parties had competed separately.[14]

To better understand the outcome of the 1960 contest in the Saar, the first regional election to be held in that *Land* since reunification, it is necessary to trace the political developments leading up to its reintegration into the West German State.

French policy in the immediate postwar period called for the permanent separation of the Saar from Germany, and the establishment of a special status for the area which would insure its political control and certain economic benefits without actual annexation of the territory into the French Republic. This goal was realized by granting the Saar an "international" political status inside an economic union with France. A constitution giving cognizance to this status was formulated by a constitutional commission and approved in December 1947 by the *Landtag* elected two months earlier.[15] Since pro-German parties were banned, the only opposition to the document came from the two Communist deputies in the fifty-member parliament. In spite of restrictions on political activity, support for the proponents of the constitution was genuine as the Saarlanders were motivated by the expectation of economic betterment at a time when the rest of Germany was gripped by severe shortages of food and economic stagnation.

The most important political party during the period of French control was the Christian People's Party, whose founder and leading spirit, Johannes Hoffmann, favored close cooperation with France. Hoffmann had been editor of the *Saarbrücken Landeszeitung* from 1929 to 1934 when he was forced into exile by the Nazis. Returning to the Saar in 1945, Hoffmann headed the commission which drew up the separatist constitution and served as Minister President from 1947 until after the 1955 *Landtag* election.[16] The CVP won 51.2 percent of the vote in 1947 and 54.7 percent in 1952; however, in 1955 following the lifting of restrictions on the organization of parties which "would not accept the autonomous status of the Saar and its constitution," the CVP total fell to 21.8 percent as most of its former support went to the pro-German CDU.[17] When the CVP merged with the CDU, Hoffmann, who had opposed the merger of the two Christian groups and the integration of the Saar into the Federal Republic, formed the Saarland People's Party (SVP), which succeeded in gaining 11.4 percent of the 1960 vote.

In contrast to the 1947 contest, when there was a minimum of pro-German agitation, German nationalists, backed by the Catholic clergy, attempted to transform the 1952 election into a plebiscite. The Saar Catholic Church, two-thirds of which fell under the jurisdiction of the Bishop of Trier, felt itself warranted in encouraging Saarlanders to boycott the polls or to cast invalid ballots because of the ban on pro-German parties (*New York Times*, December 2, 1952). Few Saarlanders boycotted the election,[18] and even though 24.5 percent of the ballots cast had been invalidated, the result was regarded as a decisive setback for those favoring integration with Germany. Of the four parties participating in the election, only the Communist Party opposed the existing status of the Saar, and few voters were willing to support the Communists under any circumstance and its following was limited to 9.5 percent.[19]

Although the Saar was not an integral part of West Germany at the time, the election results, nevertheless, had an important influence on German foreign policy. While Adenauer refused to recognize the outcome as a legitimate expression of the will of the Saarlanders, he was aware that German-French antagonism could affect the Government's drive to win ratification of the Bonn peace contract and the EDC treaty. His attacks were therefore leveled at Saar Minister President Hoffmann rather than at the French, whose Foreign Minister Schuman had suggested Europeanization for the Saar the previous July. The French were hopeful that Adenauer would accept this solution in view of the election results (*New York Times*, December 2, 1952). Subsequent negotiations between France and Germany led to agreement on October 23, 1954 on a European Statute, which, if approved, would have continued the Saar's autonomous international status until the conclusion of a peace treaty. In a popular referendum, held the following year, the Saarlanders rejected the Statute by a two-thirds majority, setting the stage for the Franco-German negotiations which were to result in a final settlement of the Saar question. On December 18, 1955, in the first free election held in the Saar since 1918, the three pro-German parties, the CDU, SPD and DPS, obtained 64.1 percent of the vote and 33 of fifty *Landtag* seats to reconfirm the results of the October referendum. The CDU, competing for the first time in a Saar election, emerged as the leading party with 25.4 percent of the votes and fourteen seats; the SPD, also entering its first Saar contest, polled a disappointing 14.3 percent.[20] Hoffmann's CVP, the Communist Party and the Saar Socialist Party stood in opposition to unification.

In January the three *Heimatbund* parties formed a common coalition under Dr. Hubert Ney (CDU), and on the last day of the month the Saar *Landtag* resolved in a declaration of principles the attachment of the Saarland to the Federal Republic. The question of reunification was settled in the Franco-German treaty of October 17, 1956, and on January 1, 1957, the Saar became politically incorporated into the German Republic with *Land* status, although economic ties with France continued until July 1959. Between the 1955 and 1960 *Land* elections merger of the SPS with the SPD and the CVP with the

CDU was accomplished; however, disappointed ambitions and personal rivalries prevented a successful unification of Christian forces, and one group under former Minister President Johannes Hoffmann formed the SVP and one under former Minister President Hubert Ney (CDU) formed the Christian National Community (CNG), both of which competed separately against the CDU in 1960. Although the total Christian vote amounted to 50.6 percent in the 1960 election in contrast to 47.8 percent in 1955, the CDU share was a mere 36.6 percent in spite of unification, as Hoffmann's SVP polled a surprising 11.4 percent. The CNG, on the other hand, received a disappointing 2.6 percent and failed to obtain representation. The election resulted in the breakup of the grand coalition which had existed between Christian and Socialist forces since 1956, as the CDU formed a government with the DPS.

Between the 1957 and the 1961 general elections the SPD bettered its previous *Land* election totals in eleven consecutive contests to push its total *Land* level vote from 33.5 percent in the third series of regional contests to 38.3 percent. In this same series of elections the CDU/CSU made major gains in the *Länder* until the fall of 1959, when a trend against the party set in. Contributing to this decline, which saw the party's nationwide vote drop to 42.1 percent after having been pushed from 36.7 percent to nearly 44 percent in earlier contests, was the issue of a successor to Adenauer and the gradual transformation of the SPD into a bourgeois party with new leaders having greater appeal to the voters. The CDU's misfortune in the Saar, however, resulted from a split in Christian-oriented ranks rather than from a shift to the Socialists. Only in Bremen did the CDU poll less than thirty percent of the votes, while the SPD polled at least that in all *Länder*. In spite of the CDU's late losses, it outgained the SPD in the fourth series of *Land* elections, increasing its regional total by 5.4 percentage points to 42.1 percent overall to the SPD's 4.8 percentage gain to 38.3 percent. The most significant outcome of the 1957-1960 regional contests was the increase in the combined Union/SPD vote from 70.2 to 80.4 percent. Only in Bremen and in the Saar did the two-party total fall below seventy percent, in Bremen because of the weakness of the Christian Democrat appeal and in the Saar for the reasons explained earlier. Absolute parliamentary majorities were won by the CDU in North Rhine-Westphalia and Rhineland-Palatinate and by the SPD in Bremen and Hamburg. In Hesse the SPD gained exactly one-half of the seats.

The continued growth of the Union and SPD left a trail of mutilated minor parties in their wake, some reduced to unrecognizable shells of their former selves. The *Zentrum*, which once played an important role in the politics of Lower Saxony and North Rhine-Westphalia failed to gain representation in those two *Länder*; the German Party lost its representation in Hamburg and Schleswig-Holstein and in 1960 was on the verge of collapse as a political force; the Refugee Party, while maintaining delegations in five *Landtage*, lost eleven seats over the third series of *Land* elections as its national support declined from 7.1 to 4.5 percent; and even the FDP, once a powerful group in several *Länder*, suffered losses over its 1953-1956 *Land* election totals in every *Land* and a drop

TABLE 5.1

THE FOURTH SERIES OF *LAND* ELECTIONS (Continued) [21]

Party	1959 Bremen		1960 Baden-Württemberg			1960 The Saar	
	Per-cent	Total Seats	Per-cent	Direct Seats	Total Seats	Per-cent	Total Seats
CDU/CSU	14.8	16	39.5	34	52	36.6	19
SPD	54.9	61	35.3	33	44 [a]	30.0	16
FDP/DPS	7.2	7	15.8	3	18	13.8	7
GB/BHE	1.9	---	6.6	---	7	---	---
DP	14.5	16	1.6	---	---	---	---
DRP	3.8	---	---	---	---	0.6	---
SVP	---	---	---	---	---	11.4	6
DDU	---	---	---	---	---	5.0	2
BdD	0.4	---	0.5	---	---	---	---
Others	2.5 [b]	---	0.7	---	---	2.6 [c]	---
Totals	100		70	121 [a]		50	

a The SPD won a single *Überhangmandate* in North Württemberg, increasing the size of the *Landtag* to 121 members.

b Denotes total for the Voter's Association against Atomic Rearmament, for Peace and Understanding.

c Denotes total for the Christian National Community (CNG).

from 11.8 to 8.1 percent in its national following, although it recovered some ground over its crushing setback in the 1957 *Bundestag* election vote in five states.[22] In no state parliament were more than five parties represented; in Berlin there were only two and in Hamburg and North Rhine-Westphalia only three. The number of parliamentary seats falling to other than the CDU/CSU, SPD and FDP declined from 161 in the third series of *Land* contests to 110 in the fourth. Of these, 49 were gained by the Refugee Party.[23]

The 1957-1960 period witnessed the breakup of the unrepresentative government coalitions in Bavaria, Hamburg, Lower Saxony and North Rhine-Westphalia, in which the strongest parliamentary group had been excluded from the government. The SPD-FDP-BHE-BP coalition in Bavaria was replaced by a combination of the CSU, FDP and BHE in October 1957, which continued to govern after the 1958 elections. A Socialist-FDP partnership became the government of Hamburg after the decline of the parties of the *Hamburg Block* in the 1957 *Land* election. The SPD was returned to the government of Lower Saxony in November 1957 after Minister President Hellwege dismissed his FDP and BHE ministers. The resulting grouping of the CDU, DP and SPD lasted until the 1959 regional election when the SPD formed a government with the FDP and BHE. In North Rhine-Westphalia the 1958 landslide victory for the CDU enabled it to form a one-party administration to replace the former Socialist-Free Democrat combination which had existed since February 1956. The 1958 success of the Christian Democrats in Schleswig-Holstein ended an eight-year period in which the *Land's* leading party was not included in the government. This situation came to an end when the CDU, by winning 33 of 69 *Landtag* seats, replaced the SPD as the leading party. Its increased strength enabled the CDU to form a majority with only the FDP as coalition partner in contrast to three parties in the previous legislative period. From September 1958 to July 1966 when the SPD was excluded from the government of North Rhine-Westphalia, the strongest parliamentary group was always a participant in the *Land* government.

In Hesse the existing Socialist-BHE coalition was continued after the 1958 *Land* contest and in Rhineland-Palatinate the CDU renewed its partnership with the FDP. The grand coalitions in Baden-Württemberg, Bremen and the Saar were not resumed. In Baden-Württemberg the all-party coalition was replaced by a CDU-FDP-BHE combination; in Bremen the SPD and FDP formed a government without the CDU; in the Saar a CDU-FDP government replaced the earlier CDU-SPD coalition. In view of the international crisis a Socialist-CDU government was formed in West Berlin after the 1958 election even though the Socialists could have governed alone.

The 1961 *Bundestag* Election

The 1961 *Bundestag* contest marked the beginning of a new era of electioneering in West Germany. No longer were there stark policy differences between the two major parties, and for the first time the West Germans were to choose between personalities rather than programs, publicized by methods which were strikingly similar to those employed in American presidential races. In the fall of 1960 the Social Democrats decided to run the popular mayor of West Berlin, Willy Brandt, instead of party chairman, Erich Ollenhauer, to go along with the party's "new look." Moreover, the SPD made use of many of the campaign techniques which had proven successful in the Kennedy campaign in the United States the previous year.

The CDU/CSU, on the other hand, entered the general election with its four-time candidate, Dr. Konrad Adenauer, in spite of his slipping popularity and the growing schism within the party which his continuance in office was causing. The Chancellor's skillful manipulation of political forces and the unwillingness of possible successors as Economics Minister Ludwig Erhard and

Franz Josef Strauss to wage a concerted effort against him enabled him to maintain the upper hand. Adenauer's continuance in office, his attacks on Brandt's person, and handling of the wall crisis in Berlin alienated numerous voters, many of whom were not yet willing to throw their support to the SPD. It was for the FDP to manipulate this sentiment by promising to enter a coalition with the CDU only and not the SPD, but without Adenauer as Chancellor. Nearly obliterated in the 1957 national election following a split in the party and the cutting off of financial support from business and industry in reaction to its hostility to Adenauer and role in bringing down the CDU administration in North Rhine-Westphalia, the divergent factions of the FDP were brought together under the able leadership of the party's new chairman, Erich Mende, himself an attractive personality and able speaker. The FDP's stand against Adenauer, but not against the CDU, was to form the foundation for its success on September 17, 1961.[24]

With a decline from 50.2 to 45.4 percent of the total national vote, the CDU lost its absolute majority in the *Bundestag*, setting the stage for the long period of bitter coalition negotiations with the FDP which followed. The negotiations with the Free Democrats had been made difficult by a pre-election pledge of FDP national chairman, Dr. Erich Mende, that his party, although favoring an alliance with the CDU/CSU over the SPD, would not support Adenauer as Chancellor. Adenauer, displaying the keen perception of political realities which had kept him in power for twelve years, manipulated the situation to his advantage and maneuvered the FDP into a corner. With *"Der Alte"* solidly backed by his own party and their own election commitment to the Union, the Free Democrats had no other alternative than to back down on their pledge against entering a cabinet headed by Adenauer. The sole victory for the FDP was the vague promise that Adenauer would step down from the Chancellorship before termination of his four-year term of office and Dr. von Bretano's replacement as Foreign Minister by Dr. Gerhard Schröder, the then federal Interior Minister.[25] Mende himself refused to accept a cabinet position in the Adenauer government.

The FDP's pledge to enter into a government partnership with the CDU/CSU only, but without Adenauer at its head, and the unity and effective organization which had developed under Mende's chairmanship had made the FDP the largest gainer in the 1961 general election with an increase from 7.7 percent of the national vote in 1957 to 12.8 percent in 1961. Many voters saw in the FDP a "watchdog" over the actions of the two dominant parties in both Bonn and the state capitals; however, the party's participation in an Adenauer-led government was considered by many to be a betrayal of trust, and the FDP was to be rudely punished in the regional contests to follow the *Bundestag* decision. In no *Land* between 1961 and 1965 were the Free Democrats able to duplicate their 1961 success and in three *Länder* they lost ground over their previous regional election totals.

While gaining over its 1957 totals in every *Land* and polling over a third of the national vote for the first time in a general election contest, the results nevertheless indicated that the electorate had not yet given full credence to the new program of the SPD, as the party was unable to duplicate on the national level its

TABLE 5.2

FOURTH *LAND* AND 1961 *BUNDESTAG* ELECTION RESULTS [24]

Land	Year and Election	CDU/ CSU	SPD	FDP	GDP [a]	DFU [b]	DRP	Other Parties
Hamburg	1957 *Land*	32.2	53.9	8.6	---	---	0.4	DP 4.1
	1961 *Bund*	31.9	46.9	15.7	1.0	3.6	0.9	---
North Rhine-Westphalia	1958 *Land*	50.5	39.2	7.1	---	---	0.5	---
	1961 *Bund*	47.6	37.3	11.8	0.9	2.0	0.5	---
Schleswig-Holstein	1958 *Land*	44.4	35.9	5.4	6.9	---	1.1	SSW 2.8
	1961 *Bund*	41.8	36.4	13.8	3.9	1.3	0.9	SSW 1.9
Bavaria	1958 *Land*	45.6	30.8	5.6	8.6	---	0.6	BP 8.1
	1961 *Bund*	54.9	30.1	8.8	3.9	1.6	0.5	---
Hesse	1958 *Land*	32.0	46.9	9.5	7.4	---	0.6	DP 3.5
	1961 *Bund*	34.9	42.9	15.2	4.1	2.3	0.6	---
West Berlin	1958 *Land*	37.7	52.6	3.8	---	---	---	SED 1.9
	1954 *Land*	30.4	44.6	12.8	2.5	---	---	SED 2.7
Lower Saxony	1959 *Land*	30.8	39.5	5.2	8.3	---	3.6	DP 12.4
	1961 *Bund*	39.0	38.7	13.2	6.1	1.3	1.6	---
Rhineland-Palatinate	1959 *Land*	48.4	34.9	9.7	1.4	---	5.1	---
	1961 *Bund*	48.9	33.5	13.2	0.5	1.5	2.3	---
Bremen	1959 *Land*	14.8	54.9	7.2	1.9	---	3.8	DP 14.5
	1961 *Bund*	27.0	49.7	15.2	4.1	3.0	1.1	---
Baden-Württemberg	1960 *Land*	39.5	35.3	15.8	6.6	---	---	---
	1961 *Bund*	45.3	32.1	16.6	2.8	2.3	0.7	---
The Saar	1960 *Land*	36.6	30.0	13.8	---	---	0.6	SVP 11.4 DDU 5.0 CNG 2.6
	1961 *Bund*	49.0	33.5	12.9	0.3	3.2	0.9	---

a The BHE and DP combined to form the GDP for the 1961 *Bundestag* election. For *Land* elections held prior to 1961, BHE (Refugee Party) figures are found under the GDP column and DP (German Party) figures in the column headed "Other Parties."

b The DFU was not founded until sometime prior to the 1961 *Bundestag* contest and therefore competed in none of the regional elections held in the 1957-1960 period.

TABLE 5.3

NATIONAL TOTALS
FOURTH *LAND* AND 1961 *BUNDESTAG* ELECTIONS [26]

Party	1957/1960 *Landtag* Elections		September 17, 1961 *Bundestag* Election		Seats
CDU/CSU	11,125,861	42.1	14,298,372	45.4	242
SPD	10,125,991	38.3	11,427,355	36.2	190
FDP/DPS	2,139,616	8.1	4,028,766	12.8	67
GB/BHE	1,185,925	4.5	870,756 [a]	2.8 [a]	---
DP	840,019	3.2			
DFU	---	---	609,918	1.9	---
BP	371,212	1.4	---	---	---
DRP	332,393	1.3	262,977	0.8	---
ZP	84,675	0.3	---	---	---
BdD	37,932	0.1	---	---	---
SSW	34,136	0.1	25,449	0.1	---
DG	28,308	0.1	27,308	0.1	---
Others	136,729	0.5	---	---	---
Totals	26,442,797		31,550,901		499

a The Refugee and German parties combined as the All-German Party (GDP) for the 1961 *Bundestag* election.

earlier successes in *Land* elections.[27] In the regional contests between 1961 and 1965, however, the Socialists were able to register gains in every state to nearly equal the following of the Union parties on the *Land* level (42.3 to the CDU/CSU's 42.7 percent), indicating that the new direction of the party was finally gaining more general acceptance.

Although the DP group in the *Bundestag* had disbanded a year prior to the 1961 *Bundestag* contest after a majority of its members had joined the CDU, the election of September 17 officially marked the parliamentary death of the party on the national level. Early in 1961 an almost frantic attempt was made by the German Party to maintain a foothold in the national political arena by merging with the Refugee Party, which had lost its national representation in 1957. The two parties together had polled 8.0 percent of the national vote four years earlier and 7.7 percent of the vote in succeeding *Land* elections; however, the merger proved a grave miscalculation when the new combination, the GDP, obtained only 2.8 percent of the 1961 total. The national decline of the party was to fore-shadow the deterioration of its appeal on the regional level and its elimination from the parliaments of all the *Länder* by 1966. The collapse of the DP, the failure of the newly organized German Peace Union (DFU), a left-oriented group appealing mainly to pacifists, former Communists and Socialists who found the new program of the SPD repugnant, to gain a large following,[28] and the drying up of the right-extremist vote instituted a three-party system of the Union parties, the Social Democrats and the Free Democrats on the national level.[29]

The 1961-1965 *Land* Elections

The regional elections following the 1961 *Bundestag* result demonstrated the ability of the SPD to compete on equal terms with the CDU/CSU. The trend against the Christian parties on the regional level which had begun in the fall of 1959 continued until the spring of 1963 when Prof. Dr. Ludwig Erhard was named Chancellor-elect. During this period the CDU/CSU lost ground in five of seven contests. Only the strong gains registered in four state elections between May 1963 and June 1965 prevented the party from losing more ground to the SPD prior to the fifth *Bundestag* election, as the Socialists increased their following over previous regional election totals in every *Land* except Bremen where the slippage was minimal.

Although the FDP failed to realized its *Bundestag* success in any *Land*, it augmented its following in all but three states to improve its overall regional position. Minor parties found the fifth series of *Land* elections especially damaging to their hopes as they lost 89 seats and had their share of the total *Land* level vote cut from 11.5 percent in the 1957-1960 period to 6.4 percent and their total representation reduced to 21 seats, all but eliminating them as a factor in *Land* politics.[30]

Indignation of the voters over the drawn-out negotiations in Bonn between the CDU/CSU and the FDP which preceded the formation of the national government coalition,[31] coupled with the successful administration of Dr. Paul Nevermann who had so ably filled the position of the popular Max Brauer upon the latter's move to Bonn,[32] brought the SPD a resounding victory in the Hamburg election of November 12, 1961, just eight weeks after the *Bundestag* decision. The CDU lost over both its *Bundestag* and 1957 *Land* election totals, while the FDP found itself deserted by many of its general election supporters, angered by the party's failure to honor its pledge not to participate in an Adenauer-headed coalition, and absorbed a 6.2 percentage loss over figures reached two months earlier. A slight gain over its previous regional election figure was small compensation for this setback (*Die Welt*, November 13, 1961).

In North Rhine-Westphalia the following July the SPD continued its upward swing and broke the CDU's absolute majority in West Germany's wealthiest, most populous state. For the first time since the war the Socialists won control of over forty percent of the *Land* vote. Again, Bonn politics were a decisive factor in the election outcome, as the uneven price and wage policy of the federal government, the lack of coordination within the national coalition, Adenauer's inconsiderate remarks concerning Berlin and the Fibag Affair involving the then Defense Minister Franz Josef Strauss had to be accounted for.[33]

The FDP, still haunted by what was considered a betrayal of trust in cooperating with Adenauer and its action of six years earlier in bringing down the government of Karl Arnold, likewise lost over its *Bundestag* and 1958 *Land* election totals.[34] The loss of its parliamentary majority in Düsseldorf forced the CDU to reach agreement with a second party, having governed alone since 1958. Although there was strong sentiment in CDU ranks for a grand coalition with the SPD, such an arrangement was not desired by Bonn, and the *Land* CDU had to swallow its bitter feelings against the FDP which had made its inclusion in the *Land* government four years earlier impossible, and a coalition modeled after Bonn was formed in Düsseldorf.[35] Angered by this development, a Social Democrat newspaper promptly labeled the new government a "coalition of losers" which was dictated by Adenauer and Ruhr industry (*Der Flüchtling*, Bonn, an SPD newspaper, August 1962).

The Socialists continued their winning pattern in the September election in Schleswig-Holstein, but in contrast to the two earlier electoral decisions, the CDU made gains over both its *Bundestag* and 1958 regional election figures to bring it within one seat of controlling a parliamentary majority. While the FDP lost nearly one-half of its *Bundestag* following, gains over its previous *Land* election figures added two seats to its *Landtag* delegation.[36] One of the outcomes of the election was the failure of the Refugee Party to poll the required five percent of the vote for representation in the *Land* which had given it political birth twelve years earlier.

Several factors influenced the Union's success in Schleswig-Holstein. Set on reversing the pattern of the two earlier elections the CDU threw some of its biggest guns into the campaign, Defense Minister Strauss, Federal Agricultural Minister Schwarz and Minister for *Bundestag* and *Länder* Affairs Merkatz, to supplement the intensive efforts of the *Land* party.[37] In spite of outside help, however, the CDU success was to a large extent an expression of the tremendous personal popularity of the then Minister President of Schleswig-Holstein, Kai-Uwe von Hassel, whose eight years in office had been a period of great progress for the northernmost *Bundesland*, which had earlier been known as the "poorhouse" of Germany (*Dithmarscher Landeszeitung*, September 24, 1962). Disagreement with the FDP caused Minister President von Hassel (CDU) to experiment with a minority government rather than renewing the previous coalition with the Free Democrats. This arrangement continued until von Hassel was called to Bonn to replace Franz Josef Strauss as Defense Minister in December 1962. A CDU-FDP coalition under Helmut Lemke (CDU) was formed shortly thereafter to establish a firmer basis for the government (*Die Welt*, January 15, 1963.)

CDU hopes that its success in Schleswig-Holstein had marked the end of its decline in public favor were rudely shattered in the election of November 11, 1962 in Hesse, as it lost heavily over both its *Bundestag* and 1958 regional election totals. On the other hand, the SPD registered its fourth consecutive gain since the *Bundestag* poll by winning an absolute majority in the *Landtag*.[38] The action of the Adenauer government in the Spiegel Affair contributed heavily to

CDU losses in Hesse; it was also to have a major influence on the Bavarian election two weeks later.[39] From the very beginning the Bavarian campaign was charged with the implication of Defense Minister Strauss, chairman of the Bavarian wing of the CDU, the Christian Social Union, in the arrest of several editors of the news magazine, *Der Spiegel*, and the election, in effect, became a referendum on Strauss. Local issues played little or no part in the campaign in which Strauss took an active part. The electoral decision gave the CSU an absolute majority in the Bavarian *Landtag*, clouding the substantial gains of the SPD over both its *Bundestag* and previous regional election totals and the CSU loss of 7.4 percentage points over the *Bundestag* election. *Die Welt*, a non-affiliated West German newspaper, in commenting on the CSU success in Bavaria, stated that most West German observers do not consider Bavaria to be an opinion barometer for the Federal Republic because of the special mentality of the people. The Spiegel Affair was not viewed with any special misgivings, there having been similar affairs in Munich (*Die Welt*, November 26, 1962).

Repercussions of the Bavarian result were felt in Bonn, making the deliberations over the formation of a new cabinet much more difficult. The CDU could not overlook the fact that the CSU victory in Bavaria was a personal one for Strauss. Had Strauss been defeated, he would have been quietly removed, but removal now became a clouded issue, the victory having strengthened his tactical position. The FDP, smarting from the loss of prestige which followed the breaking of its pledge in the *Bundestag* campaign not to participate in a government headed by Adenauer, held its ground against Strauss's continuation in office, and Strauss was replaced by von Hassel in the new cabinet in Bonn (*Die Welt*, December 12, 1962).

While West Berlin was not the most accurate barometer of German public opinion because of its international position at the time and did not participate in national election contests, the overwhelming Socialist victory in the election of February 17, 1963, nevertheless, was consistent with trends registered in the other *Länder*, and was to have an influence on the succession crisis in the CDU.[40] Because of the heavy losses suffered in West Berlin, the CDU there decided to go into the opposition and the SPD formed a working relationship with the FDP in the *Land* administration (*Die Welt*, April 1, 1963).

The outcome of the March election in Rhineland-Palatinate was an unexpected success for the Social Democrats as they polled 40.7 percent of the vote in what had been one of the CDU's most reliable strongholds to break the Union's majority in the *Land* parliament.[41] In view of its large gain, the SPD made a strong bid to unseat the leading CDU by offering the small FDP four of eight cabinet posts. However, negotiations between the two parties broke down over the question of confessional freedom in the educational program, the SPD not being interested in half measures (*Die Welt*, April 25, 1963), and the already existing working arrangement between the CDU and the FDP was continued in the formation of the government.

The Union's setback in Rhineland-Palatinate could be traced directly to the operation of affairs in Bonn rather than to poor administration on the part of the

Land government, in spite of differences between the two coalition partners with regards to cultural policies. The aftermath of the *Spiegel Affair*, the antipathy of Adenauer towards his Vice Chancellor, Ludwig Erhard, and especially the uncertainty over the succession to the Chancellorship, the split in the party over the country's course in foreign affairs, the behavior of the party on the steel pipe embargo and doubts on the future development of the German economy, all had their impact on the minds of the voters in influencing their decisions (*Die Welt*, April 2, 1963).

The End of the Adenauer Era

Following setbacks in Berlin and Rhineland-Palatinate the CDU saw the need for a prompt solution of the succession crisis, the uncertainly over the Chancellorship proving to be a heavy political liability for the party. The only two successes for the party in two years had been personal triumphs for other than Adenauer, namely von Hassel in Schleswig-Holstein and Strauss in Bavaria. The naming of Erhard as Adenauer's successor in April was to have a dramatic effect on the Lower Saxony outcome of May 19, 1963. Although all three of the national parties increased their representation in the *Land* parliament, as support for the splinter parties virtually collapsed, the CDU was the greatest beneficiary with a 6.9 percentage gain over its 1959 total.[42] Biggest victim of the contest was the reconstituted German Party, which, four years earlier, had gained twenty *Landtag* seats, nine by direct election. The CDU had placed its major emphasis on DP strongholds during the campaign, in addition to having many of the former top DP candidates in leading positions on its lists, to win over most of the DP's former supporters.[43] Yet, in spite of the DP reservoir, the halting of its decline in a *Land* which had never been a CDU domain was a victory in itself. A second victim, the Refugee Party, suffering from earlier losses in Schleswig-Holstein and Bavaria and lacking a *Bundestag* faction with which to focus its appeal, was deserted by most of its former adherents and lost its *Landtag* representation, bringing Lower Saxony into line with the federal model of three parties.[44] The SPD, in registering its eighth consecutive gain since the *Bundestag* election, came within two seats of winning an absolute parliamentary majority.

Strengthened by its large increase in support in the Lower Saxony contest, the CDU made strong representations in an effort to reach an agreement with the FDP and freeze the Socialists out of the government. The FDP, however, decided on a continuation of its already existing partnership with the SPD, since a CDU-FDP coalition would have placed the government on a very unstable basis (*Die Welt*, May 31, 1963).

The political climate created by the clarification of the succession question continued to benefit the CDU in the Bremen election of September 29, 1963, as the party nearly doubled its 1959 *Land* election total in spite of the general feeling about a telephone-tapping affair which precipitated stormy debate in Bonn and in the *Länder*. CDU gains were in first line at the expense of the former German Party,[45] as the SPD scored a resounding, but not surprising, victory in its traditional stronghold. The Socialists maintained their absolute majority in the *Land* parliament by winning practically the same percentage of the total vote as in 1959, namely 54.7 percent compared with 54.9 percent four years earlier; however, the operation of the d'Hondt formula caused the SPD to lose four seats.[46] While the CDU failed in its objective of breaking the Socialist majority, it succeeded in halting the SPD advance, the Bremen result being the first election in the *Länder* since the 1961 *Bundestag* decision in which the Socialists failed to register an increase in support.

The only real surprise of the Bremen election was the ability of the newly organized German Party in the State of Bremen (*Deutsche Partei im Lande Bremen*) to exceed the five percent minimum requirement.[47] Although carrying the same name as the party which four years earlier had received 14.5 percent of the *Land* vote, the new Bremen DP stood farther to the right of its predecessor and was fully independent of the German Party which participated in the 1963 *Land* election in Lower Saxony in an effort to continue the conservative tradition of the old DP. The nucleus of the new Bremen group consisted of five deputies of the old German Party who did not desert to other parliamentary groups during the legislative period.[48] Supported by right-wing elements of the old DP and former adherents of the right-extremist DRP, which did not participate in the 1963 contest, the success of the Bremen DP in gaining four *Bürgerschaft* seats marked the first election since 1959 that a right-extremist group had gained representation in a *Land* parliament.[49] Elements of the Bremen DP were instrumental in the formation of the National Democratic Party (NPD), which participated in a *Bundestag* election for the first time in 1965. *Bürgerschaft* members Friedrich Thielen and Otto Theodore Brouwer were party chairman and party presidium member respectively.[50]

Less than three weeks following the Bremen result, Ludwig Erhard succeeded Konrad Adenauer as Chancellor of West Germany; however, it was not until six months later in the election of April 26, 1964, in Baden-Württemberg that an expression of public sentiment on the change of leadership could be registered. The Christian Democrat 6.7 percentage gain over 1960 *Land* election results was interpreted as a vote of confidence in Erhard's administration as well as for himself, especially since the campaign, in which Erhard actively took part, placing his prestige on the line, emphasized national rather than local issues. Moreover, while the Socialists increased their vote total by 2.0 percentage points, they lost ground to the CDU in the highly-industrialized areas of the state which in earlier elections had been Socialist strongholds.[51] With little more than a promise to run the economy better than the CDU which built it and possibly harmed by their leader's agreement to open the Berlin wall during the Christmas period, the SPD suffered a moral defeat. While the Free Democrats lost in support over both *Bundestag* and previous *Land* election totals in their traditional center of strength, the major victim of the election was the Refugee Party which, by failing to meet the five percent requirement, lost all of its representation to mark the fourth occasion since 1961 that it had been eliminated from a *Land* parliament.[52] Following seven weeks of coalition negotiations, agreement was reached by the CDU and FDP on a joint ministry.

The last *Land* election to be held prior to the fifth *Bundestag* contest took place June 27, 1965, in the Saar. The Social Democrats, encouraged by their success in the 1964 *Kommunal* elections in which they outpolled the Christian Democrats 39.9 to 37.4 percent, had hoped to replace the CDU as the *Land's* leading party. However, Socialist expectations failed to materialize as the CDU gained 42.7 percent of the *Land* vote in contrast to their total of 40.7 percent. Nevertheless, the SPD's 10.7 percentage gain over 1960 figures was its most spectacular increase in any of the *Länder* and demonstrated the ability of the party to attract large support in predominantly Catholic areas. The failure of the left-oriented DDU to meet the five percent requirement and the drop in support for the Saarland People's Party from 11.4 percent in 1960 to 5.2 percent, indicating little appeal for its separatist stand, pointed out the hopelessness of parties lacking national organization under existing conditions in West Germany.[53]

The results of the regional contests held between the 1961 and 1965 *Bundestag* decisions catapulted the Social Democratic Party into a position of near equality with the Christian Union parties on the *Land* level. By making gains in all but one election while the CDU/CSU was losing ground in four,[54] the Socialists increased their portion of the total regional vote from 38.3 percent in the 1957-1960 period to 42.3 percent while the Union parties gained only from 42.1 to 42.7 percent.[55] Most important for the CDU, however, was the apparent reversal of the trend against the party which had begun in the fall of 1959 and remained almost unabated until the spring of 1963 when Ludwig Erhard was named as Chancellor-elect. Four straight *Land* successes following that move enabled the CDU/CSU to register the small gain in its overall regional totals for the fifth series of *Land* elections and remain slightly ahead of the Socialists.

The two most evident political developments of the fifth series of *Land* elections were the tendency for the German electorate to limit its choices to the three parties with national representation, the CDU/CSU, SPD and FDP, resulting in the gradual reproduction of the national model of three parties in the *Länder*, and the re-emergence of the Social Democratic Party as an effective challenger to the Union parties. While all splinter parties lost ground between 1961 and 1965, having their parliamentary representation drop from 110 seats at the beginning of the period to only 21 at the end, all three Bonn parties increased their overall regional representation and pushed their portion of the national vote from 88.5 to 93.6 percent.[56] The ability of the FDP to secure representation in all *Länder*, including West Berlin, and to increase its overall *Land* following from 8.1 to 8.6 percent indicated an apparent stabilization around a three-party system. The CDU/CSU, SPD and FDP were at the time represented in all *Land* parliaments; in only five states did a fourth party gain seats, meaning that the politics of the *Länder* as well as of the national government revolved around these three parties. In 1965 it appeared that a party system of two large and one

TABLE 5.4

THE COMPOSITION OF THE *LANDTAGE* BY PARTY
DECEMBER 1965

Land	Year	CDU/ CSU	SPD	FDP	GDP	Others	Total Seats	Number of Parties Receiving Representation
	1961	36	72	12	---	---	120	3
Hamburg	1957	41	69	10	---	---	120	3
North	1962	96	90	14	---	---	200	3
Rhine-	1958	104	81	15	---	---	200	3
Westphalia								
Schleswig-	1962	34	29	5	---	1 SSW	69	4
Holstein	1958	33	26	3	5	2 SSW	69	5
	1962	28	51	11	6	---	96	4
Hesse	1958	32	48	9	7	---	96	4
	1962	108	79	9	---	8 BP	204	4
Bavaria	1958	101	64	8	17	14 BP	204	5
	1963	41	89	10	---	---	140	3
West Berlin	1958	55	78	---	---	---	133	2
Rhineland-	1963	46	43	11	---	---	100	3
Palatinate	1959	52	37	10	---	1 DRP	100	4
Lower	1963	62	73	14	---	---	149	3
Saxony	1959	51	65	8	13 [a]	20 DP [a]	157	5
	1963	31	57	8	---	4 DP	100	4
Bremen	1959	16	61	7	---	16 DP	100	4
Baden-	1964	59	47	14	---	---	120	3
Württem-	1960	52	44	18	7	---	121	4
berg								
	1965	23	21	4	---	2 SVP	50	4
The Saar	1960	19	16	7	---	6 SVP 2 DDU	50	5

a The party composition of the Lower Saxony *Landtag* at the beginning of 1963 following the disintegration of the German Party as most of its members deserted to the CDU was: CDU 69, SPD 66, FDP and BHE ten each and the DP two. The Refugee (BHE) and German parties did not fuse into the GDP in Lower Saxony on the *Land* level.

Note that the differences in sizes of the *Land* parliaments between successive elections resulted from the addition of one or more *Überhangmandate* to either the CDU or SPD in cases where they won more direct seats than their proportional entitlement. See Chapter VIII of this study.

small party would continue for many years, with the FDP holding the balance between the two major parties in the absence of an absolute majority.

While some of the Socialist gains in the 1961-1965 period undoubtedly resulted from public reaction to the several crises and scandals which shook the Bonn government following the 1961 *Bundestag* election and Adenauer's continuance in office as well as the traditional trend against the party in power in off-year elections, the ability of the SPD to improve its following in predominantly agricultural and Catholic districts, traditional CDU strongholds, and among the young adult element indicated that many voters for the first time had accepted the Social Democratic Party as a satisfactory alternative to the CDU.[57] That numerous Catholic districts no longer viewed the SPD as a representative of atheism was demonstrated by Socialist successes in the heavy Catholic sections of Bavaria, Rhineland-Palatinate and the Saar.

In spite of the significant shifts in public sentiment in West Germany between 1961 and 1965, the coalition patterns already existing in the *Länder* remained virtually the same. The Refugee Party was no longer part of the ministries in Baden-Württemberg, Bavaria and Lower Saxony because of its loss of representation in those states; however, in Hesse it continued to participate in a partnership with the SPD until 1966.

In Bavaria the CSU formed a coalition with the Bavarian Party, dropping the FDP which had participated in the previous government. In Baden-Württemberg, North Rhine-Westphalia, Rhineland-Palatinate, the Saar and Schleswig-Holstein the CDU was in coalition with the Free Democrats. In the last three mentioned states the coalitions were extensions of previous partnerships, while in North Rhine-Westphalia the CDU, which governed alone from 1958 to 1962, brought the FDP into a working relationship following the loss of its parliamentary majority. In Berlin the FDP was brought into the Socialist government after the CDU decision to go into the opposition following the 1963 election. In Bremen, Hamburg and Lower Saxony the previously existing SPD-FDP administrations were continued following the respective regional elections; however, in Lower Saxony FDP opposition to Socialist efforts to consummate a concordat with the Vatican concerning the establishment of parochial schools and their financing with public funds forced an end to the SPD-FDP government in that *Land*. This rupture resulted in the establishment of a grand coalition between the SPD and the CDU, the only example of cooperation between the two dominant parties in the government of any of the *Länder* prior to the 1965 *Bundestag* election.[58]

The 1965 *Bundestag* Election

With so many factors seemingly working in its favor, the 1965 *Bundestag* election presented the SPD with its best opportunity since 1949 to break the domination of the CDU over national affairs.[59] The split within Christian Democratic ranks, unsettling developments within the country's economy, the seeming indecisiveness of the government's foreign policy and the FDP's national campaign against CSU chairman Franz Josef Strauss appeared to aid

TABLE 5.5

NATIONAL TOTALS
FIFTH *LAND* AND 1965 *BUNDESTAG* ELECTIONS [60]

Party	1961-1965 *Landtag* Elections		September 19, 1965 *Bundestag* Election		Seats
CDU/CSU	11,817,303	42.7	15,524,067	47.6	245
SPD	11,718,642	42.3	12,813,185	39.3	202
FDP	2,378,479	8.6	3,096,736	9.5	49
GB/BHE	698,389	2.5	---	---	---
DRP/NPD [a]	138,433	0.5	664,187	2.0	---
DFU/DDU	435,712	1.6	434,188	1.3	---
BP	234,939	0.8	---	---	---
DG/AUD	38,649	0.1	52,637	0.2	---
SVP/CVP	30,739	0.1	19,832	0.1	---
Others	215,971 [b]	0.8	15,605	0.0	---
Totals	27,707,256		32,620,437		496

a Totals for the Bremen DP have been included in this figure because of its close relationship with the DRP and the NPD.

b Of this total 97,764 votes were polled by the Lower Saxony DP, 76,070 votes by the Center Party in North Rhine-Westphalia.

Socialist chances. Public opinion polls taken a few days before the election gave both the SPD and the CDU/CSU 45 percent of the national vote[61] in a campaign fought along lines surprisingly similar to those in American election contests, with both major candidates stumping the country at a pace fast enough to tire the most ardent followers. Erhard stuck to one major theme throughout the campaign, the accomplishments of his party since 1949 and his own part in them. The outcome of the fifth national election contest clearly demonstrated the reluctance on the part of the German voter to change horses in midstream in face of unprecedented prosperity, no matter how appealing, responsible and competent the other party had shown itself to be. Although not obtaining a parliamentary majority, the CDU pushed its national total from 45.5 to 47.6 percent, while the SPD fell far short of its expected goal with 39.3 percent of the West German vote, only a 3.1 percentage increase over 1961.

The failure of the CDU to gain a *Bundestag* majority again made necessary a coalition government in Bonn. Although the possibility of a grand coalition with the SPD was expressed by several leading Christian Democratic leaders, including former Chancellor Konrad Adenauer, during the campaign, the CDU formed a government with the only other party to obtain national representation, the FDP, which had polled 9.5 percent of the national vote and had been coalition partners of the CDU in the previous national government. Although the election goal of the FDP was to prevent either one of the two largest parties from obtaining a national majority, party chairman Mende clearly committed his party to a coalition with the CDU during the campaign.[62] While failing to match its 1961 *Bundestag* success, the FDP increased the nationwide vote received in the *Land* balloting between the two general elections by nearly one percent and its 1957 *Bundestag* total by nearly two percentage points. Moreover, between 1961 and 1965 the FDP was able to strengthen its position in all but three *Land* parliaments, demonstrating the holding power of the party and what appeared at the time to be a stabilization around a three-party system of the CDU/CSU, SPD and FDP, made evident by the disintegration of the German and Refugee parties and the inability of such splinter parties as the DFU and the NPD/DRP to gain a foothold on the regional or national levels. Even the elections in the first half of 1966 showed no change in this trend, with the only successes for splinter parties limited to local elections where the small size of the electoral districts made minor local successes possible.[63] All but 6.4 percent of the total national vote cast in the 1961-1965 regional contests fell to the three nationally represented parties, and in the 1965 *Bundestag* election this figure was reduced to 3.6 percent. In the Hamburg election of March 27, 1966, the three-party vote amounted to 95.8 percent and in the July election in North Rhine-Westphalia to 99.7 percent. While the FDP lost a third of its support in the Hamburg election, it gained ground in the Rhine and Ruhr, indicating no early breakdown in the existing party system. More importantly, however, was the continued surge forward of the Social Democratic Party. In Hamburg it pushed its total from 57.4 to 59.0 percent and in North Rhine-Westphalia from 43.3 to 49.5 percent to replace the CDU as the leading party in Düsseldorf and come within a hair of gaining an absolute majority of the seats. Nevertheless, this victory in West Germany's largest state, which contained one-third of the country's population, enabled the SPD to become the leading party on the regional level. The fruits of victory, however, were denied the party as the CDU and FDP with a mere 101 of 200 seats formed a ministry without the leading Socialists (*Die Welt*, July 12 and 26, 1966) This unrepresentative coalition, however, lasted only a short period of time, being replaced in December 1966 by an SPD-FDP cabinet.

The year 1966 marked two decades since the first *Landtag/Bürgerschaft* elections had been held, a period during which democratic institutions slowly evolved following the collapse of the Nazi dictatorship to become firmly established in the West German State. No longer were regional or national election competitions between ten or more serious political challengers subscribing to a wide variety of political philosophies, but contests between three nationally-organized parties of broad appeal whose holding of office in no way threatened the democratic nature of the country. With the contraction in the number of parties gaining representation, assisted by the institution of percentage barriers,

TABLE 5.6

FIFTH *LAND* AND 1965 *BUNDESTAG* ELECTION RESULTS[64]

Land	Year and Election		CDU/ CSU	SPD	FDP	GB/ BHE [a]	DFU/ DDU [b]	DRP/ NPD	Other Parties
Hamburg	1961	*Land*	29.1	57.4	9.6	---	2.9	0.9	---
	1965	*Bund*	37.6	48.3	9.4	---	2.7	1.8	---
North Rhine-Westphalia	1962	*Land*	46.4	43.3	6.9	0.4	2.0	---	ZP 0.9
	1965	*Bund*	47.1	42.6	7.6	---	1.3	1.1	
Schleswig-Holstein	1962	*Land*	45.0	39.2	7.9	4.2	1.2	---	SSW 2.3
	1965	*Bund*	48.2	38.8	9.4	---	1.0	2.4	---
Hesse	1962	*Land*	28.8	50.8	11.5	6.3	2.5	---	---
	1965	*Bund*	37.7	45.9	11.9	---	1.8	2.5	---
Bavaria	1962	*Land*	47.5	35.3	5.9	5.1	0.9	---	BP 4.8
	1965	*Bund*	55.5	33.2	7.3	---	1.1	2.7	---
West Berlin	1963	*Land*	28.8	61.9	7.9	---	---	---	SED 1.4
	1958	*Land*	37.7	52.6	3.8	3.3	---	---	SED 1.9
Rhineland-Palatinate	1963	*Land*	44.4	40.7	10.1	---	1.3	3.2	---
	1965	*Bund*	49.3	36.7	10.2	---	1.2	2.5	---
Lower Saxony	1963	*Land*	37.7	44.9	8.8	3.7	0.6	1.5	DP 2.7
	1965	*Bund*	45.8	39.8	10.9	---	0.8	2.5	---
Bremen	1963	*Land*	28.9	54.7	8.4	0.2	2.7	---	DP 5.2
	1965	*Bund*	34.0	48.5	11.7	---	2.7	2.7	
Baden-Württemberg	1964	*Land*	46.2	37.3	13.1	1.8	1.4	---	---
	1965	*Bund*	50.0	33.0	13.1	---	1.6	2.0	---
The Saar	1965	*Land*	42.7	40.7	8.3	---	3.1 [b]	---	SVP 5.2
	1965	*Bund*	46.8	39.8	8.6	---	1.5	1.8	CVP 1.4

a GDP denotes the combination of the BHE and DP, which, however, was not accomplished in all *Länder*, necessitating the placing of DP figures under the column labeled "Other Parties." The DP which won 5.2 percent of the Bremen vote in 1963 had no connection with the party of the same name which formerly had held national and regional representation.

b The DDU, ideological partner of the DFU, competed only in the Saar, making DFU participation in that *Land* unnecessary.

both national and regional governments were able to demonstrate a high degree of stability, in contrast to the Weimar period.

Nevertheless, a number of developments in 1966 were to place the national consensus under considerable stress. The postwar economic expansion began to unwind, coupled with rapidly-increasing prices. Moreover, frustrations over the Federal Government's inability to make any progress towards reunification of the country and the back seat to which the West German State had relegated itself in world affairs, America's apparent neglect of her European allies as she became increasingly involved in Asia and the growing attractiveness of France's de Gaulle as a means of freeing the country from an apparent dependence on the United States all contributed to a growing nationalist sentiment in West Germany. Protests against the course of German politics which had ordinarily been expressed through the SPD now became most vividly expounded in the electoral successes of the right-extremist National Democratic Party (NPD) and in a growing nationalism within the three major parties themselves. Appeals for radical solutions were attractive to over one and a half million voters in the regional contests to follow the 1965 *Bundestag* vote, but the great majority of Germans continued to place their faith in the actions of the three mainstream-parties to resolve the immediate issues facing the country.

Endnotes to Chapter V

1 The hope of the GDP to meet the five percent limitation for representation was not groundless as the German and Refugee parties had together polled 8.0 percent of the 1957 *Bundestag* vote and 7.7 percent of the ballots cast in the regional contests held between 1957 and 1960.

2 Of the 20 member DP delegation sent to the Lower Saxony parliament in 1959 only two remained loyal to the party by the end of the legislative period. In Bremen eleven of sixteen members deserted the party prior to the 1963 *Land* election. The German Party which won four seats in the Bremen *Bürgerschaft* in 1963 was fully independent of the old DP, although the five members of the DP which remained loyal to the party formed the nucleus of the new party.

3 In the regional contests which followed the 1961 *Bundestag* election the GDP lost its representation in the parliaments of Baden-Württemberg, Bavaria, Lower Saxony and Schleswig-Holstein. In the 1966 *Land* election in Hesse the party obtained only 4.3 percent of the vote to lose its last foothold on the regional level.

4 Between 1961 and 1965 the FDP made gains in every *Land* except Baden-Württemberg, North Rhine-Westphalia and the Saar to push its regional totals from 8.1 to 8.6 percent and in the 1965 *Bundestag* contest it polled 9.5 percent of the national vote.

5 Willy Brandt was elected to replace the deceased Ollenhauer as party chairman in early 1964, thus uniting the party chairmanship and Chancellorship candidate in one person.

6 The SPD increased its Hamburg following from 45.2 percent in 1953 to 53.9 percent in the 1957 *Land* election. The CDU obtained 32.2 percent of the 1957 vote.

7 The Hamburg organization of the SPD has preferred limited participation of the national party in its election campaigns.

8 In the 1947 *Land* contest the Socialists polled 32.0 percent of the vote, in 1950 32.3 percent, in 1954 34.5 percent and in 1958 39.2 percent. The death of former CDU Minister President Karl Arnold in the middle of the campaign prevented the SPD from making even more extensive gains and helped the CDU to win a *Landtag* majority in the 1958 state election.

9 Adenauer's assumption that Erhard was his most likely successor contributed to his hesitancy to make arrangements for the succession.

10 Changes in the SPD's foreign and defense policies also contributed to the party's upward swing. Khrushchev's threat to West Berlin undoubtedly forced a complete rethinking of the SPD's approach to the German question.

11 The Communist Party had received 5.0 percent of the Bremen vote in 1955, whereas the SPD increased its support by 7.1 percentage points. On the other hand, the German Party total fell by 2.1 percentage points, that of the FDP by 1.5 percentage points.

12 *Die Welt*, May 17, 1960. The 1960 *Land* election in Baden-Württemberg marked the end of the grand coalition which had existed between the CDU and the SPD since the fall of 1953.

13 The SPD and the SPS together polled 20.1 percent of the 1955 Saar total; the 1960 vote for the Socialists was 30.0 percent.

14 The CDU polled 25.4 and the CVP 21.8 percent of the 1955 vote. The 1960 total for the CDU was 26.6 percent, with 11.4 percent going to the SVP, and 2.6 percent to the CNG, both of which refused to go along with the merger of the CVP with the CDU. At the end of the legislative period (1960) after the unification of the CDU with the CVP and the SPD with the SPS, including desertions and splits and the outlawing of the Communist Party, the CDU held 22 seats, the DPS 13, the SPD eight and seven members, including former Minister President Hubert Ney and three adherents, belonged to no *Fraktion*.

15 The three parties supporting the Saar constitution were the CVP, SPS and DPS which polled 51.2, 32.8 and 7.6 percent of the vote respectively. The Communists, who opposed the document, obtained 8.4 percent in the 1947 *Land* election.

16 *The International Who's Who 1961 and 1962*, (London, 1961): 443 and *Current Biography 1950*, (New York, 1951): 246-248.

17 The CDU had not been allowed to compete in the two earlier *Land* contests because of the specific ban on pro-German parties.

18 A turnout of 93.1 percent was recorded in the 1952 contest.

19 The Christian People's Party, major proponent of the existing status of the Saar, increased its vote total to 54.7 percent, the Saar Socialists polled 32.4 percent to nearly duplicate their 1947 following, but the DPS total fell to 3.4 percent to disqualify it from representation. *Ergebnisse der Landtagswahlen 1952 und 1955 in den Wahlkreisen*, Saarland Statistical Office, pages unnumbered.

20 *Ergebnisse der Landtagswahlen 1952 und 1955 in den Wahlkreisen*, Saarland Statistical Office, pages unnumbered, and *Die Welt*, December 19, 1955.

21 Election figures are taken from *Die Wahl zur Bremischen Bürgerschaft am 29. September 1963*, Bremen Statistical Office: 11; *Die Wahl zum Landtag von Baden-Württemberg am 15. Mai 1960*; Baden-Württemberg Statistical Office: 12-20; and *Saarland in Zahlen*, "*Die Wahlen im Saarland am 4. Dezember 1960*," Saarland Statistical Office: 10-15.

22 The FDP suffered a loss of nearly 900,000 votes over the third series of *Land* elections and 52 *Landtag* seats. In West Berlin it failed even to qualify for representation. The drying up of financial support and the split in the party resulting from its withdrawal from the national coalition and role in bringing down the CDU government in North Rhine-Westphalia and siding with the Socialists contributed to the party's decline.

23 The only parties other than the CDU/CSU, SPD, FDP and Refugee Party to obtain parliamentary representation in the 1957-1960 *Land* contests were the German Party in Bremen and Lower Saxony, the Bavarian Party in Bavaria, the DRP in Rhineland-Palatinate, the SSW in Schleswig-Holstein and the SVP and DDU in the Saar. The BP had witnessed a steady drop in support from 17.9 percent in 1950 to 13.2 percent in 1954 and 8.1 percent in 1958. The DRP, because of an adverse economic situation among the wine growers in the state, managed to poll 5.1 percent of the Rhineland-Palatinate vote to gain one seat. Nationally the DRP more than doubled the support it had received in the third series of *Land* election, not because of any increase in its appeal, but because it competed in every *Land* with the exception of Baden-Württemberg in contrast to only three states in the 1953-1956 period. The SSW, party of the Danish minority in Schleswig-Holstein, gained two seats by virtue of its exclusion from the *Land's* five percent clause. The SVP in the Saar was formed around the followers of Johannes Hoffmann who had opposed the Saar's unification with the Federal Republic, and the DDU in that same state gained support from former adherents of the Communist Party which had polled 6.6 percent of the 1955 Saar vote.

24 Figures are from the several *Land* statistical offices and the Federal Statistical Office.

25 The maneuvering which enabled Adenauer to hold his position as Chancellor is described by Peter Merkle in "Equilibrium, Structure of Interests and Leadership: Adenauer's Survival as Chancellor," *American Political Science Review*, LVI (September, 1962): 634-650.

26 Figures are from the several *Land* statistical offices and the Federal Statistical Office. National totals for the *Land* elections represent the sum of votes for each party in the ten states.

27 During the first five series of *Land* elections, while in the opposition in Bonn, the SPD made consistently better showings in *Land* than in national elections, with the reverse being true for the CDU/CSU. When the CDU/CSU was in opposition in Bonn between 1969 and 1982, it too did better in *Land* than in federal elections while outpolling the Socialists in those regional contests. The *Land* elections following the 2002 *Bundestag* poll again demonstrated this phenomenon as the voters utilized these contests to express their judgment on the economic restructuring policies of the Schröder administration by delivering the Socialists setbacks in all regional decisions between the 2002 and the 2005 general elections. Some observers have attributed this phenomenon to the

importance of foreign policy on the national level, where, during the early years of the *Bundesrepublik* the CDU program appeared more in agreement with the demands of the postwar period, even when the voters were satisfied with the regional administrations headed by Socialist premiers. Moreover, the party or parties in opposition are free from responsibility for controversial actions and crises or scandals on the national level, and public reaction to Bonn/Berlin policies have tended to benefit opposition parties in regional contests.

28 Prior to the establishment of the Berlin Wall, which severely hurt its chances at the polls, many observers feared that the DFU would exceed the five percent minimum for representation. As it turned out the party obtained only 1.9 percent of the national vote, reaching a high of 3.6 percent in Hamburg.

29 The 1961 *Bundestag* election is analyzed in Samuel Barnes, *et. al.*, "The German Party System and the 1961 Federal Election," *American Political Science Review*, LVI (December 1962): 899-914.

30 The representation of no party other than the CDU/CSU, SPD and FDP extended beyond a single *Land*, and the highest vote total polled by any of the splinter parties was the 6.3 percent received by the Refugee Party (GDP) in 1962 in Hesse.

31 The coalition negotiations had continued seven weeks before agreement was reached.

32 Max Brauer had been *Bürgermeister* of Hamburg from 1946 to 1953 and again from 1957 to the end of 1960. In 1961 he won a *Bundestag* seat.

33 Strauss was accused by *Der Spiegel*, a West German news periodical, of having misused his position as Defense Minister by recommending that the United States use Fibag, a private contractor, to build a housing development for the American Army in Bavaria. Strauss was later absolved of the charges.

34 The stand of Federal Finance Minister Heinz Starke (FDP) against wage increases for the civil service and miners as a means of balancing the budget likewise hurt the party.

35 The left-oriented Katzer wing of the CDU in North Rhine-Westphalia, including the son of the former Minister President of the *Land*, Karl Arnold, held that a coalition with the SPD would be closest to the voters' wishes. Minister President Meyers (CDU) had announced his willingness to bargain with the SPD, and the Socialists expressed their willingness to participate in such a coalition (*Dithmarscher Landeszeitung*, July 10, 1962).

36 The promise made by Erich Mende, national party chairman of the FDP, during the campaign, that the five Free Democrat ministers would leave the Bonn government in the fall of 1963 if Adenauer failed to retire at that time did not restore the party's *Bundestag* election following.

37 The triumphal visit of French President Charles de Gaulle to Germany earlier in the month (September 1962) on the decision in Schleswig-Holstein is difficult to measure, but it could only have helped the sagging prestige of the CDU.

38 Although the Socialists gained 51 of 96 *Landtag* seats, they continued their already existing partnership with the GDP, which was spared the fate of its sister organization in Schleswig-Holstein, after the election.

39 Several editors of the weekly news periodical, *Der Spiegel*, a West German publication similar to *Time* and *Newsweek*, were placed in prison on charges of treason concerning the publication of certain military information. The government's handling of the affair and especially the part which Franz Josef Strauss, Federal Defense Minister, played in it caused a storm throughout West Germany and eventually led to his replacement as Defense Minister by Kai-Uwe von Hassel, the then Minister-President of Schleswig-Holstein.

40 In spite of its special status, West Berlin was treated as if it were one of its *Länder* by the Federal Republic and was represented by non-voting delegates in both the *Bundestag* and *Bundesrat*.

41 The CDU controlled the government of Rhineland-Palatinate from the formation of the state in 1946 to 1991, a period during which it obtained absolute parliamentary majorities six times, in 1955, 1959, 1971, 1975, 1979 and 1983. The SPD did not become the leading party in the state until 1991. Between 1991 and 2006, when it won a majority of *Landtag* seats, it was in a coalition with the FDP. From 2006 to 2011 it governed alone, and since 2011 with the Greens.

42 The CDU viewed its large increase in support as public approval of the designation of Erhard as heir-apparent to Adenauer.

43 Despite its efforts to regain its former position in *Land* politics, few observers had given the DP much of a chance following the disintegration of the *Landtag* party during the legislative period, when eighteen of its twenty members deserted to the CDU. The DP polled a mere 2.7 percent of the 1963 vote in contrast to 12.4 percent four years earlier to lose all representation.

44 From the first regional elections in 1947 to 1963 Lower Saxony suffered from a fragmented legislature, with six parties obtaining representation in 1947, ten in 1951, eight in 1955 and five in 1959.

45 The Christian Democrats held that their success in Bremen could not be explained solely by their gains among former DP adherents; the result, they claimed, was a clear "no" to the Socialists' drive to power and a personal success of Erhard (*Die Welt*, October 1, 1963).

46 In 1959 the Socialists benefited from the large number of votes polled by the splinter parties, which, however, received no representation by failing to meet the five percent minimum requirement. The vote for the splinter parties amounted to a mere 2.9 percent in 1963 in contrast to 8.6 percent four years earlier.

47 In the 1959 *Land* election the DP received as many seats as the CDU, but 11 of the 16 original deputies of the party deserted to other *Landtag* groups during the course of the legislative period, six to the CDU, four to the FDP and one to the SPD. What then became known as the German Party in the State of Bremen was formed around the five representatives who remained true to the party (*Die Welt*, September 30, 1963).

48 Twenty of the 100 members of the Bremen parliament were chosen from Bremerhaven, eighty from Bremen proper. The DP received only 4.4 percent of the Bremerhaven vote, making it ineligible for the distribution of seats in that portion of Bremen. On the basis of its 5.3 percent of the vote in Bremen proper, the party received four seats. The DP challenged this division of seats as being contrary to the *Land* constitution, claiming that the distribution of seats should be on the basis of the total *Land* vote,

which was 5.2 percent, making the party eligible for an additional seat and *Fraktion* status in the *Land* parliament. (Five representatives were needed to form a *Fraktion*, thus disqualifying the DP from representation on the committees of the *Bürgerschaft*; *Die Welt*, October 7, 1963.)

49 The DRP had obtained a single seat in the *Landtag* of Rhineland-Palatinate in 1959. In the 1963 election it failed to exceed the five percent minimum for representation in that *Land*.

50 Although the NPD failed to gain national representation in the 1965 general elections, it had local successes in Schleswig-Holstein and Bavaria in March 1966 and in November it obtained 7.9 percent of the vote and eight seats in Hesse and 7.4 percent and fifteen seats in Bavaria.

51 The CDU won 44 of seventy direct mandates, ten more than in 1960 and nine at the expense of the SPD.

52 The GDP polled 1.8 percent of the vote in contrast to 6.6 percent in 1960. Defection of two of its representatives to the CDU and one to the SPD shortly before the election partially contributed to the party's defeat.

53 The DDU polled 3.1 percent of the vote in contrast to 5.01 percent in 1960. Following the 1965 *Land* election in the Saar the two SVP representatives left their party and became partyless members of the *Landtag*. They were invited by the CDU to join its *Fraktion* (*Die Welt*, October 5, 1965).

54 If West Berlin is included, the CDU registered losses in five *Länder*.

55 In the *Land* elections held between 1961 and 1965 (excluding West Berlin which did not compete in *Bundestag* elections) the CDU polled 11,817,303 votes to the Socialists' 11,718,642, or a difference of less than 100,000.

56 Representation for the Refugee Party alone dropped from 49 to six seats as it lost all representation in four *Länder* and one seat in Hesse.

57 The SPD also benefited from the difficulties in coordinating the national coalition and from the very real split in Christian Democratic ranks, which Erhard's accession to power failed to eliminate. The antipathy of the Adenauer wing of the party towards Erhard and the divergent views within the party on West German's course in foreign affairs—as between European unity or strong attachments with the United States, between England and France, or a small as opposed to a large Europe—fomented further dissension. Adenauer's retention of the CDU chairmanship until early 1966 only tended to perpetuate these differences.

58 Between March 1963 when the SPD-CDU coalition broke down in West Berlin and the formation of the red-black government in Lower Saxony in May 1965 no grand coalition had existed in any of the *Länder*.

59 In the regional elections held between the 1961 and the 1965 *Bundestag* contests the SPD had made spectacular gains, pushing its national vote total to 42.3 percent in contrast to the CDU's 42.7 percent figure. With its new program and leadership it hoped to replace the CDU as West Germany's leading, though not majority party.

60 Figures are from the several *Land* statistical offices and the Federal Statistical Office.

61 The last poll of the EMNID Institute (Bielefeld) before the election gave 45 percent of the national vote to the CDU/CSU, 45 percent to the SPD, seven to the FDP and three percent to the various splinter parties (*Die Welt*, September 18, 1965).

62 When the question of a possible alignment with the SPD was brought up at a press conference held in Hamburg September 1, 1965, FDP chairman Erich Mende stated that only a severe collapse of the CDU coupled with large gains by the SPD and the FDP, indicating widespread lack of confidence in Erhard, would cause his party to consider a coalition with the Socialists.

63 The NPD, for example, while polling only 2.1 percent of the Bavarian vote in the *Kommunal* elections of March 13, 1966, gained 8.4 percent in Bayreuth, 8.2 percent in Erlangen and 7.3 percent in Nuremberg. In local elections held the same day in Schleswig-Holstein the party polled an average of 10.5 percent in the eleven communities in which it competed, although its *Land*-wide vote was minimal (*Der Spiegel*, April 4, 1966: 30-31).

64 Figures are from the several *Land* statistical offices and the Federal Statistical Office.

CHAPTER VI

State and National Elections from 1965 to Reunification

Between the 1965 and 2009 *Bundestag* balloting a total of 140 regional elections took place in the German *Länder*, 76 of these after reunification in 1990, including thirty in the five states of the former German Democratic Republic (DDR) and a united Berlin. The outcomes of these regional election contests were influenced by a number of political developments, three of which are of special significance. One was the ability of the Social Democratic Party to contest the early predominance of the CDU/CSU on both regional and national levels. A second was the entry into the political arena of several important challengers to the three-party cartel of the CDU/CSU, SPD and FDP which had emerged from the first five series of *Land* elections and which had made the Free Democrats the only available (or acceptable) coalition partner of the CDU/CSU or SPD in the absence of a parliamentary majority or grand coalition between the two major parties. The third was the impact on state and national politics of the addition of the five eastern provinces and the east sector of Berlin to the Federal Republic following the demise of the Communist-led DDR in 1990.

The Two-And-A-Half Party System

From the first elections in 1946 to 1965 the CDU/CSU was the dominant party in the western part of Germany on both regional and national levels. With the exception of the period between the first and second *Bundestag* elections (1949-1953), when the political right was fragmented (a situation which favored the SPD), it was the most important party in *Land* politics and outpolled all other political groupings in the first five national elections. In 1953 and 1957 it won absolute *Bundestag* majorities when Chancellor Konrad Adenauer was at the height of his popularity. In the ten *Land* elections held between 1961 and 1965, however, the Socialists were able to close the gap separating the two parties to less than 100,000 votes, and, with major gains in the states of North Rhine Westphalia and Hesse following the 1965 *Bundestag* election, were able to outpoll the CDU/CSU 42.5 to 42.0 percent in the regional contests held between 1966 and 1968. Then, to deal with the national crisis facing the country in 1966 they were brought into the national government for the first time in a grand coalition with the CDU/CSU. With the resurgence in their fortunes they were able to form the national government in coalition with the FDP from 1969 to 1982, first under Willy Brandt and then under Helmut Schmidt. Once again, after an interlude of sixteen years, during which the CDU/CSU and FDP controlled the national agenda under Dr. Helmut Kohl, the SPD from 1998 to 2005 took on the responsibility for national policy, this time in coalition with the Greens. Following the inconclusive results of the 2005 *Bundestag* election it continued to participate in the national government as junior partner with the CDU/CSU under Dr. Angela Merkel in the country's second grand coalition. The CDU/CSU/SPD partnership continued for four years until the 2009 general election when the Free Democrats obtained sufficient seats to make a black/yellow combination possible, again under Dr. Angela Merkel as Federal Chancellor.

In contrast to fluctuations on the national level, the CDU/CSU has been the leading vote-getter on the regional level in every series of *Land* elections since 1969, with its *Land* following exceeding fifty percent twice and falling below forty percent only two times in the eleven series of regional contests held between 1969 and 2009, that being between the 1998 and 2002 and between the 2005 and 2009 *Bundestag* elections. In contrast, the Socialists have never obtained a majority of the votes polled in any series of regional contests and in only six of the seventeen cycles of regional contests held since 1946 have they been able to obtain as much as forty percent of the vote. A Social Democrat, however, has headed the government of every state with the exceptions of Baden-Württemberg and Bavaria of the old *Länder* and Saxony and Thuringia of the new states since 1969.

The three-party cartel of the CDU/CSU, SPD and FDP which had emerged from the first five series of *Land* elections (1946-1965) was initially challenged by the electoral successes of the right-extremist National Democratic Party (NPD) between 1966 and 1968 when it polled 5.3 percent of the nation-wide regional vote to gain representation in seven of the ten *Land* parliaments. The threat proved to be short-lived, however, as the party failed to bridge the five percent barrier in the 1969 *Bundestag* race and lost its participation in all seven state parliaments in the regional elections held between 1969 and 1972 when its total regional vote fell below two percent. The right-extremist vote remained minimal until the 1990s when several parties of the radical right succeeded in gaining representation in six states, but neither the Republicans, the German People's Union (DVU) nor a reformed NPD has been able to duplicate the early success of the NPD in any series of *Land* contests. The combined national vote of the NPD, DVU and Republicans amounted to only 2.1 percent in the 2005 *Bundestag* election and 2.0 percent in 2009. None of these extremist parties has been an acceptable coalition partner in any of the *Land* ministries.

The black-red-yellow cartel remained basically intact until the early 1980s when a series of groupings which became known as the Greens gained a sufficient following to become a fourth force in German politics. The success of the NPD in the late 1960s had not seriously impacted the three-party vote which dropped only from 93.5 to 92.7 percent of the regional total in the 1965/1969 period, pointing out that NPD gains had come primarily at the expense of splinter groupings rather than from the three institutionalized parties. The three-party vote reached a peak during the 1972-1976 series of regional contests when it amounted to 98.2 percent of ballots cast and did not fall below ninety percent until the first series of regional contests following reunification in 1990.

A new and more lasting challenge to the black-red-yellow constellation emerged in the late 1970s when a strong environmental movement found expression in the formation of a number of groupings under a variety of names, including the Alternative List for Democracy and Environmental Protection, the Green List Hesse, the Green List for Environmental Protection, etc, which ultimately became known as the Greens following amalgamation in 1993.[1] Following successes in local elections, these assemblages entered candidates in four regional contests in 1978, but failed to exceed the five percent vote total required for the awarding of seats in any of them, their best showing being the 3.9 percent polled in Lower Saxony. Their first regional success came in the October 7, 1979 *Bürgerschaft* balloting in Bremen when two separate environmental combinations polled 6.5 percent of the votes to gain four seats for the Bremen Green List (BGL). There followed a second triumph in the March 18, 1980 election in Baden-Württemberg when a Green grouping polled 241,303 votes (5.3 percent) to place six deputies in the state parliament. The movement was less successful in regional balloting in the Saar and North Rhine-Westphalia just prior to the fall 1980 *Bundestag* election in which it gained only 1.5 percent of the vote nation-wide. In spite of these set-backs, the various environmental groupings polled 991,628 or 3.0 percent of the total regional vote while gaining seats in two state parliaments in the ten regional elections held between 1978 and 1980.

In the four *Land* elections held between the 1980 and 1983 *Bundestag* polls, the various Green groupings qualified for representation in three states, reaching a high of 8.0 percent of the Hessian vote and outpolling the FDP in all four states. In the 1983 general election it polled 5.6 percent of ballots cast to send 28 delegates to Bonn to join the three established parties. In the ten *Land* elections held between 1983 and 1986 environmental groupings gained seats in six state parliaments and outpolled the Free Democrats in nation-wide totals by 175,000 votes to firmly replace the FDP as the country's third party on the regional level.

Between 1961 and 1983 when the Greens gained national representation for the first time, only the CDU/CSU, SPD and FDP were represented in the *Bundestag*, and, in the federal states, with the collapse of the Refugee Party in 1966, all regional ministries between 1966 and 1985, in the absence of an absolute majority by a single party, were coalitions between the CDU/CSU and FDP or SPD and FDP except in the rare case of a grand coalition as in Lower Saxony and Baden-Württemberg. The first opportunity for a Green grouping to participate in a *Land* ministry came in 1985 when one coalesced with the SPD in the state of Hesse for fourteen months.[2] By the end of 2009 the Greens, at one time or another, had obtained representation in every *Land* parliament with the single exception of Mecklenburg-Vorpommern and had participated in the ministries of ten of the sixteen states and of the national government with the SPD from 1998 to 2005 before being excluded from every *Land* government and the national coalition during the course of 2005.[3] This situation changed when a Socialist/Greens government was formed in Bremen in 2007, followed by a CDU/Greens coalition in Hamburg in 2008, and a CDU/FDP/Greens combination in the Saar in 2009, a Socialist/Greens minority government in North Rhine-Westphalia in 2010, an SPD/Greens partnership in Rhineland-Palatinate and a Greens/Socialist ministry in Baden-Württemberg in 2011, headed by the first Greens' Minister-President, Winfried Kretschmann. The red/Green alliance in Bremen was continued after the May 2011 *Bürgerschaft* election, placing the Greens in five ministries with the breakup of the CDU/Greens coalition in Hamburg in November 2010.

Another challenge to the early black-red-yellow constellation arose in 1990 with the reintegration of the eastern provinces of the former Reich into the German state. Competing under the nomenclature of the Party of German Socialism (PDS), the former Communist Party of East Germany became an important factor in the eastern provinces of Brandenburg, Mecklenburg-Vorpommern, Saxony, Saxony-Anhalt and Thuringia, as well as in a united Berlin. In regional elections held since 1990 it has outpolled the FDP and Greens in all six states, the SPD in Saxony in 1999, 2004 and 2009; in Saxony-Anhalt in 2002, 2006 and 2011; and in Thuringia in 1999, 2004 and 2009; and the CDU by 100,000 votes in Brandenburg in both 2004 and 2009. In the regional contests held between 1998 and 2002 it nearly equaled the nation-wide totals of the Free Democrats and Greens in spite of lackluster showings in the Western states, and in the twelve regional ballotings between 2002 and 2005 it polled only 150,000 fewer votes than the FDP. In the fifteen provincial elections held between the 2005 and 2009 *Bundestag* contests, competing as *Die Linke* following its merger with the WASG, it outpolled the Free Democrats and Greens to solidify itself as the third party on the regional level. At the end of 2009 the Leftists participated in the governments of Berlin and Brandenburg with the SPD, but had partnered with the Socialists in Mecklenburg-Vorpommern from 1998 to 2006.

In the 2005 *Bundestag* election it entered into an alliance with Oskar Lafontaine's left-oriented Alternative Choice for Work and Social Justice (WASG, *Wahlalternative Arbeit und Soziale Gerechtigkeit*) to form *Die Linke* (the party of the left), and by appealing to former Communists and left-wing Socialists in the West who were angered by the economic reform measures taken by the Schröder government and to its traditional base in the eastern provinces of Germany, it polled 8.7 of the national vote to replace the Greens as the fourth party on the national level. Oskar Lafontaine had been Lord Mayor of Saarbrücken, a former Socialist minister-president of the Saar, the SPD candidate for the chancellorship in 1990 and Finance Minister for a short time in the first Schröder Cabinet. By transforming the confined PDS into a national party of the left, the success of this alliance changed the political landscape in Germany by adding a fifth player and upsetting existing coalition patterns. Neither a Red/Green nor a Black/Yellow combination could produce a working majority in the *Bundestag* and neither grouping was willing to work with this new force, leaving a grand coalition between the CDU/CSU and SPD, only the second since 1949, as the sole working alternative in Berlin (*Stern*, September 15 and 22, 2005). The party's success in the 2008 *Land* election in Hesse likewise threw traditional coalition patterns into turmoil when it obtained 5.1 percent of the vote and six *Landtag* seats. Following a year of governing in minority status, the CDU was able to partner with the FDP after the successful rerun election of January 18, 2009, which gave a CDU/FDP combination a working majority of 66 of 118 *Landtag* seats. Again, in the Saar in the August 2009 regional contest, the entry of *Die Linke* into the parliament prevented either a CDU/FDP or an SPD/Greens alliance from providing a working majority, necessitating bringing the Greens into a three-party coalition with the Christian Democrats and Liberals, the first such association of its kind on the regional level. In the May 2010 state election in North Rhine-Westphalia the success of *Die Linke* put traditional coalition patterns into disarray for a third time. The dilemma was temporarily overcome by the formation of a Socialist/Greens minority ministry, tolerated by the Leftists.

The three-party vote of the CDU/CSU, SPD and FDP which had reached a peak of 98.2 percent in the 1972-76 series of *Land* elections and 99.1 percent in the 1972 and 1976 *Bundestag* elections fell to 81.6 percent in the twelve regional contests held between 2002 and 2005, to 73.1 percent in the fifteen regional polls between 2006 and 2009, and to 71.4 percent in 2009 *Bundestag* balloting, indicating a continual weakening of traditional party appeal.

The 1966-1968 *Land* Elections

Following the 1965 *Bundestag* election the CDU/CSU again formed a government coalition with the Free Democrats in Bonn rather than with the SPD in spite of the urging of several prominent Christian Union leaders. In the regional elections to follow, the Socialists continued to be the major recipient of electorate dissatisfaction and were able to extend their string of gains on the *Land* level to 26 out of 27 contests, including major wins in Hamburg, North Rhine-Westphalia and Hesse to produce the SPD's best *Land*-level showing since the first regional elections were held in 1946, enabling it to become the leading party on the regional level for only the second time. The Erhard government fell apart following the withdrawal of four FDP ministers from his cabinet on October 27, 1966, shortly before the regional balloting in Hesse and Bavaria.[4] This led to the formation of a grand coalition between the CDU/CSU and SPD under CDU Chancellor Dr. Kurt Kiesinger, who had been Minister President of Baden-Württemberg prior to his elevation to the Chancellorship[5] The SPD's participation in a coalition with the CDU/CSU in December 1966 in what *Der Spiegel* called a *"Kartell der Angst"* (an anxiety cartel), however, changed the SPD's position from outsider to insider and no longer a relevant beneficiary of voter disenchantment with Bonn politics. As a result, beginning with the election of April 23, 1967 in Rhineland-Palatinate the SPD suffered a string of four consecutive setbacks prior to the 1969 general election.

The formation of the "Black-Red" coalition in Bonn greatly complicated the concept of opposition, since dissatisfaction could be expressed only in the small FDP, itself a part of the Bonn "establishment" for many years or in the NPD, which was not represented in Bonn. The FDP had hoped to benefit from its new status in the opposition, but, instead, suffered setbacks in three of the five regional elections to follow the establishment of the CDU/CSU/SPD coalition. While losing only one seat in the November 6, 1967 election in Hesse, it lost all nine representatives in the Bavarian parliament in the November 20th election of that year. (In the nine *Land* elections held between 1965 and 1969 it suffered setbacks in six of them.) The setbacks were attributed by some observers to a backlash from voters angry at its precipitating a breakdown in the coalition with the CDU and to a shift of the protest vote to the NPD.

The fear of a CDU/CSU-SPD cartel dominating German political life without opposition was cleverly exploited by NPD propagandists (*Der Spiegel*, November 17, 1966, March 1, 1967, March 20, 1967 and April 3, 1967), and the party became the major beneficiary of the difficulties confronting the new coalition in Bonn. The National Democratic Party (NPD) was formed in November 1964 in anticipation of participation in the 1965 *Bundestag* election. In that first attempt at national representation the party polled only 2.0 percent of the West German vote in spite of placing candidates in 247 of the country's 248 electoral districts. It was undeterred, but following several local successes it polled only a disappointing 3.5 percent of the vote in the March 7, 1966 election in Hamburg, insufficient to gain representation. The party decided not to compete in the July 10, 1966 election in North Rhine Westphalia, West Germany's most populous state, because of its disastrous showing there in the 1965 general election. However, capitalizing on the Erhard government's steady decline in public favor, an unbalanced federal budget, an economic slowdown and public dissatisfaction over the growing likeness of the three parties which dominated West German political life, it was able to portray itself as the only clear choice, not an echo. It also exploited growing impatience over the question of reunification and the desire of many Germans to steer a more independent course in foreign affairs, independent of American influences, and the political criticism brought about by the withdrawal of the FDP from the national coalition shortly before the voting in Hesse and Bavaria. The NPD's first major success came in the November 6, 1966 balloting in Hesse when it gained 7.9 percent of the *Land's* vote to place eight representatives in the state parliament. (This initial breakthrough for the NPD in no way interfered with the establishment of a stable government in Hesse as the SPD gained an absolute majority of seats in the state *Landtag*.) The party's good fortune in Hesse was followed by successes in Bavaria (7.4 percent), Schleswig-Holstein (5.8 percent), Rhineland-Palatinate

(6.9 percent), Lower Saxony (7.0 percent), Bremen (8.0 percent) and Baden-Württemberg (9.8 percent) during the course of 1967 and the early part of 1968.

The electoral gains of the NPD created widespread concern both within and outside West Germany, because of the party's right-extremist tendencies and the presence within its ranks of numerous former Nazi party members. (The September 8, 1965 issue of *Der Spiegel* noted that twelve of the NPD's eighteen-member executive committee had been active Nazis.) Its nationalistic appeal, its exploitation of the fears and disappointments being felt by many Germans during a period of rapid political and economic transition, Chancellor Erhard's lack of decisiveness and failure to provide effective leadership and condemnation of the three established parties were upsetting. While some quarters discounted the party's upswing as a temporary phenomenon, a Poujadist-type success, others called for the party's outlawing, as an embarrassment to the Federal Republic's international image, seeing it as a contemporary of the banned Socialist Reich Party (SRP) in a more respectable form. West Germans had not witnessed a challenge from right-extremist groups since the successes of the Socialist Reich Party in the 1951 state elections in Lower Saxony and Bremen (11.0 percent in Lower Saxony and 7.7 percent in Bremen). That party was declared illegal the following year because of its apparent totalitarian character and from 1953 to 1965, with growing prosperity, extremist sentiment lay virtually dormant or was wasted on a variety of splinter groupings, including Alfred Schneider's German Worker's Party (DAP) and August Haussleiter's German Community Party (DG).

The need for a new party, uncontaminated by the symbols of the past and capable of operating in a society which had come to take democracy for granted, to unite the fragmented elements of the Right was recognized by Adolf von Thadden, a representative of the German Rightist Party in the first *Bundestag* and later chairman of the German Reich Party, and he set about to organize a unified movement of the right-wing. So sensitive was the party at being called a neo-Nazi movement that it threatened to sue any newspaper which attempted to label it as such, calling attempts to call them neo-Nazis "efforts by the licensed parties to stifle competition and prevent any disruption of the present system." Friedrich Thielen, Bremen cement manufacturer and chairman of the right-oriented German Party in the State of Bremen which had gained four seats in the Bremen parliament in 1963 was chosen as national chairman with von Thadden as his chief deputy. The party entered candidates in 247 of the 248 *Bundestag* constituencies (*Der Spiegel*, April 4, 1966: 39) but succeeded in gaining only 664,187 votes or 2.0 percent in its first national competition.

The rise of the NPD after fourteen years of impotence among right-wing movements presented the three established parties with the greatest threat to their positions since the rise of the Refugee Party and the Socialist Reich Party in the early 1950s. It replaced the FDP as the third party in Bavaria in 1966 and in Lower Saxony in 1967, giving rise to fears that the NPD rather than the FDP would play a balancing role between the two major parties in the absence of a majority by either the SPD or CDU/CSU or a grand coalition, thereby eliminating the possibility of a democratic alternation of power (Culver, *Idaho Issues*, 1967). Ultimately between 1966 and 1968 the NPD obtained 1,516,868 votes or 5.3 percent of the regional total, a following which, if duplicated on the national level would have given the party from 27 to 30 *Bundestag* seats in 1969. But torn by dissention between Thielen and von Thadden over the direction of the party and deserted by numerous key followers, coupled with more effective leadership in Bonn under the Black-Red coalition headed by Dr. Kurt Kiesinger, the party failed to duplicate its regional successes in the 1969 federal election.[6]

Because of its orientation, the party was an unacceptable coalition partner of the established parties and did not become part of the government in any of the states. Moreover, its vote total had little impact on the followings of the three established parties, which saw their combined vote nationwide fall by less than one percent. The NPD vote totals did not prevent the SPD from winning majorities in Bremen, Hamburg and Hesse or the CSU in Bavaria and the formation of coalitions without the NPD in the other states.

With the grand coalition in Bonn providing more effective leadership, the threat posed by the NPD proved to be short-lived. In the 1969 *Bundestag* contest it polled a disappointing 4.3 percent of the national vote, insufficient for representation, and in the regional balloting between the 1969 and 1972 general elections its following fell to only 1.9 percent of the total vote to lose its seats in all seven states where it had been represented. Although continuing to contest later elections, and gaining access to the parliaments of Saxony and Mecklenburg-Vorpommern in 2004 and 2006 and holding onto its representation in Saxony in the 2009 state election, albeit at a reduced level, the party has not been a serious player in *Land* politics as have the Greens and the PDS/*Die Linke*. It entered candidates in six of the twelve *Land* elections held between the 2002 and 2005 general balloting, but succeeded in gaining representation only in Saxony where it polled 9.2 percent of the vote. It scored a second success in the 2006 contest in Mecklenburg-Vorpommern to gain six legislative seats with 7.3 percent of the ballots cast and kept eight of its twelve seats in Saxony balloting in 2009.

A competing right-extremist party, the German People's Union (DVU), has been more successful in recent years, gaining 5.6 percent of the vote and six seats in Bremen in 1991, 6.3 percent of the vote and six seats in Schleswig-Holstein in 1992, 12.9 percent of the vote and 16 seat in the 1998 *Land* election in Saxony-Anhalt, 5.3 percent of the vote and five seats in the 1999 election in Brandenburg, 6.1 percent of the vote and six seats in Brandenburg in 2004 and 2.7 percent of the vote and one seat in Bremen in 2007. Over the years the effectiveness of the DVU has been hurt by internal conflict and resignations, and it lost all six of its seats in Brandenburg as a result of its poor showing in the 2009 state election.

A third right-extremist party, the Republicans, has also had mixed results since gaining 7.5 percent of the vote and eleven seats in West Berlin in 1989. The Berlin success was followed by gains of 10.9 percent and 15 seats in 1992

TABLE 6.1

THE SIXTH SERIES OF *LAND* ELECTIONS 1965-1969 [7]

Land and Date	Valid Votes	CDU/CSU	SPD	FDP	NPD	Others
Hamburg March 27, 1966	947,802	284,501 30.0 (38)	558,754 59.0 (74)	64,887 6.8 (8)	36,645 3.9 (-)	FSU (0.3)
North Rhine- Westphalia June 10, 1966	8,542,493	3,653,184 42.8 (86)	4,226,604 49.5 (99)	633,705 7.4 (15)	Did Not Compete	Center (0.2)
Hesse November 6, 1966	2,827,633	746,495 26.4 (26)	1,442,093 51.0 (52)	294,074 10.4 (10)	223,415 7.9 (8)	BHE 4.3
Bavaria November 20, 1966	5,270,340	2,537,171 48.1 (110)	1,844,487 35.8 (79)	269,566 5.1 (0) [a]	390,907 7.4 (15)	BP 3.4
Schleswig- Holstein April 23, 1967	1,233,816	567,555 46.0 (34)	486,124 39.4 (30)	72,795 5.9 (4)	71,561 5.8 (4)	SSW 1.9 (1) [b]
Rhineland- Palatinate April 23, 1967	1,843,959	861,142 46.7 (49)	679,177 36.8 (39)	155,089 8.3 (8)	127,680 6.9 (4)	DFU 1.2
Lower Saxony June 4, 1967	3,571,558	1,491,092 41.7 (63)	1,538,776 43.1 (66)	245,368 6.9 (10)	249,197 7.0 (10)	DFU 0.8
Bremen October 1, 1967	405,901	119,647 29.5 (32)	186,795 46.0 (50)	42,731 10.5 (10)	35,894 8.8 (8)	DFU 4.2
Baden- Württemberg April 28, 1968	3,884,617	1,718,261 44.2 (60)	1,124,096 29.0 (37)	560,145 14.4 (18)	381,569 9.8 (12)	
Totals	28,528,119	11,979,048 42.0	12,086,906 42.4	2,338,360 8.2	1,516,868 5.3	606,937 2.1

a The FDP failed to meet the ten percent requirement in a single administrative
district.

b The Danish minority party is exempted from the five percent requirement.

and 9.1 percent and 14 seats in 1996 in Baden-Württemberg. Between 1990 and
1994 it entered candidates in fourteen state elections and polled over one million
votes, but its only success was in Baden-Württemberg. It lost its representation
in the Southwest state in the 2001 election and failed to qualify for seats in 2006
when it polled only 2.5 percent of the vote.[8] In the 2009 *Bundestag* contest it
received less than one percent of second votes.

The 1966-1969 "Black-Red" alliance proved to be more beneficial to the
CDU/CSU than to the Socialists as the Christian Democrats made gains in four
of the five *Land* elections to follow its formation. Nevertheless, by virtue of its
strong showing in Hamburg, North Rhine-Westphalia and Hesse prior to the

formation of the Black-Red ministry in Bonn, the SPD was able to become the leading party on the regional level for only the second time with 42.4 percent of the vote to the Union parties' 42.0 percent.

With the ability of the NPD to gain representation in seven of the ten West German states, four parties were now represented in half of the *Land* parliaments, with the National Democrats replacing the Refugee Party as the fourth faction in the Hessian *Landtag*. A system of three parties existed in Hamburg, where the NPD failed to qualify for seats with only 3.9 percent of the vote in the 1966 *Bürgerschaft* election, in North Rhine-Westphalia where the National Democrats did not compete in view of their poor showing there in the 1965 *Bundestag* contest, in Bavaria where the NPD replaced the FDP as third party, and the Saar which did not compete in this series of regional contests because of its five-year election cycle. Schleswig-Holstein had five parties by virtue of the exemption of the party of the Danish minority, the SSW, from the five percent restriction for representation.

The 1969 *Bundestag* Election

The grand coalition of the CDU/CSU and SPD led by Christian Democrat Dr. Kurt Kiesinger survived to the end of the legislative session in 1969. The *Bundestag* election of that year pitted the incumbent against Willy Brandt who had been Deputy Chancellor and Foreign Minister in the Kiesinger cabinet. In a surprising showing following four consecutive regional election setbacks prior to the September 28, 1969 balloting, the SPD produced its best national election outcome, even surpassing its best regional election totals in the 1966-1968 period. Nevertheless, with 42.7 percent of the vote, the Socialists fell behind the

TABLE 6.2

**THE SIXTH SERIES OF *LAND* ELECTIONS AND 1969
BUNDESTAG ELECTION** [9]

Party	1965-1968 *Land* Elections		September 28, 1969 *Bundestag* Election		Seats
CDU/CSU	11,979,048	42.0	15,195,187	46.1	242
SPD	12,086,906	42.4	14,065,716	42.7	224
FDP	2,338,360	8.2	1,903,422	5.8	30
NPD	1,516,868	5.3	1,422,010	4.3	0
Others	606,937	2.1	127,181	1.1	0
Totals	28,528,119	100.0	32,713,516	100.0	496

CDU/CSU whose combined total represented 46.1 percent of ballots cast countrywide, a slight setback from the total of 47.6 percent gained in 1965. The FDP was the election's biggest loser, with its total falling from 9.5 percent in 1965 to 5.8 percent, its worse showing in six *Bundestag* contests. However, with the failure of the National Democrats to bridge the five percent barrier, the FDP maintained its position as one of only three parties to be represented in the *Bundestag* and, with neither the CDU/CSU nor the SPD able to gain a majority, held the balance of power between the two in the absence of a continuation of the coalition between the two major parties. Not wishing to be locked out of the government for another four years, the Free Democrats, following good relations with the SPD in several states, including populous North Rhine-Westphalia, threw their support to the Socialists to form the first national administration headed by a Socialist Chancellor.

The 1970-1972 *Land* Elections

Between the 1969 and 1972 *Bundestag* ballotings, ten elections were held in the West German states. It was the first time since the formation of the Federal Republic that regional contests were held with a Socialist-led national government sitting in Bonn. In the opposition on the national level for the first time, the CDU/CSU was in a position to be the major beneficiary of dissatisfaction with actions of the national administration, and, with the collapse of NPD appeal, it made gains in all ten contests, winning absolute majorities in five states (Baden-Württemberg, Bavaria, Rhineland-Palatinate, the Saar and Schleswig-Holstein) and pushing its nationwide regional vote total to 48.3 percent, its best showing in regional contests since elections were first held in 1946. CDU/CSU gains, however, were not at the expense of the ruling Socialists, but primarily at the expense of the NPD, which lost representation in all seven of the states in which it had delegates, and the FDP. With 42.3 percent of the vote, the SPD held its own on the regional level, making gains in six of the ten elections and winning absolute majorities in Bremen, Hamburg and Lower Saxony. (The Socialists also won an absolute majority in West Berlin in the November 22, 1970 contest).[10]

The Free Democrats, on the other hand, while regaining representation in Bavaria, lost ground in eight of ten states and was no longer represented in the parliaments of Lower Saxony, the Saar and Schleswig-Holstein, as its nationwide following fell from 8.2 to 6.4 percent. Its worse regional election showing of the postwar period was attributed to disapproval by former party supporters of the party's move to the left and participation with the Socialists in the national government.

With the failure of the NPD to win a seat in any *Land* parliament, as its regional vote total fell to 1.9 percent, and the absence of the FDP from the parliaments of Lower Saxony, the Saar and Schleswig-Holstein, only two parties were represented in the Lower Saxony and the Saar legislative bodies and three

TABLE 6.3

THE SEVENTH SERIES OF *LAND* ELECTIONS 1970-1972 [11]

Land and Date	Valid Votes	CDU	SPD	FDP	NPD	Others
Hamburg March 22, 1970	1,003,104	329,337 32.8 (41)	554,455 55.3 (70)	70,875 7.1 (9)	27,312 2.7 (-)	DKP 1.7 (-)
Lower Saxony June 14, 1970	3,875,828	1,771,698 45.7 (74)	1,792,942 46.3 (75)	169,457 4.4 (-)	124,675 3.2 (-)	DKP (0.4)
North Rhine- Westphalia June 14, 1970	8,677,827	4,020,186 46.3 (95)	3,996,808 41.6 (94)	478,420 5.5 (11)	94,043 1.1 (-)	DKP 0.9 (-)
The Saar June 14, 1970	643,903	308,107 47.8 (27)	262,492 40.8 (23)	28,167 4.4 (-)	22,020 3.4 (-)	DKP 2.7 (-)
Hesse November 8, 1970	3,141,816	1,247,301 39.7 (46)	1,442,094 45.9 (53)	317,323 10.1 (11)	94,254 3.0 (-)	DKP 1.2 (-)
Bavaria November 22, 1970	5,621,554	3,172,300 56.4 (124)	1,871,380 33.3 (70)	312,280 5.6 (10)	162,823 2.9 (-)	BP 1.3 (-)
Rhineland- Palatinate March 21, 1971	2,026,372	1,012,847 50.0 (52)	821,350 40.5 (42)	120,444 5.9 (6)	53,882 2.7 (-)	DKP 0.9 (-)
Schleswig- Holstein April 25, 1971	1,421,034	737,120 51.9 (40)	582,420 41.0 (32)	54,099 3.8 (-)	18,822 1.3 (-)	SSW 1.4 (1)
Bremen October 10, 1971	441,791	139,423 31.6 (34)	244,470 55.3 (59)	31,509 7.1 (7)	12,561 2.8 (-)	DKP 3.1 (-)
Baden- Württemberg April 23, 1972	4,750,637	2,513,808 52.9 (65)	1,784,416 37.6 (45)	424,685 8.9 (10)	No NPD	KPD 0.5 (-)
Totals	31,603,866	15,252,127 48.3	13,352,827 42.3	2,007,359 6.4	610,392 1.9	381,161 1.2

in all other *Land* parliaments. In Schleswig-Holstein the third party was the Danish SSW, which, with 1.4 percent of the vote total received a single seat by virtue of its exemption from the five percent clause. Hesse and North Rhine-Westphalia were the only states in which a single party did not hold an absolute majority of the seats, greatly facilitating the formation of governing ministries.

The 1972 *Bundestag* Election

Two events caused the seventh *Bundestag* election to be held nearly a year earlier than the four-year legislative cycle would have demanded. First, Rainer Barzel, the CDU's faction leader in the *Bundestag*, attempted in April 1972 to bring down the SPD/FDP government through a constructive vote of non-confidence. The move failed, however, by the slim margin of two votes. But later in the year Chancellor Willy Brandt, himself, put forward the confidence question, and when there was no majority, requested the federal president to dissolve the federal parliament, leading to the general election ten months early.

Having obtained nearly half of the nation-wide regional vote in elections held between 1969 and 1972 there were expectations that the CDU/CSU, with Rainer Barzel as Chancellor-candidate, would emerge as the leading party in the general election held November 19, 1972. However, the SPD, helped by the favorable reception of Willy Brandt's "*Ostpolitik*," which served to normalize relations between West Germany and the East Block states, received 45.8 percent of the national vote to the CDU/CSU's 44.9 percent, marking the first time that the Socialists were able to outpoll the Union parties in national balloting. The only other party to gain representation in Bonn, the Free Democrats, with an improved 8.4 percent of the vote, again sided with the Socialists. With the NPD following falling to less than one percent and no other grouping of consequence arising to challenge the status quo, the total vote received by the three established parties reached 99.1 percent, the highest total in any national election, giving added credence to a continuation of a three-party system into the foreseeable future. Willy Brandt was succeeded as Federal Chancellor by Helmut Schmidt May 16, 1974 when the unmasking of a top aid as an East German spy forced his resignation and placed a chill on relations between the eastern and western parts of Germany.

TABLE 6.4

**THE SEVENTH SERIES OF *LAND* ELECTIONS AND 1972
BUNDESTAG ELECTION** [12]

Party	1970-1972 *Land* Elections		November 19, 1972 *Bundestag* Election		Seats
CDU/CSU	15,252,127	48.3	16,806,020	44.9	225
SPD	13,352,827	42.3	17,175,169	45.8	230
FDP	2,007,359	6.4	3,129,982	8.4	41
NPD	610,392	1.9	207,465	0.6	-
DKP/KPD	243,370	0.8	113,891	0.3	-
Others	137,791	0.4	27,223	0.1	-
Totals	31,603,866		37,459,750		496

The 1974-1976 *Land* Elections

In the regional contests held between the 1972 and 1976 *Bundestag* elections, the CDU/CSU continued to benefit from its opposition status, increasing its vote share in nine of ten state elections (the only exception being Schleswig-Holstein) to bring its regional gains to 19 in 20 successive contests since the formation of the SPD/FDP coalition in 1969. For the first time in regional balloting it gained over half of the nationwide vote, a 51.4 percent share, bettering even its best *Bundestag* election showing of 50.2 percent in 1957. Absolute majorities were won in Baden-Württemberg, Bavaria, Rhineland-Palatinate and Schleswig-Holstein; it replaced the Socialists as the leading party in Hesse and Lower Saxony and remained the leading party in

TABLE 6.5

THE EIGHTH SERIES OF *LAND* ELECTIONS 1974-1976 [13]

Land and Date	Valid Votes	CDU	SPD	FDP	NPD	Others
Hamburg March 3, 1974	1,044,750	423,912 40.6 (51)	469,912 44.9 (56)	113,930 10.9 (13)	7,992 0.8 (-)	DKP 2.2 (-)
Lower Saxony June 9, 1974	4,297,693	2,098,096 48.8 (77)	1,852,797 43.1 (67)	302,165 7.0 (11)	27,581 0.6 (-)	DKP 0.4 (-)
Bavaria October 27, 1974	5,639,293	3,500,776 62.1 (132)	1,704,563 30.2 (64)	293,267 5.2 (8)	60,872 1.1 (-)	BP 0.8 (-)
Hesse October 27, 1974	3,230,420	1,528,793 47.3 (53)	1,394,123 43.2 (49)	238,726 7.4 (8)	32,713 1.0 (-)	DKP 0.9 (-)
Rhineland- Palatinate March 9, 1975	2,120,481	1,143,360 53.9 (55)	817,018 38.5 (40)	118,762 5.6 (5)	22,942 1.1 (-)	DKP 0.5 (-)
Schleswig- Holstein April 13, 1975	1,504,683	758,227 50.4 (37)	603,360 40.1 (30)	107,042 7.1 (5)	8,123 0.5 (-)	SSW 1.4 (1)
North Rhine Westphalia May 4, 1975	10,261,205	4,828,554 47.1 (95)	4,630,995 45.1 (91)	689,623 6.7 (14)	32,281 0.4 (-)	DKP 0.5 (-)
The Saar May 4, 1975	706,238	347,094 49.1 (25)	295,406 41.8 (22)	52,100 7.4 (3)	4,774 0.7 (-)	DKP 1.0 (-)
Bremen September 28, 1975	430,391	145,308 33.8 (35)	209,802 48.7 (52)	55,739 13.0 (13)	4,781 1.1 (-)	DKP 2.1 (-)
Baden- Württemberg April 4, 1976	4,536,515	2,573,147 56.7 (71)	1,510,012 33.3 (41)	353,754 7.8 (9)	42,927 0.9 (-)	DKP 0.5 (-)
Totals	33,771,669	17,347,267 51.4	13,487,988 39.9	2,325,108 6.9	244,986 0.7	366,320 1.1

North Rhine-Westphalia and the Saar. It also made gains in both Bremen and Hamburg, but could not keep the Socialists from maintaining their leading position in those two states. [14]

With its honeymoon wearing thin, the SPD lost ground in every *Land* with the exception of the Saar. Only in Bremen did it win a majority of the seats as its ten-state following sank from 42.3 to 39.9 percent. The replacement of Willy Brandt by Helmut Schmidt in 1974 failed to stem the losses. The SPD's partner in Bonn, the FDP, fared much better as it made gains in five of the ten West German states and was returned to the parliaments of Lower Saxony, the Saar and Schleswig-Holstein to again be represented in all ten state legislative bodies. It picked up an additional 318,000 *Land*-level votes to push its regional following to 6.9 percent. With most of the vote of disaffected voters being absorbed by the cartel parties, minor groupings were able to obtain only 1.8 percent of ballots cast, with the fading NPD total falling to less than one percent. The 98.2 percent of the vote won by the CDU/CSU, SPD and FDP in these regional contests was the highest level reached in any series of *Land* elections.

With the FDP returning to the parliaments of Lower Saxony, the Saar and Schleswig-Holstein, there were no longer any two-party states, and all state legislative bodies were comprised of three factions, with the exception of Schleswig-Holstein where the party of the Danish minority was awarded a single seat by virtue of its exemption from the five percent clause.

The 1976 *Bundestag* Election

Building on its strong following in regional elections, the CDU/CSU, with Dr. Helmut Kohl, Minister President of Rhineland-Palatinate, as its Chancellor

TABLE 6.6

**THE EIGHTH SERIES OF *LAND* ELECTIONS AND
1976 *BUNDESTAG* ELECTION [15]**

Party	1972-1976 *Land* Elections		October 3, 1976 *Bundestag* Election		Seats
CDU/CSU	17,347,267	51.4	18,394,801	48.6	243
SPD	13,487,988	39.9	16,099,019	42.6	214
FDP	2,325,108	6.9	2,995,085	7.9	39
NPD	244,986	0.7	122,661	0.3	-
KPD/DKP	205,865	0.6	141,295	0.4	-
Others	160,455	0.5	69,639	0.2	-
Totals	33,771,669		37,822,500		496

candidate, polled 48.6 percent of the national vote to the Socialists' 42.6 percent in the general election held October 3, 1976. Ordinarily the largest party in the parliament is able to form the government, but the FDP, the only other party to gain representation with 7.9 percent of the vote, again kept the Christian parties out of leadership in Bonn by siding with the Socialists under Helmut Schmidt. With the West German voter seemingly comfortable with the positions of the three older parties, the share of the national vote falling to them again reached 99.1 percent.

The 1978-1980 *Land* Elections

In the ten *Land* elections held between the 1976 and 1980 *Bundestag* elections, the CDU/CSU, although the only party in opposition in Bonn, suffered setbacks in all ten states, and its national following declined from 51.4 to 48.7 percent. Nevertheless, it won absolute majorities in Baden-Württemberg, Bavaria, Lower Saxony, Rhineland-Palatinate and Schleswig-Holstein and outpolled the SPD in Hesse. In contrast, the SPD, riding on the growing popularity of Chancellor Helmut Schmidt, made gains in eight of the ten states, winning absolute majorities in Bremen, Hamburg and North Rhine-Westphalia and replacing the CDU as the leading party in the Saar, as its share of the nationwide regional vote increased from 39.9 to 41.5 percent. Its coalition partner, the Free Democrats, however, suffered setbacks in seven of the ten states to register their weakest *Land*-level following in the postwar period, with only 5.9 percent of ballots cast, and lost their representation in Hamburg, Lower Saxony and North Rhine-Westphalia.

A new force in German politics appeared during this series of regional contests to challenge the three-party cartel which had existed for nearly two decades. A variety of environmentally-oriented groups contested every election with the exception of Rhineland-Palatinate. Although the movement, which became known as the Greens, was successful in gaining representation only in Bremen where it won four seats in the 1979 election and Baden-Württemberg where it won six seats in 1980, the ability of this new grouping to poll nearly one million votes, 2.9 percent of the total, which otherwise would have gone to the three established parties, was disturbing to the three party hegemony of the CDU/CSU/SPD/FDP. In spite of the entry of this new player to the political arena, the vote of the three originally-licensed parties still amounted to 96.1 percent of the regional total. With the CDU/CSU and SPD winning absolute majorities in eight of the ten states, there was need for coalitions only in Hesse and the Saar where Green groupings were not represented. In Hesse, the FDP coalesced with the SPD and in the Saar with the CDU.

With the FDP having lost its representation in Hamburg, Lower Saxony and North Rhine-Westphalia, only two parties were represented in their respective legislative bodies, while in Bavaria, Hesse, Rhineland-Palatinate and the Saar there was a three party system of the CDU/CSU, SPD and FDP. With the entry

TABLE 6.7

THE NINTH SERIES OF *LAND* ELECTIONS 1978-1980 [16]

Land and Date	Valid Votes	CDU	SPD	FDP	Green List	Others
Hamburg June 4, 1978	958,397	360,409 37.6 (51)	493,340 51.5 (69)	45,903 4.8 (-)	33,279 3.5 (-)	DKP 1.0 (-)
Lower Saxony June 4, 1978	4,088,183	1,989,326 48.7 (83)	1,723,638 42.2 (72)	171,514 4.2 (-)	157,733 3.9 (-)	NPD 0.4 (-)
Hesse October 8, 1978	3,422,967	1,574,565 46.0 (53)	1,516,374 44.3 (50)	225,916 6.6 (7)	68,459 2.0 (-)	NPD 0.4 (-)
Bavaria October 15, 1978	5,734,048	3,391,046 59.1 (129)	1,799,740 31.4 (65)	355,874 6.2 (10)	105,489 1.8 (-)	NPD 0.6 (-)
Rhineland-Palatinate March 18, 1979	2,184,540	1,094,480 50.1 (51)	923,965 42.3 (43)	139,248 6.4 (6)	- -	NPD 0.7 (-)
Schleswig-Holstein April 29, 1979	1,568,833	757,664 48.3 (37)	653,982 41.7 (31)	90,131 5.2 (4)	38,009 [a] 2.4 (-)	SSW 1.4 (1)
Bremen October 7, 1979	406,911	129,985 31.9 (33)	201,129 49.4 (52)	43,730 10.7 (11)	26,449 6.5 (4)	KPD 0.8 (-)
Baden-Württemberg March 16, 1980	4,513,009	2,407,798 53.4 (68)	1,468,873 32.5 (40)	374,633 8.3 (10)	241,303 5.3 (6)	DKP 0.3 (-)
The Saar April 27, 1980	694,745	305,584 44.0 (23)	315,432 45.4 (24)	47,977 6.9 (4)	19,945 2.9 (-)	DKP 0.5 (-)
North Rhine-Westphalia May 11, 1980	9,818,518	4,240,885 43.2 (95)	4,756,103 48.6 (106)	489,225 4.98 (-)	291,378 3.0 (-)	KPD 0.3 (-)
Totals	33,390,151	16,251,742 48.7	13,852,576 41.5	1,984,151 5.9	982,044 2.9	319,638 1.0

a Green List Schleswig-Holstein

of the Greens into the parliaments of Bremen and Baden-Württemberg a four-party system existed in these two states, while in Schleswig-Holstein, where a Green List obtained only 2.4 percent of the vote, the fourth party was the party of the Danish minority, the SSW.

The 1980 *Bundestag* Election

For the *Bundestag* election of October 3, 1980 the CDU/CSU selected Franz Josef Strauss, Minister President of Bavaria and former federal defense minister, to run against incumbent Helmut Schmid for the federal

TABLE 6.8

THE NINTH SERIES OF *LAND* ELECTIONS AND
1980 *BUNDESTAG* ELECTION [17]

Party	1978-1980 *Land* Elections		October 5, 1980 *Bundestag* Election		Seats
CDU/CSU	16,251,742	48.7	16,897,659	44.5	226
SPD	13,852,576	41.5	16,260,677	42.9	218
FDP	1,984,151	5.9	4,030,999	10.6	53
Green Lists	982,044	3.0	569,589	1.5	-
DKP/KPD	97,049	0.3	71,600	0.2	-
NPD/DRP	89,694	0.3	68,096	0.2	-
Others	132,895	0.4	40,361	0.1	-
Totals	33,390,151		37,822,500		497

chancellorship. While the Union parties outpolled the Socialists 44.5 to 42.9 percent, the drop of four percentage points from the 1976 following was attributed in part to the wide-ranging negative image of the Union candidate, while the SPD's modest gain was ascribed to Helmut Schmidt's general popularity. The results confirmed the staying power of the three established parties as the new challenger, the Greens, was unable to capture more than 1.5 percent of the vote in their first attempt at national representation, only half of the following gained in the previous regional contests. They could not even gain five percent of the vote in their two bastions of strength, Baden-Württemberg and Bremen, where they had won representation in *Land* election contests, giving the impression that the grouping would fade much as the Refugee Party and the NPD had before it. At the same time, the party which had the most to lose should a fourth grouping gain a strong footing, the FDP, which appeared on the brink of extinction after the regional contests leading up to the general election, won a new lease on life with its best showing since 1961. Although the CDU/CSU remained the largest party in the *Bundestag*, the Free Democrats, with a 10.6 percent following, again sided with the Socialists under Chancellor Helmut Schmidt to form a fourth SPD/FDP administration in Bonn. However, this red-yellow combination was to last only two more years, as the FDP, concerned over its falling national image and the growing power of the environmental movement, decided to swing its support to the opposition CDU/CSU. With the failure of the Greens to gain a national footing, the three-party cartel of the CDU/CSU, SPD and FDP remained intact with 98.0 percent of the nationwide vote.

The 1982 *Land* Elections

Only five regional contests were held between the 1980 and 1983 *Bundestag* elections because of the shortened legislative period caused by the withdrawal of the Free Democrats from the national coalition in October 1982 and the need for a voter mandate on the new CDU/CSU/FDP partnership in Bonn. The federal legislative period, reduced to only 29 months, has been the shortest in the history of the Federal Republic. While the number of *Land* elections during the course of 1982 were too few to provide a more general picture of public opinion, the results demonstrated an increasing voter disenchantment with the SPD/FDP combination in Bonn and ultimately influenced the decision of the Free Democrats to abandon their arrangement with the Socialists.

The first regional balloting following the 1980 *Bundestag* election took place in Lower Saxony March 21, 1982, in which the CDU, in addition to winning a majority of parliamentary seats, also received an absolute majority of the votes (50.7 percent), a feat that the Socialists were unable to accomplish in ten election periods. Then, in the Hamburg contest of June 6, it outpolled the Socialists for the first time in a stand-alone vote, gaining 56 seats to the Socialists' 55.[18] The setback for the SPD was heavily influenced by the resignation of Lord Mayor Hans Ulrich Klose (following strong internal party differences) over his support of opponents to the building of the planned Brokdorf nuclear power plant (*Hamburg Abendblatt Chronik* 1982: 583). He was replaced by Klaus von Dohnanyi, who, following the election in which the Socialists lost their majority status, attempted to negotiate an agreement with the Greens, who had entered the Hamburg *Bürgerschaft* for the first time. The attempt was unsuccessful because the SPD could not accept the newcomers' terms. With the Free Democrats again failing to qualify for representation, the leading Christian Democrats also were unable to form a government, since they too, at the time, could not work with the Greens. This led to a minority government under von Dohnanyi, which was tolerated by the Greens until new elections could be held December 19, 1982.

The Christian Union parties experienced minimal losses in Hesse on September 26 and in Bavaria October 10th, but remained the leading grouping in the two states. The victory in Bavaria marked the sixth time in a row that the CSU, the CDU's sister party, was able to win an absolute majority of seats in the state parliament. The Socialists lost ground in each of the first three elections in this period before making a slight gain in Bavaria. Then, on October 22, 1982, four FDP ministers resigned from the Schmidt cabinet to force the first and only successful constructive vote of non-confidence at the national level in postwar German history. The FDP decision to side with the Christian parties placed the Socialists in the opposition in Bonn for the first time since 1966 when they entered into a grand coalition with the CDU/CSU. The fifth and final state election of the period was held in Hamburg December 19, 1982, a balloting made necessary by the difficulties in forming a stable government in the *Hansastadt* following the inconclusive results of the June *Bürgerschaft* election. Now in the opposition in Bonn, the Socialists won an absolute majority of votes and seats and were able to govern alone.

During this set of elections, the Free Democrats regained representation in the Lower Saxony *Landtag*, but lost their delegations in both the Hessian and Bavarian parliaments and failed to obtain seats in either of the two Hamburg contests. These setbacks, coupled with the success of the Greens which succeeded in entering the legislative bodies of Lower Saxony, Hesse and Hamburg for the first time, weighed heavily on the party's decision to seek a new course and opt for a change in Bonn where it held the balance of power. The FDP's overall total of only 4.0 percent was its worse showing in any series of *Land* elections. Bringing down its coalition with the Socialists in Bonn was a gamble, since there were still nearly two years remaining in the legislative session.

Recovering from their setback in the 1980 *Bundestag* election, the Green groupings registered nearly as many votes in four states in 1982 as in the nine states in which they had entered candidates between June 1978 and May 1980. Importantly, they outpolled the third ranking FDP by 300,000 votes to now be represented in five of the ten West German state parliaments. Moreover, public opinion polls showed the FDP in danger of being replaced as the pivotal player in Bonn as it had been for two decades.

A number of factors led to the collapse of the SPD/FDP coalition in Bonn. There was disagreement within Socialist ranks over the stationing of Pershing II missiles on West German soil to counter the emplacement of new intermediate-range missiles in the Soviet Union, and the FDP began to draw away from the Socialists on economic policy. In addition, the threat posed by a growing environmental movement to replace the FDP as the "*Zunglein an der Wagge*" caused it to consider a change in strategy. It was Chancellor Schmidt's rejection of the austere economic measures proposed by FDP economics minister Otto von Lambsdorff on September 17, 1982, one week before the *Land* election in Hesse, to deal with the economic downturn and a growing budget deficit that triggered the withdrawal of four FDP ministers from the Schmidt cabinet and brought about the collapse of the coalition. A constructive vote of non-confidence brought Dr. Helmut Kohl into the chancellorship as Schmidt's replacement.

The move ultimately backfired for the Free Democrats as the party, seen as a betrayer, lost its parliamentary delegations in six consecutive *Land* elections, three prior to the 1983 *Bundestag* balloting and three directly thereafter to reduce its representation to only three of the ten West German *Länder* and its elimination from all *Land* ministries before recovering in the September 25, 1983 election in Hesse. Nevertheless, it still held the balance of power in Bonn. (For an in-depth analysis of the 1982 change in Bonn, see Arthur Lupia and Kaare Strøm, *American Political Science Review*, "Coalition Termination," September 1995: 648-650.)

TABLE 6.9

THE TENTH SERIES OF *LAND* ELECTIONS 1982 [a] [19]

Land and Date	Valid Votes	CDU	SPD	FDP	Greens	Others
Lower Saxony March 21, 1982	4,178,510	2,118,137 50.7 (87)	1,526,346 36.5 (63)	246,959 5.9 (10)	273,338 6.5 (11)	DKP 0.3 (-)
Hesse September 26, 1982	3,465,493	1,580,265 45.6 (52)	1,483,231 42.8 (49)	107,430 3.1 (-)	279,639 8.0 (9)	DKP 0.4 (-)
Bavaria October 10, 1982	6,083,601	3,545,722 58.3 (133)	1,938,485 31.9 (71)	215,091 3.5 (-)	279,344 4.6 (-)	NPD 0.6 (-)
Hamburg [b] December 19, 1982	1,032,813	398,518 38.6 (48)	530,117 51.3 (64)	26,485 2.6 (-)	70,501 6.8 (8)	DKP 0.4 (-)
Totals	14,760,417	7,642,642 51.8	5,478,179 37.1	595,965 4.0	902,822 6.1	140,809 1.0

a Because of the shortened general election interval of only 29 months, only five regional elections were held between 1980 and 1983, two of them in Hamburg.

b The June 6, 1982 *Bürgerschaft* election in Hamburg did not produce a majority for either the SPD or the CDU, and a working relationship with the Greens, the only other party to receive representation, proved unachievable, necessitating the follow-up election in December. The results of the June 1982 contest are noted below. To have included both Hamburg elections in the totals would have distorted the standings of the several parties. Because the June election result provided for only a provisional, short-time government, the December election was included in the total.

Land and Date	Valid Votes	CDU	SPD	FDP	Greens	Others
Hamburg June 6, 1982	955,865	413,361 43.2 (56)	408,261 42.7 (55)	46,364 4.9 (-)	73,404 7.7 (9)	DKP 0.6 (-)

The elections created a two-party system of the CSU and SPD in Bavaria, where neither the FDP nor the nascent Greens were able to obtain representation, a three party system of the CDU, SPD and Greens in Hesse and Hamburg and a four-party order in Lower Saxony. In the limited number of elections, the CDU/CSU polled 51.8 percent of ballots cast, the SPD 37.1 percent, the Greens 6.1 percent and the FDP, in its worse showing since the first elections were held after World War II, only 4.0 percent. Just one percent of the vote fell to various splinter groups.

The 1983 *Bundestag* Election

Having become Chancellor in October 1982 by virtue of the FDP decision to withdraw from its coalition with the SPD and without a mandate from the voters, the 1983 national election, held March 6th, became a referendum on Helmut Kohl only five months after he had assumed the leading national office. In that election the voters responded favorably by giving the CDU/CSU 48.8 percent of the national vote, an improvement of 4.3 percentage points over their 1980 following, to carry every state with the exception of the SPD strongholds of Bremen and Hamburg. The Socialists, with Hans-Jochen Vogel as their chancellor-candidate, experienced a drop in support from 42.9 to 38.2 percent, the FDP from 10.6 to 7.0 percent. While the Greens entered the *Bundestag* for the first time with 5.6 percent of ballots cast, the Free Democrats found some relief in having polled over a half million more votes than the new challenger. Although receiving a third fewer ballots than in 1980, the FDP, with 34 seats, was able to insure a working majority for a continuation of the black/yellow alliance. A coalition with the SPD would not have provided a parliamentary majority and neither major party was ready to partner with the then radical Greens.

TABLE 6.10

THE TENTH SERIES OF *LAND* ELECTIONS AND 1983 *BUNDESTAG* ELECTION [20]

Party	1982 *Land* Elections		March 6, 1983 *Bundestag* Election		Seats
CDU/CSU	7,642,642	51.8	18,998,545	48.8	244
SPD	5,478,179	37.1	14,865,801	38.2	193
FDP	595,965	4.0	2,706,942	7.0	34
Greens	902,822	6.1	2,167,431	5.6	27
DKP	41,466	0.3	64,986	0.2	-
NPD	34,828	0.2	91,095	0.2	-
Others	64,515	0.4	45,887	0.1	-
Totals	14,760,417		38,940,687		498

The 1983-1986 *Land* Elections

Regional parliamentary elections were held in all ten West German states between the 1983 and 1987 *Bundestag* contests. The first regional balloting

TABLE 6.11

THE ELEVENTH SERIES OF *LAND* ELECTIONS 1983-1986 [21]

Land and Date	Valid Votes	CDU/CSU	SPD	FDP	Greens	Others
Rhineland-Palatinate March 6, 1983	2,515,393	1,306,090 51.9 (57)	995,795 39.6 (43)	88,189 3.5 (-)	113,809 4.5 (-)	NPD 0.1 (-)
Schleswig-Holstein March 13, 1983	1,662,472	814,557 49.0 (39)	726,632 43.7 (31)	35,832 2.2 (-)	59,358 3.6 (-)	SSW 1.3 (1)
Bremen September 25, 1983	410,240	136,635 33.3 (37)	210,632 51.3 (58)	18,828 4.6 (-)	37,742 [a] 9.2 (5)	6,403 0.2
Hesse September 25, 1983	3,373,853	1,329,298 39.4 (44)	1,558,720 46.2 (51)	356,413 7.6 (8)	199,057 5.9 (7)	DKP 0.3 (-)
Baden-Württemberg March 25, 1984	4,650,186	2,412,085 51.9 (68)	1,507,088 32.4 (41)	333,386 7.2 (8)	372,374 8.0 (9)	DKP 0.3
The Saar March 10, 1985	704,901	262,975 37.3 (20)	346,595 49.2 (26)	70,713 10.0 (5)	17,642 2.5 (-)	Rep. 3.4 (-)
North Rhine-Westphalia May 12, 1985	9,479,440	3,463,656 36.5 (88)	4,942,346 52.1 (125)	565,413 6.0 (14)	431,371 4.6 (-)	76,374 0.8 (-)
Lower Saxony June 15, 1986	4,293,146	1,903,559 44.3 (69)	1,807,157 42.1 (66)	257,873 6.0 (9)	303,308 7.1 (11)	DKP 0.1 (-)
Bavaria October 12, 1986	5,677,200	3,166,867 55.8 (128)	1,559,562 27.5 (61)	214,395 3.8 (-)	427,177 7.5 (15)	Rep. 3.0 (-)
Hamburg November 9, 1986	959,137	402,681 41.9 (54)	400,402 41.7 (53)	45,680 4.8 (-)	99,779 10.4 (13)	DKP 0.2 (-)
Totals	33,725,968	15,198,403 45.1	14,054,929 41.7	1,986,722 5.9	2,061,617 6.1	424,297 1.3

a The total is for three "Green" groupings, only one of which qualified for seats.

coincided with the March 6, 1983 general election and, coincidentally, took place in Rhineland-Palatinate, the state which Chancellor Kohl had headed for ten years. In that election the CDU won both an absolute majority of the votes and seats, even bettering the support it received the same day in the national contest 51.9 percent to 49.6 percent. The SPD, now in the opposition in Bonn, was able to win the same number of seats as in 1979, but with a smaller following, as neither the FDP with 3.5 percent of the vote nor the Greens with 4.5 percent were able to qualify for seats. Interestingly, the FDP total was only half of the 7.0 percent it polled in *Bundestag* balloting the same day. In the Schleswig-Holstein balloting a week later the CDU again won an absolute majority of seats (but not of the votes). The Socialists also made modest gains as neither the Free Democrats nor the Greens qualified for representation.

Within a half year of these elections voter opinion began to swing away from the CDU. Although the party made a small gain in Bremen in the September 25th election, the SPD expanded its hold on the state parliament with 51.3 percent of ballots cast, and, in an election held the same day in Hesse, replaced the CDU as the state's leading party as the Christian Democrat total fell from 45.6 percent in 1982 to 39.4 percent. Setbacks for the CDU/CSU continued in Baden-Württemberg (although it kept its absolute majority in the *Land* parliament), the Saar (where the Socialists won an absolute majority of seats for the first time), North Rhine-Westphalia (where the Socialists won an absolute majority of votes and seats for the first time), Lower Saxony (where it lost its absolute majority while remaining the *Land's* leading party) and Bavaria (while maintaining its absolute majority in the *Land* parliament). The string of six consecutive, but not crucial, setbacks ended in the November 9, 1986 election in Hamburg when the CDU outpolled the Socialists in their stronghold 41.9 to 41.7 percent. In spite of a reversal of support prior to the Hamburg decision, the CDU/CSU, nevertheless, won absolute majorities in Rhineland-Palatinate, Schleswig-Holstein, Baden-Württemberg and Bavaria, remained the leading party in Lower Saxony and replaced the Socialists as the major faction in Hamburg. With 45.1 percent of the regional vote the Union parties remained ahead of the Socialists, who, with gains in six states, polled 41.7 percent of the ten election total and won absolute majorities in North Rhine-Westphalia, Bremen and the Saar.

Following a string of six straight setbacks and loss of representation in five of the ten states, the FDP, beginning with the September 25, 1983 balloting in Hesse, experienced gains in six of the next seven *Land* contests, enabling it to regain representation in Hesse, the Saar and North Rhine-Westphalia to add to its existing representation in Baden-Württemberg and Lower Saxony. While these successes improved its national standing, it was, nevertheless, outpolled by the Greens (who polled over two million votes for the first time) by 75,000 votes nationwide. The Greens, in spite of their newly-won success, were able to add only Bavaria to the states in which they were represented, bringing the total to six, as they continued to fail to exceed the five percent barrier in Rhineland-Palatinate, Schleswig-Holstein, the Saar and North Rhine-Westphalia. In 1985 they were brought into a *Land* ministry for the first time in Hesse with the SPD.

Of significance was the continued limited appeal of right-extremist groups, amounting to less than one percent of the regional vote cast nationwide. The best percentage showing was the 3.4 percent gained by the Republicans in the Saar in the March 10, 1985 *Land* election. That same party obtained 171,490 votes in the October 1986 election in Bavaria, but that was only 3.0 percent of the statewide total and no rightist party obtained representation in any of the state parliaments. In spite of the entry of the Greens into the political arena, the vote falling to the CDU/CSU, SPD and FDP still amounted to 92.3 percent of ballots cast.

The 1987 *Bundestag* Election

The eleventh *Bundestag* election was held January 25, 1987. It took place following a string of six setbacks in the previous seven regional elections for the CDU/CSU, and there was concern within Union ranks that a continuation of the trend would have serious consequences for their factions on the national level. While the Union parties did witness a drop in their national following from 48.8 to 44.3 percent, they remained the largest grouping in the federal parliament, as the Socialists, with Johannes Rau, the popular Minister President of North Rhine-Westphalia, as their leading candidate, saw their total fall moderately to 37.0 percent from 38.2 percent. These outcomes were poorer than in the previous series of *Land* elections for both parties.

The major gainers were the two smaller groupings, the FDP, which pushed its nationwide following from 7.0 to 9.1 percent, and the Greens who pushed their total from 5.6 percent in 1983 to 8.3 percent. For the FDP, which had failed to gain representation in five of the ten West German state parliaments and had looked headed for extinction after having been outpolled by the Greens in regional balloting, the ability to poll over five percent of ballots cast in every state and to stay ahead of the Greens by 315,000 votes in the general election was especially gratifying. It again entered into a coalition with the CDU/CSU. A combination with the SPD would have been insufficient to provide a *Bundestag* majority. As in the previous regional contests, the vote falling to right-extremist

TABLE 6.12

THE ELEVENTH SERIES OF *LAND* ELECTIONS AND 1987 *BUNDESTAG* ELECTION [22]

Party	1983-1986 *Land* Elections		January 25, 1987 *Bundestag* Election		Seats
CDU/CSU	15,198,403	45.1	16,761,572	44.3	223
SPD	14,054,929	41.7	14,025,763	37.0	186
FDP	1,986,722	5.9	3,440,911	9.1	46
Greens	2,061,617	6.1	3,126,256	8.3	42
Rep./NPD	232,863	0.7	227,054	0.6	-
DKP	40,424	0.1			
Others	151,010	0.4	285,763	0.7	
Totals	33,725,968		37,867,319		497

groupings continued to be less than one percent. Nevertheless, because of the improvement by the Greens, the proportion of ballots cast for the CDU/CSU, SPD and FDP declined to 90.4 percent, the lowest since the 1957 general election.

The 1987-1990 *Land* Elections

The eleven regional contests held between the 1987 and the 1990 *Bundestag* elections were the last to take place prior to reunification and before the five eastern states and a united Berlin were added to the Federal Republic and could have an impact on election outcomes.[23] Four of these elections, in the Saar, Lower Saxony, North Rhine Westphalia and Bavaria occurred after the fall of the Berlin wall and the one in Bavaria after reunification had been achieved. One of the eleven elections was a re-run in Schleswig-Holstein made necessary by the revelation of the "Barschel Affair" involving political spying and breaking the confidentiality of tax returns (see page 313). In these contests the CDU continued to lose ground, suffering setbacks in eight of the ten states to run its string of losses to thirteen in the last fifteen *Land* elections before registering a minor gain in the May 13, 1990 balloting in North Rhine-Westphalia. In this set of regional contests the anticipation of reunification was of little help to Chancellor Kohl's party. Nevertheless, the Union groupings gained absolute majorities in Baden-Württemberg and Bavaria, remained the largest party in Rhineland-Palatinate and regained its status as leading party in Hesse. The SPD did little better, gaining ground in only four of the ten states and remaining behind the CDU/CSU in total regional votes with 41.0 percent to the CDU/CSU's 43.1 percent. However, it ended the period as the leading party in six states, four by absolute majorities (Bremen, North Rhine-Westphalia, the Saar and Schleswig-Holstein) and, with the addition of Berlin's four votes and by replacing the CDU in Schleswig-Holstein and Lower Saxony, took control of the *Bundesrat*, the upper house of the West German parliament, for the first time in June 1990 with 24 votes to the CDU/CSU's eighteen.[24] The Socialist triumph in Lower Saxony in May 1990 provided the new Minister-President Gerhard Schröder with a base from which he was able to ascend to the federal Chancellorship in 1998.

The Free Democrats, following their comeback in the 1987 *Bundestag* election, improved their standings in seven of the ten state elections and returned to the parliaments of Bavaria, Bremen, Hamburg and Rhineland-Palatinate to now be represented in every West German state with the single exception of Schleswig-Holstein. However, they still remained behind the Greens in the total regional vote, who, by polling 6.2 percent of ballots cast to the FDP's 6.0 percent and placing delegates for the first time in the parliaments of Rhineland-Palatinate and North Rhine-Westphalia were now represented in eight of the ten *Bundesländer*, the only exceptions being the Saar and Schleswig-Holstein.

Other than the single seat won by the right-wing German People's Union (DVU) in Bremen by virtue of its strength in the Bremerhaven portion of the

TABLE 6.13

THE TWELFTH SERIES OF *LAND* ELECTIONS 1987-1990 [25]

Land and Date	Valid Votes	CDU	SPD	FDP	Greens	Others
Hesse April 5, 1987	3,314,648	1,395,712 42.1 (47)	1,332,721 40.2 (44)	259,212 7.8 (9)	311,488 9.4 (10)	DKP 0.3 (-)
Rhineland- Palatinate May 17, 1987	2,177,314	981,412 45.1 (48)	844,241 38.8 (40)	158,964 7.3 (7)	128,653 5.9 (5)	NPD 0.8 (-)
Hamburg May 17, 1987	984,573	398,686 40.5 (49)	442.670 45.0 (55)	64,389 6.5 (8)	69,148 7.0 (8)	9,680 0.9
Bremen September 13, 1987	389,800	91,334 23.4 (25)	196,903 50.5 (54)	39,078 10.0 (10)	39,839 10.2 (10)	DVU 3.4 (1)
Baden- Württemberg March 20, 1988	4,876,493	2,391,937 49.1 (66)	1,562,205 32.0 (42)	285,830 5.9 (7)	382,881 7.9 (10)	NPD 2.1 (-)
Schleswig- Holstein [a] May 8, 1988	1,566,837	521,264 33.3 (27)	857,956 54.8 (46)	69,620 4.4 (-)	44,898 2.9 (-)	SSW 1.7 (1)
The Saar January 28, 1990	694,101	231,983 33.4 (18)	377,502 54.4 (30)	39,113 5.6 (3)	18,380 2.6 (-)	Rep. 3.4 (-)
Lower Saxony May 13, 1990	4,216,296	1,771,974 42.0 (67)	1,865,267 44.2 (71)	252,615 6.0 (9)	229,846 5.5 (8)	Rep. 1.5 (-)
North Rhine- Westphalia May 13, 1990	9,291,975	3,410,045 36.7 (89)	4,644,341 50.0 (122)	535,655 5.8 (14)	469,098 5.0 (12)	Rep. 1.8 (-)
Bavaria October 14, 1990	5,549,456	3,046,757 54.9 (127)	1,441,004 26.0 (58)	286,669 5.2 (7)	356,051 6.4 (12)	Rep. 4.9 (-)
Totals	33,061,493	14,241,104 43.1	13,564,810 41.0	1,991,145 6.0	2,050,282 6.2	1,214,152 3.7 [b]

a The constitutional crisis in Schleswig-Holstein caused by the "Barschel Affair" made necessary a re-run of the September 13, 1987 *Land* election. See page 311 and footnote 23 on page 159. Results of the September 13, 1987 election are noted below.

b Within this total are 739,208 (2.2 percent) votes for the right-extremist parties, the Republicans, NPD and DVU and 26,001 for the KPD/PDS.

Land and Date	Valid Votes	CDU	SPD	FDP	Greens	SSW	Others
Schleswig- Holstein September 13, 1987	1,550,036 76.6%	660,484 42.6 (33)	701,124 45.2 (36)	81,113 5.2 (4)	60,408 3.9 (0)	23,316 1.5 (1)	23,591 1.5 (0)

city-state, which is treated as a separate unit in figuring the distribution of seats, right-extremist parties could seat delegates in no other West German state. (The Republicans did poll 90,222 votes in the 1989 election in West Berlin to gain eleven deputies in the city parliament, but, at the time, the divided city was not included in nationwide totals.) Right-extremist parties did, however, triple their following over the previous series of *Land* elections to gain 2.2 percent of the national vote, the largest total registered since the 1965-1969 period. The Republicans with 269,308 (4.9 percent) votes in Bavaria and 171,867 (1.8 percent) votes in North Rhine-Westphalia accounted for most of that gain.

With the recovery of the FDP coupled with gains by the Greens, a four-party system emerged in seven of the ten states, the only exceptions being the Saar where the Greens failed to gain representation, leaving just three factions in the *Landtag*, Schleswig-Holstein where neither the FDP nor the Greens qualified for seats, but where the SSW was the third party and Bremen, where, in addition to the four nationally-represented groupings, the DVU held a single seat. This series of *Land* elections marked the last period in which the combined CDU/CSU/SPD/FDP vote exceeded ninety percent, as the Greens, the rightist parties, the PDS in the eastern provinces and a number of splinter groupings such as the German Communist Party, Familie and the Bavarian Party pulled that proportion down below ninety percent in elections held after reunification.

TABLE 6.14

THE TWELFTH SERIES OF *LAND* ELECTIONS AND 1990 *BUNDESTAG* ELECTION [26]

Party	1987-1990 *Land* Elections		December 2, 1990 *Bundestag* Election		Seats
CDU/CSU	14,241,104	43.1	20,358,096	43.8	319
SPD	13,564,810	41.0	15,545,366	33.5	239
FDP	1,991,145	6.0	5,123,233	11.0	79
Greens	2,050,282	6.2	1,788,200	3.8	(-)
KPD/PDS[a]	26,001	0.1	1,129,578	2.4 [a]	17
Rep./NPD/DVU	739,208	2.2			
Others	448,943	1.4	2,511,299 [b]	5.4	8[b]
Totals	33,061,493		46,455,772		662

a KPD totals for *Land* elections only. In 1990 the 5% clause applied separately to East and West.

b In this total are 559,207 votes and eight seats for the *Bündnis 90* in the eastern states.

Endnotes to Chapter VI

1 Founded in 1977 as the GLU (the Green List), the new association pushed for environmental protection, including the elimination of nuclear power plants as a source of energy generation in Germany. For an interesting discussion of the rise of the Greens, particularly on the local level, refer to Thomas Scharf, *The German Greens* (Berg Publishers Limited, 1994).

2 The SPD/Greens alliance in Hesse was followed by a working arrangement between the two parties in West Berlin from January 1989 until shortly before the 1990 *Bundestag* vote.

3 After a two-year absence from any ministry, the Greens were brought into a coalition with the SPD in Bremen in June 2007 and with the CDU in Hamburg in May 2008 following an extended period of negotiations. The Hamburg partnership was the first between the CDU and Greens on the regional level. A second case of cooperation between CDU and Greens factions occurred in the Saar following the inconclusive balloting in the August 30, 2009 *Land* election. The combination between CDU, FDP, and Green factions which was hammered out was also a first of its kind on the regional level. Christian Democrat Peter Müller continued as Minister President under the new partnership. Beginning in July 2010 the Greens participated in a minority government with the Socialists in North Rhine-Westphalia and in 2011 in an SPD-led coalition in Rhineland-Palatinate and Baden-Württemberg where they provided the first Green Minister-President.

4 The setback of the CDU in North Rhine-Westphalia, Germany's most populous state, on July 10, 1966 in an election in which the Socialists came within two seats of a majority helped to trigger the collapse of the Erhard Chancellorship. The SPD victory was seen as a protest against the economic policies of the Erhard administration which hurt the Ruhr industries.

5 The Free Democrat faction in the *Bundestag* signaled a readiness to support a coalition with the SPD, with Willy Brandt as Chancellor, but the Socialists decided on a grand coalition because of the need for a larger majority to attack the major problems facing the country.

6 Following the defection of Franz Florien Winter, chairman of the party's Bavarian organization, over the party's godlessness, the party was again shaken in March 1967 when national party chairman Thielen summarily expelled his deputy Adolf von Thadden, party propaganda chief Otto Hess and six other party functionaries from the party. A shocked central committee requested Thielen to resign for "stabbing the party in the back." Thielen refused to step down and was himself suspended as party chairman. Von Thadden and seven other expelled party functionaries were reinstated and Wilhelm Gutman, state chairman of Baden-Württemberg, was made chairman to replace Thielen (*Der Spiegel*, March 13 and 20, 1967).

7 The table is based on election results provided by the various state statistical offices or taken from individual reports on the separate elections such as *Wahl zum Bayerischen Landtag am 20. November 1966, Bayerischen Statistischen Landesamt,* 1967.

8 The Republicans were founded in 1983 as a party "right of the middle." It first entered candidates in the 1986 Bavarian *Land* election in which it pulled 3.0 percent of

the vote. It had little success until the 1989 election in West Berlin in which it gained 7.5 percent of the vote and eleven seats, the first breakthrough for a right-extremist group since 1968.

9 The table is based on data taken from *Wahlhandbuch für die Bundesrepublik Deutschland*, Claus A. Fischer (Hrsg), 1990.

10 The SPD's successes were strongly influenced by Chancellor Brandt's *"Ostpolitik"* in which he recognized the existence of a "Second Germany." "Even when two states exist, they are still for one another." A treaty signed in December 1972 recognized this in law.

11 The table is based on election results provided by the various state statistical offices or taken from individual reports on the separate elections such as *Die Wahl zum Niedersächsischen Landtag am 14. Juni 1970, Niedersächsisches Landesverwahltungsamt - Statistik, 1970.*

12 The table is based on data taken from *Wahlhandbuch für die Bundesrepublik Deutschland*, Claus A. Fischer (Hrsg), 1990.

13 The table is based on election results provided by the various state statistical offices or taken from individual reports on the separate elections in the various states.

14 In spite of the CDU's ability to outpoll the SPD in Hesse 47.3 to 43.2 percent, in Lower Saxony 48.8 to 43.1 percent and in North Rhine-Westphalia 47.1 to 45.1 percent, the Socialists, nevertheless, were able to maintain control of the administration of the three states by virtue of their coalitions with the Free Democrats.

15 The table is based on data taken from *Wahlhandbuch für die Bundesrepublik Deutschland*, Claus A. Fischer (Hrsg), 1990.

16 The table is based on election results provided by the various state statistical offices or taken from individual reports on the separate elections in the various states, such as *Wahl zur Bürgerschaft und zu den Bezirksversammlungen am 4. Juni 1978, Statistischen Landesamt der Freien and Hansastadt Hamburg, 1979.*

17 The table is based on data taken from *Wahlhandbuch für die Bundesrepublik Deutchland*, Claus A. Fischer (Hrsg), 1990.

18 In the 1953 *Bürgerschaft* election in Hamburg the CDU had combined with the FDP, DP and Refugee Party to defeat the Socialist government of Max Brauer. The combination, known as the Hamburg Block, succeeded in gaining 50.0 percent of the vote and a majority of seats. The total of CDU support within the combination probably did not exceed 35 percent (*Hamburg Abendblatt Chronik*, 1981: 583).

19 The table is based on election results provided by the various state statistical offices or taken from individual reports on the separate elections in the various states.

20 The table is based on data taken from *Wahlhandbuch für die Bundesrepublik Deutschland*, Claus A. Fischer (Hrsg), 1990.

21 The table is based on election results provided by the various state statistical offices or taken from individual reports on the separate elections in the various states.

22 The table is based on data taken from *Wahlhandbuch für die Bundesrepublik Deutschland*, Carl A. Fischer (Hrsg), 1990.

23 Two elections were held in Schleswig-Holstein during the twelfth series of *Land* elections, September 13, 1987 and May 8, 1988. The first contest gave the SPD a small advantage, 45.2 to 42.6 percent, but the CDU was able to form a ministry with the Free Democrats without a stable majority. However, as a result of the constitutional crisis caused by the Barschel Affair involving political spying and breaching the confidentiality of tax returns new elections were held in May 1988. Reacting to the scandal, voters gave the SPD a resounding victory with 54.8 percent of the vote to the CDU's 33.3 percent.

24 The Socialists took control of Schleswig-Holstein following their victory in May 1988 and of Lower Saxony following the election of May 13, 1990. Bremen, Hamburg, North Rhine-Westphalia and the Saar were already in their column and Berlin was added in June 1990.

25 The table is based on election results provided by the various state statistical offices or taken from individual reports on the separate elections such as *Zwölfte Landtagswahl in Bayern am 14. Oktober 1990, Bayerischen Landesamt für Statistik und Datenverarbeitung*, 1990.

26 The table is based on *Der Bundeswahlleiter, Results of the Election to the 12th German Bundestag am 2. Dezember 1990.*

CHAPTER VII

State and National Elections from Reunification to the Present

The 1990 *Bundestag* Election

The unification of the territory of what was formerly the German Democratic Republic (DDR) with the ten western states of the *Bundesrepublik* in 1990 opened a new chapter in German politics, necessitating not only the framing of new constitutions and introduction of democratic institutions in the five new provinces, but the integration of a people which had known only totalitarian rule for 57 years into a non-authoritarian framework. Thuringia was the first of the new states to draft a constitution, but it had to be withdrawn as being irreconcilable with the Basic Law. (A replacement was formulated and approved by popular referendum the same day as the 1994 *Landtag* election.) In all other eastern provinces, constitutions were drawn up and approved by the state's respective parliaments, without going to the people.[1]

The *Bundestag* election of December 2, 1990 was the first national poll to include the eastern provinces of Germany. The expansion of the electorate by over twelve million new voters and the addition of 138 seats to the federal parliament, raising the count to 662, posed a major challenge to the western parties which hoped to win the affection of a people who had lived under two dictatorial regimes for over five decades. Would these newly enfranchised Germans give the majority of their support to the western democratic parties or to the successor of the former Communist Socialist Unity Party (SED), the Party of Democratic Socialism (PDS)? Instead of ten states, there were now sixteen, with Brandenburg, Mecklenburg-Vorpommern, Saxony, Saxony-Anhalt, Thuringia and a united Berlin added to the election equation. The outcomes of elections in the East would not only change the party composition of the *Bundestag*, but, through democratically-elected governments in the *Länder*, also that of the *Bundesrat*, now expanded to 69 members.

The SPD selected Oskar Lafontaine, former Lord Mayor of Saarbrücken and minister president of the Saar since 1985, as its candidate to run against Christian Democrat Helmut Kohl who was seeking his third mandate as federal Chancellor. In this first all-German election the western parties fought hard for eastern voter support. In the end, the CDU/CSU, riding on the euphoria of reunification, was able to win the largest share of the new voters in the east to

TABLE 7.1

**RESULTS OF THE *BUNDESTAG* ELECTION OF
DECEMBER 2, 1990** [2]

Party	Valid Second Choice Votes	Percentage	*Bundestag* Seats
Total	46,455,772	100.0	662
SPD	15,545,366	33.5	239
CDU	17,055,116	36.7	} 319
CSU	3,302,980	7.1	
Greens	1,788,200	3.8	0
B90/Gr	559,207	1.2 [a]	8
FDP	5,123,233	11.0	79
PDS	1,129,578	2.4 [a]	17
Others	1,952,092	4.2	0

a Both the *Bündnis* 90 and PDS obtained seats in the 12th *Bundestag* by virtue of the eastern and western provinces being considered as separate districts for the application of the five percent restriction on representation. Although the PDS received only 2.4 percent of the vote nationwide, its total in the eastern provinces was 9.9 percent. *Bündnis* 90/Greens competed only in the eastern provinces and exceeded the five percent barrier in that section of the country.

emerge as the leading party in all five eastern provinces and nationwide with 43.8 percent of the vote to the Social Democrat's 33.5 percent, in spite of the entry of a new force of the left into the political arena. For this first election in a united Germany, the west and east were divided into two separate districts for the application of the five percent restriction on representation, enabling the PDS with only 2.4 percent of the national poll, but with 9.9 percent of ballots in the eastern provinces, to place seventeen delegates in the *Bundestag*. The PDS's poor showing of less than one percent in the west occurred in spite of its endeavor to distance itself from the central domination practices of the SED and to develop a democratic conception of socialism in the tradition of Marx and Engels and not of Stalin and the former East German leaders Walter Ulbricht and Erich Honecker. According to a party statement, "the Stalinist type of socialism is dead, but not socialism as an alternative to capitalism" (*First all German Election*, **Inter Nationes**, 1990: 45). The SPD secured less of a following in the east than hoped for and suffered a 3.5 percentage loss over its 1987 *Bundestag* showing. The Greens, who had received 8.3 percent of ballots cast in

1987, suffered a stunning setback in the new environment to lose their *Bundestag* representation and to have their environmental interests represented in Bonn only by virtue of the ability of their counterpart in the eastern provinces, *Bündnis* 90/Gr, to secure eight seats.[3]

The singular winner in the election was the FDP which boosted its national following from 9.1 percent in 1987 to 11.0 percent, making gains in every state except the Saar and polling 12.9 percent of the eastern vote. As in *Land* elections held between 1987 and 1990, rightist parties nearly quadrupled their share of the national vote, but their combined total of only 2.4 percent fell far short of qualifying any of them for representation. The Republicans were able to compete in the eastern provinces by virtue of a ruling handed down by East Germany's supreme court which negated a *Volkskammer* resolution banning the party (*First All German Election*, **Inter Nationes,** 1990: 45). With the Socialist total falling far below forty percent, a CDU/FDP ministry under Helmut Kohl was the only possible combination for a stable government outside of a grand coalition of the two major parties. Chancellor Helmut Kohl, for his important role in bringing about the reunification of the two parts of Germany, has become known as the "Reunification Chancellor."

The 1990-1994 *Land* Elections

Elections were held in fourteen of the now sixteen German states between the 1990 and 1994 federal polls. The only exceptions were North Rhine Westphalia and the Saar which had five-year legislative cycles. Five of the first *Landtag* elections of this period took place October 14, 1990 in the eastern provinces of Brandenburg, Mecklenburg-Vorpommern, Saxony, Saxony-Anhalt and Thuringia, seven weeks prior to the *Bundestag* balloting, but, for comparative purposes are included as part of the 13th series of regional contests. A sixth election in the east was held December 2, 1990 (the same day as the *Bundestag* election) in a unified Berlin, the first democratic balloting to take place there since 1946 which included the entire city. The CDU, with 42.9 percent of the eastern vote, emerged as the leading party in five of the six new states, conceding only Brandenburg to the Socialists who won a disappointing 26.3 percent of eastern region ballots. (Only in Saxony did a single party, the CDU, gain an absolute majority of seats). In spite of the region's Communist past, the PDS, successor to the once powerful SED which ruled the area while under Soviet occupation, competing in democratic elections for the first time, polled only 11.1 percent of the region-wide vote and was neither the leading nor second party in any of the states, even falling behind the FDP in Saxony-Anhalt, where the Free Democrats had their best showing at 13.5 percent. While polling far less than the hoped-for 25 percent, the PDS, nevertheless, gained representation in all six eastern provinces. This was to be the party's worst showing in any series of *Land* contests, as continued high unemployment and feelings on the part of former DDR citizens of being second class citizens enlarged the ranks of its supporters, pushing its vote total in the east from a little over one million in the 1990-1994 regional contests to nearly two million in the *Land* elections which took place between the 1998 and 2002 *Bundestag* elections. By 2004 it was able to outpoll the SPD in Thuringia and Saxony and the CDU in Brandenburg, and, with 23.7 percent of the eastern vote, to replace the SPD as that area's second party behind the CDU. In the elections held between 2006 and 2009, the SPD was able to recover its status as second party in the east by gaining 23.2 percent of ballots cast to the PDS/*Die Linke's* 21.5 percent.

Encouraging was the limited support given to right-extremist groups, in contrast to the west where they gained their largest following since the 1965-69 series of *Land* contests. But this too would change in future elections in the eastern provinces, as the same conditions and feelings which nourished a strong leftist vote also caused the right-extremist vote to surge in later election contests. With 83.6 percent of the vote, this was the high mark for the four western parties in the east. The Free Democrats gained seats in all six state parliaments with 7.6 percent of the regional vote, while "Green" groupings, competing under different labels, won seats in all of the eastern states with the single exception of Mecklenburg-Vorpommern with 6.8 percent of ballots cast. These were high points for both the Free Democrats and the Greens in the east until the fifth series of regional elections (2006-2009) when the Free Democrats polled 8.2 percent of the regional total and the Greens duplicated their earlier 6.8 percent share. Five parties were represented in all of the eastern *Land* parliaments with the exception of Mecklenburg-Vorpommern where, with the absence of the Greens, four were present.

Suspicious of the democratic process or, at least, unaccustomed to it, voters in the east turned out in far fewer numbers than in the western provinces, except for Berlin where two-thirds of the voters had experienced democratic elections since 1946.

The first election to be held in the western part of Germany following the 1990 *Bundestag* decision took place January 20, 1991 in Hesse where the CDU suffered a minor loss of support, but sufficient to enable the SPD to replace it as the state's leading party, 40.8 to 40.2 percent, and to take over the reigns of government in coalition with the Greens, supplanting the earlier CDU/FDP combination. The PDS, still a regional party, made no attempt to contest this first regional election in the west since reunification. (Note that for comparative purposes the Bavarian election of October 14, 1990 was included in the previous series of regional contests. The PDS did not enter candidates in that election either.) Both the FDP and Greens won seats while polling slightly fewer votes than in 1987. Nine weeks later the CDU suffered a major setback in Rhineland-Palatinate, the state once governed by federal chancellor Kohl, as the SPD with 44.8 percent of the vote to the CDU's 38.7 percent became the leading party in Mainz for the first time since 1947. Both the FDP and Greens gained representation in the *Landtag*, but in contrast to Hesse, the Socialists chose to form a government with the Free Democrats rather than with the Greens.

TABLE 7.2

THE FIRST *LAND* ELECTIONS IN THE EASTERN PROVINCES [4]

Land and Date	Valid Votes	CDU	SPD	FDP	Greens	PDS	Others
Brandenburg Oct. 14, 1990	1,273,906 67.1	374,572 29.4 (27)	487,134 38.2 (36)	84,501 6.6 (6)	117,963 6.4 (6)	170,804 13.4 (13)	Rep 1.1 (-)
Mecklenburg-Vorpommern Oct. 14, 1990	895,999 64.7	343,447 38.3 (29)	242,147 27.0 (21)	49,104 5.5 (4)	37,336 2.2 (-)	140,397 15.7 (12)	Rep 1.0 (-)
Saxony Oct. 14, 1990	2,633,422 72.8	1,417,332 53.8 (92)	502,722 19.1 (32)	138,376 5.3 (9)	147,543 [a] 5.6 (10)	269,420 10.2 (17)	
Saxony-Anhalt Oct. 14, 1990	1,412,512 65.1	550,815 39.0 (48)	367,254 26.0 (27)	190,800 13.5 (14)	74,696 5.3 (5)	169,319 12.0 (12)	Rep 0.6
Thuringia Oct. 14, 1990	1,398,777 71.7	634,769 45.4 (44)	318,490 22.9 (21)	129,543 9.3 (9)	90,643 6.5 (6)	136,099 9.7 (9)	Rep 0.8
Berlin Dec. 2, 1990	2,019,198 80.8	815,382 40.9(101)	614,075 30.4 (76)	143,080 7.1 (18)	188,730 [b] 9.3 (23)	184,820 9.2 (23)	Rep 3.1 (-)
Totals	9,633,814	4,136,315 42.9	2,531,822 26.3	735,404 7.6	656,911 6.8	1,070,859 11.1	502,503 5.2 (-)

a Represents the vote in Saxony of a list combination of the *Neues Forum* and *Bündnis 90.*

b In 1990 the Greens and *Bündnis 90/*Gr competed separately in Berlin with the Greens receiving 100,839 votes and 12 seats, the *Bündnis/*Gr 87,891 votes and 11 seats.

The CDU suffered yet another setback in Hamburg June 2, 1991, as the SPD won an absolute majority of seats with 48.0 percent of ballots cast. The CDU's 35.1 percent was its worst showing in Hamburg since 1970, causing its mayoral candidate to resign (*Hamburger Abendblatt Chronicle;* 1998: 606). Both the FDP and Greens obtained representation, and because of the SPD's narrow margin in the *Bürgerschaft,* Lord Mayor Voscherau made a coalition offer to the FDP, which decided not to participate because of its poor showing. The CDU ended its losing streak with major gains in the Bremen election of September 29, 1991 to break the SPD's majority in the city parliament. But, with 38.8 percent to the Christian Democrat's 30.7 percent, the Socialists remained the city's leading party and formed a "traffic light" coalition with the FDP and Greens. In addition to the Free Democrats and Greens the right-extremist DVU, which had won a single seat in the Bremen *Bürgerschaft* in 1987, was able this time to gain six seats with 6.2 percent of the vote. The next two *Land* elections were held April 5, 1992 in Baden-Württemberg and Schleswig-Holstein. The CDU suffered a major setback in the Southwest state to lose its parliamentary majority for the first time in twenty years, as much of conservative support swung to the right-extremist Republican Party which, with

10.9 percent of the vote, sent sixteen delegates to the state parliament. (The Republicans had contested the elections in Hesse, Rhineland-Palatinate and Hamburg, as well as those in the eastern provinces with the exception of Saxony, but were unable to exceed the five percent barrier to representation in any of those states. Its initial success had come in Berlin in the 1989 election when it won 7.5 percent of the vote and eleven seats in the then divided city). The CDU, however, remained the largest party in the *Landtag* as the SPD also lost ground and formed a coalition with the Socialists, since the eight seats won by the FDP were insufficient to provide a working majority. In Schleswig-Holstein that same day the CDU made minor gains, but was unable to prevent the SPD from gaining an absolute majority of seats for a second time in a row, albeit by a narrower margin. A major surprise in the election was the ability of the German People's Union (DVU) to duplicate its Bremen success by winning six seats with 6.3 percent of the vote. While both the FDP and SSW gained seats, the Greens failed for the fifth consecutive time to exceed the five percent threshold for representation in the state.

The September 19, 1993 election in Hamburg, nearly two years prior to the end of the legislative term, was a result of a suit brought by Marcus Wegner, a former CDU rebel, challenging the fairness of the CDU's inner-party nomination process prior to the 1991 *Bürgerschaft* election. The Hamburg Constitutional Court upheld Wegner's claim in a decision rendered May 4, 1993, ruling the 1991 election invalid because the CDU, contrary to inner-party democracy, nominated an insufficient number of candidates (*Hamburgische Justizverwaltungsblatt*, 1992-1993 *Jahrgang*: 56-78). Shortly after the decision Herr Wegner founded a new grouping, the STATT Party, to contest the September election. In the balloting both the CDU and SPD suffered substantial losses, registering their lowest totals since the first elections were held in 1946, and the FDP lost its representation in the *Bürgerschaft*, as the voters revolted against the three established parties and gave the Greens 13.5 percent of the vote, double their 1991 total, and 13.2 percent to three protest groupings, Wegner's STATT Party, the right-wing Republicans and DVU. Of these, however, only the STATT Party, with 5.6 percent of ballots cast, qualified for seats in the legislature. Although their vote totals were insufficient to secure seats in the city parliament, the Republicans and DVU succeeded in electing representatives to three of the district assemblies into which Hamburg is divided (*Hamburger Abendblatt*, September 20, 1993). Having lost its majority by a wide margin the SPD attempted to broker a coalition with the Greens, but ultimately turned to the STATT Party as coalition partner when negotiations with the Greens broke down.

The last two elections to be held prior to the 1994 *Bundestag* balloting took place in Lower Saxony on March 13, 1994 and Bavaria September 25, 1994. In Lower Saxony the CDU again lost ground while the Socialists, with a small gain, won an absolute majority of seats in the state parliament. The Greens with 7.4 percent of the vote were the only other grouping to gain representation, as both the Free Democrats and Republicans failed to exceed the five percent hurdle. In Bavaria the CSU experienced a small percentage loss, but continued to win an absolute majority of both votes and legislative seats. The Socialists made significant gains, but their total of 30.1 percent fell far short of the CSU's 52.8 percent. With 6.1 percent of the vote the Greens were the only other party to qualify for representation, as the FDP following fell to 2.8 percent. While the right-extremist Republicans outpolled the Free Democrats by over 60,000 votes, their 3.9 percent share was also insufficient for representation.

Although the CDU/CSU lost ground in six of the eight western states in which regional elections were held, it remained the leading party in the west and, coupled with its strong showing in the eastern provinces, remained the leading party nationwide with 42.1 percent of the vote, winning absolute majorities in Bavaria and Saxony and emerging as the leading party in five other states. While the SPD lost ground in four of the eight western provinces and won fewer votes nationwide than the CDU/CSU with 33.9 percent of the total, it held absolute majorities in five states and was the leading party in four more. After losing control of the *Bundesrat* for a short period following the elections of October 14, 1990 in the east, the Socialists regained control as the CDU stumbled in Hesse, Rhineland-Palatinate and Lower Saxony. The FDP, with 5.9 percent of the national vote ended the period with representation in every *Land* with the exceptions of Bavaria, Hamburg and Lower Saxony while the Greens, recovering from their dismal *Bundestag* showing with 7.3 percent of ballots cast, was represented in every *Landtag* with the exceptions of Mecklenburg-Vorpommern, the Saar, and Schleswig-Holstein. The PDS, which secured over one million votes, was represented in all six eastern provinces, but in none of the western states. Right-extremist parties polled the largest number of votes since the 1965-69 period when the NPD sent shock waves through the West German political system by gaining representation in seven of the ten western states, only to fade in the following series of *Land* elections. Although the Republicans obtained over one million votes, 539,014 of them in Baden-Württemberg, it secured representation only in that one state, while the DVU, with far fewer votes, won seats in two states, Bremen and Schleswig-Holstein. In none of these states were the rightist parties significant players. The only other minor party to gain representation, the STATT Party, is difficult to categorize except that it originated out of an internal opposition group within the CDU, what former Hamburg Lord Mayor Ole von Beust called "an illegitimate child of the Hamburg CDU" (*Zeitschrift für Parlaments-fragen, Jahrgang* 2002-2003: 45). The party, attempting to gain a national following as a protest against the established party system, entered candidates in the March 13, 1994 election in Lower Saxony, the June 26, 1994 contest in Saxony-Anhalt, the October 16, 1994 elections in the Saar and Thuringia and in the competition for *Bundestag* seats, but failed to gain representation in any of those states or in the federal parliament. Wegner's authoritarian leadership style led in November 1994 to his dismissal as chair of the Hamburg faction of the party and he left the party in August 1995. The grouping foundered during the 1993-97 legislative session over internal conflicts, and in the 1997 city council election it was repudiated

TABLE 7.3

THE 1991-1994 *LAND* ELECTIONS IN THE WESTERN PROVINCES [5]

Land and Date	Valid Votes	CDU/CSU	SPD	FDP	Greens	Rep.	Others
Hesse Jan. 20, 1991	2,974,872 70.8%	1,195,965 40.2 (46)	1,214,909 40.8 (46)	220,115 7.4 (8)	262,161 8.8 (10)	49,320 1.7 (0)	
Rhineland-Palatinate April 21, 1991	2,125,407 73.9%	822,449 38.7 (40)	951,695 44.8 (47)	146,400 6.9 (7)	137,139 6.5 (7)	43,480 2.0 (0)	
Hamburg [a] June 2, 1991	819,773 66.1%	287,467 35.1 (44)	393,414 48.0 (61)	44,460 5.4 (7)	59,262 7.2 (9)	9,959 1.2 (0)	PDS 0.5
Bremen Sept. 29, 1991	370,148 72.2%	113,512 30.7 (32)	143,576 38.8 (41)	35,087 9.5 (10)	42,096 11.4 (11)	5,594 0.9 (0)	DVU 6.2 (6)
Baden-Württemberg April 5, 1992	4,949,199 70.1%	1,960,018 39.6 (64)	1,454,477 29.4 (46)	291,199 5.9 (8)	467,781 9.5 (13)	539,014 10.9 (15)	NPD 0.9
Schleswig-Holstein April 5, 1992	1,487,909 71.7%	503,510 33.8 (32)	687,427 46.2 (45)	82,953 5.6 (5)	74,014 4.97 (0)	18,225 1.2 (0)	DVU 6.3 (6) SSW (1) [b]
Hamburg Sept. 19, 1993	844,902 69.6%	212,186 25.1 (36)	341,688 40.4 (58)	35,236 4.2 (0)	114,263 13.5 (19)	40,856 4.8 (0)	STATT Party 5.6 (8) [a]
Lower Saxony March 13, 1994	4,250,584 73.8%	1,548,231 36.4 (67)	1,881,283 44.3 (81)	188,826 4.4 (0)	314,438 7.4 (13)	158,875 3.7 (0)	STATT Party 1.3 (0)
Bavaria Sept. 25, 1994	5,834,941 67.8%	3,081,944 52.8 (120)	1,753,310 30.1 (70)	163,653 2.8 (0)	356,866 6.1 (14)	227,085 3.9 (0)	
Totals [a]	22,812,833	9,513,098 41.7	8,480,091 37.2	1,172,693 5.1	1,713,757 7.5	1,051,552 4.6	881,642 3.9
Fourteen State Totals [c]	32,440,647	13,649,413 42.1	11,011,913 33.9	1,908,497 5.9	2,370,668 7.3	1,156,528 3.6	2,343,628 7.2

a The totals above include the 1991 election in Hamburg rather than the 1993 rerun.

b The Danish minority party SSW received one seat with 28,245 votes (1.9 percent) only because of its exemption from the five percent barrier.

c The "Others" total includes 1,055,259 (3.3%) votes for the PDS.

when the voters gave it only 3.8 percent of the vote. What protest vote was left in the *Hansastadt* was expressed four years later when the Schill Party, riding on a law and order platform, won 19.4 percent of the vote to place 25 deputies in the Hamburg parliament.

The entrance of several new players into the political arena after 1990 further complicated ministry building in those states where no majority party was present. But in the eight states requiring coalitions, governments were formed involving only the four western democratic parties with the single exception of Hamburg where the SPD coalesced with the STATT Party. At the end of the thirteenth series of *Land* elections a three party system existed in three western states, Bavaria, Lower Saxony and the Saar, while four parties were represented in six states and five parties in the remaining seven. During this series of *Land* elections the proportion of the vote falling to the CDU/CSU, SPD and FDP fell below ninety percent for the first time in over three decades.

The 1994 *Bundestag* Election

Dr. Helmut Kohl was again the chancellor candidate for the CDU/CSU in the 1994 *Bundestag* election, matching the four candidacies of Dr. Konrad Adenauer who led the party's ticket in 1949, 1953, 1957 and 1961 before stepping down in the middle of his term in 1963 in favor of Dr. Ludwig Erhard. The Socialists, having been in the opposition since 1982 when the withdrawal of the FDP brought about the collapse of the red-yellow coalition in Bonn, challenged Kohl with the Minister President of Rhineland-Palatinate, Rudolf Scharping. The party had been split between several equally strong contenders, including Rudolf Scharping, Johannes Rau, Minister President of North Rhine-Westphalia, and Oskar Lafontaine who had been the party's candidate in 1990, possibly weakening its appeal, since no grouping within the party could be completely satisfied no matter who was selected. (The designated SPD Chancellor candidate Björn Engholm, Minister President of Schleswig-Holstein, had resigned his position as national party chairman and Chancellor candidate,

TABLE 7.4

RESULTS OF THE *BUNDESTAG* ELECTION OF OCTOBER 16, 1994 [6]

Party	Valid Second Choice Votes	Percentage	*Bundestag* Seats
SPD	17,140,354	36.4	252
CDU	16,089,960	34.2	} 294
CSU	3,427,196	7.3	
Greens	3,424,315	7.3	49
FDP	3,258,407	6.9	47
PDS	2,066,176	4.4	30
REP	875,239	1.9	0
STATT Party	63,354	0.1	0
Others	760,173	1.6	0
Total	47,105,174	100.0	672

along with his premiership, in May 1993 upon disclosures that he had pre-knowledge of the spying that led to the Barschel scandal, leaving the SPD candidacy wide open). In the early stages of the campaign Scharping was ahead of Kohl in voter sentiment, but as the German economy improved the Chancellor slowly caught up and overtook his challenger.[7] Although the SPD bettered its 1990 following by nearly three percentage points to 36.4 percent, the CDU/CSU gained a 41.5 percent share of ballots cast to remain the country's largest party and was again able to form a majority with its coalition partner since 1982, the FDP, which lost over a third of its 1990 *Bundestag* following, but, with 6.9 percent of the vote, could still play a balancing role. Even though the Greens outpolled the Free Democrats in a strong recovery from their 1990 setback, their total of 7.3 percent was insufficient to provide a majority in combination with the Socialists and neither would an SPD/FDP grouping have produced a working majority.[8] The PDS, still a purely regional party, received 19.8 percent of the eastern vote, but only 0.8 percent of the western total for a national aggregate of 4.4 percent. Still benefiting from the two district arrangement, it was able to place thirty deputies from the eastern states in the *Bundestag*. Rightist parties, which had had considerable success in regional elections, were able to poll only 1.9 percent of the national vote, with the Republicans' total of 875,239 votes also falling behind 1990-1994 regional numbers.[9]

The 1994-1998 *Land* Elections

The first of the second series of *Land* elections to be held in the eastern provinces of Germany took place June 26, 1994 in Saxony-Anhalt, followed by balloting September 11, 1994 in Brandenburg and Saxony, October 16, 1994 in Mecklenburg-Vorpommern and Thuringia and October 10, 1995 in Berlin. (Although the first three of these contests were held prior to the federal election of October 16, 1994, they are, for comparative purposes, included in this series of *Land* elections while the Bavarian election of September 25, 1994 was counted in the previous series). In Saxony-Anhalt, the CDU following fell from 39.0 to 34.4 percent, enabling the SPD, with a gain from 26.0 to 34.0 percent to come within 4,000 votes and one seat of equaling its position. While the Greens succeeded in defending their five member legislative faction, the FDP, the CDU's coalition partner from 1990 to 1994, lost over three-quarters of its earlier following to be eliminated from the state parliament, causing the CDU/FDP coalition under Christoph Bergner to be replaced by an SPD/*Bündnis* 90/Greens minority ministry under Socialist Reinhard Höppner which governed under a toleration agreement with the PDS, strengthened by a surge in its following from 12.0 to 19.9 percent.

In Brandenburg the SPD enhanced its leading position by winning an absolute majority of votes and seats as CDU support fell to 18.7 percent, only 72 votes ahead of the PDS whose total increased from 13.4 percent in 1990 to an equal 18.7 percent. Neither the FDP nor the Greens qualified for representation. In Saxony, the CDU fared better, winning an absolute majority of the votes for the second time in a row, while the PDS following rose from 10.2 to 16.5 percent of ballots cast to nearly replace the SPD, which gained 16.6 percent, as the state's second party. Neither the New Forum which had polled 147,543 votes and gained ten seats in 1990 nor its environmental counterpart, the Greens, was able to win legislative seats. The FDP was also eliminated from the legislature following a loss of over 100,000 votes from its 1990 total. In Mecklenburg-Vorpommern both CDU and SPD basically repeated their 1990 results with the CDU remaining the state's leading party with 37.7 percent to the Socialist's 29.5 percent. Neither the FDP nor the Greens qualified for seats, but the PDS continued to gain ground with a fifty percent increase over its 1990 following to 22.7 percent. Without a majority, and, in the absence of the Free Democrats from the *Landtag*, the CDU formed a grand coalition with the SPD as the only alternative to an undesirable linkup with the leftist PDS. In Thuringia the CDU total dropped from 45.4 to 42.6 percent, but it remained the state's leading party as the Socialists could gain only 29.8 percent of ballots cast. Again, the FDP and Greens failed to exceed the five percent barrier for representation, while the PDS, reflecting continued discontentment among East Germans, nearly doubled its support to 16.6 percent. The failure of the Free Democrats to gain representation brought an end to the existing CDU/FDP coalition, necessitating a new party combination. The SPD undertook extended negotiations with the PDS to form a minority government with their tolerance as in Saxony-Anhalt, but when this strategy failed, the CDU formed a coalition with the Socialists as the only alternative to an objectionable alliance with the PDS. Dr. Bernhard Vogel (CDU) continued as Minister President under this arrangement.

The last election to be held in the eastern provinces during the fourteenth series of *Land* elections took place October 10, 1995, in Berlin, which was on a five-year legislative cycle. In that election all three of the old established parties of the west, the CDU, SPD and FDP, lost heavily while the Greens and PDS made substantial gains. However, the CDU remained the city's leading party by outpolling the SPD 37.4 to 23.6 percent while the FDP was eliminated from the city's parliament with a 2.5 percent total. In contrast, the Greens, with 13.2 percent of the vote, registered their best showing since first entering candidates in 1979, and the PDS improved its following from 9.2 percent in 1990 to 14.6 percent. In spite of setbacks by the two major parties, they continued the grand coalition which had been in existence since reunification in 1990.

In the eastern provinces the CDU again emerged as the leading party region-wide and in five of the six states, but with a smaller following than in 1990, having suffered setbacks in five of the elections. In contrast, the SPD improved its regional standing by registering gains in five of the six provinces to poll nearly thirty percent of the regional total, but remained the leading party only in Brandenburg. The FDP lost heavily by obtaining only a third of its 1990 vote total and lost representation in all six states. The Greens also witnessed a major decline in support to secure representation only in Berlin and Saxony-

Anhalt. The PDS was the big winner, making gains in all six eastern states to bring its regional total to 17.6 percent. While the Republicans entered candidates in all six eastern provinces, they received only 1.5 percent of the total regional vote and failed to obtain a single mandate. With the weakness of the Free Democrats and Greens, only three parties (CDU, SPD and PDS) were represented in the parliaments of Brandenburg, Mecklenburg-Vorpommern, Saxony and Thuringia, while four parties were represented in Berlin and Saxony-Anhalt where the Greens were the fourth party.

The first *Land* election in this series to be held in the western states took place in the Saar in conjunction with the 1994 *Bundestag* balloting. In that election the Socialists won an absolute majority of *Landtag* seats for the third time in a row in spite of a moderate drop in support. The CDU made gains from 33.4 to 38.6 percent, but remained far behind the SPD. The FDP continued its slide in public favor and lost its representation while the Greens became eligible for *Landtag* seats for the first time after four tries. In Hesse four months later the CDU, again running neck and neck with the Socialists, regained its position as the *Land's* leading party by experiencing a smaller loss than its major rival. The FDP, which had failed to qualify for legislative seats in seven successive *Land* elections, succeeded in maintaining its delegation in the Hessian *Landtag* by duplicating its 1991 support level of 7.4 percent. The Greens made major gains to place an additional three delegates in the state parliament. Although losing its leading faction status, the SPD was able to continue governing as a result of expanded Greens' support.

Elections were held May 14, 1995 in both North Rhine-Westphalia and Bremen. In Germany's most populous state the SPD suffered a minor setback to lose its majority status in the *Landtag*, but remained the state's leading party, as the CDU made only minor gains to 37.7 percent. The election's major winner was the Greens who, with 10.0 percent of the vote, doubled their legislative representation, while the FDP, whose total dropped to 4.0 percent lost its fourteen seats in the Düsseldorf parliament. The Socialists continued their hold on the state by forming a ministry with the strengthened Greens, a cooperation which became a test case for the coalition of the two on the national level in 1998. In Bremen the CDU came within 3,000 votes of replacing the SPD as the city's leading party to equal the Socialists' 37 seat count. The FDP continued its decline by failing to obtain five percent of the vote in either Bremen proper or in Bremerhaven, while the Greens added to their representation by winning 13.1 percent of the vote. Influencing the election outcome for the three older parties was the ability of a protest grouping, the AFB (*Arbeit für Bremen und Bremerhaven*), to siphon off 10.7 percent of the vote and gain twelve of the city's 100 delegates. But the entry of the AFB into the political arena also caused the right-extremist DVU, which had been recipient of the protest vote in earlier elections, to lose its representation, as its vote total fell from 6.2 percent in 1991 to 2.5 percent. The PDS, in an attempt to gain a following in the West, ran candidates in the Bremen election, but, with only 8,174 votes (2.37 percent),

TABLE 7.5

THE SECOND SERIES OF *LAND* ELECTIONS IN THE EASTERN PROVINCES [10]

Land and Date	Valid Votes	CDU	SPD	FDP	Greens	PDS	Others
Saxony-Anhalt	1,134,430	390,077	386,020	40,560	57,739	225,243	Rep. 1.4
June 26, 1994	54.9	34.4 (37)	34.0 (36)	3.6 (-)	5.1 (5)	19.9 (21)	STATT 0.3
Brandenburg	1,072,019	200,700	580,422	23,541	31,033	200,628	Rep. 1.1
Sept.11, 1994	56.3	18.7 (18)	54.1 (52)	2.2 (-)	2.9	18.7 (18)	
Saxony	2,063,926	1,200,052	342,695	36,062	85,497	339,576	Rep.
Sept. 11, 1994	58.4	58.1 (77)	16.6 (22)	1.7 (-)	4.1 (-)	16.5 (21)	Forum
Thuringia	1,425,247	606,797	421,247	45,814	64,183	236,466	Rep 1.3
Oct. 16, 1994	75.3	42.6 (42)	29.6 (29)	3.2 (-)	4.5 (-)	16.6 (17)	Forum
Mecklenburg-Vorpommern	977,867	368,206	288,431	37,498	36,035	221,814	Rep.1.0
Oct. 16, 1994	72.8	37.7 (30)	29.5 (23)	3.8 (-)	3.7 (-)	22.7 (18)	NPD 0.3
Berlin	1,669,186	625,005	393,245	45,391	219,990	244,196	Rep. 2.7
Oct. 10, 1995		37.4 (87)	23.6 (55)	2.5 (-)	13.2 (30)	14.6 (34)	
Totals	8,342,675	3,390,837	2,412,060	228,866	494,477	1,467,923	348,512
		40.6	28.9	2.7	5.9	17.6	4.2

failed to qualify for *Bürgerschaft* seats. The Socialists formed a grand coalition with the CDU, which continued through the 2007 election.

Elections were held March 24, 1996 in three states, Baden-Württemberg, Rhineland- Palatinate and Schleswig-Holstein. In Baden-Württemberg the CDU continued to dominate the balloting with 41.3 percent of the vote. The results for the Christian Democrats represented a small gain, while the Socialists experienced a significant decline to 25.1 percent, their worst showing since the formation of the Southwest state in 1952. The Free Democrats, competing in their traditional stronghold, won 9.6 percent of the vote to better their 1992 following and register their strongest showing in 28 years. This was only the second time in this series of regional contests that they were able to gain representation. The Greens also gained ground with 12.1 percent of the vote, recording their highest total in the state since first entering candidates in 1980. A disturbing development was the ability of the right-extremist Republicans to retain their delegation in the state parliament, in spite of polling over 100,000 fewer votes than in 1992. This outcome was in contrast to the NPD's inability to follow up on its 1966-68 successes in any state until 2004. The Christian Democrats' control over *Land* policies was continued through a coalition with the Free Democrats.

In Rhineland-Palatinate the SPD emerged as the leading party for only the second time since 1947 with 39.8 percent of the vote to the CDU's 38.7 percent. Both the FDP and Greens retained their representation on slightly better results over 1991. Although the Republicans campaigned heavily in Rhineland-Palatinate, with only 3.5 percent of ballots cast, they were unable to duplicate their success the same day in Baden-Württemberg. The Socialists continued their existing combination with the FDP under Kurt Beck (SPD), who had replaced Rudolf Scharping as that state's premier after the 1994 *Bundestag* balloting. In Schleswig-Holstein the SPD lost its majority in the *Landtag*, but remained the leading party even though the CDU improved its total by 3.4 percentage points to narrow the political gap. The FDP maintained its representation in the *Land* parliament to complete a day with three successes to give it a breather from the long string of setbacks which it had experienced. The right-wing DVU failed to duplicate its 1991 success and lost its six legislative seats. With a slightly stronger following, the party of the Danish minority was able to place two delegates in the Schleswig-Holstein parliament, the largest number since 1958. Having lost its majority in the *Landtag*, the SPD, following difficult negotiations, formed a ministry with the Greens, which entered the state parliament for the first time with 8.1 percent of ballots cast after five unsuccessful attempts.

It was not until eighteen months later that another regional contest was held. In that election in Hamburg, September 21, 1997, the Socialists experienced their worst showing since 1946, gaining only 36.2 percent of the vote, a setback which caused Lord Mayor Henning Voscherau to resign his position in favor of Ortwin Runde, who had been serving as Finance Senator. The SPD, nevertheless, outpolled the CDU to remain the city's leading party as the CDU was able to increase its following only from 25.1 to 30.7 percent. The FDP, with a 3.5 percent result, again failed to secure seats in the legislature, while the Greens registered their largest total (13.9 percent) since first entering candidates in the *Hansastadt* in 1978. The STATT Party which had fabricated a surprising entry into the political arena in 1993 and which had been a partner of the SPD in the Hamburg government for four years was eliminated from the *Bürgerschaft* when it received only 3.8 percent of the votes. There was fear that the right-extremist German People's Union, the DVU, would exceed the five percent barrier to representation, and its 4.977 percent of ballots cast came within 233 votes of gaining six seats (*Frankfurter Allgemeine Zeitung*, September 22,1997). The party did, however, qualify for representation in four of the seven district assemblies in Hamburg (*Zeitschrift für Parlamentsfragen, Jahrgang* 1998-2000: 47).

A poll taken after the election demonstrated strong public support for a grand coalition between the Socialists and the CDU over one with the Greens, but looking forward to the *Bundestag* election the next year, an alliance with the Greens was favored as a model for an SPD/Greens partnership in Bonn (*Frankfurter Algemeine Zeitung*, September 23, 1997).

The last three elections prior to the 1998 *Bundestag* balloting were held in Lower Saxony March 1, 1998, Saxony-Anhalt April 26, 1998 and Bavaria

September 13, 1998. In Lower Saxony, in a contest that was to determine the future of SPD leadership, the Socialists produced their best showing since the first *Landtag* election in 1947 to gain an absolute majority of seats in the state parliament. The election, which had become a referendum on Minister President Gerhard Schröder, catapulted him into the position of being the strongest candidate to lead the Socialists in the general election some six months later (*Frankfurter Allgemeine Zeitung*, March 3, 1998). Schröder, premier of Lower Saxony since 1990, was subsequently selected at the April meeting of the SPD to lead it as Chancellor-candidate against Helmut Kohl, who was seeking his fifth term in office.

Schröder took advantage of Chancellor Kohl's personal involvement in the campaign by claiming that the modest setback experienced by the CDU from 36.4 percent in 1994 to 35.9 percent in 1998 coupled with his party's gain indicated a strong wish by the voters for a change in Bonn after September 27, 1998 (*Hamburger Abendblatt*, March 2, 1998). Jürgen Tritten of the Greens, which managed to send twelve delegates to the *Landtag* in spite of a modest setback, called the election outcome a signal for a red/green coalition in the Federal capital. The FDP, with 4.9 percent of the vote, again failed to elect any representatives. In a state where right-extremist groups had found fertile ground in the past, the Republicans, with 2.8 percent of the vote, fell far short of the support needed to gain representation in the state parliament.

In Saxony-Anhalt eight weeks later the Socialists replaced the Christian Democrats as the state's leading party by winning 47 of the 49 direct seats with 35.9 percent of the vote. In contrast, the CDU suffered one of its worst setbacks in this series of *Land* elections as its following declined from 34.4 to 22.0 percent. While neither the FDP nor the Greens succeeded in winning *Landtag* seats, the PDS was able to hold its own, gaining an additional 68,000 votes even as its percentage fell moderately from 19.9 to 19.6 percent on a major increase in voting participation. With unemployment in the state at 18.9 percent at the time of the election, a major beneficiary was the right-extremist German *Volksunion* (DVU), which obtained 12.9 percent of the vote to place 16 deputies in the state parliament. This was the highest percentage total received by any right-extremist party in a major election in the postwar period, but the party was to play an insignificant role in the parliament. The CDU setback was viewed by the SPD as a further sign that the country was ready for a change in Bonn. With the forbearance of the PDS, the Socialists, absent the Greens, were able to continue their minority government under Reinhard Höppner after the election (Andersen and Woyke, 2003, 370).

In Bavaria the CSU continued to dominate the politics of the state by winning an absolute majority of votes and legislative seats for the eighth time since 1970 with 52.9 percent of ballots cast, a small improvement over 1994 *Land* election totals. SPD support slipped from 30.1 to 28.7 percent to again remain far behind the Christian Socialists. The Greens, with 5.7 percent of the vote, secured representation for the fourth time in a row, while the FDP failed to place deputies in the state legislature for a second consecutive time with its worse showing in any postwar *Land* election in Bavaria. At 1.7 percent, it was outpolled by both the Republicans who gained 3.6 percent of the vote and an independent voter grouping which won 3.7 percent.

Although the CDU/CSU remained the leading party on the regional level during the 1994-1998 series of *Land* elections with 40.8 percent of the nationwide vote to the Socialists' 36.2 percent, the SPD, by virtue of winning absolute majorities in the Saar, Brandenburg, North Rhine-Westphalia and Lower Saxony and forming favorable coalitions with either the FDP or Greens in several states where it had no majority, was able to keep control of the *Bundesrat,* the upper house of the federal parliament, 41 to 26. With six, rather than three or four parties, competing for the voters' favor, it was becoming increasingly difficult for a single party to gain a parliamentary majority. The SPD and CDU/CSU together gained majorities in six of the sixteen states in contrast to as many as in eight of the ten states during the 1976-1980 period.

While the Greens polled over three million votes in the two parts of Germany for the first time to secure representation in eleven of the sixteen states, the Free Democrats, with nearly a million and a half fewer votes (1,860,984 to the Greens' 3,328,729), gained seats in only four of them, none in the East, with 4.6 percent of the nation-wide total, to mark one of its worst showings in regional competition since World War II. The future of the party appeared precarious.

The CDU emerged as the leading party in four eastern provinces and Berlin, polling 40.6 percent of the vote to the Socialists' 28.9 percent in that region. While the CDU's followings in the East and West were nearly equal, the SPD did significantly better in the western states (38.1 to 28.9 percent in the East), as much of its potential support in the new *Länder* was absorbed by the successor to the Communist SED, the left-oriented PDS. (In the West the PDS competed in only two states during the 1994-1998 series of regional contests, that of Bremen, where it received only 8,174 votes or 2.37 percent and Hamburg, where it gained 5,350 votes, or less than one percent, and was not a factor in limiting SPD strength). Of significance was the FDP's loss of over two-thirds of its earlier support in the six eastern provinces from 735,404 votes (7.6 percent) in the first series to only 228,866 (2.7 percent) in the second to forfeit representation in all six states. The party did somewhat better in the West with 5.2 percent of ballots cast. The Greens, with a third less votes in the East, lost their delegations in Brandenburg, Saxony and Thuringia, but in the western states they had an overall 8.9 percent following and seated delegations in all ten parliaments. The PDS was the big gainer in a region troubled by high unemployment, pushing its totals from 11.1 to 17.6 percent on an increase of nearly 400,000 votes and improving its representation in all six eastern states. In contrast to the western states, where the Republicans polled nearly a million votes and secured fourteen seats in the Baden-Württemberg *Landtag*, the right-extremist following in the East remained limited during the first two series of *Land* elections as most dissatisfaction was expressed in the PDS vote. However, in the first election of the third round of contests in the new states the DVU, on

TABLE 7.6

THE 1994-1998 *LAND* ELECTIONS IN THE WESTERN PROVINCES[11]

Land and Date	Valid Votes	CDU/CSU	SPD	FDP	Greens	Others
The Saar Oct. 16, 1994	688,910 83.5	265,843 38.6 (21)	340,116 49.4 (27)	14,251 2.1 (0)	38,081 5.5 (3)	Rep. 1.4
Hesse Feb. 19, 1995	2,768,821 66.3	1,084,146 39.2 (45)	1,051,452 38.0 (44)	206,173 7.4 (8)	309,897 11.2 (13)	Rep. 2.0
North Rhine- Westphalia May 14, 1995	8,294,235 64.0	3,124,758 37.7 (89)	3,816,639 46.0 (108)	332,634 4.0 (0)	830,861 10.0 (24)	Rep. 0.8
Bremen May 14, 1995	344,440 68.6	112,301 32.6 (37)	115,001 33.4 (37)	11,607 3.4 (0)	44,977 13.1 (14)	AFB 10.7 (12) PDS (2.4)
Baden- Württemberg Mar. 24, 1996	4,784,061 67.5	1,974,366 41.3 (69)	1,198,959 25.1 (39)	458,482 9.6 (14)	580,636 12.1 (19)	Rep. 437,186 9.1 (14)
Rhineland- Palatinate Mar. 24, 1996	2,063,707 70.8	798,259 38.7 (41)	821,510 39.8 (43)	184,401 8.9 (10)	142,716 6.9 (7)	Rep. 3.5 (0)
Schleswig- Holstein Mar. 24, 1996	1,501,995 71.8	559,070 37.2 (30)	597,729 39.8 (33)	85,225 5.7 (4)	121,913 8.1 (6)	DVU (4.3) SSW 2.5 (2)
Hamburg Sept.21, 1997	822,899 68.7	252,414 30.7 (46)	298,144 36.2 (54)	28,741 3.5 (0)	114,689 13.9 (21)	DVU (4.98) STATT (3.8)
Lower Saxony Mar. 1, 1998	4,316,890 73.8	1,550.523 35.9 (62)	2,068,960 47.9 (83)	209,710 4.9 (0)	304,254 7.0 (12)	Rep. (2.8) STATT (0.7)
Bavaria Sept. 13, 1998	6,093,954 69.8	3,223,882 52.9 (123)	1,750,950 28.7 (67)	100,894 1.7 (0)	346,228 5.7 (14)	Rep. 219,072 3.6 (0)
Totals [a]	31,679,912	12,945,562 40.9	12,059,460 38.1	1,632,118 5.2	2,834,252 8.9	2,208,520. 7.0
Sixteen State Total	40,022,587	16,336,399 40.8	14,471,520 36.2	1,860,984 4.6	3,328,729 8.3	4,024,955 [b] 10.1

a The *Land* election of April 26, 1998 in Saxony-Anhalt is not included in this table since it took place in the eastern part of Germany and is to be found in the third series of *Land* elections in the eastern provinces (Table 7.8).

b This total includes 1,481,447 ballots cast for the PDS (3.7%) and 1,120,969 for the Republicans (2.8%), of which 437,186 was polled in Baden-Württemberg.

April 26, 1998 gained 12.7 percent of ballots cast in Saxony-Anhalt, a portent of future gains by right-extremist groupings in the East. (In the 1994 *Land* election in Saxony-Anhalt the Republicans had received only 1.4 percent of the vote on 15,478 ballots).

The 1998 *Bundestag* Election

With a dynamic, articulate candidate in the person of Gerhard Schröder, a growing unemployment rate and a nation getting tired of Helmut Kohl after sixteen years in office, the Socialists won a major victory in the September 27, 1998 *Bundestag* election, gaining 40.9 percent of the national vote to the CDU/CSU's 35.1 percent, only the second time the SPD was able to outpoll the Christian parties in a national election contest. Having coalesced with the Greens, which polled 6.7 percent of the national vote, in several *Land* parliaments, the SPD did not have to turn to the Free Democrats, who won 6.2 percent of the vote in their worst national showing since the 1949 *Bundestag* election, to form a government. With 345 of the 669 *Bundestag* seats, the new coalition had a comfortable margin to set national policy for the next four years. While the SPD had participated in a national coalition for sixteen years, from 1966 to 1982, this was the first time since entering the political arena in 1979, that the Greens were able to share directly in national decision-making. Joseph (Joschka) Fischer, who had molded the Greens into a more modern, pragmatic party from its earlier, more radical beginnings, became deputy chancellor and foreign minister, and, ultimately, one of Germany's most popular politicians. With the emergence of a fourth alternative in German politics, the FDP was absent from a national coalition for the first time in 29 years.

The PDS, the only other party to obtain seats in the fifteenth *Bundestag,* gained 5.1 percent of the vote to seat 36 delegates. Most of its support came

TABLE 7.7

**RESULTS OF THE *BUNDSTAG* ELECTION OF
SEPTEMBER 27, 1998** [12]

Party	Valid Second Choice Votes	Percentage	*Bundestag* Seats
Total	49,947,067	100.0	669
SPD	20,181,269	40.9	298
CDU	14,004,908	28.4	198
CSU	3,324,480	6.7	47
Greens	3,301,624	6.7	47
FDP	3,080,955	6.2	43
PDS	2,515,454	5.1	36
REP	906,383	1.8	0
DVU	601,192	1.2	0
Pro DM	430,099	0.9	0
NPD	126,571	0.3	0

from the new states, where it polled 21.6 percent of the vote in contrast to only 1.1 percent in the western part of the country. There was a relatively strong, if fragmented, right-extremist vote, but, even if combined, the 1,637,146 ballots cast for the Republicans, DVU and NPD amounted to only 3.3 percent of the national total, far short of the support required for representation.

The political arms of the federal government and certain ministries moved from Bonn to Berlin in 1999. The first seating of the *Bundestag* in Berlin was April 19, 1999. Half of the ministries and federal civil servants remained in Bonn.

The 1998-2001 *Land* Elections

Between the 1998 and 2002 *Bundestag* contests regional elections were held in fourteen of the sixteen federal states, the only exceptions being Lower Saxony and Bavaria which had introduced five-year legislative terms. For comparative purposes the vote totals of the Saxony-Anhalt election of April 26, 1998, discussed earlier, are included in this series of elections even though it was held five months prior to the general election.

In the balloting in Mecklenburg-Vorpommern the same day as the *Bundestag* contest, the SPD, helped by its national success, replaced the CDU as that state's leading political party with 34.3 percent of the vote, as the CDU total slipped from 37.7 to 30.2 percent. The PDS with a modest increase to 24.4 percent of ballots cast was the only other party to gain representation in the state legislature as neither the Free Democrats nor the Greens could overcome the five percent hurdle. The outcome led to the formation of the first coalition in Germany between the Socialists and the PDS under Minister President Harald Ringstorff (SPD), replacing a grand coalition of the CDU and SPD led by Christian Democrat Dr. Berndt Seite and marking the PDS's initial entry into the *Bundesrat* (Andersen and Woyke: 2003, 331 and Olsen, 2000: 12-20).

Both the CDU and SPD made gains in the February 5, 1999 election in Hesse, but the Christian Democrats increased their lead over the Socialists sufficiently to overturn the existing red/green coalition, and form a ministry with the Free Democrats, who barely slipped into the parliament with 5.1 percent of the vote, following a significant drop in support at the polls. The Greens, which also experienced a significant loss of support, from 11.2 to 7.2 percent, were the only other party to gain representation in the Hessian *Landtag*. In Bremen four months later both the SPD and CDU increased their vote totals with the SPD remaining the city-state's leading party with a 42.6 percent share to the CDU's 37.1 percent. The FDP again failed to gain representation, while the Greens sent ten delegates to the Bremen *Bürgerschaft* on a diminished following over 1995. The only other party to receive representation was the right-extremist DVU which secured one seat with 3.0 percent of the vote by virtue of overcoming the five percent hurdle in the city-part of Bremerhaven. The PDS made a second attempt to gain entry to the Bremen city council, but without success, as it polled only 8,418 votes (2.89 percent). Lord Mayor Henning Scherf continued his amicable working arrangement with the CDU in forming a government for the city.

On September 5, 1999 regional elections were held in both Brandenburg and the Saar. In Brandenburg the SPD emerged as the leading party as it had in the first two *Land* elections in the state, but with a drop in support from 54.1 to 39.3 percent it lost its absolute majority in the *Landtag*, while the CDU improved its following from 18.7 to 26.5 percent. The major gainer was the PDS which pushed its vote total from 18.7 to 23.3 percent. Neither the FDP nor the Greens could generate a sufficient following to gain representation, but the right-extremist German People's Union (DVU) succeeded in bridging the five percent hurdle to place five delegates in the *Landtag*. Having lost its absolute majority and not wishing to form an alliance with the PDS, SPD Minister President Manfred Stolpe fashioned a grand coalition with the CDU.

In the Saar the same day the CDU with 45.5 percent of the vote to the Socialists' 44.4 percent, gained an absolute majority of seats in the state legislature, replacing the SPD which had governed the state with absolute majorities since 1985. No other party was able to bridge the five percent barrier to representation, producing a rare example of a two-party parliamentary body. Noteworthy was another failed attempt by the PDS to win a following in a western state, receiving less than one percent of the Saar vote.

In Thuringia one week later the CDU won an absolute majority of both votes and seats to strengthen its position as the *Land*'s leading party. The SPD, now responsible for national policy, was no longer the beneficiary of dissatisfaction within the electorate, and lost 11.1 percentage points to be replaced by the PDS, which polled 21.3 percent of the vote, as that *Land*'s second party. Neither the FDP nor the Greens qualified for representation, even being outpolled by the right-extremist DVU, which, however, also failed to qualify for representation. The CDU formed a one-party government under Dr. Bernhard Vogel.

In the September 19th election in Saxony the CDU won an absolute majority of votes for the third time since reunification in 1990, while the SPD registered one of its lowest showings in any regional contest with only 10.7 percent of ballots cast. The major recipient of the Socialists' poor showing was the PDS which boosted its *Land* following from 16.5 to 22.2 percent. Again, as in four previous elections held in the eastern provinces, both the FDP and Greens failed to qualify for seats. It was especially embarrassing for the FDP, which, with only 1.1 percent of the vote, was outpolled by the right-extremist Republicans and National Democratic Party and by the Pro-DM Party.

On October 10, 1999 the CDU emerged as the leading party in Berlin, as it had in the seven previous elections in the city-state, with a 40.8 percent vote total. The SPD, hurt by the competition from the PDS for its vote in the eastern sector of the city since reunification, registered its worst following since the first elections were held in the city in 1946. The dimension of the setback is clearly demonstrated in the distribution of direct mandates, 46 for the CDU, thirty for the PDS, which won a 17.7 share of the votes, two for the Greens and none for the SPD. The Greens/Alternative List secured eighteen seats with 9.9 percent of the vote, while the Free Democrats again failed to qualify for representation. Without the FDP as a potential coalition partner, the CDU renewed its existing alliance with the SPD. The combination, however, failed to outlive the legislative period, when on June 16, 2001, with the legislative term less than half over, the SPD and Greens, with the help of the PDS, forced the CDU under Lord Mayor Eberhard Diepgen (CDU) out of the government on a constructive vote of non-confidence (the first in Berlin's postwar history) following a series of scandals, placing the Berlin administration under SPD leadership for the first time in ten years.

On February 24, 2000 in Schleswig-Holstein the SPD registered its first major gain following five straight setbacks in this series of *Land* elections to remain the state's leading party with 43.1 percent of the vote, while the CDU experienced a minor loss, only its second in nine regional contests. Both the FDP and Greens secured representation along with the SSW which had its best showing in 46 years to secure three seats in the Schleswig-Holstein parliament. The Socialists continued their existing coalition with the Greens.

In the May 14, 2000 election in North Rhine-Westphalia the SPD lost 3.2 percentage points, but remained the state's leading party with 42.8 percent of the vote to the CDU's 37.0 percent, and continued to maintain its hold on Germany's most populous state in alliance with the Greens, which polled 7.1 percent of ballots cast. The FDP returned to the *Landtag* after a five-year absence with a 9.8 percent share of the votes, its best showing in the Rhine and Ruhr in 46 years. The PDS again made an attempt to develop a following in a western state, but could do no better than attract 1.1 percent of the voters.

No new elections were held for over ten months until March 25, 2001 when voters in Baden-Württemberg and Rhineland-Palatinate went to the polls. In the Southwest State both the CDU and SPD made gains, with the Socialists recording their best effort since 1976 with a 33.3 percent vote total. The CDU, however, maintained its grip on the state with a 44.8 share and success in winning all of its 63 seats by direct election, a total which fell just three seats short of providing an absolute majority in the state legislature. Both the FDP and Greens secured a sufficient following to be represented, but on weakened support. However, the Republicans, who had obtained legislative seats in the two previous *Land* elections, lost their delegation when they obtained only 4.4 percent of the vote. Lacking a majority, the CDU continued its coalition with the Free Democrats.

Benefiting from the growing personal popularity of SPD Minister President Kurt Beck, the Socialists made major gains in Rhineland-Palatinate to widen their grip on the state, but fell two seats short of a parliamentary majority. This marked the third time in succession that the SPD was able to outpoll the CDU, which gained 35.3 percent of the vote, in this heavily Catholic *Land.* Both the FDP and Greens qualified for representation, but rather than following the Berlin model, the Socialists continued their working relationship with the Free

Democrats which had flourished over a ten-year period. The election marked a significant comeback for the FDP, which had now registered its fourth straight success after having been locked out of five *Land* parliaments in a row.

The Hamburg election of September 23, 2001 was strongly influenced by the law and order appeal of former district court (*Amtsgericht*) judge Ronald Schill in a city which Schill claimed to be "the capital of criminality." (In a poll taken in the city shortly before the election, 56 percent of respondents listed "criminality" as the most important issue facing Hamburg). One year prior to the election Schill had formed the *Partei Rechtsstaatlicher Offensive* (the aggressive law and order party) most commonly known as the Schill Party after its founder. Its share of the votes (19.6 percent) was greater than that gained by any splinter party in any state since the advent of the Refugee Party in Schleswig-Holstein in 1950.[13] Schill's success was attributed to his personalization of the party and emphasis on internal security This was the first time since World War II that a party carried the name of its founder and the country's first party of the personality (*Zeitschrift für Parlamentsfragen, Jahrgang* 2002-2004, 43-47). The SPD had entered the election having controlled the city for 44 successive years, either alone or in coalition with a second party, and hoped to be rewarded for its economic successes. Although the SPD outpolled the CDU by over ten percentage points to better its 1997 performance and remain the *Land's* leading party, the CDU, while experiencing its second worse showing since 1946, was able to form a coalition with the Schill Party and Free Democrats, who polled 5.1 percent of the vote to reenter the *Bürgerschaft* after being locked out for two legislative sessions. Ole von Beust became only the second Christian Democrat *Bürgermeister* in postwar Hamburg, with Schill serving as vice-mayor (*Zweite Bürgermeister*). (The coalition broke up before the end of the legislative session over scandalous remarks by Schill against Mayor von Beust, but not before von Beust had established himself as one of Hamburg's most popular mayors, enabling the CDU to win an absolute majority for the first time in the 2004 election). The Greens, although losing over a third of their 1997 following, was the fifth party to obtain representation in the election. Following its success in Hamburg the Schill Party, called a "one theme" protest grouping, attempted to gain a national following, but attracted only 4.5 percent of voters in Saxony-Anhalt in the April 21, 2002 election, 1.7 percent of Mecklenberg-Vorpommern voters on September 22, 2002 and less than one percent of *Bundestag* voters the same day. In 2004, with 3.1 percent of ballots, it was voted out of the Hamburg *Bürgerschaft.*

The October 21, 2001 election in Berlin was made necessary by the collapse of the grand coalition between the CDU and SPD in June over a controversial mixture of CDU party expenditures, a bank scandal and budgetary crisis and the need to legitimize the replacement minority ministry of the SPD and Greens which had been supported by the PDS. The controversies brought a resounding defeat to the Christian Democrats and propelled the SPD into the leading position in the German capital for the first time in 26 years. The CDU lost 17.1 percentage points from 40.8 to 23.7 percent, while the Socialists under Lord

TABLE 7.8

THE THIRD SERIES OF *LAND* ELECTIONS IN THE EASTERN PROVINCES [14]

Land and Date	Valid Votes	CDU	SPD	FDP	Greens	PDS	Others
Saxony-Anhalt April 26, 1998	1,494,023 71.5	328,829 22.0 (28)	536,048 35.9 (47)	63,195 4.2 (0)	48,469 3.2 (0)	293,271 19.6 (25)	DVU 12.9 (16)
Mecklenburg-Vorpommern Sept. 27, 1998	1,084,611 79.4	327,948 30.2 (24)	371,885 34.3 (27)	17,062 1.6 (0)	29,240 2.7 (0)	264,299 24.4 (20)	DVU 2.9 (0) NPD 1.1 (0) Rep. 0.5 (0)
Brandenburg Sept. 5, 1999	1,102,360 54.3	292,634 26.5 (25)	433,521 39.3 (37)	20,472 1.9 (0)	21,410 1.9 (0)	257,309 23.3 (22)	DVU 5.3 (5) NPD 0.7 (0)
Thuringia Sept. 12, 1999	1,161,129 59.9	592,474 51.0 (49)	214,801 18.5 (18)	13,001 1.1 (0)	21,617 1.9 (0)	247.908 21.3 (21)	DVU 3.1 (0) Rep. 0.8 (0)
Saxony Sept. 19, 1999	2,164,072 61.4	1,231,253 56.9 (76)	232,311 10.7 (14)	23,369 1.1 (0)	55,809 2.6 (-)	480,317 22.2 (30)	Rep.1.5 (0) NPD 1.4 (0)
Berlin [a] Oct. 21, 2001	1,623,338 68.1	385,692 23.7 (35)	481,772 29.7 (44)	160,953 9.9 (15)	148,066 9.1 (14)	366,292 22.6 (33)	Rep. 1.3 (0) NPD 0.9 (0)
Totals	8,629,533	3,158,830 36.6	2,270,338 26.3	298,052 3.5	324,611 3.8	1,909,396 22.1	668,306 7.7

a The 2001 election in Berlin was the second to be held during the third series of regional contests in the eastern provinces. The October 10, 1999 balloting in Berlin is covered on pages 180-181. In the 1999 election the CDU gained 40.8 percent of the vote and 76 seats, the SPD 22.4 percent and 42 seats, the PDS 17.7 percent and 33 seats, the Greens 9.9 percent and 18 seats and the FDP 2.2 percent which disqualified it for seats.

Mayor Klaus Wowereit gained 7.3 percentage points to 29.7 percent. The FDP and PDS were also beneficiaries of the CDU's difficulties, with the FDP gaining 7.7 percentage points to reenter the Berlin *Abgeordnetenhaus* on a 9.9 percent following and the PDS 4.9 additional percentage points to record a 22.6 percent share of the vote. The Greens were able to retain their representation in spite of a small drop in support to 9.1 percent. The psychological split between the eastern and western sections of the city was apparent in the ability of the PDS to obtain 47.6 percent of the East Berlin vote and 32 direct seats, in contrast to less than ten percent and no direct seats in the western districts (Anderson and Woyke, 2003: 303). An attempt to form a traffic-light coalition of the SPD, Greens and FDP faltered and, following successful negotiations with the PDS, an SPD/PDS ministry was formed under Socialist Klaus Wowereit as Lord Mayor.

The last regional contest to take place prior to the 2002 *Bundestag* election was held April 21, 2002 in Saxony-Anhalt. In that election the CDU, gaining 15.3 percentage points to a 37.3 share of ballots cast, made a major comeback to

TABLE 7.9

THE 1999-2001 *LAND* ELECTION IN THE WESTERN PROVINCES[15]

Land and Date	Valid Votes	CDU	SPD	FDP	Greens	Others
Hesse Feb. 5, 1999	2,800,372 66.4	1,215,783 43.4 (50)	1,102,544 39.4 (46)	142,845 5.1 (6)	201,194 7.2 (8)	Rep. 2.7 (0) NPD 0.2 (0)
Bremen June 6, 1999	291,091 60.1	108,050 37.1 (42)	123,875 42.6 (47)	7,327 2.5 (0)	25,958 8.9 (10)	DVU 3.0 (1) PDS 2.9 (0)
The Saar Sept. 5, 1999	557,337 68.7	253,856 45.5 (26)	247,311 44.4 (25)	14,259 2.6 (0)	18,106 3.2 (0)	Rep. 1.3 (0) PDS 0.8 (0)
Schleswig- Holstein Feb. 27, 2000	1,464,096 69.5	515,421 35.2 (33)	630,728 43.1 (41)	111,649 7.6 (7)	91,389 6.2 (5)	SSW 4.1 (3) PDS 1.4 (0) NPD 1.0 (0)
North Rhine- Westphalia May 14, 2000	7,336,411 56.7	2,712,176 37.0 (88)	3,143,179 42.8 (102)	721,558 9.8 (24)	518,295 7.1 (17)	Rep. 1.1 PDS 1.1
Baden- Württemberg March 25, 2001	4,530,763 62.6	2,029,806 44.8 (63)	1,508,358 33.3 (45)	367,580 8.1 (10)	350,383 7.7 (10)	Rep. 4.4 (0)
Rhineland- Palatinate March 25, 2001	1,833,846 62.1	647,238 35.3 (38)	820,610 44.7 (49)	143,427 7.8 (8)	95,567 5.2 (6)	Rep. 2.4 (0)
Hamburg Sept. 23, 2001	850,068 71.0	223,015 26.2 (33)	310,362 36.5 (46)	43,214 5.1 (6)	72,771 8.6 (11)	Schill 19.4 (25)
Totals	19,663,984	7,705,345 39.2 [a]	7,886,967 40.1 [a]	1,551,859 7.9	1,273,663 6.5	1,246,150 6.3
Fourteen State Totals	28,293,517	10,864,175 38.4	10,157,305 35.9	1,849,911 6.5	1,598,274 5.6	3,823,852 [b] (13.5)

a Note that the CDU total would have been higher and the SPD total lower had a *Land* election been held in Bavaria during the interval between *Bundestag* elections.

b Of this total 2,025,564 (7.2%) was received by the PDS and 926,572 (3.3%) by right extremist groupings.

regain its earlier status as the *Land*'s leading party. In contrast, the Socialists lost as much as the CDU gained to register their worst showing since the first *Land* election in the state in 1990, even falling below the 20.4 percent cast for the PDS. The turnaround is best illustrated in the direct election count. In 1998 the

Socialists won 47 of 49 direct seats, while in 2002 the Christian Democrats won 48 of the 49 direct seats. The FDP was also a big winner in the election, not only returning to the state parliament after being locked out for two legislative sessions, but, with 13.3 percent of the vote, nearly duplicating its 1990 following. The right-extremist DVU, which had won a surprising sixteen seats with a 12.9 percent share of the vote in 1998, was racked by internal discord and resignations during the legislative session and did not run candidates in the 2002 election. The Greens, with 2.0 percent of ballots cast, again failed to qualify for representation, even though Saxony-Anhalt had been burdened by the greatest environmental damage of all of the new states. The party of Ronald Schill, which had made such a spectacular entry into the political arena in Hamburg just seven months earlier, failed to duplicate its earlier success, gaining only 4.5 percent of the Saxony-Anhalt vote. As a consequence of the SPD setback, the Socialist-led minority government of Reinhard Höppner was replaced by a CDU/FDP coalition, under Christian Democrat Professor Dr. Wolfgang Böhmer.

In the fifteenth series of *Land* elections, the CDU/CSU, in the opposition for the first time in sixteen years, made gains in five of the first seven regional contests to be held following the 1998 *Bundestag* election; however, after the unclear transfer of party campaign funds to foreign accounts became public the CDU/CSU suffered setbacks in five of the next seven ballotings. Nevertheless, it maintained its standing as the leading party on the regional level with 38.4 percent of total votes cast to the SPD's 35.9 percent, down from a 40.8 percent share in the previous series of *Land* elections because of the absence of a contest in Bavaria, which provides the Christian parties with a large proportion of their support, during the interval. Although the Socialists outpolled the Christian parties 40.1 to 39.2 percent in the eight western states, the Union maintained its overall predominance by gaining 36.6 percent of the eastern vote to the Socialists' 26.3 percent. Even though no longer in the opposition on the national level, the SPD managed gains in nine of the fourteen elections, improving its western state totals, but losing ground to the PDS in the eastern provinces.

After being locked out of all but four of the *Land* parliaments in the previous series of regional contests, the FDP, now in the opposition in Bonn, experienced a major comeback to gain representation in four additional states and increase its regional following from 4.6 to 6.5 percent. Its gains came mainly in the western states, where its level of support rose from 5.2 to 7.9 percent, as the party benefited from the CDU/CSU finance stigma. Following setbacks in the six eastern provinces and the Saar and a small gain in Schleswig-Holstein, Jürgen Möllemann, who competed with Dr. Guido Westerwelle for the party leadership, was successful in energizing the North Rhine-Westphalian FDP, resulting in a more than doubling of its following to 9.8 percent in the 2000 *Land* election. Möllemann ultimately lost out to Westerwelle, who was elected FDP chairman in May 2001, with a program aimed at presenting the party as a "young, dynamic and unspent" force in German politics. The FDP was returned to the *Landtag* of North Rhine-Westphalia in May 2000, to the

Hamburg *Bürgerschaft* in September 2001, and to the Berlin parliament the next month. In April 2002 it was also returned to the Saxony-Anhalt *Landtag*. An exuberant Westerwelle spoke of polling eighteen percent of the vote in the fall *Bundestag* election. (It gained less than half that total.) The Greens, now a participant in the national government for the first time, lost a third of their regional following to mark the first time since 1980 that they were outpolled by the Free Democrats in *Land* contests. They lost their representation in the Saar and failed to win seats in any of the eastern states outside of Berlin during the interval, but continued to be represented in ten of the sixteen state parliaments. The PDS remained strictly a regional party, gaining 22.1 percent of the eastern vote, but less than one percent of western ballots. In the East it nearly doubled the vote polled in the first series of *Land* elections following reunification to seriously impact SPD support. In the West it entered candidates in only five states, Bremen, Hamburg, North Rhine-Westphalia, Schleswig-Holstein and the Saar, with its best following of 2.89 percent coming in Bremen. As a result, it had little influence on SPD support in the western states. Nevertheless, because of its strength in the six eastern states the PDS outpolled both the FDP and Greens to become the third party in this series of *Land* elections. Right-extremist parties polled less than one million votes with the DVU winning the largest share in the East, the Republicans the largest share in the West. While the 462,101 votes received in the West amounted to only 2.3 percent, in the East the 464,471 ballots represented 5.4 percent of a much smaller electorate, with the DVU gaining sixteen seats in the Saxony-Anhalt *Lantag* in 1998.

The 2002 *Bundestag* Election

For the *Bundestag* election of September 27, 2002, Gerhard Schröder, federal Chancellor since 1998, was selected to lead the SPD in its effort to continue the party's hold on the national government, while the CDU/CSU turned to Edmund Stoiber, Minister President of Bavaria and leader of the Christian Social Union, the CDU's sister party in Bavaria, rather than to Helmut Kohl who had been discredited over a series of campaign finance scandals in which he was alleged to have participated. The Socialists were highly vulnerable because of the party's failure to control growing unemployment, or to resolve severe budgetary problems and deficits which exceeded European Union guidelines. The party had also suffered several election setbacks in the states, including in the country's most populous unit, North Rhine-Westphalia, in the just completed series of contests, to bring its regional following down to 35.9 percent, the lowest regional showing since the 1953-1957 period when CDU-Chancellor Konrad Adenauer's popularity was at its peak. Public opinion polls predicted a solid CDU/CSU victory. Two events, however, appear to have altered the tide to the Chancellor's favor, even though he failed to cut unemployment from around four million by 500,000 during his four years in office as promised. First, Schröder, an aggressive campaigner, demonstrated strong and effective leadership in quickly responding to the emergency caused by the flooding of Elbe River cities, including Dresden and Magdeburg. Second, following the American President's call for support of an invasion of Iraq, Schröder announced his intention not to provide German troops, as in Afghanistan, calling it an ill-conceived "adventure" unsupported by credible intelligence sources. He would, however, allow fly-over rights and unrestricted use of NATO bases in Germany. In spite of denunciation by the Bush administration and various Republican Party spokesmen, Chancellor Schröder had little choice in his decision. Such a move would not have been supported by his coalition partner, the Greens, and public opinion polls at the time demonstrated overwhelming public opposition to such an involvement. (Neither United Nations nor American investigators found any evidence of the existence of weapons of mass destruction in Iraq, giving support to the German Chancellor's position. The American President, on a visit to Stralsund, Germany in May 2006 indicated that he now understood Germany's position on the Iraq incursion.)

Rather than a landslide for the Christian parties, the election turned out to be one of the closest in postwar German history with the SPD outpolling the CDU/CSU by only 6,000 out of nearly 48 million votes cast, but the Socialists carried twelve of the sixteen states, being outpolled by the CDU/CSU only in Bavaria, Baden-Württemberg, Rhineland-Palatinate and Saxony. With the

TABLE 7.10

RESULTS OF THE *BUNDESTAG* ELECTION OF SEPTEMBER 22, 2002 [a] [16]

Party	Valid Second Choice Votes	Percentage	*Bundestag* Seats
Total	47,996,480	100.0	603
SPD	18,488,668	38.5	251
CDU	14,167,561	29.5	190
CSU	4,315,080	9.0	58
The Greens	4,110,355	8.6	55
FDP	3,538,815	7.4	47
PDS	1,916,702	4.0	2
Schill	400,476	0.8	0
Republicans	280,671	0.6	0
NPD	215,232	0.4	0

a Twenty other splinter groupings competed in the 2002 general election, but their combined second choice vote of 462,920 amounted to less than one percent of the total.

SPD's coalition partner, the Greens, polling 8.6 percent of the vote and gaining 55 seats to register their best national showing, the red/green combination held a bare majority of 306 seats to 297 seats for the opposition. The FDP, hurt by the scandal arising from seemingly anti-Semitic statements made by North Rhineland-Westphalia state chairman Jürgen Möllemann, gained a disappointing 7.4 percent of the vote and 47 seats, insufficient to make a CDU/CSU-FDP alliance workable. The PDS carried 16.9 percent of the eastern vote, but only 1.1 percent of ballots cast in the western provinces to gain but 4.0 percent of the vote nationwide and was able to place only two representatives in the *Bundestag* through direct election. Had the PDS obtained five percent of the vote and received thirty seats or had Schröder's coalition partner not outpolled the FDP, the chaotic situation which occurred following the 2005 outcome would have presented itself three years earlier. The Schill Party, only a year away from its Hamburg success, failed to attract a national following and polled only 400,476 (0.8 percent) votes. In contrast to 1998, when right-extremist parties received 1,634,146 votes, neither the NPD nor the Republicans could exceed even one percent of ballots cast and less than 500,000 ballots together.

The 2002-2005 *Land* Elections

Regional elections were held in only twelve of the sixteen German states between the 2002 and 2005 *Bundestag* polls because of the shortened legislative session caused by Chancellor Schröder's decision to call for new general elections one year early following a string of eleven straight setbacks for his party in regional contests occasioned primarily by a widespread unfavorable reaction to his controversial reform initiatives aimed at dealing with continued high unemployment (especially in the eastern provinces where it was approaching twenty percent) and curbing the excesses in the nation's various social and welfare programs which were creating unacceptable budget deficits. Although given a mandate to govern for four years, but lacking a strong base to make the necessary changes, there were fears that the red/green coalition in Berlin would collapse within a few months. Finance Minister Hans Eichel blamed much of the country's poor performance on the costs of reunification running at over seventy billion dollars a year (*The Wall Street Journal*, December 23, 2002). Schröder offered to resign during a meeting of SPD leaders at the end of 2002, but, realizing the consequences of a new election at a time of declining popularity of both party and Chancellor, the offer was not accepted (*The Chicago Tribune*, December 29, 2002).

The first *Land* contest in the new election period was held in Mecklenburg-Vorpommern the same day as the *Bundestag* balloting. Benefiting from the same issues that helped their cause in the national contest the Socialists made major gains, pushing their share of the votes from 34.3 to 40.6 percent to mark their best showing in that state since reunification. The gains came primarily at the expense of the PDS, which saw its support fall from 24.4 percent in 1998 to 16.4

percent, and not the CDU which experienced a small gain to 31.4 percent. Neither the FDP nor the Greens qualified for representation, but the Free Democrats could take heart in being able to triple their vote over 1998 to 4.7 percent, portending a surge in support which was to give them a 9.6 percentage share of ballots four years later. All splinter parties did poorly. The NPD, which was to poll a surprising 7.3 percent of the vote in the 2006 *Land* election, received less than one percent of the vote in 2002. With only three parties represented in the *Landtag*, the SPD continued its working arrangement with the PDS.

Having barely won a new mandate at the national level and registered a better than expected outcome in Mecklenburg-Vorpommern the SPD now faced an increasingly skeptical public in the remaining regional contests prior to the next *Bundestag* election. Beginning with *Land* elections in Hesse and Lower Saxony on February 2, 2003 the SPD experienced its poorest showing in any series of regional contests since the first elections were held in 1946, falling below a 30 percent share of the votes for the first time. In the former Socialist stronghold of Hesse the SPD's vote fell from 39.4 to 29.1 percent, and in Lower Saxony from 47.9 percent (an absolute majority) to 33.4 percent, the party's poorest showing in either state since the first postwar elections. In contrast, the CDU gained an absolute majority of seats in the Hessian *Landtag* for the first time with 48.8 percent of ballots cast and a near majority in Lower Saxony with 48.3 percent, its highest total in 21 years, winning 91 of 100 direct seats. The loss in Lower Saxony was especially painful for Chancellor Schröder since it was in that state that he had built up his political career prior to taking over the office of Federal Chancellor in 1998. The loss also gave the CDU and its partners a firm majority in the federal *Bundesrat* as the CDU formed a ministry with the Free Democrats.

Both the FDP and the Greens made gains in the two states with the FDP returning to the Lower Saxony parliament for the first time in two legislative sessions. Although in partnership with the Socialists in the national government, the Greens did not suffer the backlash aimed at the Chancellor's party, and in Hesse increased their position from 7.2 to 10.1 percent and in Lower Saxony from 7.0 to 7.6 percent. The Greens' success was partly due to the personal popularity of party chairman Joschka Fischer who, as Foreign Minister, guided the nation's foreign policy. The right-extremist Republicans ran candidates in both states, but obtained only 1.3 percent of the vote in Hesse and 0.4 percent in Lower Saxony. The Schill Party, still hoping to make a national impact, obtained only 0.5 percent of the vote in the former state and 1.0 percent in the latter. The PDS polled less than one percent of the vote in Lower Saxony.

In the May election in Bremen the Socialists, in a grand coalition with the Christian Democrats under the popular SPD mayor Henning Scherf since 1995, held their own with 42.3 percent of ballots cast while the CDU suffered a major loss of support, dropping below thirty percent for the first time since 1987. In stark contrast to its February successes, the FDP following fell below five percent for the third consecutive legislative session, but it qualified for a single seat by virtue of its ability to exceed the five percent barrier in Bremerhaven where representation is figured separately. In this same manner the right-extremist DVU with only 2.3 percent of the total Bremen vote was able to place a single representative in the Bremen *Bürgerschaft,* while the Schill Party with a larger following than either of them at 4.4 percent placed no representatives. The Greens were the big winner with a fifty percent increase in support from 8.9 to 12.8 percent to send twelve deputies to a smaller *Bürgerschaft,* reduced from 100 to 83 members for the first time. The PDS, with only a 1.7 percent following, again failed to win a seat. Lord Mayor Scherf continued his working relationship with the CDU.

On September 21, 2003 Bavarian voters gave Minister President Edmund Stoiber and his Christian Social Union a resounding victory with 60.7 percent of the votes, exceeded in postwar elections in Bavaria only by the 62.1 percent given to Dr. Alfons Goppel in 1974. The SPD, on the other hand, suffered its worse setback in Bavaria since elections were held in the postwar period with only 19.6 percent of the vote, while the FDP failed for the third legislative session in a row to qualify for seats. Again, unharmed by its participation in the national coalition, the Greens pushed their share of votes from 5.7 to 7.7 percent. Nearly ten percent of votes cast fell to a variety of splinter parties, including the Free Voters (FW) with 4.0 percent, campaigning as an alternative to the CSU, the Republicans with 2.2 percent and the Bavarian Party (BP), which had entered every election since 1950, with 0.8 percent.

The election of February 29, 2004 in Hamburg was held less than two and a half years into the legislative session because of a falling-out between Lord Mayor Ole von Beust and Ronald Schill, the leader of the CDU's coalition partner, over scandalous remarks made by Schill over the mayor's sexual orientation and a controversial appointment (*Spiegel Jahres-Chronik* 2004: 56). The usually liberal and tolerant Hamburg voters in this traditionally red city handed von Beust's Christian Democrats a resounding victory and their first absolute majority with 47.2 percent of ballots cast, absorbing most of the vote which had been given to the renegade Schill Party in 2001, reducing its share of votes from 19.4 to 3.1 percent and eliminating it from the Hamburg parliament (*Zeitschrift für Parlamentsfragen, Jahrgang* 2002-2004: 253-254). Other than the Schill controversy, the CDU was helped by dissatisfaction with SPD reform measures in Berlin. The popular von Beust was called "Ole Superstar" by *Der Spiegel* magazine, and in 2005 was named the outstanding mayor for his efforts in turning Hamburg into a boom city (See *Stern,* "Boomtown Hamburg," May 5, 2006). The usually dominant Socialists saw their support decline from 36.5 percent in 2001 to 30.5 percent, their worst performance in the *Hansastadt* in the postwar period in spite of the appearance of Chancellor Schröder in Hamburg nine days before the election. Support for the FDP, which had also been in coalition with the CDU since 2001, fell to 2.8 percent, causing it to lose its parliamentary representation. The Greens, continuing their surge in voter confidence, upped their share of the Hamburg vote from 8.6 to 12.3 percent. The PDS failed to compete in this election. With its majority, the CDU was able to form a one-party ministry under Ole von Beust.

In the *Land* election in Thuringia June 13, 2004 both the CDU and SPD lost ground. Although its total fell from 51.0 to 43.0 percent of the vote, the CDU remained the state's largest party and maintained a bare majority of seats in the legislature by winning 39 of 44 direct mandates, while the SPD total dropped from 18.5 to 14.5 percent, its worst showing in four elections in the state. The major benefactor was the PDS which increased its position from 21.3 to 26.1 percent to again place ahead of the Socialists in voter favor. The Greens continued their surge by more than doubling their vote total, which at 4.5 percent, was still insufficient to be awarded seats. With most of the protest vote falling to the PDS, the Republicans with 2.0 percent and the NPD with 1.6 percent failed to qualify for seats.

In the September 5, 2004 election in the Saar the CDU made a modest improvement in its position with 47.5 percent of the vote to increase its majority in the state parliament by one seat. The SPD, in contrast, recorded its poorest following since 1960, with a drop from 44.4 to 30.8 percent of the vote. Both the FDP and Greens returned to the state legislature by barely exceeding the five percent hurdle for representation. The Greens registered their best showing since first entering candidates in the Saar in 1980 and continued to improve on earlier elections for the eighth consecutive time. The NPD waged a strong campaign, but its 4.0 vote total was insufficient to gain representation.

Elections were held September 19, 2004 in both Brandenburg and Saxony. In Brandenburg the SPD suffered yet another significant loss from 39.3 to 31.9 percent, but with the CDU experiencing an almost equal setback from 26.5 to 19.4 percent, the Socialists remained the *Land*'s leading party. A major beneficiary of the decline of the two major parties was the PDS which, with 28.0 percent of the vote, not only outpolled the CDU, but came close to equaling the SPD share. It was significant that the Party of Democratic Socialism won more direct seats, 23 of 44, than either the SPD or CDU which won seventeen and four direct seats respectively. Although improving on their 1998 election totals, neither the FDP nor the Greens secured sufficient votes to be eligible for representation. The rightist DVU not only held on to its representation in the *Landtag,* but improved its position from 5.3 to 6.1 percent of the vote. With limited coalition possibilities, the Socialists continued their arrangement with the CDU.

In Saxony the same day the SPD was nearly reduced to a splinter party, its 9.8 percent share of ballots cast representing its worst showing in any state election held since 1946. Most embarrassing was that its support was only slightly above the 9.2 percent registered by the right-extremist NPD, a party which had received only 1.4 percent of voters' second choice ballots five years earlier. The CDU, which had won absolute majorities in the three previous *Land* elections, also suffered a major setback, seeing its following falling from 56.9 percent in 1999 to 41.1 percent. It did, however, win 55 of the state's 60 direct seats to remain the state's leading party, but it now had to form an alliance with the FDP which was returned to the legislature after being excluded for two legislative periods. The PDS with 23.6 percent of the vote made a small improvement over its 1999 standing, while both the FDP and Greens returned to the state parliament. The Greens with 5.1 percent of the vote continued their recovery streak. With the splintering of the vote, Saxony became, at the time, the only state in which six parties were represented in its parliament in spite of the *Sperrklausel*.

With the Socialists experiencing a steady decline in voter favor, the elections of February 20, 2005 in Schleswig-Holstein and May 22, 2005 in North Rhine-Westphalia became crucial readings of public sentiment for their party, not only because they governed both states in coalition with the Greens, but because North Rhine-Westphalia was the country's most populous state. Schleswig-Holstein had been led by Germany's first woman minister president, Heide Simonis, since 1993. In spite of her popularity, with public opinion polls demonstrating a preference for her sixty to thirty percent over the CDU's leading candidate Peter Harry Carstensen, she was burdened by the declining national image of her party. In the election the SPD total dropped to 38.7 percent, its worse showing since the 1958 balloting, to lose its leading position to the Christian Democrats who polled 40.2 percent of the vote. Both the Free Democrats and Greens won four seats apiece, while the party of the Danish minority, the SSW, gained two (*Die Welt*, February 21, 2005). Coalition building was complicated by the fact that neither a CDU/FDP nor an SPD/Greens combination could provide a working parliamentary majority because of the SSW's two seats. Minister President Simonis attempted to lead a minority government for two months with the forbearance of the SSW, but little could be done to deal with the many problems facing the state. As a result, a grand coalition of the CDU and SPD was formed in April 2005 under Minister President Peter Harry Carstensen (CDU) to place the government on a more stable basis with 59 of 69 seats (*Die Welt*, April 18, 2005 and *Dithmarscher Landeszeitung*, April 19, 2005).

The election in North Rhine-Westphalia three months later became the most important test for the Schröder government in Berlin because of the size of the state's electorate. The Socialists had governed the state since 1966, from 1980 to 1995 with absolute majorities and after 1995 in coalition with the Greens. In polling only 37.1 percent of the vote, the SPD registered its worse performance in the Rhine and Ruhr in over fifty years, while the CDU, with 44.8 percent, recorded its best result since 1975. The CDU victory ended the last SPD/Greens ministry on the regional level, removing the Greens from all *Land* governments, but securing a constitutional majority for the CDU in the federal *Bundesrat* in coalition with the FDP. Although the Greens outpolled the Free Democrats in the election, the margin was less than one thousand votes and both parties received 12 seats with 6.2 percent of ballots cast. This was the first election in which the seat total in the *Landtag* was set at 180 members, down from 200, exclusive of compensating mandates. An attempt by the PDS to gain a following in the Rhine and Ruhr failed miserably when it polled only 72,982 votes, less than one percent of the total. More significant was the entry of a new party

TABLE 7.11

THE 2003-2005 *LAND* ELECTIONS IN THE WESTERN PROVINCES[17]

Land and Date	Valid Votes	CDU/CSU	SPD	FDP	Greens	Others
Hesse Feb. 2, 2003	2,734,992 64.6	1,333,863 48.8 (56)	795,576 29.1 (33)	216,110 7.9 (9)	276,276 10.1 (12)	Rep. (1.3) Schill (0.5)
Lower Saxony Feb. 2, 2003	3,984,009 67.0	1,925,055 48.3 (91)	1,330,156 33.4 (63)	323,107 8.1 (15)	304,532 7.6 (14)	Rep. (0.4) PDS (0.5)
Bremen May 25, 2003	291,766 61.3	86,819 29.8 (29)	123,480 42.3 (40)	12,294 4.2 (1)	37,350 12.8 (12)	DVU 2.3 (1) PDS (1.7)
Bavaria Sept. 21, 2003	5,124,368 57.1	3,108,932 60.7 (124)	1,006,133 19.6 (41)	131,866 2.6 (0)	396,525 7.7 (15)	Rep. (2.2) FW [a] (4.0)
Hamburg Feb. 29, 2004	824,128 68.7	389,170 47.2 (63)	251,441 30.5 (41)	23,373 2.8 (0)	101,227 12.3 (17)	Schill (3.1) NPD (0.3)
The Saar Sept. 5, 2004	441,628 55.5	209,690 47.5 (27)	136,224 30.8 (18)	22,842 5.2 (3)	24,830 5.6 (3)	PDS (2.3) NPD (4.0)
Schleswig-Holstein Feb. 20, 2005	1,434,805 66.6	576,095 40.2 (30)	554,879 38.7 (29)	94,935 6.6 (4)	89.387 6.2 (4)	SSW 3.6 (2) PDS (0.8) NPD (1.9)
North Rhine-Westphalia May 22, 2005	8,243,372 63.0	3,695,806 44.8 (89)	3,059,074 37.1 (74)	508,354 6.2 (12)	509,219 6.2 (12)	WASG (2.2) PDS (0.9) NPD (0.9)
Totals Percent of Vote	23,079,068	11,325,430 49.1	7,256,263 31.4	1,332,881 5.8	1,739,340 7.5	1,425,154 6.2

a The Free Voters (FW) grouping in Bavaria campaigns as an alternative to the CSU.

founded by Oskar Lafontaine, former minister president of the Saarland and SPD candidate for the federal chancellorship in 1990, into the political arena, the WASG (or Electoral Alternative for Social Justice; *Die Welt*, May 23 and 24, 2005). Although the party polled only 181,886 votes (2.2 percent), it presaged the formation of an electoral alliance with the PDS under the designation *Die Linke* which entered the 2005 *Bundestag* election and gained 8.7 percent of the national vote, possibly preventing the SPD from equaling or exceeding the totals of the combined CDU/CSU vote in that election.

The election setback in North Rhine-Westphalia caused federal Chancellor Gerhard Schröder, frustrated by the lack of support for his reform policies, both outside and within his own party, to call for new elections in September 2005, one year short of the constitutional term. In contrast to 1982, when the government of Helmut Schmidt was brought down by the withdrawal of the FDP from the governing coalition, Schröder's decision was not caused by a non-supporting Greens party, but by a presumed lack of confidence by the German voter. (No further *Land* elections were held between May 22 and September 19, 2005, when the sixteenth *Bundestag* election took place).

In the twelve elections held between the 2002 and 2005 *Bundestag* contests the CDU/CSU made gains in eight of them, most importantly in the large states of Bavaria, Hesse, Lower Saxony and North Rhine-Westphalia, to increase their regional totals from 38.4 in the previous series of fourteen *Land* elections (1998-2002) to 46.4 percent, the Christian parties' best showing since the 1980s. The SPD, on the other hand, following an initial success in Mecklenburg-Vorpommern, suffered eleven consecutive setbacks to record its worst performance on the regional level in the postwar period, with 29.6 percent of the vote. In contrast, the Greens, although partners of the Socialists in the national government, improved their following in ten of the twelve election contests to be represented in twelve of the sixteen state parliaments and recover their position from the PDS and FDP as the third largest party in *Land* politics with 6.9 percent of the vote. Much credit for the Greens' success was attributed to the foreign policy successes of party chairman Joschka Fischer, who was not blamed for domestic problems. Nevertheless, the poor showing of the SPD was responsible for the elimination of the Greens from the ministries in all of the states in which they had participated with the Socialists, including North Rhine-Westphalia, Lower Saxony, and Schleswig-Holstein. The FDP did not benefit as much from its opposition status as did the CDU/CSU, witnessing a drop in its overall totals from 6.5 to 5.6 percent, even though it made gains in nine of the twelve elections and polled 6.2 percent of the eastern vote. It regained representation in the Saar, Saxony and Saxony-Anhalt, but lost it in Hamburg to end the period with delegations in eleven of the sixteen state legislative bodies. Although polling only 2.1 percent of ballots cast in the twelve regional contests, right-extremist groups had limited success in three states, including the NPD with 9.2 percent in Saxony, and the DVU with 6.1 percent in Brandenburg and 2.3 percent in Bremen for which it received a single seat by virtue of exceeding the five percent hurdle in Bremerhaven. In a by-election held only in the Bremerhaven portion of Bremen July 6, 2008 the right-conservative *Bürger in Wut* group also received a single seat (see page 201).

Because of the stigma attached to the PDS in the western states of being a successor to the Communist-led SED, it realized little support there and was

TABLE 7.12

THE FOURTH SERIES OF *LAND* ELECTIONS IN THE EASTERN PROVINCES[18]

Land and Date	Valid Votes	CDU/CSU	SPD	FDP	Greens	PDS	Others
Saxony-Anhalt [a]	1,160,985	433,521	231,732	154,145	22,696	236,485	Schill 52,589
April 21, 2002	56.5	37.3 (48)	20.0 (25)	13.3 (17)	2.0 (-)	20.4 (25)	4.5 (-)
Mecklenburg-Vorpommern	970,031	304,125	394,118	45,676	25,402	159.065	Schill 1.7
Sept. 22, 2002	70.6	31.4 (25)	40.6 (33)	4.7 (-)	2.6 (-)	16.4 (13)	NPD 0.8(-) Rep.0.3(-)
Thuringia	1,010,578	434,088	146,297	36,483	45,649	263,717	Rep. 2.0
June 13, 2004	53.8	43.0 (45)	14.5 (15)	3.6 (-)	4.5 (-)	26.1 (28)	NPD 1.6
Brandenburg	1,169,005	227.036	372,956	38,887	42,107	326,923	DVU
Sept. 19, 2004	56.4	19.4 (20)	31.9 (33)	3.3 (-)	3.6 (-)	28.0 (29)	6.1 (6)
Saxony	2,080,135	855,203	204,438	122,605	106,771	490,488	NPD
Sept. 19, 2004	59.6	41.1 (55)	9.8 (13)	5.9 (7)	5.1 (6)	23.6 (31)	9.2 (12)
FiveState Totals	6,390,734	2,253,973 35.3	1,349,541 21.1	397,796 6.2	242,625 3.8	1,476,678 23.1	670,121 10.5
Twelve-State Totals [b]	28,308,817	13,145,882 46.4	8,374,072 29.6	1,576,532 5.6	1,959,269 6.9	1,361,352 4.8	1,891,710 [c] 6.7

a Saxony-Anhalt is included in Table XII since the election of April 21, 2002, even though held five months prior to the fifteenth *Bundestag* contest, was the fourth election held in that state.

b The twelve-state totals include only those elections held between the fifteenth and sixteenth general elections without Saxony-Anhalt totals.

c Of this total, 606,474 votes fell to the three right-extremist parties, DVU, NPD and Republicans, 311,835 (4.9%) in the East, and 294,639 (1.3%) in the West for a nationwide figure of 2.1 percent.

outpolled by the Greens and FDP in overall totals. But in the five new states where elections were held, it not only far outdistanced the Greens and Free Democrats with 23.1 percent of the vote, but replaced the SPD, which received a 21.1 percent share, as the region's second largest party, while the CDU remained the area's most important grouping with 35.3 percent of ballots cast. In the fourth series of *Land* elections in the East the FDP succeeded in gaining representation only in Saxony and Saxony-Anhalt with an area-wide total of 6.2

percent, while the Greens placed delegates only in the Saxony *Landtag* with a 3.8 percent eastern-state following. Somewhat disturbing was the ability of right-extremist parties (NPD, DVU and Republicans), while having little success in the west (only 1.3 percent of ballot cast), to outpoll the Greens in the East with a 4.9 percent total, with the DVU winning 6.1 percent of the vote and six seats in Brandenburg and the NPD 9.2 percent and twelve seats in Saxony. This was blamed on continuing high unemployment in the area encompassed by the former DDR and feelings on the part of residents of being second class citizens within a unified Germany.

The 2005 *Bundestag* Election

Following eleven straight setbacks in regional balloting, including in the country's largest state, Chancellor Gerhard Schröder, a day after the results in North Rhine-Westphalia were confirmed, made the decision to call new *Bundestag* elections one year prior to the end of the constitutional term. The move was both surprising and unprecedented, since it seemed apparent that the SPD would risk certain defeat at the polls, and the move was questioned by numerous observers. Nevertheless, the decision was supported by Federal President Köhler and the federal courts. But the Christian parties were having difficulties of their own in deciding on a chancellor-candidate to lead the party and finding consensus on ways to address the country's economic difficulties. Edmund Stoiber, Minister President of Bavaria, hoped for a second chance, having only narrowly lost to Schröder in 2002. Moreover, Bavarian voters had given him overwhelming support in the *Land* election two years earlier. His major competition came from Dr. Angela Merkel, former Minister for Women and Youth (*Frauen und Jugend*) in the Kohl government after reunification, CDU General Secretary in 1998 and Party chairperson since 2000. The choice to lead the party fell to Dr. Angela Merkel, the first woman Chancellor candidate and the first easterner. With SPD support nearly seventeen percentage points below that of the CDU/CSU in the most recent series of regional contests, and with public opinion polls as late as two weeks prior to the election showing CDU/CSU support of over forty percent and fifty percent for a CDU/CSU/FDP combination, in contrast to less than forty percent for the SPD/Greens coalition, the outcome appeared certain for a Merkel victory. Chancellor Schröder, a tireless campaigner and powerful speaker, fought back. Merkel was criticized for her lackluster speaking style, her seeming inability to smile. Moreover, she was burdened by the proposals of prospective Finance Minister Prof. Dr. Paul Kirchhof from the University of Heidelberg who pushed for a single tax of 25 percent on income and an end to government subsidies. Although Merkel did not personally endorse these proposals, Schröder used them to his advantage by challenging the unfairness of rich and less affluent paying at the same rate and to warn voters that CDU/CSU reform initiatives might be more unsettling than those proposed by his administration.

TABLE 7.13

RESULTS OF THE *BUNDESTAG* ELECTION OF SEPTEMBER 18, 2005 [19]

Party [a]	Valid Second Choice Votes	Percentage	*Bundestag* Seats
Total	47,287,988	100.0	614
SPD	16,194,665	34.2	222
CDU	13,136,740	27.8	180
CSU	3,494,309	7.4	46
FDP	4,648,144	9.8	61
Die Linke	4,118,194	8.7	54
Greens	3,838,326	8.1	51
NPD	748,568	1.6	0
REP	266,101	0.6	0

a Twenty-three other parties participated in the election, but their total amounted to less than two percent of the vote.

Rather than a runaway win, the CDU/CSU outpolled the SPD by less than one percent and Schröder carried twelve of the sixteen states, but strong margins in Bavaria and Baden-Württemberg enabled the CDU to remain ahead of the Socialists in the final vote tally. Observers held that the SPD might have outpolled the CDU/CSU had it not been for the entry into the political arena of a new political grouping, *Die Linke*, an alliance between the PDS and the WASG under former Socialist Minister President of the Saar, Oskar Lafontaine, which won 8.7 percent of the vote, pulling much of the SPD's left wing over to its side.

The inconclusive outcome created a confused situation in which neither a CDU/CSU/FDP combination nor an SPD/Greens alliance could constitute a working majority in the *Bundestag*. Neither of these two grouping wished to work with *Die Linke*, which opposed any reform, nor was a CDU/CSU/FDP/Greens or an SPD/Greens/FDP combination possible because of irreconcilable differences. The only alternative became a grand coalition between the two major parties, the CDU/CSU and the SPD. Schröder, having come from behind and having outpolled the Christian parties in twelve of the sixteen states attempted to retain the chancellorship, but ended up retiring from politics. Following five weeks of negotiations a CDU/CSU/SPD government was formed with Dr. Merkel as Chancellor, Socialist Franz Müntefering as deputy chancellor and the Socialists awarded most of the choice ministries, including foreign affairs and finance. Public opinion polls initially indicated strong support for the combination as the only way for Germany to resolve the many issues facing the country. This was only the second time Germany was governed by an alliance between the two major parties and the first time that the country was led by a woman Chancellor. [20]

The 2006-2009 *Land* Elections

Between the 2005 and the 2009 *Bundestag* elections, regional contests were held in fifteen of the German states, including two (Brandenburg and Schleswig-Holstein) which took place the same day as the 2009 general election. The only exception in this series of state contests was North Rhine-Westphalia where the state parliament was chosen May 9, 2010.

These ballotings took place under circumstances quite different from those in which *Land* elections were held between 1969 and 2005. First, for only the second time, the two major parties, the CDU/CSU and SPD, were participating in a common national government, and dissatisfaction with the policies of the national administration could no longer be expressed through one of them, but only through one of the three smaller parties, the FDP, Greens or *Die Linke* which together controlled 166 of 614 seats in the *Bundestag*, somewhat over a quarter of delegates. This was in contrast to a single party, the FDP, which, with 49 of 496 seats, comprised the total opposition on the national level in the 1966-1969 period, although dissent was expressed in seven of the state legislative bodies through the National Democratic Party (NPD) at the time.

Second, this was the first series of elections since the early 1950s in which the far left, organized in *Die Linke*, was strong enough to challenge the position of the older political groupings nationally. Prior to 2005 the Socialists did not have to compete for the far-left vote in the western states. But after 2005, with the amalgamation of the PDS with Oskar Lafontaine's WASG into *Die Linke,* the new combination succeeded in winning representation in six of the western provinces, Bremen, Hesse, Lower Saxony, Hamburg, the Saar, and Schleswig-Holstein, skimming off votes which might otherwise have gone to the Socialists. With five nationally organized parties now competing for the voters' favor, traditional coalition patterns were put into disarray, in the absence of the now rare case of a single party able to obtain a majority of parliamentary seats. From 1966 to 1985 the FDP was the only available or acceptable coalition partner with which to build a majority. Even with the advent of the Greens the CDU could coalesce with the FDP and the SPD with either the Greens or FDP, except in the rare instance of an SPD/PDS alliance as in Berlin and Mecklenburg-Vorpommern. With the exception of Rhineland-Palatinate where the SPD succeeded in gaining a majority in the 2006 state election, new coalitions had to be constructed in the fourteen other states, in Baden-Württemberg, Bavaria, Hesse, Lower Saxony, Saxony, and Schleswig-Holstein the CDU/CSU with the FDP; in Saxony-Anhalt, Thuringia and Mecklenburg-Vorpommern the CDU and the SPD; in Bremen the SPD with the Greens; in Berlin and Brandenburg the SPD with the PDS/*Die Linke*; in Hamburg the CDU with the Greens, the first combination of its kind on the regional level; and in the Saar the CDU with the FDP and Greens, also the first combination of its kind on the regional level. In Hesse, the task of building a government after the 2008 state election was complicated by the fact that neither a CDU/FDP nor an SPD/Greens partnership could provide a majority since *Die Linke* controlled six balancing seats, and neither the CDU nor the SPD at first was willing to partner with the Leftist party because of irreconcilable differences. As a result, former Minister President Roland Koch, whose party had lost its majority status, was forced into a minority government as *Land* manager (*Geschäftsführer*). In the fall of 2008, however, Socialist leader Andrea Ypsilanti attempted to oust Koch with an SPD/Greens combination tolerated by *Die Linke*, but the attempt failed when four Socialist delegates refused to back the arrangement (*Die Welt*, November 16, 2008). The dilemma could be resolved only through new elections, which took place January 18, 2009. By winning 46 seats, all by direct election, the CDU was able to provide the necessary majority by partnering with the Free Democrats who won twenty of the *Landtag's* 118 seats.

Third, being part of the national government, the SPD could not capitalize on any mistakes made by the coalition in Berlin. The jockeying over leadership succession also harmed the party's image, from Müntefering to Platzeck to Beck, back to Müntefering and, since November 2009, to Sigmund Gabriel. It was difficult for the voters to know what the party alone stood for. Moreover, there were the international successes of Chancellor Angela Merkel and her general popularity which helped sustain the Union base. The replacing of the controversial Kurt Beck with Franz Müntefering as party head and the naming of Frank Walter Steinmeier, Germany's foreign minister, as Chancellor candidate for the 2009 *Bundestag* election failed to curb the general decline of the SPD in voter favor.

The first *Land* election following the 2005 federal poll took place in Baden-Württemberg on March 26, 2006 where the CDU was able to hold its own with 44.2 percent of the vote, failing to win a parliamentary majority by only one seat. In contrast, SPD support fell by 8.1 percentage points, marking its second worse showing in the Southwest state and causing its lead candidate to resign. Both the FDP and Greens increased their standing, while the WASG, with a 3.1 percent share of the vote, and the Republicans with 2.5 percent, failed to qualify for representation. The existing CDU/FDP coalition was continued.

In an election held the same day in Rhineland-Palatinate, the Socialists won an absolute majority of parliamentary seats with 45.6 percent of the vote, as neither the Greens nor the WASG or Republicans were able to exceed the five percent hurdle. Although the SPD had been the largest faction since 1991, this was the first time that it had elected a majority of representatives. The victory ultimately catapulted the *Land's* Minister President, Kurt Beck, into the national chairmanship of the SPD.

In Saxony-Anhalt, in yet another election held on March 26th, the CDU maintained its position as the state's leading party, as the Socialists recovered only modestly from their 2002 setback and were outpolled by *Die Linke* 24.1 to 21.4 percent. Neither the Greens nor the right-oriented DVU qualified for seats.

With the existing CDU/FDP alliance unable to provide a working majority and a CDU/*Die Linke* combination out of the question, the only alternative was a partnership with the SPD under Christian Democrat Dr. Wolfgang Böhmer.

In the Berlin election of September 17, 2006 the CDU failed to make the hoped-for comeback, losing 2.4 percentage points, while the Socialists made a small gain to 30.8 percent. With the two major parties barely exceeding half of ballots cast, the FDP, Greens and *Die Linke* all obtained representation and 13.5 percent of the vote fell to various minor groupings, including 3.9 percent for *die Graue* and 2.9 for the WASG, which competed separately from the PDS. Had the 40,504 votes cast for the WASG gone to the PDS, the PDS would have received 16.3 rather than 13.4 percent of the vote and an equivalent increase in its delegation. In spite of strong representations by the national parties for a grand coalition in the Berlin city government, Lord Mayor Klaus Wowereit felt it was important to continue the existing coalition with the PDS to help integrate the two parts of the city.

In the Mecklenburg-Vorpommern election held the same day as the Berlin contest, both the CDU and SPD lost ground as the two-party share dropped from 72.0 percent in 2002 to 59.0 percent. The Socialists maintained their leading position while the FDP was returned to the legislature with 9.6 percent of the vote after an absence of twelve years. The Greens failed for the fifth time to gain entrance into the *Land* parliament while the PDS/*Die Linke* kept the same number of seats with a 16.8 percent vote total. The NPD, after failing in four earlier attempts to gain representation, obtained 7.3 percent of ballots cast and six seats in a state which at the time registered the highest unemployment rate in the Federal Republic at 18.9 percent (*Die Welt am Sonntag*, September 17, 2006). Since a continuation of the existing SPD/PDS coalition would have provided only a one-seat margin in the *Landtag*, Minister President Harald Ringstorff opted to form a grand coalition between the two major parties to place the government on a more stable basis in order to combat the influences which gave rise to the NPD success. Again, as in Berlin, the WASG organization in Mecklenburg-Vorpommern made the decision to compete separately from *Die Linke* (*Hamburger Abendblatt*, May 8, 2006). The party, however, received only 4,281 votes (0.5 percent) in the election.

In the Bremen balloting of May 13, 2007 the SPD maintained its position as the city's major party, but, at 36.7 percent, its share of the votes was the second lowest in sixteen postwar elections. The CDU share fell almost as much in its worse showing in twenty years. On the other hand, the FDP, with 6.0 percent of the vote, increased its representation, while the Greens recorded their best total in any regional election with a 16.5 percent share. The big surprise was the ability of *Die Linke* to gain representation in a western state for the first time with 8.4 percent of the vote. The DVU, with only 2.74 percent of ballots cast, again sent one delegate to the city parliament because of its concentrated strength in Bremerhaven. Although a continuation of the grand coalition which had been in existence since 1995 was possible, the CDU, in view of its poor showing, decided not to participate in a Socialist-led government. Lord Mayor

Jens Böhrnsen, therefore, turned to the Greens and an alliance was approved in June 2007, the first time in two years that the Greens had been part of any regional ministry. In a by-election held July 6, 2008 in Bremerhaven the right-conservative BIW (*Bürger in Wut* -Angry Citizens) which had lacked one vote in the 2007 election of being eligible for representation, obtained 2,336 ballots or 5.29 percent to gain a single *Bürgerschaft* seat. Following the 2007 decision, the group had requested a recount which led to a by-election to settle the matter. The SPD was obliged to vacate a single seat to make room for the BIW representative (*Berliner Morgenpost*, July 8, 2008 and *Wikipedia, Bürger in Wut*, 2010).

Regional elections were held in both Hesse and Lower Saxony on January 27, 2008. While the CDU lost ground in Lower Saxony, so did the Socialists, and a 42.5 percent share of the vote coupled with the FDP's 8.2 percent insured a continuation of the existing black/yellow coalition.[21] For the second time *Die Linke* was able to gain seats in a western legislative body, this time with 7.1 percent of the vote. The only other party to secure representation was the Greens who made a small gain over their 2003 *Land* election total. This was the first election to be held in a smaller *Landtag* of 135 members.

While a two-party ministry was possible in Lower Saxony, this was not the case in Hesse where the CDU lost its absolute majority, suffering a 12.0 percentage point drop while the Socialists gained 7.6 percentage points to equal it in the number of legislative delegates. With *Die Linke* securing six seats, neither a CDU/FDP nor an SPD/Greens combination could provide a working majority, throwing traditional coalition patterns into turmoil. Irreconcilable differences prevented the formation of a grand coalition and there were insufficient conciliatory moves to build a three party coalition of either the CDU/FDP/Greens or the SPD with the FDP and Greens. As a result, Christian Democrat Roland Koch continued his government in minority status. Following the failed attempt by SPD head Andrea Ypsilanti to put together an SPD/Greens ministry tolerated by *Die Linke*, new elections were held in January 2009 to resolve the coalition dilemma, resulting in a CDU/FDP majority under Koch.

The ninth *Land* election in this interval took place February 24, 2008 in Hamburg, where the CDU had held a majority of seats for four years. The SPD had hoped to break the CDU grip by gaining enough seats to form a coalition with the Greens, but *Die Linke* was able to skim off sufficient votes that otherwise might have gone to the Socialists to enter a western state parliament for the fourth straight time. Since the Free Democrats failed to gain representation, Lord Mayor Ole von Beust, in a rare move, turned to the Greens who had won 9.6 percent of ballots cast. Having been stirred by former U.S. Vice President Albert Gore's film, "An Inconvenient Truth," the mayor was willing to attempt an arrangement with the Greens. Negotiations continued for several months over school organization, the fate of a coal-fired power plant and the deepening of the Elbe River to allow larger ships to reach the Hamburg Port, leading to the first CDU/Greens partnership on the regional level in May 2008.

The tenth election in this series of regional contests was held in Bavaria

September 28. Hurt by the leadership struggle over a successor to Edmund Stoiber, state bank investment losses and the party's assumed resistance to reform, the Christian Social Union lost its majority status for the first time in 46 years as its vote total fell by 17.3 percentage points over 2003 results. The Socialists, however, failed to benefit from this setback as its own following declined by a percentage point. The major winners were the Greens, the Free Democrats (who were returned to the Bavarian *Landtag* for the first time in four legislative sessions), and the Free Voters (FW), which, running as an alternative to the CSU, gained 10.2 percent of the vote. Although supported by nearly a quarter million voters, *Die Linke*, with 4.4 percent of ballots cast, failed to gain representation in a fifth western state (*Die Welt*, September 29 and 30, 2008). The outcome forced minister president Günther Beckstein to resign in favor of rival Horst Seehofer. Without a majority, the CSU, not wishing to coalesce with the FW which had siphoned off many of its supporters, turned to the Free Democrats to form a government.

A second regional election was held in Hesse January 18, 2009 to resolve the confused situation caused by the entrance of a Leftist faction to the state parliament in the election of the previous January. In this rerun contest, the CDU experienced a small gain to 37.2 percent to obtain 46 seats, all by direct election. In contrast, the Socialist total fell by over a third to 23.7 percent to reduce the party's *Landtag* delegation to 29 seats. Both the FDP and Greens made major gains, 16.2 percent of ballots cast and twenty mandates for the Liberals, 13.7 percent and seventeen mandates for the Greens. The Leftists were able to retain their six seats with 5.4 percent of the vote. The combination of 46 CDU and twenty FDP representatives enabled Minister President Roland Koch to form a stable two-party black/yellow majority in the Hessian *Landtag*, which had been enlarged by eight seats as a result of the awarding of four balancing seats to offset the CDU's four *Überhang* mandates.

Three regional elections, in the Saar, Saxony and Thuringia, were held August 30, 2009, one month prior to the seventeenth *Bundestag* balloting. The Saar contest was strongly influenced by personalities, as Oskar Lafontaine, who had won absolute majorities for the SPD in the 1985, 1990 and 1994 *Land* elections before a falling-out with his former party, attempted to make a comeback as the first Leftist head of a state government. He was opposed by two equally strong contenders, Minister President Peter Müller (CDU), whose party held a majority in the state parliament, and Socialist Heiko Mass, whose party's goal was to replace the CDU as the state's leading faction.

Although the *Die Linke* failed in its attempt to emerge from the election as the state's principal grouping, it did obtain 21.3 percent of the vote, the largest following for the party in any of the ten western states, and its success contributed to a major setback for both the CDU and SPD. The Christian Democrats suffered a 13.0 percentage slide to lose their majority status in the legislature while the Socialist experienced a drop in their share of ballots cast from 30.8 to 24.5 percent. However, with 34.5 percent of the vote, the Union remained the leading faction. Other than *Die Linke*, the Free Democrats made major gains, nearly doubling their following from 5.2 to 9.2 percent to gain two additional legislative seats. The Greens registered a small gain to retain their three seats in the *Landtag* while support for the right-extremist NPD fell from the 4.0 reached in 2004 to only 1.5 percent (*Süddeutsche Zeitung*, September 1, 2009).

By splintering the vote, the Leftist success made coalition building in the state highly problematical, since the CDU could no longer govern alone and an alliance with the FDP was insufficient to provide a legislative majority. Minister President Müller had been on bad terms with the Socialists, ruling out a grand coalition, and a combination with *Die Linke* was out of the question, leaving a three-party combination the only alternative if Müller was to remain in power. The outcome placed the Greens in a position of being king-maker. Following two months of negotiations the first "Jamaica" (black/yellow/Green) coalition of the CDU/FDP/Greens was hammered out with the Greens awarded two ministries and concessions were made to the Greens on university student tuition, the building of coal-driven power plants and education (*Hamburger Abendblatt*, November 5, 2009 and *Die Welt am Sonntag*, November 10, 2009).

In an election held the same day in Thuringia the CDU suffered a second major setback, losing its parliamentary majority as its following sank from 43.0 to 31.2 percent of the vote, its poorest showing in the five elections held in the state since reunification. Partial blame for the loss was placed on Minister President Dieter Althaus, who had been in a skiing accident earlier in the year which killed a woman skier, and whose leadership style was criticized within his party. The enormity of the downslide can be measured in the direct-seat count. While the CDU had won 39 of 44 direct mandates in 2004, it won only 28 in 2009. The Leftists, on the other hand, with a 27.4 percent share of the vote, were able to up their direct mandate count from five to fourteen seats. Never a strong contender in Thuringia, the Socialists, nevertheless, were able to raise their vote share from 14.5 to 18.5 percent which gave them eighteen seats to the CDU's thirty and the *Die Linke's* 27. While the CDU was experiencing a major loss, the FDP and Greens were both returned to the Thuringia *Landtag* after a fifteen-year absence (*Süddeutshe Zeitung*, September 1, 2009).

Although a Socialist/Leftist combination could have provided a majority with 45 of 88 seats, such an alliance, in addition to being unstable, would have placed Leftist Bodo Ramelow into the premiership as his was the larger of the two parties, a situation repugnant to the Socialists. With intense political criticism over Althaus' continuation in office, the CDU turned to the former Protestant minister and faction head, Christine Lieberknecht to head the party. A ministry with the SPD was eventually formed with Lieberknecht as Premier and Socialist Christoph Matschie as her deputy, marking the third grand coalition to be formed in this series of regional contests, the others being in Mecklenburg-Vorpommern and Saxony-Anhalt. No one from Althaus' former government was awarded a post in the new ministry (*Hamburger Abendblatt*, November 5, 2009). This was only the second time that a woman was selected as the executive head of a state, the only other premier being Heide Simonis who served as Minister President of Schleswig-Holstein from 1993 to 2005.

In Saxony, the CDU fared better than in the other two elections held August 30, 2009, experiencing only a minor setback from 41.1 to 40.2 percent, while gaining three additional seats by winning 58 of the state's sixty direct mandates. The Socialists recovered modestly from their worst regional election result in the 2004 balloting from 9.8 to 10.4 percent. The biggest gainer, as in the Saar and Thuringia, was the FDP which increased its following from 5.9 to 10.0 percent, nearly outpolling the SPD. By doubling their count of representatives from seven to fourteen, the Free Democrats were able to provide the necessary mandates to make a continuation of the black/yellow ministry possible with Christian Democrat Stanislaw Tillich remaining as state premier. The Greens made a small gain to pick up three additional seats, while support for *Die Linke* slipped from 23.6 to 20.6 percent. Of significance was the decline in the NPD following from 9.2 percent to 5.6 percent to cut the party's *Landtag* representation from twelve to eight seats. Because of the CDU's success in single member districts, the size of the Saxony parliament had to be raised from 120 to 132 members (*Süddeutsche Zeitung*, September 1, 2009 and *Wahl zum 5. Sächsischen Landtag 2009, Landeswahlleiterin des Statistischen Landesamtes der Freistaates Sachsen*).

The last two contests in the seventeenth series of regional elections were held in Brandenburg and Schleswig-Holstein, the same day as the seventeenth *Bundestag* poll. In Brandenburg all three of the state's leading factions, the SPD, CDU and *Die Linke*, lost ground as voters turned to the Greens and Free Democrats, neither of which had been represented in the state parliament since 1994. The Greens gained five seats on a 5.7 percent share of ballots, the Liberals seven seats on a 7.2 percent share. The right-extremist German People's Union (DVU) which had won six seats on 6.1 percent of the vote in 2004 lost its entire delegation when its following fell to 1.1 percent. A second rightist grouping, the NPD, also had little success, receiving 2.6 percent of ballots cast.

Although falling behind the Socialists with 27.2 percent of second votes, the Leftists, nevertheless, won 21 of 44 direct seats to the Socialists' nineteen. The Christian Democrats with a 19.8 percent share gained sufficient mandates to make a continuation of the existing grand coalition with the Socialists possible, but Minister President Mathius Platzek surprisingly, and in the face of severe criticism, turned to *Die Linke* as coalition partner in the interest of reconciliation (*Brandenbürgerishe Landeszentrale für Politische Bildung*, October 27, 2009 and *Die Welt*, October 29, 2009). On November 6, 2009 Platzek was reconfirmed as Minister President. Ever since its establishment, the red/red coalition in Brandenburg has been troubled by the disclosure that six of the *Die Linke's* 26-member parliamentary delegation had *Stasi* ties. Two of these, *Landtag* Vice-President Gerlinde Stobrawa gave up her office, but not her seat, while Leftist delegate Renate Adolph resigned from the legislature (*"Pulverfass Stasi," Dithmarscher Landeszeitung*, December 1, 2009).

The regional election in Schleswig-Holstein was moved forward five months as a result of the collapse of the grand coalition which had existed

TABLE 7.14

THE FIFTH SERIES OF *LAND* ELECTIONS IN THE EASTERN PROVINCES [22]

Land and Date	Valid Votes	CDU	SPD	FDP	Greens	PDS/*Linke*	Others
Saxony-Anhalt March 26, 2006	902,254 44.4	326,721 36.2 (40)	192,754 21.4 (24)	60,209 6.7 (7)	32,117 3.6 (0)	217,295 24.1 26)	DVU 3.0 (0)
Berlin Sept. 17, 2006	1,377,355 58.0	294,026 21.3 (37)	424,054 30.8 (53)	104,584 7.6 (13)	180,865 13.1 (23)	185,185 13.4 (23)	WASG 2.9 (0)
Mecklenburg-Vorpommern Sept. 17, 2006	818,061 59.1	235,350 28.8 (22)	247,312 30.2 (23)	78,440 9.6 (7)	27,642 3.4 (0)	137,253 16.8 (13)	NPD 7.3 (6)
Saxony Aug. 30, 2009	1,797,349 52.2	722,983 40.2 (58)	187,261 10.4 (14)	178,867 10.0 (14)	114,963 6.4 (9)	370,359 20.6 (29)	NPD 5.6 (8)
Thuringia Aug. 30, 2009	1,054,297 56.2	329,302 31.2 (30)	195,363 18.5 (18)	80,600 7.6 (7)	64,912 6.2 (6)	288,915 27.4 (27)	NPD 4.3 (0)
Brandenburg Sept. 27, 2009	1,388,722 67.0	274,825 19.8 (19)	458,840 33.0 (31)	100,123 7.2 (7)	78,550 5.7 (5)	377,112 27.2 (26)	NPD 2.6 (0)
Six State Totals Percent	7,338,038	2,183,207 29.8	1,705,584 23.2	602,823 8.2	499,049 6.8	1,576,119 21.5	771,256 10.5

between the CDU and SPD since April 2005. A running feud between CDU Minister President Peter Harry Carstensen and SPD faction head Rolf Stegner had made continued cooperation impossible (see Franziska Reich's *"Friesenerz und Fliegenträger," Stern,* August 2009).

In the September contest the CDU emerged as the leading party with 31.5 percent of the vote in spite of an 8.7 percentage loss over 2005 totals. The Socialists, however, suffered an even greater loss from 38.7 to 25.4 percent, to the lowest level in any regional election held in the state since 1947. As in Brandenburg the same day, the Liberals and Greens were the big winners. The FDP pushed its share of the vote from 6.6 to 14.9 percent, the Greens from 6.2 to 12.4 percent. The party of the Danish minority, the SSW, also made sufficient gains to place four delegates in the *Landtag. Die Linke* entered the Schleswig-Holstein parliament for the first time with a 6.0 percent share of the vote and six seats to now be presented in six of the ten western provinces and causing Schleswig-Holstein to become the third state, along with Bremen and Saxony, to have six parties represented in its legislature. With the addition of 26 additional seats as a result of the CDU's ability to win 34 of the state's forty direct mandates, the size of the legislature had to be raised to 95 members. With 49 of the 95 seats (34 CDU, 15 FDP) the Union was able to produce a majority with the Liberals to replace the defunct black/red ministry. Christian Democrat Carstensen was reelected Minister President October 27, 2009 (*"Carstensen bleibt Minister President,"* NDR-Online, October 27, 2009).

The validity of the election results was challenged by the four opposition parties which had polled 27,500 more votes than the two government parties, but which had received only 46 seats in the distribution to the CDU/FDP total of 49. A perfect balance would have given the opposition one more seat than that of the two government parties. There has been a move by the opposition to reduce the number of direct seats from forty to thirty to prevent a recurrence of the distortion created by the addition of *Überhang* and compensating (*Ausgleich*) mandates (*Dithmarscher Landeszeitung*, November 3 and 20, 2009).[23]

Hurt by a series of scandals involving the country's business elite and various local issues (*Wall Street Journal*, March 4, 2008), the CDU/CSU experienced a decline in support in all fifteen of the regular contests held between the 2005 and 2009 *Bundestag* elections, losing their majority status in five of the *Land* parliaments. Although the Socialists made minor gains in seven of these elections, the Union parties outpolled the SPD in ten of them to remain the leading party on the regional level with 37.4 percent of the nationwide vote to the Socialists' 26.8 percent. With only 64.2 percent of ballots cast, this marked the smallest level of support for the two major parties in regional balloting since the second series of provincial elections between 1949 and 1953.

While the two major parties were losing ground, the smaller parties were gaining an ever-larger share of the vote, amounting to as much as half of ballots cast in several states (50.3 percent in Thuringia, 49.4 percent in Saxony and 47.9 percent in Berlin where the Leftist party was strong). As a result, it was only the second time since the late 1950s that the Union parties polled less than forty percent of the vote in regional competition, and the Socialists registered their lowest share since the first state elections were held in the western states in the 1946-1947 period. The Free Democrats, with 8.9 percent of the regional vote, by adding Brandenburg and Thuringia, were now represented in every state legislative body with the single exception of Hamburg. The Greens, on the other hand, with 8.6 percent of regional totals, also by adding Brandenburg and Thuringia, were now represented in thirteen of the sixteen German states, the only exceptions being Mecklenburg Vorpommern, Rhineland-Palatinate and Saxony-Anhalt. Although losing voter share in the eastern provinces, the major gainer in the seventeenth series of *Land* elections was the Leftist Party which, by gaining representation in six of the ten western states, to now be represented in twelve *Landtage*, pushed its regional total from 4.8 to 9.5 percent to place ahead

TABLE 7.15

THE 2006-2009 *LAND* ELECTIONS [24]

Land and Date	Valid Votes	CDU	SPD	FDP	Greens	PDS/ WASG *Die Linke*	Others
Baden-Württemberg Mar. 26, 2006	3,960,615 53.4	1,748,766 44.2 (69)	996,207 25.2 (38)	421,994 10.7 (15)	462,889 11.7 (17)	121,733 [a] 3.1 (-)	Rep. 2.5 (0)
Rhineland-Palatinate Mar. 26, 2006	1,753,110 58.2	574,329 32.8 (38)	799,377 45.6 (53)	140,865 8.0 (10)	81,411 4.6 (0)	44,826 [b] 2.6 (0)	Rep. 1.7 (0)
Saxony-Anhalt Mar. 26, 2006	902,254 44.4	326,721 36.2 (40)	192,754 21.4 (24)	60,209 6.7 (7)	32,117 3.6 (0)	217,295 24.1 (26)	DVU 3.0 (0)
Berlin Sep. 17, 2006	1,377,355 58.0	294,026 21.3 (37)	424,054 30.8 (53)	104,584 7.6 (13)	180,865 13.1 (23)	185,185 13.4 (23)	WASG 2.9 (0)
Mecklenburg-Vorpommern Sep. 17, 2006	818,061 59.1	235,350 28.8 (22)	247,312 30.2 (23)	78,440 9.6 (7)	27,642 3.4 (0)	137,253 [a] 16.8 (13)	NPD 7.3 (6)
Bremen May 13, 2007	276,022 57.6	70,832 25.7 (23)	101,417 36.7 (32)	16,497 6.0 (5)	45,524 16.5 (14)	23,296 8.4 (7)	DVU 2.74 (1) BIW 0.8 (1)
Lower Saxony Jan. 27, 2008	3,425,426 57.1	1,456,742 42.5 (68)	1,036,727 30.3 (48)	279,826 8.2 (13)	274,221 8.0 (12)	243,361 7.1 (11)	NPD 1.5 (0)
Hesse[25 c] Jan. 27, 2008	2,742,959 64.3	1,009,775 36.8 (42)	1,006,264 36.7 (42)	258,550 9.4 (11)	206,610 7.5 (9)	140,769 5.1 (6)	Rep. 1.0 (0)
Hamburg Feb. 24, 2008	777,531 63.5	331,067 42.6 (56)	265,516 34.1 (45)	36,953 4.8 (0)	74,472 9.6 (12)	50,132 6.4 (8)	27,103 3.5
Bavaria Sep. 28, 2008	5,306,137 57.9	2,301,980 43.4 (92)	986,218 18.6 (39)	423,614 8.0 (16)	499,556 9.4 (19)	230,878 4.4 (0)	(FW) 10.2 (21)
The Saar Aug. 30, 2009	534,793 67.6	184,537 34.5 (19)	131,241 24.5 (13)	49,064 9.2 (5)	31,516 5.9 (3)	113,664 21.3 (11)	NPD 1.5 (0)
Saxony Aug. 30, 2009	1,797,349 52.2	722,983 40.2 (58)	187,261 10.4 (14)	178,867 10.0 (14)	114,963 6.4 (9)	370,359 20.6 (29)	NPD 5.6 (8)
Thuringia Aug. 30, 2009	1,054,297 56.2	329,302 31.2 (30)	195,363 18.5 (18)	80,600 7.6 (7)	64,912 6.2 (6)	288,915 27.4 (27)	NPD 4.3 (0)
Brandenburg Sep. 27, 2009	1,388,722 67.0	274,825 19.8 (19)	458,840 33.0 (31)	100,123 7.2 (7)	78,550 5.7 (5)	377,112 27.2 (26)	2.6 NPD DVU
Schleswig-Holstein Sep. 27, 2009	1,603,374 73.6	505,612 31.5 (34)	407,643 25.4 (25)	239,338 14.9 (15)	199,367 12.4 (12)	95,732 6.0 (5)	SSW 4.3 (4)
Fifteen State Total	27,725,717	10,366,847	7,436,194	2,469,524	2,374,615	2,640,530	2,438,007
Percent of Vote		37.4	26.8	8.9	8.6	9.5	8.8

a In Berlin and Mecklenburg-Vorpommern the WASG competed separately from *Die Linke*.

b In Rhineland-Palatinate the Left competed under the WASG designation.

c The inconclusive results of the January 27, 2008 election in Hesse necessitated a rerun poll which took place January 18, 2009 with the following outcome: (see top of next page)

Land and Date	Valid Votes	CDU	SPD	FDP	Greens	*Die Linke*	Others
Hesse Jan. 18, 2009	2,591,872 61.0%	963,763 37.2 (46)	614,648 23.7 (29)	420,426 16.2 (20)	356,040 13.7 (17)	139,074 5.4 (6)	97,921 3.8 (0)

of the Liberals and Greens as the third party on the regional level.

Right-extremist parties continued to be on the defensive. While the National Democrats succeeded in gaining six seats in the Mecklenburg-Vorpommern parliament, the DVU lost its entire delegation in Brandenburg when its following fell from 6.1 to 1.1 percent in 2009 balloting and NPD support fell from 9.2 to 5.6 percent in Saxony to cause the party to lose four seats. In Bremen, the DVU held on to its single mandate only by virtue of exceeding the five percent barrier in Bremerhaven. The most votes polled by a rightist group were the 100,834 cast for the National Democrats in Saxony, giving the party eight seats.

This series of elections produced a three-party system only in Rhineland-Palatinate, while four parties gained representation in Baden-Württemburg, Hamburg and Saxony-Anhalt, five in Bavaria, Berlin, Brandenburg, Hesse, Lower Saxony, Mecklenburg-Vorpommern, the Saar, and Thuringia, six in Schleswig-Holstein and Saxony, and, after the by-election of July 2008 in Bremerhaven, seven in Bremen.[26]

The 2009 *Bundestag* Election

From its very beginning the unnatural coalition between the Union parties and the SPD in Berlin had a troubled existence, and there were a number of discussions by the two partners with the three smaller parties to determine what other alternatives were possible. However, the alliance held together for four years because there was no real alternative. As the campaign drew to a close, CDU Chancellor Angela Merkel, because of her personal popularity, continued to be favored over her Socialist opponent, Foreign Minister Frank Walter Steinmeier, by a wide margin, even as her party was taking a beating in regional contests. However, in the last two weeks of this lackluster contest for voter support, especially following the single television debate between the two major candidates, it appeared that the Socialists might narrow the gap and prevent Chancellor Merkel from achieving her desired CDU/CSU/FDP majority. Nearly four million fewer voters went to the polls to register the poorest turnout in any national election with a 70.8 percent total. Rather than a close contest as in 2005 when the parties were separated by less than one percentage point and the Socialists emerged as the leading party in twelve of the sixteen states, the SPD suffered its worse general election outcome in the sixty-year history of the Federal Republic with a disappointing 23.0 percent of ballots cast, emerging as the leading party only in Bremen. And the share of the votes garnered by the two major parties was under sixty percent for the first time (*The Economist*, October 3-9, 2009). The Socialists were especially hurt by the desertion of many former supporters to the Greens and *Die Linke*, both of which registered their best general election results.

Although the Union following was less than public opinion polls indicated, due partially to less than robust support in Bavaria, it carried thirteen of the sixteen states and its 33.8 total was less than a percentage point under its 2005 showing. The strong outcome for its desired coalition partner, the FDP, which registered its best general election result with 14.6 percent of the vote, provided the necessary margin to end the grand coalition. (The two groupings controlled a comfortable margin with 332 of the *Bundestag's* 622 seats.) The Greens also made significant progress to 10.7 percent, but its gains were insufficient to offset the 11.2 percentage decline experienced by the Socialists. *Die Linke*, now a nationally organized political force, polled 11.9 percent of the vote to remain ahead of the Greens in national vote totals. Encouraging in the face of a severe financial crisis was the limited support given to right-extremist parties, which, combined, received only 2.0 percent of the national total, less than their combined totals in the 2005 general election.

Following several weeks of negotiations, a CDU/CSU/FDP ministry was formed with Dr. Angela Merkel as Chancellor and Free Democrat Dr. Guido Westerwelle as Deputy Chancellor and Foreign Minister.

TABLE 7.16

RESULTS OF THE *BUNDESTAG* ELECTION OF SEPTEMBER 27, 2009 [27]

Party	Valid Second Choice Votes	Percentage	*Bundestag* Seats
Total	43,357,542	100.0	622
CDU	11,824,794	27.3	194
CSU	2,830,210	6.5	45
SPD	9,988,843	23.0	146
FDP	6,313,023	14.6	93
Greens	4,641,197	10.7	68
Die Linke	5,153,884	11.9	76
Pirates	845,904	2.0	-
NPD	635,437	1.5	-
Republicans	193,473	0.4	-
Others [a]	930,777	2.1	-

a Nineteen other parties participated in the election, receiving 930,777 votes or 2.1 percent of the total.

The 2010-2011 *Land* Elections

The only regional election to be held in 2010 took place May 9th in Germany's most populous state, North Rhine-Westphalia. The election was of considerable importance to the governing coalition in Berlin since a strong Socialist showing could upset the party balance in the Federal *Bundesrat*, thereby undermining support for the Black/Yellow coalition. In that contest, while failing to regain its earlier position as leading party in the Rhine and Ruhr, the SPD came within 6,000 votes of equaling the CDU's share of ballots cast to win a comparable number of seats in the *Landtag* and break the CDU/FDP majority in Düsseldorf. Again, as earlier in Hesse and the Saar, the entrance of *Die Linke* into the parliament complicated coalition building, since neither a CDU/FDP nor an SPD/Greens combination could produce the needed majority, and both groupings ruled out cooperation with the Leftists. Discussions between the CDU and SPD on a grand coalition or on a combination of the CDU/FDP and Greens or the SPD with the FDP and Greens proved unfruitful. As a consequence, the Socialists, in association with the Greens which had made major gains in the election, came within one seat of forming a majority in the *Landtag*. This enabled Socialist leader Hannelore Kraft to negotiate a minority government with the Greens which would be tolerated by *Die Linke*, with Kraft serving as Minister President (*Die Welt*, May 10, 2010 and *Frankfurter Allgemeine FAZ.NET*, July 14, 2010).

In the February 20, 2011 *Bürgerschaft* election in Hamburg the Social Democrats experienced a second major comeback by winning an absolute majority of seats and elevating Socialist Olaf Scholz into the mayorship. The outcome was strongly influenced by the withdrawal of the Greens from its coalition with the CDU in November, forcing Lord Mayor Christoph Ahlhaus (CDU) to govern in minority status until new elections could be held. The Greens did not benefit from their move, making only a small gain to 11.2 percent and failing to prevent the Socialists from winning a parliamentary majority, thereby ending their hope to influence policy in a Socialist-led ministry. Ahlhaus' CDU, however, took the brunt of voter disaffection, losing 20.7 percentage points over its 2008 following to register its worse showing in the postwar period. The Socialists, on the other hand, gained 14.3 percentage points to record their best result since 1982. The FDP registered a small gain to reenter the *Bürgerschaft* for the first time since 2004, but its total of 6.7 percent was insufficient to offset Union losses. The Leftists duplicated their 2008 results with 6.4 percent of ballots cast. Voter turnout was the lowest in Hamburg postwar history, blamed on the difficulties in dealing with the new electoral system which gave each voter up to twenty choices (*Die Welt*, February 21 and 22, 2011).

In the March 20, 2011 election in Saxony-Anhalt the SPD made a small gain, but insufficient to prevent the CDU from remaining the state's largest faction. The Greens, with 7.1 percent of the vote, reentered the parliament for the first time since 1998, but their following was too small to be a major player in the state and the grand coalition between the CDU and SPD was continued under Christian Democrat Dr. Reiner Haseloff, who succeeded retiring Prof. Dr. Wolfgang Böhmer as Minister-President. *Die Linke* held its own over 2006 totals and outpolled the Socialists with 23.7 percent of the vote to the SPD's 21.5 percent. The FDP, with 3.8 percent of ballots cast, lost its representation (*Statistisches Landesamt Sachsen-Anhalt*, 2011). A week later in Rhineland-Palatinate the outcome was not as gratifying for the Socialists as they lost their parliamentary majority, while remaining marginally ahead of the CDU with 35.7 percent of the vote to the CDU's 35.2 percent. Kurt Beck remained Minister-President, however, by coalescing with the Greens, who, benefiting from the Fukushima reactor tragedy in Japan, were returned to the state parliament after a five-year absence with a 15.4 percent following. Neither the Free Democrats nor the Leftists qualified for seats, leaving only three parties in the state parliament (*Landeswahlleiter Rheinland-Pfalz, Wahlergebnis* 2011*).

That same day the CDU lost control of Baden-Württemberg for the first time in 58 years to a combination of the Greens and SPD, while remaining the largest party with 39.0 percent of the vote. In that election, the Greens, helped not only by the Fukushima disaster, but by the conflict over the central railroad station project, Stuttgart 21, obtained 24.2 percent of the vote to outpoll the SPD, in its best showing in any election, and, with the SPD, formed the first ministry headed by a Greens' Minister President, Winfried Kretschmann (*Financial Times Deutschland*, May 13, 2011). The FDP, although losing half of its 2006 following, was able to remain in the state legislature with 5.3 percent of the vote. *Die Linke*, with a 2.8 percent total, failed to qualify for seats (*Landeszentrale für politische Bildung Baden-Württemberg, Landtagswahl* 2011). In the May 22, 2011 balloting in Bremen, the SPD remained the leading party with 38.6 percent of the vote while the Greens continued their surge to replace the CDU as the state's second party. The DVU did not compete as a separate grouping in the election, but the BIW (*Bürger in Wut*) retained its single seat in the Bremen *Bürgerschaft* by virtue of polling 7.1 percent of the vote in Bremerhaven which is considered as a separate unit in the division of seats. The FDP continued its decline in voter favor by failing to qualify for seats as in Saxony-Anhalt and Rhineland-Palatinate. The party hoped that its change in national leadership would enhance future chances. The existing Socialist-Greens combination was continued under Lord Mayor Jens Böhrnsen (SPD).

According to Prof. Dr. Joachim Krause of the University of Kiel, the success of the Greens in Bremen and earlier elections was due in large measure to the panic caused by the reactor catastrophe in Fukushima. He warned, however, that if an energy collapse results from their efforts to close all nuclear plants, the voters could quickly go the other way (*Norddeutsche Rundschau*, May 24, 2011).

TABLE 7.17

THE 2010-2011 *LAND* ELECTIONS

Land and Date	Valid Votes	CDU	SPD	FDP	Greens	*Die Linke*	Others
North-Rhine Westphalia May 9, 2010	7,760,546 59.3	2,681,700 34.6 (67)	2,675,818 34.5 (67)	522,229 6.7 (13)	941,162 12.1 (23)	435,627 5.6 (11)	504,010 6.5 (0)
Hamburg [a] Feb. 20, 2011	696,568 57.3	753,805 21.9 (28)	1,667,804 48.4 (62)	229,804 6.7 (9)	384,502 11.2 (14)	220,428 6.4 (8)	Pirates 2.1 NPD 4.6
Saxony-Anhalt Mar. 20, 2011	993,175 51.2	322,897 32.5 (41)	213,586 21.5 (26)	38,172 3.8 (0)	70,906 7.1 (9)	234,917 23.7 (29)	FW 2.8 NPD 4.6
Baden-Württemberg Mar. 27, 2011	4,981,114 66.3	1,942,404 39.0 (60)	1,151,859 23.1 (35)	262,500 5.3 (7)	1,205,508 24.2 (36)	139,700 2.8 (0)	Pirates 2.1 NPD 1.0
Rhineland-Palatinate Mar. 27, 2011	1,867,593 61.8	658,211 35.2 (41)	666,666 35.7 (42)	79,363 4.2 (0)	288,341 15.4 (18)	56,040 3.0 (0)	FW 2.3 NPD 1.1
Bremen May 22, 2011	264,472 57.5	265,844 20.3 (20)	504,333 38.6 (36)	31,127 2.4 (0)	293,440 22.5 (21)	73,681 5.6 (5)	48,475 [b] BIW (1)
Six State Totals		35.1	31.1	5.8	15.9	5.6	6.5

a In Hamburg and Bremen, each voter casts multiple votes, for a party list and for individual candidates, greatly increasing the number of votes noted in the table. In Hamburg, each voter has ten choices for *Bürgerschaft* seats, ten for district seats.

b The *Bürger in Wut* (BIW) group received one seat in the Bremen *Bürgerschaft* by virtue of its 7.1 percent following in Bremerhaven which is considered separately for the distribution of seats.

Endnotes to Chapter VII

1 Through Article 2 of the state installation law (*Ländereinführungsgesetz von 22, Juli* 1990) the legislatures of the five new federal states were authorized to prepare constitutions, since, during the first legislative period (1990-1994), they were simultaneously legislatures and constituent assemblies. Legally-binding constitutions were subsequently drawn up and approved by the respective state legislative bodies, with the exception of Thuringia, where the draft was submitted to popular referendum at the same time as the October 16, 1994 *Land* election (Andersen and Woyke, 2003: 379 and 383).

2 *Der Bundeswahlleiter*, Results of the Election to the 12th German *Bundestag* on 2.

December 1990.

3 The Greens' debacle was due in large measure to radical elements in its program, which appeared irrelevant to the new situation in Europe created by the collapse of the eastern Communist regimes. The party was hostile to German reunification, cool to European integration, called for the dissolution of NATO, for the closing down of all nuclear power facilities, for the introduction of a 31-hour work week to combat unemployment and for the introduction of other controversial measures aimed at reducing environmental degradation (*First All German Election*, **Inter Nationes**, 1990: 41-44). The western and eastern Green alternative groupings did not merge until 1993.

4 The table is based on election results provided by the various state statistical offices or taken from individual reports on the separate elections such as *Wahlen in Berlin am 2. Dezember 1990*, *Statistisches Landesamt* Berlin, December 1991.

5 The table is based on data provided by the several German statistical offices in the western states, from the federal election directory (*Bundeswahlleiter*) and from reports from the individual states, such as *Analyse der Hamburger Wahlen am 2. Juni 1991*, *Statistisches Landesamt der Freien und Hansastadt* Hamburg, 1991.

6 *Der Bundeswahlleiter, First and Second Votes in the 1994 Bundestag Election*, 1994.

7 An analysis of shifts in German public opinion during the 1994 *Bundestag* election campaign is provided by Wolfgang G. Gibowski in "Germany's General Election in 1994," *Germany's New Politics: Parties and Issues in the 1990s* (Oxford, UK:, Berghahn Books, 1995): 105-130.

8 The "deradicalization" or reorientation of the Greens' program and campaign strategy following their stunning setback in the 1990 federal election which resulted in the party's 1994 comeback is analyzed by Hans-Georg Betz in "Alliance 90/Greens," *Germany's New Politics: Parties and Issues in the 1990s* (Oxford, UK, Berghahn Books, 1995): 203-254.

9 A thorough coverage of the 1994 *Bundestag* election campaign and its outcome is found in *Germany's New Politics: Parties and Issues in the 1990s* (Oxford, U.K., Berghahn Books, 1995).

10 The table is based on data taken from the federal election directory web site (*Bundeswahlleiter)* and from materials supplied by the various state statistical offices.

11 The table is based on statistical data provided by the various state statistical offices.

12 The results are taken from the federal election directory web site, *Bundestag 1998-Bundesergebnis*, 1998.

13 The *Block der Heimatvertriebenen und Entrechteten,* most commonly known as the Refugee Party, representing the special interests of the masses of refugees and expellees from the East, entered the political arena in the Schleswig-Holstein *Land* election of July 9, 1950, gaining 23.4 percent of the vote and securing 15 of 69 seats to become the second strongest faction in the parliament.

14 The table is based on data obtained from the federal directory website (*Bundeswahlleiter*) and from publications of the various *Land* statistical offices.

15 Election results are based on statistics from the various state statistical offices

and from the federal election directory.

16 Election data comes from *Wahl zum 15. Deutschen Bundestag am 22. September 2002* and *Bundestagwahl 2002 -Ergebnisse in den Bundesländern* from the federal election directory.

17 The table is based on statistical data from the various state statistical offices and from the federal election directory web site.

18 Election results are based on statistical data provided by the various state statistical offices and from the federal election directory.

19 Statistics for the 2005 general election come from *Wahl zum 16. Deutschen Bundestag am 18. September 2005- Gesamtergebnis* from the federal election directory web site and from *Die Welt* (Hamburg) newspaper.

20 A grand coalition between the CDU/CSU and the SPD had governed the country under Christian Democrat Kurt Kiesinger from 1966 to 1969.

21 All 68 of the CDU's seats in 2008 were won by direct election. In the 2003 *Land* election the CDU also won all of its 91 seats by direct election and none from the *Land* list in a larger parliament of 183 seats.

22 The table is based on data from *Der Bundeswahlleiter* and from the statistical offices of the several States.

23 The Schleswig-Holstein parliament normally has 69 seats, but because of the ability of the CDU to win 34 of forty direct mandates, eleven more seats than its proportional total, to these eleven seats were added fourteen balancing mandates and an additional seat to give the parliament an uneven count. In its reaction to challenges to the distribution of seats in the Schleswig-Holstein *Landtag* after the 2009 election, the State Supreme Court ruled that new balloting must take place no later than the fall of 2012 (*Financial Times Deutschland*, February 25, 2011). A May 2012 date has been set for the new election.

24 The table is based on data from *Der Bundeswahlleiter* and from the statistical offices of the several States.

25 Two regional contests were held in Hesse during the interval between the 2005 and 2009 general elections, one January 27, 2008, the second January 18, 2009. In the first contest the CDU lost its absolute majority in the Hessian *Landtag*, and because of the entrance of the Leftists into the parliament for the first time, neither a CDU/FDP combination with 53 seats nor a Socialist/Greens alliance with 51 seats could provide a working majority in the 110-member parliament, forcing Minister President Roland Koch to govern in minority status. Two attempts by the SPD during the course of 2008 to produce the necessary majority in cooperation with the Greens and *Die Linke* failed when four members of the SPD delegation refused to support a ministry which included the Leftists. This necessitated the second election in which the CDU and Liberals together were able to gain sufficient seats to establish a stable government. (See third footnote to Table 7.15.)

26 See Chapter X for a discussion of ministry changes resulting from the outcomes of the seventeenth series of regional elections.

27 Table 7.16 is based on *"Endgültiges Ergebins Der Bundestagwahl 2009, Bundeswahlleiter,* 9/30/2009 and 10/24/2009.

CHAPTER VIII

State and National Electoral Systems

Of the many factors which have operated to influence political developments in Germany since the first elections were held in 1946, few have been as significant as the electoral arrangements adopted. Because of the existence of a federal system, these arrangements have taken on a wide variety of forms. While there is a five percent restriction on both the state and national levels to qualify for representation, in the *Länder* there are differences in the length of the legislative cycle, either four or five years, in the size of the various legislative bodies and in the manner in which seats are distributed, whether on a strictly proportional basis from a *Land* list or through a mixed arrangement under which a set number of representatives (usually from one-half to seventy percent) are elected from single-member districts by simple majority vote with the remaining seats allocated to achieve an overall proportional result. But whatever the dissimilarities, all electoral systems on both the state and national levels are essentially proportional in nature.[1]

Not only do electoral systems determine the manner in which votes are counted, they influence to a considerable degree the voting behavior of the electorate, the character of the party system produced, the degree to which various shades of public opinion are reflected in the legislative body and the representativeness and stability of the various state and national governments formed. It is therefore understandable that the Western Occupying Powers and the original licensed parties showed great concern over the form of the first postwar electoral systems. For the German political parties, particularly those with only limited appeal, the systems adopted were a matter of political life or death.

Early Electoral Arrangements

The electoral arrangements established for the first *Land* elections in 1946/1947 reflected the differing policies of the Western Allies. The Americans and French made no attempt to change the basic character of the systems which had earlier existed in the areas under their control, resulting in the reintroduction of proportional systems in Bavaria, Hesse, and Württemberg-Baden in the American zone and Rhineland-Palatinate, South Baden and Württemberg-Hohenzollern in the French zone and the Saar which had a special status under French control.[2] The British, however, out of fear that the Germans would reestablish a system of proportional representation based on party lists which they abhorred, were unwilling to leave the decision of an electoral system to the Germans themselves, and undertook to introduce the Anglo-American system of direct election by simple majority ballot.[3] Although the Germans in the British areas of occupation showed little desire to resurrect the electoral system of the Weimar Republic, neither did they like the unrepresentative character of the British system. Eventually a compromise arrangement was worked out which combined proportional representation with the simple majority ballot. From sixty to eighty percent of the seats were to be chosen by direct election with the remaining seats distributed proportionally among the contending parties from reserve lists according to one or the other of two schemes.[4] In Bremen, Hamburg and Schleswig-Holstein the total *Land* vote for each party was not taken into consideration in determining the allocation of indirect seats. Rather, the votes of all losing candidates (*Reststimmen*) as well as the numerical difference between the winning candidate and the highest unsuccessful candidate in each constituency (*Mehrstimmen*) were credited to the reserve list, and the totals arrived at for each party determined the distribution of seats from the reserve list.[5] The number of seats already won by direct election did not figure in the indirect entitlement.[6] This system favored those parties which did especially well in direct election, and enabled the Social Democratic Party to gain an absolute majority of the seats in Bremen, Hamburg and Schleswig-Holstein with less than an absolute majority of the votes.[7]

In Lower Saxony and North Rhine-Westphalia a proportion of the seats were filled directly by simple majority ballot as in the previously mentioned system, but instead of distributing reserve list seats according to a formula which accounted for the losing and excess votes of each party, they were distributed among the qualifying parties in such a manner as to correct any discrepancies caused by the results in single member constituencies. In basing the allocation of indirect seats on the total *Land* vote, the final authorization for each party approximated that which would have been obtained had all, not merely a portion, of the seats been apportioned by proportional representation.[8] If a party won more seats by direct election than it otherwise would have been entitled to in the proportional allocation, the number of seats in the *Landtag* was increased to allow the party to retain the excess seats (*Überhangmandate*).

Although the first electoral laws in the British zone were not purely German as were those in the American and French zone *Länder*, the British system has had one of the most enduring influences on German politics of the reforms introduced by the Western Allies in the postwar period. After 1948 the system of combining proportional representation with the simple majority ballot began to attract attention in *Länder* outside the British zone, and became the model for seven of the West German *Länder* and the Federal parliament.[9]

National Electoral Arrangements

For the first *Bundestag* balloting in 1949, provisions were made for a legislative body of 402 members, with 242 seats to be filled by direct election and 160 by proportional representation from state party lists in a roughly 60:40 arrangement. To be represented, a party was required to obtain a minimum of five percent of the vote in an individual state or win a single member district outright. Because the restriction applied to each separate state rather than to the three Western zones as a whole, ten parties were able to send delegates to the first *Bundestag*. Had the limitation applied nationally, five of the groupings, the Communists, the Center Party, the German Rightist Party, the Economic Reconstruction Union (WAV), and the South Schleswig Voters Association, would not have qualified for seats (Elmer Plischke, *Contemporary Governments of Germany*, 1969).

Beginning in 1953, a 50:50 ratio between direct and indirect seats was instituted with 242 seats filled by election from single member districts and a like number chosen by proportional representation from party reserve lists, raising the size of the *Bundestag* to 484 members. This ratio has been continued in all subsequent national polls. In addition to the ratio change, the five percent restriction was applied to the country as a whole rather than to a party's standing in the individual states, although a party could obtain representation by winning a direct mandate. This new provision reduced the number of parties obtaining *Bundestag* representation to six. In 1957 the size of the federal parliament was raised temporarily to 497 to accommodate the incorporation of the Saar into the Federal Republic in January of that year. In that election the number of parties qualifying for seats fell to four, with the German Party (DP) qualifying only by virtue of its ability to meet the direct seat requirement. In every general election between 1961 and 1980, with 248 seats to be selected by direct mandate and 248 from party reserve lists, only three parties (the CDU/CSU, SPD and FDP) were represented in the *Bundestag*, as it was not until 1983 that a fourth party, the Greens, succeeded in gaining entrance to the federal parliament.

With the incorporation of the area encompassed by the former East German State into the Federal Republic in 1990, the number of *Bundestag* seats was expanded by 138. With balancing mandates the size of the first all-German parliament was raised to 662 members. For this first election including the five eastern provinces and the eastern sector of Berlin, the five percent restriction for representation was applied to the eastern and western parts of the country separately, and not to the country as a whole, enabling the PDS (successor to the Communist SED in the East) with only 2.4 percent of the country-wide vote, but with 9.9 percent of ballots cast in the eastern provinces, to obtain seventeen seats in the now expanded federal legislature. The two-district arrangement remained in place for the 1994 federal election, making it possible for the PDS to obtain thirty seats with a 4.4 percent following nationwide (David Conradt, *et. al.*, *Germany's New Politics*, 1995). In 1998, helped by a strong following in the eastern states, the PDS exceeded the five percent barrier for the first time to place 36 delegates in the federal parliament. In 2002, however, with the five percent requirement applying to the vote nationally and not to the individual states, the PDS, with only 4.0 percent of the countrywide vote, failed to qualify for reserve list seats, but gained two mandates through direct election. In 2005, competing in combination with Oskar Lafontaine's WASG as *Die Linke*, the Leftist following expanded to 8.7 percent of the vote qualifying it for 54 seats. For the 2009 general poll 298 seats were to be filled by direct election, 298 over party lists. Because of the ability of the CDU/CSU to win more direct seats (218 of 298) than a straight percentage allocation of the vote would have allowed, the *Bundestag* had to be expanded to 622 delegates through excess and balancing seats. Again, as in 2005, five parties, the CDU/CSU, SPD, FDP, *Die Linke* and Greens, gained parliamentary representation.

Present Electoral Systems in the States

The governments of the *Länder* are based on the parliamentary system, and except for Bavaria, the state legislatures are unicameral.[10] Initially the parliamentary term in all *Länder* with the exception of the Saar was four years. However, first with North Rhine-Westphalia in 1970 and Saxony and Thuringia in 1994 the legislative cycle in all states with the exceptions of Bremen, Hamburg, Mecklenburg-Vorpommern and Saxony-Anhalt has been extended to five years. The question of a five-year term has been brought up in Hamburg, but a definitive move in that direction has yet to be made. The number of seats to be filled in each *Landtag* (*Abgeordnetenhaus* in Berlin and *Bürgerschaft* in Bremen and Hamburg) ranges from 51 in the Saar to 181 in North Rhine-Westphalia.[11] While several states, including Hesse, Mecklenburg-Vorpommern, Hamburg and the Saar have increased the size of their respective parliaments from earlier levels, the trend in recent years has been to reduce their sizes. Eight of the sixteen German states have done so since 1998. The Bavarian *Landtag* which had consisted of 204 delegates since 1950 was reduced to 180 delegates in 1998 and the Bremen *Bürgerschaft*, which had had [12] 100 members since the addition of Bremerhaven in 1947, was reduced to 83 in 2003. North Rhine-Westphalia lowered its *Landtag* membership from 200 to 181 for the 2005 *Land* election and Lower Saxony from 155 to 135 for the 2008 regional contest.

Parliamentary seats are distributed either on a straight proportional basis as in Bremen and the Saar or a certain number of deputies (70.7 percent in North Rhine-Westphalia, two-thirds in Schleswig-Holstein, one half in Hesse, Saxony, Saxony-Anhalt, etc.)[13] are elected directly from single member constituencies with the remaining seats distributed according to various modifications of proportional representation from party lists. In spite of the simple majority ballot in these states, the whole election takes place in a proportional setting and seats are allocated as if all seats, not merely the number prescribed, were to be distributed on a proportional basis.[14] Only if a party is able to win a higher number of seats by direct vote than it would be entitled to under proportional representation could it receive the larger number of seats.[15] Initially neither Bavaria nor Rhineland-Palatinate provided for the so-called *Überhangmandate* in their electoral laws. In Bavaria when a party received a larger number of direct mandates than its percentage of the vote in a *Regierungskreis* would otherwise warrant under the proportional allocation of seats, the elected candidate of the same party having the smallest number of votes in a single member constituency within the *Kreis* had to give up his/her seat. The electoral laws in both *Länder* today make provision for the additional seats.

With the exceptions of Baden-Württemberg and North Rhine-Westphalia, the voter in states employing a mixed system casts two votes, one for a candidate in one of the legislative constituencies and one for a party from a *Land* or electoral district list. Voters in the Saar and Bremen up to 2011 cast only a single ballot by virtue of the fact that seats were allocated on the basis of a proportional formula.

The advantage of electing some of the members from single member districts is that some of each party's deputies have a closer relationship to their voters. On the other hand, the mixed system produces two classes of representatives, the "constituency" member and the "reserve list" member. The former is in a better position to take an independent stand on an issue if he/she can win votes on the basis of his/her personality in spite of party doctrine; the latter is dependent on the party for his/her seat and has little direct contact with the people. Yet, the reserve list allows outstanding party members who are unwilling to stand the rigors of a campaign to get elected to office. Not beholden to a constituency, the reserve list member can take a broad view of party policy. Too often, however, the party lists may be filled with party functionaries, who because of lack of color do not compete in the constituencies, but are able to slip into office through the efforts of others. The reserve list may be the only manner in which members of the smaller parties can get elected to office. In fact, almost all seats of parties other than the CDU/CSU, SPD and PDS/*Die Linke* are filled through the reserve lists. Because the non-Communist vote in the eastern provinces is fragmented between a number of contenders, the PDS has been highly successful there in winning direct mandates, even with a limited following. In the 2004 regional election in Brandenburg, for example, with 28.0 percent of the ballots cast, the PDS was able to win 23 of 44 direct mandates (in 2009 it was victorious in 21 of 44 districts with 27.2 percent of ballots cast) and in Berlin in 2001 it gained 32 of 78 direct seats, more than either the SPD or CDU with 22.6 percent of the city-wide vote.

The electoral laws of most *Länder* with mixed systems allow the name of a candidate to appear on both the ballot of a constituency and on the *Land* list, thus giving the party leaders a reasonable chance of being elected even if unsuccessful in a single member constituency. If a candidate wins his constituency, his/her name is passed over in the assignment of reserve list seats, allowing the next candidate on the list to be elected. It is, however, quite possible for a party to win such a landslide in single member constituencies, as did the CDU in Lower Saxony in the 2003 *Land* election (all of its 91 seats by direct election) and CDU in Saxony in the 2009 state contest (all of its 58 seats by direct election) that it is ineligible for seats from the reserve list. In such a case, an important party leader who was unsuccessful in a constituency would lose his/her second chance to be elected and would have to wait until a by-election offers another opportunity to gain a seat in the *Landtag.* Yet, some states make no provision for by-elections. In Baden-Württemberg a substitute candidate, whose name appears directly on the ballot, is elected along with the main candidate and assumes the seat in case of death, resignation, loss of eligibility, etc. of the main candidate, making a by-election unnecessary.[16] Vacancies in constituencies in some *Länder* are filled from the unused balance of the reserve list prepared for the previous election[17] or they remain unoccupied if the party list is used up. [18]

In order to prevent the multiplying effect which is usually associated with proportional representation, a provision, first adopted in the American zone *Länder* and now a part of all *Land* electoral systems, was introduced which required that a party obtain a minimum percentage of the total *Land* vote in order to be eligible for representation in the state parliament.[19] Prior to 1974 in Bavaria a party had to receive ten percent of the vote in at least one of the seven administrative districts into which the state is divided to be considered for representation. This led to some unusual representational glitches, on the one hand making it possible for a party with localized strength to obtain representation with less than five percent of the total *Land* vote, and, on the other, denying representation to a party which received five percent of the *Land* vote, but failed to gain the necessary ten percent in any of the seven administrative districts. In 1962 the Bavarian Party with 4.8 percent of the statewide vote obtained eight seats by virtue of its 10.3 percent following in a single district, Lower Bavaria, but in that same election the Refugee Party with 5.1 percent of the ballots cast received no representation because of its failure to obtain the necessary ten percent in an administrative district. In the first *Land* election in Bavaria in 1946 the Communist Party with 6.1 percent of the vote became the first victim of the ten percent requirement. Then in 1966 the FDP with 5.1 percent of the ballots cast also obtained no seats in the Bavarian *Landtag* because of the ten percent requirement. These unrepresentative outcomes led to the change in 1974 which eliminated the ten percent requirement and instituted a straight five percent state-wide limitation. Until 1998 101 of the 204 seats in the Bavarian *Landtag* were filled from single member districts. Since then it has been 92 of 180 seats.

In **Bremen** the *Land* is divided into two electoral districts, Bremen proper and Bremerhaven. It is only necessary to gain five percent of the vote in one of these parts to be considered for representation. Under this provision it is possible, as in Bavaria prior to 1974, for a party to obtain representation with less than five percent of the total *Land* vote. The German People's Union (DVU) because of its concentrated strength in Bremerhaven received one seat in 1987 with only 3.4 percent of the total *Land* vote and a single representative with 3.0

percent in 1999. In the 2003 election it again obtained one seat with only 2.3 percent of ballots cast, while in that same election the FDP needed a 4.2 percent vote total to gain its single mandate and the Schill Party with 4.4 percent was locked out of representation altogether because of its failure to obtain the necessary five percent in either one of the two electoral districts. In like manner the DVU gained a single seat in 2007 with 2.74 percent of the *Land* vote.[20] In 2008 in a by-election held only in Bremerhaven, the *Bürger in Wut* gained a single seat with a 5.27 percent following and again in 2011 with 7.1 percent of the Bremerhaven vote.

The only other exception to the *Sperrklausel* is found in Schleswig-Holstein, where the party of the Danish minority, the South Schleswig Voters' Association has been exempted from the five percent limitation which applies to all other parties in the state.[21] As a result of this exemption, the SSW, which has not received at least five percent of the *Land* vote since 1950, has been able to send at least one representative to Kiel in every legislative session, with the exception of 1954 prior to the enactment of the special provision. In the *Landtag* election of February 20, 2005 the party received 3.6 percent of ballots cast and two mandates. Because of the fragmented political situation produced by that election, it held the balance of power between an SPD/Greens and a CDU/FDP coalition, and the minority government of the SPD/Greens headed by Socialist Heide Simonis lasted only two months before being replaced by a more stable grand coalition between the Christian Democrats and Social Democrats in April 2005 under CDU Minister President Peter Harry Carstensen.[22] This new combination challenged the exemption of the SSW from the *Sperrklausel*. In 2009 the SSW was awarded four seats on a 4.3 percent vote total. It is also possible for a party to obtain representation in several states, including Berlin and Schleswig-Holstein, by winning a direct mandate even if it fails to meet the five percent requirement. For the first elections in Schleswig-Holstein in 1947, a party had to win at least one single member constituency to qualify for reserve list seats, no matter whether its total vote was five or twenty percent. As a result the FDP, Communists and German Conservative Party failed to qualify for seats even without a five percent clause.

Since its institution in the first elections minor parties have challenged the *Sperrklausel* as undemocratic and contrary to the principle of equality guaranteed in the Federal Basic Law,[23] preventing the representation of a wide variety of opinions which is the very essence of democracy. Hence, these various groups have not hesitated to bring their argument before the German courts. However, such restrictive measures have been upheld by the constitutional courts of the *Länder*, and their constitutionality was firmly established by the Federal Constitutional Court in its decision of July 8, 1959, upholding Article 5, paragraph 2, of the Hamburg electoral law of December 6, 1956, which required that a party receive at least five of 100 of the total valid votes to be eligible for the division of seats in the Hamburg *Bürgerschaft*.[24] Moreover, the Constitutional Court in the same decision upheld prohibitions against the combination of lists, which, if allowed, would have defeated the purpose of the *Sperrklausel*, that of eliminating the splinter parties.[25] Nevertheless, it is interesting to note that, as a result of the percentage limitation, some ten percent of German voters have found themselves unrepresented in the regional legislatures, by as much as 16.5 percent in Thuringia and 14.6 percent in Brandenburg after the 2004 *Land* elections in those two states, including supporters of the FDP and Greens. It has, therefore, been argued that the five percent clause prostitutes the very purpose of proportional representation and, in effect, works to maintain the status quo by deterring new parties, whether democratic or not, from gaining representation in the *Landtage*. It is further argued that elimination of restrictive clauses would in no way endanger the political stability of the *Land* governments. The absence of a percentage limitation did not prevent Lower Saxony from forming stable governments prior to 1959 when a five percent *Sperrklausel* was reintroduced. Even prior to 1959 the portion of the vote falling to all parties failing to poll five percent of the vote was only 8.2 percent in 1951 (for which such parties obtained a mere ten of 158 seats) and 6.9 percent in 1955 (for which nine seats were awarded). Although the non-qualifying vote amounted to just 3.9 percent in the 1959 *Landtag* election, all of the parties which had exceeded five percent of ballots cast in 1955 were again represented in the parliament. The loss of appeal by the German and Refugee parties in Lower Saxony after 1959 caused their decline, not the reestablishment of the five percent limitation.[26] On the other hand, the five percent clause did not prevent the Greens and the PDS/*Die Linke* from becoming important players in German politics or for protest groupings such as the Schill Party in Hamburg in 2001 and various right-extremist parties, including the DVU, NPD and Republicans, from gaining representation in several states between 1989 and 2006. Restrictive clauses did not prevent six parties from gaining representation in Saxony in 2004, in Bremen in 2007 and Schleswig-Holstein in 2009. Nevertheless it is interesting to speculate how many of the 150 different parties which have competed for seats in the various state elections since 1946/1947 would have gained representation in the absence of the *Sperrklausel*.[27]

The FDP, which had been an early beneficiary of the *Sperrklausel* in that the five percent limitation had helped to eliminate competitors to its position as balancer between the CDU/CSU and SPD until the advent of a powerful environmental movement, has itself become victim of restrictive clauses in the *Länder* in a number of recent elections. It failed to gain representation in the three *Land* contests held in Brandenburg and Thuringia prior to the 2009 state elections, was unrepresented in Hamburg between 2004 and 2011 when it was returned to the *Bürgerschaft,* and was unsuccessful in fifteen other elections between 1994 and 2009.[28]

Another measure to restrict the growth of splinter parties is the requirement in each *Land* that a party prove a certain degree of support in a constituency, administrative district or *Land* before being allowed to enter a party list or a candidate in a single member constituency. Parties already represented in the *Land* parliament or in the *Bundestag* need merely the signatures of the party executive committee in the constituency, district or *Land*, whichever the case may be or a relatively small number of signatures of eligible voters to enter candidates on the ballot. New or non-represented parties must have a democratically elected executive committee, a written charter and program, not clash with Article 21, paragraph 2, of the Federal Basic Law,[29] and be able to obtain a specified number of signatures, which in every case exceeds the requirement for represented parties. Because of differences in the number of deputies to be elected, the population of the *Land* and the electoral systems, the minimum number of signatures required in each *Land* to place candidates on the ballot differs widely.[30] Some *Länder* require a minimum number of signatures for both constituency candidates and the entering of reserve lists. Others require only one or the other. The requirement that a party have entered candidates in all single member constituencies to be eligible for *Land* list seats has been abandoned by the *Länder* because it appeared to contravene a ruling of the Federal Constitutional Court concerning the guarantee of equal opportunity for all parties and voters associations in elections.[31] Nevertheless, even without a *Land* list requirement in mixed systems, a party is forced to enter candidates in a large number of constituencies if it is to have any chance of meeting the minimum vote requirements for representation. Independents must obtain the same number of signatures in constituencies as parties to be placed on the ballot. The only chance for independent candidates to gain representation in the *Landtag* is to win a single member constituency outright; only parties and voter associations can enter *Land* lists. In those *Länder* with straight proportional systems independents are excluded from the ballot. Since 1946 no independent candidates have succeeded in getting elected to a *Land* parliament and independents are of importance only in local elections.[32]

A straight proportional system exists only in the Saar, since Bremen changed to a mixed system in 2011, whereby there are 48 list and 35 personal representatives. **Rhineland-Palatinate** utilized a straight proportional system, under which 100 seats were allocated between qualified parties within each of seven election districts, until 1991 when it switched to a mixed system wherein 51 of 101 seats are chosen directly, and 50 indirectly from *Land* lists, and Hamburg changed from a proportional to a mixed scheme in 2004 under which voters cast from three to five votes to fill 71 of 121 seats.[33]

In spite of the absence of the simple majority ballot in the electoral systems of Bremen and the Saar, wide differences exist between the two *Länder*. In Bremen the *Land* is divided into two units, Bremen proper and Bremerhaven, with each unit being considered separately for the proportional division of seats and for the meeting of the five percent requirement. The Saar, while divided into three separate districts for the proportional distribution of seats, applies the five percent requirement to the entire *Land*.

The electoral system of no other *Land* has witnessed so many changes as that of **Hamburg**. For the first *Bürgerschaft* election held October 13, 1946, the city was divided into 21 districts, each of which elected four deputies by simple majority, made possible by giving each voter four votes. In addition to the 84 seats filled by direct election, 26 seats were distributed among the participating parties according to a complicated formula which involved adding the votes of the losing candidates of a party and the numerical difference between the winning candidates and the highest unsuccessful candidates in each constituency to establish a quota for the proportional division of seats. Because of the general dissatisfaction with this British-imposed system, two major changes were made in the electoral law regulating the *Bürgerschaft* election of October 16, 1949, in Hamburg. Most important was the establishment of single member constituencies in which each voter had a single vote. Secondly, the number of seats in the *Bürgerschaft was* increased from 110 to 120 and the count of direct seats reduced from 84 to 72, thereby raising the number of deputies to be elected over the *Land* list from 26 to 48 and establishing a 60:40 ratio between the two categories of seats. Although the d'Hondt formula replaced the more complicated Hare system in figuring the proportional allocation of seats, the practice of counting only *Rest-* and *Mehrstimmen* in the calculation was retained.[34] In 1952 a five percent requirement for representation was instituted and, then, between 1957 and 2004 elections were held under a straight proportional arrangement.[35] Beginning in 1991 the number of seats in the *Bürgerschaft* was raised from 120 to 121. The electoral law of 2004, as amended in 2006, returned the *Hansastadt* to a mixed system which had existed prior to 1957, whereby 71 seats are filled by direct election in seventeen voting districts, each having from three to five seats, with each voter having from three to five choices which could be given to a single candidate (cumulative voting) or spread over candidates from different parties (*panaschieren*). Fifty additional seats are distributed in such a manner as to produce a proportional balance between parties which have obtained at least five percent of the *Land* vote. The total number of seats may be raised through *Überhang-* and *Ausgleich*-mandates should a party or parties win more seats by direct election than its proportional allocation would allow (*Gesetz zur Änderung des Gesetzes über die Wahl zur hamburgischen Bürgerschaft vom 19. Oktober 2006).*[36] The 2008 *Bürgerschaft* election was held under this altered system, but a new electoral law passed in June 2009 following a citizen initiative, while retaining the 50/71 ratio between indirect and direct seats, gave each voter ten choices, five of which could be given to a single candidate or spread over as many as five candidates, even of different parties, on a *Land* list which included candidates of all parties and voter associations. On a separate red ballot the voter could cast the other five votes for candidates within one of the seventeen electoral districts into which the city was divided, and from which three to five representatives are elected. The five percent clause for the city remains in effect. The goal of the 2009 law was to give voters more influence over the personal composition of the Hamburg parliament (*Das neue Wahlrecht zur Hambürgischen Bürgerschaft und der Bezirksversammlungen, Landeszentrale für politische Bildung,* Hamburg, 2010).

Except for the introduction of absentee balloting in 1963 and the reduction of its legislature from 100 to 83 members for the 2003 election, the electoral system of **Bremen** remained basically unchanged from 1947 to 2011, when a voter was able to cast multiple ballots.[37] The *Bürgerschaft* elected in 1946 had eighty members, but the addition of Bremerhaven (formerly Wesermünde) to the *Land* required increasing the size of the parliament to 100, with eighty deputies representing Bremen proper, twenty Bremerhaven. Moreover, a proportional system was instituted to replace the mixed system which had been employed in 1946, with each voter limited to a single vote.

Under the present system Bremen proper and Bremerhaven form two distinctly independent electoral districts for the proportional allocation of seats. The result in one of the districts has no influence on the other, with the five percent limitation applying to each separate district and not to the *Land* as a whole.[38] A party may choose to compete solely in one district, and if it obtains at least five percent of the vote in that district, it is eligible for seats in the particular district irrespective of its total *Land* vote. In this manner a party obtaining five percent of the Bremerhaven vote is eligible for a single seat in the *Bürgerschaft* even though its total *Land* vote amounts to only one percent.

In 1963 the German Party in the *Land* of Bremen polled 5.2 percent of the total *Land* vote and obtained four of the eighty seats allotted to Bremen proper where its support amounted to 5.34 percent. However, by gaining only 4.4 percent of ballots cast in Bremerhaven, the party was ineligible for a seat in that electoral district. Had the distribution of seats been on the basis of the total *Land* vote, the DP would have received five instead of four seats. In 1987, 1999, 2003 and 2007 the DVU gained a single seat in Bremerhaven because of its concentrated strength there even though its *Land* totals were under five percent.[39] The FDP likewise gained a single seat in 2003 with 4.2 percent of the total *Land* vote because of its ability to meet the five percent test in Bremerhaven, while the Schill party with 4.4 percent of total *Land* ballots received no representation. In a 2008 by-election the *BIW* received a single seat in Bremerhaven with less than one percent of the *Land* vote by virtue of its 5.29 percent following in that portion of the city-state. In like manner it received one seat in 2011 with 7.1 percent in Bremerhaven. For 2011 Bremen adopted a mixed list and personal multiple voting system with 48 list and 35 personal representatives.

The **Saar**, which elects 51 deputies, has maintained a proportional system since its first *Land* election in 1947. The present electoral system, as modified in 1960, 1980 and 1988, divides the *Land* into three electoral districts and allots fifteen seats to Neunkircken, fifteen to Saarbrücken and eleven to Saarlouis. The seats in each district are distributed on a proportional basis according to the results in the separate districts. A second separate allocation of the ten *Land* list seats is made on the basis of the total *Land* vote. In contrast to Bremen, a party must obtain five percent of the total *Land* vote, not merely that of a separate district, to be eligible for the distribution of either district or *Land* list seats. Thus, the party receiving ten percent of the vote in Saarlouis would lose its entitlement of one seat if its *Land* total fell below the five percent figure. On the other hand, since it is possible for a party to receive five percent of the vote in each separate district without qualifying for a single district seat, the district results are corrected by the second allocation of seats which is based on the total *Land* vote. The DDU in 1960, for example, although gaining 5.02 percent of the total *Land* vote, could gain no seats in any of the three districts, but was awarded two *Land* list seats. The remaining eight *Land* list seats were distributed among other qualifying parties in such a manner as to achieve a proportional balance between them. Thus, the final result is as if all of the seats had been allocated on the basis of the total *Land* vote in a single distribution.

Prior to 1960 no *Land* list seats existed. Instead, each of the three districts had a larger number of seats, Saarbrücken nineteen, Neunkircken eighteen and Saarlouis thirteen. Any discrepancies in the district results remained uncorrected. The present system is a definite aid to the smaller parties. Under the previous system most splinter parties would have been effectively eliminated even without a five percent clause.[40]

A mixed system combining the simple majority ballot with proportional representation for the selection of *Landtag* deputies is employed in fourteen of the sixteen German states, Baden-Württemberg, Bavaria, Berlin, Brandenburg, Hamburg, Hesse, Lower Saxony, Mecklenburg-Vorpommern, North Rhine-Westphalia, Rhineland-Palatinate, Saxony, Saxony-Anhalt, Schleswig-Holstein and Thuringia. The practice of electing some deputies from single member districts and a specified number by proportional representation was initially introduced in the British zone *Länder*, but was quickly adopted by the *Länder* in the former American zone of occupation, and, after 1990, by all five provinces of the former German Democratic Republic. Bremen between 1947 and 2011 and Hamburg between 1957 and 2004, however, abandoned the arrangement.[41]

In **Baden-Württemberg** seventy of the 120 deputies are elected directly from single member districts, fifty from reserve lists according to the d'Hondt formula of highest average.[42] The *Land* is divided into four administrative districts (*Regierungsbezirke*), North Württemberg, North Baden, South Baden and South Württemberg-Hohenzollern each of which forms a separate independent electoral unit. Allocation of seats is based on the vote totals of each party in the separate districts. The total *Land* vote is of consequence only in determining which parties have met the five percent requirement and are thereby eligible for seats in the separate districts. Since a party may obtain five percent of the *Land*-wide vote without gaining a single direct seat, a specified number of seats is set aside in each district to correct any imbalance between the parties created by the constituency results, and the final allocation in each district is as if all seats in the districts had been distributed on a proportional basis. In case a party receives more direct seats than accorded to it by the proportional allocation in the district, provision is made for the so-called *Überhangmandat*. With each district an independent unit, additional seats may be awarded in any or all of the four districts, and the count of representatives is raised over 120 until a proportional balance between the parties is reached in each.[43] In 2011 the CDU won sixty of the *Land's* seventy direct mandates with 39.0 percent of the statewide vote, thirteen more than would have been allotted under a straight proportional distribution in the four districts. To compensate for the CDU's additional seats and produce a proportional balance, *Ausgleich* mandates were awarded, raising the total number of deputies in the Baden-Württemberg *Landtag* from 120 to 138.[44]

Berlin employed a proportional system for the first four elections of its House of Representatives (*Abgeordnetenhaus*).[45] Its first election, held October 20, 1946, encompassed all of Berlin, including the Soviet sector. The 130 deputies were elected on a proportional basis from the twenty districts into which the city was divided. With the breakdown in cooperation between the four occupying powers and threatened with continual harassment by Communist demonstrators, the Berlin parliament on September 6, 1948, moved its seat from the Soviet Sector to West Berlin, minus its Communist delegation. The Soviets reacted by establishing a new municipal parliament in East Berlin November 30, 1948, making the split between the two parts of the city complete. Because of a prohibition on the part of the Soviet authorities Berlin's second municipal election was held only in the Western sectors of the city and a total of 98 deputies from the twelve Western districts were elected to office, the 32 seats allotted to the Soviet Sector having been deducted from the total of 130. Again, principles of proportional representation were followed in distributing parliamentary seats. In 1950 the size of the Berlin *Abgeordnetenhaus* was expanded to 200 members, with the number of deputies to be elected from the twelve districts in West Berlin determined by the ratio of the West Berlin population to the total Berlin population. In both 1950 and 1954 the West Berlin parliament, without the allocation for the eastern sector of the city, consisted of 127 members chosen on a proportional basis.[46]

Under the proportional system in existence in Berlin prior to 1958, a quota was established by adding together the votes of all qualifying parties and dividing the figure obtained by the number of seats to be distributed. The resulting quota was then divided into the vote totals received by the parties in each of the twelve districts into which the city was divided.[47] In 1954 110 of the 127 seats were distributed in this manner, but this number was not fixed. Since the quota would not go evenly into party totals in each district, the remainders of each party in the twelve districts were added together for a second division of seats according to the d'Hondt formula. The number of seats to be distributed in this manner was determined by subtracting the number of seats already allocated by quota from the total number of *Landtag* seats. In 1954 seventeen seats were awarded in the second division. The only advantage of the district system as employed in Berlin up to 1954 was that deputies from the *Kreis* list could have a closer relationship with the voters in each of the districts.

In 1958 Berlin adopted an electoral system combining proportional representation with the simple majority ballot. The number of deputies to be elected was increased to 133 (134 in 1963), eighty of which were to be chosen from single member districts.[48] Each of the twelve administrative districts of the city formed a constituency block made up of a certain number of single member districts determined by the percentage of the total West Berlin population living in the block. The Berlin *Senat* determined the number of direct seats each constituency block could elect and the boundaries of those single member districts. In addition to the seats filled by direct election, a certain number of reserve list seats were allotted to each constituency block (*Wahlkreisverband*) to balance any discrepancies in the distribution of direct seats.[49] Excess seats could be awarded in any or all of the constituency blocks if a party happened to be able to win more seats by direct election than it otherwise would be entitled to under proportional representation. In 1963 the SPD gained a single *Überhangmandat* in Wilmersdorf, two in Zehlendorf and one in Steglitz after winning all eighty direct seats. The imbalance created by the awarding of excess seats caused the process of equalization to be carried one step further through the use of *Ausgleichmandate*.[50] In 1963 the CDU received a single *Ausgleichmandat* in Zehlendorf and one in Steglitz. The awarding of these six extra seats increased the size of the Berlin *Abgeordnetenhaus* to 140 members.[51]

Prior to the addition of the eastern sector of Berlin to the city in 1990 the *Abgeornetenhaus* consisted of 119 members, 71 of whom were elected from single member constituencies within the city's twelve electoral districts. In the election of January 29, 1989 that number had to be raised to 138 to compensate for the addition of nineteen *Überhang-* and *Ausgleich* mandates. The election of December 2, 1990 was the first to be held in a united Berlin since 1946. With the accession of the former Soviet sector to the city the number of delegates to be elected was raised to 200, 120 from single member districts and eighty from party lists. Because seventeen *Überhang-* and 24 *Ausgleichmandaten* had to be awarded to create a proportional balance between the parties in that election, the size of the Berlin parliament was increased to 241 members.[52] The current electoral law calls for a legislative body of at least 130 delegates, 78 of which are to be elected directly from single member constituencies and 52 from party lists. In the election of October 21, 2001 the PDS won 32 direct seats, the SPD 26, the CDU nineteen, and the Greens one. Again, eleven seats were added to the parliament to effect an overall proportional distribution of seats, bringing the total number of seats in the 2001-2006 Berlin parliament to 141. In the 2006 Berlin election 78 seats were again filled by direct election, but 71 over party lists because of nineteen additional balancing seats.

Hesse: A proportional system was established for the first *Landtag* election in Hesse, held December 1, 1946. Hesse was one of the first *Länder* to adopt a restrictive clause; however, all four contending parties easily exceeded the five percent limitation in this first election. The division of the ninety *Landtag* seats was determined by the number of times an established election quota could be divided into the party vote in each of the fifteen districts into which the *Land* was divided. Since the quota did not go evenly into each party's total in the various districts, the remainders from all the districts were compiled for a second division of seats from the *Land* list. Again, the quota was employed to distribute the remaining seats. If all seats were not filled by quota in the second division, they were awarded to the parties with the largest remaining vote totals.[53] Sixty-two seats were allocated on the basis of the district results, 28 in the second allocation from the *Land* list.[54]

Hesse's present system of combining simple majority and proportional systems was first employed in the *Landtag* election of November 19, 1950. Of the eighty deputies elected in that year, 48 were chosen from single member constituencies, 32 from party reserve lists on the basis of a party's total of *Mehr* and *Reststimmen*. In 1954, a 50:50 ratio between direct and indirect seats was established to replace the earlier 60:40 ratio by raising the number of reserve list seats to 48 and increasing the size of the *Landtag* to 96 seats. Indirect seats were allocated to reflect the total *Land* vote rather than the totals of excess and lost votes credited *Land*-wide to the party as in 1950. The electoral system of Hesse has remained basically the same since 1954, except that the number of seats in the Hessian *Landtag* was raised to 110 in 1970, with the earlier 50:50 ratio between direct and indirect seats being maintained, and in 2003 the legislative period was increased from four to five years. Under the current electoral law the voter casts two votes, one for a candidate in one of the 55 constituencies into which the *Land* is divided and one for a party list for the 55 indirect seats. In the 2003 regional election the CDU won 53 of the 55 direct seats and three indirect seats to hold an absolute majority in the Hessian parliament. This advantage was lost in the 2008 *Land* election in which both CDU and SPD won 42 mandates.[55] In the 2009 rerun election in Hesse the CDU won 46 of the 55 direct seats with only 37.2 percent of the vote, necessitating the addition of eight seats to the *Landtage* to produce a proportional balance. The CDU was able to form a ministry with the FDP which won twenty seats.

The British zone *Länder* of **Lower Saxony, North Rhine-Westphalia** and **Schleswig-Holstein** adopted mixed systems for their first *Landtag* elections held April 20, 1947. In Lower Saxony 95 of 149 deputies were to be elected from single member districts by simple majority ballot, in North Rhine-Westphalia 150 of 200 deputies and in Schleswig-Holstein 42 of seventy deputies, with the remaining seats distributed between the qualifying parties in such a manner as to produce a proportional balance between them. Although a party was to be able to retain all seats won by direct election regardless of its total *Land* vote, only those parties polling a minimum of five percent of the state-wide vote would be qualified for seats from the reserve list.[56] Provision for the so-called *Überhangmandate* or *Mehrsitz* was made in the electoral laws of Lower Saxony and North Rhine-Westphalia. Under the 1947 law in Lower Saxony the number of *Mehrsitze* was limited to nine so that in no case could the size of the *Landtag* exceed 158 members. North Rhine-Westphalia established a similar restriction on the number of additional seats; however, the size of the *Landtag* could be increased by as many as fifty seats.[57] The method of dividing reserve list seats employed in Schleswig-Holstein prior to 1954 did not require the use of *Überhangmandate* in either the 1947 or 1950 *Land* elections. Since changing in 1954 to the method of indirect seat allocation already in use in Lower Saxony and North Rhine-Westphalia, excess seats have been allowed in Schleswig-Holstein. In 1947 in North Rhine-Westphalia the CDU won 92 direct seats although its 37.5 percent of the vote entitled it to only 76 mandates. This success in single member districts necessitated the awarding of sixteen

Überhangmandate and increasing the size of the *Landtag* to 216 members. Again in 1950 fifteen additional seats were awarded because of the ability of the CDU to win 93 direct seats to increase the size of the *Landtag* to 215 members. Not until 1985 when the SPD won 125 seats by direct election did additional seats have to be awarded in North Rhine-Westphalia, raising the size of the *Land* parliament in that year to 227. In 2005 six extra seats were awarded.[58]

No *Mehrsitze* were awarded in the 1947 *Landtag* election in Lower Saxony; however, in 1951, the SPD did so well in single member districts as to gain the maximum number of *Mehrsitze*, necessitating an increase in the size of the *Landtag* to 158 seats. In 1955 the limitation on the number of *Mehrsitze* was removed, but thereafter the number of seats added to the legal size of the *Landtag* was to be double the count of *Mehrsitze*, all but eliminating any advantage gained by a party which won more seats directly than it would be entitled to in the proportional allocation. In winning five direct seats in excess of its proportional entitlement in the 1955 regional election the SPD pushed the size of the *Landtag* to 159 members. Again in 1959 the SPD won four *Mehrsitze* and the number of seats in the *Landtag* was increased by eight to 157 after compensating with *Ausgleich* seats to achieve a proportional balance between the parties.[59] No additional seats were awarded in the next five *Land* elections. In 1974 the number of seats in the Lower Saxony *Landtag* was raised from 149 to 155, with 100 seats elected by simple majority ballot and 55 from party lists. In the 1982 *Land* election sixteen additional seats were awarded, in 1994 six and in 1998 two. In 2003 the number of excess seats reached 28 as the CDU won 91 of the 100 direct seats, fourteen more than its proportional allocation. Fourteen additional seats had to be distributed to effectuate a proportional balance. For the 2008 *Land* election the size of the Lower Saxony *Landtag* was reduced to 135 members with 87 seats filled directly and 48 over party lists. Again, the final seat total was raised to 152 to compensate for *Überhang-* and *Ausgleich* mandates resulting from the CDU's ability to win 68 direct seats, eight over its proportional allotment.

Although the ratio between direct and indirect seats has remained basically the same in Lower Saxony and North Rhine-Westphalia since the first *Land* elections were held, the former has both raised and lowered the size of its *Landtag*, from 149 to 155 members in 1974 and then to 135 for the 2008 *Land* election, while the latter lowered its legislative membership from 200 to 181 for the 2005 regional contest. Schleswig-Holstein, on the other hand, has changed both the ratio between direct and indirect seats and the size of its parliament several times. The first *Landtag* in the Horizon State consisted of seventy seats, 42 filled by direct election and 28 from party reserve lists in a 60:40 ratio. In 1950 the count of direct seats was raised to 46 and that of indirect seats decreased to 23 to produce a 2:1 ratio and reduce the size of the *Landtag* to 69 members. A further change was made in 1954 when the count of direct seats was lowered to 42, and, in order to maintain the size of the *Landtag* at 69 deputies, the number of reserve list seats was set at 27. The method of apportioning seats from the *Land* lists was also altered in 1954 to reflect the total

Land vote of each party rather than the sum of a party's lost and excess ballots in the single member constituencies.[60] In 1958 an agreement was reached with the Danish minority to exempt the SSW from the five percent restriction which applied to all other parties. Following the failure of the SSW to gain more than 3.5 percent of the total *Land* vote in the 1954 *Landtag* election, the Danish minority was granted the right to appoint two advisors to work with the *Landtag's* Committee for Danish Minority Affairs (*Ausschuss für Angelegenheiten der Dänischen Minderheit*) until the 1958 election.[61] Under the exemption from the five percent clause the SSW gained two seats with 2.8 percent of the total vote in 1958 and has gained at least a single seat in the Schleswig-Holstein legislature since 1958. In the 2005 *Landtag* election, the SSW obtained 3.6 percent of the *Land* vote and two seats in the *Land* parliament, in 2009 four seats with 4.3 percent of the vote.

For the 1967 regional election the size of the Schleswig-Holstein *Landtag* was raised to 73 members, with 44 seats to be filled by direct election, 29 from party lists. In 1983 the number of direct seats was left at 44, but the count to be elected over the party lists was raised to 30, establishing a legislative body of 74 members. The SPD, by winning seven seats more than its proportional entitlement by direct election in 1992 and 2000, coupled with the need to award balancing seats, pushed the total number of mandates in the two years to 89. For the 2005 election the size of the *Landtag* was reduced to 69 seats with 46 filled by direct vote and 23 over the *Land* list to again produce a 2:1 ratio between the two categories of seats.[62] No excess seats were awarded in 2005. In 2009 because of the success of the CDU in single member districts the size of Schleswig-Holstein *Landtag* was raised to 95 seats to compensate for the CDU's *Überhangmandate*.

For their first *Landtag* elections following reunification in 1990 all five of the new *Länder* adopted mixed electoral systems combining the simple majority ballot with selection from party lists. In **Brandenburg** 44 of 88 delegates are elected directly from single member constituencies, 44 from *Land* lists. For the 1990 contest in **Mecklenburg-Vorpommern** 33 of 66 seats were filled by direct election, 33 indirectly. However, beginning in 1994 the number to be chosen by simple majority ballot was raised to 36, with 35 chosen from *Land* lists. For the first *Landtag* election in **Saxony** eighty of 160 seats were chosen from single member constituencies, with an additional eighty from party reserve lists. These numbers were reduced to sixty direct and sixty indirect seats for the 1994 and later *Landtag* ballotings. In **Saxony-Anhalt** 45 of 89 seats (lowered from 49 of 99 seats prior to the 2006 regional election) and 44 of 88 seats in **Thuringia** are filled directly with the remainder elected from party lists. Each voter in these five states casts two votes, one for a specific candidate in a single member district and one for a party list. Should a party win more direct seats than its proportional entitlement would allow, *Überhang-* and *Ausgleich* mandates are awarded to effect a proportional balance between the qualifying parties. In the 2009 parliamentary election in Saxony, the CDU won 58 of sixty direct mandates necessitating increasing the size of the legislature by twelve seats, and in 2011 in Saxony-Anhalt sixteen additional seats had to be awarded to compensate for the CDU's ability to win 41 of 45 direct seats with 32.5 percent of the vote. Neither Brandenburg nor Thuringia have followed the examples of Mecklenburg-Vorpommern, Saxony-Anhalt and Saxony of either raising or lowering the size of their legislative bodies.

Initially the legislative term of all five new states was four years, but in 1994 Brandenburg, Saxony and Thuringia changed the legislative period to five years, while Mecklenburg-Vorpommern and Saxony-Anhalt have retained the four year cycle. A five percent restrictive clause for representation appears in the electoral law of the five new *Länder*. Voting turnout in the five eastern provinces has tended to be lower than in the original German states. Following strong turnouts in the first elections held in the new *Länder* participation has been unspectacular. In the most recent elections (2006-2009), the turnout exceeded sixty percent only in Brandenburg (67.0 percent) and was as low as 44.7 percent in Saxony-Anhalt in the 2006 state contest.

Voting Qualifications

Before becoming eligible to vote residents of Germany must meet certain statutory requirements relating to age, length of residency and legal status. Since each *Land* in the Federal Republic has the responsibility for establishing voting requirements for regional and local elections, some differences are to be found between the *Länder* regarding eligibility. Women have the same right to vote as men in all *Länder*.

Prerequisites for voting in *Landtag* elections include being registered in a particular voting district, having reached the age of eighteen by election day (sixteen-year-olds are able to vote in local contests in seven states, but only in Bremen in regional elections, beginning in 2011; the age of eighteen continues to be the requirement in national contests), having resided a certain number of days in the particular state (usually three months, but as little as sixteen days in North Rhine-Westphalia), not having been disenfranchised through criminal conviction or being declared mentally incompetent and being German within the meaning of Article 116, paragraph 1 of the Federal Basic Law.[63] One of the complaints made by Germans of the first electoral laws in several of the *Länder* was the stipulation that an individual have reached voting age several weeks or even months before the election date. For example, in Hamburg, an individual was required to have reached the age of 21 years by May 12, 1946 for the *Bürgerschaft* election of October 13, 1946, or five months earlier.[64] There was also a wide range in residency requirements for eligibility. In North Rhine-Westphalia it was 35 days, while in Bavaria it was one full year, which effectively disenfranchised most refugees and expellees who had fled to that state.[65] Large numbers of voters were disenfranchised in the period immediately following the Second World War because of their connections with the National Socialist regime.[66]

Because elections in the *Länder* are held on varying dates over a period of four or five years and residency requirements are three months or less, it was possible for individuals to establish residency and participate as voters or run for office is several of the states. In order to correct this abuse the *Länder* established the requirement that a person prove his/her primary residence (*Hauptwohnsitz*) not merely residence or present abode (*Wohnsitz oder gewöhnlicher Aufenhalt*) to be in the state.[67]

The Future

Over the past 65 years the German *Länder* have made numerous changes in their electoral systems. The four-year legislative term has been replaced by a five-year cycle in most states; the size of various legislative bodies has either been expanded as in the case of Hesse, Mecklenburg-Vorpommern and the Saar or reduced as in Bavaria, Bremen, Lower Saxony, North Rhine-Westphalia and Saxony; in several states employing mixed electoral systems the ratio between members elected from single member constituencies and those from *Land* lists has been altered; Bremen abandoned its earlier mixed system for a straight proportional arrangement while Rhineland-Palatinate dropped its straight proportional format for one which combines the simple majority ballot with election from party lists; and Bavaria discarded its ten percent in an administrative district requirement for representation in favor of a five percent *Land*-wide restrictive clause. Hamburg, after discarding its earlier mixed system for a proportional one, returned to a mixed, personalized voting arrangement in 2004. This personalized system was amended in 2009 as previously mentioned. And it is possible that the future will bring about other changes.

An electoral arrangement which has found little support in Germany is the Anglo-American system of simple majority balloting. Adoption of the simple majority system for the election of all representatives would effectively eliminate minor parties from representation in all of the *Landtage* with the exception of Berlin and the eastern provinces where the PDS/*Die Linke* has succeeded in winning large numbers of direct seats. In the 2004 election in Brandenburg, for example, the PDS won 52.3 percent of the direct seats as the CDU, SPD and other parties splintered the vote. A simple majority ballot would have made the PDS the majority party in Brandenburg were it not for the balancing performed by the *Land* list seats. In those states with strong PDS/*Die Linke* representation, a first-past-the-post system would make a grand coalition between the CDU and SPD, in the absence of a parliamentary majority by one of them, the only alternative to a combination with the left-oriented PDS/*Die Linke*. This could prove disadvantageous to the CDU which has shown little interest in allying with the successor to the former Communist SED, while the SPD has formed a government with the PDS/*Die Linke* in Berlin since 2001, in Mecklenburg-Vorpommern from 1998 to 2006, and in Brandenburg since 2009. Nevertheless, the CDU/CSU remains the dominant party on the regional level as it has in fifteen of seventeen series of regional election contests since the end of Would War II, and the simple majority ballot would favor it in most of the *Länder* and prevent the Socialists, without the ability to form a coalition with a third party, from governing in all but a few states. For this reason the Socialists, along with the Free Democrats, Greens and other minor parties have good reason to oppose any change in the present proportional order. [68]

The proportional nature of *Land* electoral systems did not prevent a three–party system of the CDU/CSU, SPD and FDP from emerging from the first five series of *Land* elections, and the five percent clause appeared to be perpetuating it until the rise of the Greens in the 1980s and the entry of the PDS as an important player in regional politics following reunification in 1990. In a limited number of cases, even the FDP became a victim of restrictive clauses in regional electoral systems and a two party system of the CDU/CSU and SPD existed for short periods of time in several of the states, Bavaria from 1982 to 1986, Hamburg from 1953 to 1957 and 1978 to 1982, Lower Saxony from 1970 to 1974 and 1978 to 1982, North Rhine-Westphalia from 1980 to 1985, Rhineland-Palatinate from 1983 to 1987, and the Saar from 1970 to 1975. After 1987 only in the Saar from 1999 to 2004 did a two-party system of the CDU and SPD emerge in any of the states. North Rhine-Westphalia came close to instituting a direct election system by having three-quarters of its *Landtag* delegates chosen by simple majority ballot. However, the provision for *Überhang-* and *Augleich* mandates essentially nullified the advantage of winning large numbers of direct seats, and on one occasion (1990) pushed the size of the *Landtag* from 200 to 237 members. The new electoral law in North Rhine-Westphalia reduces the proportion of direct seats to 70.7 percent from 75 percent.

One advantage of the minimum requirement for representation in national and regional electoral laws is that it has tended to limit representation to those parties with wide appeal and national organization. Parties which have appealed to narrow ideological, regional or group interests or have failed to modify their programs to reflect the changing political sentiment of the electorate have found difficulty in exceeding the minimum vote requirement for parliamentary representation. Moreover, the five percent provision of the federal electoral law, by applying to the total national vote rather than to the vote in each state, discriminates against those parties lacking national organization, since even if a party has developed considerable strength in a particular *Land* it is unable to secure the minimum nationwide vote or to secure direct seats in competition with the nationally-organized parties. The federal electoral law forces those parties desiring to compete successfully on the national level to develop a nationwide organization. The result is the nationalization of the scope of existing parties, and the voters, in the habit of voting for the national parties become reluctant to support purely local parties except in protest. Moreover, locally-based parties lack the financial resources to compete with the national ones, and as national issues continue to overshadow issues of a purely local or regional nature in most regional contests, the lack of national representation places any splinter party, old or new, at a distinct disadvantage in building up a local base.

Nevertheless, the *Sperrklausel* has proven not to be an insurmountable barrier to groupings with more than local appeal as witnessed by the success of the Greens and PDS/*Die Linke*.

Endnotes to Chapter VIII

1 As herein used, an electoral system is the total legal framework governing the election of representatives to public office, including the qualifications for voting and for holding office, the frequency of elections, the stipulations for the preparation and administration of elections, by-elections and repeat elections, the replacement of deputies, the form of the ballot and the manner in which votes are counted and seats distributed.

2 One significant innovation in the electoral systems of Bavaria and Hesse was the provision that a party obtain a specific minimum percentage of the vote to be eligible for the proportional division of seats. In Hesse a party was required to obtain at least five percent of the total *Land* vote; in Bavaria the requirement for representation was ten percent of the vote in at least one of the five (later seven) administrative districts into which the *Land* was divided. American authorities did place certain restrictions on the Germans with respect to qualifications for voting and requirements for becoming a candidate for office. Men and women had to be given equal rights of voting and being elected to office, residence requirements could not exceed one year in the area involved, German nationality had to be a requirement for voting and persons formerly residing outside of Germany would have the right to vote as German nationals if otherwise qualified (*Germany, 1947-1949: The Story in Documents*, Department of State; Washington, 1950: 164).

3 The British blamed the weaknesses of the Weimar Republic on a multiplicity of parties, the lack of close contact between representatives and constituents and the power of the party hierarchy which the list system of proportional representation sustained. Raymond Ebsworth in *Restoring Democracy in Germany* holds that the introduction of the mixed electoral system more than any other innovation helped to break the power of the party headquarters. Although a candidate still requires the approval of his party for nomination, the party organizers soon came to see that it was useless to nominate "party hacks" who had no following with the voters.

4 In Hamburg 84 of 110 seats, in Bremen 64 of eighty seats, in Lower Saxony 95 of 149 seats, in North Rhine-Westphalia 150 of 200 seats, and in Schleswig-Holstein 42 of seventy seats were filled by direct election in the first *Bürgerschaft* or *Landtag* elections. Only in Bremen and Hamburg were deputies elected directly from multi-member constituencies in which each voter had as many votes as deputies to be chosen.

5 In Schleswig-Holstein the d'Hondt formula was employed in allocating the 28 reserve list seats; in Bremen and Hamburg a quota was established by dividing the number of reserve list seats (sixteen in Bremen, 26 in Hamburg) plus one into the total sum of *Mehr* and *Reststimmen* of all parties. The number of times this quotient plus one could be divided into each separate party total determined a party's indirect representation.

6 In Bremen from three to five deputies were elected directly from each constituency depending on the population of each; in Hamburg each of 21 constituencies

elected four deputies apiece; in Schleswig-Holstein only one deputy was elected from each constituency.

7 The SPD obtained 47.6 percent of the vote in Bremen, 43.1 percent in Hamburg, and 43.8 percent in Schleswig-Holstein. Had this manner of distributing reserve list seats been employed in Lower Saxony and North Rhine-Westphalia, the SPD in the former and the CDU in the latter would have gained absolute majorities in the respective *Landtage* in the 1947 parliamentary elections.

8 See pages 18, 19, and 24 for a more detailed description of this system.

9 Of the *Länder* originally employing a mixed system, only Bremen and Hamburg reverted back to straight proportional arrangements, Bremen in 1947, Hamburg in 1957. However, Hamburg in 2004 returned to a modified mixed system, not unlike the multimember arrangement that existed for the first *Bürgerschaft* election in 1946. Rhineland-Palatinate, originally under French control, continued with a proportional arrangement until 1991 when it was replaced by a mixed system under which 51 of 101 seats are filled by direct vote. At the end of 2010 only Bremen and the Saar employed straight proportional arrangements. In 2011 Bremen moved to a mixed list and personal multiple voting system.

10 The second chamber in Bavaria, called the Senate (*Senat*), employs a system of functional representation. In spite of its right to introduce bills and to give legislative advisory opinions, the Senate has no real veto authority and enjoys little authentic legislative power.

11 Baden-Württemberg elects 120 deputies, Bavaria 180, Berlin 130. Brandenburg 88, Bremen 83, Hamburg 121, Hesse 110, Lower Saxony 135, Mecklenburg-Vorpommern 71, North Rhine-Westphalia 181, Rhineland-Palatinate 101, the Saar 51, Saxony 120, Saxony-Anhalt 89, Schleswig-Holstein 69 and Thuringia 88. These numbers can be increased by the addition of *Überhangmandates* and *Ausgleichmandates*.

12 Hesse raised the size of its *Landtag* from 96 to 110 members for the 1970 election, the Saar from fifty to 51 following a political stalemate resulting from the outcome of the 1975 *Land* election, and Hamburg from 120 to 121 for the 1991 election.

13 The proportion of seats filled directly in Baden-Württemberg is seventy of 120 (58.3 percent), in Bavaria 92 of 180 (51.1 percent), in Berlin 78 of 130 (sixty percent), in Brandenburg 44 of 88 (fifty percent), in Hamburg 71 of 121 (58.7 percent), in Hesse 55 of 110 (fifty percent), in Lower Saxony 87 of 135 (64.4 percent), in Mecklenburg-Vorpommern 36 of 71 (50.7 percent), in North Rhine-Westphalia 128 of 181 (70.7 percent), in Rhineland-Palatinate 51 of 101 (50.5 percent), in Saxony sixty of 120 (fifty percent), in Saxony-Anhalt 45 of 89 (50.6 percent), in Schleswig-Holstein 46 of 69 (66.7 percent) and in Thuringia 44 of 88 (fifty percent).

14 Almost all seats awarded to other than the CDU, SPD, PDS/*Die Linke* and the Greens result from the second or proportional allocation from party lists.

15 No great advantage results from doing especially well in single member districts, since any proportional imbalance is corrected through the awarding of *Ausgleich* mandates (equalization mandates).

16 See *Landtag von Baden-Württemberg*, 2006.

17 Replacement of deputies elected indirectly is usually from the unused balance of the party's *Land* list.

18 The Federal Constitutional Court in Karlsruhe ruled in November 1953 that the naming of substitute candidates by the *Landtage* from among the three nominees put up by the party executive committee when no candidates are left on the reserve list is contrary to the directness of the election and was an after-the-fact appointment of candidates. The Court could not accept the principle of appointing deputies who were unknown to the voters and were therefore in no position to represent them (*Die Wahl zur Bürgerschaft und zu den Bezirksausschussen am 1. November 1953,* Hamburg Statistical Office: 128).

Hamburg is the only exception to the practice of leaving seats unoccupied. The seat goes to the candidate of another party which was next in line in the d'Hondt division of seats.

19 The first restrictive clauses appeared in 1946 in the electoral systems of Bavaria and Hesse. In 1947 Bremen, Lower Saxony, North Rhine-Westphalia and Schleswig-Holstein incorporated similar clauses into their electoral laws and all other *Länder* have since followed suit. Lower Saxony dropped the five percent requirement for its 1951 and 1955 *Land* elections but reinstated it in 1959. All of the new states have had restrictive clauses since 1990.

20 The DVU had gained 5.36 percent of Bremerhaven ballots to qualify for the one seat.

21 Without its exemption from the *Sperrklausel,* the party of the Danish minority would not have been represented in the Schleswig-Holstein *Landtag* after 1954.

22 The two seats received by the SSW in the 2005 *Land* election with 3.5 percent of ballots cast greatly complicated traditional coalition patterns as neither an SPD/Greens nor a CDU/FDP alliance could provide a working majority (*Die Welt,* April 15, 2005).

23 Three clauses of the Basic Law come into question: Article 3, paragraph 1, guaranteeing the equality of all persons before the law; Article 19, paragraph 1, requiring that a law apply generally and not solely to an individual case; and Article 28, paragraph 1, guaranteeing the equality of the vote.

24 The following reasoning was applied to the case by the Federal Constitutional Court: "If it were to be concluded that every vote is equal, then the five percent clause would be unacceptable. However, legally speaking and in theory, the *Sperrklausel* must be held valid in spite of the delineation it places on the value of each vote. The legislature may, especially on important political grounds such as the maintenance of a workable parliament and the orderly formation of governments, circumscribe the principle of voting equality within certain limits to hinder an excessive splintering of the parliament. That such a restriction on voting equality is necessary has been proven by the Weimar Republic, especially in its last years, as well as by the Third and Fourth French Republics. The limitation on the equality of the vote through the *Sperrklausel* is a legitimate measure as long as it stays 'within allowable limits.' It is thereby determined that the five percent restriction represents no violation to the principle of voting equality. This restriction is not discriminatory, applying to all parties alike. There is no restriction on the right to vote through the *Sperrklausel.*"

This case is described in detail in *Die Wahl zur Bürgerschaft und zu den Bezirksausschüssen am 10. November 1957,* Hamburg Statistical Office: 184-190.

25 Although every *Land* electoral system forbids the combination of lists, the Court's decision does not rule out a true fusion of two or more parties as was accomplished in 1961 by the German and Refugee parties, nor does it forbid electoral alliances in which the parties forming the alliance mutually agree not to run candidates against each other in certain constituencies. An alliance, federation or bloc such as that formed in 1953 by the CDU, FDP, DP and BHE under the title Hamburg Bloc, in which all four of the parties maintained their separate identity would be illegal today.

26 In the case of the SSW in Schleswig-Holstein it can be argued that parliamentary representation, even the possession of a single seat in the *Landtag*, gives the party a *raison d'etre*, which without would cause it eventually to lose whatever support it has. This can also be said of the DVU in Bremerhaven/Bremen.

27 To illustrate, in the 2006 *Land* election in Berlin an additional six parties would have been eligible for reserve list seats had there been no restrictive clause, the *Graue* (the Grays) with five seats, the WASG with four seats, the NPD with three seats, and the Republicans, *Tierschutz* (Animal Protection) and *Eltern* (Parents) parties with one representative each. These six groupings polled 162,312 votes or 11.8 percent of the total and together would have received fifteen seats which would have reduced the numbers awarded to the qualifying parties.

Other than the requirement that a party obtain a specified number of signatures in a constituency, administrative district or *Land* to indicate a minimum degree of support as a requisite to the entering of candidates on the ballot, a system which allows reserve list seats to be distributed in districts smaller in size than the *Land* as a whole such as earlier in Bavaria, Rhineland-Palatinate and the Saar would effectively deny representation to most splinter parties even without a five percent clause. For example, the system of districts prevented the DRP from obtaining more than a single seat in the Rhineland-Palatinate *Landtag* in 1959, even though it received 5.1 percent of the total *Land* vote which would have entitled it to five seats had the whole *Land* served as a single district for the proportional allocation of seats. Had the DRP's total fallen much below five percent, it would have received no seats even had there been no five percent clause. The requiring of a deposit from each candidate in the constituencies of those *Länder* employing mixed systems, to be forfeited unless the candidate obtains a minimum percentage of the constituency vote as in Britain, could also serve to restrict splinter parties.

28 The Free Democrats were unsuccessful in the 1994, 1998 and 2003 elections in Bavaria; the 1995 and 1999 elections in Berlin; the 1995, 1999, 2003 and 2011 elections in Bremen; the 1994, 1999 and 2004 elections in Brandenburg; the 1993, 1997, 2004 and 2008 elections in Hamburg; the 1994 and 1998 elections in Lower Saxony; the 1994, 1998 and 2002 elections in Mecklenburg-Vorpommern; the 1995 election in North Rhine-Westphalia; the 1994 and 1999 elections in the Saar and Saxony; the 1994, 1998 and 2011 elections in Saxony-Anhalt; the 1994, 1999 and 2004 contests in Thuringia; and the 2011 election in Rhineland-Palatinate.

29 Article 21, paragraph 2, of the Federal Basic Law makes illegal "parties, which by reason of their aims or the behavior of their adherents, seek to impair or destroy the free democratic basic order or to endanger the existence of the Federal Republic of Germany."

30 In Baden-Württemberg new and non-represented parties must submit petitions carrying the signatures of at least 150 eligible voters in each constituency in which it

intends to place a candidate on the ballot. In Bavaria the requirement is 500 signatures in an administrative district for parties not presently represented in the *Landtag*, twenty signatures for parties which are represented. In Berlin forty signatures in a single member constituency are required to place a candidate on the ballot, but to be eligible for the division of reserve list seats a party must place a candidate in every constituency of a constituency bloc (*Wahlkreisverband*), twelve in number and each electing from four to ten deputies by simple majority ballot, unless presently represented by at least five deputies in the Berlin House of Representatives. New or non-represented parties in Bremen must obtain 1,000 signatures to enter lists in both Bremen and Bremerhaven, both of which are considered as completely independent units. Hamburg requires 500 supporters in the whole *Land* for new and non-represented parties. In Hesse fifty signatures in a constituency is sufficient to place a candidate on the ballot; however, 1,000 signatures in the whole *Land* is required to enter a *Land* list. Twenty signatures are required in a constituency in Lower Saxony to place a candidate on the ballot. In North Rhine-Westphalia 100 signatures are needed in a constituency, 1,000 to submit a *Land* list. These requirements do not apply to parties presently represented in the *Landtag*.

31 Prior to 1962 in Hesse and 1963 in Lower Saxony a party must have entered candidates in all single member constituencies in order to qualify for the submission of *Land* lists and be eligible for seats therefrom. Three parties were excluded from entering *Land* lists in Lower Saxony in 1959 for having failed to meet the constituency requirement. Hesse has substituted the constituency requirement with one of a thousand signatures *Land*-wide.

32 Two independents were elected to the Bremen *Bürgerschaft* in 1946, but none were returned to the parliament in 1947 or since.

33 Prior to 1991 Rhineland-Palatinate was divided into seven districts, each of which was awarded a specified number of seats depending on the population in each. A proportional division of 100 seats was made within each of the separate districts.

34 See *Die Wahl zur Bürgerschaft und zu den Bezirksausschussen am 16. Oktober 1949, Sondernummer 5*: pages 4 and 88 for a description of these changes.

35 The change to a proportional system was pushed through by the Hamburg Block, a party alliance formed in 1953 by the CDU, FDP, DP and the BHE to defeat the SPD at the polls. Having succeeded in controlling the government, the grouping hoped to reduce the advantage of the Social Democrats who were consistently strong in single member districts. The SPD acquiesced to the change and did not revert back to direct election during the time it controlled the Hamburg government, as it was able to win absolute majorities under the proportional system in 1957, 1961, 1966, 1970, 1978, 1982 and 1991. The CDU also won an absolute majority under the existing proportional arrangement in 2004 prior to the change to the present mixed system.

36 The mixed system was instituted by a CDU-controlled *Bürgerschaft*, but failed to provide the Union party with a majority in the 2008 *Land* election, necessitating the formation of a coalition government and the establishment of the first Black/Green ministry on the state level. The new election law passed in 2009 has been criticized as being confusing to the voters, leading to reduced voter participation and invalid ballots. In fact 530,000 eligible voters failed to show up at the polls in 2011 in contrast to 349,000 in the 2001 *Bürgerschaft* election (*Hamburger Abendblatt*, February 25, 2011).

37 For the first *Bürgerschaft* election in 1946 the city of Bremen was divided into sixteen districts, each of which elected from three to five deputies by simple majority vote. The voters in each of these districts could cast from three to five votes depending on the number of deputies to be elected from each district. Sixty-four of the eighty seats were filled by direct election, sixteen from reserve lists by proportional representation according to the same system employed for the first *Bürgerschaft* election in Hamburg.

Bremen never experienced a system of single member districts, in that in the 1946 *Bürgerschaft* election deputies were elected from multimember constituencies in which each voter had from three to five votes.

38 The application of the five percent barrier to Bremen proper and Bremerhaven separately enabled the DVU to gain access to the Bremen parliament with less than five percent of the total *Land* vote on four occasions, in 1987, 1999, 2003 and 2007, and the *BIW* in the 2008 re-run and in the 2011 *Burgerschaft* election.

39 Only in 1991 did the DVU exceed the five percent barrier with 6.2 percent of the *Land*-wide vote enabling it to send six deputies to the Bremen *Bürgerschaft*.

40 Had the 1955 electoral system applied to the 1960 election the DDU would still have qualified for two *Landtag* seats. However, had it received 576 less votes in Saarbrücken, it would have received no seats even had there been no five percent clause, although its *Land* total would have amounted to 4.7 percent. Had the same vote total been cast, but the 1934 votes had fallen in district Saarlouis, rather than in Neunkircken and Saarbrücken, the DDU would have obtained no seats even with the five percent clause.

41 Bremen opted for a straight proportional system following its merger with Bremerhaven in 1947 with each part considered separately for the application of the five percent restriction and the proportional division of seats. This arrangement continued to 2011. Hamburg, on the other hand, employed a proportional system from 1957 to 2004. The 2008 *Land* election was the first to be held under a system of multimember districts under which 71 seats are filled directly.

42 The number of seats in Baden-Württemberg may be increased above 120 when more direct seats are won by a party than its proportional entitlement, in which case balancing seats must be provided to maintain a proportional balance between eligible parties. In 2006 nineteen additional seats were awarded as the CDU gained more seats directly than its proportional allotment would allow.

43 Twenty-six additional seats were awarded in 1992, 35 in 1996, eight in 2001, nineteen in 2006 and eighteen in 2011 in Baden-Württemberg.

44 Had mandates been awarded on a straight proportional basis, the CDU in 2001 would have received 57 instead of the 63 it received through direct election.

45 A mixed system was first introduced in Berlin in 1958 with eighty of 127 seats filled by direct vote.

46 The electoral law set the size of the Berlin parliament at 200 members with 127 to be elected from the three western sectors and 73 from the eastern sector. Because of the non-participation of East Berlin in the elections, the western portion elected only the 127 deputies. The unfilled seats were set aside for the representatives of East Berlin should city-wide elections be held again.

47 The twelve districts are Charlottenburg, Kreuzberg, Neukölln, Reinickendorf, Schöneberg, Spandau, Steglitz, Tempelhof, Tiergarten, Wedding, Wilmersdorf and Zehlendorf.

48 Each *Wahlkreisverband* elected from four to ten deputies from single member districts, Charlottenburg eight, Kreuzberg seven, Neukölln ten, Reinickendorf eight, Schöneberg seven, Spandau six, Steglitz seven, Tempelhof five, Tiergarten four, Wedding eight, Wilmersdorf six and Zehlendorf four.

49 The number of deputies to be elected from the reserve lists of a district was not a constant figure as the count of deputies in each *Wahlkreisverband* could be raised by the addition of *Überhang-* and *Ausgleichmandates*.

50 The small number of deputies elected from each constituency block necessitates the provision for the *Ausgleichmandat*.

51 See *Unterlagen für die Vorbereitung und Durchführung der Wahlen zum Berliner Abgeordnetenhaus und zu den Bezirksverordnetenversammlungen am 17. Februar 1963, Senator für Inneres*, Ref. IH, and *Endgültiges Ergebnis der Berliner Wahlen am 17. Februar 1963, Senator für Inneres*, Number 15.

52 In the 1995 election the size of the Berlin parliament was increased only to 206 members. With the reduction in the size of its parliament, the number of deputies elected in 1999 was 169, in 2001 141 and in 2006 149.

53 To establish the election quota, the *Land*-wide vote of each eligible party was totaled and divided by ninety (the number of *Landtag* seats). The resulting quota, 17,882 in this case, was then divided into the party totals in the fifteen districts (*Wahlkreise*), each of which elected a varying number of representatives depending on the amount of valid ballots cast in the district. For example, District VII in which 75,693 votes were cast, elected three *Wahlkreis* representatives; District XI elected ten representatives on the basis of 209,024 votes cast. The remainders of each party in the fifteen districts were compiled and a second division determined the distribution of *Land* list seats.

54 The 1946 Hessian electoral system is described in *Staat und Wirtschaft in Hessen*, Heft 1, Hessen Statistical Office, 1947: 20-26.

55 In the 2008 *Land* election the CDU following slipped from 48.8 to 36.8 percent. The 3,511 vote margin over the SPD, with 36.7 percent of ballots cast, was insufficient to give the CDU an additional seat.

56 Schleswig-Holstein did not adopt a five percent clause until 1950. For the 1947 election a direct seat requirement limited the number of parties gaining representation in the *Landtag*. Unless a party could win in a single member constituency, it was ineligible for the distribution of reserve list seats regardless of its percentage of the *Land*-wide vote. Thus, a party able to win a single direct seat with three percent of the vote qualified for indirect seats, whereas a party with ten percent of the vote and unable to win a direct seat was left unrepresented. Only the SPD, CDU and the SSV (Danish Minority Party) gained seats in the first *Landtag* as a result of this requirement, and even in the absence of a five percent clause the FDP with 4.97 percent of the ballots cast, the Communist Party with 4.7 percent, and the German Conservative Party (DKP) with 3.1 percent failed to gain representation. The direct seat requirement was retained for the 1950 election except that parties obtaining at least five percent of the *Land* vote were also eligible for reserve list seats.

The 1947 electoral law in Lower Saxony provided that a party, to be eligible for the reserve list allocation, had to gain either five percent of the *Land* vote or win at least one direct seat. By winning a single direct seat the Center Party in 1947 became eligible for five *Land* list seats in addition to its direct mandate even though it polled only 4.1 percent of the total *Land* vote. Both of these restrictions were deleted from the electoral laws governing the 1951 and 1955 *Land* elections in Lower Saxony, and not until the 1959 election was a five percent clause reestablished.

57 Because of the possibility of a party winning a large number of direct seats with a small percentage of the total vote such limitations on the size of the *Landtag* appeared necessary in 1947; however, they have since been eliminated as a system of relatively few parties developed.

58 The number of additional seats awarded in North Rhine-Westphalia was 37 in 1990, 21 in 1995 and 31 in 2000.

59 In 1959 the SPD had been entitled to 61 seats, but it had already won 65 direct mandates. The SPD was able to retain the four excess seats; however, the other parties were able to participate in the division of four extra seats to equalize the effect of the *Mehrsitze* on the proportional nature of the election. See *Die Wahl zum Niedersächsischen Landtag am 19. April 1959*, Heft 7, Lower Saxony Administrative Office—Statistics, 1959: 5 and 15.

60 These numerous changes in the Schleswig-Holstein electoral system were prompted by political considerations. Because of its ability to do well in single member constituencies in the 1947 *Land* election, the SPD hoped to increase its advantage in future elections by raising the number of direct seats from 42 to 46. The Socialist plan came to naught in the 1950 *Land* election as an electoral alliance formed by the CDU, FDP and DP, through a united effort, were able to win 31 direct seats. Unable to gain any seats from the reserve list in 1950 because of their failure to enter candidates in all 46 constituencies, the bourgeois parties in a coalition with the Refugee Party changed the system of apportioning reserve list seats to reflect the total *Land* vote.

61 The exemption from the five percent clause granted to the Danish minority has been challenged by the major parties on a number of occasions without success.

62 Only one additional seat was added to the Schleswig-Holstein *Landtag* as a result of the outcome of the 1996 *Land* election.

63 This provision of the Federal Basic Law reads as follows:

> Unless otherwise provided by law, a German within the meaning of this Basic Law is a German who possesses German citizenship or who has been admitted to the territory of the German Reich as it existed on December 31, 1937, as refugee or expellee of German stock or as the spouse or descendant of such person.

Doubtful cases of nationality have been clarified in the federal laws of February 22, 1955, and May 17, 1956, entitled "Regulations of Questions of Nationality."

64 The physical difficulties surrounding the holding of these first elections made such discrepancies unavoidable; however, they had been eliminated by the second series of elections.

65 Returning prisoners-of-war were exempted from the residency requirement. The federal electoral law stipulates a residency period of three months.

66 As a result of denazification proceedings Germans were classified under five categories established by the Allied Control Council, with penalties and sanctions imposed upon the individual determined by the category under which he is placed. Major offenders (*Hauptschuldiger*) and offenders (*Belasteter*) were ineligible to hold any public office, to vote, to run for election and were forbidden to be politically active in any way or to be members of a political party. Lesser offenders, sometimes designated as probationers, were placed on probation for a period of at least two years, but normally not more than three years. For the period of the probation, at the discretion of zone commanders, lesser offenders could be denied the right to vote, the capacity to be elected and the right to be politically active in any way or to be members of a political party. In general, the restrictions on this category of individuals were removed by 1949. Those classified as followers could not at first stand for election at any level but could vote. No sanctions were applied against those placed in the fifth category, persons declared exonerated by a tribunal. See Control Council Directive No. 38 of October 12, 1946, entitled "The Arrest and Punishment of War Criminals, Nazis, and Militarists and the Internment, Control and Surveillance of Potentially Dangerous Germans," in *Documents on Germany Under Occupation 1945-1954*, Royal Institute of International Affairs: 168-179.

A report made in June 1947 indicated that in the American zone 1,600 persons had been classified as major offenders, 21,900 as offenders, 106,100 as lesser offenders, 482,700 as followers and 18,300 as exonerated (*Germany 1947-1949*, Dept. of State: 111).

In Hamburg 14,633 individuals or 1.48 percent of those eligible to vote were disenfranchised for the election of October 13, 1946. For the election of December 1, 1946, in Hesse 134,091 or 5.3 percent were disqualified on political grounds.

67 In Rhineland-Palatinate a person who has several residences may vote only in the community designated as his/her primary residence, and if from another *Land*, he/she will be registered only upon declaration of his/her present abode as permanent residence. Individuals may be fined or sentenced to prison for periods of up to six months for giving false information at the time of registration in most *Länder*.

68 A straight simple majority system would eliminate all or most opposition in those *Länder* where a single party is especially strong, as in Baden-Württemberg, Bavaria, Bremen, and Saxony. For example the CDU won 58 of sixty direct seats in Saxony in the 2009 *Land* election and 69 of seventy direct seats in the 2006 *Land* election in Baden-Württemberg. Had there been no balancing seats, the possibility of a one-party legislature is apparent. In highly competitive states such as Berlin, Lower Saxony and North Rhine-Westphalia there would be a chance for a change in governments, as both CDU and SPD have demonstrated their ability to win a majority of direct mandates in past elections. With five nationally-organized parties fragmenting the vote, it is possible in some states for a party with limited support to win a majority of direct seats as the PDS did in the 2004 *Land* election in Brandenburg with only 28.0 percent of ballots cast. The current system increases the possibility of an alternation in power and for the participation of competing agendas in policy-making as parties which could never gain sufficient support to control a ministry on their own are able to share in governance in coalition with one or two other parties.

CHAPTER IX

Elections and the Party System

Although as many as seven different political groupings are represented in one state parliament (Bremen), six in two others, and five in the *Bundestag* today, German political life on both the regional and national levels since the end of World War II has been dominated by two nationally-organized, non-doctrinaire parties of wide-appeal, the Christian Democratic/Christian Social Union and the Social Democratic Party. This has occurred in spite of modified proportional systems in all of the states and on the federal level, which, in most cases, allow parties which are able to obtain at least five percent of the state or national vote to obtain parliamentary representation. The share of the nationwide regional vote for the CDU/CSU and SPD reached a high of ninety percent between 1969 and 1980 and 91.2 percent for the two parties in 1976 *Bundestag* balloting. This share began to fall with the entrance of the Greens and PDS/*Die Linke* into the political arena coupled with a resurgent FDP, but as late as the 2002-2005 period the two *Volks* parties were still able to command over three-quarters of the German vote. Since 2005 there has been a dramatic drop in support for the two major parties, with their national share falling to 64.2 percent in the 2006-2009 series of regional elections and to only a 56.7 percent share in the 2009 general election. Between 1965 and 2005 one or the other of the two major parties was able to win an absolute majority of legislative seats in 62 of 133 *Land* elections (46.4 percent). But in the most recent series of regional contests (2006-2009) the Union parties lost their majority status in Bavaria, Hamburg, Hesse, the Saar and Thuringia, leaving only Rhineland-Palatinate controlled by a single party, the SPD. On the national level the CDU/CSU gained parliamentary majorities in 1953 and 1957, and came close to gaining half of *Bundestag* seats in 1965 and 1983, but in the last two national contests, 2005 and 2009, CDU/CSU support has barely exceeded one-third of ballots cast. While the role of the two major groupings has diminished since 2005, no ministry since 1946 on either the state or national level has been formed without the participation of either the CDU/CSU or SPD, and the executive heads of the various states, with only three exceptions, have been either a member of the Union parties or a Social Democrat and all of the country's eight Chancellors, from Adenauer to Merkel, have either been a Christian or Social Democrat. Although the two-party vote fell below fifty percent in the 2009 balloting in the state of Thuringia, it is highly unlikely that a ministry involving only a coalition of the smaller parties will ever be formed on either the state or national level. [1]

Regional and National Party Developments 1946-1965

The licensing policies of the Occupying Powers, especially the initial prohibitions on expellee and refugee political movements and right-extremist groupings, limited the first partisan elections in most of the *Länder* to contests between the original anti-fascist parties, the CDU/CSU, SPD, the Liberals and the Communists.[2] In the French zone, where no minor parties were authorized, these four parties polled all of the vote in the 1947 elections; in the American zone, where several minor parties, notably the WAV in Bavaria, were licensed, the four-party total amounted to 96.1 percent; only in the British zone, where licensing policies were less rigid, did large numbers of parties appear, and the vote falling to other than the four major political organizations was significant, amounting to 14.2 percent of the zonal total. In West Germany as a whole, all but 8.4 percent of the vote in these first elections fell to the four originally-licensed parties.

In addition to the licensing policies of the Occupying Powers, restrictive clauses appearing in the electoral laws of several of the states served to limit the number of parties receiving parliamentary representation.[3] In Schleswig-Holstein the direct seat requirement in the 1947 electoral law prevented all but three parties from gaining seats in the *Landtag*. In seven other states (Baden, Bavaria, Hamburg, Hesse Rhineland-Palatinate, Württemberg-Baden and Württemberg-Hohenzollern) restrictive clauses, licensing policies, the manner of distributing parliamentary seats or a combination of these factors held the number of parties obtaining representation to four, in North Rhine-Westphalia to five and in Bremen and Lower Saxony to six. With the exception of the 1946 election in Bremen, independents have been unable to win parliamentary seats in any of the states.[4]

Already in the first series of regional elections the West German voter demonstrated a strong preference for the two major party organizations, the CDU/CSU and the SPD, which together polled 72.7 percent of the three-zonal vote and emerged as the two strongest parties in every *Land*.[5] Only four parties other than the CDU/CSU, SPD, KPD and Liberals received representation in the various state parliaments and their followings were strictly regional in nature, not extending beyond two *Länder*.[6] By the time of the first *Bundestag* election in 1949, however, the lifting of most restrictions on political activity,[7] the changed complexion of the electorate, swollen by returning prisoners of war, refugees and expellees from the East, enfranchised individuals who had been barred from voting because of their connections with National Socialism and youth voting for the first time, and the absence of strong integrating forces at the national level contributed to a splintering of the political arena.[8]

No less than ten separate parties obtained representation in the first *Bundestag*, the largest parliamentary group being the CDU/CSU which polled 31.0 percent of the West German vote.[9] The application of the five percent requirement in the first federal electoral law to the individual states rather than to countrywide totals of each party enabled a number of strictly regional groups, such as the Bavarian Party and WAV in Bavaria and the SSV in Schleswig-Holstein, to gain *Bundestag* representation.[10]

The fragmentation in the first general election held August 14, 1949, was most apparent in the American and British zone *Länder*, least in the French zone because of the continuation of strict licensing policies. The combined vote of the Union parties and SPD fell to 60.2 percent and the total vote falling to other than the four originally-licensed parties increased from the 8.4 percent figure reached in the first series of regional contests to 22.2 percent in the first general election.[11] Only in Württemberg-Hohenzollern in the French zone did the two-party vote increase; in Bavaria it dropped by 28.9 percentage points as both the CSU and the SPD failed to poll as much as thirty percent of the vote.

The fragmentation which characterized the first general election continued into the second series of regional contests. The most significant fracturing force was the emergence in 1950 of a fifth party of national scope, the BHE, a purely interest movement which appealed to the unassimilated refugees and expellees and other groups which had suffered from the war and felt disenfranchised.[12] The entry of a powerful refugee movement, committed neither to bourgeois nor to socialist philosophies, into the political arena hindered the development of a kind of two-party system which had been developing around the bourgeois-socialist cleavage. A second important party development of the period between the first and second general elections was the success of the Socialist Reich Party (SRP) in two states. In contrast to the nation-wide success of the Refugee Party, the SRP could build up a sufficient following only in Bremen and Lower Saxony to gain parliamentary representation.[13] Increased strength of the German Party in the *Länder* of the British zone and the success of the particularistic Bavarian Party, competing in a Bavarian state election for the first time in 1950, contributed to a further splintering of the *Landtage* in those states.[14]

The three-zonal totals of the CDU/CSU and the SPD in the second series of regional contests amounted to only 60.4 percent, a drop of 12.3 percentage points from the two-party following in the first series of *Land* elections, although nearly duplicating totals of the 1949 general election.[15] No less than fifteen different parties obtained seats in the various *Landtage*, ten in the Lower Saxony parliament alone.[16] This splintering occurred in spite of restrictive clauses in the electoral laws in all states but Hamburg and Lower Saxony. Because the process of fragmentation fractured the Right more than the Left, the CDU/CSU, of the two major parties, suffered the greatest loss of support and witnessed a drop from 37.7 percent in the 1946/1947 regional contests to 28.0 percent in the 1949-1952 *Land* elections. This period marked the lowest ebb for the CDU/CSU in any series of regional contests and enabled the Socialists, whose *Land* totals dropped only from 35.0 to 32.4 percent, to replace the Union parties as the leading grouping on the regional level.[17]

In contrast to the Weimar period in which a multiplicity of parties was perpetuated by economic, social and political instability, a backward movement in the number of parties gaining parliamentary representation on both the countrywide and regional levels set in after 1952/1953. The outlawing of the neo-Nazi SRP in 1952 and the Communist Party in 1956,[18] together with the general loss of support for all extremist groups as a result of growing economic and political stability, the tightening of election law requirements for parties to get on the ballot and to obtain representation, the growing personal popularity of Chancellor Konrad Adenauer and acceptance of his programs and the general integrating influence of national politics contributed to this trend, and by 1957, other than the CDU/CSU, SPD and FDP, only the Refugee and German parties continued to play an important role in regional political developments.

In the 1953 *Bundestag* election the CDU/CSU clearly established itself as the dominant party on the national level as it polled 45.2 percent of the West German vote and won every state with the exception of the Socialist strongholds of Bremen, Hamburg and Hesse. A return to the earlier movement towards a modified two-party system was clearly evident as the combined CDU/CSU/SPD vote rose to 74.0 percent, over thirteen percentage points greater than in the 1949 *Bundestag* election and in the second series of regional contests. Moreover, with the Free Democrats receiving 9.5 percent of ballots cast and the KPD 2.2 percent, the vote falling to other than the four originally-licensed parties dropped to 14.3 percent and *Bundestag* representation was reduced to six parties, one of which, the Center Party (*Zentrum*), owed its three seats to the goodwill of the CDU in North Rhine-Westphalia, creating a more manageable political body on the federal level.[19]

In the regional contests held between 1953 and 1956 the countrywide vote total of the CDU/CSU and SPD increased to 70.2 percent, nearly matching the two-party following of the first *Land* elections, but falling short of the 1953 general election totals. The most spectacular gains were registered by the Union parties which, riding the crest of Chancellor Adenauer's national popularity, regained their leading position in regional level competition.[20] The four largest parties, the CDU/CSU, SPD, FDP and GB/BHE (the Communist Party having fallen into relative insignificance after 1949) polled all but 10.9 percent of the West German vote, and the number of separate parties obtaining representation in the various state parliaments shank from 15 to nine. Of the five parties of national scope, only the CDU/CSU, SPD and FDP held seats in all states, the Refugee Party was represented in six *Länder*, the KPD in two.[21] Of the regional parties, the German Party gained seats in four *Land* parliaments, the *Zentrum* in two and the Bavarian and German Reich Party in one each.[22] The excessive splintering which characterized the second series of regional contests was limited to Lower Saxony, where the continued absence of a minimum require-ment for representation allowed eight groupings to obtain parliamentary seats. In no other state legislative body were more than five parties represented.[23]

The 1957 general election not only gave a single party an absolute majority of the countrywide vote for the first time in German democratic history,[24] it marked the end of national political life for the Refugee Party and the *Zentrum*, leaving only four parties represented in the *Bundestag*.[25] The two-party vote increased to 82.0 percent and all but 10.3 percent of the countrywide vote was polled by the CDU/CSU, SPD and FDP. The success of the CDU's foreign and domestic programs served to isolate the Social Democratic Party, whose class character and policy of neutrality towards the West failed to gain the goodwill of the West German voter; however, the Socialists' overwhelming defeat in the 1957 *Bundestag* poll was to have a far-reaching influence on the future course of the party, forcing it to make changes which were to narrow the differences between it and the Union parties and make it more competitive on the national level.

The movement in the states towards what was slowly becoming a three-party (or which some observers called a two and a half party) system of the CDU/CSU, SPD and FDP (a trend which continued into the early 1980s when it was challenged by the first successes of various Greens groupings) became even stronger in the interval between the 1957 and 1961 *Bundestag* contests as the two-party total of the CDU/CSU and SPD increased to 80.4 percent,[26] 10.2 percentage points more than in the previous series of regional elections, and the vote falling to other than the CDU/CSU, SPD and FDP declined to just 11.5 percent. Although the Free Democrats and Refugee Party lost a third of their earlier regional-level followings, the FDP maintained its representation in all ten West German state parliaments, but lost 36 *Landtag* seats on diminished vote shares, while the BHE retained its seats in five state legislative bodies, also with fewer representatives.[27]

Although the number of different parties receiving parliamentary representation increased from nine to ten in the elections held between 1957 and 1960, in spite of the outlawing of the Communist Party and the extinction of the Center Party in Lower Saxony and North Rhine-Westphalia, it did not represent a return to the splintering of the early 1950s. Rather it was primarily a reflection of the unstable political situation in the Saar and the provision in the new Schleswig-Holstein electoral law which exempted the party of the Danish minority, the SSW, from the five percent minimum requirement which applied to all other parties.[28] Only five parties gained representation in more than one state. The CDU/CSU, SPD and FDP held seats in all ten state parliaments,[29] the Refugee Party in five and the German Party in two, although the DP increased its overall following by over 200,000 votes by entering candidates in a number of South German states without success. Nevertheless the DP failed to retain its representation in Hamburg and Schleswig-Holstein.[30] The Bavarian Party gained fourteen seats in Bavaria, the DRP a single seat in Rhineland-Palatinate,[31] the SSW two seats in Schleswig-Holstein and the CVP and the DDU six and two seats respectively in the Saar.[32] The followings of these five splinter parties were strictly limited, the CVP in the Saar being the largest, and none participated in a state ministry.

The incorporation of a five percent clause in the electoral law governing the 1959 state election in Lower Saxony reduced representation in that *Land* to five parties to bring it into line with the party systems in the other states. In addition to Lower Saxony, five parties were represented in the *Landtage* of Bavaria, the Saar and Schleswig-Holstein, four in the legislatures of Baden-Württemberg, Bremen, Hesse and Rhineland-Palatinate and three in Hamburg and North Rhine-Westphalia.

Although the regional elections held between 1957 and 1960 indicated a sharp decline in the fortunes of the Refugee and German parties, it was not until the 1961 *Bundestag* balloting and the *Land* contests held between 1961 and 1966 that the two parties ceased to be a factor in federal and regional politics. The elimination of these two groupings from all *Landtage* and the lack of success of such new parties as the German Peace Union (DFU) in gaining a foothold in any of the states was to produce by the end of 1965 a three-party system in a majority of the states to duplicate the model which had been established in Bonn in the 1961 *Bundestag* election.[33]

The desertion of a majority of the German Party deputies in the *Bundestag* to the CDU/CSU in the second half of 1960 marked the death of the DP as a parliamentary group in Bonn; however, in early 1961 the DP merged with the Refugee Party, which had lost its *Bundestag* representation four years earlier in an attempt to regain its former position in national politics. During the merger negotiations between the DP and GB/BHE, representations were made to the FDP to participate in the formation of a Third Force, an alliance of the small parties. FDP chairman, Erich Mende, however, wisely refused the offer. The merger of such widely diverse groups, one performing the role of a pressure group for refugee and expellee interests, the other serving conservative and often right-wing interests, proved to be a grave miscalculation, and the combination, known as the GDP (*Gesamt Deutsche Partei*), obtained only 2.8 percent of the 1961 *Bundestag* vote.[34]

The Three-Party Era in the *Bund* and *Länder*

In 1965 the GDP, the designation retained by the Refugee Party, did not compete in the fifth *Bundestag* contest as a separate entity and lost its last remaining foothold on the *Land* level when it received only 4.3 percent of the vote in the November 6, 1966 election in Hesse. The German Party groups in Bremen and Lower Saxony were plagued by mass desertions after 1961, and by the 1963 *Land* elections were but skeletons of their former selves, with only five of the 16 deputies remaining loyal to the party in Bremen and two of the twenty in Lower Saxony. While the DP failed to make a comeback in Lower Saxony in the 1963 *Land* election, a new party, known as the German Party in the State of Bremen, was formed around the five DP members who had remained true to the party, and the group succeeded in gaining four seats in the 1963 *Bürgerschaft* election in Bremen.[35]

Not only were the 1961-1965 regional elections damaging to the cause of the German and Refugee parties, they put all splinter groups into full retreat. The DDU in the Saar and the DRP in Rhineland-Palatinate failed to qualify for representation, and the Bavarian Party in Bavaria, the SSW in Schleswig-Holstein and the CVP in the Saar all lost parliamentary seats, demonstrating the difficulty at the time for parties which appealed to narrow regional or group interests to gain representation. By the end of 1965 splinter parties held seats in the parliaments of only five states and in no case did their representation extend beyond a single *Land*. In Schleswig-Holstein the fourth party, the Danish SSW, existed only because of its exemption from the five percent clause;[36] in Bavaria the Bavarian Party, with 4.8 percent of the vote, gained representation only because of the particular operation of the state's electoral system;[37] in Bremen the fourth party was the right-wing German Party in the State of Bremen which gained 5.2 percent of the 1963 vote; in Hesse the rapidly fading Refugee Party polled 6.3 percent in 1962 balloting to give it four additional years of life before its elimination in 1966;[38] and in the Saar the Christian People's Party was able to win two seats in the 1965 *Land* election. In the five other states a three-party

TABLE 9.1

**NATIONWIDE PARTY TOTALS IN THE
FIRST FIVE SERIES OF *LAND* ELECTIONS** [39]

	1946/47 *Land* Elections	1949/52 *Land* Elections	1953/56 *Land* Elections	1957/60 *Land* Elections	1961/65 *Land* Elections
CDU/CSU	37.7	28.0	36.7	42.1	42.7
SPD	35.0	32.4	33.5	38.3	42.3
FDP/DVP	9.5	12.2	11.8	8.1	8.6
KPD/DFU	9.4	3.8	3.0	....	1.6 [a]
GB/BHE	....	8.2	7.1	4.4	2.5
DP/NLP	2.6	3.2	2.4	3.2	0.4
ZENTRUM	3.4	2.8	1.2	0.3	0.3
DRP/DKP/ SRP/NPD	0.4	3.6	0.6	1.5	0.5
Others	2.0	5.9	3.7	2.2	1.1
CDU/CSU/SPD Totals	72.7	60.4	70.2	80.4	85.0
CDU/CSU/SPD/ FDP vote	82.2	72.6	82.0	88.5	93.6

a This figure represents the countrywide total for the left-oriented German Peace Union.

system of the CDU/CSU, SPD and FDP prevailed.

The decline of all splinter parties after 1953 strengthened the clustering around three nationally-organized parties on both the regional and countrywide levels, and between 1961 and 1965 the CDU/CSU, SPD and FDP increased their share of the total *Land* level vote from 88.5 percent in the fourth series of regional contests to 93.6 percent.[40] At the same time the *Bundestag* totals of the three groupings swelled from 94.4 percent in 1961 to 96.4 percent in 1965, limiting splinter group support to a mere 3.6 percent. Thus, by 1965 the German party system was no longer characterized by numerous ideological, regional and class groupings, but by three bourgeois middle-of-the-road parties of wide appeal.

This early clustering around three parties was the result of a number of economic, political and social factors. One was the minimum requirement for representation found in state and federal electoral laws. While preventing an excessive multiplication of parties it could not explain why West German voters prior to the 1980s limited their choices to these three groupings, since even under the five percent clause it was still possible for seven or more parties to obtain representation under what were basically proportional systems. The hurdle did not prevent seven political groupings from obtaining representation in the 1951 Bremen election nor six in Saxony in the 2004 and 2009 *Land* ballotings, or six in the 2009 regional poll in Schleswig-Holstein. It did not prevent the National Democratic Party (NPD) from gaining representation in seven of the ten state parliaments between 1966 and 1968 nor for the Greens to gain a foothold in most of the state parliaments and *Bundestag* in the 1980s or for the PDS (*Die Linke*) and various right-extremist groups to obtain seats in various state parliaments after 1990. It ultimately did not protect the three-party monopoly which dominated West German politics between the early 1960s and early 1980s. The NPD's success proved to be transitory as the party failed to gain national representation in the 1969 *Bundestag* election and lost all of its *Landtag* seats during the 1969-1972 series of regional contests, and its emergence had little impact on the share of the countrywide vote received by the three established parties, which together polled 92.7 percent of ballots cast in the regional contests held between the 1965 and 1969 general elections and 94.5 percent of the 1969 *Bundestag* vote.

The leveling effects of the Nazi dictatorship, the influx of large numbers of expellees and refugees from the East and the commonality of problems facing the German people after the war, which were vigorously dealt with by the Adenauer administration, contributed to an early clustering. Arnold Heidenheimer, writing in the 1960s, stressed the polarization of German politicians into pro-Adenauer and anti-Adenauer camps during his fourteen-year tenure in office (1949-1963).[41] Moreover, economic prosperity and the electorate's sense of well-being tended to deideolize German politics and the three major parties reflected this development in their concern for the problems of today rather than the goals of tomorrow. The universality of the CDU/CSU appeal, a reflection of the coalition nature of the party in economic, social and cultural spheres, and the quality of its leadership early made the Union parties the dominant political group in postwar Germany. To make it competitive with the all-encompassing nature of the CDU/CSU, the Social Democrats developed a liberal bourgeois program of wide appeal of their own and presented attractive leaders in the persons of Willy Brandt and Helmut Schmidt. The FDP, while never able to approach the following of the CDU/CSU and SPD, likewise moderated its position on many issues, presented attractive personalities like Erich Mende and Walter Scheel and reorganized in the direction of a well-defined liberal party to enhance its national appeal and by 1965 firmly established itself as a democratic Third Force and an alternative to the two major parties. The similarities between the three nationally-organized parties became so marked as to cause opponents to label them *Drillinge* (triplets). By 1965 the CDU/CSU, SPD and FDP had come to resemble the pragmatic, non-ideological groupings which characterized the Anglo-American party systems of the period. Ossip K. Flechtheim, writing in 1963, noted that the three parties had accommodated themselves to the social capitalistic status quo, standing no longer as movements of dynamic innovation with a concern for the possibilities, opportunities and demands of tomorrow, but as organizations of conservative preservation, bound to the dynamic ideas, customs and judgments of today and yesterday. He considered the decline of the small parties to be not just an interlude, but an irresistible trend, and that with the need for mammoth organization, the success of a new party was a near impossibility.[42]

The consensus which had slowly developed in the early postwar years in the western part of Germany, however, was not to last forever, and Flechtheim's prognostication was challenged within a few years as a result of growing economic troubles, dissatisfaction with the apparent listlessness and indecisiveness of the Bonn parties and developments beyond Germany's borders over which the parties had little or no control. By stressing the absence of choice between the three established parties and the lack of an effective opposition in Bonn following the formation of the grand coalition between the CDU/CSU and SPD in late 1966, the NPD polled 1,516,877 votes (5.3 percent of the regional total) in eight elections held between 1966 and 1968 to gain seats in seven of the state parliaments.[43]

This added a fourth party to the CDU/CSU/SPD/FDP cartel in Hesse, Lower Saxony, Bremen, Rhineland-Palatinate, and Baden-Württemberg. In Schleswig-Holstein the NPD became the fifth grouping along with the SSW and in Bavaria it replaced the FDP as the third party. It failed to gain representation in Hamburg and did not compete in North Rhine-Westphalia, both of which maintained a three-party system. In Hesse the Refugee Party lost its representation and in Bremen the right-wing German Party was replaced by the NPD. The SPD, benefiting from dissatisfaction with the CDU/CSU/FDP coalition in Bonn in the elections held prior to allying itself with the Union parties in the national government, became the leading party on the regional level for only the second time with 42.4 percent of ballots cast to the CDU/CSU's 42.0 percent.

In spite of the entry of the NPD into the political arena, the regional totals for the CDU/CSU, SPD and FDP amounted to 92.7 percent, only slightly less than in the previous series of *Land* elections, as most of the NPD's support came, not at their expense, but from former supporters of various minor groupings such as the Refugee and German parties and an important share of the over three million new voters.[44] Building on its regional success the NPD hoped to gain a foothold on the federal level in the 1969 *Bundestag* election. However, it was able to poll only 4.3 percent of the West German vote to fail to qualify for seats, and in the ten state elections held between the 1969 and 1972 general balloting its regional support fell to only 1.9 percent and it lost its representation in all seven state legislative bodies. With its elimination from all state parliaments a three-party system of the CDU/CSU and SPD and FDP was reestablished. In seven of the ten West German states they were the only parties represented. In Lower Saxony and the Saar the FDP failed to gain representation and a two-party system emerged. In Schleswig-Holstein the third party was the SSW as the Free Democrats failed to qualify for seats. The only minor party in any of the states was the SSW which existed only because of its special exemption from the five percent clause. In spite of the FDP's setback in three of the states, the three party total in the 1969-1972 series of regional contests increased to 96.9 percent, exceeding general election totals for the first time since the first series of regional elections. It also marked the first time that the two-party total of the CDU/CSU and SPD exceeded ninety percent of regional ballots cast. The CDU/CSU, now in the opposition in Bonn following the formation of the SPD/FDP government in 1969 under Willy Brandt, regained its status as the leading vote-getter on the regional level, a position it has held ever since.

In the ten regional contests held between the 1972 and 1976 general elections the small party of the Danish minority in Schleswig-Holstein was again the only political grouping other than the CDU/CSU, SPD and FDP to gain representation in the state legislative bodies. With a modest recovery in support, the FDP was returned to the parliaments of Lower Saxony, the Saar and Schleswig-Holstein, to be represented in all ten West German states once more. A three-party system existed in every state with the exception of Schleswig-Holstein where the SSW, with one seat, was a fourth party. The NPD total declined to less than one percent, and for all splinter parties to only 1.8 percent, as the three major parties captured 98.2 percent of the regional vote. This marked the smallest share of the vote falling to other than the CDU/CSU, SPD and FDP in any series of regional elections and the largest share, 91.3 percent, polled by the two major parties. This also marked the first time that a party, the CDU/CSU, no longer in power in Bonn, polled over fifty percent of the vote in a series of *Land* elections covering all ten West German states.

Beginning with the June 4, 1978 balloting in Hamburg a new movement, arising out of the failure of the three established parties to address a variety of environmental issues, began to challenge the three-party cartel. In contrast to the NPD phenomenon which faded after one series of regional contests, the various

Land organizations which came to be known as the Greens have demonstrated a permanency which has continued to this day. The movement failed to gain sufficient followings in its first five attempts to place representatives in a state legislature. Success finally came in Bremen in the October 7, 1979 election when two groupings under the Bremen Green list polled 6.5 percent of the vote to gain four seats in the Bremen *Bürgerschaft*. Five months later another Green grouping polled 5.3 percent of the Baden-Württemberg vote to win six legislative seats. The movement failed to qualify for seats in the last two *Land* elections prior to the 1980 *Bundestag* vote.

With a vote total in the 1978-1980 regional elections amounting to only half of the FDP following, the entry of the Greens did not immediately challenge the three-party cartel. Nevertheless, it was an auspicious start, and the ballot share of the three established parties declined to 96.1 percent, that of the two major parties to 90.2 percent. For the Free Democrats to lose their representation in Hamburg, Lower Saxony and North Rhine Westphalia as a result of a drop in support from 6.9 to 5.9 percent, the entrance of a new force into the political arena was disturbing. Nevertheless, the FDP losses enabled a two-party system of the CDU and SPD to be established in those three states while a three party system continued in Bavaria, Hesse, Rhineland-Palatinate and the Saar. In Schleswig-Holstein the SSW was the fourth party, in Bremen and Baden-Württemberg a Greens grouping was the fourth faction.

The Greens failed in their first attempt to gain national representation in the 1980 *Bundestag* election, polling only 1.5 percent of the countrywide vote, as the vote for the three-party cartel totaled 98.0 percent, for the CDU/CSU and SPD 87.4 percent. The SPD with 42.9 percent of the overall vote continued to lead the country in coalition with the Free Democrats. Only five elections were held between the 1980 and 1983 general elections (one a rerun in Hamburg), as a result of the decision by the federal FDP to abandon its coalition with the Socialists in Bonn after only two years, supposedly to stem the party's decline in regional balloting. The decision proved disastrous for the party as the voters reacted negatively to the move, and it lost its representation in Hesse, Bavaria and Hamburg and reached its lowest ebb of support in any series of regional elections with only 4.0 percent of ballots cast. In contrast, the Greens added Lower Saxony, Hesse and Hamburg to the states in which they were represented and outpolled the Free Democrats by nearly 300,000 votes in the contests to mark an end to the three party monopoly on the regional level which had lasted for twenty years. This left the Free Democrats represented in only five of the state parliaments, matching the number of state delegations amassed by the Greens. As a result, Lower Saxony now had a four-party system, Hesse and Hamburg a legislature of three parties with the Greens replacing the FDP, and Bavaria joined North Rhine-Westphalia as a *Land* with only the two major parties represented. With elections in only half of the West German states, the Greens and SSW remained the only parties other than the CDU/CSU, SPD and FDP to have representation. In spite of the FDP's weakened status, the three-party vote still amounted to 92.9 percent and the vote of the two major parties to

88.9 percent, as the CDU/CSU captured over half of all ballots cast for the second time.

In the March 6, 1983 general election the Greens, with 5.6 percent of the national vote, made their initial entry into the federal parliament, marking the first time since 1960 that more than three parties were represented in the *Bundestag*. While the FDP outpolled the Greens in the national balloting, it continued to lose ground to them in regional contests, and in the ten elections held between the 1983 and 1987 general elections the Greens continued to hold on to their third party status on the regional level with 6.1 percent of the vote to the FDP's 5.9 percent. By obtaining representation in Bavaria for the first time with 7.5 percent of ballots cast they increased their number of state delegations to six, but remained unrepresented in North Rhine-Westphalia, Rhineland-Palatinate, Schleswig-Holstein and the Saar. In spite of falling behind the Greens in regional support the FDP was able to maintain its number of state delegations at five, losing Rhineland-Palatinate and Bremen, while regaining representation in Hesse and North Rhine-Westphalia. The Greens and SSW were again the only parties to be represented in the various state parliaments other than the CDU/CSU, SPD and FDP.

The three-party system in the states was now no longer reflective of the Bonn model which had existed from 1961 to 1983, but one which could just as well be black, red and green as black, red and yellow. In Bavaria, Bremen and Hamburg the third party was the Greens and in North Rhine-Westphalia and the Saar the Free Democrats. All four of the now nationally-organized parties were represented in Baden-Württemberg, Hesse and Lower Saxony. A two-party system of the CDU and SPD existed in Rhineland-Palatinate and would have existed in Schleswig-Holstein were it not for the one seat held by the party of the Danish minority in that state. In spite of the Greens' success, the share of the total regional vote polled by the two major parties amounted to 86.8 percent as the SPD, now in the opposition in Bonn, was able to close the gap between it and the CDU/CSU in regional support. Nevertheless, the Union parties remained the leading grouping on the regional level with 45.1 percent of the ten-state vote to the Socialists' 41.7 percent. The vote total of the CDU/CSU, SPD and FDP amounted to 92.7 percent as support for other than the now four national parties was limited to only 1.3 percent.

In the last general election to be held prior to reunification, January 25, 1987, the Greens increased their national following by nearly fifty percent, but support for the Free Democrats also expanded to enable them to remain the third largest party in Bonn with 9.1 percent of the total vote. The CDU/CSU again emerged as the largest grouping and its leader, Dr. Helmut Kohl, continued to head the national government in coalition with the FDP. The three older parties gained 90.4 percent of the vote, with the vote of the CDU/CSU and SPD alone falling to 81.3 percent.

In the ten state elections held between the 1987 and 1990 general ballotings, a true four-party system emerged in the *Länder* as the Greens gained representation in North Rhine-Westphalia and Rhineland-Palatinate for the first time, to now have delegations in eight of the ten states, while the Free Democrats, with only 59,000 fewer votes than the Greens, returned to the parliaments of Bremen, Hamburg, and Rhineland-Palatinate to also be represented in eight of the West German states.[45] Consequently, a four-party system was established in seven of the *Länder*, the only exceptions being the Saar, where the Greens failed to qualify for seats, Schleswig-Holstein where neither the Greens nor the Free Democrats gained representation (but where the SSW was the third party), and Bremen where a fifth grouping, the right-oriented German People's Union (DVU) gained one seat by virtue of its concentrated strength in Bremerhaven, which is recognized as a separate jurisdiction in the application of the five percent requirement. It was the first time since the late 1960s that a right-extremist party was able to obtain a seat in any state legislative body, even though it polled but 3.4 percent of the total Bremen vote. Only in the Saar did the traditional three-party model of the CDU/CSU, SPD and FDP emerge. The CDU/CSU again outpolled the Socialists in regional vote totals, as the two major parties together obtained 84.1 percent of ballots cast. With a 90.1 percent vote total, this was to be the last time that the share polled by the CDU/CSU, SPD and FDP was to exceed ninety percent in provincial elections. Of note in this election series was the ability of right-extremist groups to gain 739,208 votes countrywide, the largest total since the NPD was the choice of over one and a half million voters in the 1965-1969 period. This figure does not include the 90,222 votes polled by the Republicans in West Berlin in

TABLE 9.2

NATIONWIDE PARTY TOTALS IN THE *LAND* ELECTIONS HELD BETWEEN 1965 AND 1990 [46]

	1966/68 *Land* Elections	1970/72 *Land* Elections	1974/76 *Land* Elections	1978/80 *Land* Elections	1982 *Land* Elections	1983/86 *Land* Elections	1987/90 *Land* Elections
CDU/CSU	42.0	48.3	51.4	48.7	51.8	45.1	43.1
SPD	42.4	42.3	39.9	41.5	37.1	41.7	41.0
FDP	8.2	6.4	6.9	5.9	4.0	5.9	6.0
GREENS	-	-	-	3.0	6.1	6.1	6.2
NPD/REP/DVU	5.3	1.9	0.7	0.3	0.2	0.7	2.2
DKP/DFU/KPD	0.3	0.8	0.6	0.3	0.3	0.1	0.1
Others	1.8	0.4	0.5	0.4	0.4	0.4	1.4
CDU/CSU/ SPD Totals	84.4	90.6	91.3	90.2	88.9	86.8	84.1
CDU/CSU/ FDP Vote	92.6	97.0	98.2	96.1	92.9	92.7	90.1

the January 29, 1989 election to place eleven deputies in the West Berlin city parliament.

The German Party System Since Reunification

The addition of the five eastern provinces and the eastern sector of Berlin to the Federal Republic in 1990 introduced a new dimension to German politics. Not only was a new party, the PDS, successor to the Communist SED, added to the political spectrum, but the voting preferences of over twelve million new voters, who had been living under dictatorial rule for 57 years, to the electorate presented a major challenge to the western democratic parties. Moreover, a restructuring of both the federal *Bundestag* and *Bundesrat* was necessitated to integrate the new states into the country's political system. The number of *Bundestag* seats was expanded from 497 to 662 members and *Bundesrat* votes from 41 to 69. In order not to upset a balance between the interests of the small and large states, the restructuring of the federal upper house, besides awarding from three to four votes to the individual eastern provinces, required giving additional votes to five of the largest western states.

The first general election in a reunited Germany took place December 2, 1990. The euphoria over reunification helped the CDU/CSU to emerge as the leading party in both the western and eastern states with 43.8 percent of the vote, while the Socialists, having to share a potential pool of voters in the East with the Party of Democratic Socialism (PDS), saw their share of ballots cast fall to 33.5 percent, marking the first time since 1953 that the combined vote of the two major parties in a general election had fallen below eighty percent. An amended electoral law, which caused the five percent clause to be applied separately to the old and new states, enabled the PDS to be awarded seventeen *Bundestag* seats with only 2.4 percent of the national vote.[47] While the Greens failed to exceed the five percent hurdle in the West, the Alliance 90/Greens overcame the barrier in the East to place eight deputies in the federal parliament. The FDP, in contrast, easily remained the third largest party nationally by expanding its countrywide following from 9.1 to 11.0 percent. Its success gave the three major national parties an 88.3 percent share of the vote. With the PDS represented in the *Bundestag* for the first time the number of parties in the federal parliament increased from four to five. Right-extremist groupings expanded their support nationwide, but with a 2.4 percent share of the total vote, none succeeded in gaining representation. The government in Bonn continued to be a coalition of the Union parties and FDP under Chancellor Helmut Kohl.

Between the 1990 and 1994 general elections, balloting took place in fourteen of the sixteen federal states. (There were no contests in North Rhine-Westphalia and the Saar by virtue of their five year legislative cycles). In the first democratic elections to be held in the new states the CDU polled 42.9 percent of the overall vote to emerge as the leading faction in every *Landtag* with the exception of Brandenburg where the Socialists led. In spite of the region's Communist past the left-oriented PDS was able to gain only a disappointing 11.1 percent of the eastern vote, far less than the anticipated 25 percent. Nevertheless, it outpolled both the Free Democrats and Greens in that region to gain representation in all of the eastern state parliaments. The FDP also gained seats in every eastern state, Green groupings in all states but Mecklenburg-Vorpommern. Although running candidates in thirteen of the sixteen states in elections held between early 1990 and 1994 the right-oriented Republicans succeeded in winning representation only in Baden-Württemberg with fifteen seats. Its 1,392,981 vote total, however, was the largest gained by a right-extremist party since the NPD polled over a million and a half votes in eight states between 1966 and 1968. Its major support came in the western states; in eastern provinces support for the party represented only 1.1 percent of ballots cast. A second right-extremist grouping, the DVU, competing in three western states, gained six seats with 6.2 percent of the vote in Bremen and six seats on 6.3 percent of ballots cast in Schleswig-Holstein. Since it did not compete nationally, its following amounted to only 162,000 votes.

The most spectacular addition on the regional scene was the ability of the STATT Party to win eight seats in the Hamburg election of September 19, 1993. The Party was founded by a young lawyer, Marcus Wegner, after the Hamburg High Court had declared the election of June 2, 1991 invalid. (The grouping's bid to obtain representation beyond Hamburg failed in four subsequent *Land* elections.)

In contrast to the 1987-1990 series of regional contests when only two political groupings other than the CDU/CSU, SPD, FDP and Greens secured *Landtag* seats, the number increased to five in the 1990-1994 series with the addition of the PDS, the STATT Party and the Republicans, to push the count of different parties to nine, the largest total represented in the various state parliaments since the 1957-1961 period. This produced an odd mixture in the various legislative bodies. Only in Lower Saxony did a three-party system exist, but the third party was the Greens and not the FDP. In Bavaria, Hesse and Rhineland-Palatinate a four-party system of the CDU/CSU, SPD, FDP and Greens emerged, but in Mecklenburg-Vorpommern, the fourth party was the PDS, not the Greens, and in Hamburg, the fourth grouping was the STATT Party as the FDP failed to retain seats gained in the 1991 election. A five-party system existed in the other ten states with the PDS being the fifth grouping in Berlin, Brandenburg, Saxony-Anhalt, Saxony and Thuringia, the DVU the fifth party in Bremen, the Republicans the fifth party in Baden-Württemberg, and in Schleswig-Holstein, where the Greens failed to qualify for seats, the fourth and fifth parties were the party of the Danish minority (the SSW) and the DVU. Of the new political groupings, only the STATT Party in Hamburg participated in a *Land* ministry, in this case with the SPD.

With the success of these new political groupings, the share of the vote falling to the two major parties declined to 76.0 percent, the smallest total polled by the Union parties and SPD together since the 1953-1956 period. The share obtained by the two major parties and the Free Democrats fell to 81.9 percent, also the smallest share for the three parties since the 1953-1956 period. Of the four nationally-organized parties, the CDU/CSU and SPD were represented in every state legislature, the FDP in every state but Lower Saxony and Hamburg (after the second *Bürgerschaft* election) and the Greens in every state but Mecklenburg-Vorpommern, the Saar, and Schleswig-Holstein. With 83.6 percent of ballots cast, this was the high mark for the four major western parties in the East, as it was for the Free Democrats and various Green groupings until the 2005-2009 period with 7.6 percent and 6.8 percent of the vote respectively in the five new states and Berlin. The PDS won seats in all five of the new states and Berlin, but had no success in the West. The representation of all of the other parties did not extend beyond a single *Land* with the exception of the DVU, which placed delegates in both the Bremen and Schleswig-Holstein legislatures.

Five parties secured representation in the 1994 *Bundestag* election, as the PDS, again benefiting from the two-district arrangement, was able to gain thirty seats, although its vote total amounted to only 4.4 percent. The CDU/CSU with 41.5 percent of the vote emerged as the leading party followed by the SPD with 36.4 percent, weakened by its poor showing in the eastern provinces, as much of the support which ordinarily would have gone to it was absorbed by the PDS. The Greens, with 7.3 percent of the national vote, became the third largest party on the national level for the first time as the FDP share of second choice ballots was only 6.9 percent. As neither an SPD/Greens alliance nor an SPD/FDP combination would provide a workable majority, the only possible grouping outside of a grand coalition between the two major parties was a cooperative arrangement between the CDU/CSU and FDP, placing Dr. Helmut Kohl in the chancellorship for the fourth time. Right-extremist parties attracted only a limited following with 1.9 percent of the countrywide vote. The two-party vote of the CDU/CSU and SPD increased modestly to 77.9 percent while the three-party share, including the FDP, fell to 84.6 percent.

In the sixteen regional contests held between the 1994 and the 1998 general elections only one new political grouping, the AFB (*Arbeit für Bremen Partei*), a purely protest organization in Bremen, was able to secure representation, as the DVU in Schleswig-Holstein with only 4.3 percent of the vote in 1996 lost its mandates and the STATT Party, with just 3.8 percent of the Hamburg vote, failed to qualify for seats in the 1997 *Bürgerschaft* election. As a result, the party count in the states fell from nine to eight. The CDU/CSU and SPD gained seats in every *Landtag*, the Greens in ten, the PDS in the five eastern provinces and Berlin and the FDP in only four western states, Baden-Württemberg, Hesse, Rhineland-Palatinate and Schleswig-Holstein. The decline of the Free Democrats in voter favor corresponded with the growing unpopularity of the Kohl administration in its fourth legislative term in which the FDP was involved. All other political groupings had their representation limited to a single *Land*, the SSW in Schleswig-Holstein, the Republicans in Baden-Wuertemberg (with a modestly smaller following than in 1992,) the DVU in Saxony-Anhalt and the AFB in Bremen. (The DVU did not send sixteen representatives to the Saxony-Anhalt *Landtag* until after the April 26, 1998 balloting in that state.) Again, the entrance of various minor groupings into the political arena changed the political makeup of virtually every *Landtag*.

With the decline of the FDP and the inability of the Greens to gain representation in any of the eastern provinces outside of Berlin, a three-party system was established in Brandenburg, Mecklenberg-Vorpommern, Saxony and Thuringia, where the third party in every case was the PDS. A three-party system also emerged in Bavaria, Hamburg, Lower Saxony, North Rhine-Westphalia and the Saar, where the Greens were the third party. In Bremen the third and fourth parties were the Greens and AFB, in Berlin the Greens and PDS, in Hesse and Rhineland-Palatinate the FDP and Greens, in Saxony-Anhalt the PDS and DVU, which gained 12.9 percent of the vote in the April 1998 state election. Five parties received representation in Baden-Württemberg where the third, fourth and fifth parties were the FDP, Greens and Republicans, and Schleswig-Holstein, where they were the FDP, Greens and SSW.

The share of the regional vote gained by the two major parties declined to 77.0 percent and the total with the Free Democrats to 81.6 percent, the lowest combined total since the 1953/1956 period. The CDU/CSU continued to outpoll all other parties in regional vote totals with 40.8 percent of ballots cast to 36.2 percent for the SPD. The Greens maintained their status as the third largest party on the regional level with 8.3 percent of the countrywide vote to 4.6 percent for the FDP. The PDS polled only 3.7 percent of the total regional vote, but with 17.6 percent in the East, it secured representation in all five of the new *Länder* and Berlin.

Five parties, the CDU/CSU, SPD, FDP, Greens and PDS, gained *Bundestag* seats in the 1998 general election, with the SPD receiving the largest share of the votes for the first time since 1972 with a 40.9 percent total to the Union parties' 35.1 percent. The Socialist victory occurred in spite of the over two and a half million votes (5.1 percent) cast for the PDS. Because of successful coalitions with the Greens in several states, including North Rhine-Westphalia and Lower Saxony, they, with 6.7 percent of the vote, rather than the Free Democrats, with 6.2 percent, were selected as the Socialists' coalition partner, marking the Greens' first participation in a national administration.

Regional elections were held in fourteen of the sixteen states in the interval between the 1998 and 2002 national elections. In spite of the tendency of voters to vote against the party in control of the national government the Socialists managed gains in nine of the fourteen contests and, although outpolled by the CDU/CSU nationally, they led in ballots cast (40.1 to 39.2 percent) in the western states to retain control of the *Bundesrat.* The FDP, now in the opposition in Bonn along with the CDU/CSU, made a strong comeback to regain representation in Berlin, North Rhine-Westphalia, Hamburg and Saxony-Anhalt and expand its delegation count to eight states, while the Greens, in coalition with the SPD in the national government, lost a third of their regional following to fall behind the Liberals in regional balloting for the first time since 1980. Although losing their representation in the Saar and failing to gain seats in any of the eastern states outside of Berlin, the Greens still had delegations in nine of the ten western states. The PDS, while winning mandates in all five of the new states and Berlin, was unable to develop a following in any of the Western *Länder.* With the Republicans failing to retain their delegation in Baden-Württemberg and the DVU in Saxony-Anhalt, right-extremist groups were represented only in Bremen where the DVU gained a single seat, and Brandenburg, where it won five mandates, in 1999 elections. As a result of internal discord and resignations during the 1998-2002 legislative period the party did not contest the 2002 election in Saxony-Anhalt. The AFB in Bremen also faded to no longer be represented in the Bremen parliament. The only new grouping to gain legislative seats during this period was the Schill Party, which, by running on a law and order platform and benefiting from the terrorist attack of September 11th in the United States, obtained 19.4 percent of the vote for the Hamburg *Bürgerschaft* September 23, 2001.

As a consequence of the changes in representation in the various state legislative bodies resulting from 1999-2001 *Land* election outcomes, including the elimination of the Republicans in Baden-Württemberg and AFB in Bremen and the addition of the Schill Party in Hamburg, only two parties, the CDU and SPD, were represented in the Saar and three in Mecklenburg-Vorpommern, Saxony and Thuringia (where the third party in all three states was the PDS), Bavaria and Lower Saxony (where the third party was the Greens). Four parties held seats in Hesse, Bremen, Brandenburg, Baden-Württemberg, North Rhine-Westphalia, Rhineland-Palatinate and Saxony-Anhalt. The CDU and SPD were represented in all seven states, while the third and fourth parties in Baden-Württemberg, Hesse, North Rhine-Westphalia and Rhine-Palatinate were the FDP and Greens, in Brandenburg the PDS and DVU, in Bremen, the Greens and DVU, and in Saxony-Anhalt the PDS and DVU. Five parties gained seats in Berlin, Hamburg and Schleswig-Holstein. In Berlin the third, fourth and fifth parties were the FDP, Greens and PDS, in Hamburg the FDP, Greens and the Schill Party and in Schleswig-Holstein the FDP, Greens and SSW. The vote total of the two major parties fell to 74.3 percent, while the three-party vote of the CDU/CSU, SPD and FDP declined to 80.8 percent.

During this period the PDS, for the first time, was brought into a *Land* government with the SPD following the regional election of September 27, 1998 in Mecklenburg-Vorpommern, and, following an unsuccessful attempt to form a traffic-light coalition with the FDP and Greens after the 2001 election in Berlin, the Socialists under Socialist Klaus Wowereit formed a second alliance with the PDS. In Hamburg Christian Democrat Ole von Beust, with only 26.2 percent of ballots cast, fashioned a three-party combination with the FDP and Schill Party to break the Socialists' grip on the city.

Five parties (the CDU/CSU, SPD, FDP, the Greens and PDS) again obtained national representation in the 2002 *Bundestag* election. However, the PDS, with its following dropping by 600,000 votes over its 1998 total, failed to qualify for reserve list seats and was represented only by virtue of winning two direct mandates in the eastern portion of Berlin. This failure to share in the proportional allocation of seats was significant, since had the PDS won thirty or more seats as in 1998 neither an SPD/Greens nor a CDU/CSU/FDP combination would have provided the necessary majority to govern and the confusion which followed the 2005 general election would have occurred three years earlier. As it was, the SPD remained the largest faction in the *Bundestag*, albeit by only 6,000 votes, and with the Greens registering their best showing in a general election with 8.6 percent of ballots cast, Chancellor Schröder was provided with a small majority to continue his red-green administration.

Because of the shortened *Bundestag* period, resulting from Chancellor Schröder's decision to call early elections, only twelve regional contests were held between the 2002 and 2005 national ballotings. Negative public reaction to his government's reform initiatives caused the Socialists to suffer setbacks in eleven of those contests, including in Germany's most populous state, North Rhine-Westphalia, and register their worse showing in regional competition since the first elections were held in 1946. In contrast, their coalition partner, the Greens, made gains in nine of the twelve elections and held their own in Schleswig-Holstein to outpoll the Free Democrats in this series of *Land* contests. In spite of these gains, which returned them to the parliaments of the Saar and Saxony, to be represented in twelve of the sixteen federal states, they were locked out of the governments of Lower Saxony, North Rhine-Westphalia and Schleswig Holstein as a result of the Socialists' poor showing, and from 2005 to 2007 participated in none of the *Land* ministries.

The CDU/CSU made gains in eight of the twelve contests to bring their regional election following to 46.4 percent to the Socialists' 29.6 percent and regain control of the *Bundesrat*. The Free Democrats, under their new leadership, continued their comeback to make gains in nine states and return delegations to the parliaments of Lower Saxony, Saxony and Saxony-Anhalt to now be represented in eleven of the sixteen states, in spite of the loss of Hamburg.

The PDS continued to be a regional party, limited to the five eastern provinces and Berlin as it failed to develop any significant following in western states. However, in the east it was able to replace the SPD as the region's second party 23.1 to 21.1 percent. As result of continuing high unemployment right-extremist parties had success in two of the eastern states, the NPD with 9.2 percent of the vote in Saxony and the DVU with 6.1 percent of the vote in Brandenburg in 2004 *Land* elections. In the western states their only success was the single seat won by the DVU in Bremerhaven.

Other than the five parties represented in the federal parliament, three splinter parties obtained seats in the *Land* legislatures during the 2002-2005 period, the NPD in Saxony, the DVU in Brandenburg and Bremen and the SSW in Schleswig-Holstein. With the Schill party failing to qualify for seats in Hamburg and the NPD entering the Saxony *Landtag* for the first time, the number of different parties obtaining representation in the state parliaments remained at eight.

There were no longer any two-party states as the FDP and Greens, along with the CDU and SPD, qualified for seats in the Saar. Three parties were represented in Bavaria and Hamburg where the third party was the Greens and in Thuringia, where the third party was the PDS. Four parties held seats in Hesse, Lower Saxony, North Rhine-Westphalia and the Saar where the third and fourth parties in every case were the FDP and Greens and Brandenburg where the third and fourth parties were the PDS and DVU. Five parties were represented in Bremen, where the third, fourth and fifth parties were the FDP, Greens and DVU and Schleswig-Holstein where the third, fourth and fifth parties were the FDP, Greens and SSW. For the first time in over forty years six parties were represented in a state legislative body, in this case, the Saxony *Landtag*, where the third, fourth, fifth and sixth parties were FDP, Greens, PDS and NPD. In the four states that did not hold elections during this interval, a four-party arrangement of the CDU, SPD, FDP and Greens existed in Baden-Württemberg and Rhineland-Palatinate and of the CDU, SPD, FDP and PDS in Saxony-Anhalt. Five parties held seats in the Berlin *Abgeordnetenhaus*, the CDU, SPD, FDP, Greens and PDS.

The two-party vote of the CDU/CSU and SPD increased modestly from 74.3 to 76.0 percent in spite of the SPD's steep decline in voter approval, as the Union parties recorded their best showing in regional competition since the early 1980s with a 46.4 percent total in the twelve elections. The three-party vote of the CDU/CSU, SPD and FDP increased to 81.6 percent.

In the 2005 *Bundestag* election the five-party constellation of the CDU/CSU, SPD, FDP, the Greens and PDS continued to be represented, but in contrast to 2002 when the PDS placed only two delegates in the federal parliament, it contested the 2005 contest in combination with Oskar Lafontaine's WASG, in an alliance known as *Die Linke*, to gain 54 seats on 8.7 percent of the national vote. The grouping's success fragmented the federal parliament, making neither a continuation of the Socialist/Greens coalition nor a CDU/CSU/FDP arrangement possible. This confused situation ultimately led to the formation of only the second grand coalition between the Union parties and the Socialists since the first general elections were held in 1949 (the first covering the period from 1966 to 1969). Holding a four-seat advantage over the Socialists, the CDU/CSU was able to have its candidate for the Chancellorship, Dr. Angela Merkel, selected to lead the country following five weeks of negotiations.

Fifteen regional elections were held in the German states between the 2005 and 2009 *Bundestag* ballotings, including two (in Brandenburg and Schleswig-Holstein) which took place the same day as the 2009 general election. With the two major parties forming the national government between these two national polls, dissatisfaction could no longer be expressed through one of them as the outparty, but only through the three smaller factions represented in Berlin, the FDP, Greens and *Die Linke*, which together controlled 27 percent of *Bundestag* seats, or through groupings outside of the federal parliament, including the several right-extremist parties and various splinter organizations, in regional polls. As a result, with over thirty percent of ballots cast falling to other than the two major parties, this was not a particularly advantageous period for the two coalition partners. The Union parties suffered setbacks, some severe, in fourteen of the fifteen regional contests, including the loss of their majority status in Bavaria, Hesse, Hamburg, the Saar and Thuringia. Although making gains in eight of the fifteen ballotings, the Socialists were unable to take advantage of the Union setbacks and, whereas the share of the regional vote falling to the CDU/CSU dropped from 46.4 to 37.4 percent, that of the Socialists slumped from 29.6 percent in the 2002-2005 period to 26.8 percent because of poor showings in several of the larger states, including Bavaria (18.6 percent of the vote) and Baden-Württemberg (25.2 percent). The singular achievement for the Socialists in this series of elections was the winning of an absolute majority of seats in the Rhineland-Palatinate *Landtag* for the first time in March 2006, an election success which contributed to Minister President Kurt Beck's temporary elevation to the national chairmanship of the SPD. While the SPD's 26.8 percent share of the regional vote was the lowest recorded in any series of regional contests, the Union total of 37.4 percent remained far above its worse recording of 28.0 percent in the second series of *Land* elections.

The Free Democrats made gains in thirteen of the fifteen elections to regain representation in Bavaria after a fourteen-year absence, in Mecklenburg-Vorpommern after a twelve-year absence, and in Brandenburg and Thuringia after fifteen-year absences to hold seats in every federal state with the single exception of Hamburg. The Greens made gains in twelve states including registering their best showing ever with a 16.5 percent share of the Bremen vote and a 13.1 percent share in Berlin, while losing their representation in Rhineland-Palatinate to now be represented in thirteen state legislative bodies. More importantly, after being shut out of all *Land* ministries for two years, the Greens became coalition partners of the Socialists in Bremen after the 2007 regional contest, and in North Rhine-Westphalia after the 2010 regional poll. In Hamburg, when the CDU lost its parliamentary majority in the 2008 election, it was brought into a coalition with the Union party, the first such arrangement between the two groupings on the regional level. This was followed by its participation in a CDU-led government of the Saar, along with the FDP, in the nation's first "Jamaica" coalition in the states. The Black/Green coalition in Hamburg broke up in November 2010 when the Greens faction surprisingly pulled out of the alliance, necessitating new elections in February 2011 which resulted in a Socialist majority government without the Greens.

The leftist party, running as the WASG in the 2006 contests in Baden-Württemberg and Rhineland-Palatinate, failed to qualify for seats in those two states, but continued to gain representation in the six eastern *Länder* of Saxony-Anhalt, Berlin, Mecklenburg-Vorpommern, Brandenburg, Saxony and Thuringia competing as *Die Linke*. The WASG ran candidates separately in both Berlin and Mecklenburg-Vorpommern rather than in combination with PDS lists. After having had little success in the western states as the PDS, *Die Linke* qualified for seats in six elections held between May 2007 and September 2009, in Bremen in May 2007, in Hesse and Lower Saxony in January 2008, in Hamburg in February 2008, in the Saar in August 2009 and in Schleswig-Holstein in

September 2009. In the September 2008 balloting in Bavaria it obtained 4.4 percent of ballots cast to fail to qualify for seats in that state. Its entry in the western states did not prevent the building of two-party coalitions in Bavaria, Bremen, Hamburg, Lower Saxony, and in Schleswig-Holstein, but in Hesse and the Saar, as the fifth party, it created a situation, as nationally in 2005, where neither a CDU/FDP combination nor an SPD/Greens alliance could provide a working majority. Although *Die Linke* agreed to tolerate an SPD/Greens minority government in Hesse after the 2008 election, two attempts were unsuccessful when the proposed arrangement failed to gain the support of several Socialist delegates (*Die Welt*, November 4, 2008). To resolve the impasse created by a fifth party, a new election was held in January 2009, the outcome of which enabled the CDU, under Roland Koch, to form a government with the Liberals. In the Saar, the situation was resolved when the Greens agreed to participate in a three-party coalition with the CDU and FDP under Christian Democrat Peter Müller. With their success in six western states and with delegations in the five eastern provinces and Berlin, the Leftists were now represented in twelve of the German *Länder*, but participated only in the governments of Berlin and the state of Brandenburg.

Right-extremist parties had mixed fortunes in this series of *Land* contests. On September 17, 2006 in Mecklenburg-Vorpommern, the NPD recorded a second success in provincial elections by winning 7.3 percent of ballots cast to add to its 2004 breakthrough in Saxony. In Bremen, the DVU continued to hold onto its single seat by virtue of its strength in Bremerhaven, while, in that same part of Bremen, a new right-conservative grouping, the BIW (*Bürger in Wut*),

TABLE 9.3

**NATIONWIDE PARTY TOTALS IN THE *LAND*
ELECTIONS HELD BETWEEN 1990 AND 2009** [48]

	1990/94 *Land* Elections	1994/98 *Land* Elections	1998/02 *Land* Elections	2002/05 *Land* Elections	2006/2009 *Land* Elections
CDU/CSU	42.1	40.8	38.4	46.4	37.4
SPD	33.9	36.2	35.9	29.6	26.8
FDP	5.9	4.6	6.5	5.6	8.9
GREENS	7.3	8.3	5.6	6.9	8.6
PDS/*DIE LINKE*	3.3	3.7	7.2	4.8	9.5
NPD/DVU/REP	4.1	3.6	3.3	2.1	1.6
OTHERS	3.4	2.8	3.1	4.5	7.2
CDU/CSU/SPD Vote Totals	76.0	77.0	74.3	76.0	64.2
CDU/CSU/SPD/ FDP Vote Totals	81.9	81.6	80.8	81.6	73.1

was able to gain a single seat in a 2008 by-election. In Brandenburg, however, the DVU lost its total delegation when its following fell to only 1.1 percent from the 6.1 share registered in 2004, and in Saxony the NPD, while maintaining its representation in the 2009 election, lost four of its twelve seats when its vote total fell from the 9.2 percent gained in 2004 balloting to 5.6 percent. Thus, at the end of 2009 right-extremist groups were represented in only three states.

A number of important changes resulted from the fifteen regional election outcomes. The Free Democrats were added to the parliaments of Bavaria, Brandenburg, Mecklenburg-Vorpommern and Thuringia, the Greens to the Brandenburg and Thuringia legislatures, the NPD to the Mecklenburg-Vorpommern parliament, *Die Linke* to the parliaments of Bremen, Hamburg, Hesse, Lower Saxony, the Saar and Schleswig-Holstein, and the Free or Independent Voters (FW), which, with 10.2 percent of the vote, seated 21 representatives in the Bavarian *Landtag*. Two important losses were the elimination of the Greens from the Rhineland-Palatinate legislature and the DVU from the Brandenburg parliament.

With these changes, three parties were represented in Rhineland-Palatinate, where the third party was the FDP, four parties in Baden-Württemberg, where the third and fourth parties were the FDP and Greens, in Saxony-Anhalt where the third and fourth parties were the FDP and *Die Linke* (PDS), and in Hamburg where the third and fourth parties were the Greens and *Die Linke*. Five parties gained seats in Bavaria, where the third, fourth and fifth parties are the FDP, Greens and the Free Voters, in Berlin, Brandenburg, Hesse, Lower Saxony, the Saar, and Thuringia where the third, fourth and fifth parties are the FDP, Greens and *Die Linke* (PDS) (replicating the federal parliament), and Mecklenburg-Vorpommern where the third, fourth and fifth parties are the FDP, *Die Linke* (PDS) and NPD. Bremen and Schleswig-Holstein became the second and third states to have six parties represented in their parliament, joining the state of Saxony. The 2008 by-election in Bremerhaven enabled a new grouping, the BIW (*Bürger in Wut*), to gain a single seat, thus raising the number of parties represented in the Bremen *Bürgerschaft* to seven. The groupings, other than the SPD and CDU, in Bremen are the FDP, the Greens, *Die Linke* and DVU; in Schleswig-Holstein, the FDP, Greens, *Die Linke* and SSW. The election outcome resulted in changes in no fewer than eleven of the fifteen states. See Chapter 10 for a description of changes in the composition of state ministries. The two and three-party vote was the lowest since the 1949/1952 period as a result of the SPD's poor showing.

Five parties were again elected to the *Bundestag* in the September 27, 2009 national balloting, with the Union parties emerging as the leading faction with a 33.8 percent share of the vote to the SPD's 23.0 percent share, the Socialists' worst general election performance in the post-war period. The Free Democrats, on the other hand, recorded their best general election total with a 14.6 percent share of ballots cast to give a black/yellow combination sufficient representation to replace the existing grand coalition between the Union parties and the SPD.

TABLE 9.4

PARTY TOTALS IN THE *BUNDESTAG* ELECTIONS
HELD BETWEEN 1990 AND 2009

	1990 *Bundestag* Election	1994 *Bundestag* Election	1998 *Bundestag* Election	2002 *Bundestag* Election	2005 *Bundestag* Election	2009 *Bundestag* Election
CDU/CSU	43.8	41.5	35.1	38.5	35.2	33.8
SPD	33.5	36.4	40.9	38.5	34.2	23.0
FDP	11.0	6.9	6.2	7.4	9.8	14.6
GREENS	3.8 [a]	7.3	6.7	8.6	8.1	10.7
PDS/*DIE LINKE*	2.4	4.4	5.1	4.0	8.7	11.9
NPD/DVU/REP	2.4	1.9	3.3	1.0	2.2	2.0
OTHERS	3.1	1.6	2.7	2.0	2.8	4.0
CDU/CSU/SPD Totals	77.3	77.9	76.0	77.0	69.4	56.8
CDU/CSU/FDP/ SPD Totals	88.3	84.6	82.2	84.4	79.2	71.4

a A counterpart of the Greens Party in the East, the *Bündnis* 90/Greens, received 1.2 percent of the national vote, but obtained eight seats by virtue of the eastern and western provinces being considered as separate districts for the application of the five percent limitation.

Die Linke outpolled the Greens again in national competition with an 11.9 percent countrywide total to the Greens' 10.7 percent, a best national showing for both parties. Dr. Angela Merkel remained as Federal Chancellor, with Free Democrat Dr. Guido Westerwelle serving as Vice Chancellor. As a result of SPD weakness, the combined CDU/CSU/SPD vote fell to 56.8 percent, the lowest for the two major parties in the seventeen *Bundestag* elections held since 1949 and far below the 90.2 percent polled by the two parties in the 1972 and 1976 general elections.

In the only election held in 2010, the CDU/FDP coalition in North Rhine-Westphalia failed to sustain itself, as CDU support fell from 44.8 to 34.6 percent and the FDP was unable to compensate for the loss. This enabled the Socialists with a 34.5 percent share of the vote and the Greens with 12.1 percent to form a minority government under Socialist Hannelore Kraft, tolerated by the Leftists who, with a 5.6 percent total, entered the North Rhine-Westphalian *Landtag* for the first time to now be represented in thirteen of the sixteen German state parliaments. Five state elections were held during the first half of 2011, the outcomes of which are discussed on pages 210-212.

The Future of the German Party System

By mid 2011 the German party system was no longer characterized by three nationally-organized groupings of wide appeal, but by five such parties, as the Greens have moved from a protest collectivity concerned primarily with environmental issues into a mini-*Volkspartei* concerned with a broad spectrum of issues, while *Die Linke*, although holding to a narrow leftist program, has moved beyond its eastern roots to become a national force represented in seven of the western states with the inclusion of the May 9, 2010 outcome in North Rhine-Westphalia to place delegates in thirteen of the sixteen state parliaments. The entry of the Greens into the political arena in the late 1970s, while reducing the number of times that the CDU/CSU or SPD could win an absolute majority of legislative seats, did not noticeably upset the coalition-building process, in which the Free Democrats played a balancing role between the Union parties and Socialists, and only in the 1990s did they play an important role in coalition-formation by making Socialist-led ministries possible in a number of *Länder*. However, the entry of a powerful leftist organization into the political arena following the fall of the wall has been upsetting to traditional coalition patterns, especially since its Communist roots has made it a less desirable coalition partner than the Greens, which in 2008 were able to conclude their first working relationship with the CDU on the regional level in Hamburg. This was followed by its participation in a three-party ministry with the Christian and Free Democrats in the Saar following the August 2009 state election. The strength of the PDS (*Die Linke*) in the eastern provinces has forced the formation of a number of grand coalitions as the only alternative to working with the leftist party, and only in Mecklenburg-Vorpommern from 1998 to 2006, Berlin since 2001 and in Brandenburg since the fall of 2009 has the PDS (*Die Linke*) participated in a *Land* government. The possibility of it tolerating a Socialist-led ministry under Andrea Ypsilanti in Hesse was too much to stomach for four SPD delegates and the anticipated working arrangement failed to materialize (*Die Welt,* November 4 and 5, 2008).

The fragmentation of the 1950s in West Germany may become the new reality of a united Germany in the 21st century. Although there are only five parties of national appeal, the success of two splinter groups (the DVU and BIW) in the Bremerhaven part of Bremen has produced a *Bürgerschaft* with seven difference assemblages in that state, while in the parliaments of Saxony and Schleswig-Holstein six factions are represented. The success of the Free or Independent Voters (FW) in Bavaria in the 2008 *Land* election portends a possible further fragmentation there. The consequences of this new splintering has been evidenced in several *Länder*. The turmoil created by the outcome of the 2008 *Land* election in Hesse, in which neither a CDU/FDP nor a SPD/Greens combination could provide a working majority because of the election success of *Die Linke* is a case in point, and it took a new election in January 2009, which resulted in a CDU/FDP majority, to cure the situation. It took a number of years for the Greens to become an acceptable coalition partner, and it may take an equally long period of time for *Die Linke* to become more widely acceptable. Combinations with the Leftists have succeeded in Berlin and Mecklenburg-Vorpommern and is an ongoing experiment in Brandenburg, but whether *Die Linke* can adjust itself to become an acceptable partner in the western states remains to be seen. Prior to 2005 the Socialists did not have to compete with a powerful leftist movement for votes in the western states, and the successes of *Die Linke* in seven of them has hurt them more than the Union, since both the SPD and *Die Linke* are competing for the same group of left-oriented voters.

Fortunately, the appeal of right-extremist parties has remained weak, and in the several states where they have gained representation their presence has not prevented the formation of stable ministries. Nevertheless, the success of such groupings as the *Freie Wähler* in Bavaria in 2008, and the Schill Party in Hamburg in 2001 and the large following of the Pirates in the 2009 general election is an indication of how fragile the German party system has become. The consensus which enabled the two major parties to capture 91.3 percent of ballots cast in the 1972-1976 period has been eroded, and in the most recent series of regional contests the two-party vote has fallen below seventy percent for the first time since the early 1950s. In Berlin, Brandenburg, and Saxony, where the PDS is strong, the two-party vote barely exceeds fifty percent and was less than half of ballots cast in the 2009 election in Thuringia. But the contraction in support for the two major parties is not limited to the eastern states. In the September 2009 regional poll in Schleswig-Holstein the two major parties polled only 56.9 percent of the statewide vote.

Should the share of votes polled by the two major parties continue to erode, it is possible in several of the states that not even a grand coalition will provide a working majority and three-party combinations as in the Saar may become more the rule than the exception. However, it is difficult to envision a situation where a government could be formed without the participation of at least one of the two major parties. Even if three or four of the minor parties together were able to poll a majority of the vote, the differences between them are so great as to make a governing coalition of the small parties highly unlikely. In the 2010 regional election in Germany's largest state, North Rhine Westphalia, both of the two major parties obtained over a third of the votes with the remaining ballots split between the Greens, Free Democrats and the Leftists. While one of the three minor parties may succeed in replacing the CDU/CSU or SPD as one of the two major factions in a state, as has already occurred in several eastern provinces, Baden Württemberg and Bremen, it is highly unlikely that the Union and/or the Socialists will be replaced as the leading groupings nationally. In most states the so-called "party of the non-voters" the "*Sofa Fraktion*" (couch faction) would be the largest grouping, and no one knows how these potential voters would vote were they to go to the polls. Rather than trying to entice supporters away from each other, the parties should concentrate on winning the allegiance of this large pool of unaffiliated individuals. In the 2006 *Land* election in Saxony-Anhalt, only 44.4 percent of eligible voters turned out to vote, and in most states some forty percent of eligible voters stay away from the polls. [49]

Endnotes for Chapter IX

1 Reinhold Meier, a Free Democrat, was Minister President of Württemberg-Baden from 1946 to 1952 and of the new state of Baden-Württemberg from 1952 to 1953, while Heinrich Hellwege, a German Party member, served as Minister President of Lower Saxony from 1955 to 1959 and Winfried Kretschmann of the Greens Party since the March 2011 *Land* election in Baden-Württemberg. There have been five Christian Democrat Chancellors (Dr. Konrad Adenauer, Prof. Dr. Ludwig Erhard, Dr. Kurt Kiesinger, Dr. Helmut Kohl and Dr. Angela Merkel) and three Social Democrat Chancellors (Willy Brandt, Helmut Schmidt and Gerhard Schröder).

2 Refugee parties were forbidden in the immediate postwar years in the belief that they would be a hindrance to the assimilation of the newcomers. All restrictions on refugee group activity were eventually removed in 1950, allowing the formation of a number of refugee political movements in that year. The Western Allies retained the authority to suspend or revoke the license of any party if its activities proved to be militaristic, undemocratic or hostile to Allied purposes.

3 Bremen, Hesse, Lower Saxony and North Rhine-Westphalia all incorporated five percent clauses into their electoral laws, with Bavaria requiring that a party obtain at least ten percent of the vote in one of the *Land's* five administrative districts to qualify for representation. Schleswig-Holstein required the winning of at least one direct seat to qualify for reserve list seats.

4 In the 1946 *Bürgerschaft* election in Bremen two independents gained seats in the constituency competition.

5 The CDU/CSU emerged as the leading party in Baden, Bavaria, North Rhine-Westphalia, Rhineland-Palatinate, Württemberg-Baden and Württemberg-Hohenzollern, the SPD as the leading party in Bremen, Hamburg, Hesse, Lower Saxony and Schleswig-Holstein. In Berlin, under four-power control, the 1946 election produced a four-party system with the Social Democrats controlling the largest bloc of parliamentary seats.

6 These included the WAV in Bavaria, the *Zentrum* in Lower Saxony and North Rhine-Westphalia, the German Party, originally the Lower Saxony State Party, in Bremen and Lower Saxony and the SSV, party of the Danish minority in Schleswig-Holstein. The Bremen Democratic People's Party could be listed as a fifth regional group; however, it later merged into the FDP as did the Social People's Service (SV) in Rhineland-Palatinate.

7 In the American zone *Länder* control over the regulation and licensing of political parties was relinquished in November 1948, and although the British did not take similar action until early 1950, few obstacles were placed in the way of new political groups, and it was in their zone that the first extreme-right political movements of the postwar period developed. The French, on the other hand, maintained strict control over political activity in their zone until 1950.

8 Prior to the formation of the first national government in 1949, West Germany had no national leaders, no national economic policy and no foreign or defense policy. Issues and personalities which were later to dominate national and regional elections alike could not yet serve as unifying elements in this first general election contest.

9 Parties receiving representation in the first *Bundestag* included the CDU/CSU (139 seats), the SPD (131 seats), the FDP/DVP (52 seats), the KPD (15 seats), the Bavarian Party (17 seats), the German Party (17 seats), the *Zentrum* (10 seats), the WAV (12 seats), the DRP (5 seats), and the SSW (1 seat). The three remaining seats were won by independents.

10 Had the present requirement of five percent of the total nation-wide vote or the winning of three direct seats for *Bundestag* representation applied to the 1949 contest, only six parties (the CDU/CSU, SPD, FDP and KPD, all of which obtained over five percent of the national vote, the Bavarian Party and the German Party, which won eleven and five direct seats respectively) would have gained national representation.

11 The largest blocks of votes falling to other than the four originally licensed parties went to the Bavarian Party (4.2 percent), the German Party (4.0 percent), the *Zentrum* (3.1 percent) and the WAV (2.9 percent), all regionally based groups.

12 The Refugee Party entered the political arena with a resounding success in the election of July 9, 1950, in Schleswig-Holstein, where refugees accounted for nearly forty percent of the population. In less than two years the party succeeded in gaining representation in six *Länder* and cabinet positions in four.

13 The SRP polled 11.0 percent of the Lower Saxony vote in the 1951 *Land* election contest and 7.7 percent of the vote in Bremen later in that year. Although the party also competed in North Rhine-Westphalia, Schleswig-Holstein and Baden-Württemberg, its highest total in any of these *Länder* amounted to 2.4 percent in Baden-Württemberg.

14 The following of the German Party increased from 448,709 votes in the first series of regional elections to 718,466 in the second. The Bavarian Party polled 17.9 percent of the 1950 Bavarian vote, hurting particularly the CSU from which it seceded.

15 The portion of the total *Land* level vote falling to other than the four originally licensed parties increased from 8.4 percent in the first series of regional contests to 23.6 percent in the second, with only the FDP of the four parties gaining ground.

16 Eight parties gained representation in the Bremen parliament, six in Schleswig-Holstein and Hamburg, five in Baden-Württemberg, Bavaria and North Rhine-Westphalia, four in Hesse and three in Rhineland-Palatinate. Other than the five parties of national scope, the CDU/CSU, SPD, FDP, KPD and BHE, representation was gained by the DP in the British zone *Länder*, the SRP in Bremen and Lower Saxony, the *Zentrum* in Lower Saxony and North Rhine-Westphalia, the BP in Bavaria, the SSW in Schleswig-Holstein, the DRP and DSP in Lower Saxony, the RSF in Hamburg, the WdF in Bremen and the DG, aided by the BHE, in Bavaria

17 The SPD emerged as the leading party in six *Länder* (Bavaria, Bremen, Hamburg, Hesse, Lower Saxony and Schleswig-Holstein), the CDU in only three (Baden-Württemberg, North Rhine-Westphalia and Rhineland-Palatinate). The Social Democrats also outpolled the CDU in the 1950 *Land* elections in West Berlin and the now defunct *Land* of Württemberg-Baden to mark two additional successes for the SPD in the interval between the 1949 and 1953 general elections.

18 The political death of the Communist Party had been sealed long before the 1956 decision of the Federal Constitutional Court. Whereas the party had been represented in the parliaments of every *Land* after the first regional contests, with the exceptions of Bavaria and Schleswig-Holstein, its representation was reduced to five *Länder* in the second series of *Land* elections and to two *Länder*, Bremen and Lower Saxony, after the third series of elections, during which period it polled a mere 3.0 percent of the total *Land* level vote. Its 2.2 percent following in 1953 had reduced it to the status of a splinter group nationally.

19 The CDU/CSU, SPD, FDP and Refugee Party all exceeded the five percent requirement for national representation in 1953; the German Party and the *Zentrum*, while failing to meet the percentage restriction, became eligible for *Bundestag* seats by winning seats in the district competition, the DP ten, the ZP one.

20 The CDU gained 36.7 and the SPD 33.5 percent of the total *Land* level vote cast between 1953 and 1956.

21 The Refugee Party was represented in all states with the exceptions of Bremen, North Rhine-Westphalia and Rhineland-Palatinate. The Communist Party gained seats in Bremen and Lower Saxony.

22 The German Party gained seats in Bremen, Hamburg, Lower Saxony and Schleswig-Holstein, the *Zentrum* in Lower Saxony and North Rhine-Westphalia, the BP in Bavaria and the DRP in Lower Saxony.

23 Five parties were represented in Bavaria, Bremen and Schleswig-Holstein, four in Baden-Württemberg, Hamburg, Hesse and North Rhine-Westphalia and three in Rhineland-Palatinate. With the dissolution of the *Landtag* groups of the Communist Party in Bremen and Lower Saxony at the end of 1956, the number of parties in those two *Länder* was reduced accordingly. Following the Saar's incorporation into the Federal Republic in 1957 the Communist Party *Fraktion* in that *Land* was also dissolved.

24 The CDU/CSU polled 50.2 percent of the national vote, gaining over half of the ballots cast in Baden-Württemberg, Bavaria, North Rhine-Westphalia, Rhineland-Palatinate and the Saar and carrying every *Land* with the exceptions of Bremen and Hamburg.

25 Only the CDU/CSU, SPD, FDP and German Party obtained seats in the third *Bundestag*. Although the Refugee Party outpolled the DP 4.6 to 3.4 percent, the Refugees failed to win any direct seats while the German Party won six. The *Zentrum* formed an alliance with the Bavarian Party, known as the Federalist Union, in an attempt to save its *Bundestag* representation. However, the combination polled less than one percent of the national vote.

26 Of this total the CDU/CSU polled 42.1 percent, the SPD 38.3 percent.

27 While gaining seats in the ten West German states, the FDP failed to qualify for representation in West Berlin in the 1958 election.

28 See Article 3, paragraph 1 of the Schleswig-Holstein electoral law for the *Land* election of September 28, 1958 (*Handbuch des Schleswig-Holsteinischen Landages, 4. Wahlperiode,* 1959:123.

29 The Refugee Party gained representation in Baden-Württemberg, Bavaria, Hesse, Lower Saxony and Schleswig-Holstein, the German Party in Bremen and Lower Saxony.

30 The German Party's following fell to 4.1 percent in Hamburg and to 2.8 percent in Schleswig-Holstein.

31 While the German Reich Party lost its Lower Saxony representation after the 1959 election which was governed by a five percent clause, it succeeded the same day in polling 5.1 percent of the Rhineland-Palatinate vote and gaining a single *Landtag* seat. The DRP's success in 1959 was attributed to the backing of numerous wine growers and small farmers who were troubled by problems of over-production of wine. See *Der Spiegel*, July 19, 1961: 20-32.

32 Disappointed ambitions and personal rivalries caused a split in Christian-oriented forces in the Saar, and one group under former Minister President Johannes Hoffmann formed the Saarland People's Party (SVP), which polled 11.4 percent of the 1960 vote. The success of the left-oriented German Democratic Union in polling 5.0 percent of the Saar vote was attributed to the closeness of heavily Communist areas in France to which the Saar had been attached, the distance from Soviet zone reality and the fact that the party served as a natural refuge for those who had given the now-outlawed Communist Party 6.6 percent of the vote in the 1955 *Land* election.

33 The German Peace Union (DFU) was founded just prior to the 1961 *Bundestag* election to represent the German Left. Its supporters included former Communists and radical Socialists, as well as a large number of pastors, professors, teachers and other pacifist-minded intellectuals. Labeled *Deutsche Freunde Ulbrichs* (German Friends of Ulbrich, the East German dictator) by opponents, it received only 1.9 percent of the 1961 *Bundestag* vote and just over one percent of ballots cast in the regional elections held between 1961 and 1965. It had better success in local contests, where it won 6.1 percent of the vote in Solingen in 1964 and was instrumental in placing a Social Democrat into the mayor's seat (*Der Spiegel*, November 25, 1964: 64).

34 In its stronghold of Lower Saxony many former DP supporters gave their support to other parties, fearing that the indigenous, conservative stand of the party had been lost in the merger.

35 The Bremen DP served as an early base for the founding of the National Democratic Party (NPD), which gained 8.8 percent of the vote in the 1967 *Bürgerschaft* election in Bremen. One of the DP representatives, Friedrich Thielen, became NPD national chairman.

36 The appeal of the Danish minority party was strongest immediately after the war when economic conditions in South Schleswig were at their worse, and there was strong agitation for union with Denmark. The Danes succeeded in capturing the *Kreise* of Flensburg, Schleswig, and South Tondern in 1946 and 9.3 percent of the total *Land* vote in the 1947 *Landtag* election. In 1962 the SSW polled only 2.3 percent of the vote, but in Flensburg its support amounted to 25 percent.

37 Although the BP polled only 4.8 percent of the total *Land* vote in 1962, it succeeded in gaining 10.3 percent of the ballots cast in Lower Bavaria, one of the *Land's* seven administrative districts, which automatically qualified it for representation.

38 The Refugee Party lost its representation in Hesse in the 1966 *Land* election when it polled 4.3 percent of the *Land* vote.

39 The figures in Table I are based on a totaling of all of the votes cast for the various parties in the regional elections held between 1946 and 1965.

40 The CDU/CSU increased its *Land* total from 42.1 to 42.7 percent, the SPD from 38.3 to 42.3 percent and the FDP from 8.1 to 8.6 percent.

41 Arnold Heidenheimer, *The Governments of Germany*: 158. The strong position which Adenauer made of the Chancellorship greatly enhanced the power of that office, although individual successors have differed in the degree to which they have exercised that power.

42 Ossip K. Flechtheim, *"Die Institutionalisierung der Parteien in der Bundesrepublik, Zeitschrift für Politik*, IX (June 1962): 97-110.

43 Norman Crossland, "The German Rearguard," *Manchester Guardian Weekly*, December 1, 1966: 7.

44 The three-party total which had amounted to 93.6 percent in the 1961-1965 series of regional contests dropped by less than one percent, although the NPD polled 5.3 percent of ballots cast in the 1965-1969 period.

45 In the *Land* elections held just prior to the 1990 *Bundestag* contest the Greens remained unrepresented only in the Saar and Schleswig-Holstein, while the Free Democrats were unrepresented in Schleswig-Holstein and in Bavaria prior to the October 14, 1990 regional poll in which they received 5.2 percent of the Bavarian vote.

46 The figures in Table II are based on a totaling of ballots cast for the various parties in the regional elections held between 1965 and 1990.

47 The PDS, successor to the Communist SED, polled 9.9 percent of the vote in the new *Länder* to qualify for *Bundestag* representation from that section of the country, but less than one percent of the vote in the western states.

48 The figures in Table III are based on the totaling of ballots cast for the various parties in the regional elections held between 1990 and 2009.

49 Support for the CDU has fallen in the new states since 1990, not because of a surge in the fortunes of the PDS (*Die Linke*), but because of disinterest on the part of the region's growing middle class (Marian Lau, *"Wo die Politik nur stört,"* Die Welt, May 13, 2008: 3).

CHAPTER X

State and National Governments in German Politics

Regional elections in Germany not only determine the party composition of the individual state legislative bodies, but, under parliamentary practice, their outcomes circumscribe the possibilities available in forming the various *Land* ministries. The political makeup of the governments established is of considerable significance in German politics since, in addition to the role of the states in the administration of federal policies and programs for which they have sole responsibility, the *Länder* play an important role in national affairs through the *Bundesrat*, the upper house of the federal parliament. With power to veto stipulated categories of legislation and to delay, if not prevent, the passage of other measures, the *Bundesrat*, if controlled by groupings other than those forming the national government, can effectively bottle up the Government's legislative program. As a delegative body rather than a popularly elected chamber, the vote in the upper house is reflective of the party composition of the several state governments. It is, therefore, not surprising that after the formation of the Federal Republic in 1949 the parties comprising the national coalition would attempt to create favorable *Bundesrat* majorities for their programs by intervening not only in regional election campaigns, but in the negotiations leading up to the formation of the *Land* ministries.[1] The efforts of Germany's first Chancellor, Konrad Adenauer, to coordinate regional and national politics and to establish governments in the states reflecting the political makeup of the Bonn government and the counter-efforts of the opposition parties often led to the formation of coalitions which were not truly reflective of the will of the voters nor headed by the most popular or influential political leaders of the state.[2]

The existence of parliamentary systems in the *Länder* makes changes in the party composition of their governments an ever-present possibility long after their initial formation, in the absence of a majority party. Strictly local issues, as the FDP opposition in Lower Saxony to the 1965 concordat with the Vatican or the controversial spending and banking affair on the part of the local CDU in Berlin in 2001, may cause a coalition crisis or the breakup of a government may be precipitated by political developments in the federal capital.

The entry of two new players to the political scene (the Greens after 1979 and the PDS/*Die Linke* after 1990) and the formation of a CDU-SPD national coalition in Berlin in 2005 changed the coalition dynamics of the *Länder*. Between 1966 and 1990, with few exceptions such as the short-lived coalition between the SPD and Greens in Hesse from 1985 to 1987, either the CDU or SPD governed alone or in combination with the FDP. While the SPD has governed with the Greens in no fewer than eleven states and with the PDS in three since 1990, the CDU/CSU has never cooperated with the PDS, and not until May 2008 in Hamburg and October in 2009 in the Saar did it form a common ministry with the Greens.

At mid 2011 only three of the sixteen German states were ruled by grand coalitions between the two major parties. The formation of a grand coalition in Saxony-Anhalt after the 2006 election was not so much a result of a decision to duplicate the existing CDU/CSU/SPD combination in Berlin at that time, but of changed party strengths in the *Landtag*. The former CDU/FDP coalition could no longer provide a working majority and the CDU had no desire to form a ministry with *Die Linke*. The CDU/CSU/SPD alliance was continued after the 2011 *Land* election. Likewise in Thuringia, with the CDU's loss of its parliamentary majority in the 2009 *Land* elections, the CDU could form a majority only by allying itself with either the SPD or *Die Linke*. Again the SPD was the preferred partner. As in these two cases where the Union has ruled out cooperation with the Leftists, grand coalitions may be the only alternative in those eastern states where *Die Linke* is especially strong. The partnership between the Free Democrats and SPD in North Rhine-Westphalia between 1966 and 1970 reflected not only fears of changes in the electoral law inimical to FDP existence but also to the opposition of the Socialist *Landtag* faction to the then grand coalition in Bonn. More recently, in spite of pressure from their national counterparts for an SPD/CDU combination in the City of Berlin after the 2006 election, Lord Mayor Klaus Wowereit (SPD) opted to continue his working arrangement with the PDS because he placed the integration of the eastern part of Berlin with the western part above national party wishes.

The Early Ministries

The military defeat of Germany in 1945 completely shattered the existing political and administrative structure of the country and placed all governmental authority in the hands of the four victorious Allies.[3] The four Military Authorities approached the task of reconstructing the fabrics of government in their various zones of occupation in widely differing fashions, both as to method and pace of devolving power to the Germans. The first *Land* level organs of government were appointed bodies, made up of independents or members of the anti-Nazi parties who had returned from exile, possessed a record of opposition to the National Socialist regime or had been cleared of responsibility for the criminal acts of the Nazi period. These provisional bodies were strictly responsible to the occupying authorities, and tenure of office was at the discretion of the zonal military government.[4]

The American Military Government for Bavaria on May 28, 1945, established the first *Land* government following the Nazi collapse, naming Friedrich Schäffer, prominent leader of the Bavarian People's Party (BVP) prior to 1933, to the post of Minister President.[5] Similar appointments followed in the American zone *Länder* of Hesse and Württemberg-Baden.[6] Until a decision could be reached on the number of states to be carved out of her zone of occupation, the most important appointments made by the British in the immediate postwar period were to the post of *Oberpräsident*, head of a former Prussian province, and mayor of the large cities in her zone.[7] By the end of 1946 delineation of the *Land* boundaries made possible the establishment of nominated governments in Lower Saxony, North Rhine-Westphalia and Schleswig-Holstein, while municipal elections in Hamburg and Bremen enabled the governments of those two *Länder* to be formed on a parliamentary basis after October 1946. The French set up directorates (*Direktorium*), state secretariats (*Staatssekretariat*) or presidiums in the areas under their control to carry on the functions of state until official *Land* governments reflecting the outcomes of the first political elections in their zone could be established.[8]

In January and February 1946 provisional parliaments (*Vorparlaments*) were formed in the three American zone *Länder*. These bodies, which were to exist only until June 30, 1946, when popularly elected constituent assemblies (*Verfassunggebenden Landesversammlungen*) replaced them, reflected an attempt to combine a mixture of political, corporate and class representation in a parliamentary body,[9] making possible the representation of various groups and interests in the absence of a general election.[10] The British appointed provisional parliaments in their zone during the course of 1946, with only Hamburg employing a system of functional representation in its first nominated *Bürgerschaft*.[11] The French were the last to establish parliamentary bodies on the *Land* level, delaying the move until after the political elections of October 1946. These bodies were not appointed, rather they were elected indirectly on a party basis by members of the municipal and county councils and served as consultative state assemblies for the purpose of drafting constitutions for their respective *Länder*.

The outcomes of the first political elections in the American zone *Länder* produced no major changes in the makeup of the nominated ministries of Bavaria, Hesse and Württemberg-Baden, and not until after the first *Landtag* elections in November and December of 1946 did the *Land* ministries reflect the relative strengths of the parties in these *Länder*. The British, on the other hand, were quick to make changes in both the nominated parliaments and in the *Land* ministries after the first political elections to correct any discrepancies in representation produced by the original appointments.[12] The French, by delaying the appointment of *Land* ministries until December 1946, could establish them on a partisan basis reflecting the party complexion of the various *Länder* under their control from the very beginning.

The appointments of the first *Land* ministries reflected the desire of the Western Allies to establish stable majorities within the *Länder* rather than to encourage the development of a political opposition. The first Maier cabinet in

Württemberg-Baden consisted of four Christian Democrats, two Social Democrats and two members of the Democratic Peoples' Party.[13] Of the licensed parties, only the Communists were excluded from the government. In Hesse the first government had a nonparty Minister President, Prof. Dr. Karl Geiler of the University of Heidelberg, three additional non-party ministers, an SPD Interior Minister and a Communist Labor Minister. On November 1, 1945, less than a month after the appointment of the first ministry, the government was reformed to include four Social Democrats, one Liberal Democrat (FDP), one Christian Democrat and one Communist in addition to four independents.[14] In Bavaria, following the removal of Friedrich Schäffer as Minister President in September 1945, the American authorities appointed Wilhelm Hoegner, a Social Democrat, over Dr. Josef Müller, leader of the liberal Catholics in the *Land*, even though it should have been obvious to political observers that the CSU, not the SPD, was the leading group in Bavaria.[15] Whereas members of the Schäffer cabinet had been selected on a non-party basis, the Hoegner cabinet was made up of four Social Democrats, two members of the CSU who acted as individuals, not as party representatives, one Communist, and two independents.[16] Müller, himself, refused to participate in the Hoegner administration.

In the British zone the first appointed cabinets in Lower Saxony, North Rhine-Westphalia and Schleswig-Holstein likewise contained ministers representing the breadth of the political spectrum.[17] In Lower Saxony, for example, the government appointed in December 1946 extended from the Lower Saxony State Party representing the right-wing landowners to the Communists who supplied a single minister. All four of the parties licensed in the French zone *Länder*, the Christian Democrats, Social Democrats, Liberals and Communists, participated in the appointed executive body of Baden, with the Liberals excluded from the cabinet in Rhineland-Palatinate, the Communists from the State Secretariat in Württemberg-Hohenzollern.[18]

The first *Landtag* elections of November and December 1946 made possible the formation of governments in the American Zone *Länder* on a parliamentary basis, with their outcomes necessitating changes in the political composition of several of the cabinets. Dr. Hans Ehard (CSU) replaced Social Democrat Wilhelm Hoegner as Minister President in Bavaria and Christian Stock (SPD) took over the same post from independent Prof. Dr. Karl Geiler in Hesse. Dr. Reinhold Maier retained his position as head of the government in Württemberg-Baden; however, numerous changes were made within the cabinet itself. The elections of October 1946 enabled responsible governments to be formed in Bremen and Hamburg; the elections of April 20, 1947 made possible the establishment of responsible governments in the other British Zone *Länder*.[19] Of the appointed heads of government in the British Zone only Wilhelm Kaisen (SPD) in Bremen and Wilhelm Kopf (SPD) in Lower Saxony retained their posts as a result of the outcomes of the First *Landtag* elections.[20] Several changes were necessitated in the administrations of the French zone *Länder* as a result of the *Landtag* elections of May 18, 1947. In Württemberg-Hohenzollern Social Democrat Prof. Dr. Carlo Schmid was replaced as President by Christian Democrat Lorenz Bock.[21] Peter Altmeier (CDU) took over the post of Minister President in Rhineland-Palatinate from his colleague Dr. Wilhelm Boden, and in Baden Leo Wohleb (CDU) continued in the post of President.

In view of the economic and political crisis of the immediate postwar period, most of the first responsible governments were coalitions, as had been the appointed ministries before them, even though individual parties in five of the *Länder* commanded absolute majorities without combining with other groups.[22] The majority party was reluctant to "go it alone" and accept full responsibility for the task of solving the pressing problems then facing the *Länder*. Not only did the party have little to gain by shouldering full responsibility for the acts of government, but the coalition system was held desirable, praiseworthy and a necessity of the moment.[23] To shun responsibility in this critical period was considered cowardice, to accept it an act of heroism. The desirability of presenting a united stand to the Occupying Powers, the real opposition to many Germans, was a further motive for party cooperation. As a result, the dominant party pattern in the governments of the *Länder* up to 1950 was a broad coalition which often encompassed all of the parties represented in the *Landtag*.[24]

Only in Schleswig-Holstein did a single party, the SPD, accept full responsibility for the conduct of government following the first *Landtag* elections, dissolving the "grand coalition" which had existed between the SPD and the CDU in the appointment period.[25] The breakup of the nine-month coalition between the CSU and the SPD in Bavaria resulted in the establishment of a second one-party government in September 1947, but for reasons quite unlike that in Schleswig-Holstein in that the initiative for the dissolution of the coalition was not taken by the majority party.[26] Differences over local policy broke up the CDU-SPD government in Baden in 1948.[27] The "grand coalitions" in Hesse, North Rhine-Westphalia, Rhineland-Palatinate and Württemberg-Baden remained in existence until the second *Landtag* elections in those *Länder*, and in Württemberg-Hohenzollern until the dissolution of that *Land* in April 1952,[28] but the coalition between the SPD and the CDU in Lower Saxony did not survive the first legislative period, breaking up in August 1950.[29] Governments were formed in the city-states of Bremen and Hamburg without CDU participation, although the coalition principle was maintained with the smaller parties.[30]

The all-party coalitions established in Lower Saxony, Rhineland-Palatinate and Württemberg-Baden far exceeded the numbers required for a legislative majority and all but excluded genuine parliamentary opposition, a requisite of democratic government, in those *Länder* in the first year or two of their existence.[31] In all three *Länder*, although no single party had an absolute majority in the parliament, the CDU and the SPD together or one of the two major parties acting in concert with a third party could have formed a stable majority.[32] In North Rhine-Westphalia a coalition representing four of the five parties holding seats in the *Landtag* was hammered out after an eight-week governmental crisis caused by the CDU refusal to participate in the formation of any government committed to the socialization of the basic industries in the Ruhr.[33] In the interval the appointed cabinet under Dr. Rudolf Amelunxen served as a caretaker government.

The SPD participated in all eleven of the initial *Land* governments established on a parliamentary basis, and at the end of the first legislative period formed part of the governments of all *Länder* with the exceptions of Baden and Bavaria. On the other hand, the Union parties never participated in the governments of Bremen, Hamburg, or Schleswig-Holstein during any part of the first legislative period and had ceased to be a member of the coalition in Lower Saxony a year prior to the second *Landtag* election in that *Land*. The Communist Party participated in the initial coalitions in Hamburg, Lower Saxony, North Rhine-Westphalia, Rhineland-Palatinate and Württemberg-Baden, but was expelled from each of these coalitions prior to the end of the first legislative period.[34] From November 1946 to January 1948 the KPD also participated in the first responsible Kaisen government in Bremen. The *Land* groups which were later to form the Free Democratic Party were initially represented in the governments of Bremen, Hamburg, Lower Saxony, Rhineland-Palatinate, Württemberg-Baden and Württemberg-Hohenzollern; however, after 1948 in Lower Saxony and Rhineland-Palatinate and after 1949 in Württemberg-Hohenzollern they no longer participated in the respective coalitions. The German Center Party was part of the coalitions in both Lower Saxony and North Rhine-Westphalia during the whole legislative period. The German Party in Lower Saxony and the WAV in Bavaria participated in the governments of those *Länder* for short periods of time.

The first *Landtag* elections found the Social Democratic Party and the CDU/CSU almost equally matched,[35] with both parties providing the governmental heads in five states and the Liberal Democrats the premier in one.[36] The policies of the occupying powers restricted any national coordination of the first *Landtag* elections, and no coordinated effort was made to effectuate a definite pattern in the party make-up of the first responsible *Land* ministries. The determining principle was the formation of a stable coalition regardless of its party composition, and with the high value placed on cooperation, these early governments were medleys of parties comprising both extremes without distinctive pattern, unless cooperation between the CDU and SPD in eight of the eleven states for varying periods of time could be regarded as such.

The creation of the Federal Republic in 1949, however, was to have a far-reaching effect on the coalition patterns in the states. The constitutional role of the upper house of the federal parliament, the *Bundesrat*, which gives it power to block stipulated categories of legislation affecting *Land-Bund* relationships, and to exercise a general suspensive veto, the use of which could be overridden only by the requisite *Bundestag* majorities, and the political relationship which placed control of *Bundesrat* delegations directly in the hands of the *Land* governments rather than in the hands of the people, made it politically desirable for the party block controlling the national government to widen its influence over legislation by attempting to institute governments in the *Länder* reflecting the Bonn cabinet as far as party make-up was concerned. The opposition parties, on the other hand, were encouraged to strengthen their position by creating a "friendly" *Bundesrat*. The very power of the *Bundesrat* in contrast to its politically emasculated predecessor, the *Reichsrat*, invited the direct intervention by the national parties in *Land* politics.

Cooperation between the CDU and the SPD which had proven so satisfactory in many of the *Länder* prior to 1949, was no longer desirable once the Socialists had been excluded from the first national government. Whereas the character of the issues handled by the *Land* governments had made cooperation between the two parties possible on the regional level, the assumption of responsibility by the Germans for such policies as foreign relations, defense, foreign trade and economic recovery made working together on the national level difficult if not impossible unless the parties were to compromise a large measure of their programs. This, the national leaders of the two parties, Christian Democrat Chairman Konrad Adenauer and Social Democrat Chairman Kurt Schumacher, who became bitter political rivals, refused to do, and in order to effect the national and international programs of his party, the new Federal Chancellor, Adenauer, set about to command a parallel majority for his coalition in the *Bundesrat*.[37] The fragmentation of the political arena during the early 1950s often created such a fluid state of affairs in some *Länder* that federal intervention was often decisive in the formation of the ministries.

The grand coalitions in Baden and Bavaria broke up prior to the formation of the Federal government; however, at the end of 1949 working arrangements between the CDU and SPD still existed in six states.[38] These too were gradually to be replaced between 1950 and 1952 by smaller coalitions between the CDU or SPD and one of the minor parties, with the exception of Hesse where the Socialists formed a one-party government.[39] Pressures from the national parties were instrumental in breaking up the relatively successful coalitions between the CDU and SPD in Hesse and North Rhine-Westphalia which the CDU *Land* groups had been quite willing to continue. In neither case, however, did Adenauer succeed in effecting the conservative coalition of the CDU and the FDP which he desired.[40] In Hamburg the CDU formed a party alliance with the FDP and the German Conservative Party, known as the Hamburg Native Alliance (*Vaterstädtischer Bund Hamburg*—VBH), for the 1949 *Land* election in an attempt to oust the Socialists in their stronghold. The effort failed as the Social Democrats won an absolute majority of the seats in the *Bürgerschaft* and formed a pure Socialist government under Max Brauer. The electoral bloc formed by the parties of the national coalition, the CDU, FDP and German Party in Schleswig-Holstein was more successful, winning 31 of 69 seats, all by direct election. Unable to form a majority on their own, the bloc parties established a government with the Refugee Party to replace the former all-Socialist ministry.

The emergence of a powerful refugee political movement in 1950 was to greatly complicate the coalition struggles of the second legislative period because of its perfect willingness to side with either bourgeois or Socialist forces for political advantage. In several of the *Länder* the political composition of the *Landtag* made it impossible to form a government without its participation. In Schleswig-Holstein the BHE supported the bourgeois parties; in Lower Saxony after the 1951 *Landtag* election it sided with the Social Democratic Party and *Zentrum* and in 1952 it made possible a left of center coalition in Baden-Württemberg which excluded the CDU. The formation of the SPD-FDP-BHE cabinet in the new Southwest State drastically altered the party composition of the *Bundesrat*, since the safe CDU *Länder* of Baden and Württemberg-Hohenzollern had been extinguished in the union of the three *Länder*.[41] Antagonisms between the CSU and the right-wing Bavarian Party, which had siphoned off a large portion of the vote which ordinarily would have gone to the CSU, made a coalition between the Union and the Socialists the only possible grouping in Bavaria following the 1950 *Land* election, but because the new coalition could not count on the complete loyalty of the CSU right wing, which would have preferred a small coalition with the Bavarian Party, the Refugee Party was added to the coalition.[42] A second coalition in which both the CDU and the SPD participated in a common government was formed in Bremen following the 1951 *Land* election contest. However, in contrast to Bavaria, there was no demanding reason for the inclusion of the CDU in the cabinet in Bremen as it controlled only nine of the 100 *Bürgerschaft* seats, whereas the SPD and the FDP commanded 55 together.[43] In Rhineland-Palatinate the Christian Democrats formed a government with the FDP to replace the grand coalition with the SPD which had existed prior to May 1951.

Nearly every *Land* witnessed a change in the party composition of its government between 1949 and 1953; however, with the exception of Schleswig-Holstein, Adenauer had been far from successful in his attempts to create a parallelogram of power for his party in the *Bundestag* and *Bundesrat*, and his single success was more than matched by the CDU's loss of Baden-Württemberg.[44] Following the overwhelming triumph of the CDU in the 1953 general elections which gave the parties of the national coalition a two-thirds majority in the *Bundestag*, intervention efforts in the *Länder* reached a new intensity as the Government parties attempted to create a similar majority in the *Bundesrat*. Within a month of the CDU national victory, strong repercussions were to be felt in the *Länder*. In a cabinet reshuffle in Baden-Württemberg, Dr. Gebhard Müller (CDU) replaced Free Democrat Dr. Reinhold Maier as Minister President, and although the new government included Socialist, Liberal and Refugee party members, the *Land's* five *Bundesrat* votes came under Christian Democratic control. The following month in Hamburg a party alliance formed by the groupings in the national government won 62 of 120 *Bürgerschaft* seats and succeeded in ousting the government of the popular Hamburg Socialist, Max Brauer. The Hamburg victory in November 1953 assured Adenauer a two-thirds majority in the *Bundesrat*, making possible the enactment of any constitutional amendment needed to implement his defense and foreign policies.[45]

Following the 1954 *Land* elections in North Rhine-Westphalia and Schleswig-Holstein, governments closely reflecting the composition of the Federal cabinet were established in those two *Länder*, enabling the national government to protect its constitutional majority in the federal upper chamber.[46] The outcome of the election in Schleswig-Holstein was of considerable significance for the course of Adenauer's foreign policy, coming as it did just a few weeks after the French rejection of the European Defense Community treaty.[47] The first major setback for Adenauer in his attempts to establish replicas of the Bonn coalition in the *Länder* came after the election of November 1954 in Bavaria. Although the CSU emerged as by far the strongest party,[48] it was excluded from the government formed in December 1954 by a coalition of the SPD, BHE, FDP and the Bavarian Party. The issue of church control over education, the exorbitant demands of the CSU, the antagonisms between the CSU and the Bavarian Party and the determination of the other parties to check the coordination attempts of the Federal Government all played a role in the formation of this unholy alliance of widely diverse elements, which cost the national government its constitutional majority in the *Bundesrat*. In that same month Adenauer's efforts to persuade the Refugee Party to join with the CDU and FDP in the formation of a government in Hesse, following the loss by the Socialists of their *Landtag* majority, came to naught as the *Land* BHE sided with the SPD in opposition to the Chancellor's wishes.[49]

The Lower Saxony election of April 1955 led to further success for Adenauer's intervention tactics, when a coalition of the CDU, DP, BHE and FDP replaced the former Socialist-Refugee Party government.[50] The following month the CDU won an absolute majority in Rhineland-Palatinate to maintain its dominant position in that *Land* and guarantee a continuation of the CDU-FDP cabinet. The SPD registered a like success in the Bremen election later in the year, winning 52 of 100 parliamentary seats. No changes were made in the previously existing government which had consisted of the SPD, the CDU and FDP. In February 1956 Adenauer's coordination efforts suffered a severe setback when growing opposition to the Chancellor's policies within the FDP, and FDP resentment to the introduction of a federal electoral law which threatened the independent existence of the party coupled with Socialist bitterness over their exclusion from the 1950 and 1954 governments in North Rhine-Westphalia in spite of their willingness to join, set the stage for the alliance between SPD and FDP groups in Düsseldorf which upset the government of Karl Arnold.[51] With the exclusion of the CDU from the cabinet in North Rhine-Westphalia a situation was reached in 1956 in which governments were in power in over half of the *Länder* in which the strongest parliamentary group did not participate,[52] although democratic practice would appear to dictate the representation of the largest parliamentary group in the government unless pressing reasons dictated its exclusion as with the Communist Party in Fourth Republic France. Ordinarily the inclusion of the largest *Fraktion* in the ministry promotes a more stable government and makes possible a more positive and effective policy. Yet, the coordination efforts of the CDU in the early 1950s produced coalitions in three of the *Länder* which did not include the major party, while the retaliatory actions of the Socialists produced two such coalitions.[53] This juggling for political advantage has not become outdated. The SPD was excluded from the Hamburg *Senat* from 2001 to 2004 even though it was the largest party and the CDU from the governments of Hesse from 1974 to 1983 and again from 1995 to 1999 and of Saxony-Anhalt from 1994 to 1998 and of Baden-Württemberg in 2011 in spite of its greater size.[54]

Within a year of the 1957 *Bundestag* election the five governments in which the largest party was not present, were replaced by ministries in which they were included.[55] In October 1957 the Hoegner (SPD) administration in Bavaria collapsed when the Bavarian and Refugee parties withdrew from the Socialist-led coalition, making possible a government comprising the CSU, BHE and FDP under Dr. Hans Seidel (CSU).[56] The following month a Socialist victory in Hamburg returned it to power in that *Land*,[57] while in Lower Saxony Minister President Hellwege (DP) dismissed the FDP and BHE ministers from his cabinet and brought the SPD into his government instead, a move precipitated by the refusal of the CDU, the largest party in the former coalition, to ally itself with right-wing elements which could have embarrassed the CDU nationally and the Federal government internationally.[58] In July 1958 the CDU won an absolute majority in North Rhine-Westphalia, dissolving the former Socialist-FDP-Center Party coalition and enabling the CDU to form a one-party government.[59] Large gains in Schleswig-Holstein and Bavaria later in the year enabled the CDU to maintain its hold on those two *Länder*. In Schleswig-Holstein a coalition was formed with the FDP, in Bavaria with the FDP and Refugee Party. While *Land* elections in Hesse and Rhineland-Palatinate produced no changes in the governments of those *Länder*, the 1959 contest in Lower Saxony enabled the Socialists to form a three-party coalition which excluded the CDU.[60] Elections in Bremen, Baden-Württemberg and the Saar in 1959 and 1960 ended the grand coalitions in those three states,[61] and between the shift in administrations in Lower Saxony in May 1959 and the fall of 1966, there was no change in party control in any of the states, resulting in a stabilization of the party ratio in the *Bundesrat* at 26 safe CDU and fifteen safe SPD votes during that period. This stabilization reflected the increasing strengths of the CDU and SPD on the regional level and the gradual elimination of all minor parties other than the FDP from the *Landtage*, curtailing most of the political maneuvering which characterized the 1950s. While the establishment of the first grand coalition on the national level in 1966 ended a seventeen year rivalry between the two major parties for control of the *Bundesrat*, it did not end efforts by the regional organizations of the parties, especially of the FDP, to block the formation of CDU-SPD governments on the *Land* level, even in opposition to their national counterparts. In North Rhine-Westphalia both the state and national leadership of the SPD favored a coalition with the CDU during the negotiations in November 1966; however, the parliamentary group of the SPD in Düsseldorf voted 73 to 21 for an alliance with the FDP in opposition to the party organization.[62] In Baden-Württemberg the following month the FDP lost out in its efforts to prevent the formation of a "Black-Red" coalition which survived through 1972. The grand coalition in Bonn was viewed from the very beginning as a temporary expedient, but it succeeded in lasting through the legislative period. Throughout this interval (1966 to 1969), the state organizations of the two major parties demonstrated that they would not be merely rubber stamps of the national parties.

At the end of 1966 a single party held an absolute majority in five states, in two of which it governed with a second party. In Hamburg and Hesse the dominant SPD governed alone; in Bremen and West Berlin it cooperated with the FDP.[63] In Bavaria the CSU formed a one-party ministry after the Bavarian Party went into the opposition in July 1966 and continued to govern alone for forty two years until 2008 when it lost its majority in the *Landtag* election of that year and formed an alliance with the Free Democrats. In all other states, the absence of a controlling majority by a single party made necessary a coalition with a second parliamentary group.[64] In Rhineland-Palatinate, the Saar and Schleswig-Holstein the CDU cooperated with the FDP or its affiliate (the DPS in the Saar). In North Rhine-Westphalia the SPD formed a common ministry with the FDP and in Baden-Württemberg and Lower Saxony it joined in grand coalitions with the CDU, in the former under a Christian Democrat premier, in the latter under a Socialist head of government. The SPD participated in the administrations of seven of the eleven states, the CDU/CSU in six and the FDP in six.[65]

While one-party ministries were formed on nine occasions in the *Länder* between 1946/47 and 1966, at the other extreme was the all-party coalition in Lower Saxony which included six parties and the four-party coalitions of North Rhine-Westphalia, Rhineland-Palatinate and Württemberg-Baden.[66] The number of parties participating in these first alliances far exceeded the amount required for a workable majority; however, beginning in 1950 a group of coalitions were formed which required the participation of up to four parties to form a stable parliamentary majority,[67] made necessary by the exclusion of the largest parliamentary group from the government. In the 1950 *Landtag* election in Schleswig-Holstein the electoral alliance between the CDU, FDP and German Party failed to produce the desired majority to dislodge the largest party, the SPD, necessitating inclusion of a fourth grouping, the Refugee Party, in the government. The decision of the Refugee Party to support bourgeois rather than Socialist forces was the decisive factor in this coalition. In the 1953 *Land* election contest in

TABLE 10.1

COMPOSITION OF *LAND* AND NATIONAL GOVERNMENTS, DECEMBER 1966

Baden-Württemberg	CDU/SPD	North Rhine-Westphalia	SPD/FDP
Bavaria	CSU	Rhineland-Palatinate	CDU/FDP
Bremen	SPD/FDP [a]	The Saar	CDU/FDP
Hamburg	SPD	Schleswig-Holstein	CDU/FDP
Hesse	SPD	Lower Saxony	SPD/CDU
West Berlin	SPD/FDP [a]	Federal Government	CDU/SPD

a Parties with an absolute majority of seats in the state legislature which chose to govern with a second party.

Hamburg the same four parties again cooperated in a partnership known as the Hamburg Block and succeeded in gaining a majority of the seats and forming a ministry without the Socialists. Two years later, in Lower Saxony, the four bourgeois parties again established a government without the leading Socialists.[68] However, in contrast to the four-party coalitions in Schleswig-Holstein and Hamburg, the Socialists were able to reenter the government before the end of the legislative period.[69] Between December 1954 and October 1957 a four-party coalition consisting of the SPD, FDP, BP and Refugee Party governed Bavaria, although in this case the inclusion of the FDP was not necessary to produce a workable majority. The negative nature of this alliance, that of excluding the leading CSU from the government, and the wide divergency of opinions within the coalition which included the strongly federalist Bavarian Party and the centralist SPD and FDP caused it to administer rather than to govern, contributing to its dissolution with over a year remaining in the legislative period. The four-party coalition which governed Baden-Württemberg from October 1953 to May 1960 was considered advisable to further unity within the newly-formed state, although a stable majority could have been achieved by the CDU in concert with either the SPD or the DVP/FDP.[70]

Three-party coalitions have been formed at some stage in every state since 1946/1947 with the exception of Hesse of the old *Länder* and Mecklenberg-Vorpommern, Saxony, Saxony-Anhalt and Thuringia of the new states, yet few required the participation of all three parties. Of the early ministries, only those in Bavaria (November 1950 to November 1954 and October 1957 to December 1958), North Rhine-Westphalia (February 1956 to July 1958) and Lower Saxony (May 1959 to June 1963) required the cooperation of all three parties to form a stable majority. Although the CSU and the SPD controlled a majority of seats in the Bavarian *Landtag* following the election of November 26, 1950, support from the CSU's right-wing, which had preferred a partnership with the Bavarian Party over the Social Democrats was uncertain, making participation of the Refugee Party in the government a necessity.[71]

With the ebbing of the fragmenting influence of numerous minor parties there were no three-party coalitions formed in any of the West German states between 1966 and 1990, and since 1990 there have been only four. A three-party *"Ampel"* coalition of the SPD, FDP and Alliance 90/Greens was formed in Brandenburg following the 1990 *Land* election, since the leading Socialists were opposed to forming a combination with either the CDU or the left-leaning PDS and the support of both the Free Democrats and Alliance 90 was needed to provide a workable majority. The next year a like red/yellow/green alliance was established in Bremen, since an SPD/Free Democrat or an SPD/Greens partnership could produce only a bare majority, neither of which was considered sufficient to provide a stable government. A third example occurred in Hamburg following the 2001 *Land* election in which three political groupings (the CDU, FDP and Schill Party) were required to exclude the leading Socialists from the government. The arrangement in Hamburg prematurely broke down nineteen months prior to the end of the legislative session over the scandalous conduct of

Schill Party leader Roland Schill.[72] The CDU/FDP/Greens combination in the Saar after the inconclusive 2009 *Land* election is the most recent example of a three-party alliance on the regional level.

Cooperation between the two major parties and the FDP has been marked by a degree of ambivalence, but in most cases the Free Democrats have sided with the largest party in the *Landtag* unless political considerations dictated otherwise. In December 1966 it cooperated with the Socialists in three states and with the Christian Democrats in three states; however, whereas it made government possible for the CDU in all three cases, only in North Rhine-Westphalia (after December 1966) was its participation necessary to provide the SPD with a working majority. Although the FDP demonstrated a greater inclination to side with the CDU on both the national and regional levels during the first twenty years of parliamentary democracy in Germany, including thirteen years in the national government, its cooperation with the Socialists in a number of states between 1946/1947 and 1966 was often decisive in putting Socialist-led ministries into power, as was the case between 1954 and 1957 in Bavaria with the help of the Bavarian and Refugee parties, between 1963 and 1965 in Lower Saxony, and between 1956 and 1958 and from December 1966 to May 1980 in North Rhine-Westphalia. Moreover, the FDP was a partner in every Socialist-led ministry in Bremen between 1946 and 1966, even though the SPD held absolute majorities during three of the five legislative sessions. This cooperation was facilitated by the conservative, non-militant character of Wilhelm Kaisen's (1946-1965) and his successor's socialism and the liberal nature of the Bremen FDP.[73] In Hamburg, the Free Democrats participated in three Socialist-led administrations between 1946 and 1966, although the Socialists commanded a legislative majority each time. Such coalitions may be explained: first, as attempts to lay the basis for cooperation in the event the dominant party should lose its majority in a subsequent election, as happened in Hamburg between 1974 and 1978 and again from 1987 to 1991 when FDP support was necessary to maintain the Socialists' hold on power; second, as continuations of a previous highly satisfactory partnership, as was the case in Bremen from 1955 to 1971 with the FDP or in West Berlin where the SPD, in spite of its majority position, governed with the FDP from 1963 to 1975 (the FDP continued to support the SPD from 1975 to 1981 after it had lost its majority); or, third, as efforts to strengthen what otherwise would have been a highly unstable or weak majority. Between 1975 and 1977 the CDU, with just half the seats in the Saar parliament, governed alone before forming a ministry with the Free Democrats and placing the government on a more stable basis. The SPD also, prior to 1969, saw its coalitions with the FDP, whether in majority status or without, as models for possible future cooperation between the two parties on the national level. Prior to 1970 there was no cooperation between the SPD and FDP in Hesse, and none prior to 1991 in Rhineland-Palatinate.[74]

Working arrangements between the SPD and FDP tended to be limited to the North German and Protestant states prior to the formation of a common government in Rhineland-Palatinate in 1991. (The SPD-FDP combination in

Rhineland-Palatinate lasted until 2006, when the Socialists won an absolute majority of *Landtag* seats.) This reflected the weakness of the Socialist cause in the highly Catholic areas of southern Germany outside of Hesse during these early years. Through 2010 the two parties had not participated in a common ministry in either the Saar or Schleswig-Holstein.

The cooperation between the two major German political parties, the CDU/CSU and the SPD, which was so common in the immediate postwar period and which took place in every West German state at some stage after 1946/1947 with the exceptions of Hamburg and Schleswig-Holstein (prior to 2005), had ceased by March 1963 with the breakup of the CDU-SPD ministry in West Berlin,[75] and no grand coalitions existed in any of the *Länder* for two years until an SPD/CDU government was formed in Lower Saxony in May 1965.[76] After the dissolution of the original grand coalitions, cooperation between the CDU and SPD was limited to Baden-Württemberg (October 1953 to May 1960), Bavaria (December 1950-December 1954), Bremen (November 1951-December 1959), Lower Saxony (November 1957-May 1959), the Saar (from its incorporation into the Federal Republic in 1957 to December 1960), and West Berlin (December 1946-November 1953 and January 1955-March 1963), where the most continuous working relationship between the two parties was found in the early postwar period, not only because the political situation encouraged a unity of effort, but because, at the time, the composition of its government had no influence on the voting in the *Bundesrat.*

The gradual demise of major party cooperation after 1949 was due not only to the coordination efforts of the Adenauer administration, but to the strong opposition of the FDP and some of the state organs of the SPD to such arrangements. The efforts to continue the coalition of Christian and Socialist forces in the Saar following the 1960 *Land* election were strongly opposed by Bonn in view of the *Bundestag* election the following year. After the 1962 regional election in North Rhine-Westphalia the CDU foresaw a possible coalition with the Socialists, and Herr Arnold (CDU), son of the former Minister President of the state, Karl Arnold, held that such a combination would be closest to the voters' wishes. Minister President Dr. Franz Meyers announced his readiness to bargain with either the SPD or the FDP in forming a government, and the SPD announced its readiness to participate in a coalition with the CDU. However, again, opposition from Bonn quashed the formation of a CDU-SPD administration in Düsseldorf. When the Socialists replaced the CDU as the leading party in the 1966 regional contest they strongly advocated the formation of a common government and went so far as to offer to retain Meyers (CDU) as Minister President. These efforts came to naught as the CDU formed a mini-coalition with the FDP, in spite of the combination's shaky one-vote margin.[77] In November 1966 a further attempt to form a grand coalition in the country's most populous state was quashed by the SPD *Landtag Fraktion* which voted for an alliance with the Free Democrats (*Der Spiegel*, December 5, 1966:47).

The SPD-CDU combination in Lower Saxony, formed in May 1965, predated the establishment of the grand coalition in Bonn and was brought about by

Free Democratic opposition within the previous government to Socialist efforts to consummate a concordat with the Vatican designed to govern the establishment of Catholic confessional schools within the *Land,* the support of those schools with public funds, the teaching of the Catholic faith in the public schools and the establishment of a Catholic faculty of theology at the University of Göttingen.[78] The grand coalition which resulted from this rupture eventually implemented the desired changes in the Lower Saxony educational code. It was terminated when the SPD won an absolute majority of seats in the Lower Saxony parliament in the 1970 *Landtag* election. The CDU-SPD partnership in Baden-Württenberg between 1966 and 1972 was an unexpected outcome of the necessity to elect a new Minister President following Dr. Kurt Georg Kiesinger's elevation to the Federal Chancellorship. The *Land* FDP decided against an automatic continuation of the existing CDU-FDP coalition in order to strengthen its demand for a Baden-Württemberg veto in the *Bundesrat* against any attempt to introduce a majority voting system on the federal level and the alteration of the *Land* education code concerning confessional schools. Informed of the FDP decision to form a coalition with the SPD rather than with his own CDU, Hans Filbinger, faced with the unhappy possibility of going into the opposition before having a chance to prove himself as Minister President, agreed to the change in the educational code, which both Socialists and Free Democrats had supported, and made other concessions to pave the way for a CDU-SPD understanding which no one had considered possible.[79] The grand coalition in Lower Saxony ended in 1970 when the Socialists obtained an absolute majority of *Landtag* seats and in 1972 in Baden-Württemberg when the CDU likewise gained a majority of seats.

With the gradual elimination of all parties other than the CDU/CSU, SPD and FDP from the *Landtage,* the increasing ability of either the Christian parties or the Socialists to control absolute majorities in the various states and the democratic and non-doctrinaire character of the FDP, making it a satisfactory partner for either of the two political giants, the necessity and even the desirability of major party cooperation faded and no new grand coalitions appeared in any of the states until 1990. While pressing economic and political issues appeared to justify a large majority on the national level in 1966 there were few arguments for major party cooperation in the *Länder*, and not one state chose to duplicate the Bonn model in spite of strong representations by the national organizations to do so. (The two grand coalitions which existed in the *Länder* at the end of 1966 were formed for reasons quite apart from national political pressures).

State and National Ministries from 1966 to 1990

With the demise of the Refugee Party in 1966 and the inability of the Bavarian Party to gain representation in the Bavarian *Landtag* after 1966, the FDP remained the only acceptable coalition partner for the two major parties for the next two decades in the absence of an absolute majority by one of them. Although the National Democratic Party (NPD) gained representation in seven of the ten state parliaments between 1966 and 1968 it was never considered an acceptable coalition candidate by either the CDU/CSU or SPD and did not participate in any of the state ministries during the period of its ascendancy. Moreover, with the ability of the two major parties to obtain ninety percent or more of ballots cast in most elections (the SPD and CDU/CSU received 90.5 percent of the votes cast in the regional elections held between the 1969 and 1972 *Bundestag* polls), there was a greater chance for one or the other of them to gain a majority of seats in the state parliaments and to govern alone. During the 1969-1972 election period and again during the 1976-1980 interval the CDU/CSU and SPD together won parliamentary majorities in eight of the ten state parliaments, and between 1966 and 1990 a single party elected a majority of representatives in 40 of the 65 regional contests (23 CDU/CSU and 17 SPD) held over the 24 year period. In Bavaria the CSU governed alone during the entire 1966-1990 period, while in Baden-Württemberg the CDU governed alone for twenty of those years, in both Rhineland-Palatinate and Schleswig-Holstein for sixteen years and in Lower Saxony for eight years. The SPD, on the other hand, formed one-party ministries in Bremen for nineteen of the 24 years, in North Rhine-Westphalia for ten years and in Berlin and Hamburg for eight years each. Where there was no majority party, the FDP demonstrated an almost equal willingness to side with the CDU or SPD. It cooperated with the SPD in Berlin from 1975 to 1981, in Bremen from 1967 to 1971, in Hamburg from 1974 to 1978 and again from 1987 to 1991, in Hesse from 1970 to 1982, in Lower Saxony from 1974 to 1976 and in North Rhine-Westphalia from 1966 to 1980. It partnered with the CDU in Hesse from 1987 to 1991, in Lower Saxony from 1977 to 1978 and again from 1986 to 1990, in Rhineland-Palatinate from 1967 to 1971 and again from 1987 to 1991, in the Saar from 1965 to 1970 and again from 1977 to 1985 and in Schleswig-Holstein from 1967 to 1971 and from 1987 to 1988. Contributing to the governing environment between 1966 and 1990 was the failure of the NPD to gain regional representation after 1968, the inability of the FDP to qualify for representation in fifteen of the 65 elections held during the 24 year period (producing a two-party system in six of the states for one or more legislative periods) and the unacceptability of the various Green factions as coalition partners in most of the states between 1979 and 1990.

Beginning with their initial success in the Bremen election of 1979 various "Green" groupings gained representation in the parliaments of Baden-Württemberg in 1980, in Lower Saxony, Hesse, and Hamburg in 1982 and Bavaria in 1986, and during this interval replaced the FDP as the third party in total votes on the regional level. In spite of its early successes, it was prevented by its seemingly radical program from being an acceptable coalition partner of the major parties. In 1982, for example, the negotiations on a possible combination between the SPD and Greens in Hamburg broke down because of irreconcilable differences (Interview with former Lord Mayor of Hamburg Klaus von Dohnanyi, *Die Welt am Sonntag*, April 21, 2008). However, in December 1985 they were brought into a Socialist-led ministry in Hesse, resolving a difficult

TABLE 10.2

COMPOSITION OF *LAND* AND NATIONAL GOVERNMENTS, DECEMBER 1989

Baden-Württemberg	CDU	5 [a]	North Rhine-Westphalia	SPD	5
Bavaria	CSU	5	Rhineland-Palatinate	CDU/FDP	4
Bremen	SPD	3	The Saar	SPD	3
Hamburg	SPD/FDP	3	Schleswig-Holstein	SPD	4
Hesse	CDU/FDP	4	West Berlin	SPD/Greens	
Lower Saxony	CDU/FDP	5	Federal Government	CDU/FDP	

a Number of votes in the *Bundesrat* by state. Of the 41 votes available, 23 could be cast by the Christian parties, 18 by the Social Democrats. Prior to reunification West Berlin could not cast a vote in the *Bundesrat*.

situation in which the SPD had governed alone for twelve months with less than a majority of seats in the parliament. The cooperation lasted only until April 5, 1987, when the CDU replaced the SPD as the *Land*'s leading party and formed a coalition with the FDP. The only other occasion during the 1980s that a Green affiliate was able to participate in a government coalition was in West Berlin with the SPD from January 29, 1989 to December 2, 1990 when the Socialist-Green ministry was replaced by a grand coalition of the CDU and SPD following the first election since 1946 encompassing the entire city. The stunning setback for the Green groupings in the 1990 *Bundestag* election set in motion a series of changes in the party program which eventually enabled it to participate in nine state ministries with the SPD during the 1990s, to partner with the SPD in two consecutive national administrations between 1998 and 2005 and to coalesce with the CDU in Hamburg in 2008 and in the Saar in 2009.[80]

It should be mentioned here that the party of the Danish minority in Schleswig-Holstein, the SSW, was the only minor political grouping other than the FDP to obtain representation in any of the state legislative bodies between 1969 and 1979. Its representation of only one or two members resulted from its exemption from the five percent clause which applied to all other parties and its role in the Schleswig-Holstein parliament was strictly limited.

At the end of 1989, prior to reunification, the SPD governed alone in four states (Bremen, North Rhine-Westphalia, the Saar and Schleswig-Holstein), with the FDP in Hamburg and with the Greens in West Berlin. The CDU/CSU formed one-party ministries in Baden-Württemberg and Bavaria and partnered with the FDP in Hesse, Lower Saxony and Rhineland-Palatinate. The Christian parties, which controlled 23 of the *Bundesrat's* 41 votes, also formed the national government with the FDP in Bonn.

State and National Ministries Since Reunification

The addition of five new states and the eastern part of Berlin to the Federal Republic in 1990 ushered in a new era in German politics. Not only were there the problems of absorbing a vast new area, which had been under totalitarian rule for 57 years, into a democratic order, but reunification brought a new player into the political arena, the Party of Democratic Socialism (PDS), successor to the former Communist SED. The eastern states also proved to be more receptive to the appeal of extremist parties, as both the DVU and NPD have won seats in eastern legislatures since reunification. Moreover, the success of the "Greens" groupings in overtaking the Free Democrats in voter favor on the regional level likewise introduced an added new calculation in coalition building. The Socialists, in the absence of a majority, no longer had to rely entirely on the Free Democrats to provide a working majority.

But the addition of two new significant players to the political arena also cut into the share of the vote which the two major *Volks* parties and the FDP had taken for granted for nearly two decades. Whereas the combined vote of the CDU/CSU and SPD consistently amounted to over 90 percent of ballots cast in the regional elections held between 1969 and 1980 (90.6 percent between 1969 and 1972, 91.3 percent between 1972 and 1976, and 90.2 percent between 1976 and 1980) and the vote of the three originally authorized parties never fell below ninety percent from 1961 to 1990, the two major parties were able to poll only 64.2 percent of ballots cast in the fifteen elections held between 2005 and 2009 and 56.8 percent in the 2009 *Bundestag* election. The three-party vote dropped from a high of 98.2 percent in the 1972-1976 period to 73.1 percent in the 2005-2009 series of *Land* elections, representing a 25.1 percentage decline in support. Moreover, whereas a single party was able to win a majority of seats in forty of 65 regional contests held between 1966 and 1990 (61.5 percent), in the 74 state elections held between 1990 and 2009 absolute majorities were obtained in only 22 of them (29.7 percent). This greatly increased the number of coalitions that needed to be formed in order to establish a working parliamentary majority. Moreover, whereas there were no three-party coalitions between 1963 and 1990, four such combinations have been formed since 1990, in Brandenburg between the SPD, FDP and Alliance 90/Greens from 1990 to 1994, in Bremen between the SPD, FDP and Greens from 1991 to 1995, in Hamburg between the CDU, FDP and Schill Party from 2001 to 2004 and between the CDU, FDP and Greens in the Saar since 2009. In addition, an alliance between the SPD and Greens was able to govern Berlin from June and December 2001 because of the tolerance of the PDS. All other ministries, in the absence of a majority, were two-party groupings between the CDU or SPD and either the FDP, Greens or PDS serving as coalition partner, with the exception of the SPD/STATT Party combination in Hamburg from 1993 to 1997. Not that Germany has returned to the political fragmentation of the early 1950s, but the fact that over a third of German voters no longer support the two major parties is a development of considerable significance complicating coalition building. Compounding the situation has been the unwillingness of the CDU to consider the PDS as a potential coalition partner or the Greens until 2008 in Hamburg and 2009 in the Saar.

Although the PDS had only nominal success in the first *Bundestag* election held in a reunited Germany and in the sixteen provincial elections which followed, by the time of the 2002-2005 regional contests it had more than doubled its eastern following from 11.1 percent in the 1990-1994 period to 23.1 percent in the elections held between 2002 and 2005 to replace the SPD as the second party in the new states and even outpoll the CDU in Brandenburg. In the most recent series of regional elections (2006-2009) the SPD has again become the second party in the eastern provinces with 23.2 percent of the vote to the Leftists' 21.1 percent. PDS success, coupled with the difficulty of the Free Democrats and Greens to build a consistent following in the east, made coalition building in that part of the country more formidable. In the absence of a parliamentary majority and without the FDP and Greens as potential coalition partners, the two major parties in several of the eastern states have been forced into a series of grand coalitions -- in Berlin between 1990 and 2001, in Mecklenburg-Vorpommern from 1994 to 1998 and since 2006, in Thuringia from 1994 to 1999 and since 2009, in Brandenburg from 1999 to 2009, in Saxony from 2004 to 2009, and in Saxony-Anhalt since 2006. At first, neither the CDU nor the SPD wished to ally itself with the PDS because of its Communist roots. However, in 1998 it was brought into a ministry for the first time with the SPD in Mecklenberg-Vorpommern, an alliance which lasted eight years, when it was replaced in 2006 by a grand coalition between the SPD and CDU. A continuation of the red/red coalition in Mecklenburg-Vorpommern was problematical in any case as an SPD/PDS combination would have provided only a slim 36 to 35 seat majority in the *Land* parliament. In June 2001 the PDS helped the Socialists bring down the scandal-ridden Christian Democrat-led government in Berlin and, following the October election, formed a government with the Socialists, a combination which was renewed following the 2006 *Land* election in spite of strong overtures by the national SPD to form a grand coalition with the Christian Democrats. Between 2007 and 2009 *Die Linke*, a combination of the PDS and WASG, gained seats in six western state parliaments. In one of those states, Hesse, it was willing to tolerate an SPD/Greens ministry, but the arrangement came to naught when four Socialist delegates failed to support it (*Die Welt*, November 9, 2008). Since July 2010 it has tolerated a Socialist/Greens minority ministry in North Rhine-Westphalia.

Although the "Greens" surged past the FDP in voter favor during the 1980s, they participated in the governments of only two states during that decade, in Hesse from 1985 to 1987 and in West Berlin from 1989 to 1990. Since 1990, however, they have cooperated with the Socialists in eleven states. In 1990 they enabled future Chancellor Gerhard Schröder to form a government in Lower Saxony to replace a CDU/FDP ministry under Dr. Ernst Albrecht. The alliance was dissolved in 1994 when the SPD won an absolute majority of seats in the state *Landtag*. Also in 1990 an eastern affiliate of the Greens, along with the

FDP, sided with the SPD in Brandenburg as the only possible combination out-side of a grand coalition between the SPD and CDU. In 1991, in an election in which the right-extremist German People's Party (DVU) obtained six seats, they combined with the Socialists and Free Democrats to provide a firm working majority in Bremen until the end of the legislative session in 1995. In Hesse in 1991, in an election in which both SPD and CDU won 46 *Landtag* seats, they partnered with the Socialists and in 1995 again made possible a Socialist-led ministry even as the Christian Democrats replaced the SPD as the state's leading party. In North Rhine-Westphalia they kept the SPD in power for ten additional years (1995-2005) after the Socialists lost their majority status. In Schleswig-Holstein they allied themselves with the SPD after both the 1996 and 2000 *Land* elections. In Saxony-Anhalt they supported a minority government under SPD leadership from 1994 to 1998, with the tolerance of the PDS. In Hamburg they cooperated with the Socialists in the SPD-led government between 1997 and 2001 and collaborated with the Socialists and PDS in bringing down the CDU-led ministry in Berlin in June 2001. These cooperative arrangements on the re-gional level helped to facilitate the establishment of the Socialist/Greens combination which governed Germany from 1998 to 2005. Following a two-year absence from any ministry, the Greens were brought into an alliance with the SPD in Bremen in 2007; in 2008 they entered into the first *Land*-level part-nership with the CDU in Hamburg and with the CDU and FDP after the 2009 *Land* election in the Saar. In 2010 they collaborated with the Socialists in a mi-nority ministry in North Rhine-Westphalia, in 2011 in a Socialist-led government in Rhineland-Palatinate and a Greens-led alliance in Baden Würt-temberg.

In spite of being a partner in the national administration from 1998 to 2005, the negative reaction to the reform initiatives of the Schröder government did not undermine support for the Greens as it did for the SPD. The Greens not only outpolled the FDP 6.9 to 5.6 percent in regional competition between 2002 and 2005, but improved on their 1998-2002 *Land* election following, due in no small measure to the popularity of their then leader, Joschka Fischer, who served as Germany's foreign minister. Nevertheless, by virtue of the declining fortunes of the SPD after the 2002 *Bundestag* election, by May 2005 they were no longer a participant in any of the *Land* ministries, and, following the setback of the SPD in the general election later in the year, they no longer participated in the nation-al government. This complete absence from direct participation in either regional or national governments was corrected in May 2007 in Bremen when they were brought into an alliance with the SPD (*Die Welt*, May 24, 2007), fol-lowed by a partnership with the CDU in Hamburg (*Die Welt*, April 28, 2008), in 2009 with the CDU and FDP in the Saar, in 2010 with the Socialists in North Rhine-Westphalia and in 2011 with the Socialists in Rhineland-Palatinate and Baden-Württemberg.

Even though the SPD allied itself most commonly with the Greens and in three states with the PDS after 1990, it also found the FDP an acceptable and willing coalition partner, and the two formed a common ministry in Rhineland-

Palatinate between 1991 and 2006, and from 1991 to 1995 the FDP participated in the three-party coalition with the SPD and Greens in Bremen. For the CDU/CSU, with two exceptions, the Free Democrats were its exclusive coalition partner in the absence of an absolute majority or a grand coalition. Not only did the two parties serve together on the national level for sixteen years (1982 to 1998), but they formed a common government in Mecklenburg-Vorpommern, Saxony-Anhalt and Thuringia between 1990 and 1994, in North Rhine-Westphalia from 2005 to 2010, in Baden-Württemberg from 1996 to 2011, in Hesse from 1999 to 2003 and again since January 2009, in Saxony-Anhalt from 2002 to 2006, and have been in coalition in Lower Saxony since 2003, Bavaria since 2008 and Schleswig-Holstein since the September 2009 state balloting. It was not until 2008 in Hamburg and 2009 in the Saar that the CDU partnered with the Greens.

Grand coalitions between the CDU/CSU and SPD which flourished in the early postwar period were no longer present in any of the states between 1972, when the working arrangement between the two major parties in Baden-Württemberg came to an end, and 1990. Since reunification, they have become a more common phenomenon, not only on the regional level, but also nationally between 2005 and 2009. The success of the PDS in the new provinces and the difficulties faced by the FDP and Greens in building up reliable eastern follow-ings, coupled with the initial reluctance of either of the two major parties to partner with the successor of the former Communist SED, made alliances be-tween the CDU and SPD, in the absence of a parliamentary majority, the only alternative in building workable majorities. As a result, grand coalitions have been formed in all five of the new states and Berlin at one time or another since 1990 and have appeared in three western states. The CDU and SPD formed a common administration in Berlin from 1990 to 2001 to assist in the reunification of the city, and grand coalitions were established in Baden-Württemberg from 1992 to 1996 because a CDU/FDP combination could not provide a workable majority, and in Mecklenburg-Vorpommern from 1994 to 1998 and since 2006, Thuringia from 1994 to 1999 and since 2009, Brandenburg from 1999 to 2009 because neither the CDU nor the SPD at the time wanted to form a common government with the PDS, and Saxony-Anhalt since 2006. A grand coalition was instituted in Bremen in 1995 since that was the choice of then Lord Mayor Henning Scherf (1995-2005). This alliance lasted until the 2007 election when the Socialists coalesced with the Greens. In Schleswig-Holstein the February 20, 2005 *Land* election gave neither a CDU/FDP nor an SPD/Greens combination a majority, since the party of the Danish minority, with two seats, held the balance between the two possible alliances. Socialist Minister-President Heide Simonis attempted a minority government for two months prior to resigning in favor of a grand coalition under Peter Harry Carstensen (CDU) in April 2005. The combi-nation lasted until after the 2009 state election when it was replaced by a CDU/FDP arrangement. At the beginning of 2011, grand coalitions existed in three states, Mecklenburg-Vorpommern (since October 2006), Saxony-Anhalt (since March 2006) and Thuringia (since October 2009). The SPD/CDU part-

TABLE 10.3

COMPOSITION OF *LAND* AND NATIONAL GOVERNMENTS, JUNE 2011

Baden-Württemberg	Greens/SPD [a]	Mecklenburg-Vorpommern	SPD/CDU
Winfried Kretschmann (Greens)		Erwin Sellering (SPD)	
Bavaria	CSU/FDP	North Rhine-Westphalia	SPD/Greens [b]
Horst Seehofer (CSU)		Hannelore Kraft (SPD)	
Berlin	SPD/*Die Linke*	Rhineland-Palatinate	SPD/Greens [c]
Klaus Wowereit (SPD)		Kurt Beck (SPD)	
Brandenburg	SPD/*Die Linke*	The Saar	CDU/FDP/Greens
Matthias Platzeck (SPD)		Peter Müller (CDU)	
Bremen	SPD/Greens	Saxony	CDU/FDP
Jens Böhrnsen (SPD)		Stanislaw Tillich (CDU)	
Hamburg	SPD [d]	Saxony-Anhalt	CDU/SPD [e]
Olaf Schulz (SPD)		Dr. Reiner Haseloff (CDU)	
Hesse	CDU/FDP [f]	Schleswig-Holstein	CDU/FDP
Volker Bouffier (CDU)		Peter Harry Carstensen (CDU)	
Lower Saxony	CDU/FDP [g]	Thuringia	CDU/SPD
David McAllister (CDU)		Christine Lieberknecht (CDU)	
Federal Government	CDU/FDP		
Chancellor Angela Merkel (CDU)			

a A Greens/SPD ministry under Winfried Kretschmann (Greens) replaced the CDU/FDP coalition under Stefan Mappus (CDU) following the March 27, 2011 *Land* election.

b Hannelore Kraft (SPD) headed a minority government in North Rhine-Westphalia following the breakup of the CDU/FDP coalition under Jürgen Rüttgers (CDU) after the May 9, 2010 state election. The SPD/Greens combination held ninety of the 181 parliamentary seats, with the eleven-member Leftist delegation tolerating the minority ministry.

c A Socialist/Greens ministry was formed following the SPD's loss of its parliamentary majority in the March 27, 2011 *Landtag* election. Socialist Kurt Beck remained as Minister-President.

d Christoph Ahlhaus (CDU) succeeded Ole von Beust as Lord Mayor of Hamburg upon von Beust's retirement in August 2010. On November 28, 2010 the Greens withdrew from the existing Black/Green coalition, causing Ahlhaus to lead a minority government until the February 20, 2011 election, in which the Social Democrats won an absolute majority of seats, placing the reins of government in the hands of Olaf Scholz (SPD).

e Dr. Reiner Haseloff (CDU) replaced the retiring Prof. Dr. Wolfgang Böhmer (CDU as Minister-President following the March 20, 2011 *Land* election. The CDU/SPD alliance was resumed.

f Volker Bouffier (CDU) was selected to replace Roland Koch (CDU) upon Koch's retirement in August 2010. The CDU/FDP coalition was continued.

g David McAllister (CDU) replaced Christian Wulff when Wulff was elected Federal President in June 2010.

nership in Bremen broke up following the 2007 *Bürgerschaft* election and the CDU/SPD alliances in Brandenburg and in Schleswig-Holstein collapsed following the 2009 polls.

Several parties other than the CDU/CSU, SPD, FDP, Greens and PDS/*Die Linke* gained legislative representation during the 1990-2010 period, but only two of them, both in Hamburg, the STATT Party from 1993 to 1997 with the SPD and the Schill Party from 2001 to 2004 with the CDU and FDP, participated in a *Land* government. These two protest parties have since faded into oblivion, but, at the time of their ascendancy had siphoned off important support from the established parties, primarily from the Christian Democrats, and their participation, with the Socialists (the STATT Party) and the CDU (the Schill Party), helped to provide a working majority. Both attempted to develop a following outside of Hamburg without success. Several extremist parties, which were organized in a number of the states, among them the DVU, NPD and Republicans, succeeded in gaining parliamentary representation in several of the *Landtage* by drawing off support from the established parties, but none of them was brought into a state ministry.

Coalition Patterns in the *Länder*

While several of the German states, notably Baden-Württemberg, Bavaria, Bremen and Saxony, have been dominated by a single party over an extended period, the majority have witnessed one or more changes in party rule. *Länder* which were once strongholds of one of the two major political factions, as Berlin, Hamburg, Hesse, and Lower Saxony were for the SPD and Rhineland-Palatinate, the Saar and Schleswig-Holstein for the CDU, have experienced an alternation in power much as has been the case between the two major parties on the national level since 1969, following control by a single party bloc for the first seventeen years of the Federal Republic's existence and a three-year interval of joint rule. Hamburg, a bulwark of Socialist strength for over fifty years, for example, gave a resounding victory (in the form of an absolute majority) to popular CDU Lord Mayor Ole von Beust in the 2004 *Bürgerschaft* election and retained him in power in the 2008 balloting. The SPD regained its earlier dominant position in February 2011 when it won a majority of *Bürgerschaft* seats. In Rhineland-Palatinate the Socialists gained the upper-hand in 1991, following 44 years of Christian Democratic leadership.

Generally speaking, the governments of the German states and the federation have exhibited considerable stability, even when coalitions have been required. This is due in part to the rather strong record of cooperation and constructive compromise between the parties.[81] In every *state* with the single exception of Hamburg the CDU/CSU and SPD have cooperated on one or more occasions in common governments since 1946/1947, although the collaborations in Bavaria, Hesse, Rhineland-Palatinate and North Rhine-Westphalia were limited to the immediate postwar period and in Schleswig-Holstein only between

2005 and 2009.[82] Moreover, the Free Democrats have participated in the governments of all of the old states at one time or another, in all but one with the CDU and in all but three with the SPD. (The FDP has played a lesser role in coalition building in the new states because of its failure to qualify for representation in over half of the regional elections held there). The Refugee Party, during its short life as a political group (1950-1966), participated in ministries as often with the SPD as with the CDU. Other than the parties of the extreme right, such as the SRP, DRP DVU, NPD and Republicans, and the Communist Party after 1948, with several exceptions, every party was a potential partner in the cabinets of the two major parties, including even renegade groupings such as the STATT Party and the Schill Party in Hamburg. However, the Greens, while serving in cabinets with the Socialists in eleven states, did not participate in a CDU/CSU-led ministry until 2008 in Hamburg. The PDS/*Die Linke* has been a partner of the SPD in three states, but never with the CDU/CSU. In spite of the entry of the Greens and PDS/*Die Linke* into the political arena the current political situation in Germany no longer permits the wide variety of coalition possibilities that existed during the 1950s nor the same type of political maneuvering which characterized that decade. Still, what has come to be a party system with five players allows for considerable variety in the forming of political alliances in the absence of a parliamentary majority by one of the two major parties.

In Bremen, a single party, the SPD, has provided leadership continuously over a span of over sixty years; in Bavaria the CSU has governed continuously since 1957, alone without a coalition partner for 44 years; and the CDU led Baden-Württemberg continuously from 1953 to 2011 when a coalition of the Greens and Socialists came to power. Other than Dr. Reinhold Maier (DVP/FDP) in Württemberg-Baden (1946-1952) and Baden-Württemberg (1952-1953), Heinrich Hellwege (DP) in Lower Saxony (1955-1959) and Winfried Kretschmann (since 2011) the parliamentary heads of government in the various *Länder* have been either Christian Democrats/Christian Social Democrats or Social Democrats.[83]

Of the original federal states, only Bremen has been led by a single party, the SPD, since the first elections in 1946. Bremen and Rhineland-Palatinate have the distinction of having had the fewest number of executive heads, only six since 1946 for Bremen, six since 1947 for Rhineland-Palatinate. Since reunification, a single party has provided the executive leadership in Brandenburg (SPD), Saxony (CDU) and Thuringia (CDU), but for far shorter periods of time. In all other states there has been at least one change in party leadership, and as often as six times in highly contested Lower Saxony.

Coalition Patterns in the Western States

Baden-Württemberg: Baden-Württemberg, formed in 1952 out of the former provinces of Baden, Württemberg-Baden, and Württemberg-

Hohenzollern was controlled by the CDU without a break between 1953 and 2011 when an alliance of the Greens and the Socialists formed the government. It has had only nine executive heads since its inception. The first exception to Christian Democratic rule came following the initial establishment of the state when Free Democrat Dr. Reinhold Maier, former Minister-President of the old Württemberg-Baden from 1946 to 1952, continued in his position in the new state for one year. Leo Wohleb (CDU) had been the first President of Baden from 1947 to 1952 and Dr. Lorenz Bock (CDU) the first leader of Württemberg-Hohenzollern from 1947 to 1948. Upon Bock's death in office he was succeeded by Dr. Gebhard Müller (CDU) who continued as Minister President until 1952 when the state was amalgamated into the new state of Baden-Württemberg.[84] The first Baden-Württemberg government was a coalition of the FDP, SPD and Refugee Party under Dr. Reinhold Maier. Christian Democrat Gerhard Müller took over the reigns of government from Dr. Maier following the CDU's historic success in the 1953 *Bundestag* election, and served in an alliance with the SPD, FDP/DVP and Refugee Party until 1958 when he was succeeded by Dr. Kurt Georg Kiesinger. The SPD and Refugee Party were dropped from the coalition in 1960 and Kiesinger continued to serve in combination with the FDP/DVP until December 1966 when he was selected to replace Ludwig Erhard as federal Chancellor. His replacement, Dr. Hans Filbinger, fearful of losing his position to an SPD-FDP combination, formed a grand coalition with the Socialists, an alliance which continued until 1972 when his party won an absolute majority of seats in the Southwest State parliament. By winning absolute majorities in five successive *Land* elections the CDU was able to govern alone between 1972 and 1992, under Filbinger until 1978 and under Lothar Späth until 1991, when Erwin Teufel became Minister President. Teufel led a one-party ministry until 1992 when the CDU lost its majority in the state parliament, forcing it to form a grand coalition with the SPD since a CDU/FDP combination could not provide a workable majority and an alliance with the Greens or the right-extremist Republicans, which won fifteen seats, was unacceptable. A partnership with the Free Democrats was resumed after the 1996 election when both the CDU and the FDP improved their combined representation from 72 to 83 seats. The CDU/FDP alliance continued until March 2011 when it was replaced by a Greens/SPD partnership. Erwin Teufel retired as Minister-President in 2005 in favor of a younger successor, Günther Oettinger. Premier Oettinger in turn was succeeded in February 2010 by Stefan Mappus when he became a European Community (EU) Commissioner. Winfried Kretschmann (Greens) became Minister-President in March 2011.

Bavaria: Other than Bremen, in no *Land* has domination by a single party been more complete than in Bavaria, where the Christian Social Union, the CDU's sister party, has emerged as the leading party in fifteen of the sixteen regional ballotings concluded since the first elections in 1946, eleven by absolute majorities. The only exception came in 1950 when much of the CSU's strength was siphoned off by the entrance of the particularistic Bavarian Party into the political arena to give a slight edge to the Socialists. And only between

1954 and 1957 did a party other than the CSU provide the Minister President, Socialist Wilhelm Hoegner, when the CSU became a victim of the SPD's efforts to thwart the coordination actions of Federal Chancellor Konrad Adenauer.[85] Since 1957 there has been an unbroken succession of CSU minister presidents, a span of over fifty years, and the CSU's record of gaining an absolute majority of parliamentary seats in eleven of the elections held since 1962, is unmatched in the Federal Republic. As a result of the stability provided by the CSU, Bavaria has been governed by only eight premiers since 1946.[86]

The state's first responsible Minister President, Hans Ehard, served from 1946 to 1954 and again from 1960 to 1962. From December 1946 to September 1947 he led a coalition with the SPD and WAV, and from September 1947 to November 1950 governed alone, only the second one-party government to be formed prior to the formation of the Federal Republic in 1949, the CSU having won an absolute majority of seats in the December 1946 *Land* election. In 1950 the CSU lost its majority, forcing Ehard to negotiate a coalition with the SPD and Refugee Party, a difficult alliance made necessary by the ability of the Bavarian Party to gain 17.9 percent of the vote which otherwise would have gone to the CSU. In 1954 the Ehard government was replaced by a four-party coalition of the SPD, Bavarian Party, FDP and Refugee Party under Socialist Wilhelm Hoegner, an alliance formed to counteract Adenauer's coordination efforts. The alliance broke up following the 1957 *Bundestag* election and a CSU/FDP/Refugee Party ministry was constructed under Christian Socialist Hanns Seidel, who served as minister president until 1960 when the state's first premier, Hans Ehard, returned to the helm for two years. This began a succession of CSU-led governments which has continued over fifty years. In the 1962 *Land* election the CSU won the first of eleven consecutive polls in which it gained an absolute majority of seats in the Bavarian parliament. In that year Dr. Alfons Goppel became minister president, a position he was to hold for the next sixteen years. Although the CSU held a majority of seats in the state parliament in 1962 and could have ruled alone, Goppel brought the Bavarian Party into his cabinet, a participation which the BP terminated in June 1966 in anticipation of the state election later in the year. Between 1966 and the fall of 2008, when it lost its majority status, the CSU governed alone, under Dr. Goppel until 1978, Franz Joseph Strauss from 1978 to 1988, Max Streibl from 1988 to 1993, Edmund Stoiber from 1993 to 2007, Günther Beckstein from 2007 to 2008 and Horst Seehofer since the fall of 2008 in an alliance with the Free Democrats. The CSU became engrossed in a leadership crisis following the 2005 *Bundestag* election when Chancellor Angela Merkel offered Edmund Stoiber the economics ministry in Berlin. Realizing that his influence on Bavarian politics would be severely diminished if he accepted a position in the federal capital, Stoiber decided to remain in Munich. This and questions concerning his leadership style eventually forced him out of office in 2007. His heir apparent, Horst Seehofer, was passed over because of an embarrassing extramarital relationship and Finance Minister Günther Beckstein became the compromise candidate for the premiership. Beckstein's tenure in office, however, lasted only one year when the party's leadership struggle, large investment losses by the Bavarian state bank and questions of party reform caused the CSU to suffer a 17.3 percentage setback over 2003 election totals, forcing Beckstein to resign. Having lost its majority status and seeking new leadership to revive the party's fortunes, the CSU reverted to Seehofer who formed a government with the Free Democrats (*Die Welt*, December 4, 2008).

Bremen: Wilhelm Kaisen served as Lord Mayor of Bremen from 1946 to 1965, with the Communist Party and the Bremen affiliate of the Liberals from October 1946 to January 1948, when the Communists were dropped, and then to 1951 with the Liberals alone. His government from 1951 to 1959 included the CDU and FDP and from 1959 to 1965 the FDP alone, even though his party, with absolute majorities in 1955, 1959 and 1963, required no coalition partner.[87] He was followed by Willy Dehnkamp who, however, served for only two years. Hans Koschnick became Lord Mayor in 1967 and served until 1985, in partnership with the FDP until 1971 and then alone until the end of his mayoralty, a tenure in office which nearly equaled that of Wilhelm Kaisen. Klaus Wedemeier succeeded him, governing alone from 1985 until 1991 when the SPD lost its majority and then with the FDP and Greens until 1995, when Dr. Henning Scherf became Lord Mayor and formed a partnership with the CDU, an alliance which continued until his retirement. He was succeeded in November 2005 by Jens Böhrnsen, who continued the grand coalition with the CDU until after the May 2007 *Land* election, when he entered into a partnership with the Greens (*Der Spiegel*, June 16, 2007). The alliance with the Greens under Böhrnsen was resumed following the May 2011 *Bürgerschaft* election.

Hamburg: The city-state of Hamburg has been governed by a Social Democrat mayor since the February 20, 2011 *Bürgerschaft* election, following over nine years of Christian Democratic rule. Between 1946 and 2001 the Socialists outpolled the CDU in fifteen of seventeen elections, winning nine by absolute majorities, and led the city continuously during that 55 year time span with the exception of the 1953-1957 legislative term when an alliance of the CDU, FDP, German and Refugee parties, known as the Hamburg Block, was able to gain a majority of seats and place Christian Democrat Dr. Kurt Sieveking in the mayor's office. Since 1946 Hamburg has been served by twelve different leaders.

Socialist Max Brauer, mayor of Altona from 1924 to 1933 before fleeing the Nazi regime and who had been in exile in China, France and the United States before returning to Hamburg after the war, became Hamburg's first elected mayor, serving from 1946 to 1953, a period of significant reconstruction for a city which had suffered 213 air attacks during the war (*Hamburger Abendblatt*, September 23, 1997). In spite of a majority in the city council, Brauer brought the FDP and the Communists into his first government. In October 1948 the KPD was dropped from his cabinet, but the partnership with the FDP was continued until the October 1949 election when he formed a one-party government. In spite of his great popularity, Brauer was voted out of office in 1953 by the *Hamburg Block* which enabled Dr. Kurt Sieveking to serve as mayor for four years. Then, from 1957 to 2001, a period encompassing 44 years, the city was governed continuously be a Socialist mayor.

Max Brauer was returned to office after the 1957 election, in which the SPD won an absolute majority of seats in the city parliament, and continued as Lord Mayor until he took a seat in the federal *Bundestag* in December 1960. He was followed by Dr. Paul Nevermann who served as mayor until June 1965 when he was forced to resign over the embarrassment caused by marital difficulties which prevented him from hosting a visit by Queen Elizabeth of England to the city. Professor Dr. Herbert Weichmann, who, like Brauer, had been in exile during the Nazi period because of his Jewish background, replaced him and served as Lord Mayor from 1965 to 1971, to be followed by Peter Schulz from 1971 to 1974. Although the Socialists held an absolute majority of seats in the city parliament between 1957 and 1974, its Senate included FDP senators from 1957 to 1965 and again from 1970 to 1974. As a consequence, when the Socialists lost their absolute majority in the 1974 city election they could count on the Free Democrats to side with them until an absolute majority was again gained in the 1978 election. Hans-Ulrich Klose succeeded Peter Schulz in 1974 and continued in office until 1981 when he became embroiled in the protests against the building of a nuclear power plant on the lower Elbe River ("*Wie Brokdorf zum Symbol wurde*," *Die Welt am Sonntag*, October 22, 2006) and was forced to resign. He was replaced by Klaus von Dohnanyi, son of Hans von Dohnanyi who was executed by the Nazis for his involvement in the plot against Hitler, who served as Lord Mayor until 1988. A year after von Dohnanyi became mayor, the SPD lost its majority, and with the failure of the FDP to gain representation and the inability of either the Socialists or the Christian Democrats to come to terms with the Greens' agenda, von Dohnanyi had no alternative but to continue governing in minority status until new elections could be held six months later. The new election in December 1982 provided him with the majority he had been seeking, enabling him to govern alone until November 1986 when the SPD again lost its majority status, forcing Dohnanyi to form a minority ministry for a second time. After six months in minority status, a new election in May 1987 returned the Free Democrats to the *Bürgerschaft*, enabling the SPD, in coalition with the FDP, to place the government on a more stable basis. In 1988 von Dohnanyi retired in favor of Henning Voscherau who continued the alliance with the Free Democrats until the 1991 election when his party won a majority of *Bürgerschaft* seats. The election, however, was invalidated by the Hamburg Constitutional Court in May 1993 because of improprieties in the CDU nomination process, and new elections were held the following September (*Hamburgische Justizverwaltungsblatt*, 1992-1993 *Jahrgang*, 56-78). In that election, the grouping which had brought the suit before the Constitutional Court, running under the designation STATT Party, won eight seats, denying the SPD its majority. However, an alliance between the STATT Party leadership and the SPD was negotiated, enabling the Socialists to remain in power for another four years under Voscherau. After the SPD experienced its worst showing since 1946 in the 1997 *Bürgerschaft* contest (*Frankfurter Allgemeine Zeitung*,

September 22, 1997), Vorscherau stepped down in favor of Finance Senator Ortwin Runde, who continued SPD rule until 2001 by forming a coalition with the once unacceptable Greens. Prior to the elevation of Ole von Beust as lead candidate for the Hamburg Christian Democrats, the CDU had been hurt by a lack of effective leadership, its failure to hinder the fraying of its right-wing and the absence of a coalition partner over a number of legislative sessions (the FDP having failed to qualify for representation between 1978 and 1987 and again between 1993 and 2001). For the 2001 election campaign a new grouping, running on a law and order platform, was formed by a former district judge, Ronald Schill, and won 19.4 percent of the vote. Although the Socialists outpolled the Christian Democrats by over ten percentage points, the Schill grouping, made up primarily of former CDU supporters, sided, along with the FDP, with the Christian Democrats, putting Ole von Beust into the mayorship. In locking out the leading Socialists, all three parties were necessary to form a workable majority. Von Beust became only the second Christian Democrat to serve as Lord Mayor in the 55 years since the first postwar elections were held in Hamburg. Difficulties between Schill and von Beust led to the calling of new elections in February 2004, nineteen months before the end of the legislative period. Although the CDU had outpolled the Socialists by small margins in two previous elections, 1982 and 1986, the 2004 election gave the CDU, running on the popularity of von Beust, an absolute majority of seats in the city parliament for the first time. Von Beust was then able to establish a one-party Senate to guide the city. However, the CDU lost its majority in the 2008 city election, necessitating the formation of an alliance with the Greens after extended negotiations. The combination marked the first time that the Christian Democrats had coalesced with the Greens on the *Land* level. Ole von Beust remained as Lord Mayor under this new arrangement, but following a setback on the school reform referendum on July 18, 2010, he announced his intention to retire August 25 after nearly nine years in office. He was succeeded by Interior Senator Christoph Ahlhaus. The Greens withdrew from its coalition with the CDU November 28, 2010, necessitating the calling of new elections, scheduled for February 20, 2011. In that election the Social Democrats won an absolute majority of seats in the *Bürgerschaft* and Socialist Olaf Scholz became the new Lord Mayor of the *Hansastadt.*

Hesse: After winning an absolute majority of seats in the Hessian *Landtag* for the first time in the 2003 regional election and governing without a partner for five years, the Hessian CDU, hurt by what seemed to be hostility towards immigrants, only barely outpolled the SPD in the 2008 contest, 36.8 to 36.7 percent. This major setback ushered in a difficult period of party negotiations, since neither a CDU/FDP nor an SPD/Greens combination could provide a working majority because of the six seats won by *Die Linke*. Roland Koch in May 2008 proposed bringing a CDU/FDP/Greens coalition into being against strong objections within his party (*Welt am Sonntag*, May 18, 2008). Failing this, he continued to head a minority government even as the lead SPD candidate, Andrea Ypsilanti, twice attempted to gain support for a ministry with the Greens tolerated by the Leftists. The two attempts failed, leading to the calling of new elections January 18, 2009. Although the CDU only barely exceeded its 2008 election total in that contest, the FDP picked up nine seats to provide Koch with his sought-after majority.

Prior to the 1999 balloting, the outcome of which enabled the Christian Democrats to establish a government with the FDP, Hesse had been dominated by the Social Democratic Party for most of the post World War II period. By winning absolute majorities in four elections and negotiating favorable alliances with a second party, even when outvoted by the CDU on four occasions, the Socialists were able to lead the state during every legislative period with the single exception of the 1987-1991 session, giving the state the early designation "Red Hesse." As a result, Hesse has had only eight premiers over a 64-year period, five Socialists and three Christian Democrats.

Following the first *Land* election in December 1946 the SPD formed a coalition with the CDU under Christian Stock (SPD), who continued as Minister President until December 1950 when he was replaced by Georg August Zinn, who remained in that position for nearly nineteen years. With a majority resulting from the 1950 *Land* election Zinn was able to govern alone during his first three years in office. From 1954 to 1966 the SPD partnered with the Refugee Party, an alliance which continued even after the Socialists won an absolute majority of seats in the 1962 state election. The SPD won an absolute majority of seats again in 1966, but its coalition partner, the Refugee Party, failed to exceed the five percent threshold, ending its life as a viable political grouping, and the SPD governed alone. Albert Osswald replaced Zinn in 1969 and served as minister president until 1976, without a partner for the first year and then in combination with the Free Democrats, after his party lost its *Landtag* majority in the 1970 regional election. He was followed by Holger Börner who served as premier from 1976 to 1987, in coalition with the FDP until 1982 and then alone in a minority ministry for one year when the FDP failed for the first time to gain representation in the 1982 state election. This situation made necessary a new election in September 1983, and, while it produced no majority party, the election enabled the SPD to recover its position as leading faction. Again, Börner led a minority government with the tolerance of the Greens (which had entered the parliament for the first time in 1982), until December 1985 when a formal coalition with the Greens was constructed, marking the first time that a Greens grouping participated in a regional ministry. Troubled by the conflict over the handling of nuclear waste from the Hanau power plant, the SPD lost its leading position in the 1987 *Land* election, enabling the CDU to form a government for the first time in the postwar period, since neither an SPD/FDP nor an SPD/Greens combination could produce a working majority. Christian Democrat Dr. Walter Wallmann, former mayor of Frankfurt, lacking a majority, formed an alliance with the Free Democrats, a combination which lasted until the January 1991 state election in which the Socialists marginally outpolled the CDU, with both being awarded 46 seats. The Greens, with ten seats, were able to provide the Socialists with the majority needed to govern. This SPD/Greens partnership under Minister President Hans Eichel, former mayor of Kassel, who later became federal Finance Minister in the Schröder cabinet, was renewed in 1995, even though the CDU once again became the state's leading party. The SPD/Greens combination in Hesse helped to demonstrate the possibility of collaboration between the two parties on the national level, a possibility which became a reality after the 1998 *Bundestag* contest. Joschka Fischer, head of the Hessian Greens, was rewarded with the post of Foreign Minister in the Schröder cabinet for his cooperation. In 1999 the Christian Democrats broke the Socialist hold on the state after the Socialists had governed for 48 of the 52 years of Hesse's existence. The CDU with 50 seats to the Socialists' 46 formed a coalition with the FDP under Roland Koch. In 2003 the CDU won an absolute majority of seats in the Hessian *Landtag* for the first time, enabling Koch's CDU to form a one-party ministry. That majority was lost in the 2008 *Land* election, forcing Koch to govern in minority status until early January 2009 when new elections made a CDU/FDP ministry possible (*FAZ.NET Wahl in Hessen*, 2009). After eleven years in office, Minister President Koch on May 25, 2010 announced to a shocked nation his intention to retire at the end of August. The Hessian CDU selected interior minister Volker Bouffier to replace him.

Lower Saxony: Once a Socialist preserve, with the SPD emerging as the state's leading party in the first seven regional contests and providing the minister president continuously from 1947 to 1976 with the exception of the 1955-1959 legislative period, Lower Saxony has become a highly competitive *Land*, with the Socialists and Christian Democrats sharing equally in being the largest parliamentary group in the twelve elections held between 1963 and 2008. The state currently has a Christian Democrat premier, David McAllister, who replaced Christian Wulff after Wulff's elevation to the Federal Presidency following his election on June 30, 2010.

Hinrich Wilhelm Kopf (SPD) was the state's first responsible minister president, leading a five-party government of the SPD, CDU, FDP, German Party and Communists between April 20, 1947 and June 9, 1948, and then a smaller coalition of the SPD, CDU and Center Party until September 18, 1950, when the CDU was dropped from the ministry. After the 1951 state election a coalition was formed with the Refugee and Center parties which lasted until December 1953 when the Center Party, with only four representatives, no longer participated. In 1955, although the SPD won the largest number of seats, a four-party bourgeois coalition of the German Party, CDU, Refugee Party and Free Democrats under Minister President Heinrich Hellwege of the German Party, was crafted as part of Adenauer's coordination efforts to interrupt Socialist rule. This bloc collapsed in November 1957 when the FDP and Refugee Party formed a faction combination and the six DRP (German Reich Party) representatives left the party. A new government which included the Socialists, along with the CDU and German Party, was then formed with Hellwege (DP) continuing as premier. The 1959 regional election placed the Socialists back in the leadership in an alliance with the Free Democrats and Refugee Party under Kopf who served as premier until his death in December 1961. The three-party combination continued under Dr. Georg Diederichs until the May 1963 *Land* election when the

Refugee Party failed to qualify for representation. The Socialist/Free Democrat ministry which was formed following the election broke down in May 1965 when the Free Democrats refused to support a concordat with the Catholic Church governing religious education in the state. With the CDU the only other faction in the *Landtag*, a grand coalition was established and the concordat approved. The coalition with the CDU was renegotiated after the 1967 regional election and continued under Diedericks until the 1970 regional election, when the SPD won an absolute majority of parliamentary seats. Numerous faction changes between 1967 and 1970 had made a new election necessary after only three years. The Socialists formed a one-party government under Alfred Kubel, as the only alternative since the CDU was the only other party to qualify for parliamentary seats and a grand coalition would have eliminated all opposition. In 1974 the CDU became the state's leading party for the first time when the Socialists lost their majority in the state parliament, but was prevented from governing until 1976 when the Socialists formed a partnership with the Free Democrats who were able to return to the parliament with eleven seats. Following Kubel's resignation as premier in February 1976 a secret ballot placed Christian Democrat Dr. Ernst Albrecht in the premiership. The CDU, lacking only one seat of providing an absolute majority, formed a minority government with the tolerance of the FDP until January 1977 when an alliance between the CDU and FDP was formalized. This grouping continued until the June 4, 1978 *Land* election when the FDP failed to gain representation and the Christian Democrats won an absolute majority of seats for the first time. Christian Democrat Dr. Ernst Albrecht, who had first become premier in February 1976, was able to govern alone from 1978 to 1986 as the CDU again maintained its majority by an even larger margin in the 1982 regional contest. In 1986 the CDU lost its majority, making necessary a partnership with the FDP until 1990 when the Socialists again emerged as the state's leading party under the leadership of Gerhard Schröder. Schröder formed a ministry with the Greens who had first entered the parliament in 1982 and continued to surmount the five percent barrier to representation. In 1994 the SPD won an absolute majority of parliamentary seats making it possible for Schröder to govern alone. In the 1998 *Land* election the Socialists again won an absolute majority of seats, in an election which propelled Schröder into the party leadership and set the stage for his selection as the SPD's candidate for the federal chancellorship. In the September general election, the SPD emerged as the largest *Bundestag* faction and Schröder became the nation's seventh chief executive. He was replaced in Lower Saxony initially by Gerhard Glogowski (1998-1999) and then by Sigmar Gabriel, who continued in that position from 1999 until the 2003 regional election in which the CDU regained its status as the state's leading party following a 14.5 percentage drop in Socialist support. Lacking one seat of a majority after having won 91 of 100 direct seats, the CDU formed a coalition with the Free Democrats under Christian Wulff (CDU). Although losing nearly six percentage points in the 2008 regional balloting, the CDU remained the state's leading party with 42.5 percent of the vote as the Socialists' total fell to 30.3 percent. Again the CDU turned to the FDP to provide a working majority with Christian Wulff continuing as minister President until June 2010 when he was elevated to the federal presidency. His position was filled by David McAllister (CDU).

North Rhine-Westphalia: North Rhine-Westphalia has been a competitive state since the first *Land* election was held in 1947, with the CDU emerging as the leading party in nine of the fifteen regional contests, the SPD in six of them, and leadership of the state has swung back and forth several times. A Christian Democrat/Free Democrat coalition governed the state until July 2010, when, in the aftermath of a major CDU setback in the May 9th regional election, the Socialists under Hannelore Kraft were able to form a minority ministry with the Greens. Prior to this change in administration, the Social Democratic Party had led the state of the Rhine and Ruhr for thirty-eight-and-a-half years from 1966 to 2005. The state's first minister president under a popularly-elected parliament was Karl Arnold who served from 1947 to 1956, at first in coalition with the SPD, the Center Party and Communists for less than ten months and then in combination with the Socialists until the June 1950 *Land* election. Following that election Arnold led a minority government for three months, but in order to place the government on a firmer basis he formed an alliance with the Center Party. Without a majority in the 1954 regional election the FDP was brought into his cabinet along with a weakened Center Party. This alliance lasted until February 1956 when the Socialists, in the first successful constructive vote of non-confidence in the Federal Republic, brought down the Arnold government, and a ministry of the SPD, the Free Democrats and Center Party under Socialist Fritz Steinhoff was formed, placing the CDU in the opposition. The coalition lasted only two years as the CDU won an absolute majority in the North Rhine-Westphalian *Landtag* in the 1958 regional poll. Because of the sudden death of Karl Arnold during the election campaign, Dr. Franz Meyers became the state's third premier. Meyers formed a one-party ministry until 1962 when the CDU lost its majority and was forced into a partnership with the FDP. In the 1966 state election the SPD became North Rhine-Westphalia's leading party for the first time, but lacked two seats of providing a workable majority, and the CDU took advantage of the situation to form a ministry with the FDP. The combination, still under Meyers, collapsed in December 1966 when the FDP sided with the Socialists to establish a new government under Socialist Heinz Kühn. Kühn was the first of four successive Socialist minister presidents to lead the state between 1966 and 2005, a span of 39 years. Kühn, himself, served as premier until 1978, in coalition with the Free Democrats throughout his tenure in office. He was replaced in 1978 by Dr. Johannes Rau who continued the alliance with the FDP until the 1980 regional poll when the Socialists won an absolute majority of seats in the state parliament. Under Rau the SPD won absolute majorities again in 1985 and 1990 and the party governed alone until 1995, when it lost its majority and enlisted the Greens as coalition partner, in what some observers called a future model for the national government. The popular Rau served as a counterbalance to the national dominance of the CDU in a premiership which lasted until 1998, a span of nearly twenty years, and in 1999 he became the Federal Republic's eighth President. He was replaced by Wolfgang Clement who served until 2002 when he joined the Schröder cabinet in Berlin. Peer Steinbrück followed him as minister president, in coalition with the Greens, until May 2005 when the Christian Democrats outpolled the SPD to gain control of the state for the first time since 1966. Conflict between the SPD and Greens in Düsseldorf and negative reaction to the Socialists' reform agenda in Berlin contributed to the CDU victory. Short of a majority, the CDU formed a coalition with the Free Democrats under Christian Democrat Jürgen Rüttgers, only the state's eighth Minister President. It was this telling setback in the Rhine and Ruhr which influenced Chancellor Gerhard Schröder's decision to call for new national elections one year early, much as the CDU's setback in the 1966 regional election in the state contributed to the fall of then Chancellor Ludwig Erhard.

The CDU and FDP lost their governing status in the May 9, 2010 state election. Coalition possibilities were thrown into disarray, since neither a CDU/FDP nor an SDP/Greens combination could provide a majority in the *Landtag* because of the entry of the *Die Linke* into the parliament. Negotiations for a grand coalition between the Christian Democrats and Socialists were attempted as well as a Jamaica coalition involving three parties. When these possibilities came to naught, Socialist Hannelore Kraft arranged a minority ministry with the Greens Party tolerated by *Die Linke*.

Rhineland-Palatinate: The CDU dominated Rhineland-Palatinate politics for the first 44 years, outpolling the Socialists in the initial eleven elections, six of which were won by absolute majorities. The first four minister presidents, including Dr. Helmut Kohl, who was the state's executive head from 1969 to 1976, were Christian Democrats. Over a sixty-four year period Rhineland-Palatinate has had only six executive heads, four Christian Democrats and two Socialists. The state's first elected premier, Dr. Peter Altmeier, served from 1947 to 1969, the longest span of time of any German state executive in a single *Land*. (Dr. Bernhard Vogel served as a minister-president for 23 years, but his time was shared between two states, twelve years, 1976-1988, as premier of Rhineland-Palatinate, and eleven years, 1992 to 2003, as executive head of Thuringia.) Although a majority could be established with either the SPD or FDP after the 1947 election, Altmeier formed an all-party combination of the CDU, SPD, FDP and Communist Party for his first ministry, a practice which was not uncommon in the first governments. The Communists and Free Democrats were dropped from the cabinet after the first year and a CDU/SPD partnership continued until 1951 when the CDU dropped the Socialists and formed a ministry with the FDP, which had pushed its following from 6.1 percent in 1947 to 16.7 percent. Altmeier continued this working relationship with the Free Democrats after the 1955, 1959, 1963 and 1967 state elections, even though his Christian Democrats won majorities in the 1955 and 1959 contests. Dr. Helmut Kohl became Minister President in 1969, after Altmeier's retirement following nearly 22 years in office. Under Kohl the CDU won absolute majorities in 1971 and 1975, and the CDU/FDP combination was abandoned in favor of a one party ministry.

When Dr. Kohl became a member of the *Bundestag* in 1976 he was followed by Dr. Bernhard Vogel who continued in that office until 1988. Under Vogel the CDU won absolute majorities in the 1979 and 1983 regional elections, continuing the one-party administration until May 1987 when the CDU lost its majority status, forcing Vogel to bring the Free Democrats into the state administration again. Dr. Vogel was replaced the next year by Dr. Carl-Ludwig Wagner who continued as minister president until the 1991 *Land* election in which the SPD became the state's leading party for the first time to end 44 years of CDU rule. Since a CDU/FDP combination could no longer provide a majority, the Free Democrats, not wanting to see the state SPD side with the Greens as had occurred earlier in Brandenburg and Hesse, supported a coalition with the leading Socialists under Rudolf Scharping. When Scharping became the SPD's candidate for the federal chancellorship in 1994, he was replaced by Kurt Beck in October of that year. The Socialist/Free Democrat partnership continued under Beck after both the 1996 and 2001 state elections but was dissolved in 2006 when the Socialists won sufficient seats in the state parliament to govern alone under Beck. In the 2011 state election the Socialists lost their parliamentary majority, leading to a combination with the Greens, again under Beck.

The Saar: The Saar, a strong Catholic state, was the preserve of the CDU from its reintegration into the Federal Republic in 1957 to 1980, when the SPD outpolled it for the first time. Today, although the CDU governs in combination with the Free Democrats and Greens in the state parliament, the Saar has been highly competitive, with the SPD obtaining over forty percent of the vote in eight of the eleven elections held since 1955, the CDU in six of those elections. Still, the Christian Democrats have led the state during nine legislative periods, including three, 1970, 1999 and 2004, in which they were supported by absolute majorities. In contrast, the Socialists won absolute majorities in the *Land* elections of 1985, 1990 and 1994.

Dr. Hubert Ney served as Minister President of the Saar prior to its rejoining the West German state in 1957.[88] Christian Democrat Egon Reinert was the first premier following the reintegration, serving from 1957 until his death in April 1959 in coalition with the SPD and the *Land* affiliate of the Liberals. He was followed by Dr. Franz Josef Röder (CDU) who served as the state's chief executive from 1959 until his death in 1979, one of the longest tenures in regional history. Initially in coalition with the SPD, the CDU dropped the Socialists following the 1960 *Land* election and formed a CDU/Liberal combination which was renewed after the 1965 regional poll. With an absolute majority in the 1970 state election and half of the seats in the 1975 contest Röder was able to govern alone until March 1977 when he brought the FDP into his cabinet to place the government on a more stable basis, following twenty-two months in a *Patt* (stalemated) situation. (To correct the possibility of this recurring, the number of seats in the Saarland parliament was raised from 50 to 51 beginning with the 1980 election.) Röder was succeeded in 1979 by Werner Zeyer who continued in office in coalition with the FDP until 1985, when the SPD won an absolute majority of seats for the first time, although it had become the leading faction in the 1980 election. With absolute majorities in the legislature after the 1985, 1990 and 1994 *Land* elections, the Socialists, under Oskar Lafontaine's leadership, were able to govern alone from 1985 to 1999. Only in the last year of that period, when Lafontaine became Finance Minister in the first Schröder cabinet, did Reinhard Klimmt (SPD) assume the duties of Minister President. In the 1999 and 2004 regional polls the CDU recovered its former leading status by winning absolute majorities and formed one-party ministries under Peter Müller after each election. In the state election held August 30, 2009, the CDU lost its majority, forcing it to partner with the FDP and Greens to form a majority, the first coalition of its kind on the state level, with Müller remaining as Minister President.

Schleswig-Holstein: The Horizon State has been highly competitive politically with the CDU and SPD each winning the largest number of seats eight times, the CDU by absolute majorities in four elections, the SPD in three. However equal this appears, Christian Democrats have provided the minister president for 44 years to the Socialists' twenty years, and since April 2005 the state has been led by Christian Democrat Peter Harry Carstensen. Schleswig-Holstein had the distinction of having had more premiers than any other state, twelve in number since 1947, until Hamburg equaled it after the 2011 election. (Berlin has had fourteen heads since 1946, but only two since its reintegration into the Federal Republic in 1990.) The state's first elected head was Socialist Hermann Lüdemann, who was the only chief executive to decide to govern alone after the first *Land* elections in 1946/1947, by virtue of his party's absolute majority in the state parliament.[89] He was followed by fellow party member Bruno Diekmann who continued one-party governance until 1950, when a bloc of bourgeois parties collaborated to form a Christian Democrat-led government, even though the SPD remained the state's leading party. This began a 37-year period of uninterrupted CDU rule.

With only 19.8 percent of the vote in the 1950 election, Christian Democrat Dr. Walter Bartram had to bring four disparate parties, his own CDU, the FDP, Refugee and German parties, together to form a workable administration. The coalition lasted for only one year, along with Bartram's services. There followed a CDU/FDP/Refugee Party combination without the German Party under Christian Democrat Dr. Friedrich Wilhelm Lübke. This alliance lasted only six months after which the CDU, in tandem with the Refugee Party, governed until the 1954 state election, remaining in power by defections from the German Party. The Socialists again polled more votes than the CDU in the 1954 *Land* contest, but both received 25 parliamentary seats, and the CDU was able to build a government with the Free Democrats and Refugee Party under Kai-Uwe von Hassel. After the 1958 election, in which the CDU outpolled the Socialists for the first time, a position it was to maintain through 1987, von Hassel governed with the FDP. Following the state election in September 1962, the CDU, lacking a majority by only one vote, formed a minority ministry, because of disagreements between von Hassel and his previous partner, the FDP, and his unwillingness to cooperate with the SPD. The minority government continued to govern Schleswig-Holstein until December 1962 when von Hassel was called to Bonn to replace the disgraced Franz Joseph Strauss as Defense Minister, ending an eight-year tenure in office.[90] He was replaced by Dr. Helmut Lemke who was more favorable to a grand coalition with the SPD, but such an arrangement was bitterly opposed by von Hassel and an alliance was formed with the FDP in January 1963 to place the government on a more stable basis. Lemke served as minister president until 1971, initially with the FDP to end the minority administration and again with the Free Democrats after the 1967 *Land* election to the end of his ministry in 1971. In 1971 the CDU won an absolute majority of seats in the state parliament for the first time and placed the state administration in the hands of Professor Dr. Gerhard Stoltenberg, who established a one-party ministry. With absolute majorities in 1975 and 1979 for the popular Stoltenberg, the CDU was able to govern alone throughout his eleven years in office, which he vacated to serve in Chancellor Helmut Kohl's initial administration. He was replaced by Dr. Uwe Barschel who continued the one-party government after the CDU won a fourth absolute majority in a row in the March 13, 1983 *Land* election. Barschel tried to continue in office as head of a minority government after the SPD replaced the CDU as the state's leading party in the September 13, 1987 state election. Implicated in an election scandal, involving spying on his Socialist opponent and breaching the confidentiality of tax returns for political advantage, which was to shake the Federal Republic and which was labeled as "Watergate in Kiel" by Germany's leading news magazine *Der Spiegel* (September 13 and 20, 1987, Volker Skierka, *"Die Affäre Barschel,"* in *Die Skandale der Republik,*1990 and Cordt Schnibben und Volker Skierka, in *Macht und Machenschaften,* 1988), Barschel resigned and left the state for Switzerland where, on October 11, 1987, he was found dead in a hotel bathtub, the cause of death remaining a mystery to this day. Barschel was followed by Christian Democrat Dr. Henning Schwarz who formed a coalition with the Free Democrats. As a result of the constitutional crisis caused by the Barschel Affair, new elections were held May 8, 1988, less than eight months into the legislative session. Reacting to the scandal in which a number of CDU players were involved, the Schleswig-Holstein voters awarded the SPD a resounding 54.8 percent of the state vote while the CDU total fell from 42.6 to 33.3 percent. The scandal led to the establishment of a constitutional and parliamentary reform commission (the first in the Federal Republic) to guard against a repeat of the activities which led to the fall of Barschel. The new Socialist premier was Björn Engholm, former Minister of Education and Science in the third Schmidt cabinet, at whom Barschel's scandalous actions had been directed. With a large parliamentary majority and both the FDP and Greens unable to exceed the five percent barrier to representation, Engholm established a one-party ministry. With a second straight majority in the 1992 *Land* election Engholm continued to govern alone until May 1993 when he resigned not only his premiership, but his position as national party chairman of the SPD and Chancellor candidate, upon disclosures that he had pre-knowledge of the spying which led to the Barschel Affair. He was replaced by Heide Simonis, the first woman minister president in any state and the first woman to hold such high elective office in the Federal Republic until 2005 when Dr. Angela Merkel became the first woman Chancellor. Simonis continued to hold that position for twelve years, initially in a one-party ministry and after the 1996 and 2000 state elections with the Greens, who gained representation in the state parliament for the first time in the 1996 election.[91] Following the state election in February 2005, in which the SPD lost its leading status to the CDU as a result of a general decline of her party in voter favor, Simonis attempted to lead a minority government with the Greens and the forbearance of the party of the Danish minority. With neither an SPD/Greens coalition nor a CDU/FDP combination able to form a majority because of the two seats gained by the SSW, a grand coalition of the CDU and SPD was formed in April 2005 under Christian Democrat Peter Harry Carstensen to place the state government on a more stable basis. Following state elections in September 2009, the grand coalition was replaced by a CDU/FDP ministry, again under Carstensen.

Coalition Patterns in the Eastern States

Berlin: In this former "Red" city, the SPD and CDU have shared political power, not only separately but together for some 25 years (from 1946 to 1953, 1955 to 1963 and from 1990 to 2001). The SPD emerged as the leading party in the first eight elections held in the city, followed by a period in which the Christian Democrats held that distinction, also in eight elections (from 1975 through 1999). The SPD then outpolled the CDU in both the 2001 and 2006 *Land* elections. The first balloting of the postwar period in Berlin took place on October 20, 1946 and covered all four sectors of the city. All four of the authorized parties, the SPD, CDU, the Liberals and the Communist SED gained representation and all four participated in the first government. As the leading party with 48.7 percent of the vote, the Socialists provided the first mayor, Dr. Otto Ostrowski, who resigned after less than a year over Soviet interference. Professor Ernst Reuter was selected as Lord Mayor in August 1947, but his selection was blocked by a Soviet veto. As a result, Frau Louise Schröder (SPD) and later Dr. Ferdinand Friedenburg (CDU) served as acting mayor until January 14, 1949 when Ernst Reuter, whose party received 64.5 percent of ballots cast the previous month, became the first mayor of West Berlin following the split of the city into two ideologically separate parts. A ministry including only the three western parties, the SPD, CDU and the Liberals was formed. A third election, including only the three western sectors of Berlin, was held December 3, 1950, with the Socialists again emerging as the city's leading party, but without a legislative majority. The coalition of the three western parties was continued with Reuter serving as Lord Mayor until his death in September 1953. He was succeeded by Christian Democrat Dr. Walther Schreiber who formed a government with the FDP without the Socialists. Schreiber continued as mayor to the end of 1954 when the SPD, again emerging as the city's leading party in the December 1954 election, combined with the CDU under Socialist Dr. Otto Suhr, who served as Lord Mayor until his death in August 1957. He was followed by the dynamic Willy Brandt, who helped his party win absolute majorities in the 1958 and 1963 West Berlin elections. In spite of the 1958 victory, Brandt continued the grand coalition with the CDU, which had been established under Dr. Suhr, until 1963, when he brought the Free Democrats in as coalition partner, in anticipation of a possible Socialist victory in the 1965 *Bundestag* election with the expected retirement of Chancellor Konrad Adenauer. That victory did not materialize, but in December 1966 a grand coalition between the CDU and SPD was constituted at the national level with Brandt as Vice Chancellor and Foreign Minister. He was replaced by Heinrich Albertz who chose to govern alone following the SPD's victory in the March 1967 three-sector election. The Socialists continued a one-party ministry after the 1971 election, but sided with the FDP when they not only failed to obtain majorities in the 1975 and 1979 contests, but lost their leading party status. Albertz served as Lord Mayor for less than a year, resigning following student protests during the visit of the Shah of Iran. He was succeeded by Dr. Klaus Schütz (October 1967-May 1977), Dietrich Stobbe (May 1977-January 1981) and Dr. Hans-Jochen Vogel from January 1981 until the May 1981 election when the CDU came within two seats of gaining an absolute majority in the city parliament. Dr. Richard von Weizsäcker (CDU), thereupon, formed a minority government with the tolerance of several FDP representatives, a state of affairs which existed for 22 months until the CDU entered into a formalized relationship with the Free Democrats. Von Weizsäcker continued as Lord Mayor until 1984 when he was chosen to be the sixth Federal President, an office he held for ten years. He was replaced by Eberhard Diepgen (CDU) who resumed the CDU/FDP partnership. The combination was renewed after the 1985 city election and continued until the January 1989 poll in which the FDP failed to qualify for representation, enabling the SPD to form a government with the Alternative List which had first gained seats in the Berlin *Abgeordnetenhaus* in 1981. This marked only the second occasion that a Green affiliate had participated in a *Land* ministry. Socialist Walter Momper assumed the post of Lord Mayor.

German reunification made necessary a new election less than two years later because of the addition of the former eastern (Soviet) sector of Berlin to the three western sectors of the city. In the December 2, 1990 balloting the enlarged electorate gave 40.4 percent of its votes to the CDU in contrast to 30.4 percent for the Socialists. But neither a CDU/FDP nor an SPD/Greens combination could provide a working majority because of the 23 seats won by the successor to the eastern Communist Party, the PDS, leaving a coalition between the two major parties as the only alternative. Eberhard Diepgen (CDU) again became Lord Mayor. The CDU/SPD coalition under Diepgen was continued after both the 1995 and 1999 all-Berlin elections and lasted until June 2001 when the partnership broke up over corruption charges against the city CDU. The Socialists under Klaus Wowereit then formed a minority government with the Greens and the toleration of the PDS which continued until October 2001 when the Berlin parliament was dissolved and new elections held. The outcome was a major setback for the CDU as it lost 17.1 percentage points while the SPD, FDP and PDS were strengthened. This enabled Wowereit to formalize a partnership with the PDS, only the second in German regional politics.[92] Following the September 2006 *Land* vote, Wowereit disavowed a combination with the CDU to come into line with the then federal model, since he considered the integration of the two parts of Berlin to be more important than national deference and continued his alliance with the PDS. With the breakup of the SPD/PDS coalition in Mecklenburg-Vorpommern after the September 2006 *Land* election, Berlin remained the only state in which the SPD and PDS cooperated (*Die Welt*, October 2, 2006), until such a combination was formed in Brandenburg after the 2009 election.

Brandenburg: In contrast to the West German states, where from fourteen to eighteen regional elections have been held in each jurisdiction (only eleven in the Saar, which, however, was not integrated into the Federal Republic until 1957), only five regional contests have taken place in four eastern states and six in Saxony-Anhalt, so there has been limited time to categorize a state politically. The SPD emerged as the leading party in all five of the elections held in Brandenburg, enabling it to provide the minister president for the entire twenty years from 1990 to 2010. In the 1990 election it polled only 38.2 percent of the vote, necessitating the formation of a three-party alliance of the SPD, FDP and the Alliance 90 (the eastern Greens) to provide a majority. In 1994 the Socialists won an absolute majority of *Landtag* seats and were able to govern alone. However, in the 1999 *Land* election they lost their majority, and, with neither the FDP nor the Alliance 90 able to qualify for seats, they formed a grand coalition with the Christian Democrats, the only party other than the PDS and right-extremist DVU to obtain parliamentary representation. Socialist Manfred Stolpe served as minister president from 1990 to June 25, 2002 when he stepped down in favor of Matthias Platzeck, former Socialist mayor of Potsdam, over charges of involvement with the *Stasis*. After the 2004 election the SPD again failed to gain a majority of seats and renewed its partnership with the CDU under Platzeck, as the FDP and Greens again failed to qualify for representation and there was no desire to establish an alliance with the PDS. In the state election held the same day as the 2009 *Bundestag* poll, the SPD once more emerged as the leading party and the CDU received sufficient support for the Socialists to continue their grand coalition with the Christian Democrats. However, Minister-President Platzeck, in the interest of reconciliation, chose to form a ministry with *Die Linke*, much to the CDU's consternation. Upon finding that six of the 26 Leftist members of the state parliament had *Stasi* connections the new coalition got off to a shaky start. Both the FDP and Greens qualified for seats after three sessions of being unrepresented, but the right-extremist DVU lost its six-seat delegation when it received only 1.2 percent of ballots cast (*Matthias Platzeck's Versucht Stasi und Linkspartei auseinander Zuhalten, Die Welt am Sonntag*, December 6, 2009).

Mecklenburg-Vorpommern: Five elections have been held in Mecklenburg-Vorpommern since 1990, with the CDU emerging as the leading party in the first two elections, the SPD in the following three, none by majority vote.

The CDU formed the first government with the Free Democrats under Dr. Alfred Gomolka, who stepped down in favor of party colleague Dr. Berndt Seite after only two years in office over the shipyard crisis. Seite continued to govern with the FDP until the 1994 *Land* election when the Free Democrats failed to qualify for seats, forcing him to form a grand coalition with the SPD. In the 1998 *Land* election the Socialists became the leading party for the first time, and Dr. Harald Ringstorff, the new minister president (SPD), established the first government in which the PDS participated (Andersen and Woyke, 2002: 331). Ringstorff continued the arrangement after the 2002 *Land* election, but, following the 2006 regional poll, the partnership with *Die Linke* (the new name for the PDS in Mecklenburg-Vorpommern) could provide only a one vote majority (36 of 71 seats), too weak to govern, considering the entry of the NPD into the parliament (*Die Welt*, October 2, 2006). The SPD/PDS ministry was, therefore, terminated in favor of a grand coalition between the SPD and CDU, with Ringstorff continuing as premier, not only to place the ministry on a stronger basis but to provide the national government with its desired constitutional majority.[93] Ringstorff retired on age grounds in October 2008 in favor of Social Minister Erwin Sellering (SPD) (*Internationale Biographisches Archiv von 6. Januar 2009*).

Saxony: The CDU has been the leading party in Saxony since the initial regional contests in 1990. The first three elections, in 1990, 1994 and 1999, were won by absolute majorities and the CDU governed alone for the first three legislative sessions under Prof. Dr. Kurt Biedenkopf, former Secretary-General of the CDU West and the first premier in an eastern province to come from the West, from 1990 to 2002. After leading his party to three legislative majorities, Minister President Biedenkopf stepped down in favor of Prof. Dr. Georg Milbradt on age grounds (Andersen and Woyke, 2003:362). In the 2004 *Land* election the CDU lost its majority in an election characterized by its fragmented outcome, with six different parties qualifying for representation. Milbradt's desired alliance with the FDP fell one seat short of a working majority, causing him to partner with the SPD, also a loser, in a combination the *Hamburger Abendblatt* (September 21, 2004) called a "coalition of losers." Dr. Milbradt, himself, was forced to step down, effective in May 2008, in favor of Stanislaw Tillich in reaction to the collapse of the Saxony State Bank stemming from speculative losses in the U.S. real estate market and its resulting purchase by the Baden-Württemberg State Bank (*Minister Präsident stüzt über seine Sachsen LB Affären*," *Die Welt*, April 15, 2008 and *Focus* April 21, 2008:34-37). The coalition with the SPD continued until the 2009 state election when the Free Democrats doubled their mandates to make a CDU/FDP combination possible, again under Tillich.

Saxony-Anhalt: Six elections have been held in Saxony-Anhalt since reunification, with the CDU emerging as the leading party in five of them, none by majority vote. The state has had a turbulent political history, with party control changing back and forth several times and six individuals serving as minister-president in a period of only twenty years. The first ministry was a coalition between the CDU and FDP with Christian Democrat Gerd Gies as premier. He was forced to step down after only eight months in office on suspicion of dishonesty and was replaced by Werner Münch, former finance minister of Lower Saxony. In 1993 Münch also had to step down over accusations of an exorbitant salary after having served as premier for only two years. He was replaced by Christoph Bergner, also of the CDU, who served until the 1994 *Land* election when the Socialists came within one seat of matching the CDU's 37 representatives in the state parliament. With the FDP failing to qualify for representation, Socialist Reinhard Höppner took advantage of the situation to form a minority government with the Alliance 90/Greens which was tolerated by the PDS. This minority government continued after the 1998 election, even as the Greens lost their representation, as a result of the ability of the SPD to outpoll the CDU for the first time and protracted PDS support. In the 2002 state election the Socialists suffered a severe setback, and, with a CDU resurgence and the FDP's ability to regain representation in the *Landtag,* a CDU/FDP government under Prof. Dr. Wolfgang Böhmer was formed. Following the March 2006 state poll a grand coalition between the CDU and SPD was crafted under Böhmer, not only as a duplication of the federal model, but because a CDU/FDP grouping alone could not produce a working majority, and there was no desire on the part of the CDU to ally itself with the *Die Linke.* Böhmer was succeeded as head of the existing CDU/SPD coalition by Dr. Rainer Haseloff (CDU) after the March 2011 *Land* election.

Thuringia: The CDU has been the dominant party in Thuringia since reunification, winning all of the five *Land* elections held since 1990, two by absolute majorities. Between 1990 and 1994 it formed a coalition with the FDP, but from 1994 to 1999 found it necessary to coalesce with the SPD when the Free Democrats failed to qualify for representation. In both 1999 and 2004 it was able to win a majority of *Landtag* seats and governed alone during both legislative periods. In spite of an appearance of considerable stability, Thuringia has been plagued by a string of cabinet crises and personnel changes in its short history. First there was the long drawn-out replacement of the state's first Minister President Josef Duchač; then the affairs leading up to the dismissal of Interior Minister Böck and Social Minister Axthelm and the personnel scandals between Interior, Justice and Finance ministers in 2002 (Johannes Kuppe in Andersen and Woyke, 2003: 381). Duchač, who had served in the last DDR government, was replaced after sixteen months by Dr. Bernhard Vogel, former Minister President of Rhineland-Palatinate from 1976 to 1988, who served as premier from 1992 to 2003. Christian Democrat Dieter Althaus succeeded Vogel as Minister President and led the CDU to a winning majority in the 2004 regional election. While Althaus survived a 2009 ski accident in which a female skier was killed due to his negligence, he did not survive the 2009 state election in which the CDU lost its majority status and was forced into a coalition with the SPD (the only alternative to an undesirable matching with *Die Linke*). Althaus was replaced by Christine Lieberknecht (CDU), only the second female to be selected as a state chief executive.

Land Coalitions and the *Bundesrat*

The original expectation that the *Bundesrat*, the federal upper chamber, would be controlled by groupings of parties other than those forming the national government was based on the assumption that the party system of the Federal Republic would resemble that of Weimar. However, when the fragmentation which characterized the early 1950s failed to be sustained and the CDU/CSU became the dominant group on both the national and regional levels, this early concept gave way to one which recognized a probable parallelogram of power in the two chambers of the federal parliament as the parties controlling the national government inevitably sought to impose similar coalition patterns in the *Länder* to control the politics of the *Bundesrat*. The coordination efforts of the Adenauer administration during the 1950s, during a period of political fragmentation, have been well-documented. But regimentation of the state ministries by the parties controlling the national government has not always been achievable nor have duplicative ministries in the *Länder* always guaranteed support for national policies in the *Bundesrat*. Financially-weak CDU-led states such as Lower Saxony, the Saar and Schleswig-Holstein often sided with Socialist delegates in the upper house to get more financial aid from horizontal financial equalization even when the federal government was controlled by a CDU/CSU-led coalition.

In contrast to the fluidity which characterized *Bundesrat* representation during the 1950s, the ability of the Christian parties to dominate regional voting for all but two election periods between 1949 and 2010 and to fashion advantageous coalitions in the absence of a majority in the various *Land* parliaments guaranteed control of the *Bundesrat* for most of Federal Republic's 62-year history, including between 1969 and 1982 when the Socialists controlled the national government in partnership with the FDP. The coordination efforts of Adenauer after 1949 insured not only a majority in the federal upper house, but an early constitutional majority. The Christian Union majority in the *Bundesrat* remained undisturbed from the middle of 1959 to December 1966 when the Socialists gained control of North Rhine-Westphalia's five *Bundesrat* votes, reducing the CDU/CSU's majority to only one vote.[94] The almost simultaneous formation of the CDU/SPD alliance in Bonn somewhat clouded the significance of this change in Düsseldorf, since it temporarily terminated the rivalry between the two parties for control of the federal upper chamber and guaranteed a parallelogram of power in the two houses. Even in December 1966, in a period of Socialist dominance in regional elections, the Socialists could count on only fifteen sure votes, the CDU/CSU on sixteen, with ten votes split between the CDU-led grand coalition in Baden-Württemberg and the SPD-led grand coalition in Lower Saxony.

The sustained domination of regional politics by the Christian parties during the entire thirteen years of Socialist rule in Bonn (1969-1982) continued to prevent SPD-led state ministries from controlling the *Bundesrat*. In July 1980, for example, with an SPD/FDP government in power on the national level, the

Christian parties could count on 26 upperhouse votes to the SPD's 15. When the Christian parties returned to power in October 1982 under Helmut Kohl they continued to control the *Bundesrat* throughout the 1980s, and at the end of 1989 could count on 23 votes in the upper house to the Socialists' eighteen. This changed in June 1990 after the Socialists regained Lower Saxony and obtained the four votes of Berlin which was granted full voting rights in the *Bundesrat* as of June 21, 1990 (*Stimmenanzahl der Länder im Bundesrat, Archiv des Bundesrates*, 2005). The Union regained control of the federal upper house when the CDU won the largest share of voters in the new states in the October 1990 provincial elections. This advantage, however, lasted only half a year as the Socialists replaced the CDU in Hesse and Rhineland-Palatinate during the first half of 1991. In the expanded upper house resulting from reunification, the SPD by July 1992 controlled 37 votes to the Christian party's 31 votes and by July 1995 the ratio had increased to 41 votes for the SPD to the CDU/CSU's 27. The Socialists continued to dominate the federal upper house throughout the second half of Helmut Kohl's tenure in office and through most of Gerhard Schröder's first term as Chancellor. The loss of Saxony-Anhalt, which carries four votes in the federal upper house, just prior to the 2002 *Bundestag* election gave the CDU 36 votes and a majority in the *Bundesrat* for the first time in over a decade. The CDU victory in Lower Saxony in February 2003 expanded that margin, and the turnovers in Schleswig-Holstein and North Rhine Westphalia in early 2005 and the increase in Hesse's delegation from four to five votes provided the CDU with a constitutional majority of 47 sure votes (46 needed), compensating for the four from Schleswig-Holstein where the two parties were in coalition, just prior to the 2005 general election. With the two major parties forming a common government after that election, the national government could ordinarily count on the Union and Socialist-controlled states and those states in which the two parties formed a common ministry. The establishment of an SPD/CDU combination in Mecklenburg-Vorpommern following the September 2006 state election gave the Union/Socialist partnership in Berlin an additional three votes and a constitutional majority to put through laws without regard for the FDP, Greens or the Left party (*Die Welt*, October 2, 2006). However, following the formation of the Socialist/Greens government in Bremen after the May 2, 2007 *Bürgerschaft* election, the national government could count on only 44 votes, whereas 46 were needed for a two-thirds majority. Support in the *Bundesrat* for the CDU/SPD coalition was further eroded by the CDU's loss of its majority in Hesse, by the establishment of a CDU/Greens combination in Hamburg and by the CDU's loss of its majority in Bavaria, the Saar and Thuringia prior to the 2009 *Bundestag* election. With the breakup of the national grand coalition, the collapse of the CDU/FDP government in North Rhine-Westphalia in 2010 and in Baden-Württemberg in 2011, and the changeover in Hamburg in February 2011, neither a Black/Yellow nor a Red/Green combination could count on a clear majority in the *Bundesrat*, expanding the power of the smaller parties.

With the two major parties increasingly dependent on one or more of the minor groupings to form a working majority in the *Länder*, any action which would prove detrimental to one or more of the states could be blocked in the *Bundesrat*. This would appear to provide an adequate counterbalance in the federal upper chamber to national policies injurious to the small parties and to the *Länder*.[95]

Endnotes to Chapter X

1 For a reflective analysis of the early interplay of national and *Land* politics on the functioning of the *Bundesrat*, see E. L. Pinney, *Federalism, Bureaucracy and Party Politics in Western Germany, The Role of the Bundesrat*, especially Chapter 4, pages 89-141.

2 The 1953 *Land* election in Hamburg is illustrative. In that year a party alliance comprising the parties of the Bonn government, the CDU, FDP, DP and BHE, succeeded in gaining an absolute majority of parliamentary seats and excluding the SPD from the government, even though with 45.2 percent of the vote it was by far the most important single parliamentary group, and its leader, Max Brauer, the single most popular Hamburg politician.

3 Policies relating to the occupation of Germany are discussed in Chapter I of this study.

4 The first dismissal of a prominent postwar appointee occurred September 28, 1945, in Bavaria when Minister President Friedrich Schäffer was removed from office. Upon his appointment in May 1945 Schäffer formed a cabinet of his political friends and assistants, maintaining that he alone bore responsibility towards the Military Government, necessitating the selection of people whom he could trust. His reactionary policy, his retention of many Nazis in office and inclusion of more and more rightist elements in his administration led to an alliance of Left Catholics, under the leadership of Dr. Joseph Müller, Social Democrats and Communists to seek Schäffer's removal. Powerless to act upon Schäffer directly and unable to force the Military Government of Bavaria to take action, the alliance had to await action by higher headquarters. The situation eventually came to the attention of General Eisenhower, resulting in Schäffer's dismissal and his replacement by Social Democrat Wilhelm Hoegner. This incident is described in Robert Neumann, "The New Political Parties of Germany," *American Political Science Review*, XL (August 1946): 755-758.

5 The British had made a number of political appointments prior to May 28, 1945; however, they were for political entities of less than *Land* size since no decision on the number and boundaries of the British Zone *Länder* had yet been determined. A *Senat* for Hamburg, not then having *Land* status, had been established as early as May 15, 1945, and on May 24, 1945, Dr. Hans Fuchs was named *Oberpräsident* of the Rhine Province, now part of the *Land* North Rhine-Westphalia.

6 The provisional government of Hesse was established October 15, 1946, with Professor Dr. Karl Geiler of the University of Heidelberg named to the post of Minister President. In Württemberg-Baden Dr. Reinhold Maier, Economics Minister of Württemberg and member of the *Reichstag* in the pre-Nazi period, was appointed the nonparty head of the provisional government and Minister of Finance in September 1945.

7 In Lower Saxony Wilhelm Kopf was initially (in 1945) appointed *Oberpräsident* of the province of Hannover and on December 9, 1946, after the definitive existence of

the *Land* Lower Saxony had been established, was named Acting Minister President. In the Rhine Military District during the course of 1945 the British appointed Dr. Hans Fuchs *Oberpräsident* of the Rhine Province and Dr. Rudolf Amelunxen *Oberpräsident* of Westphalia. Following the formation of the four zones of occupation and the resulting reduction in size of the area under British administration, the province North Rhine was formed with Dr. Robert Lehr, former mayor of Düsseldorf, taking over the post of *Oberpräsident* in October 1945. Dr. Amelunxen became Acting Minister President of North Rhine-Westphalia in July 1946. The British appointed Theodore Steltzer *Oberpräsident* of Schleswig-Holstein in November 1945 and as Minister-President August 23, 1946. Rudolf Petersen was named mayor of Hamburg May 15, 1945, and Erich Vagts mayor of Bremen June 6, 1945.

8 In South Baden, for example, civil servants from the previous administration were appointed by the French to head such administrations as Interior, Finance, Education, etc. under the title of Ministerial Director (*Ministerialdirektor*). The heads of the various administrations rotated as chairmen under the title of President of the Baden *Land* Administration (*Gazette Officielle*, Nr. 6 vom 19.8. 1945 S. 13).

9 Of the 124 representatives of the first nominated parliament established in Württemberg-Baden, twelve came from each of the four parties then approved (CDU, SPD, DVP and KPD), while others came from occupational groups, town and rural districts, churches and universities (Dolf Sternberger, "Parties and Party Systems in Postwar Germany," *The Annals*; CCLX (November 1948): 26).

10 There having been no elections to register the relative strengths of the parties, the Allies had only pre-Nazi election figures to rely on and sometimes their guesses were wide of the mark. The employment of a system of corporate and political representation was one method of avoiding the necessity of estimating party strengths. These appointed bodies, however, had no true legislative power.

11 Of the 81 members of the Hamburg *Bürgerschaft* which met for the first time February 27, 1946, thirteen represented the *Senat*, seventeen came from the five licensed political parties (six Social Democrats, six Communists, three Free Democrats, one Christian Democrat, and one member of the Lower Saxony State Party), four from churches, sixteen represented labor unions, eight business and trade, six professions and science, one agriculture, three property owners, five women groups, six political divisions of Hamburg and two political prisoners.

12 In North Rhine-Westphalia, for example, the British overestimated the strengths of the SPD and KPD and underestimated that of the CDU in the first appointed *Landtag*. The second appointed *Landtag* which met for the first time in December 1946 reflected the results of the September and October elections and the CDU gained 26 seats for a total of 92 of the 200 seats, the SPD lost five seats and the KPD fifteen seats. Six additional seats were lost by the Center Party.

13 The first appointed government in Württemberg-Baden was strongly criticized for overrepresenting the Liberal Democrats, considered numerically and organizationally the weakest of the licensed parties, and completely excluding the Communists. The two Liberal Democrat (DVP) members of the cabinet were to be among the important German leaders of the postwar period. Dr. Theodor Heuss, Minister of Culture and Education, became the Bonn Republic's first President, serving in that capacity from 1949 to 1959, and Dr. Reinhold Maier was Minister President of Württemberg-Baden from 1945 until the *Land* was dissolved in 1952 and of the new *Land* of Baden-

Württemberg for eighteen months. He was also a prominent leader of the liberal wing of the FDP after its founding in 1948, and its national leader for three years.

14 *"Hessens Nachkriegskabinette,"* in *Handbuch des Hessischen Landtags* (*V. Wahlperiode*), Hessen Center for Political Education: 117-118. Those ministers without party affiliation either took on a party designation or were gradually replaced by party members during the course of 1946, and before the nominated government was replaced by the first responsible government following the elections of December 1946 it was made up of five Social Democrats, two Christian Democrats, one Free Democrat, one Communist and one independent. Dr. Geiler, who maintained his non-party status continued in the post of Minister President until January 5, 1947, when he was replaced in that position by Social Democrat Christian Stock.

15 Even after the first political elections of April, May and June of 1946 had indicated the dominant position of the CSU in Bavaria, Hoegner was retained in his post until after the first *Landtag* election in December 1946. The only change in the Hoegner cabinet was the replacement of the single Communist minister by a CSU minister.

16 Schäffer had chosen his own friends to fill the cabinet posts, except for two Social Democrats who were appointed directly by the Military Government. One of the two non-party members of the first Hoegner cabinet was Prof. Dr. Ludwig Erhard, who held the post of Economics Minister in Bavaria from October 1945 to December 1946.

17 Two Christian Democrats, two members of the NLP, one Free Democrat, one Communist and four Social Democrats, including Minister President Wilhelm Kopf, sat on the first appointed cabinet in Lower Saxony. Three Social Democrats, two Communists, one Free Democrat, two independents and two members of the Center Party, including Minister President Dr. Rudolf Amelunxen, comprised the first nominated cabinet of North Rhine-Westphalia. In Schleswig-Holstein the first nominated cabinet headed by Theodor Steltzer (CDU) consisted of four Christian Democrats, three Social Democrats and one Communist. The results of the local elections of September and October 1946 led to the rebuilding of the Amelunxen cabinet in North Rhine-Westphalia and the Steltzer cabinet in Schleswig-Holstein. The first appointed government in Lower Saxony was not established until December 1946, necessitating no changes. The second Amelunxen cabinet was expanded to include five Christian Democrats and the Communists lost one of their two positions. No posts were held by independents. The one Communist was dropped from the second Steltzer cabinet in Schleswig-Holstein and the ten posts in the cabinet were distributed equally between the CDU and the SPD.

18 The first provisional government of Rhineland-Palatinate, formed December 4, 1946, and consisting of six Christian Democrats, including Minister President Dr. Wilhelm Boden, two Social Democrats and one Communist Minister, reflected the strengths of the parties represented in the constituent assembly, itself based on the results of the September and October elections. Members of the cabinet were appointed by the French Military Government from proposals from the authorized political parties. The first Directorate appointed by the French in Baden in 1945 and enlarged in 1946 consisted of both party and non-party members who rotated as head of this executive body under the title of President of the Baden *Land* Administration. This Directorate was replaced December 2, 1946, by a State Secretariat (*Staatssekretariat*) consisting of six State secretaries and four State commissioners appointed by the Military Government from proposals made by the authorized political parties. Leo Wohleb (BCSV) was named President of the Secretariat which included three BCSV, two SPD, two Democratic Party, one

Communist and two non-party members. This body served as the provisional government of Baden until a new government could be formed on the basis of the results of the *Landtag* election of May 18, 1947.

Prof. Dr. Carlo Schmid (SPD) was appointed *Land* director of the State Secretariat of Württemberg-Hohenzollern October 10, 1945, a body made up of two Christian Democrats, two Social Democrats and one non-party member. The Secretariat, enlarged December 4, 1946, to include four CDU and two SPD members and one DVP member, was again headed by Prof. Schmid, who served in that position until July 22, 1947, when Dr. Lorenz Bock became President of Württemberg-Hohenzollern.

19 The first Bremen *Senat* was appointed June 6, 1945, with independent Erich Vagts serving as mayor of the city. On August 1, 1945, Wilhelm Kaisen (SPD) replaced Vagts and served as *Bürgermeister* without interruption for twenty years until his retirement July 17, 1965. The British appointed four members each from the SPD, BDV and KPD and five independents to the first *Senat*. In November 1946 the *Senat* was reformed to reflect the results of the first *Bürgerschaft* election held the previous month. The SPD took eight *Senat* posts, the BVD three and the KPD one.

The British established a non-party *Senat* for the City of Hamburg May 15, 1945. Rudolf Petersen was named as Hamburg's first postwar mayor. In February 1946 the Hamburg *Senat* was reformed on a party basis with Herr Petersen (CDU) retaining the post of *Bürgermeister*. The new *Senat* included six Social Democrats, four Christian Democrats, two Communists and one Free Democrat. This nominated executive body served to assist the British authorities until November 1946 when the first responsible *Senat* was established under Social Democrat Max Brauer, who had been mayor of Altona from 1924 to 1933 and had returned to Germany after thirteen years in exile to accept the important post of *Bürgermeister* of Hamburg ("*Übersicht über die Senate der Freien und Hansestadt Hamburg seit 1945*," State Press Agency, July 1963: 2-3).

20 In Hamburg Christian Democrat Rudolf Petersen was replaced by Social Democrat Max Brauer. In North Rhine-Westphalia Karl Arnold (CDU) took over the post of Minister President from Dr. Rudolf Amelunxen (Center Party), and in Schleswig-Holstein Social Democrat Hermann Lüdemann replaced Christian Democrat Theodor Steltzer. As a result of the first *Landtag* and *Bürgerschaft* elections Social Democrats headed the governments of all British Zone *Länder* with the exception of North Rhine-Westphalia. In the appointment period many of the first political posts went to Social Democrats, not only because the British Labour Party was in power at the time, but large numbers of Socialists had been exiled in Britain during the Nazi period and many who remained in Germany had a splendid anti-Nazi record. As a result, the British felt they could rely on the Socialists more than any other party. Moreover, the Socialists showed a willingness to cooperate with the British. Some of these Socialists were among the most prominent leaders of the postwar period—Wilhelm Kaisen, Wilhelm Kopf, Hermann Lüdemann, etc.

21 Schmid had been retained in his post after the rebuilding of the cabinet in December 1946 even though the September and October elections had indicated the inferior position of the SPD in Baden.

22 A single party held an absolute majority of the seats in Baden, Bavaria, Hamburg, Schleswig-Holstein, Württemberg-Baden and prior to October 1947 in Bremen, yet only in Schleswig-Holstein did the majority party, the SPD, form a one-party government from the outset. The coalitions in Baden and Bavaria later broke down and the CDU

formed one-party ministries in those two *Länder* prior to the formation of the national government.

23 A government formed of more than one party when an absolute majority of the seats in the parliament is controlled by one of them, is not a coalition in the true sense of the term since the majority party is always in a position of dominance and the other parties are placed in subservient roles if they wish to remain in the coalition. Only where there is no majority party does cooperation become mandatory, and one party dominates only at the risk of destroying the coalition. The "grand coalition" between the CSU and the SPD in Bavaria was dissolved in 1947 on just these grounds even though CSU Minister President Hans Ehard desired a continuation of the partnership. The four Social Democrat ministers in the cabinet were forced to resign against their will by a decision of the state committee of the party on the grounds that a real coalition required that the partners be dependent on each other, with neither having a majority (Sternberger, *The Annals*, CCLX (November, 1948): 27-28).

24 All-party coalitions were formed in Lower Saxony, Rhineland-Palatinate and Württemberg-Baden. This meant that no less than six parties were represented in the Lower Saxony government established in June 1947, and four parties in the governments of Rhineland-Palatinate and Württemberg-Baden formed in July 1947 and in December 1946 respectively. In Lower Saxony the original coalition consisted of four SPD, two CDU, two DP and single ministers from the FDP, KPD and Center Party. The Communist minister was dropped from the cabinet in February 1948 and the DP and FDP ministers the following June in the reconstitution of the government. Participation of the CDU in the cabinet ended in August 1950 leaving a small coalition of the Social Democrat and Center parties, enlarged by *Fraktion* desertions, in control of the government until the 1951 *Landtag* elections. Wilhelm Kopf held the post of Minister President throughout the entire legislative period.

In Rhineland-Palatinate the CDU, SPD, KPD and Democratic Party (now FDP) participated in the government formed in July 1947. The Communist and Democratic Party ministers were dismissed from the coalition April 7, 1948, and the resulting CDU-SPD coalition was maintained under Minister-President Peter Altmeier until the 1951 *Landtag* elections.

The CDU, SPD, DVP and KPD formed the government of Württemberg-Baden from December 16, 1946, to July 27, 1948, when the single Communist minister was expelled from the cabinet. The other three parties continued in coalition under Minister President Dr. Reinhold Maier until the 1950 *Landtag* election.

25 The mixed electoral system had enabled the Socialists to control 43 of 70 seats in the Schleswig-Holstein *Landtag* in the election of April 20, 1947. The all-Socialist government was headed by Hermann Lüdemann, *Oberpräsident* of Lower Silesia from 1928 to 1932 and Deputy Minister President and Interior Minister in the second Steltzer cabinet, from April 1947 to August 1949 and by Bruno Diekmann from August 1949 to September 1950 when the premiership passed to Christian Democrat Dr. Walter Bartram.

26 See footnote 23 of this chapter for a comment on the move of the Social Democratic Party in Bavaria. The coalition formed December 21, 1946, in Bavaria had included the CSU, the SPD and the Economic Reconstruction Association (WAV), with the WAV providing a single minister. FDP opposition to the *Land* constitution had ruled it out of the government. WAV leader and Bavarian Denazification Minister Alfred Loritz, was dropped from the cabinet in July 1947 on black market charges, and in September 1947 the Four Socialist ministers withdrew from the cabinet to end coalition

government in Bavaria. Controlling 104 of the 180 seats in the *Landtag*, an all-CSU government was established and continued to govern Bavaria until the 1950 *Landtag* elections.

27 The government formed in July 1947 under President Leo Wohleb had included only Christian Democrat and Social Democrat ministers, with the Socialists holding two cabinet posts. The CDU (formerly Baden Christian Peoples' Party) controlled 34 of the sixty *Landtag* seats and no search for other coalition parties was made necessary by the dissolution of the coalition.

28 In Hesse no parties other than the SPD and the CDU participated in the coalition. Opposition to the constitution had ruled out any participation of the FDP in the government and a Socialist coalition with the Communist Party would not have provided a firm basis of government. In North Rhine-Westphalia all parties with the exception of the FDP participated in the government formed in June 1947. Following the dismissal of the two Communist members of the cabinet in February 1948 the Arnold cabinet consisted of CDU, SPD and Center party ministers in a coalition which continued until the 1950 *Landtag* election. Rhineland-Palatinate started out with an all-party government, but after April 1948 the CDU and the SPD alone comprised the government. The DVP remained a part of the coalition of Württemberg-Baden during the entire legislative period, supplying the Minister President. The single Communist minister had been dropped from the government in July 1948. The initial coalition in Württemberg-Hohenzollern was formed by the CDU, SPD and the DVP; however, after September 1949 the DVP ceased to be a participant in the government. Württemberg-Hohenzollern was the only *Land* in which a "grand coalition" between the CDU and the SPD survived where one of the two parties held an absolute majority in the *Landtag*.

29 See footnote No. 24 of this chapter.

30 In Bremen the government formed in November 1946 was a coalition of the SPD, which then held an absolute majority in the *Bürgerschaft*, the BDV and the Communist Party. After January 1948 the SPD and the BDV formed a government in which the SPD no longer held a majority.

The Socialists formed a government with the FDP and the Communist Party from 1946 to 1949 under Mayor Max Brauer who had returned to Germany after thirteen years of exile in Austria, China and the United States. Throughout this legislative period the SPD held an absolute majority in the *Bürgerschaft*.

31 A governmental crisis lasting six weeks resulted in the establishment of the all-party coalition in Lower Saxony, even though the SPD could have formed a majority with any of the other parties. Eventually the KPD, DP, FDP and CDU ministers in that order left or were dismissed from the coalition, making possible a vigorous opposition. After April 1948 the Communist and Liberal parties formed an opposition in Rhineland-Palatinate and in Württemberg-Baden a weak opposition was formed by the Communist Party following its expulsion from the cabinet in July 1948.

32 For a critique of the coalition system as it operated in the West German *Länder* in the immediate postwar period, see Sternberger, *The Annals*, CCLX (November, 1948): 25-30.

33 A coalition of the SPD, KPD and Center Party, the three parties favoring the British plan for the socialization of all Ruhr industry, would have given the government a three-vote majority; however, aware they would have to answer the appeals and demands

of food demonstrators, the Left-Wing parties reconsidered their ambition to form a government in North Rhine-Westphalia without the CDU, the largest party in the *Landtag*, and retreated in their demand for immediate socialization to allow Karl Arnold to form a government.

34 Communist ministers were dismissed from the various ministries during the course of 1948 when the breakdown in East-West cooperation became apparent. Many of the non-Moscow trained Communists had favored genuine cooperation with the other parties in the immediate postwar period, but as orders began to filter through from the East, they became less cooperative and those who would not go along were purged from the party.

35 The CDU/CSU had received 37.7 percent of the nation-wide vote in the first series of *Land* elections, the SPD 35.0 percent.

36 The Socialist heads of government were Wilhelm Kaisen in Bremen, Max Brauer in Hamburg, Christian Stock in Hesse, Wilhelm Kopf in Lower Saxony and Hermann Lüdemann in Schleswig-Holstein. Heads of government of the Union parties included Leo Wohleb in Baden, Dr. Hans Ehard in Bavaria, Karl Arnold in North Rhine-Westphalia, Peter Altmeier in Rhineland-Palatinate and Dr. Lorenz Bock in Württemberg-Hohenzollern. In Württemberg-Baden Liberal Democrat Dr. Reinhold Maier served as the only non-Socialist, non-Christian/Social Democrat Premier, although his party, the DVP, was only the third largest group in the *Landtag*.

37 In 1949 only three states (Baden, Bavaria and Württemberg-Hohenzollern) with eleven *Bundesrat* votes were safely CDU/CSU; three additional states (Bremen, Hamburg and Schleswig-Holstein) with ten *Bundesrat* votes were safely SPD, while the five other states with 22 votes were in the doubtful category. By June 1955, at the height of Adenauer's coordination efforts, the CDU controlled six states with 26 *Bundesrat* votes, the SPD three with twelve votes. None were in the doubtful category.

38 These states were Hesse, Lower Saxony, North Rhine-Westphalia, Rhineland-Palatinate, Württemberg-Baden and Württemberg-Hohenzollern.

39 The grand coalition in Lower Saxony broke up in August 1950, eight months prior to the second *Landtag* election. In Hesse, North Rhine-Westphalia and Württemberg-Baden the coalitions between the two parties dissolved following the 1950 *Land* elections in those states, and in Rhineland-Palatinate following the 1951 *Land* election contest. The coalition in Württemberg-Hohenzollern dissolved in 1952 with the amalgamation of the three Southwest states into the new *Land* of Baden-Württemberg.

40 Chancellor Adenauer, following the 1950 *Land* election in North Rhine-Westphalia, had attempted to force a coalition between his CDU and the right-wing FDP. Minister President Arnold (CDU), however, resisted these pressures and formed a temporary government with the small *Zentrum*, a coalition which was to last four years.

41 Intense discord within the CDU in Baden-Württemberg had caused its share of the vote to fall to 35.9 percent in 1952 in contrast to 44.9 percent in the elections held in the three *Länder* in 1946 and 1947. Maier, in excluding the Christian Democrats from his cabinet, pointed out that the serious dissention within the CDU would have made an FDP-CDU government too unstable. Prior to the formation of Baden-Württemberg the CDU could count upon the three *Bundesrat* votes of both Baden and Württemberg-Hohenzollern, the SPD upon the four *Bundesrat* votes of Württemberg-Baden; however, the amalgamation of the three *Länder* into a single Southwest State reduced the size of

the *Bundesrat* from 43 to 38 members and placed the five *Bundesrat* votes of the new *Land* in the doubtful category. For the influence of this change on the operation of the *Bundesrat* and especially the struggle over ratification of the EDC treaties, see Pinney, 1963: 119-127.

42 *5th Quarterly Report on Germany,* October 1-December 31, 1950, Office of the U.S. High Commissioner for Germany: 36. A government excluding both the Socialists and the Bavarian Party would not have had a majority in the Bavarian *Landtag.*

43 CDU participation in the Kaisen government in no way endangered the Socialist vote in the *Bundesrat.* Socialist cooperation with the Free Democrats in Bremen was a continuation of a working arrangement which had proven satisfactory since the establishment of the first *Bürgerschaft.*

44 The SPD had won absolute majorities in both Hamburg and Hesse, where it formed pure Socialist governments, established governments in concert with the FDP and CDU in Bremen and with the BHE and *Zentrum* in Lower Saxony and participated in the coalitions in Bavaria and Baden-Württemberg where its presence was required for a majority. On the other hand, the CDU controlled the governments of North Rhine-Westphalia with the *Zentrum,* Rhineland-Palatinate with the FDP, Schleswig-Holstein with the DP, FDP and BHE and Bavaria with the SPD and BHE, but where it was dependent on Socialist goodwill. The CDU had polled only 28.0 percent of the nation-wide vote cast in the *Land* elections held between the first and the second *Bundestag* contest in contrast to the SPD's 32.4 percent. The Socialists were the leading party in six *Länder,* the CDU in only three. In no *Land* did the CDU alone gain an absolute majority of the seats.

45 Hamburg's three votes gave the Bonn coalition 26 of the 38 votes in the *Bundesrat.*

46 Following the 1954 election in North Rhine-Westphalia the SPD had announced its willingness to accept pro-Adenauer votes in the *Bundesrat* if it were brought into a CDU-led government; however national interests dictated the FDP and *Zentrum* as coalition partners.

47 A government consisting of the CDU, FDP and Refugee Party was formed in Schleswig-Holstein although the SPD remained the strongest party in the *Land.*

48 The CSU had gained 38.0 percent of the *Land* vote in contrast to 28.1 percent for the second place SPD.

49 Of Hesse's 96 *Landtag* seats, the SPD controlled 44, the CDU and FDP together 45, placing the balance between the two groupings in the hands of the Refugee Party. The events in Bavaria and Hesse were a severe blow to Adenauer's hopes for quick approval of the Saar and Paris agreements in the *Bundesrat.* The latter would have granted virtual sovereignty to West Germany and brought her into NATO.

50 The exclusion of the leading SPD from the government in Lower Saxony restored a two-thirds majority for the Bonn government in the *Bundesrat.*

51 A running account of the events leading up to the ouster of the Arnold government in North Rhine-Westphalia in 1956 is found in Heidenheimer, *American Political Science Review* (September 1958): 813-815 and 821-823 and Pinney, 1963: 103-109.

52 The largest parliamentary group did not participate in the cabinets of five of the nine *Länder*. The leading Socialists were excluded from the governments of Hamburg from November 1953 to November 1957, Lower Saxony from May 1955 to November 1957, and Schleswig-Holstein from August 1950 to September 1958 when the CDU became the strongest *Landtag* group. The Christian Democrats were excluded in the same manner from the governments of Bavaria from December 1954 to October 1957 and North Rhine-Westphalia from February 1956 to July 1958. From April 1952 to October 1953 the leading CDU had been excluded from the government in Baden-Württemberg, and from October 1953 to January 1955 the largest parliamentary group, the SPD, had been excluded from the government in Berlin. Until 1966 in North Rhine-Westphalia no government was again formed in any of the *Länder* in which the strongest party did not participate.

53 Several of these coalitions were criticized as merely administering, not governing.

54 In the 2001 *Land* election in Hamburg the SPD had received 36.5 percent of the vote to the CDU's 26.2 percent. This necessitated the establishment of a three-party coalition of the CDU, FDP and Schill Party to provide a working majority. In Hesse, the CDU outpolled the Socialists 47.3 to 43.2 percent in the 1974 *Land* election, 46.0 to 44.3 percent in the 1978 *Land* contest, 45.6 to 42.8 percent in the 1982 election and 39.2 to 38.0 in the 1995 regional contest, but the SPD, by combining with the Free Democrats in the earlier period and with the Greens from 1995 to 1999, succeeded in retaining control of the state administration. In the 1994 regional contest in Saxony-Anhalt, the CDU received 34.5 percent of ballots cast to the SPD's 34.0 percent, but the Socialists were able to form a minority government with the Greens and PDS tolerance.

55 In Schleswig-Holstein there was no change in party control, rather, the second party, the CDU, became the leading party as a result of the 1958 regional election. In 1954 the SPD had polled 33.2 percent of the vote to 32.2 percent for the CDU. In 1958, while the CDU total surged to 44.4 percent, the Socialist figure increased only to 35.9 percent.

56 The governmental change in Bavaria was interpreted as the first major repercussion of the overwhelming victory of the CDU in the *Bundestag* election of September 1957.

57 The SPD gained 53.9 percent of the *Land* vote and an absolute majority in the Hamburg *Bürgerschaft*. In spite of its dominant position the Free Democrats were brought into the Socialist administration.

58 The stand of the Lower Saxony CDU was directed primarily at the *Land* FDP which included former Nazis within its ranks and had considered combining with the right-wing DRP on a state basis.

59 The CDU won 104 of 200 *Landtag* seats. The election campaign in the Rhineland was marred by the sudden death of CDU leader Karl Arnold shortly before the election. His death was thought to have contributed to the Christian Democrat success at the polls.

60 The Socialist-Refugee party coalition in Hesse and the CDU-FDP administration in Rhineland-Palatinate were continued, while the CDU-SPD-DP government in Lower Saxony was replaced by one containing Socialist, Free Democrat and Refugee party members.

61 In Bremen the Socialists formed a coalition with the FDP, in Baden-Württemberg the CDU coalesced with the FDP and BHE and in the Saar with the DPS/FDP. Elimination of the GDP from the *Landtag* in the 1964 regional election in Baden-Württemberg ended its participation in that state's government, while events in December 1966 established a CDU-SPD coalition in Stuttgart.

62 *Der Spiegel*, December 19, 1966: 40-41.

63 Prior to the 1966 *Land* elections the SPD governed with a second party in both Hamburg and Hesse. In Hamburg the FDP unilaterally decided not to continue participation in the state administration after suffering extensive election losses. In Hesse the GDP lost its representation in the *Landtag*, and the Socialists decided against seeking another coalition partner. Between 1962 and 1966 none of the majority parties had chosen to govern alone.

64 At the end of 1966 the parliamentary executive of every state was either a Social or Christian Democrat. The Socialist heads of government included Willy Dehnkamp in Bremen, Dr. Herbert Weichmann in Hamburg, Georg August Zinn in Hesse, Dr. Georg Diederichs in Lower Saxony, Heinz Kühn in North Rhine-Westphalia and Heinrich Albertz in West Berlin. Christian Democrat heads included Hans Filbinger in Baden-Württemberg, Alfons Goppel in Bavaria, Peter Altmeier in Rhineland-Palatinate, Dr. Franz Josef Röder in the Saar and Dr. Helmut Lemke in Schleswig-Holstein.

65 Prior to May 1965 the FDP had been represented in the governments of every state but Bavaria and Hesse. The formation of grand coalitions in Baden-Württemberg and Lower Saxony and its decision not to continue its partnership with the Socialists in Hamburg after the 1966 regional election reduced the number to six.

The Free Democrats participated in governments with the Socialists in both Rhineland-Palatinate and the Saar for brief periods of time; however, in both cases the CDU, not the SPD, headed those governments. Disagreement on policies concerning confessional and Christian non-denominational schools was a major factor in making an SPD-FDP coalition in Rhineland-Palatinate impossible following the 1963 *Land* election, although the SPD offered four of eight cabinet posts to the FDP in an attempt to woo it away from the CDU.

66 See footnote No. 24 of this chapter.

67 See footnote No. 52 of this chapter.

68 By the end of 1966, in not a single state was the leading parliamentary group excluded from the government, although this had occurred in seven states during the 1950s and in North Rhine-Westphalia from July to November 1966. Those who were critical of FDP cooperation with the CDU at the time are reminded that with the single exception of North Rhine-Westphalia, the Free Democrats were consistent through 1969 in siding with the largest legislature faction, whether on the state or national level.

69 Although the Socialists reentered the Lower Saxony government as the leading party in November 1957, German party leader Heinrich Hellwege retained the position of Minister President.

70 The four-party coalition in Baden-Württemberg in which both the CDU and the SPD participated from 1953 to 1960 was considered a necessary means of achieving unity in the newly formed state. The same considerations were influential in CDU-SPD cooperation in the Saar until 1960.

71 Between July 1960 and June 1964 in Baden-Württemberg a three-party coalition was formed between the CDU, FDP and the Refugee Party; however, the CDU and the FDP alone controlled seventy of the 121 parliamentary seats, making inclusion of the BHE in the government unnecessary. From December 1946 to July 1947 three parties, the CSU, SPD and WAV, participated in the Bavarian government, even though the CSU could have formed a government on its own from the very beginning. The three-party government in Bavaria from December 1958 to December 1962 was a continuation of the previous ministry which had governed since 1957; however, in the later period the CSU could have formed a stable government with either the FDP or BHE. Between 1946 and 1948 in Greater Berlin and 1948 and 1953 in West Berlin all governments included the three Western democratic parties, the SPD, CDU and FDP, although the SPD with either of the two other parties could have formed a majority, and from 1948 to 1950 could have governed alone. The international status of Berlin and its position as a symbol of resistance to Communist attempts to snuff it out as an island of freedom demanded the cooperation of the democratic parties in the immediate postwar period; however, since 1953 the governments in West Berlin or a united Berlin have included only one or two parties with the exception of the period between June and December 2001 when the SPD and Greens ruled with PDS tolerance. Bremen's first responsible government, functioning from November 1946 to January 1948, consisted of the SPD, BDV and the KPD, although the Socialist's parliamentary majority required the cooperation of neither party. From November 1951 to December 1959 the SPD formed the government of Bremen with the CDU and FDP, although from 1951 to 1955 it could have formed a majority with a second party and from 1955 to 1959 could have governed alone. In Hamburg the Socialists governed with the FDP and KPD from 1946 to 1949 in spite of a parliamentary majority, and in Lower Saxony they combined with the Refugee Party and the small *Zentrum* from 1951 to 1953, although inclusion of the ZP was not required for a majority. Again in Lower Saxony from 1957 to 1959 the CDU and the SPD together controlled sufficient seats to govern in an administration also including the German Party. Likewise, in North Rhine-Westphalia from 1954 to 1956 the CDU and FDP were in no way dependent upon the *Zentrum* for a majority. In the Saar after its incorporation in 1957 the CDU with either the SPD or the DPS could have formed a workable majority.

72 In the 2001 *Bürgerschaft* election the SPD polled 36.5 percent of the vote to the CDU's 26.2 percent. A combination between the CDU and FDP alone provided only 39 of the 61 seats needed to govern. The renegade Schill Party with 25 seats provided the necessary margin.

73 Cooperation between the SPD and FDP continued after Kaisen's retirement until 1971, but was not resumed until the 1991-1995 legislative session under an *Ampel* coalition which included the Greens.

74 Cooperation between the Socialists and FDP in Hesse lasted twelve years, from 1970 to 1982, when the Free Democrats failed to qualify for seats, and in Rhineland-Palatinate from 1991 to 2006, when the SPD won an absolute majority in the *Landtag*.

75 In 1949 prior to the formation of the national government, regional ministries which included both the SPD and the CDU existed in Hesse, Lower Saxony, North Rhine-Westphalia, Rhineland-Palatinate, West Berlin, Württemberg-Baden and Württemberg-Hohenzollern. For some months at the beginning of the first legislative period in Baden and Bavaria both major parties participated in a common government.

76 *Die Welt*, May 20, 1965. The SPD/CDU coalition in Lower Saxony resulted from the unwillingness of the Free Democrats to support a concordat with the Catholic Church governing religious education in the state. Political observers interpreted the concordat as an attempt by the Lower Saxony SPD to increase its support among Catholic voters in the *Land*; however, the results of the 1965 *Bundestag* election in Lower Saxony indicated that the concordat had little or no influence on the election outcome.

77 The SPD had won 99, the CDU 86 of the 200 *Landtag* seats in the July election. In the voting for Minister President, Meyers fell one short of the necessary 101 votes to elect on the first ballot as one CDU deputy abstained in the secret election. Meyers was chosen on the second ballot, in which only a majority of the deputies actually voting was required to elect. See *Die Welt*, July 12, 13 and 26, 1966.

78 See footnote No. 76 of this chapter.

79 The events leading up to this coalition are described in *Der Spiegel*, December 19, 1966: 40-41.

80 After having gained access to the *Bundestag* for the first time in 1983 and increased its following to 8.3 percent in the 1987 general election, the Greens' stunning setback in 1990 signaled the need to revise its appeal if it was to regain a national foothold. To demonstrate the severity of the party's loss of support, the various *Land* organizations had polled 2,050,282 votes in the ten regional contests held between the 1987 and 1990 *Bundestag* polls, but only 1,788,200 votes (3.8 percent) in an election which encompassed all sixteen German states.

81 A combination of legal and political factors have also been responsible for this stability. First, neither the Minister President nor the Cabinet as a whole may dissolve the *Landtag*. Moreover, executive stability is insured through constitutional stipulations prescribing that in the event a Minister President dies, resigns or is forced out of office, his successor must be elected within a certain period of time or the *Landtag* must be dissolved (Bavaria, Hesse and Rhineland-Palatinate), or which required the constructive vote of non-confidence, under which the executive can be dismissed by a vote of non-confidence only if accompanied by the election of a successor. The requirement in the electoral laws of all *Länder* that a party obtain a specific percentage of the vote to be eligible for representation likewise enhances stability by minimizing political fragmentation in the legislature.

82 The absence of defense and foreign policy matters as a concern of the states prior to 1949 helped to make cooperative efforts between the CDU and SPD possible on the regional level during the period when their international programs were far apart.

83 Dr. Reinhold Maier served as Minister President of Württemberg-Baden from his appointment by the Military Government in 1945 until the *Land* was dissolved in 1952, at which time he took over the post of Minister President for the new *Land* of Baden-Württemberg, continuing in that position until October 1953. German Party Leader Heinrich Hellwege was Minister President of Lower Saxony from May 1955 until May 1959. The CDU or the SPD alone or the two parties together participated in the above-noted governments. Winfried Kretschmann became the first Green Party Minister-President following the March 2011 *Land* election in Baden-Württemberg.

84 Dr. Reinhold Maier (DVP/FDP) served as Baden-Württemberg's first Minister President from April 1952 to October 1953 when he was replaced by Dr. Gebhard Müller (CDU), who continued in the post of Premier until November 1958 when he was elected

President of the Federal Constitutional Court. His successor, Dr. Kurt Georg Kiesinger (CDU), held the premiership until he became Federal Chancellor in December 1966. Hans Filbinger (CDU) succeeded Kiesinger. Prior to the establishment of the *Land* Baden-Württemberg in 1952, Leo Wohleb (CDU) served as State President of Baden from 1947 until the dissolution of the state five years later. Dr. Lorenz Bock (CDU) held the post of President of Württemberg-Hohenzollern from July 1947 until his death in August 1948 when he was succeeded by Dr. Gebhard Müller (CDU) who continued as President until the incorporation of the state into Baden-Württemberg in 1952. Dr. Reinhold Maier (DVP/FDP) was Minister President of Württemberg-Baden during the entire appointment period and from December 1946 until April 1952 on a responsible basis.

85 In Bavaria Dr. Hans Ehard (CSU) served as Minister President from December 1946 to December 1954 when a coalition of the SPD, FDP, BP and Refugee Party under Wilhelm Hoegner (SPD) excluded the leading CSU from the government. A reorientation of political forces enabled the CSU to form a coalition with the FDP and the Refugee Party before the end of the legislative period and Hoegner's successor, Dr. Hanns Seidel (CSU), took over the premiership in October 1957 and continued in that post until 1960.

86 The Christian Social Union won an absolute majority of seats in the Bavarian *Landtag* in 1962, 1966, 1970, 1974, 1978, 1982, 1986, 1990, 1994, 1998 and 2003.

87 In Bremen Wilhelm Kaisen (SPD) held the post of *Bürgermeister* from his initial appointment to the post by the British in August 1945 until his retirement in July 1965 when he was succeeded by Willy Dehnkamp (SPD). Kaisen was the second appointed *Bürgermeister* of Bremen, his predecessor, Erich Vagts (Ind.), serving in that position for less than two months, from June 6, 1945, to July 31, 1945.

88 Johannes Hoffmann, leader of the Christian People's Party, served as Minister President from 1947 until replaced by Dr. Hubert Ney (CDU) after the 1955 *Landtag* election.
Dr. Ney (CDU) was Minister President at the time of the Saar's incorporation into the Federal Republic, but resigned shortly thereafter (March 25, 1957). His successor, Egon Reinert (CDU), was Premier from June 1957 until his death in April 1959.

89 Several factors were responsible for the early successes of the SPD in Schleswig-Holstein, chief among them being the early difficulties faced by the CDU in making inroads in this heavily Protestant state, the fragmentation of the political Right, the image of the SPD as a respectable party in a state which had held strong Nazi sympathies in an earlier period and the presence of a large refugee population which saw in the Socialists their best hope for a redistribution of the wealth as a means of compensation for their losses in the East.
The Social Democrats won an absolute majority of *Landtag* seats in 1947, enabling them to form a one-party government until 1950 when an alliance of the parties of the Bonn government (CDU, FDP, and DP) broke the Socialist majority and formed a government with the Refugee Party. In 1950 the Socialists gained more seats than any other party, and in 1954 they outpolled all other parties, but gained the same number of seats as the CDU (25) under the d'Hondt distribution. Again the leading party was excluded from the government by a coalition of the CDU, FDP and the Refugee Party.
Hermann Lüdemann (SPD) held the post of Minister President of Schleswig-Holstein from April 1947 to August 1949, and his successor, Bruno Diekmann (SPD), until September 1950 when a four-party coalition of the CDU, DP, FDP, and BHE under Dr. Walter Bartram (CDU) formed a government without the leading SPD. A cabinet

crisis led to Bartram's replacement in June 1951 by Friedrich-Wilhelm Lübke (CDU), who continued in the premiership until October 1954 when he was succeeded by Kai-Uwe von Hassel (CDU).

90 Strauss was removed for his implication in the Spiegel Affair (*Die Welt*, December 14, 1962).

91 A Green list of candidates had been entered in every regional election in Schleswig-Holstein since 1979, but the grouping failed in its first five attempts to exceed the five percent barrier to representation. In the 1996 contest it received 8.1 percent of ballots cast and six seats in the state parliament.

92 The first SPD/PDS alliance existed in Mecklenburg-Vorpommern between 1998 and 2006 when it was replaced by a grand coalition between the Socialists and the CDU.

93 The grand coalition in Mecklenburg-Vorpommern provided the national coalition with 47 *Bundesrat* votes, 46 votes being necessary for a two-thirds majority. That majority was lost the following May when the Socialists coalesced with the Greens in Bremen and was further eroded when the CDU partnered with the Greens after the 2008 *Bürgerschaft* election in Hamburg.

94 From 1959 to the end of 1966 the CDU controlled 26, the SPD 15 *Bundesrat* votes. Following the change of administration in North Rhine-Westphalia the party ratio stood at 21 CDU and twenty SPD votes.

95 The *Bundesrat,* for example, refused to approve the controversial Federal Criminal Office (BKA) bill for combating terrorism which had passed the *Bundestag.* The small parties in those states where the CDU governed with the FDP or Greens opposed the law (*Die Welt*, November 29, 2008).

CHAPTER XI

Reflections on German Elections

Emerging from the trauma of a totalitarian dictatorship and a destructive war, Germany has evolved into one of the world's most stable and effective democracies. In spite of the basically proportional nature of its federal and state electoral laws, a modified two-party system, currently under stress, developed on both the national and regional levels, and the country's two leading political groupings, the Christian Union parties and the Social Democratic Party have alternated in power or governed together under only eight chancellors over a 62-year period. Among its leaders, Dr. Konrad Adenauer (CDU), Germany's first chancellor, served in office for fourteen years (1949-1963), Dr. Helmut Kohl (CDU) for sixteen years (1982-1998), Helmut Schmidt (SPD) for eight years (1974-1982), and Gerhard Schroeder (SPD) for seven years (1998-2005), providing both stability and continuity in government at the national level.[1] This compares most favorably with Great Britain, the world's oldest democracy, which has witnessed seven changes in party control since 1949 under thirteen prime ministers, only two of whom, Margaret Thatcher (Conservative Party) and Tony Blair (Labour Party) served as long as ten years.[2] Continuity in foreign policy has likewise been assured through only seven foreign ministers, one of whom, Hans-Dietrich Genscher, served under both Socialist and Union chancellors for eighteen years, 1974-1992 (*Die Welt am Sonntag*, October 21, 2006).[3]

Large credit for the vitality of the German state rests with Dr. Konrad Adenauer and Ludwig Erhard who took over a defeated, devastated, divided and despised country and for seventeen years, guided its destiny, leading the western part of the country to full sovereignty, political stability, economic recovery and to a respected status in the world community. They established a sound foundation on which their successors could build, and today it is safe to say that a tradition of democratic practices has become firmly established with voters demonstrating a degree of sophistication usually characterized by much older democracies.

The non-doctrinaire approach of *"Der Alte"* (a nickname given to Dr. Adenauer) to political and economic problems, his strong personality and capacity to comprehend political power, the all-encompassing nature of the Union parties' program and their ability to attract a diversity of elements coupled with the success of Ludwig Erhard's economic policies completely altered the conditions under which political contests in Germany had traditionally been fought. Rival parties either had to accommodate themselves to the changed situation or perish. The result during the first fifteen years of the Republic was a steady decline in the number of political groupings obtaining national and regional representation, leading by the early 1960s to a three party system on both the national and regional levels. However, as the CDU/CSU, SPD and FDP came more and more to resemble each other, segments of the population which felt unrepresented have been able to form a base from which to challenge the older established parties The result has been a declining share of the vote falling to the three originally-licensed parties and more to fourth, fifth and even sixth groupings, such as the Greens, *Die Linke* and various right-extremist groups.

The dominating influence of economic reconstruction, the resettlement of millions of uprooted expellees and refugees from the East, the need to compensate victims of National Socialist injustices and foreign policy decisions relating to the Cold War early pushed issues of a strictly local nature into the background, and *Land* election campaigns after 1949 came increasingly to be fought on national rather than on regional issues. Moreover, as the national parties attempted to control *Bundesrat* majorities through the domination of *Land* politics, regional elections assumed a plebiscitary character, a vote for or against the major party in control of the federal government, a vote for or against the sitting Chancellor. The national parties not only actively sought to influence regional election outcomes but also the make-up of the various state governments. The eleven straight regional election setbacks for the SPD between 2002 and 2005, for example, were directly related to voter resistance to the reform initiatives taken by the SPD/Greens government in Berlin, leading to Chancellor Schröder's decision to call for national elections one year early.

Many of the same forces which shaped the national political scene also influenced regional politics, but local issues and the particular characteristics of the individual *Land* electorates guaranteed that at least some of the states would be controlled by parties different from those controlling the national administration and produce stability on the regional level not unlike that found on the national sphere. It has not been uncommon for a state premier or Lord Mayor, whether Unionist or Socialist, to remain in office longer than any federal chancellor. Dr. Peter Altmeier (CDU) served as Minister President of Rhineland-Palatinate for a period of 22 years, from 1947 to 1969, while both Johannes Rau (SPD) in North Rhine Westphalia (1978-1998) and Franz Josef Röder (CDU) in the Saar (1959-1979) held their state's leading office for twenty years. Other long-serving state heads include Wilhelm Kaisen (SPD), Lord Mayor of Bremen from 1946 to 1965, August Zinn (SPD), Minister President of Hesse from 1951 to 1969, Hans Korschnik (SPD), Lord Mayor of Bremen from 1967 to 1985, Hans Goppel (CSU), Minister President of Bavaria from 1962 to

1978, Kurt Beck (SPD), Minister President of Rhineland-Palatinate from 1994 to the present, Erwin Teufel (CDU), Minister President of Baden-Württemberg from 1991 to 2005, Oskar Lafontaine (SPD), Minister President of the Saar from 1985 to 1998, Matthias Platzeck, Minister President of Brandenburg from 1992 to the present, and Heidi Simonis (SPD), Minister President of Schleswig-Holstein from 1993 to 2005. In October 2007 Edmund Stoiber (CSU) stepped down as Minister President of Bavaria after having led Bavaria for fourteen years.

In spite of the lengthy tenure in office of a number of regional leaders, the German voter has not been reluctant to vote a party or party coalition out of power or support one of the numerous protest groupings which have emerged over the years, if the political situation warranted it, whether because of disenchantment with a party's national policies or purely local issues. The abrupt turnaround in the fortunes of the Schleswig-Holstein CDU in 1988 after 37 years of continuous rule followed the election scandal involving Minister President Uwe Barschel, a humiliation from which it took seventeen years for the Christian Democrats in that *Land* to recover (*Dithmarscher Landeszeitung*, "CDU Krise durch Barschel Affair," October 5, 2007). Likewise, the financial scandal in 2001 involving the Berlin CDU cost the party its leading position after ten years in power, a disgrace from which it has yet to recover.

In the last fifty years every state with the exceptions of Bavaria, Brandenburg, Bremen, Saxony and Thuringia has witnessed at least one change in party control. In several highly competitive states like Lower Saxony and North Rhine Westphalia change in party control has occurred four or five times. In other states domination by a single party has been broken only after an extended period. The SPD interrupted CDU control of the Saar for the first time in 1985 after thirty years of continuous Christian Democratic rule, and in 1991 it came to power in Rhineland-Palatinate after 44 years of CDU governance. The CDU, on the other hand, broke Socialist control of Hesse in 1987 after being in the opposition for over forty years, while in Hamburg it took over the reigns of government in 2001 after being out of power for 44 years. The CDU victory in North Rhine-Westphalia in 2005 enabled it to replace the SPD after having been out of favor since 1966. The stability which has been demonstrated in most of the state governments has been due in large measure to the non-doctrinaire character of the country's major parties, including the Greens after 1994, and, with few exceptions, such as the Greens' opposition to nuclear power, alteration in party control has not resulted in earth-shaking change.

The German political scene has been characterized by a high level of tolerance and high office is not automatically closed to a competent political figure because of divorce, sexual orientation or stand on certain controversial religious issues as is so often the case in the United States. A recent Chancellor has been married four times and a foreign minister, who was also party leader, five times. And several married chancellors and ministers have had mistresses. Having a child out of wedlock did not prevent a high-profile politician from becoming premier of a German state. The recent chair of the Free Democratic

Party (FDP) and Germany's current foreign minister, Dr. Guido Westerwelle, as well as the Lord Mayor of Berlin and former Lord Mayor of Hamburg, have male companions. Klaus Vorwereit, Lord Mayor of Berlin, in spite of openly having a male partner, has been portrayed in several of Germany's leading news magazines as a potential future chancellor candidate (*Stern*, September 12, 2007, *Der Spiegel* 8, 2007) and the recently retired Lord Mayor Ole von Beust of Hamburg was named the country's outstanding mayor in 2005 for his leadership in turning Hamburg into a "boom city" (*Stern*, May 5, 2006), and leading his party, the CDU, in 2004 to his party's first absolute majority in this strongly Socialist city. While that majority was lost in 2008, von Beust formed a coalition with the Greens, remaining as Lord Mayor of the *Hansastadt* until his retirement in August 2010. By 2010 a number of developments had placed the Black/Green partnership in Hamburg under stress, including a large budget shortfall, a major cost overrun in the Elbe Philharmonic project and public opposition to the Black/Green coalition's school reform measure, which led to a controversial referendum on the issue. In a bitter setback, the school reform plan was overturned in a vote held July 18, 2010. That same day von Beust announced his intention to retire the end of August after nearly nine years in office (*Spiegel Online* July 18, 2010).

Religious orientation is also not a drawback as the country has had both Catholic and Protestant chancellors and state premiers. Dr. Konrad Adenauer, the country's first Chancellor, was a devout Catholic, attending the small church in his native Rhöndorf on the Rhine on a regular basis. He has been ranked along with Otto von Bismarck as one of Germany's most important political figures. In October 2007 Hans Beckstein became the first Protestant premier of strongly Catholic Bavaria. Although serving as premier for only one year, the CSU's decline in voter favor in the 2008 state election and Beckstein's subsequent resignation had nothing to do with his religious orientation.

Whatever one's personal life or orientation, the important factors in German politics are competence and credibility.

Just as Angela Merkel has been the only female federal Chancellor, Heidi Simonis, Minister President of Schleswig-Holstein from 1993 to 2005, had been the sole female head of a state government until October 2009 when Christine Lieberknecht (CDU) replaced Dieter Althaus as minister president in Thuringia (*Hamburger Abendblatt*, October 30, 2009), and Hannelore Kraft replaced Jürgen Rüttgers (CDU) in North Rhineland-Westphalia in July 2010, although as head of a minority government coalition (*FAZ.NET*, July 14, 2010). Annegret Kramp-Karrenbauer has been chosen to succeed Peter Müller as Minister-President of the Saar in fall 2011, making her the fourth female to hold such high office (*Welt am Sonntag*, January 23, 2011). A number of other women, however, have aspired to that high state office.[4] In both 2001 and 2006 Ute Vogt stood as the Socialist candidate for minister president in Baden-Württemberg, but lost out to Erwin Teufel in 2001 and to Günther Oettinger in 2006. Vogt, however, was voted deputy chair of the national SPD in 2003 and served in that position until October 2007 when she stepped down in favor of Andrea Nahles

(*Der Spiegel*, September 17, 2007 and October 12, 2007). The SPD in both Lower Saxony and Hesse supported a woman candidate for the premiership in the 2008 state elections and Hannelore Kraft faced Jürgen Rüttgers (CDU) in the 2010 state election in North Rhine-Westphalia, ultimately becoming that state's premier.[5] In Bavaria, CSU *Landrat* Gabriele Pauli, a strong critic of the direction of her party, stood as a candidate for the leadership of the Christian Social Union to replace retiring Edmund Stoiber, but received only two percent of the vote of party delegates at the September 29, 2007 meeting of the party, losing out to Erwin Huber who received 57 percent of ballots cast (*Der Spiegel*, November 10, 2007). Pauli subsequently bolted to the *Freie Wähler* (FW) and became a member of the Bavarian parliament in 2008 following the first regional election success of the grouping. As a result of that same election Barbara Stumm (CSU) became the first woman in Bavaria to be elected *Landtag* president. Claudia Roth is co-chairperson of the Greens Party.

Both the Greens and *Die Linke* have made a special effort to balance their party lists between male and female candidates. In Schleswig-Holstein, for example, six of twelve *Landtag* representatives of the Greens, three of six Leftist delegates and two of four SSW delegates are women. In the Schleswig-Holstein *Landtag* as a whole, 35 of 95 (36.8 percent) representatives are women (six of fourteen FDP, nine of 25 SPD and nine of 34 CDU delegates). In Hamburg, 41 of the 121 (33.9 percent) *Bürgerschaft* representatives are women, including half of the Green and Leftist delegates. It is interesting to note that for the 2011 *Bürgerschaft* election in Hamburg, the lead candidates of all three minor parties, the Greens, FDP and *Die* Linke, were women, Anja Hajduk for the Greens, Katja Suding for the FDP and Dora Heyenn for the Leftists (*Welt am Sonntag*, January 16, 2011).

In contrast to the ability of an individual with little or no political experience to become governor or even president in the United States, this is not the case of Germany, where a person must have proven himself or herself over a number of years before being designated as a candidate for high office. The longest serving chancellor of Germany, Helmut Kohl, for example, joined the Christian Democratic Union in 1947, became a member of the Rhineland-Palatinate *Landtag* in 1959, chairman of the CDU *Fraktion* in the state parliament in 1963, Minister President of Rhineland-Palatinate in 1969, serving in that capacity until 1976 when he became a member of the *Bundestag* and chairman of the Union parties before becoming Chancellor of the Federal Republic in 1982 (*First All German Election*, **Inter Nationes**, 1990) . Executive heads of the various states likewise must have first proven themselves as party leaders and members of the state parliaments before ascending to the state's highest office. It is interesting to note how many state executives have become federal ministers and even chancellors and federal presidents. Six of Germany's eight chancellors gained their experience on the state or local level. Dr. Konrad Adenauer was Lord Mayor of Cologne prior to the Nazi take-over in 1933; Dr. Kurt Kiesinger was Minister President of Baden-Württemberg before being elevated to the Chancellorship in 1966; Willy Brandt was Lord Mayor of Berlin,

Helmut Schmidt Interior Senator in Hamburg, Dr. Helmut Kohl Premier of Rhineland-Palatinate and Gerhard Schröder Minister-President of Lower Saxony prior to becoming Chancellor in 1998. Johannes Rau, probably the most successful state premier, led Germany's most populous state, North Rhine-Westphalia, for twenty years before becoming Federal President in 1999. Dr. Richard von Weizsächer was Lord Mayor of West Berlin prior to his elevation to the federal presidency in 1984.

Germany is no longer the homogeneous country that it once was. It is now the home of some 6,717,000 residents of foreign birth according to 2004 census figures. The largest grouping, numbering 1,764,313, have a Turkish background, followed by 826,504 Asians and 548,194 Italians. Of the 6.7 million, 65.3 percent are from European Union countries and an estimated 3.3 million are Muslims. The integration of the Muslim population has been a special concern since, as in Berlin and Cologne, many Muslims live in ghettoized conditions and the Islamists among them are inclined to place Muslim law and practices above the German Basic Law, creating an unacceptable two sets of standards.[6] This and the proliferation of mosques in a Christian country has produced numerous tensions. It is estimated that in Hamburg alone there are over sixty-six mosques for the over 130,000 Muslims living in the city. Plans to construct a mosque with a 175-foot high minaret in the city created a storm there (*Welt am Sonntag*, October 4, 2007). A large mosque seating 1,000 was opened in Duisburg-Marxloh in October 2008.

A 2008 study indicated that the Turkish population in Germany was the least integrated of newcomers, while those from European Union countries have the best record of integration. Although Turkish political leaders have not formed a minority party of their own, the Greens have made a concentrated effort to attract the eligible Turkish voter. It was through the Greens that Cem Oezdemir became the first *Bundestag* representative of Turkish ancestry in 1994. Called the "Turkish Obama," he has not only become the leader of the Greens in Hesse, but co-chair of the national party with Claudia Roth (*Husumer Nachrichten*, November 28, 2008). In spite of his calling for the teaching of Turkish in the schools, his party made major gains in the January 2009 *Land* election in Hesse. In April 2010 Aygül Özkan, a lawyer/manager and Christian Democratic representative in the Hamburg *Bürgerschaft,* became the first ethnic Turk to hold a ministerial post in a state government, in this case, Social Minister in Lower Saxony (*Die Zeit*, April 22, 2010: 2). In Hamburg, the son of Iranian immigrants, Daniel Ilkhanipour, rose to the leadership of the Hamburg Jusos (young Socialists), and by a 45 to 44 vote, won the right to be the SPD's direct seat candidate for the 2009 *Bundestag* contest over favorite Niels Annen.

Right-extremist groups have readily exploited the fear of foreigners in their campaign rhetoric, especially when birth rates for "non-native" groups have far surpassed the native German replacement level. There have been acts of violence by some right-extremists, including several prominent murders, but most supporters of extremist groups frown from violent actions, since they do not foster general sympathy for their rightist causes (*Stern*, October 29, 2007).

Although gaining limited representation in three states between 2004 and 2007, support for right extremist groups in the most recent state and national elections has been minimal. In the 2009 state contest in Brandenburg, the DVU, which had polled 6.1 percent of the statewide vote in 2004 to gain six legislative seats, lost its entire delegation when its vote total fell to 1.1 percent, far below the five percent minimum required for representation. Also in 2009, support for the NPD in Saxony fell from the 9.2 percent reached in the 2004 state election to 5.6 percent, causing it to lose four of its *Landtag* seats. In 2009 *Bundestag* balloting the three most prominent right-extremist parties, the NPD, Republicans and DVU, together polled 874,835 votes or only 2.0 percent of the total national vote, with support for the NPD in its stronghold of Saxony falling to 4.0 percent of ballots cast (*Süddeutsche Zeitung*, October 1, 2009 and *Bundeswahlleiter BTW_BUND_09/ergebnisse/lande* 10.24.2009.)

Failing to have the National Democrats declared unconstitutional by the Federal Supreme Court in 2003 over their racist program and the violent acts of some of their members, several state interior ministers, among them Uwe Schünemann of Lower Saxony, have turned to having the party barred from receiving public campaign funds. In 2007 the NPD received 1,448,500 Euros (somewhat over two million dollars), representing 40 percent of the party's expenses. The argument is that if Germans have to live with the extremists, they shouldn't have to finance their activities with public funds. Groupings which threaten the basic order of the Federal Republic can be excluded from participation in public funding (*Neue Presse Hannover*, "*Keine Steuergelder für die NPD?*" November 20, 2008).[7] In May 2008 former Interior Minister Wolfgang Schäuble (CDU) banned two right extremist groups whose members continue to deny the murder of Jews during the Third Reich (*Financial Times Deutschland*, May 8, 2008).

A new scandal involving public funding enveloped the NPD in 2009. The party was charged with overestimating its expenses by 870,154 Euros for which it became eligible for a state subsidy of 270,000 Euros. Should the charges be substantiated, the party would not only have to refund the grant, but pay a penalty of 1.7 million Euros ("*Frisierte Spenden*," *Der Spiegel*, November 9, 2009: 15.)

The new CDU/CSU/FDP government in Berlin has been faced with a number of challenges which will require not only strong federal-state cooperation, but cooperation with other countries in Europe and with the United States to resolve. In addition to the global financial crisis and the Euro emergency caused by the Greek state's near bankruptcy and financial problems in Ireland, there are the problems of an aging population with its consequent drain on public resources and one of the lowest birth rates in the world which, if not reversed, will lead to a significantly smaller and older population.[8] Based on calculations from the Federal Statistical Office, Germany, with only 651,000 births in 2009, recorded the smallest number of children born in the country in the sixty-year history of the Federal Republic (*Welt am Sonntag*, May 23, 2010). In addition, various social and economic developments have led to rising income inequality in the population and to the development of a statistical *"Unterschicht"* amounting to fifteen percent of the population in the midst of relative prosperity.[9] Education reform, an overburdened health care system, large state debt (Berlin alone carries a debt of over sixty billion Euros – over $80 billion dollars), the continuing cost of reunification, and Germany's controversial commitment to NATO forces in Afghanistan are other challenges facing the country. Germany has attempted to address these problems, including increasing the retirement age to 67 years in spite of strong resistance from within and outside the government.

A drawback in the German system has been the difficulty in getting things done. There can be *"kleine Schritte"* (small steps) as Willy Brandt once put it, but no "great leaps forward." Chancellor Gerhard Schröder showed great courage in trying to reform policies which were stifling economic progress and his party was severely punished at the polls for his initiatives. In contrast, Chancellor Helmut Kohl, who lacked a reform agenda, was able to remain Chancellor for sixteen years. Partial privatization of the federal railway system was blocked not by rancor between the CDU/CSU and SPD administration, but by a coalition of unions and Socialist politicians, coupled with the economic downturn. Progress, as a result, comes in increments. Jürgen Rüttgers, Christian Democrat Minister President of North Rhine-Westphalia from 2005 to 2010, summed up the problem with his comment that "continual reform endangers the inner unity of the country (*Die Welt am Sonntag*, June 8, 2008).

The 2009 *Bundestag* election enabled the Union parties to drop the Socialists as their coalition partner and form a government at the national level with the Free Democrats, with Dr. Angela Merkel continuing as federal Chancellor.[10] The severe setback for the SPD, which recorded its worse showing since general elections were first held in 1949 is faced with the task of rebuilding its base in the face of growing competition from the Greens and *Die Linke*. Replacing Kurt Beck as party chair, in spite of his efforts to stave off the challenge of the Leftists, with the party's seasoned warrior Franz Müntefering in October 2008 failed to prevent the *Bundestag* debacle. To set a new tone, the SPD, on November 13, 2009 at its party convention in Dresden, selected former Minister President of Lower Saxony Sigmar Gabriel as its new party chair with a 94.2 percent vote to replace retiring Franz Müntefering, in the hope that he could provide the necessary leadership for a party revival (*Hamburger Abendblatt*, November 14-15, 2009). The outcome of the May 2010 regional election in North Rhine-Westphalia proved to be a modest comeback in that state over 2009 *Bundestag* results for the party as was the February 2011 outcome in Hamburg.

The general election of September 27, 2009 again produced a *Bundestag* inhabited by five parties. While the Free Democrats, the Greens and *Die Linke* made major gains, the CDU/CSU experienced a modest loss, but insufficient to alter its position as the largest party in the federal parliament. In contrast, SPD support dropped from 34.2 to 23.0 percent. Both the Christian Union parties and the Socialists need to regain their earlier positions as innovators if they are to stem the fragmentation besetting the German political system. More important to their future success rests in mobilizing the non-voters, the so-called *Sofa Fraktion* (couch faction), which in some states outnumber the votes cast for either of the two major parties or the two major parties together.

In May 2009 Germany was faced with the selection of a new federal President. The three candidates for the high office were the existing office holder Horst Köhler (CDU), Prof. Dr. Gesine Schwann (SPD) and Peter Sodann (*Die Linke*). Although President Köhler had the highest approval rating of the three (69 percent to Schwann's fifteen percent) prior to the balloting, the vote was considered to be close as the President in Germany is not selected by direct election, but by the 612 (622 in the 2010 vote) members of the then existing *Bundestag* and an equal number of electors representing the *Länder*, with 613 (623 in 2010 voting) required for election (*Stern*, May 20, 2009). In the balloting which took place May 13, 2009, Horst Köhler was selected over Dr. Schwann for a second term on the first ballot (*Die Welt am Sonntag*, May 24, 2009). After only one year in office, President Köhler surprisingly announced his resignation on May 31, 2010. The abrupt relinquishment of office followed the publication of controversial remarks he made after a visit to Afghanistan relating to Germany's military role in the world (*Die Welt*, June 1, 2010). A scathing article by Horst Lübke in the May 31, 2010 issue of *Der Spiegel* may have influenced his decision. This set in motion procedures established to select a replacement, while Jens Böhrnsen, Lord Mayor of Bremen and *Bundesrat* President, served as head of state during the interim period. To succeed Köhler, the Union parties and Free Democrats selected Lower Saxony's Minister President Christian Wulff as their candidate while the SPD and Greens supported independent Joachim Gauck, civil rights activist and the first federal commissioner of the Stasi Archives. The Leftists chose Ms. Luc Jochimsen, a member of parliament and former editor-in-chief of Hessen Public Radio, as their nominee. In a vote held June 30, 2010 Christian Wulff was not elected Germany's tenth President until the third ballot, as not all Black/Yellow delegates were initially willing to support their parties' choice. (With 623 votes required to elect, Wulff had received only 600 votes on the first ballot and 615 on the second; on the third and deciding ballot he obtained the support of 625 delegates to Gauck's 494, while the 121 supporters of Ms. Jochimsen abstained following her withdrawal from the final balloting (*Frankfurter Allgemeine FAZ.NET*, July 1, 2010 and *News Aktuell*, June 30, 2010).

Within a period of several weeks in the middle of 2010 the image of the Union was severely shaken by a series of political developments. First was the setback for the party in the May 9th state election in North Rhine-Westphalia which led to the replacement of Minister-President Jürgen Rüttgers by Socialist Hannelore Kraft and the ultimate impact of this change on voting in the *Bundesrat*. This was followed by the announced retirement of one of the party's most important leaders, Roland Koch, Minister-President of the State of Hesse. Then, at the end of May, President Horst Köhler suddenly resigned, necessitating the selection of a new head of state. A fourth shock occurred July

18th when Lord Mayor of Hamburg Ole von Beust, one of Chancellor Merkel's closest allies, made known his intention to retire the end of August. Thus, within less than a year, the CDU, through retirement, reassignment or decline in public favor, lost six of its state leaders (Günther Oettinger in Baden-Württemberg who became a European Union commissioner in January, Ole von Beust in Hamburg and Roland Koch in Hesse who decided to retire, Jürgen Rüttgers who was replaced as Minister-President in North Rhine-Westphalia, and Christian Wulff in Lower Saxony who was elevated to the position of Federal President. Earlier Dieter Althaus had been replaced as Minister-President by colleague Christine Lieberknecht in Thuringia). In spite of these seemingly damaging developments ("Wave of Resignations Dangerous for Merkel," *Spiegel Online*, August 18, 2010) and a series of electoral setbacks, Chancellor Merkel was elected party chair for the sixth time in November 2010 and faces no major challenger within her party with the retirement of Roland Koch as Minister-President of Hesse and the resignation of Karl-Theodor zu Guttenberg from the federal cabinet.

The success of the Free Voters (FW) in the 2008 *Land* election in Bavaria coupled with the ability of the grouping to outpoll all of the other parties put together in local elections in Thuringia and public opinion polls indicating that 45 percent of respondents could support the grouping posed the possibility of a sixth force in German politics.[11] Of some comfort to the established parties was the inability of the FW to obtain more than 1.6 percent of the vote in the January 2009 *Land* election in Hesse, only 3.9 percent in the August 2009 balloting in Thuringia and 2.9 percent in the March 2011 contest in Saxony-Anhalt. Nevertheless, the willingness of the German voter to support groupings such as the Free Voters and the Pirates (which polled 845,904 votes in the 2009 *Bundestag* election), the continuing success of *Die Linke* and low voter turnouts in most states demonstrate how far trust in the established parties has eroded since the 1980s.

On the regional level, Germans may have to get used to governments of varying colors. Robin Alexander writing about the political fragmentation that has occurred in the *Bundesrepublik* since the early 1980s sees the move to a five or six party system as good for democracy. The fear that the country is returning to the fragmentation of the Weimar Republic or to an Italian condition, he feels, is ill-founded. "The smaller parties are not splinter groups, but represent large, solid elements from the middle. They are not so far apart as to make compromise impossible." He sees the new particularism as a challenge, not a catastrophe (Robin Alexander, "*Mut zum Partikularism*," *Die Welt*, September 30, 2008). As fewer and fewer states are able to provide a legislative majority for a single party, the possibilities in coalition-building become wide open, as has been seen in Hamburg, where the CDU governed with the Greens for eighteen months, in Berlin and Brandenburg where the Socialists govern with *Die Linke*,[12] in Bavaria where the CSU has had to form a partnership with the Free Democrats after having governed alone for over forty years, and in the Saar where the first Jamaica coalition of the CDU, FDP and Greens on the *Land* level has been negotiated (*Hamburg Abendblatt*, November 13, 2009). German democracy has overcome numerous challenges in the past. Its extensive, if overstretched, social net and the fact that the housing bubble which triggered the world financial crisis is absent in the Federal Republic will help the country to resolve its problems no matter which party or parties are in control of the national and state governments.[13]

Endnotes to Chapter XI

1 Dr. Konrad Adenauer held the position of Chancellor from 1949 to 1963, Prof. Dr. Ludwig Erhard from 1963 to 1966, Dr. Kurt Georg Kiesinger from 1966 to 1969, Willy Brandt from 1969 to 1974, Helmut Schmidt from 1974 to 1982, Dr. Helmut Kohl from 1982 to 1998, Gerhard Schröder from 1998 to 2005 and Dr. Angela Merkel since September 2005.

2 Margaret Thatcher served as British Prime Minister from 1979 to 1990 and Tony Blair from 1997 to 2007. Blair was replaced by Gordon Brown in May 2007. After two years in office, Brown was succeeded by David Cameron of the Conservative Party in May 2010.

3 Dr. Konrad Adenauer assumed the posts of both Chancellor and Foreign Minister of the new Federal Republic from 1949 to 1951. He was followed by Franz Blücher who served from 1951 to 1955, Heinrich von Bretano (CDU) from 1955 to 1961, Gerhard Schröder (CDU) from 1961 to 1966, Willy Brandt (SPD) from 1966 to 1969, Walter Scheel (FDP) from 1969 to 1974, Hans-Dietrich Genscher (FDP) from 1974 to 1992, Klaus Kinkel (CDU) from 1992 to 1998, Joschka Fischer (Greens) from 1998 to 2005, Frank-Walter Steinmeier (SPD) from 2005 to 2009 and Dr. Guido Westerwelle since September 2009.

4 Chancellor Angela Merkel brought a number of women into her 2005-2009 cabinet including Brigitte Zypries (CDU) who headed the Justice Ministry, Ulla Schmidts (SPD) the Health Ministry, Ursula von der Leyen (CDU) the Family Ministry, Heidmarie Wieczorek-Zeuls (SPD) the Development Aid Ministry, and Annette Schavan (CDU) the Education and Research Ministry. Ilse Aigner (CSU) became the seventh woman in the then Merkel cabinet when she was named to replace Horst Seehofer (who became Minister President of Bavaria) as Agricultural Minister. Several changes were made after the 2009 *Bundestag* election to reflect the change in the party makeup of the national government, including bringing in the youngest woman in German history in a ministerial post, Kristina Köhler (32 years of age), Minister of Family Affairs.

5 The attempt to form a government headed by Andrea Ypsilanti with Greens support and toleration by *Die Linke* failed because four SPD parliamentary representatives would not support the arrangement. In a move contrary to party democracy the four dissidents were punished for not following the party line. They were no longer allowed to sit with party colleagues, their membership privileges were withdrawn and two of the dissidents are no longer allowed to speak or make proposals at party meetings (*Focus*, November 17, 2008). Ypsilanti, herself, while remaining faction leader and party chair, stepped down as top candidate in favor of Thorston Schäfer-Gümbel (*Welt am Sonntag*, November 9, 2008). The leadership change failed to prevent the Socialists from suffering their worst setback in Hesse since the first elections were held in 1946 in the January 18, 2009 *Land* election.

6 Although there is nothing in the Koran which legitimizes "honor killings," it has been reported that 47 Muslim women were victims of "honor killings" in Germany between 2000 and 2006, demonstrating that tribal practices from the homeland have not been eradicated after long residence in Germany ("My Family, My Killers," *The Sydney Morning Herald*, February 3, 2008).

7 A party need receive only one percent of votes cast in a *Landtag* election to be eligible for public funding. Eighteen groupings, including the NPD, currently receive public support in regional contests.

8 With a birthrate of only 1.36 children per female, the number of deaths in Germany each year has exceeded the number of births. With fewer workers to support an aging population, an advisory board of experts has recommended raising the retirement age for most workers to 69 from the current 67 (*"Sachverständigenrat empfielt Rente mit 69,"* *Frankfurter Allgemeine* Zeitung, May 19, 2011). See Prof. Dr. Hans-Jürgen Block, *"Die demographische* Zeitbombe," (2003) for a discussion of Germany's population problem. Dr. Block sees the German population declining to around 75 million by 2050. While this total is similar to the population count in 1960, the population will be older, with fewer employable individuals having to support an ever-larger group of retirees. The worse case scenario would be 100 workers for every 75 retirees by 2050, resulting in social system bankruptcy. While immigration can help the situation, there is a need to increase the birthrate to the replacement levels found in France and the United States. The recent increase in the retirement age of 67 years will be helpful in defusing the problem. A more recent commentary on Germany's population problem is found in Thomas Houzeroth and Dorothea Siems *"Neue Eltern braucht die Republic: Geburtenabsturz sprengt die Sozialsysteme,"* *Welt am Sonntag*, May 23, 2010: 1.

9 In Germany 61.1 percent of net wealth is held by the richest ten percent, while the lowest fifty percent holds only 3.2 percent of the wealth. The average worth in the western states is 101,208 Euro as opposed to only 30,723 Euro in the East (*Das Parlament*, September 14, 2009, from the German Institute for Economic Research).

10 Although he lost out to Angela Merkel, Frank-Walter Steinmeier had been the first chancellor candidate not to have held elective office. He was chief-of-staff to Chancellor Gerhard Schröder before becoming Foreign Minister in the Merkel cabinet in 2005. Before the *Bundestag* election, he was the second most popular German politician behind Chancellor Merkel and a constituency was found for him in Brandenburg for that election (*The Economist*, September 13-19, 2008: 59-60).

11 The Free Voters see themselves as the *Volks* Party of the future with aspirations of replacing the SPD as the second largest faction in Bavarian politics, a status which they have already achieved on the local level in that state (*Die Welt*, January 5, 2010).

12 A working relationship between the Union and the PDS/*Die Linke* should not be completely ruled out. At least in the eastern provinces they have cooperated in a number of cities. In Schwerin, the capital of Mecklenburg-Vorpommern, the CDU and *Die Linke* work together under a leftist mayor, Angelika Gramkow, who won a run-off election against Socialist Gottfried Timm September 28, 2008 with 50.5 percent of the votes. The former CDU Lord Mayor had been recalled in April (*Die Welt*, September 30, 2008). There is also local cooperation in Magdeburg, Meissen and Dresden, but there are no such partnerships on the regional level (*Der Spiegel*, September 29, 2008).

13 The most serious threat to the viability of the Federal Republic was not posed by

any of the right-extremist parties, which could be fought at the ballot box, but by the Red Army Faction (RAF) Baader-Meinhof gang of terrorists or urban guerillas which terrorized the country between 1972 and 1989. The proposed release of one of the main terrorists, Christian Klar, who was implicated in nine high-level assassinations, in January 2009 following 26 years in prison created a storm of protests. The terrorist danger was overcome, including the heroic rescue of passengers in Africa in 1977 from an aircraft hijacked by the gang. One of Germany's leading news magazines, *Der Spiegel*, covered the history of the RAF in a five-issue series, September 10, 17, 24 and October 1 and 8, 2007. A film has also been produced about this anxious period in German history, as well as a book by Stefan Aust under the title *Baader-Meinhof.*

This and other difficult challenges have not deterred the development of a strong democratic tradition in the Federal Republic, and Germany celebrated the sixtieth anniversary of its constitution, the Basic Law, on May 22, 2009. To this juncture in German history, the President of the Federal Supreme Court, Hans-Jürgen Papier, called the Basic Law as being "the basis for sixty years of democracy, the rule of law, freedom and social peace" (*Husumer Nachrichten*, May 22, 2009). The *Länder* have played an important role in that accomplishment.

APPENDIX I

Electoral System Devised for 1946 British Zone Elections

For the 1946 local elections in the British zone a system was devised which combined proportional representation with the simple majority ballot. From sixty to eighty percent of the seats were filled by direct election with the remaining seats distributed proportionally among the contending parties from a reserve list on the basis of the totals arrived at by adding together the votes of

FIGURE I

<table>
<tr><td colspan="5" align="center">District I[1]</td></tr>
<tr><td></td><td align="center">Name</td><td align="center">Address</td><td align="center">Party</td><td align="center">Vote</td></tr>
<tr><td>1.</td><td>Büch, Rudolf</td><td>Hmb.-Lokstedt, Bachstraße 35</td><td>SPD</td><td>16,091</td></tr>
<tr><td>2.</td><td>Delfs, Carl</td><td>Hmb. 13, Gustav-Falke-Str. 5</td><td>RSF</td><td>655</td></tr>
<tr><td>3.</td><td>Dibbern, Max</td><td>Hmb.-Niendorf, Fritz-Reuter-Str., 15</td><td>FDP</td><td>7,874</td></tr>
<tr><td>4.</td><td>Ebert, Werner</td><td>Hmb.-Lokstedt 1, Osterfeldstr. 70</td><td>FDP</td><td>7,782</td></tr>
<tr><td>5.</td><td>Fahl, Marianne</td><td>Hmb. 36, St.-Anschar-Platz 1</td><td>RSF</td><td>269</td></tr>
<tr><td>6.</td><td>Haarmeyer, Robert</td><td>Hmb. 30, Hoheluftchaussee 75</td><td>CDU</td><td>11,005</td></tr>
<tr><td>7.</td><td>Heise, Wilhelm</td><td>Hmb. 30, Bismarckstr. 108</td><td>SPD</td><td>15,473</td></tr>
<tr><td>8.</td><td>Höcker, Johann</td><td>Hmb. 20, Loogestieg 11</td><td>KPD</td><td>3,611</td></tr>
<tr><td>9.</td><td>Kannengiesser, Alexander</td><td>Hmb.-Lokstedt 2, Teutonenweg 1</td><td>KPD</td><td>3,532</td></tr>
<tr><td>10.</td><td>Karpinski, Carl</td><td>Hmb.-Fuhlsbüttel, Resedenweg 14</td><td>SPD</td><td>15,240</td></tr>
<tr><td>11.</td><td>Knabl, Alois</td><td>Hmb.-Schnelsen, Pinneberger Str.</td><td>CDU</td><td>10,592</td></tr>
<tr><td>12.</td><td>Lohmann, Max</td><td>Hmb. 19, Emilienstr. 78</td><td>DKP</td><td>346</td></tr>
<tr><td>13.</td><td>Luerssen, Georg</td><td>Hmb.-Schnelsen, Grotwisch</td><td>UNAB</td><td>413</td></tr>
<tr><td>14.</td><td>Petersen, Hans</td><td>Hmb.-Niendorf, An der Lohe. 10/12</td><td>FDP</td><td>7,271</td></tr>
<tr><td>15.</td><td>Piehl, Walter</td><td>Hmb. 28, Wilhelmsburger Str. 86</td><td>KPD</td><td>3,437</td></tr>
<tr><td>16.</td><td>Prinz, Frieda</td><td>Hmb. 4, Wilhelminenstr. 45</td><td>RSF</td><td>246</td></tr>
<tr><td>17.</td><td>Rachow, Helmuth</td><td>Hmb.-Lokstedt, Walderseestr. 14</td><td>CDU</td><td>10,492</td></tr>
<tr><td>18.</td><td>Richter, Johannes</td><td>Hmb.-Lokstedt, Clematisweg 8</td><td>SPD</td><td>14,963</td></tr>
<tr><td>19.</td><td>Scharfenberg, Gerhard</td><td>Hmb.-Warwisch, Wohnschiff, Saale</td><td>RPD</td><td>134</td></tr>
<tr><td>20.</td><td>Schleicher, Alfred</td><td>Hmb.-Niendorf, Fuhlsbütteler Weg, Kolonie Broockkamp 13</td><td>KPD</td><td>3,332</td></tr>
<tr><td>21.</td><td>Schwartau, Max</td><td>Hmb.-Lokstedt, Königstr. 8</td><td>DKP</td><td>300</td></tr>
<tr><td>22.</td><td>Wasmus Dr.-Ing., Adolf</td><td>Hmb.-Niendorf, Am Gehege 9</td><td>FDP</td><td>7,241</td></tr>
<tr><td>23.</td><td>Wollesen, Albert</td><td>Hmb.-Lokstedt, Lindenallee 8</td><td>CDU</td><td>10,278</td></tr>
</table>

the party's losing candidates (*Reststimmen*) and the numerical difference between each of the party's winning candidates and the highest unsuccessful candidate in each constitutency (*Mehrstimmen*). To illustrate, for the 1946

FIGURE II

<table>
<tr><td colspan="5">District XX[2]</td></tr>
<tr><td></td><td>Name</td><td>Address</td><td>Party</td><td>Vote</td></tr>
<tr><td>1.</td><td>Apfelstedt, Else</td><td>Hamburg-Blankenese, Godeffroystraße 43</td><td>UNAB</td><td>612</td></tr>
<tr><td>2.</td><td>Becker, Maria</td><td>Hamburg-Blankenese, Kastanienweg 25</td><td>FDP</td><td>6,480</td></tr>
<tr><td>3.</td><td>Bremer, Gertrud</td><td>Hamburg-Blankenese, Richard-Dehmel-Str. 1</td><td>KPD</td><td>2,628</td></tr>
<tr><td>4.</td><td>Damkowski, Martha</td><td>Hamburg-Rissen, Eckerkamp 33</td><td>SPD</td><td>11,967</td></tr>
<tr><td>5.</td><td>Grönig, Willy A.</td><td>Hamburg-Blankenese, Elbchaussee 78</td><td>CDU</td><td>12,029</td></tr>
<tr><td>6.</td><td>Haarmeyer, Adolf</td><td>Hamburg-Blankenese, Friedrich-Ebert-Str. 30</td><td>CDU</td><td>11,872</td></tr>
<tr><td>7.</td><td>Heydorn, Heinz-Joachim</td><td>Hamburg-Rissen, Suurheid 3</td><td>SPD</td><td>11,981</td></tr>
<tr><td>8.</td><td>Kalbitzer, Helmut</td><td>Hamburg-Blankenese, Baurspark 4</td><td>SPD</td><td>11,780</td></tr>
<tr><td>9.</td><td>Kessner, Otto</td><td>Hamburg-Blankenese, Sülldorfer Landstraße 19</td><td>RSF</td><td>260</td></tr>
<tr><td>10.</td><td>Langhoff, Wilhelm</td><td>Hamburg-Blankenese, Caprivistraße 19</td><td>FDP</td><td>6,364</td></tr>
<tr><td>11.</td><td>Pohlmann, Georg</td><td>Hamburg-Blankenese, Schenefelder Landstr. 94</td><td>KPD</td><td>2,511</td></tr>
<tr><td>12.</td><td>Prošek, Wenzel</td><td>Hamburg-Blankenese, Schenefelder Landstr. 94</td><td>RSF</td><td>187</td></tr>
<tr><td>13.</td><td>Reimann, Frieda</td><td>Hamburg-Gr. Flottbek, Kleiberweg 18</td><td>KPD</td><td>2,476</td></tr>
<tr><td>14.</td><td>Remmele, Dr. Adam</td><td>Hamburg 24, Hammer Landstraße 38</td><td>SPD</td><td>11,582</td></tr>
<tr><td>15.</td><td>Rohde, Gustav</td><td>Hamburg-Blankenese, Strandweg 19</td><td>RSF</td><td>191</td></tr>
<tr><td>16.</td><td>Stephan, Paul</td><td>Hamburg-Lurup, Sprützmoor 85</td><td>RSF</td><td>188</td></tr>
<tr><td>17.</td><td>Stephan, Walter</td><td>Hamburg-Blankenese, Bahnhofstraße, 52</td><td>KPD</td><td>2,404</td></tr>
<tr><td>18.</td><td>Sternberg, Gustav</td><td>Hamburg-Blankenese, Wulfsdal 31</td><td>FDP</td><td>6,238</td></tr>
<tr><td>19.</td><td>Thiede, Adolf</td><td>Hamburg-Blankenese, Elbchaussee 99</td><td>CDU</td><td>11,552</td></tr>
<tr><td>20.</td><td>Thomsen, Dr. Hans</td><td>Hamburg-Blankenese, Wilhelmsallee 9</td><td>FDP</td><td>6,359</td></tr>
<tr><td>21.</td><td>Wendt, Otto</td><td>Hamburg-Blankenese, Frenssenstraße 90</td><td>CDU</td><td>11,427</td></tr>
</table>

Bürgerschaft election in Hamburg, 84 seats were filled directly from 21 multi-member districts, 26 seats on the basis of a party's *Mehr-* and *Reststimmen.* In District I (see Figure I), for example, the SPD won all four direct seats, since its candidates obtained the four highest vote totals; however, each of the four winning candidates exceeded the total of the highest unsuccessful candidate by several thousand votes. In figuring the distribution of seats from the reserve list, not only were the votes of all of the losing candidates totaled, but also the votes of the four SPD candidates over 11,005 (the total of the highest unsuccessful candidate in the constituency) or 17,747 votes. The totaling of the two categories of votes is accomplished for all 21 constituencies, giving the party figures for the whole city. The sum arrived at by totaling the figures of all parties were divided by the number of reserve seats plus one as in the Hare system (26 plus 1 in the case of Hamburg) with one added to the result to establish a quota. Each party received as many seats from the reserve list as the quota could be divided into its total sum of *Mehr-* and *Reststimmen.*

In order to institute a personality election rather than one based on the party name, the British listed candidates in alphabetical order. This innovation failed to prevent block voting and was discriminatory between candidates of the same party on the alphabetical list. To illustrate, in Figure I, the top SPD candidate received 16,091 votes, the second 15,473, the third 15,240 and the fourth 14,963. In other words, the top SPD candidate received 1,128 more votes than the last one. The same phenomenon held for the candidates of all other parties. In this particular district one's alphabetical ranking had no adverse effect on the results. District XX (see Figure II), however, where the outcome was close, showed a different pattern: the two top SPD candidates on the alphabetical list gained seats, but the last two listed candidates of the party lost out to the two top-listed CDU candidates, not because they were less popular with the voters, but because their names happened to be Kalbitzer and Remmele rather than Damkowski and Heydorn. In the same manner Christian Democrats Grönig and Haarmeyer won seats as Thiede and Wendt lost because of their more favorable position on the alphabetical list. The election, in effect, proved to be as much a contest of the alphabet as of the parties.[3]

[1] Figures are from *Die Bürgerschaftswahl am 13. Oktober 1946*, Hamburg Statistical Office: 27.

[2] *Ibid.*, page 33.

[3] See page 16 of *Die Bürgerschaftswahl am 13. Oktober 1946* for a frank criticism of this British innovation.

APPENDIX II

Chronological Table of *Land* and *Bundestag* Elections

Date			*Land*
1946:	13	October	Bremen and Hamburg
	20	October	Berlin
	24	November	Württemberg-Baden
	1	December	Bavaria and Hesse
1947:	20	April	Lower Saxony, North Rhine-Westphalia and Schleswig-Holstein
	18	May	Baden, Rhineland-Palatinate and Württemberg - Hohenzollern
	5	October[a]	The Saar
	12	October	Bremen
1948:	5	December	West Berlin
1949:	14	August	First *Bundestag* Election
	16	October	Hamburg
1950:	18	June	North Rhine-Westphalia
	9	July	Schleswig-Holstein
	19	November	Hesse and Württemberg-Baden
	26	November	Bavaria
	3	December	West Berlin
1951:	29	April	Rhineland-Palatinate
	6	May	Lower Saxony
	7	October	Bremen
1952:	9	March	Baden-Württemberg
	30	November[a]	The Saar
1953:	6	September	Second *Bundestag* Election
	1	November	Hamburg
1954:	27	June	North Rhine-Westphalia
	12	September	Schleswig-Holstein
	28	November	Bavaria and Hesse
	5	December	West Berlin

1955:	24	April	Lower Saxony
	15	May	Rhineland-Palatinate
	9	October	Bremen
	18	December[a]	The Saar
1956:	4	March	Baden-Württemberg
1957	15	September	Third *Bundestag* Election
	10	November	Hamburg
1958:	6	July	North Rhine-Westphalia
	28	September	Schleswig-Holstein
	23	November	Bavaria and Hesse
	7	December	West Berlin
1959:	19	April	Lower Saxony and Rhineland-Palatinate
	11	October	Bremen
1960:	15	May	Baden-Württemberg
	4	December	The Saar
1961:	12	March	Baden-Württemberg (repeat election)
	17	September	Fourth *Bundestag* Election
	12	November	Hamburg
1962:	8	July	North Rhine-Westphalia
	23	September	Schleswig-Holstein
	11	November	Hesse
	25	November	Bavaria
1963:	17	February	West Berlin
	31	March	Rhineland-Palatinate
	19	May	Lower Saxony
	29	September	Bremen
1964:	26	April	Baden-Württemberg
1965:	27	June	The Saar
	19	September	Fifth *Bundestag* Election
1966:	27	March	Hamburg
	10	June	North Rhine-Westphalia
	6	November	Hesse
	20	November	Bavaria
1967:	12	March	West Berlin
	23	April	Schleswig-Holstein and Rhineland-Palatinate

	4	June	Lower Saxony
	1	October	Bremen
1968	28	April	Baden-Württemberg
1969:	28	September	Sixth *Bundestag* Election
1970:	22	March	Hamburg
	14	June	Lower Saxony
	14	June	North Rhine-Westphalia and the Saar
	8	November	Hesse
	22	November	Bavaria
1971	14	March	West Berlin
	21	March	Rhineland-Palatinate
	25	April	Schleswig-Holstein
	10	October	Bremen
1972	23	April	Baden-Württemberg
	19	November	Seventh *Bundestag* Election
1974	3	March	Hamburg
	9	June	Lower Saxony
	27	October	Bavaria and Hesse
1975:	2	March	West Berlin
	9	March	Rhineland-Palatinate
	13	April	Schleswig-Holstein
	4	May	North Rhine-Westphalia and the Saar
	28	September	Bremen
1976	4	April	Baden-Württemberg
	3	October	Eighth *Bundestag* Election
1978	4	June	Hamburg and Lower Saxony
	8	October	Hesse
	15	October	Bavaria
1979	18	March	Rhineland-Palatinate, West Berlin
	29	April	Schleswig-Holstein
	7	October	Bremen
1980	16	March	Baden-Württemberg
	27	April	The Saar
	11	May	North Rhine-Westphalia
	5	October	Ninth *Bundestag* Election

1981	10	May	West Berlin

1982	21	March	Lower Saxony
	6	June	Hamburg
	26	September	Hesse
	10	October	Bavaria
	19	December	Hamburg[b] (rerun election)

1983	6	March	Rhineland-Palatinate
			Tenth *Bundestag* Election
	13	March	Schleswig-Holstein
	25	September	Bremen and Hesse

1984	25	March	Baden-Württemberg

1985	10	March	The Saar and West Berlin
	12	May	North Rhine-Westphalia

1986	15	June	Lower Saxony
	12	October	Bavaria
	9	November	Hamburg

1987	25	January	Eleventh *Bundestag* Election
	5	April	Hesse
	17	May	Rhineland-Palatinate and Hamburg
	13	September	Bremen and Schleswig-Holstein

1988	20	March	Baden-Württemberg
	8	May	Schleswig-Holstein[c]

1989	29	January	West Berlin

1990	28	January	The Saar
	13	May	Lower Saxony and North Rhine-Westphalia
	14	October	Bavaria, Brandenburg, Mecklenburg-Vorpommern, Saxony, Saxony-Anhalt and Thuringia
	2	December	Berlin
			Twelfth *Bundestag* Election

1991	20	January	Hesse
	21	April	Rhineland-Palatinate
	2	June	Hamburg
	29	September	Bremen

1992	5	April	Baden-Württemberg and Schleswig-Holstein

1993	19	September	Hamburg[d] (rerun election)

1994	13	March	Lower Saxony
	26	June	Saxony-Anhalt
	11	September	Brandenburg and Saxony
	25	September	Bavaria
	16	October	Mecklenburg-Vorpommern, the Saar and Thuringia
			Thirteenth *Bundestag* Election
1995	19	February	Hesse
	14	May	Bremen and North Rhine-Westphalia
	10	October	Berlin
1996	24	March	Baden-Württemberg, Rhineland-Palatinate and Schleswig-Holstein
1997	21	September	Hamburg
1998	1	March	Lower Saxony
	26	April	Saxony-Anhalt
	13	September	Bavaria
	27	September	Mecklenburg-Vorpommern
			Fourteenth *Bundestag* Election
1999	5	February	Hesse
	6	June	Bremen
	5	September	Brandenburg and the Saar
	12	September	Thuringia
	19	September	Saxony
	10	October	Berlin
2000	27	February	Schleswig-Holstein
	14	May	North Rhine-Westphalia
2001	25	March	Baden-Württemberg and Rhineland-Palatinate
	23	September	Hamburg
	21	October	Berlin[e]
2002	21	April	Saxony-Anhalt
	22	September	Mecklenburg-Vorpommern
			Fifteenth *Bundestag* Election
2003	2	February	Hesse and Lower Saxony
	25	May	Bremen
	21	September	Bavaria
2004	29	February	Hamburg
	13	June	Thuringia

	5	September	The Saar
	19	September	Brandenburg and Saxony
2005	20	February	Schleswig-Holstein
	22	May	North Rhine-Westphalia
	18	September	Sixteenth *Bundestag* Election
2006	26	March	Baden-Württemberg, Rhineland-Palatinate and Saxony-Anhalt
	17	September	Berlin and Mecklenburg-Vorpommern
2007	13	May	Bremen
2008	27	January	Hesse and Lower Saxony
	24	February	Hamburg
	28	September	Bavaria
2009	18	January	Rerun Election in Hesse
	30	August	The Saar, Saxony, and Thuringia
	27	September	Brandenburg and Schleswig-Holstein Seventeenth *Bundestag* Election
2010	9	May	North Rhine Westphalia
2011	20	February	Hamburg
	20	March	Saxony-Anhalt
	27	March	Baden-Württemberg
	27	March	Rhineland-Palatinate
	22	May	Bremen

a Elections held under French auspices prior to the incorporation of the Saar into the Federal Republic in 1957.

b The June 6, 1982 *Bürgerschaft* election in Hamburg did not produce a majority for either the SPD or CDU, and a working relationship with the Greens, the only other party to receive representation, proved unachievable because of irreconcilable differences, necessitating the follow-up election in December which gave the Socialists a commanding majority in the *Bürgerschaft*.

c The constitutional crisis in Schleswig-Holstein resulting from the "Barschel Affair" made necessary a rerun of the September 13, 1987 *Land* election.

d A rerun election in Hamburg became necessary when the Hamburg high court voided the June 2, 1991 election because of an illegal nomination process.

e The second election in Berlin resulted from a constructive vote of non-confidence in the governing CDU and the need to place the resulting minority government on a more stable basis.

APPENDIX III

Dates of *Bundestag* and *Landtag/Bürgerschaft* Elections By State

BUNDESTAG

1. 14 August 1949
2. 6 September 1953
3. 15 September 1957
4. 17 September 1961
5. 19 September 1965
6. 28 September 1969
7. 19 November 1972
8. 3 October 1976
9. 5 October 1980
10. 6 March 1983
11. 25 January 1987
12. 2 December 1990
13. 16 October 1994
14. 27 September 1998
15. 22 September 2002
16. 18 September 2005
17. 27 September 2009

WÜRTTEMBERG-BADEN

1. 24 November 1946
2. 19 November 1950

BADEN

1. 18 May 1947

WÜRTTEMBERG-HOHENZOLLERN

1. 18 May 1947

BADEN-WÜRTTEMBERG
(following unification in 1952)

1. 9 March 1952
2. 4 March 1956
3. 15 May 1960
4. 26 April 1964
5. 28 April 1968
6. 23 April 1972
7. 4 April 1976
8. 16 March 1980
9. 25 March 1984
10. 20 March 1988
11. 5 April 1992
12. 24 March 1996
13. 25 March 2001
14. 26 March 2006
15. 27 March 2011

BAVARIA

1. 1 December 1946
2. 26 November 1950
3. 28 November 1954
4. 23 November 1958
5. 25 November 1962
6. 20 November 1966
7. 22 November 1970
8. 27 October 1974
9. 15 October 1978
10. 10 October 1982
11. 12 October 1986
12. 14 October 1990
13. 25 September 1994
14. 13 September 1998
15. 21 September 2003
16. 28 September 2008

BERLIN

1. 20 October 1946 [a]
2. 5 December 1948
3. 3 December 1950
4. 5 December 1954
5. 7 December 1958
6. 17 February 1963
7. 12 March 1967
8. 14 March 1971
9. 2 March 1975
10. 18 March 1979
11. 10 May 1981
12. 10 March 1985
13. 29 January 1989
14. 2 December 1990 [a]
15. 10 October 1995 [a]
16. 10 October 1999 [a]
17. 21 October 2001 [a]
18. 17 September 2006 [a]

BRANDENBURG

1. 14 October 1990
2. 11 September 1994
3. 5 September 1999
4. 19 September 2004
5. 27 September 2009

a Designates elections held in all four sectors of Berlin, in 1946 and since 1990.

BREMEN

1. 13 October 1946
2. 12 October 1947
3.   7 October 1951
4.   9 October 1955
5. 11 October 1959
6. 29 September 1963
7.   1 October 1967
8. 10 October 1971
9. 28 September 1975
10. 7 October 1979
11. 25 September 1983
12. 13 September 1987
13. 29 September 1991
14. 14 May 1995
15. 6 June 1999
16. 25 May 2003
17. 13 May 2007
18. 22 May 2011

HESSE

1.   1 December 1946
2. 19 November 1950
3. 28 November 1954
4. 23 November 1958
5. 11 November 1962
6.   6 November 1966
7.   8 November 1970
8. 27 October 1974
9.   8 October 1978
10. 26 September 1982
11. 25 September 1983
12. 5 April 1987
13. 20 January 1991
14. 19 February 1995
15. 5 February 1999
16. 2 February 2003
17. 27 January 2008
18. 18 January 2009

MECKLENBURG-VORPOMMERN

1. 14 October 1990
2. 16 October 1994
3. 27 September 1998
4. 22 September 2002
5. 17 September 2006

HAMBURG

1. 13 October 1946
2. 16 October 1949
3.   1 November 1953
4. 10 November 1957
5. 12 November 1961
6. 27 March 1966
7. 22 March 1970
8.   3 March 1974
9.   4 June 1978
10. 6 June 1982
11. 19 December 1982
12. 9 November 1986
13. 17 May 1987
14. 2 June 1991
15. 19 September 1993
16. 21 September 1997
17. 23 September 2001
18. 29 February 2004
19. 24 February 2008
20. 20 February 2011

LOWER SAXONY

1. 20 April 1947
2.   6 May 1951
3. 24 April 1955
4. 19 April 1959
5. 19 May 1963
6.   4 June 1967
7. 14 June 1970
8.   9 June 1974
9.   4 June 1978
10. 21 March 1982
11. 15 June 1986
12. 13 May 1990
13 13 March 1994
14. 1 March 1998
15. 2 February 2003
16. 27 January 2008

NORTH RHINE-WESTPHALIA

1. 20 April 1947
2. 18 June 1950
3. 27 June 1954
4.   6 July 1958
5.   8 July 1962
6. 10 June 1966
7. 14 June 1970
8.   4 May 1975
9. 11 May 1980
10. 12 May 1985
11. 13 May 1990
12. 14 May 1995
13. 14 May 2000
14. 22 May 2005
15. 9 May 2010

<table>
<tr><td>

RHINELAND-PALATINATE

1. 18   May 1947
2. 29   April 1951
3. 15   May 1955
4. 19   April 1959
5. 31   March 1963
6. 23   April 1967
7. 21   March 1971
8. 9   March 1975
9. 18   March 1979
10. 6   March 1983
11. 17   May 1987
12. 21   April 1991
13. 24   March 1996
14. 25   March 2001
15. 26   March 2006
16. 27   March 2011

</td><td>

SAXONY

1. 14   October 1990
2. 11   September 1994
3. 19   September 1999
4. 19   September 2004
5. 30   August 2009

</td><td>

SCHLESWIG-HOLSTEIN

1. 20   April 1947
2. 9   July 1950
3. 12   September 1954
4. 28   September 1958
5. 23   September 1962
6. 23   April 1967
7. 25   April 1971
8. 13   April 1975
9. 29   April 1979
10. 13   March 1983
11. 13   September 1987
12. 8   May 1988
13. 5   April 1992
14. 24   March 1996
15. 27   February 2000
16. 20   February 2005
17. 27   September 2009

</td></tr>
<tr><td>

THE SAAR

1. 5   October 1947 [b]
2. 30   November 1952 [b]
3. 18   December 1955 [b]
4. 4   December 1960
5. 27   June 1965
6. 14   June 1970
7. 4   May 1975
8. 27   April 1980
9. 10   March 1985
10. 28   January 1990
11. 16   October 1994
12. 5   September 1999
13. 5   September 2004
14 30   August 2009

</td><td>

SAXONY-ANHALT

1. 14   October 1990
2. 26   June 1994
3. 26   April 1998
4. 21   April 2002
5. 26   March 2006
6. 20   March 2011

</td><td>

THURINGIA

1. 14   October 1990
2. 16   October 1994
3. 12   September 1999
4. 13   June 2004
5. 30   August 2009

</td></tr>
</table>

b The first three elections in the Saar were held under French auspices prior
to reintegration into the Federal Republic in 1957.

APPENDIX IV

Berlin Elections Prior to Reunification

Date of Election	Valid Votes	CDU	SPD	FDP/ LDP	SED/ SEW[a]	Others
Oct. 20, 1946[b]	2,128,677	462,425	1,015,609	149,722	412,582	
	92.3	22.2 (29)	48.7 (63)	9.3 (12)	19.8 (26)	
Dec. 5, 1948	1,331,270	258,664	858,461	214,145	-	
	86.3	19.4 (21)	64.5 (60)	16.1 (17)	-	
Dec. 3, 1950	1,464,470	361,050	654,211	337,589	-	DP 53,810 (3.7)
	90.4	24.7 (34)	44.7 (61)	23.1 (32)	-	BHE 31,918 (2.2)
Dec. 5, 1954	1,535,893	467,117	684,906	197,204	41,375	DP 75,321 (4.9)
	91.8	30.4 (44)	44.6 (64)	12.8 (19)	2.7 (-)	BHE 39,236 (2.6)
Dec. 7, 1958	1,616,508	609,097	850,127	61,119	31,572	DP 53,912 (3.3)
	92.9	37.7 (55)	52.6 (78)	3.8 (-)	2.0 (-)	
Feb. 17, 1963	1,554,967	448,459	962,197	123,382	20,929	-
	89.9	28.8 (41)	61.9 (89)	7.9 (10)	1.3 (-)	
Mar. 12, 1967	1,459,044	479,945	829,694	103,973	29,925	AUD 15,507
	86.2	32.9 (47)	56.9 (81)	7.1 (9)	2.1 (-)	1.1 (-)
Mar. 14, 1971	1,448,953	553,422	730,240	122,310	33,845	
	88.9	38.2 (54)	50.4 (73)	8.4 (11)	2.3 (-)	
Mar. 2, 1975	1,375,522	604,007	585,605	97,969	25,105	BFD 46,691
	87.8	43.9 (69)	42.6 (67)	7.1 (11)	1.8 (-)	3.4 (-)
Mar. 18, 1979	1,284,596	570,174	548,060	103,609	13,744	AL 47,642[c]
	85.4	44.4 (63)	42.7 (61)	8.1 (11)	1.1 (-)	3.7 (-)
May 10, 1981	1,262,166	605,265	483,778	70,529	8,176	AL 90,653
	85.3	48.0 (65)	38.3 (51)	5.6 (7)	0.6 (-)	7.2 (9)
Mar. 10, 1985	1,245,004	577,867	402,875	105,209	7,731	AL 132,484
	83.6	46.4 (69)	32.4 (48)	8.5 (12)	0.6	10.6 (15)
Jan. 29, 1989	1,200,672	453,211	448,203	47,153	6,875	AL 141,529
	79.6	37.7 (55)	37.3 (55)	3.9 (-)	0.6	11.8 (17)
						Rep. 90,222
						7.5 (11)

a The SED (Socialist Unity Party) was the name for the Communist Party of the Soviet sector of Berlin and of eastern Germany. The grouping competed in West Berlin carrying the SED label until the 1971 election when it used the SEW designation or Socialist Unity Party West Berlin. The party received less than one percent of the vote in the last three ballotings in the then divided city.

b The October 12, 1946 election was the first and only contest to encompass all four sectors of Berlin until the December 2, 1990 balloting following reintegration of the Soviet sector of the city into the Federal Republic.

c AL or Alternative List represents one of the early environmental groupings which later formed the basis of the "Greens" Party.

APPENDIX V

Sample Ballots

Stimmzettel

für die Wahl zur Bürgerschaft in Hamburg am 29. Februar 2004

Hier

Ihre Stimme für die

Bürgerschaftswahl

(Nur einen Wahlvorschlag ankreuzen)

1	**Sozialdemokratische Partei Deutschlands** Thomas Mirow, Dr. Dorothee Stapelfeldt, Walter Zuckerer, Aydan Özoguz	SPD	◯
2	**Christlich Demokratische Union Deutschlands** Ole Freiherr von Beust, Dr. Michael Freytag, Birgit Schnieber-Jastram, Berndt Röder	CDU	◯
3	**Partei Rechtsstaatlicher Offensive** Dirk Nockemann, Norbert Frühauf, Mario Mettbach, Manfred Silberbach		◯
4	**BÜNDNIS 90/DIE GRÜNEN, Landesverband Hamburg, Grün-Alternative-Liste** Christa Goetsch, Christian Maaß, Antje Möller, Dr. Willfried Maier	GRÜNE/GAL	◯
5	**Freie Demokratische Partei** Reinhard Soltau, Burkhardt Müller-Sönksen, Rosa-Felicitas Pauly, Leif Schrader	FDP	◯
6	**REGENBOGEN – Für eine neue Linke** Heike Sudmann, Yavuz Fersoglu, Annette Sawatzki, Berno Schuckart-Witsch	REGENBOGEN	◯
7	**Feministische Partei Die Frauen** Rita Saager, Martina Schikora, Irina Lahrssen, Christiane Busse	DIE FRAUEN	◯
8	**DIE GRAUEN – Graue Panther** Peter Hoffman, Herbert Hoffmann, Andreas Bornholt, Klaus Nispel	GRAUE	◯
9	**Nationaldemokratische Partei Deutschlands** Ulrich Harder, Jan Zimmerman, Martin Dembowsky, Peter Schäfer-Hansen	NPD	◯
10	**Pro Deutsche Mitte** Ronald Barnabas Schill, Imke Noack, Katrin Freund, Richard Braak	Pro DM/Schill	◯
11	**Partei Bibeltreuer Christen** Ernst Seng, Jürgen Rubarth, Thomas Pusch, Jan Pahl	PBC	◯
12	**OLIVIA-JONES.DE** Oliver Knöbel (Künstlername: Olivia Jones)	OLIVIA-JONES.DE	◯
13	**Deutscher BürgerBund** John Wurthmann, Stefan Thören, Torsten Wulf	BürgerBund	◯
14	**Akpolat – Zukunft braucht Wahrheit** Mustafa Akpolat	MUSTAFA	◯
15	**SOSwasserterm.de** Thomas Rüsch, Alexander Brabandt, Jörg Stange, Claudia Herbst		◯
16	**Ökologisch-Demokratische Partei** Angela Zeck, Nadine Laws, Thomas Spindler, Hannes Zöllner	ödp	◯

Stimmzettel

für die Wahl zum Deutschen Bundestag
Im Wahlkreis 2 Nordfriesland – Dithmarschen-Nord
Am 27. September 2009

Sie haben 2 Stimmen

hier 1 Stimme
für die Wahl
eines / einer Wahlkreis-
abgeordneten

Erststimme

hier 1 Stimmen
für die Wahl
einer Landesliste (Partei)
- maßgebende Stimme für die Verteilung der
Sitz insgesamt auf die einzelnen Parteien -

Zweitstimme

#	Erststimme				Zweitstimme	#
1	**Fecke**, Hanno Geschäftsführer Rosendahler Weg 17 25866 Mildstedt	**SPD** Sozialdemokratische Partei Deutschlands	○	○ SPD	**Sozialdemokratische Partei Deutschlands** Dr. Ernst Dieter Rossmann, Bettina Hagedorn, Franz Thönnes, Gabriele Hiller-Ohm, Sönke Rix	1
2	**Liebing**, Ingbert Bürgermeister a.D., MdB Terpstig 45 g 25980 Sylt	**CDU** Christlich Demokratische Union Deutschlands	○	○ CDU	**Christlich Demokratische Union Deutschlands** Dr. Johann David Wadephul, Dr. Ole Schröder, Michaela Pries, Wolfgang Börnsen, Gero Storjohann	2
3	**Schmück**, Ulrich Dipl.-Informatiker Westerstr. 1 25774 Lunden	**FDP** Freie Demokratische Partei	○	○ FDP	**Freie Demokratische Partei** Jürgen Koppelin, Dr. Christel Happach-Kasan, Sebastian Blumenthal, Christine Aschenberg-Dugnus, Klaus-Peter Eberhard	3
4	**Seehausen**, Valentin Schüler Tegelring 32 25899 Niebüll	**GRÜNE** BÜNDNIS 90/DIE GRÜNEN	○	○ GRÜNE	**BÜNDNIS 90/DIE GRÜNEN** Ingrid Nestle, Dr. Konstantin von Notz, Dr. Valerie Wilms, Arfst Wagner, Monika Obieray	4
5	**Voß**, Harry Außendienstmitarbeiter Breslauer Str. 13 25746 Heide	**DIE LINKE** DIE LINKE	○	○ DIE LINKE	**DIE LINKE** Cornelia Möhring, Raju Sharma, Esther Hartmann, Sascha Thomas, Susanne Vogel-Vitzthum	5
6	**Kaehne**, Arne Dachdecker Norderende 45 25885 Oster-Ohrstedt	**NPD** Nationaldemokratische Partei Deutschlands	○	○ NPD	**Nationaldemokratische Partei Deutschlands** Uwe Schäfer, Jens Lütke, Thomas Wulff, Ingo Stawitz, Kay Oelke	6
				○ MLPD	**Marxistisch-Leninistische Partei Deutschlands** Maria Meyer, Matthias Salomon, Andrea Hähner, Jürgen Wischnat	7
				○ DVU	**DEUTSCHE VOLKSUNION** Renate Erna Köhler, Ingeborg Anna Lobocki	8
				○ PIRATEN	**Piratenpartei Deutschland** Klaus Günter Petersdorf, Adrian Müller, Ulrich König, Sven Wolfgang Jörns, Hans-Heinrich Piepgras	9
				○ RENTNER	**Rentner-Partei-Deutschland** Hartmut Keller, Peter Bing, Helmut Lemke	10
11	**Albertson**, Sönke Angestellter Hostrup 13 25884 Viöl	**KANN WAS**	○			

Stimmzettel

für die Wahl zum Schleswig-Holsteinischen Landtag
am 27. September 2009
im Wahlkreis 8 Dithmarschen-Nord

Sie haben 2 Stimmen

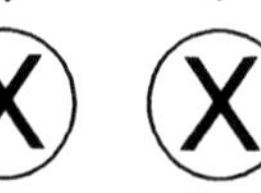

hier 1 Stimme
für die Wahl
einer / eines Wahlkreis-
abgeordneten

hier 1 Stimme
für die Wahl
einer Landesliste (Partei)
- maßgebende Stimme für die Verteilung
der Sitze auf die einzelnen Parteien

Erststimme   Zweitstimme

#	Erststimme	○	○	Partei	Zweitstimme	#
1	**Jasper, Karsten** Geschäftsführer/MdL Tellingstedt, Haupstraße 17 25866 Mildstedt **CDU**	○	○	CDU	**Christlich Demokratische Union Deutschlands** Peter Harry Carstensen, Dr. Christian von Boetticher, Herlich Marie Todsen-Reese, Rainer Wiegard, Frank Sauter	1
2	**Buder, Detlef** Lehrer Büsum, Am Oland 24 **SPD**	○	○	SPD	**Sozialdemokratische Partei Deutschlands** Dr. Ralf Stegner, Dr. Gitta Trauernicht, Lothar Hay, Birgit Herdejürgen, Jürgen Weber	2
3	**Jensen, Renate** Oecotrophologin Heide, Louisenstraße 23 **FDP**	○	○	FDP	**Freie Demokratische Partei** Wolfgang Kubicki, Dr. Ekkehard Klug, Dr.Heinrich Garg, Günther Hildebrand, Anita Klan	3
4	**Dräger, Holger** Dipl. Wirtschaftsingenieur Wiemerstedt, Waldweg 5 **GRÜNE**	○	○	GRÜNE	**BÜNDNIS 90/DIE GRÜNEN** Monika Heinold, Dr. Robert Habeck, Maria-Elisabeth Fritzen, Andreas Tietze, Anke Erdmann	4
			○	SSW	**Südschleswigscher Wählerverband** Anke Spoorendonk, Lars Harms, Silke Hinrichsen, Flemming Meyer, Jan Hundsdörfer	5
			○	NPD	**Nationaldemokratische Partei Deutschlands** Jens Lütke, Ingo Stawitz, Uwe Schäfer, Kevin Stein, Kay Oelke	6
			○	FAMILIE	**Familien-Partei Deutschlands** Werner Lahann, Matthias Kortum, Hilke Rohlfshagen, Oliver Mrozewski, Thomas Vollbracht	7
8	**Steinhardt, Karlheinz Hermann** Rentner Heide, Heimkehrerstraße 27b DIE LINKE	○	○	DIE LINKE	**DIE LINKE** Antje Jansen, Heinz-Werner Jezewski, Ellen Streitbörger, Ulrich Schippels, Ranka Prante	8
9	**Schoer, Eva** Selbstständige Kauffrau Oldenburg, Mühlenkamp 23 FW-SH	○	○	FW-SH	**Freie Wähler Schleswig-Holstein** Malte Tech, Helmut Andresen, Andreas Hagenkötter, Karin Honeriah, Wolfgang Fuß	9
			○	IPD	**Interim Partei Deutschland DAS REICHT!** Manuel Kraschinski, Jens Winzentsen, Jan Hildebrandt, Heinrich Schomacker, Reinhardt Groß	10
	Stock, Heiko Student Flensburg, Harnis 2 PIRATEN	○	○	PIRATEN	**Piratenpartei Deutschland** Anika Tanck, Ulrich König, Philipp Stern, Klaus Petersdorf, Adrian Müller	11
			○	RRP	**Rentnerinnen und Rentner Partei** Michael Suck, Hans-Dieter Döring, Dr. Klaus Beese, Horst Kozielski, Dr. Rolf Tetzlaff-Gahrmann	12
			○	RENTNER	**Rentner-Partei Deutschland** Martin Wnuck, Bernd Bassler, Hartmut Keller, Wolfgang Lichtner, Klaus Willmann	13
14	**Horn, Franz-Harro** Dipl. Ing./Landwirt Tating-Ehst, Ehst 7 **Parteilos**	○				14

Bibliography

Public Documents

1. GERMAN FEDERAL GOVERNMENT

Bundesarchiv, *Westdeutschland 1945-1950*, Koblenz, 1956.

Bundesrat: Handbuch der Deutsches Bundesländer, Bonn, 1964.

> *Handbuch des Bundesrates 1994/95, C. H. Beck. München, 1994.*

> *Handbuch des Bundesrates 1995/96, Nomos Verlag, Baden-Baden, 1995.*

> *Handbuch des Bundesrates 2002/2003, Nomos Verlag, Baden-Baden, 2003*

> *The German Bundesrat*, Roco-Druck Gmbh, Wolfenbüttel.

Bundestag, Deutscher, "Die Regierungen der Bundesrepublik seit 1949," Dokument 590/3 (L Nr 900), January 1, 1965.

Deutschland, Press and Information Office of the Federal Government, Bonn (1990-2000 issues).

Facts About Germany, Press and Information Office of the Federal German Government (Prof. Helmut Arntz), Steiner Verlag, Wiesbaden, 1962.

Facts About Germany, Bertelsmann Lexicon Verlag, Cologne, 1988.

Facts About Germany, Societäts-Verlag, Frankfurt/Main, 1993.

Federal Ministry for Expellees, Refugees and War Victims, *Facts Concerning the Problem of the German Expellees and Refugees*, Bonn, 1961.

German Information Center, *Germany in Europe*, New York, 1963.

Inter Nationes, Bonn.

> First All-German Election: Germany Elects the 12th German *Bundestag* on December 2, 1990, Bonn, 1990.

> The Heads of Government of the Sixteen Constituent States in Germany, No. 750, Bonn, 1995.

> From a Planned to a Market Economy, by Karl Zuwadgky, No. 750, Bonn, 1995.

> The Political Parties in the German *Bundestag*, No. 720, Bonn, 1992.

> Sixteen States, One Country, by Conrad Reuter, No. 720, Bonn, 1992.

Jahrbuch des Bundesrepublik 1992/93, Emil Hübner und Horst H. Rohefs, Verlag C. H. Beck, München, 1992.

Jahrbuch des Bundesrepublik 1996/97, H. H. Rohefs, und Ursel Schäfer, Verlag C. H. Beck, München, 1996.

Press and Information Office of the German Federal Government, *The Bulletin*, Bonn, (selected issues 1954-1966).

> ⸻, *Germany Reports*, Wiesbaden, 1953.

> ⸻, *The German State Yesterday, Today and Tomorrow*, extract from *Germany Reports*, 4th edition, 1964), Wiesbaden, 1964.

Press Office German Diplomatic Mission, *Handbook of German Affairs*, New York, 1954.

Statistisches Bundesamt, *Ergebnisse früheren Budestags- und Landtagswahlen nach Ländern*, Stuttgart und Mainz, 1964.

__________, *Handbook of Statistics for the Federal Republic of Germany*, Stuttgart und Mainz, 1964.

__________, *Statistisches Jahrbuch für die Bundesrepublik Deutschland*, Stuttgart und Mainz, Vols. 1-13 (1952-1964).

__________, *Vergleichszahlen aus früheren Wahlen für die neuen Bundestagswahlkreise*, Stuttgart and Mainz, 1964.

Ergebnisse früheres Bundestag- und Landtagswahlen nach Ländern, Verlag W. Kohlhammer Gmbh Stuttgart, 1965.

Statistisches Jahrbuch 1991 für das vereinte Deutschland, Metzler/Pöschal, Wiesbaden 1991

Wahlbuch für die Bundesrepublik Deutschland 1946-1989, 1. und 2. Halb Band, Verlag Ferdinand Schoeningh, Paderborn, 1990.

The Week in Germany, German Information Center, New York (various issues).

Zeitschrift für Parlamentsfragen, Jahrgänge 2002 und 2004 (Vol. 33-35) V.S. Verlag für Sozialwissenschaften, 2004.

2. THE GERMAN *LÄNDER*

Baden-Württemberg, Statistisches Landesamt, *Die Parlamentswahlen in Baden-Württemberg seit 1952*, Stuttgart, 1964.

Die Wahl zum Landtag von Baden-Württemberg am 15, May 1960, Stuttgart, 1960.

Die Wahl zum vierten Deutschen Bundestag am 17. September 1961, Stuttgart, 1962.

Die Wahl zum Landtag von Baden-Württemberg am 26. April 1964, Stuttgart, 1964.

Die Wahl zum Landtag von Baden-Württemberg am 28. April 1968, Stuttgart, 1969.

Die Wahl zum Landtag von Baden-Württemberg am 23. April 1972, Stuttgart, 1972.

Wahl zum Landtag von Baden-Württemberg am 4. April 1976 (Band 230), Stuttgart, 1976.

Wahl zum Landtag von Baden-Württemberg am 16. März 1980 (Band 280), Stuttgart, 1980.

Wahl zum Landtag von Baden-Württemberg am 25. März 1984 (Band 330), Stuttgart, 1984.

Landtag von Baden-Württemberg 11. Wahlperiode, Neue Darmstädter Verlag, 1992.

Bavaria: *Bayerisches Landesamt für Statistik und Datenverarbeitung:*

"Zusammensetzung der Bayerischen Staatsregierung" München, 1964.

Wahl zum Bayerschen Landtag am 20. November 1966 (Heft 277c), München, 1967.

Kommunalwahlen in Bayern am 27. März 1960, München, 1961.

Vierte Bundestagswahl in Bayern am 17. September 1961, München, 1962.

Wahl zum Bayerischen Landtag am 25. November 1962, München, 1963.

Zwölfte Landtagswahl in Bayern am 14. Oktober 1990, München, 1990.

Berlin: *Statistisches Landesamt Berlin:*

West Berlin, *"Ergebnisse der Berliner Wahlen 1919 bis 1933 und 1946 bis 1954"* in *Die Wahlen am 5. Dezember in West Berlin,* Berlin Statistical Office, 1955.

Senator für Inneres, Unterlagen für die Vorbereitung und Durchführung der Wahlen zum Berliner Abgeordnetenhaus und zu den Bezirksverordnetenversammlungen am 17. Februar 1963, Berlin-Wilmersdorf, 1963.

Endgültiges Ergebnis der Berliner Wahlen am 17. Februar 1963, Berlin-Wilmersdorf, 1963.

West Berlin, *Statistisches Landesamt, Die Wahlen in Berlin (West) am 17. Februar 1963,* Berlin-Schöneberg, 1963.

Die Berliner Wahlen 1946 bis 1971, Sonderheft 233, Berlin, 1975.

Die Wahlen am 2. März 1975 in Berlin (West), Berlin, 1977.

Wahlen in Berlin (West) 1979 und 1981 (Sonderheft 345), Berlin, 1981.

Die Wahlen zum Abgeordnetenhaus und zu den Bezierksverordnetenversammlungen am 10. März 1985 in Berlin (West), Berlin, 1985.

Die Wahlen zum Abgeordnetenhaus und zu den Bezirksverordnetenvesammlungen 29. January 1989. Berlin, 1989.

Wahlen in Berlin am 2. Dezember 1990, Endgültiges Ergebnis der Wahl zum ersten Gesamtberliner Abgeordnetenhaus, Berlin, 1991.

Landeswahlleiter Berlin, Wahlen in Berlin am 17. September 2006 (Wahl zum Abgeordnetenhaus und Volksentscheid in der Verfassung von Berlin).

Bremen, *Senatskanzlei, "Bekanntmachung des Wortlauts des Wahlgesetzes für die Burgerschaft (Landtag)" und "Bekanntmachung des Wortlauts der bremischen Landeswahlordnung," Gesetzblatt der Freien Hansestadt Bremen,* Bremen, 1963.

Bremen, *Statistisches Landesamt, Die Wahl zum Vierten Bundestag am 17. September im Lande Bremen,* Bremen, 1962.

Die Wahl zur Bremischen Bürgerschaft am 29. September 1963, Bremen, 1964.

Bremen Statistische Berichte: Ergebnisse der Bürgerschaftswahlen 1947 bis 1991 nach Wahlbereichen, Bremen, 1991.

Wahl der Bremischen Bürgerschaft am 29 September 1991, Bremen, 1991.

Hamburg, *Statistisches Landesamt der Freien und Hansastadt Hamburg:*

Hamburg, *Statistisches Landesamt, Die Bürgerschaftswahl am 13. Oktober 1946*, Hamburg, 1947.

Die Wahl zum ersten Bundestag am 14. August 1949, Hamburg 1950.

Die Wahl zur Bürgerschaft und zu den Bezirksausschüssen am 16. Oktober 1949, Hamburg, 1950.

Die Wahl zum zweiten Bundestag am 6. September 1953, Hamburg, 1954.

Die Wahl zur Bürgerschaft und zu den Bezirksausschüssen am 1. November 1953, Hamburg, 1955.

Die Wahl zum Bundestag am 15. September 1957, Hamburg, 1958.

Die Wahl zur Bürgerschaft und zu den Bezirksausschüssen am 10. November 1957, Hamburg, 1959.

Die Wahl zum Bundestag am 17. September 1961, Hamburg, 1962.

Die Wahl zur Bürgerschaft und zu den Bezirksausschüssen am 12. November 1961, Hamburg, 1963.

Die Wahl zur Bürgerschaft und zu den Bezirksversammlungen am 27. März 1966, Hamburg, 1967.

Die Wahl zur Bürgerschaft und zu den Bezirksversammlungen am 22. März 1970, Hamburg, 1971.

Die Wahl zur Bürgerschaft und zu den Bezirksversammlungen am 3. März 1974, Hamburg, 1974.

Wahl zur Bürgerschaft und zu den Bezirksversammlungen am 4. Juni 1978, Hamburg, 1979.

Wahl zur Bürgerschaft und zu den Bezirksversammlungen am 6. Juni 1982, Hamburg, 1982.

Wahl zur Bürgerschaft und zu den Bezirksversammlungen am 19. Dezember 1982, Hamburg, 1983.

Wahl zur Bürgerschaft und zu den Bezirksversammlungen am 9. November 1986, und am 17. Mai 1987 (Heft 148), Hamburg, 1987.

Ergebnisse der Bürgerschaftswahlen seit 1946, Hamburg, 1988.

Analyse der Hamburgerwahlen am 2. Juni 1991, Hamburg, 1991.

Hamburg, *Staatliche Pressestelle, "Übersicht über die Senate der Freien und Hansestadt Hamburg seit 1945,"* Hamburg, 1963.

Hesse:

Hessen, Statistisches Landesamt, "Volksentscheid und Landtagswahl in Hessen am 1. Dezember 1946," Staat und Wirtschaft in Hessen, Heft 1, 1947.

Handbuch des Hessischen Landtags 18. Wahlperiode 2009-2014, NDW, 2009.

Hessen Büro des Landtags, Handbuch des Hessiwschen Landtags (5. *Wahlperiode*), Wiesbaden, 1963.

Hessische Landeszentrale für politische Bildung, Handbuch des Hessischen Landtags, Wiesbaden, 1963.

Hessisches Ministerium des Innern, Leitfaden für die Vorbereitung und Durchführung der Wahl zum vierten Bundestag am 17. September 1961 im Lande Hessen, Wiesbaden, 1961.

Leitfaden für die Vorbereitung und Durchführung der Landtagswahl im Lande Hessen am 11. November 1962, Wiesbaden, 1962.

Gemeinde- und Kreiswahlen in Hessen am 25. Oktober 1964, Wiesbaden, 1964.

Lower Saxony: *Niedersächsisches Landesverwaltungsamt Statistik:*

Endgültiges Ergebnis der Wahl zum Niedersächsischen Landtag am 20. April 1947, Hannover, 1947.

Die Wahl zum Niedersächsichen Landtag am 19. April 1959, Hannover, 1959.

Die Wahl zum Niedersächsichen Landtag am 19. Mai 1963, Hannover, 1963.

Die Briefwähler in Niedersachsen, April 1966, Statistische Monatshefte für Niedersachsen.

Die Wahl zum Niedersächsischen Landtag am 4. Juni 1967, Hannover 1967, *Teil 1 und 2.*

Wahl zum Niedersächsischen Landtag am 14. Juni 1970, Hannover, 1970, *Teil 1 und 2.*

Wahl zum Niedersächsischen Landtag der 8. Wahlperiode am 9. Juni 1974, Hannover, 1974.

Wahl zum Niedersächsischen Landtag der 9. Wahlperiode am 4. Juni 1978, Hannover, 1978.

Wahl zum Niedersächsischen Landtag der 10. Wahlperiode am 21. März 1982, Hannover, 1982

Wahl zum Niedersächsischen Landtag der 11. Wahlperiode am 15. Juni 1986, Hannover, 1986.

Wahl zum Niedersächsischen Landtag der 12. Wahlperiode am 13. Mai 1990, Hannover, 1990.

Wahl zum Niedersächsischen Landtag am 27.01, 2008, Niedersächsisches Landeswahlleiter, 2008.

"Abgeordnetenbewegung im Niedersächsichen Landtag," "Landtagswahlen in Niedersachsen 1947-1963," and *"Übersicht über die vom Niedersächsichen Landtag seit 1946 gebildeten Landesregierungen,"* information sheets made available by the Lower Saxony Office for Statistics, 1965.

North Rhine-Westphalia, *Landesregierung, "Gesetz zur Änderung des Landeswahlgesetzes," "Bekanntmachung der Neufassung des*

Landeswahlgesetzes," "Landeswahlordnung," und "Landtagswahl 1962 – Wahlausschreibung," Gesetz- und Verordnungsblatt für das Land Nordrhein-Westfalen, Düsseldorf, 1962.

Nordrhein-Westfalen, *Landtag, Handbuch des Landtags Nordrhein Westfalen (5. Wahlperiode)*, Düsseldorf, 1962.

Wahlen zu den Vertretungen der Kreisfreien Städte und Landkreise in Nordrhein-Westfalen 1964 und 1961, Düsseldorf, 1964.

"Wahlen in Nordrhein-Westfalen nach dem zweiten Weltkrieg," information sheets made available by the Land Statistical Office of North Rhine-Westphalia, 1965.

North Rhine-Westphalia: *Landesamt für Datenverarbeitung und Statistik Nordrhein-Westfalen:*

Landtagswahl am 14.6 1970, Düsseldorf, 1970.

Landtagswahl 1975 (4. Mai), Düsseldorf, 1975.

Landtagswahl 1980 (11. Mai), Düsseldorf, 1980.

Landtagswahl in Nordrhein-Westfalen 1985 (12. Mai), Düsseldorf, 1985.

Landtagswahl in Nordrhein-Westfalen 1990 (13. Mai), Düsseldorf, 1990.

Rheinland-Pfalz, *Landeswahlleiter, Wegweiser für die Landtagswahl am 31, März 1963*, Bad Ems, 1962.

Rheinland-Pfalz, *Statistisches Landesamt, Die Wahlen und Volksabstimmungen in Rheinland-Pfalz in den Jahren 1946/1947*, Bad Ems, 1948.

Die Kommunalwahlen am 9. November 1952 in Rheinland-Pfalz, Bad Ems, 1953.

Ergebnisse der Landtagswahlen am 18. Mai 1947 u. 29. April 1951 sowie der Bundestagswahl am 6. September 1953, Bad Ems, 1955.

Ergebnis der Wahl zum zweiten Bundestag am 6. September 1953, Bad Ems 1953.

Endgültiges Ergebnis der Landtagswahl am 15. Mai 1955, Bad Ems, 1955.

Endgültiges Ergebnis der Wahl zum dritten Bundestag am 15. September 1957 in Rheinland-Pfalz, Bad Ems 1957.

Die Landtagswahl am 19. April 1959, Bad Ems, 1959.

Die Kommunalwahlen vom 23. Oktober 1960, Bad Ems, 1960.

Die Wahl zum vierten Deutschen Bundestag in Rheinland-Pfalz, Bad Ems, 1961.

Die Wahl zum Landtag am 31. März 1963, Bad Ems, 1963.

Die Kommunalwahlen vom 25. Oktober 1964, Bad Ems, 1964.

Geschichtliche Entwicklung von Rheinland-Pfalz, Bad Ems, 1963.

Landtagswahl am 31. März 1963, Bad Ems, 1963.

Landtagswahl am 23. April 1967, Bad Ems, 1967.

Landtagswahl am 21. März 1971, Bad Ems, 1971.

Landtagswahl am 9. März 1975, Bad Ems, 1975.

Landtagswahl am 18. März 1979, Bad Ems, 1979.

Landtagswahl am 6. März 1983, Bad Ems, 1983.

Landtagswahl am 17. Mai 1987, Bad Ems, 1987.

Landtagswahl am 21. April 1991, Bad Ems, 1991.

Saarland, *Statistisches Landesamt des Saarlandes*

"*Gesetz Nr. 723 zur Änderung der Verfassung des Saarlandes. vom 29. September 1960," und "Gesetz Nr. 724 über die Wahl des Landtages des Saarlandes (Landtagswahlgesetz – LWG). vom 29. September 1960*," *Amtsblatt des Saarlandes*, Saarbrücken, 1960.

Die Gemeinderatswahl am 27. März 1949, Saarbrücken, 1952.

Ergebnisse der Landtagswahlen 1952 und 1955 in der Wahlkreisen, Saarbrücken, 1956.

Ergebnis der Gemeinderatswahl am 27. März 1949 und der Landtagswahl am 18. Dezember 1955, Saarbrücken, 1956.

Die Wahlen im Saarland am 4. December 1960, Saarbrücken, 1961.

Die Endgültigen Ergebnisse der Bundestagswahl am 17. September 1961, Saarbrücken, 1961.

Die Ergebnisse der Wahlen in Saarland 1964 bis 1976, Saarbrücken, 1977.

Landtag des Saarlandes 10. Wahlperiode des Saarlandes: Herausgegeben vom Präsident des Landtags, 1992.

Schleswig-Holstein:

Landeswahlleiter für Schleswig-Holstein unter Mitwirkung des Statistischen Landesamts, Die Landeswahlen in Schleswig-Holstein vom 20. April 1947, Kiel, 1947.

Der Praesident des Schleswig-Holsteinischen Landtages, Handbuch des Schleswig-Holsteinischen Landtag (6. Wahlperiode), Kiel, 1967.

Sekretariat des Schleswig-Holsteinischen Landtages, Handbuch des Schleswig-Holsteinischen Landtages (4. Wahlperiode), Kiel, 1959.

Schleswig-Holstein: *Statistisches Landesamt:*

"*Landtagswahl am 9. Juli 1950," Statistisches Jahrbuch Schleswig-Holstein*, Kiel, 1951.

Die Landtagswahl am 12. September 1954, Kiel, 1955.

Ergebnis der Wahl zum Schleswig-Holsteinischen Landtag am 28. 9. 1958, Kiel, 1958.

Endgültiges Ergebnis der Gemeinde- und Kreiswahlen in Schleswig-Holstein am 25. Oktober 1959, Kiel, 1960.

Die Wahl zum 4. Deutschen Bundestag am 17.9. 1961 in Schleswig-Holstein, Kiel, 1961.

Gemeinde- und Kreiswahlen in Schleswig-Holstein am 11. März 1962, Kiel, 1962.

Die Landtagswahl am 23. 9. 1962 in Schleswig-Holstein, Kiel, 1962.

Die Landtagswahl am 23. April 1967 in Schleswig-Holstein, Kiel 1967.

Die Landtagswahl am 25. April 1971 und Nachwahl im Wahlkreis 5 am 16.5. 1971, Kiel, 1971.

Landtagswahl am 13. April 1975, Kiel, 1975.

Landtagswahl am 29. April 1979, Kiel, 1979.

Die Landtagswahl am 13. März 1983, Kiel, 1983.

Die Landtagswahl am 13. September 1987, Kiel, 1987.

Die Landtagswahl am 8. Mai 1988, Kiel, 1988.

Bundestagswahl in Schleswig-Holstein am 2. Dezember 1990, Kiel, 1991.

Landtagswahl in Schleswig-Holstein am 5. April 1992, Kiel, 1992.

Landtagswahl in Schleswig-Holstein 20.02, 2005, Wahlanalysis Konrad Adenauer Stiftung, Berlin, 2005.

3. UNITED STATES

Advisory Commission on Intergovernmental Relations, *Studies in Comparative Federalism: West Germany* (M-128), U.S. Government Printing Office, Washington, D.C., July 1981.

United States Department of State, *German Democratic Republic*, U.S. Government Printing Office, Washington, D.C., June 1987: 1-8.

Department of State, *Germany 1947-1949: The Story in Documents*, Pub. 3556, Washington, Government Printing Office, 1950.

ECA Technical Assistance Commission, *The Integration of Refugees into German Life*, Report submitted to the Chancellor of the Federal Republic of Germany, March 21, 1951.

Office of Military Government, U.S. Sector, Berlin, *A Four Year Report July 1, 1945-September 1, 1949*, OMGUS: Berlin Sector, 1950.

Office of the U.S. High Commissioner for Germany, *Germany's Parliament in Action*, Frankfurt (Main), HICOG, 1950.

__________, *Quarterly Report on Germany*, Ten Reports, September 21, 1949-March 31, 1952, Bad Godesberg/Mehlem, HICOG, 1949-1952.

Party Publications and Newspapers

1. CDU PUBLICATIONS AND NEWSPAPERS

Bundesgeschäftsstelle der CDU, *The CDU: Geschichte, Idee, Program, Statut*, Bonn, 1962.

Presse- und Informationsdienste der CDU Deutschlands, *Deutsches Monatsblatt*, Bonn, 1965 issues.

CDU Schleswig-Holstein, *Wort und Bild,* Organ des Landesverbandes Schleswig-Holstein der CDU, Kiel, August/September 1962.

2. DFU PUBLICATIONS AND NEWSPAPERS

Bundesvorstand der Deutschen Friedens-Union, *Wahlprogramm der DFU für die Bundestagswahl 1965*, Köln, 1965.

Wahrheiten (Wahlillustrierte der Deutschen Friedens-Union), Köln, 1965.

"Das Sind die Ziele der Deutschen Friedens-Union," Köln, 1961.

3. FDP PUBLICATIONS AND NEWSPAPERS

Bundesparteileitung der FDP, *Politiker Stehen Rede und Antwort*, Bonn, 1965.

The Programme of the Free Democratic Party (Adopted and promulgated by the Eighth Regular Party Congress in Berlin, on 26 January 1957), Bonn, no date.

FDP Landesverband Hamburg, *Die Freie Stadt*, Hamburg, 1965-1966 issues (newspaper published twice a month by the *Land* FDP).

Liberale in der Verantwortung: *Vorgeschichte und Entwicklung der FDP*, Hamburg, 1964.

Freie Demokratische Partei, Liberale in der Verantwortung, Wirtschaft-und Sozialpolitik Verlag Gmbh, Hamburg, 1964.

4. NPD PUBLICATIONS AND NEWSPAPERS

Thielen, Fritz, *Grundsätze unserer Politik im neuen Bundestag* (Eine Rede des NPD-Parteitages 1965), Hannover, 1965.

NPD, Bundesgeschäftsführung, *Das Manifest der NPD*, Hannover, 1965.

Deutsche Nachrichten, Hannover, Sonderdruck I-IV, 1965 (newspaper of the National Democratic Party).

5. SPD PUBLICATIONS AND NEWSPAPERS

Vorstand der Sozialdemokratischen Partei Deutschlands, *Grundsatz Program* (Godesberg Programm vom November 1959), Bonn, 1965.

Wahlen in Gemeinden und Kreisen 1964, Bonn, 1965.

Der Flüchtling, Bonn, August 1962 (Socialist monthly prepared for distribution to refugees and expellees).

Das Regierungsprogramm der SPD, Bonn, 1961.

SPD Berlin, *Berliner Stimme*, Berlin, July-September 1965 issues.

SPD Schleswig-Holstein, Landesvorstand, *Schleswig-Holstein Post*, Kiel, selected issues 1962-1965.

Non-Party Newspapers, Periodicals and Internet

dw-world.de/politik (Deutsche Welle)

Dithmarscher Landeszeitung (Heide), newspaper serving the West coast of Schleswig-Holstein, selected issues 1949-2010.

en.wikipedia.org/topstories

Focus, German news magazine (selected issues 2005-2011).

Frankfurter Allgemeine Zeitung (various issues 1990-2011).

    www.faz.net/s/homepage

German Tribune, The (Hamburg), a weekly review of the German Press, 1965-1966.

Hamburger Abendblatt (various issues 1954-2011).

    abendblatt.de/politik/Deutschland

Hamburgisches Welt Wirtschafts Institut Update (Hamburg), Various Issues 2005-2011.

Liberale Studenten-Zeitung (Bonn), organ of the federal executive committee of the Liberal Student Federation of Germany, June 1955.

Manchester Guardian Weekly (Manchester), selected issues 1962-1966.

Newsweek (selected issues 1946-1966).

New York Times (selected issues 1946-2010).

Spiegel, Der (Hamburg), weekly news periodical, selected issues 1960-2011.

    spiegel.de/politik/deutschland

Stern (Hamburg) German news periodical (selected issues 1960-2011).

    stern.de/politik/deutschland

Süddeutsche Zeitung, Die (Munich) (various issues 1993-2011).

Time (selected issues 1946-2010).

Welt Zeitung, Die (Hamburg), various issues from April 2, 1946 to 2011, including *Die Welt am Sonntag*.

Books

Andersen, Uwe and Wichard Woyke, *Handwörterbuch des politische System der Bundesrepublik Deutschland (5. Auflage)*, Leske und Budrich, Opladen, 2003.

Beyer, Helmut, *Der Niedersächsische Landtag in den fünfziger Jahren*, Hannover, Droste, 1980.

Brunswig, Hans, *Feuersturm über Hamburg*, Motorbuch Verlag, Stuttgart, 1983.

Carr, Jonathan, *Election Year 1994: Continuity and Change in the German Political Parties*, American Institute for Contemporary German Studies, the John Hopkins University, 1994.

__________, *Federalism, Bureaucracy, and Party Politics in Western Germany*, 1961.

Chamberlin, William Henry, *The German Phoenix*, New York: Duell, Sloan and Pearce, 1963.

Claxton, Carol, *Bremen: The Story of the Free Hanseatic City*, Appel Verlag, Bremen, 1954.

Conradt, David, *et. al., Germany's New Politics: Parties and Issues in the 1990s*, Berghahn Books, Providence, R.I. 1995.

Decker, Frank *und* Viola Neu, *Handbuch der Deutschen Parteien, Verlag für Sozialwissenschaften, 2006.*

Duverger, Maurice, *Political Parties*, London: Methuen and Co. Ltd., 1954.

Ebsworth, Raymond, *Restoring Democracy in Germany*, London: Stevens and Sons Ltd., 1960.

Edinger, Lewis J., *Politics in Germany*, Little, Brown and Company, 1968.

Ego, Anneliese, *Herbert und Elsbeth Weichmann*, Christians Verlag, Hamburg, 1998.

Fischbach, Günter, *DDR Almanac '89: Daten, Information, Zahlen,* Verlag Bonn Aktuell, Stuttgart, 1989.

Fischer, Claus A. (Hrsg.), *Wahlhandbuch für die Bundesrepublik Deutschland,* 1990.

German Information Center, *The Basic Law of the Federal Republic of Germany*, 1961.

Hartmann, Jürgen (ed.), *Handbuch der Deutschen Bundesländer*, Campus Verlag, Frankfurt/Main 1994.

Heidenheimer, Arnold, *Adenauer and the CDU*, the Hague: Matinus Nijhoff, 1960.

__________, *The Governments of Germany*, New York: Thomas Y. Crowell Co., 1961.

__________, *The Governments of Germany (Third Edition)*, Thomas Y. Crowell Company, New York, 1971.

Helms, Ludger (ed.), *Institutions and Institutional Change in the Federal Republic of Germany*, St. Martins Press, Inc., New York, 2000.

Hiscocks, Richard, *Democracy in Western Germany*, London: Oxford University Press, 1957.

Hofmann, Robert, *Geschichte der Deutschen Parteien,* Piper Verlag, *München.*

Höller, K. *Wahlatlas. 1987/88 Bundesgebiet Deutschland*, Hotler und Zwick Verlag Gmbh, 1988.

Jäckel, Hartmut, *Wahlführer 1969*, R. Piper & Co. Verlag, München, 1969.

Johnson, Nevil, *Government in the Federal Republic of Germany*, Penquin Press, GB, 1973.

Kästner, Friedrich, *Neues Hamburg, Zeugnisse vom Wiederaufbau der Hansastadt,* Hamburg: Hammerich und Lesser, 1947.

Katzenstein, Peter, *Policy and Politics in West Germany: The Growth of a Semi-Sovereign State*, Temple University Press, Philadelphia, 1988.

Keesing's Contemporary Archives, London: Keesing's Publications Ltd., selected volumes 1949-1956.

Krekel, Michael, *Konrad Adenauer: Profiles of the Man and the Politics, Stiftung Bundeskanzler-Adenauer Haus*, 1999.

Leigien, R. *The Four Power Agreements on Berlin*, Carl Heymanns Verlag, Berlin, 1961.

Litchfield, Edward H. (ed.), *Governing Postwar Germany*, Ithaca: Cornell University Press, 1953.

Lüth, Erich, *Stadtstaat Hamburg*, Hamburg: Gerhard Müller KG, 1963.

Menzel, E., *et al*, *Verfassungsregister*, Teil I: Deutschland, Koblenz, no date.

Merkatz, Hans Joachim von, and Wolfgang Metzner, *Germany Today*, Frankfurt (Main): Alfred Metzner Verlag, 1954.

Nagel, John David, *The National Democratic Party*, University of California Press, Berkeley, 1970.

Oppen, Beate Rurm von (ed.), *Documents on Germany Under Occupaton 1945-1954*, London: Oxford University Press, 1955.

Pinney, Edward L., *Federalism, Bureaucracy and Party Politics in Western Germany: The Role of the Bundesrat*, Durham, North Carolina: The University of North Carolina Press, 1963.

Plischke, Elmer, *The West German Federal Government*, Office of the U.S. High Commission for Germany, Bad Godesberg, 1952.

__________, *Contemporary Government of Germany*, Boston: Houghton Mifflin Company, 1961.

__________, *Contemporary Governments of Germany (Second Edition)*, Houghton Mifflin Company, Boston, 1969.

Pollock, James K., et al., *German Democracy at Work*, Ann Arbor: University of Michigan Press, 1955.

Pollock, James K., James H. Meisel and Henry L. Bretton (eds.), *Germany Under Occupation: Illustrative Materials*, Ann Arbor: George Wahr Publishing Co., 1949.

Rothe, Anne (ed.), *Current Biography*, New York, The H. W. Wilson Co., selected volumes 1948-1962.

Rudzio, Wolfgang, *Das politische System der Bundesrepublik Deutschland (5. Auflage)*, Leske und Budrich, Opladen, 2000.

Rytleweski, Ralf und Manfred Opp di Hipt, *Die Bundesrepublik Deutschland in Zahlen, 1945/49-1980*, Verlag D. H. Beck München, 1981.

Scharf, Thomas, *The German Greens: Challenging the Consensus*, Berg Publishers Limited, Oxford, U.K., 1994.

Schulz, Werner and Ludger Wolmer, *et. al. Entwicklung statt abwickeln*, Christoph Links Verlag, Berlin, 1992.

Smith, Gordon, *et. al.*, *Developments in German Politics*, Duke University Press, Durham, 1992.

Sonne, H. Christian, *The Integration of Refugees into German Life*, ECA Technical Assistance Commission, Bonn, 1951.

Stahl, Walter (ed.), *Deutsche Tatsachen*, Hamburg: Gruner Druck Gmbh., 1954.

__________, *Meet Germany*, Hamburg: Gruner Druck Gmbh., 1-12 editions, 1954-1966.

__________, *The Politics of Postwar Germany*, New York: Frederick A. Praeger, 1963.

Steinberg, S. H. (ed.), *The Statesman's Yearbook*, London: Macmillan and Co. Ltd., 1946-1965/1966 issues.

Thilenius, Richard, *Die Teilung Deutschland,* Rowahlt Taschenbuch Verlag Gmbh, Hamburg, 1957.

Werner, Christian K., *Rechts-Links,* Hohwacht Verlag, Bad Godesberg, 1963.

Articles/Papers

Alexander, Robin, *"Mut zum Partikularism,"* *Die Welt* (September 30, 2008).

Amery, C., "No Fun in Bavaria," *The Nation*, 203 (December 12, 1966): 637-639.

Arndt, Adolf, "Status and Development of Constitutional Law in Germany," *Annals of the American Academy of Political and Social Science*, 260 (November 1948): 1-9.

Barnes, Samuel, *et al.*, "The German Party System and the 1961 Federal Election," *American Political Science Review*, LVI (December 1962): 899-914.

Bolten, Seymour, "Military Government and the German Political Parties," *Annals of the American Academy of Political and Social Science*, 267 (January 1950): 55-67.

Brecht, Arnold, "Re-establishing German Government," *Annals of the American Academy of Political and Social Science*, 267 (January 1950): 28-42.

Carey, Jane Perry Clark, "Political Organization of the Refugees and Expellees in West Germany," *Political Science Quarterly*, 66 (June 1951): 191-215.

Childs, David, "The Revival of the German Right," *Contemporary Review*, 209 (September 1966): 127-136.

Crowell, Richard S., "Rightist Extremism in Postwar West Germany," *Western Political Quarterly*, XVII (June 1964): 284-293.

Culver, Lowell W., "Land Elections in West German Politics," *The Western Political Quarterly*, Vol. XIX, No. 2, June 1966: 304-336.

Culver, Lowell W., "The Reemergence of Right Extremism in West Germany," *Idaho Issues*, No. I, 1967: 1-18.

Edinger, Lewis J., "Electoral Politics and Voting Behavior in West Germany," *World Politics*, XIII (April 1961): 471-484.

Flechtheim, Ossip K., *"Die Institutionalisierung der Parteien in der Bundesrepublik,"* *Zeitschrift für Politik*, IX (June 1962: 97-110).

Frankland, E. Gene, "From Protest to Power: Green Party Organization," (paper delivered at the Annual Meeting of the American Political Science Association in Atlanta, Georgia, September 4, 1999).

Heidenheimer, Arnold, "Federalism and the Party System: The Case of Western Germany," *American Political Science Review*, LII (September 1958): 809-828.

Kirchheimer, Otto, "German Democracy in the 1950s," *World Politics*, XIII (January 1961): 258-259.

Lohse, Ezkart, *"Der Realpolitiker Fischer,"* (*Frankfurter Allgemeine Zeitung*, March 8, 1999: 3).

Long, Wellington, "Changing Scene in Bonn," *American-German Review*, 33 (October/November 1966): 13-15.

Lupia, Arthur and Kaare Strom, "Coalition Termination and the Strategic Timing of Parliamentary Elections," *American Political Science Review*, 89 (September 1995): 648-650.

Merkle, Peter H., "Executive-Legislative Federalism in West Germany," *American Political Science Review*, LIII (September 1959): 732-741.

__________, "Equilibrium, Structure of Interests and Leadership: Adenauer's Survival as Chancellor," *American Political Science Review*, LVI (September 1962): 634-650.

Merry, E. Wayne, "Eastern Germany in Search of Itself," *Current History*, 109 (March 2009): 112-118.

Moscowitz, Moses, "The Political Reeducation of the Germans: The emergence of Parties and Politics in Württemberg-Baden," *Political Science Quarterly*, LXI (December 1946): 535-561.

Neumann, Robert G., "The New Political Parties of Germany," *American Political Science Review*, XL (August 1946): 749-759.

__________, "New Constitutions in Germany," *American Political Science Review*, XLII (June 1948): 448-468.

Oezdemir, Cem, "From Foreigners to Germans," *Inter Nationes*, Bonn, 1995.

Olsen, Jonathan, "The Schwerin Model: The Red-Red Government in Mecklenburg-West Pomerania," (paper delivered at the annual meeting of the American Political Science Association in Atlanta, Georgia, September 4, 1999).

Poguntke, Thomas, "*Bündnis 90/die Grünen*," in Niedermayer (ed.) *Intermediäre Strukturen in Ostdeutschland*, Leske und Budrich, Opladen, 1996: 87-112.

Pollock, James K., "American Policy Toward Germany: The Political Situation," *Foreign Policy Reports*, 23 (November 1, 1947): 198-206.

Schellenger, H. Kent, Jr., "The German Social Democratic Party After World War II: The Conservatism of Power," *Western Political Quarterly*, XIX (June 1966): 251-265.

Schmokel, Wolfe W., "Germany and the Common Market," *Current History*: 45 (November 1963): 283-288.

Sternberger, Dolf, "Parties and Party Systems in Postwar Germany," *Annals of the American Academy of Political and Social Science*, 260 (November 1948): 10-31.

Sturm, Roland, "Government at the Center," in *Developments in German Politics*: Duke University Press Books, 1992.

Index